For

Yasmin, Alastair, Alex, James, Emilia and Raphael Liz,
Grainne, Iris, and Laurence

CORE TEXT SERIES

Company Law

Eleventh edition

ALAN DIGNAM

Professor of Corporate Law, School of Law, Queen Mary University of London
and Honorary Member, 7 King's Bench Walk Chambers

JOHN LOWRY

Emeritus Professor of Commercial Law, Faculty of Laws,
UCL; Honorary Fellow, Monash University; and Visiting Professor of Commercial Law,
University of Hong Kong

OXFORD
UNIVERSITY PRESS

OXFORD

UNIVERSITY PRESS

Great Clarendon Street, Oxford, OX2 6DP,
United Kingdom

Oxford University Press is a department of the University of Oxford.
It furthers the University's objective of excellence in research, scholarship,
and education by publishing worldwide. Oxford is a registered trade mark of
Oxford University Press in the UK and in certain other countries

Eighth edition 2014
Ninth edition 2016
Tenth edition 2018

Impression: 1

Published in the United States of America by Oxford University Press
198 Madison Avenue, New York, NY 10016, United States of America

British Library Cataloguing in Publication Data
Data available

Library of Congress Control Number: 2020939151

ISBN 978-0-19-884845-5

Printed in Great Britain by
Bell & Bain Ltd., Glasgow

Preface

Company law is a difficult subject. We know this because each year our student feedback tells us so. There are two reasons for this. First, company law has become a quasi-core subject with students choosing it because they regard it, not unnaturally, as an essential requirement for pursuing a career as a commercial lawyer. The fact that many students may not have the skills best suited to studying company law never seems to put students off and is often at the root of a poor to mediocre performance in the exams. So what are the essential skills needed? A good knowledge of contract, a proper understanding of equity, good statutory and common law interpretation skills, and a certain flexibility of mind needed to deal with the legal creation of corporate personality. With this base of skills a student will be equipped to deal with the hazardous waters of company law. If you think you don't have these essential skills then put this book down and rethink your options. Choose subjects based around the skills you have already identified as your strongest. It is best to do this now rather than suffer through an unhappy year of company law.

The second reason that students find company law difficult is that it is not until the end of the course that they see how the various parts of company law fit together. This is because company law is much like a jigsaw puzzle made up of smaller pieces that fit together to form a larger picture. Unfortunately, unlike a jigsaw puzzle you don't get a picture on the box to guide you. It is therefore not until the end of the course that the full company law picture is revealed, often too late for a really good understanding of the subject to emerge. It is our intention in this book to go as far as we can to provide that picture on the box to guide the company law student.

The book is structured fairly broadly around the University of London External LLB syllabus for Company Law on the basis that it represents the typical company law curriculum to be found in most UK undergraduate courses. However, given the burgeoning nature of the subject, not every part of that syllabus is covered by us. As a means of producing a manageable sized text that meets the objectives of the *Core Text Series*, we focus on those areas which are encountered in the company law courses we both teach. Where emphasis is accorded to certain topics above others this reflects our particular interests and our combined teaching experience rather than any subliminal message concerning the importance of those areas within the curriculum. Part I of the book seeks to guide the reader through the fundamental principles which underlie company law and those areas of the law which are necessarily encountered when a company is first brought into existence. Part II focuses on what goes on behind the corporate veil; it considers constitutional matters, classes of shares, and shareholders' rights and remedies. Part III examines issues of authority that arise when business is conducted through a company. It deals with how power is allocated to transact with outsiders, the company's principal organ of management, and the duties of directors. Emphasis is also given to corporate governance and how the corporation can be best accommodated within the various corporate theories that have been developed over the last two hundred years or so. Of course, somewhat appropriately, we also, in our final chapter, deal with the end of the company. At the end of each individual chapter there is a list of 'Further Reading' which we have selected as particularly useful for fleshing out the topic just covered. Additionally we have provided an extended list of reading for each chapter in the Select Bibliography at the end of the book. If we have discussed an article or book in a chapter the full reference to it will be found in either the Further Reading or the Select Bibliography.

Students of the subject will soon learn that company law has been in a state of flux over recent decades even without the uncertainty surrounding Brexit. A major review of company law by the Department of Trade and Industry (DTI, now the Department for Business, Energy and Industrial Strategy (BEIS)) began in 1998 which culminated in the Companies Act 2006. Although more than a decade on from the Act, it is very important that any student of company law has extensive knowledge of this review project as it provides a detailed account of the nuts and bolts of company law. The various consultation papers and the *Final Report* of the DTI's Company Law Review Steering Group (CLRSG) are available at https://webarchive.nationalarchives.gov.uk/20090609014658/http://www.berr.gov.uk/whatwedo/businesslaw/co-act-2006/clr-review/page22794.html. The *Final Report* forms the basis of the Government's 2002 and 2005 White Papers as well as much of the Companies Act 2006. These are also available at the same web address, and hard copies will most certainly be available in a good law library or, if you lack access to a library, from the Stationery Office. The proposals of the CLRSG, the Government's response, and, of course, the ensuing Companies Act 2006 are discussed where they impact on each individual chapter, but we also expect students to go through these documents themselves.

We would particularly like to thank the following for their support and comments on this work: Michael Bridge, Michael Bryan, Rob Chambers, Rod Edmunds, Michael Galanis, Jennifer Hill, Lusina Ho, Magdalena Latek, Ernest Lim, Andrea Lista, James Penner, Ian Ramsay, and David Tomkin. We owe a particular debt of gratitude to Sheila Shirley, Janette Monk, and Nerys Evans at QM for their tireless support as well as Andria Alexandrou for her research assistance. Needless to say, our thanks go to the School of Law at Queen Mary, University of London and to the Faculty of Laws at UCL and HKU for their support, and to the generations of students who have taught us much about the complexities of company law. We also thank Jessica Lehmani and all at OUP for their support in bringing this new edition to fruition.

Primary authorship of each chapter is as follows: Alan Dignam contributed Chapters 1, 2, 3, 5, 8, 12, 15, and 16; John Lowry contributed Chapters 4, 6, 7, 9, 10, 11, 13, 14, and 17.

We have tried to state the law as at 2 April 2020.

Alan Dignam and *John Lowry*
London

New to this edition

- *Antuzis v DJ Houghton Catching Services Ltd* [2019] EWHC 843 (QB)
- *BTI 2014 LLC v Sequana SA* [2019] EWCA Civ 112
- *Burnden Holdings (UK) Ltd v Fielding* [2019] EWHC 1566 (Ch)
- *Pantiles Investments Ltd v Winckler* [2019] EWHC 1298 (Ch)
- *Parr v Keystone Healthcare Ltd* [2019] EWCA Civ 1246
- *Popely v Popely* [2019] EWHC 1507 (Ch)
- *Re Sprintroom Ltd; Prescott v Potamianos* [2019] EWCA Civ 932
- *Rossendale BC v Hurstwood Properties (A) Ltd* [2019] EWCA Civ 364
- *Waldron v Waldron* [2019] EWHC 115 (Ch)
- *Global Corporate Ltd v Hale* [2018] EWCA Civ 2618
- *Instant Access Properties Ltd v Rosser* [2018] EWHC 756 (Ch)
- *LRH Services Ltd (In liquidation) v Trew* [2018] EWHC 600 (Ch)
- *Re Edwardian Group Ltd; Estera Trust (Jersey) Ltd v Singh* [2018] EWHC 1715 (Ch)
- *Sevilleja Garcia v Marex Financial Ltd* [2018] EWCA Civ 1468
- *Terry v Watchstone Ltd* [2018] EWHC 3082 (Comm)
- *Toone v Robbins* [2018] BCC 728
- *VB Football Assets v Blackpool FC* [2017] EWHC 2767 (Ch)
- *Brett v Migration Solutions Holdings Ltd* [2016] EWHC 523 (Ch)
- Latest UK Corporate Governance Code and Stewardship Developments 2020
- Wates Corporate Governance Principles for Large Private Companies
- Shareholder Rights Directive II (SRD II)

Guide to using the book

There are a number of features throughout the textbook designed to help you in your studies.

SUMMARY

Introduction
Statutory examples
Veil lifting by the courts
Classical veil lifting, 1897–1966
The interventionist years, 1966–1989
Back to basics, 1989–present
Tortious liability
Parent company personal injury tortious liability
Commercial tort

Chapter summaries highlight what will be addressed in each chapter, so you are aware of the key learning outcomes for each topic.

FURTHER READING

This chapter links with the materials in Chapter 3 of *Hicks Company Law* (Oxford, OUP, 2011, xl +649p).

Freedman and Finch, 'Limited Liability Partnerships: Have Pockets" Debate?' [1997]*JBL* 387.

Grantham, 'The Doctrinal Basis of the Rights of Company SI

Ireland et al, 'The Conceptual Foundations of Modern Com

Pettit, 'Limited Liability—A Principle for the 21st Century' [1

At the end of each chapter is a list of recommended **further reading**. These suggestions include books and journal articles, and will help to supplement your knowledge, and develop your understanding of key topics.

SELF-TEST QUESTIONS

1   Explain how the separate personality of the company

2   Why is *Salomon* an important case?

3   Was justice done in the *Macaura* case?

4   Do shareholders own the company?

5   What determines the market price of a share?

Each chapter concludes with a selection of **self-test questions**. These allow you to check your understanding of the topics covered, and help you engage fully with the material in preparation for further study, writing essays, and answering exam questions.

Acknowledgements

Special thanks to the Financial Reporting Council for allowing us to reproduce extracts from the UK Corporate Governance Code and the Stewardship Code.

Contents

Table of cases

Table of legislation

Paragraph numbers in bold type indicate where a section of the Act is set out in part or in full.

PART I

Fundamental Principles

1 Introduction to company law

SUMMARY

Forms of business organisation
The sole trader
The partnership
The company

Forms of business organisation

1.1 It may be helpful at this early stage to explore an overview of company law by examining the company's place within the various forms of business organisation. In order for us to get some comparative perspective on the relative merits of each type of organisation we need first to set some criteria to judge them by. In essence business organisations are about the effective combination of three things. First, you need capital (money) so a key question in evaluating a form of business organisation is, does it facilitate investment in the business? Second, no business venture is guaranteed to succeed and so the second key question is whether the form of business organisation mitigates or minimises the risk involved in the venture. The third question to ask relates to the fact that wherever you have money, risk, and people combined there is potential for disagreement, so does the form of business organisation provide a clear organisational structure?

The sole trader

1.2 The sole trader is the amoeba of the business organisation world. As the name implies it is a one-person operation where someone just operates on their own. There are no legal filing requirements, they just go into business on their own. Sole traders usually provide the capital with personal savings or a bank loan. They contract in their own name and have personal liability for all the debts of the business. Legally there is no distinction between the sole trader's personal and business assets and so if the business goes badly the creditors can go after his or her home, car, or other assets in satisfaction of the business debt. As the business is just one individual there is little risk of disagreement (unless the person is schizophrenic) and so there is no need for a formal organisational structure. The sole trader therefore is adequate for a single person with capital but is unsuitable for larger scale investment. The risk to the sole trader of doing business is large but there is no need for a formal organisational structure.

The partnership

1.3 Our hypothetical sole trader's business has been doing very well and there are a number of investors who are willing to provide further capital to expand the business. At this point the trader feels the need for a more complex form of business organisation to facilitate the expansion of the business. Here the trader might consider a partnership. The Partnership Act 1890, s 1 defines a partnership as 'the relationship which subsists between persons carrying on a business in common with a view of profit'. As you can see, this is a very broad definition. Therefore a partnership can come about by oral agreement, it can be inferred by conduct, or it can be a formal written agreement specifying the terms and conditions of the partnership. There is no formal process of becoming partners—if you behave as partners the law will deem you are partners, even if you have no idea what a partnership is (see *Khan v Miah* (2000)). The minimum membership required for a partnership is (obviously) two and the maximum is, since 2002, unlimited (prior to that it was 20 unless you were a professional firm (solicitors, accountants etc) who could exceed the maximum number). The assets of the firm are also owned directly by the partners. This as we will see later is very different from a company where the shareholders do not own the company's assets.

1.4 A partnership which does not expressly exclude the Partnership Act 1890 will be governed by it. This can sometimes be a problem for those who are unaware that they are partners, as under the Act each partner is entitled to: participate in management, an equal share of profit, an indemnity in respect of liabilities assumed in the course of the partnership business, and not to be expelled by the other partners. A partnership will also end on the death of a partner. Because of the nature of partnerships it is normal for those who are aware they are entering such an association to modify the Partnership Act and draft a complex partnership agreement. Law firms in particular have very complex partnership agreements governing their operation. This means that the management structure, profit sharing, and the life of the partnership can be made to fit any situation.

1.5 What cannot be achieved through a partnership agreement is limited liability, because under the Partnership Act each partner is jointly and severally liable for the debts and obligations of the partnership incurred while he or she is a partner. So if a partner runs away with the clients' funds each individual partner is legally responsible for the whole debt, not just a proportion of it. There are however two types of partnership that allow limitation of liability. The first type was created by the Limited Partnership Act 1907 and allows certain partners to have full limited liability. These partners gave rise to the term 'sleeping' partners as they take no active part in the running of the partnership. These types of partnerships have become increasingly common in recent years due to their popularity with the investment fund industry. This popularity as an investment vehicle has led to the amendment of the 1907 Act to specifically facilitate its use as an investment vehicle (The Legislative Reform (Private Fund Limited Partnerships) Order 2017). The second type was created by the Limited Liability Partnerships Act 2000 and allows for partners in these entities to achieve limited liability up to a point. It allows liability to be limited for general trading debts but individual partners are not able to limit their personal liability for a negligent act they themselves have committed. This type of partnership (LLP) was designed to allow large professional partnerships (law and accountancy firms) to achieve some measure of protection for partners who were not involved in a negligent act. In recent years as the ability of the LLP to facilitate capital raising and asset sales has become more apparent they have increasingly been used outside the law and accountancy fields.

1.6 A general partnership does therefore facilitate investment as it allows partners to pool their funds. The risk for partners however is larger than for shareholders in a limited liability company (although reduced in an LLP) but is at least shared by all the partners. The organisational structure is very flexible as the partnership agreement can facilitate almost any situation. Indeed, while we will see that the registered company dominates the business landscape, the partnership should be more attractive to small businesses given the above. It would seem however that factors such as limited liability and the positive reputational effects of operating through a company outweigh the other advantages of partnerships.

The company

1.7 Another alternative for our entrepreneur is to form a registered company. As our entrepreneur is pursuing a commercial venture he/she would be forming a company limited by shares (that is a company where the liability of the shareholders for the debts of the company is limited to the amount unpaid on their shares (see Chapter 2)). There are other types of company (the company limited by guarantee and the community interest company for example) which are designed for charitable or public interest ventures. A company limited by shares is the normal type of commercial company formed to pursue a business venture.

— If commercial venture company limited by shares

1.8 Setting up a company is governed by the Companies Act 2006 (CA 2006), ss 7–15 and is a relatively simple process. Our entrepreneur is required to provide the Registrar of

Companies with the constitution of the company (this contains the internal rules of the company called the articles of association and any objects clause limiting the power the company may have, see later), a memorandum of association stating that the subscribers intend to form a company and become members, and an application for registration containing the company name, its share capital, the address of its registered office, whether it's a private or public company, that the liability of its members is limited, a statement of the company's directors' names and addresses, and a statement of compliance with the CA 2006. The continuing purpose of registering these documents was to provide certain key information that could be accessed by the general public or government agencies if necessary. For example, concerns about complex company ownership discouraging investment and facilitating crime or tax evasion led to the introduction of statutory guidance in 2017 to expand the public register to ensure that Persons with Significant Influence or Control (PSC) appear on the public register (https://assets.publishing.service.gov.uk/government/uploads/system/uploads/attachment_data/file/675104/psc-statutory-guidance-companies.pdf). A PSC includes an individual holding more than 25 per cent of the shares or voting rights of the company, an individual who could appoint or remove a majority of the board, or an individual who could or does exercise significant influence over the company. It also covers an individual behind a trust or firm that if it were an individual would fulfil these criteria. The PSC register is a public one but if the information is likely to be misused a request can be made for it to be given protected status. This has become increasingly common with the public registers in recent decades as fears that public information could be abused have led to restrictions on its public availability. For example between April 2002 and the introduction of the CA 2006 directors could apply to have their names and addresses removed from the memorandum under provisions introduced by the Criminal Justice and Police Act 2001, if they could show they were at risk of potential or actual violence or intimidation. Media reports claim that tens of thousands of directors have done so in order to protect themselves. The CA 2006, s 165 amended the Criminal Justice and Police Act 2001 by allowing all directors to choose to have a service address (which may be the company's registered office) on the public record rather than a residential one. The Small Business, Enterprise and Employment Act 2015 (SBEEA 2015), s 96 also allows directors and major shareholders to withhold their full date of birth information from the public record (they still have to disclose the month and year but not the exact day). Furthermore the Register of Shareholders is no longer public but can be accessed on request when done so for a proper purpose, i.e. not to harass, threaten, or intimidate (see CA 2006, ss 116–118 and *Burry & Knight Ltd & Another v Knight* (2014)).

1.9 Prior to 1992 at least two people had to subscribe to become shareholders in a private company (see paras **1.14-1.16** on public and private companies). As a result of the Twelfth EC Company Law Directive (89/667), implemented in 1992, private companies could be formed with a single member but public companies still needed at least two members. The CA 2006, s 7 now provides for single-person private and public companies. Thus our entrepreneur, if he or she wished, could skip the stint as a sole trader and go straight to forming a company.

The memorandum and constitution

1.10 Under the previous Companies Acts the memorandum formed part of the company's constitution. Now, however, s 8 of the CA 2006 has reduced the memorandum of association to a more limited function. The memorandum is now a simple document providing certain basic information and key declarations to the public which state that subscribers wish to form the company and agree to become members taking at least one share each. The subscribers to the memorandum are those who agree to take some shares or share in the company thus becoming its first members. If the application to the Registrar is successful the subscribers become the first members of the company and the proposed directors become its first directors. Under the previous Companies Act 1985, the total amount of share capital that could be issued to investors had to be stated in the memorandum. In the CA 2006, s 10 the provisions have been streamlined and now only require a statement of the total number and nominal value of shares to be taken on formation by the subscribers to the memorandum of association. Additionally any rights associated (see Chapter 9 on class rights) with those shares must be stated along with the paid up and unpaid amount on each share (if any). The value given to each share is known as its 'par' or 'nominal' value. This is both a matter of convenience to facilitate the issue to the shareholders and a method of protecting the value of shares already issued as there are restrictions on issuing shares below their nominal value (indeed it is a criminal offence, see CA 2006, s 542 and Chapter 7). Additionally, the Insolvency Act 1986, s 74 deems the nominal value or any amount paid above the nominal value to be the limit of the shareholders' liability in an insolvency. If the shares are paid for immediately they are described as fully paid but shares may also be issued partly paid or even unpaid. In the case of partly paid and unpaid shares the shareholder can be called upon to pay for them at a later date (companies do however need to declare the aggregate amount unpaid on their shares—SBEEA 2015, s 92). Shares may be also be paid for in goods and services and not necessarily in cash.

1.11 Taking a simple example let's say the share capital of our entrepreneur's newly formed company is £10,001 subdivided into shares of £1 each. Our entrepreneur subscribed for 5,001 shares on registration and thus is now a member of the company holding 5,001 shares in the company at a nominal value of £1 each. In purchasing the shares she paid for half with cash and the rest are unpaid with an agreement that they are to be paid for in three years' time. Other investors in the company subscribed for a total of 5,000 shares and now are members of the company holding shares of that amount. It is important to note that in our entrepreneur's company she has majority voting rights by virtue of her 5,001 shares. This gives our entrepreneur the ability by simple majority (a voting majority of more than half the votes) to elect or remove someone from the board (see para **1.12**).

1.12 The company's constitution or articles of association are a set of rules governing the running of the company. They form the core of the organisational structure of the company—the board of directors (the management committee or organ) and the general meeting (the shareholders' committee or organ)—and generally allocate the powers of each organ. Those forming the company can provide their own set of articles but a model set of articles (historically these articles have been called the Table A Articles of Association but are referred to as the model articles in the CA 2006) is provided by the CA 2006, s 20 as a default for those setting up a company. In reality, however, the model articles have been generally adopted with some slight amendments. Once the company is up and running the CA 2006, s 21 provides that the articles may be altered if three-quarters of the members (a special resolution) vote to amend the articles. Additionally the CA 2006, s 168 gives members the right by simple majority (more than 50 per cent of the shareholders who vote, vote for the resolution) to remove a director for any reason whatsoever. Thus the articles and the Companies Act place the shareholders at the centre of the corporate power structure.

1.13 The articles, according to s 33 of the CA 2006, bind the members of the company, creating a statutory contract between the members themselves and between each member and the company (although, as we will see in Chapter 8, this gets quite complicated). If all the documentation is in order then the Registrar will issue a certificate of incorporation and the company will then come into existence.

Public and private companies

1.14 The Companies Act 2006 recognises a distinction between two different types of company: private companies where the investment is usually provided by the founding members either through their personal savings or from bank loans, and public companies where the intention is to raise large amounts of money from the general public. While this is the key difference there are others.

1.15 Private companies, obviously, are private. The vast majority of companies in the UK are private companies. The law assumes a closer relationship between the members in a private company than in a public company and so private companies commonly restrict the membership of their company (to those approved of by the directors) in the articles of association. In essence if a member wishes to leave the company by selling their shares or a member has died, the directors have a say in who replaces them, if anyone. There may also be a pre-emption clause in the articles which means that if a member wishes to sell their shares they must first offer the shares to the other members. Private companies have also historically been able to adopt an elective regime (CA 1985, s 379A) which recognised that often in private companies the directors and the members of the company are one and the same and so requirements for meetings, timing of meetings, and laying of accounts can be suspended to streamline the operation of the private company (additionally in the old Table A articles, article 53 allowed a more informal decision-making process). One of the main intentions of the reform process leading to the CA 2006 was to reform company law to suit small private companies and so many of the problematic requirements for private companies to hold meetings etc have been done away with in the 2006 Act (the annual general meeting (AGM) requirements for example do not apply to private companies, see CA 2006, Part 13, Chapter 14 and CA 2006, s 288 provides for an expanded written resolution regime for private companies). Private companies cannot invite the general public to buy shares (CA 2006, s 755), but they also, unlike public companies, have no minimum capital requirements. The members only need to come up with a nominal amount. £1 or even 1p would suffice and even then the member could purchase the shares unpaid (plus the registration fee for the Companies Registrar) in order to form the company. The members of a private company have limited liability and so the word limited or 'Ltd' must appear after the company's name. Members thereby are liable only for the amount unpaid on their shares and not for the debts of the company.

1.16 Public companies have the aim of securing investment from the general public and can advertise the fact they are offering shares to the public. In doing so the company must issue a prospectus (see Chapter 5) giving a detailed and accurate description of the company's plans. Because the general public are involved and need to be protected the initial capital requirements for a public company are more onerous than for a private one. There is a minimum capital requirement ('the authorised minimum') of £50,000 (CA 2006, s 763). While there is no formal limitation on public companies having restrictions on transfer of shares similar to those that apply to private companies, any such restriction would be highly unusual, given that one of the reasons for forming a public company is to raise money from the general public and such a restriction would discourage them. In any case if the public company is listed on the stock exchange any restrictions on transfer will be prohibited. Note here that public companies are not necessarily listed on the stock exchange. A listing is essentially a private contractual arrangement between a public company and the stock exchange (in the UK the London Stock Exchange (LSE) is itself a listed public company) to gain access to a very sophisticated market for its shares. Some public companies do however exist outside the stock exchange listing system—Sir Alan Sugar's Amstrad plc being a high-profile example. The application for registration for a public company must state that it is public and, as with private companies, the liability of the members is limited thus the words public limited company (PLC or plc) must come at the end of its name (CA 2006, s 58(1)) both as a statement that the members' liability is limited and to tell those dealing with it that it is authorised to secure investment from the general public.

So why would our entrepreneur form a company?

1.17 Using our criteria of facilitating investment, minimising risk, and providing an organisational structure the registered company seems to perform well. It is specifically designed as a capital-raising vehicle. The subdivision of shares allows for a very large number of investors to become members of the company. Those members have limited liability which minimises their risk. This in theory makes raising capital easier as individuals may feel more secure in their investment. Limited liability is also said to increase the entrepreneurial spirit of the directors, encouraging them to take risks in the knowledge the shareholders will not lose their houses or cars if the business venture fails. A company is also impervious to death, and shares are also in theory transferable and so particularly in public companies easily convertible into cash. The company is designed to potentially have a large number of participants and so has a formal constitution outlining its basic organisational and power structure. Technically, the people who control the company are the shareholders. They buy shares in the company which entitle them to certain control rights exercised through the shareholder organ, the general meeting. However, the running of the company cannot be effected by a large number of members as such control would be cumbersome and so they elect people to do it, the directors. The directors operate through the second organ of the company, the board of directors. The shareholders appoint or remove directors by simple majority vote (more than 50 per cent of the votes actually voted) at the general meeting.

1.18 However, our entrepreneur with her/his investors already identified may not have so much to gain from the corporate form. This brings us to a particular problem with the registered company. The statutory model has historically assumed a separation of ownership and control. That is, it assumes that the shareholders are residual controllers exercising control once a year at the AGM and that the day-to-day management of the business is carried out by professional managers (directors). For large companies this is the case but for the vast majority of companies in the UK this separation of ownership from control does not exist (see Chapters 13 and 15).

1.19 Freedman (1994) found that 90 per cent of all companies were small private concerns (as our entrepreneur's company would be). She also suggested that for small businesses the corporate form and the regulatory requirements that went with it were burdensome. It was also costly, as they had to employ professional advice to deal with these requirements. One assumed advantage to the small business, that of limited liability, was also negated by the practice of banks requiring the shareholders to provide guarantees for bank loans (a common source of finance among small businesses). Thus any debts owed to the banks could be reclaimed from the personal assets of the shareholders. In Freedman's study one of the major reasons that business people incorporated was the perceived benefits of having the word 'Ltd' after the company's name, namely, that it conferred prestige, legitimacy, and credibility on the venture. This may also be the key determinant for our entrepreneur.

1.20 Let us take a look at how the statutory model of the company and its surrounding case law operates in a large company. The AGM is held primarily to elect the directors to the board. The directors will be a mix of professional managers (executive directors) and non-executive (independent outsiders) (see Chapters 13 and 16). The executive directors will normally have a small shareholding but not usually a significant one. The shareholders are also provided with an annual report from the directors outlining the performance of the company over the past year and the prospects for the future (this is rather like a report card on their performance). At the heart of the report are the accounts certified by the auditor (an independent accountant who checks over the accounts prepared by the directors, see Chapter 16). Between the AGMs the directors run the company unencumbered by the shareholders. In a large company the board of directors will be more like a policy body which sets the direction the company goes in but the actual implementation of that direction will be carried out by the company's employees. In carrying out their function the directors stand in a fiduciary relationship with the company. They therefore owe a duty to act bona fide in the interests of the company (this generally meaning the shareholders' interests) and not for any other purpose (such as self-enrichment, see further Chapter 14). The employees who are authorised to carry out the company's business are the company's agents and therefore the company will be bound by their actions (see Chapter 12).

1.21 The same company law model applies to a small company but with significant differences in effect. The shareholders and directors will often completely overlap. The same people will also be the only employees of the company. To take the example of a two-person company, the two shareholders will also be the two directors and the two employees. There is no separation of ownership from control, the shareholders are the managers, and therefore most of the historical statutory assumptions about the company's organisational structure will not hold. Given that one can also form one-person companies the statutory assumption begins to take on farcical proportions. However the elective regime, as we explained earlier, had historically attempted to address this problem by allowing a 'quasi-partnership' or 'close company' (a company with few participants who know each other well) like this to do away with some of the more onerous aspects of the statutory model and the CA 2006 has significantly improved the difficulties close companies faced in using the company. The courts have also tried where possible to recognise and make allowances for these 'quasi-partnership' type companies (see *Ebrahimi v Westbourne Galleries Ltd* (1973); see further Chapter 11).

1.22 The differences in the types of business that use the statutory model featured heavily in the Company Law Review Steering Group (CLRSG) *Final Report* (2001), Chs 2 and 4. The CLRSG recommended that the statutory requirements for decision making, accounts and audit, constitutional structure, and dispute resolution be simplified. They also recommended that legislation on private companies should be made easier to understand. In particular there should be a clear statement of the duties of directors. The White Paper (*Modernising Company Law* (2002)) that followed the *Final Report*, the Consultative Document published in March 2005 (*Company Law Reform* (2005)), and the CA 2006 all carried through this focus on the 'quasi-partnership' company with a 'think small first' emphasis. However, it is still not clear more than a decade later if this focus has been entirely successful as the reform process has continued with further streamlining reforms such as the abolition of the annual return (an annual update on the company's shareholders, officers, and capital) in the SBEEA 2015.

1.23 Private companies present another problem. In a nutshell private companies, because there is often a close relationship between the participants, have more potential for those participants to have disagreements. In these cases company law and the constitution of the company can be problematic for a minority shareholder who has fallen out with the majority. Company law presumes, somewhat unhelpfully for an oppressed minority shareholder, that the company operates through its constitutional organs. In order for the company to operate, either the board of directors makes a decision or if it cannot then the general meeting can do so. It can, however, happen that a majority of shareholders holding 51 per cent (simple majority voting power) of the shares in the company could act to the detriment of the other 49 per cent. A 51 per cent majority would allow those members to elect only those who support their policies to the board. Thus the 49 per cent shareholder would be unrepresented on the board and powerless in the general meeting.

1.24 To take an example, X Ltd has three shareholders, Ron, Cathy, and Freeda. The share capital of X is 30 shares of £1 each. Ron, Cathy, and Freeda hold ten shares each. All three are directors and employees of X Ltd. Things go well for a few years but increasingly Ron and Cathy feel that Freeda is no longer contributing much to the company. They decide not to re-elect Freeda to the board of directors and having removed her from the board they transfer all the assets of X Ltd to Y Ltd (a company in which only Ron and Cathy have a shareholding) for a fraction of its real value.

1.25 In this situation Freeda has no constitutional power to block this asset-stripping exercise. She has no voice on the board (even if she did she could be outvoted by the others) and is powerless in the general meeting. Even though there appears to be also a breach of fiduciary duty, as Ron and Cathy are using their directorial powers to benefit themselves and not the company, only the board or the general meeting can instigate an action to remedy the situation (see Chapter 14). Ron and Cathy are unlikely to support an action against themselves. Thus the constitution of the company can be used to facilitate what is known as a 'fraud on the minority'. These situations are also made more acute in private companies where the oppressed minority shareholder cannot sell their shares without board approval and is thus trapped. Although the courts quickly came up with a limited exception to enforcing the constitutional structure (*Foss v Harbottle* (1843), see Chapter 10) there has always been a continuing tension between enforcing the constitutional structure (allowing directors to run the company unimpaired by factions among the shareholders) and protecting minority shareholders against genuinely fraudulent transactions. Eventually a statutory remedy was introduced (CA 2006, s 994 and CA 2006, Part 11) to make it easier for shareholders to bring an action. Additionally the CLRSG and the Government have been keen to encourage companies to use forms of Alternative Dispute Resolution for minority shareholder problems (see Chapter 11).

1.26 Thus, while the company is designed as an investment vehicle, with limited liability for its shareholders and a clear organisational structure, it is designed for ventures where there is an effective separation of ownership from control and thus has been largely unsuitable for the majority of its users who are small businesses. Even given the reforms in the CA 2006 and over the last decade or more, which focus more on small business needs, in many ways the partnership would be more suitable for our entrepreneur and less onerous for small businesses generally, especially given that limited liability is rarely a reality for these types of business. The removal in 2002 of the 20-partner limit has certainly enhanced the capital-raising ability of the general partnership. However, the continued use of the corporate form by small companies seems secure given the prestige attached to the tag 'Ltd'.

FURTHER READING

This chapter links with the materials in Chapters 1, 2, and 7 of **Hicks and Goo's Cases and Materials on Company Law** (Oxford, OUP, 2011, xl +649p).

Company Law Reform (Cm 6456, 2005) (Consultative Document, March 2005), ch 5, http://webarchive.nationalarchives.gov.uk/+/http:/www.dti.gov.uk/cld/WhitePaper.pdf.

Davies and Worthington, Gower and Davies' Principles of Modern Company Law, 10th edn (Sweet & Maxwell, 2016), Part 1: Introductory 1.2–1.13: Types and Functions of Companies.

Freedman, 'Small Businesses and the Corporate Form: Burden or Privilege?' [1994] MLR 555.

Freedman and Godwin, 'Incorporating the Micro Business: Perceptions and Misperceptions' in Hughes and Storey (eds) Finance and the Small Firm (London, Routledge, 1994).

Henning, 'The Company Law Reform Bill, Small Businesses and Private Companies' [2006] 27 Co Law 97.

Modern Company Law for a Competitive Economy: Final Report (2001), chs 2 and 4, http://webarchive.nationalarchives.gov.uk/+/http://www.dti.gov.uk/cld/final_report/prelims.pdf.

Modernising Company Law (Cm 5553, 2002), Part II, http://webarchive.nationalarchives.gov.uk/+/http://www.dti.gov.uk/companiesbill/prelims.pdf.

SELF-TEST QUESTIONS

1   Compare and contrast the various forms of business organisation discussed in this chapter.

2   Why has the partnership fallen out of use by small businesses?

2 Corporate personality and limited liability

SUMMARY

Introduction
Corporate personality
Salomon and the logic of limited liability
Some other good examples of the consequence of separate personality
Members, shareholders, and the ownership of the corporation

Introduction

2.1 In this chapter we explore the concept of separate corporate personality and the related issue of limited liability. These concepts are at the core of company law. A good understanding of them is essential to understanding what company law is about. Unfortunately, the metaphysical nature of corporate personality in particular often caused difficulties for students. Our advice here is to read the first section on corporate personality. If you feel you have grasped the concept then move on to the rest of the chapter and the rest of the book. If you have read the corporate personality section and don't understand it, relax, breathe deeply, take some time to think about it but when you feel able—read the section again. Don't worry if you have lots of questions about corporate personality—many of the questions will be answered in the following section on limited liability—all you need at this stage is an understanding that the company has a tangible existence within our legal system and will be treated as having rights and obligations just like you and I.

Corporate personality

2.2 Human beings are generally legal persons—that is, they are subject to the legal system in which they find themselves. While that legal system imposes obligations on the legal person it also confers rights. When dealing with humans who are legal persons we have little difficulty with the concept, generally viewing them as one and the same. This is however incorrect and is often at the root of students' misunderstanding of corporate personality. Children for example, while they are human beings, are commonly excluded from having full legal personality until they cease being children. It is important for now if you are to understand legal personality to keep the human and the legal person separate. In essence humanity is a state of nature and legal personality is an artificial construct which may or may not be conferred (see, this is where the flexibility of mind we discussed in the preface comes in).

2.3 So, if humanity is not necessary for legal personality it follows that it is possible for legal personality to be conferred on non-humans. Some societies for example attribute legal personality to religious icons. The icon itself is therefore treated as having rights and obligations within the legal system. A logical extension of this separation of humanity from legal personality is that groups of humans who are engaged in a common activity could attempt to simplify their joint activity by gaining legal personality for the venture. This is the origin of the corporation.

2.4 The most successful groups to attain legal personality were religious orders. Their motive was relatively simple. If a religious order could obtain legal personality the complications that regularly arose when an abbot died, over the passing of the order's land to the new abbot, would fall away. The conferring of legal personality would mean that the religious order as a legal personality would hold the land in its own name and as it was not human and therefore not subject to weaknesses of the flesh, such as death, the death of an individual head of the order had no effect on the life or land of the legal personality of the order. As the main beneficiary of these land disputes with religious orders was the Crown (through death taxes levied on what the Crown deemed to be the abbot's lands), the conferring of legal personality was necessarily tied directly to a concession from the Crown, in the form of a charter or grant, 'incorporating' (from the Latin 'corpus' meaning body, so literally meaning to 'create a body') the order.

2.5 Over time the process of corporatisation through charters extended to local authorities and crucially commercial organisations such as Guilds of Merchants. The changing nature of the power relationship between Parliament and the Crown was also reflected in the way a charter was obtained. As Parliament became more powerful the grants had to be first confirmed by Parliament and eventually a charter could only be granted by an Act of Parliament. By the start of the 18th century there was an active market in the trading of shares in these companies. However a period of irrational speculation in these markets led to a stock market crash known as the South Sea Bubble (after the South Sea Company formed in 1711 and which became most associated with speculative behaviour). Clumsy attempts by the Government to intervene to check the speculative mood caused panic and led to the crash in which many investors were ruined. The Bubble had an enormous effect on the granting of charters over the following century because officials were very wary of granting them and when they did they often placed restrictive conditions in the grant.

2.6 This forced businesses to take things into their own hands and so the use of the trust as an instrument to confer many of the privileges of incorporation became commonplace. Over time these unincorporated 'deed of settlement' companies became instruments through which fraud was easily committed and the Government was forced to intervene. After a number of ineffectual attempts at statutory intervention Parliament passed a series of statutes that to this day still form the framework of company law in the UK. The Joint Stock Companies Act 1844 provided for incorporation by simple registration, provided safeguards against fraud by insisting on full publicity, and provided a Registrar of Companies to hold the public documents provided by the companies.

2.7 One problem remained—the Act of 1844, while it conferred corporate status, still held members liable for the company's debts. (You will encounter the terms 'member' and 'shareholder' throughout this and other texts as well as the case law and the Companies Acts. It is important to note that shareholders are also members and members are shareholders of the company. The use of the word 'member' emphasises that not only do members provide capital to the company, they also have rights and obligations to the company and to each other over the life of the company, just as 'members' of a swimming club or football club have rights and obligations to the club and its other members, see further in para **2.33**.) This remained a problem as charter companies and deed of settlement companies had achieved limitations on members' liability. In the case of charter companies this was through the Act that granted them and in the case of deed of settlement companies it was through its legal complexity.

2.8 The logical follow-on from the creation of a separate legal personality is that it is just that, a separate legal personality capable potentially of suing and being sued in its own name, of holding property in its own name, and logically, therefore, of making profits and losses that are its own and not those of its members (shareholders). This issue which should be framed as the 'no liability' issue was framed rather in terms of 'limited liability' (shareholders' liability would be limited to the unpaid amount of their shares) because that was the mechanism already used for charter companies under previous Acts of Parliament.

2.9 Note here that we need to be careful with these concepts, separate legal personality and limited liability are not the same thing—limited liability is the logical consequence of the existence of a separate personality. However, just as humans can have restrictions imposed on their legal personality (for example, children, the mentally ill, or foreign nationals) a company can have legal personality without limited liability if the statute confers it in that way (this is still possible today by forming a registered unlimited company (CA 2006, s 3(4))).

2.10 It was not until the Limited Liability Act 1855 (the provisions of which were almost immediately subsumed into the Joint Stock Companies Act 1856) that limited liability was provided, as well as a simplification of the registration requirements for incorporation. Thus whenever anyone deals with a limited company in the UK they are met with the warning; 'Ltd' in the case of a private company or 'PLC' for a public company attached to the company's name to signify that the members of this company have limited liability. In other words they are not liable for the debts of the company—so be careful.

2.11   Note here that the 'Ltd' or 'PLC' refers only to the members' liability and not that of the company. The company itself is liable for its debts but once its assets are exhausted the creditors cannot go after the members' assets. Remember that the legal personality of the members and the company are separate. The corporate assets belong to the company and the members' assets are their own.

2.12   Until the Joint Stock Companies Act 1856 the corporation had been the privilege of large-scale business ventures and those with influence in Parliament or at the Royal Court. From this point onward the company somewhat unexpectedly became a viable form of business organisation for all types and size of business venture. As a result company law emerged as a distinct and important area of law. This was partly because despite humanity not being an essential requirement for legal personality most law is designed for application to humans and that became a problem in need of a solution. Companies are not human, they need to act through humans and so accommodations had to be made to agency principles, fiduciary and statutory obligations, and rights. Occasionally where no accommodation could be made, specific statutory intervention aimed at regulating the corporation was necessary. Thus, for the past 160 years or so as the company has grown in economic importance, so too has the body of law we call company law.

Salomon and the logic of limited liability

2.13   The ease with which business ventures could get access to corporate status created an unexpected problem. Small businesses began to avail themselves of the corporate form. These small businesses were far from the large-scale ventures envisaged by the framers of the 19th-century companies legislation and so a question as to their legitimacy remained. It was only a matter of time before the courts would be called to decide on their legitimacy.

Salomon v Salomon & Co (1897)

2.14   Mr Salomon carried on a business as a leather merchant. In 1892 he formed the company Salomon & Co Ltd, Mr Salomon, his wife, and five of his children holding one share each in the company. The members of the family did not intend taking an active role in the business but rather only held the shares because the Companies Acts required at that time that there be seven shareholders. Mr Salomon was also the managing director. If we freeze things at this point it is important to note that Mr Salomon had two businesses. One is the original sole trading shoe business. The other is the newly registered company which has seven shareholders and Mr Salomon as managing director. What Mr Salomon did next is crucial to our understanding of the implications of corporate personality and limited liability. The newly incorporated company purchased the sole trading leather business.

2.15   Note that the reality of this transaction was that Mr Salomon the sole trader negotiated a purchase price with Mr Salomon the managing director of Salomon and Co Ltd. As a result the price Mr Salomon the managing director paid for the shoe business was a little on the high side. The business was valued by Mr Salomon at £39,000; this was not an attempt at a real valuation but what Mr Salomon seemed to think it was worth. This was however a fantastical amount for a shoe and boot business in the east end of London—the equivalent in today's prices of £3,464,426.97 using the retail price index to calculate back to 1892. After all, who was Mr Salomon, managing director, to argue? However, the real genius of Mr Salomon was in the way he structured the transaction. The price was paid in £10,000 worth of debentures giving a charge over all the company's assets, £20,000 in £1 shares and £9,000 cash. Mr Salomon also at this point paid off all the creditors of the sole trading business in full. Mr Salomon thus was the vast majority shareholder with 20,001 shares and his family holding the six remaining shares. Additionally, because of the debenture, he was a secured creditor which is also very important.

2.16   A debenture is simply a document creating or evidencing a debt (see further, Chapter 6). In company law however the agreements tend to be fairly complex. If a company needs a loan but a bank or other lender has some concern about the company's ability to repay they can create a debenture which secures the debt in two possible ways. First, a fixed charge could be created conferring an interest in or over an asset of the company. If the company breaches the terms of the debenture then the lender can take the asset and sell it to pay off the debt owed. A normal house mortgage is an example of a common fixed charge. The bank agrees to lend a prospective buyer the money to buy a house only if the buyer agrees to pay the money back over a certain period of time plus a certain interest rate. The buyer also agrees to restrictions on their power to sell the house and that if they fail to pay the money back as agreed the bank can take the house and sell it to pay off the debt. Similarly, if a company has fixed assets like property or machinery then it can do the same. In general the debenture holder has contractual rights against the company but if the transaction is secured it also creates rights in the corporate property. Note this is something that shareholders do not have (see paras **2.30** onwards).

2.17   Certain companies however may not have fixed assets (or they may already have fixed charges in place but need to borrow more) but because of the nature of their business they have valuable moveable assets. Any retail business will have moveable assets (its stock, for example) that are valuable. This brings us to our second type of secured lending—the floating charge. Over time lenders met the needs of these businesses with valuable stock by accepting a charge over a class of assets. So a retail outlet could get a loan from a bank secured by a charge over all its stock. This type of charge is necessarily more flexible as the company needs to be able to sell the stock and replace it as needs be. This is after all the core of its business. Thus there can be nothing in the debenture restricting sale of the assets. This is why it is described as secured over a class of assets; it can't be secured over a specific asset as they are constantly changing. If the company does breach the debenture agreement the charge is said to 'crystallise' and it fixes upon the specific assets in the stockroom. At this point the company cannot sell any of the assets. A floating charge is a less secure type of lending because the lender has no way of knowing whether the assets left in the stockroom when the charge 'crystallises' will cover the debt owed. The lender will compensate for this additional risk by charging a higher rate of interest (see further Chapter 6).

2.18   Returning now to Mr Salomon. While on the ground almost nothing about the shoe trading business had changed except the sign outside containing the word 'Ltd', legally everything had changed. Before the change in legal status the customers and suppliers contracted with Mr Salomon the sole trader, who was liable for all the debts of the company. After incorporation and the sale of the business to Salomon and Co Ltd the customers and suppliers contracted with the company through its managing director, Mr Salomon (same face, different personality). Mr Salomon's personal liability for the debts of the business had changed completely from unlimited liability as a sole trader to limited liability as a shareholder in the company. Not only was Mr Salomon not liable for the debts of the company but as managing director of the company he had also granted himself a secured charge over all the company's assets. Thus, if the company failed not only would Mr Salomon have no liability for the debts of the company but whatever assets were left would be claimed by him in satisfaction of his debt.

2.19   You may sense already, given that more than 120 years later he is featuring in a company law text, that things did not go to plan for Mr Salomon. Almost immediately after the change in the legal status of the business the company had trading difficulties and Mr Salomon had to sell his debenture to raise money for the business. This just delayed the inevitable and after only a year trading as Salomon and Co Ltd the debenture holder enforced the security over the assets of the company and the company was placed into insolvent liquidation. However, there were not enough assets left to pay off all the creditors and so the debenture holder, Mr Broderip, sought to challenge the validity of the transaction to convert the legal status of the business into a company and sought to make Mr Salomon personally liable for the debts of the company.

2.20   Mr Broderip alleged that the company was but a sham and a mere 'alias' or agent for Mr Salomon. The Court of Appeal upheld this claim and in doing so they looked at the motives of the promoters (Mr Salomon) and the members (Mr Salomon and his family) of the company. The focus of the Court of Appeal's concern was that the six family members never intended to take a part in the business and only held the shares to fulfil a technicality required by the Companies Acts. Kay LJ considered that:

> [t]he statutes were intended to allow seven or more persons, bona fide associated for the purpose of trade, to limit their liability under certain conditions and to become a corporation. But they were not intended to legalise a pretended association for the purpose of enabling an individual to carry on his own business with limited liability in the name of a joint stock company.

2.21 Mr Salomon was thus liable to indemnify the company against its trading debts. Mr Salomon appealed to the House of Lords and at this point the liquidator of Salomon and Co Ltd (an official appointed by the court to carry out the statutory liquidation process, in effect to see what assets are left and divide them up among the creditors. This may also involve taking or defending legal actions—see Chapter 17) took over the litigation from Mr Broderip on behalf of the general body of creditors. The House of Lords unanimously reversed the Court of Appeal decision. It held that the company was validly formed according to the Companies Acts which only required that there be seven members, holding one share each. There was nothing in the Act about bona fides. The motives of the shareholders were irrelevant unless there was fraud involved. The business thus belonged to the company and not to Salomon. Salomon was an agent of the company, not the company his agent. In giving his reasons for overturning the decision of the Court of Appeal, Lord Macnaghten stated:

> [t]he company is at law a different person altogether from the subscribers . . .; and, though it may be that after incorporation the business is precisely the same as it was before, and the same persons are managers, and the same hands receive the profits, the company is not in law the agent of the subscribers or trustee for them. Nor are the subscribers, as members liable, in any shape or form, except to the extent and in the manner provided by the Act.

2.22 The importance of the case lies in the consequences which flow from the decision. First, the fact that some of the shareholders are only holding shares as a technicality is irrelevant, the machinery of the Companies Acts may be used by an individual to carry on what is in economic reality his business. This also had the less obvious effect of facilitating investment in large companies where shareholders could purchase shares for speculative purposes safe in the knowledge that participation in the company was not a prerequisite for limited liability. Second, a company formed in compliance with the regulations of the Companies Acts is a separate person and not per se the agent or trustee of its controller. Third, the use of debentures instead of shares can further protect investors.

2.23 It is worthwhile reading both the Court of Appeal and the House of Lords' decisions. The contrast in their positions is stark. The Court of Appeal took a more moralistic approach to the case before it and was clearly disturbed at the individual avoidance of responsibility for one's debts. This is odd given that there was no doubt that large businesses could have limited liability or even seven persons who formed to '*bona fide*' associate and run a business. They seem however uncomfortable with this position in the context of an effective one-person company. In effect they think it amounts to a fraud in that they use the words 'defeated', 'defraud', 'pretended', 'mischief', 'perverting', and 'cheating' to describe Mr Salomon's activities. They place the emphasis on what they see as the combined bad faith of the nominee members and the overvaluation and are of the view that if Parliament had intended one-person nominee companies it would have said so and not specified seven members. The House of Lords on the other hand restricted itself to asking if the Act was complied with. The Act required seven members—the company had seven members—therefore the company was validly formed and the protections of the Companies Acts would apply. They also seemed to have a more favourable view of Mr Salomon. It is also worth noting that neither the Court of Appeal nor the House of Lords could refer to the parliamentary reports (Hansard) to see what Parliament intended, as the courts were forbidden from doing this until *Pepper v Hart* (1993). Had they been able to do so they would have found that in fact the seven-member requirement had been chosen to avoid its use by very small businesses. In other words the Court of Appeal was right in its assumption.

2.24 Clearly Mr Salomon had been clever in understanding the implication of the registration requirements of the Companies Acts but it is the nominal family shareholding and the transaction to sell the sole trading concern that cause the disquiet. This concern has little to do with the formation procedures of the Companies Acts but rather the fact that Mr Salomon owned (both directly and through nominees) and controlled both businesses. It is his exercise of control combined with his claim to limited liability that is at the heart of the case. If it were a large company in which he was a small shareholder there would be no problem. It is his ownership and control of the business that causes the challenge to the validity of the formation of the company and the Court of Appeal to find Mr Salomon liable.

2.25 In a way, although the two decisions are starkly different the outcomes may be attributable both to what part of Mr Salomon's behaviour is emphasised and the court's view of its role. On the one hand, the overvaluation of the business seems outrageous, but on the other Mr Salomon used the cash part of the transaction to pay off the sole trading concern's existing creditors. Thus the creditors at the time of the liquidation had only ever dealt with the business as a company and were not in any way victims of some unseen switch. Mr Salomon had also sold his debenture in order to keep the business going. In the end the House of Lords tended to view the overvaluation in a less harsh light than the Court of Appeal, Lord Macnaghten describing it as 'a sum which represented the sanguine expectations of a fond owner rather than anything that can be called a businesslike or reasonable estimate of value'. Had Mr Salomon not paid off his creditors and put his own money into the company in a futile attempt to keep it going, the House of Lords' view of Mr Salomon's behaviour might have been very different, as would the subsequent history of company law. Additionally the Court of Appeal and the House of Lords seem to be engaged in very different analytical pursuits. The Court of Appeal is partly attempting to work out what Parliament intended with its seven-member requirement while the House of Lords takes the view that it is simply to obey the will of Parliament, i.e. seven means seven.

2.26   From this point on the separateness of the corporate personality from its members became firmly embedded as a principle of British company law. In particular it had time to become embedded because until the House of Lords changed the rules under which it operated in 1966 it was not possible for the House of Lords to overrule itself. Therefore any attempts to strike at the principle were tangential and exceptional. After that time however, as we shall see in Chapter 3, the guarantee of separateness became less assured.

Some other good examples of the consequence of separate personality

Lee v Lee's Air Farming (1961)

2.27   Mr Lee incorporated a company, Lee's Air Farming Limited, in August 1954. The nominal capital of the company was £3,000 divided into 3,000 shares of £1 each. Mr Lee held 2,999 shares, the final share being held by a solicitor for Mr Lee because the New Zealand Companies Act required two shareholders. Mr Lee was also the sole 'governing director' for life. Thus, as with Mr Salomon, he was in essence a sole trader who now operated through a corporation. Mr Lee was also specifically appointed as an employee in the company's articles of association which stated:

> *33. The company shall employ the said Geoffrey Woodhouse Lee as the chief pilot of the company at a salary of £1,500 per annum from the date of incorporation of the company and in respect of such employment the rules of law applicable to the relationship of master and servant shall apply as between the company and the said Geoffrey Woodhouse Lee.*

2.28   Mr Lee therefore wore three hats as far as the company was concerned. He was the vast majority shareholder, he was the sole governing director for life, and he was an employee of the company. In March 1956, while Mr Lee was working, the company plane he was flying, stalled and crashed. Mr Lee was killed in the crash leaving a widow and four infant children who were totally dependent on him.

2.29   The company as part of its statutory obligations had been paying an insurance policy to cover claims brought under the Workers' Compensation Act 1922. The widow claimed she was entitled to compensation under the Act as the widow of a 'worker'. The issue went first to the New Zealand Court of Appeal who found that he was not a 'worker' within the meaning of the Act and so no compensation was payable. The case was appealed to the Privy Council in London. They emphasised that the company and Mr Lee were distinct legal entities and therefore capable of entering into legal relations with one another. As such they had entered into a contractual relationship for him to be employed as the chief pilot of the company. They found that he could in his role of governing director give himself orders as chief pilot. It was therefore a master and servant relationship and so he fitted the definition of 'worker' under the Act. The widow was therefore entitled to compensation.

Macaura v Northern Assurance Co (1925)

2.30 Mr Macaura was the owner of the Killymoon estate in County Tyrone. In December 1919 he agreed to sell to the Irish Canadian Saw Mills Ltd all the timber, both felled and standing, on the estate in return for the entire issued share capital of the company, to be held by himself and his nominees. He also granted the company a licence to enter the estate, fell the remaining trees, and use the sawmill. By August 1921, the company had cut down the remaining trees and passed the timber through the mill.

2.31 The timber, which represented almost the entire assets of the company, was then stored on the estate. On 6 February 1922 a policy insuring the timber was taken out in the name of Mr Macaura. On 22 February a fire destroyed the timber on the estate. Mr Macaura then sought to claim under the policy he had taken out. The insurance company contended that he had no insurable interest in the timber as the timber belonged to the company and not Mr Macaura. The case passed through the Northern Ireland court system, during which time allegations of fraud were made against Mr Macaura but never proven. Eventually in 1925 the issue arrived before the House of Lords who, agreeing with the insurance company, found that the timber belonged to the company and that Mr Macaura even though he owned all the shares in the company had no insurable interest in the property of the company. Lord Wrenbury, agreeing with the insurance company's contention, stated that a member:

> even if he holds all the shares is not the corporation and . . . neither he nor any creditor of the company has any property legal or equitable in the assets of the corporation.

Just as corporate personality facilitates limited liability by having the debts belong to the corporation and not the members it also means that the company's assets belong to it and not the shareholders. Thus corporate personality can be a double-edged sword.

Members, shareholders, and the ownership of the corporation

2.32 You may at this point, having read the synopsis of the *Macaura* decision, be somewhat confused about what exactly a share in a company is. Didn't Mr Macaura effectively just swap the timber for the shares? Aren't the shares just a paper representation of the timber given that they are worth the same amount? So, if he sold 10 per cent of the shares wouldn't they be worth 10 per cent of the value of the timber? These are all good questions the answers to which we will explore in the following section.

2.33 As we briefly discussed in the first section of this chapter, the words 'member' and 'shareholder' are used interchangeably in company law. The word shareholder in particular can be misleading because it seems to imply that a shareholder owns a share of the company. Additionally, newspapers often refer unhelpfully to shareholders as the 'owners' of the company. In one sense this is correct as a shareholder does own a share of the participation rights in the company (right to vote, attend meetings, participate in a dividend etc) but shareholders do not own a share of the company's property. It may be better for your own understanding at this point therefore to use the term 'member' rather than shareholder because it conveys a better sense of their rights and obligations.

2.34 Let us take the example of a swimming club of which you are a member. You have certain rights to participate in the club. An obvious right would be the use of the swimming pool but you may also have voting rights to elect members of the committee to run the club. If another member breaks the rules of the club you can complain to the management committee who will enforce the rules and may even punish the other member. You do not, however, as a member of the swimming club own a part of the club's property. You may swim in lane number 4 twice a day every day but in no way do you own all or part of lane number 4. This is the case even if you work out that your expensive membership fee is exactly equivalent to the value of one lane in the swimming pool.

2.35 The same is roughly true where you are a member of a company. As a member you have shares in the company which entitle you to participate in the company as a member. As such you have such entitlements as are conferred on members by the Companies Acts and the articles of association. Broadly these are rights to information, attendance at meetings, voting, and dividends if there are any.

Dispersed shareholdings

2.36 A further complication for our understanding of membership of a company occurs where the shares become easily transferable. If there is a ready market for shares (for example, where a company is listed on the stock exchange) then a value can easily be attributed to the rights attached to a share in a company. When this is done there is a connection (it is not a legal one) between the assets of the company and a share in the company. The following example will hopefully illustrate this.

2.37 M plc is a listed company, that is, its shares are traded on the stock exchange (see Chapter 5). It has 10 million shares in circulation with a nominal value of £1 each. The shares trade today on the stock exchange at £2 each. How can there be such a difference between the nominal value of the shares and the market value? Note that the nominal or par value of the shares refers only to the value attributed to them to achieve a convenient subdivision of the share capital. That price represents only the minimum price they can be issued for and may or may not be the price they actually were issued for (see Chapter 7 and Chapter 8). For the following example however let us assume that the nominal value and the issue price are the same. As we will see there is no necessary connection between the assets of the company and the value of the shares but for our purposes here let us say that on the day the company issued the shares the assets of the company were equal to £10 million. That is, the only asset of the company was the capital contributed by the shareholders. The following is a short hypothetical trading history of the company.

Year one

1 May: M plc issues 10 million shares at a nominal value of £1 each and the directors issue a statement that the capital is to be used to fund an organic farming venture. The company's assets = £10 million.

2 May: M plc shareholders begin to sell shares on the stock exchange at £1.10. The shares rise as the market likes the idea of investing in organic farming. Nominal value of shares £1. The company's assets = £10 million. Economic value of shares if all sold today at market price = £11 million.

Year two

The shares have traded in the range of £1.10–£1.20 all the previous year.

2 January: A new managing director is appointed to M plc who announces that the company will sell its organic business and invest the proceeds in a high-tech venture to develop fuel cells for cars. The shares' price shoots up to £2 as the market likes the dynamic new managing director and his ideas. Nominal value of shares £1. The company's assets = £11 million after the sale of the organic farm. Economic value of shares if all sold today at market price = £20 million.

3 June: A similar company developing fuel cells announces that its first test of its prototype fuel cell has failed. M plc shares crash to £1.50. Nominal value of shares £1. The company's assets after initial investment in fuel cells = £9 million. Economic value of shares if all sold today at market price = £15 million.

Year three

The shares have slowly floated down to trade at 80p as no news emerges as to progress on fuel cells.

5 April: Managing director's new enormous salary is announced causing outraged shareholders to sell their shares. The market price goes to 75p. Nominal value of shares £1.

The company's assets after more investment in fuel cells = £5 million. Economic value of shares if all sold today at market price = £7.5 million.

6 July: Government announces that it will provide funding for companies to develop solar power initiatives and not fuel cells. The market price of M plc crashes to 25p. Nominal value of shares £1. The company's assets decline with expenditure to = £4.5 million. Economic value of shares if all sold today at market price = £2.5 million.

10 September: A rumour goes around that Z Ltd has spotted that the economic value of the shares of M plc is less than its asset value and intends to buy up all the shares in the company and sell off all the assets. Market price goes to 30p. Nominal value of shares £1. The company's assets = £4.3 million. Economic value of shares if all sold today at market price = £3 million.

20 September: No bid emerges and the share price goes back to 25p. The company's assets = £4.2 million. Economic value of shares if all sold today at market price = £2.5 million.

2.38 As we can see from the example of M plc the asset value of the company is just a small part of the equation that determines market price. Many factors affect the price others will pay, including managerial skill, assets, corporate strategy, similar companies' share price fluctuations, rumours, general economic conditions, government intervention etc. What is being traded is not a paper representation of a percentage of the assets of the company owned by the shareholders. Shareholders do not own any of the company's property. When they trade shares they are trading a bundle of rights that someone else thinks may grow in value or provide them with income (through dividend payments from the company) or both.

2.39 To add an additional layer of complexity, although our most visible companies have transferable shares listed on the stock exchange, the vast majority of companies in the UK are private companies. Private companies as we noted in Chapter 1 commonly restrict the right of members to transfer shares. As a result the right to sell your shares is not even a common feature of the bundle of rights that attaches to a share.

2.40 It is important to note that one of the rights that is part of the bundle that a share represents is the right to participate in a dividend. Dividends are normally paid at the discretion of the board of directors. If in any year the board decide that not only have they enough money to finance their plans for the future but they have some left over they may distribute it to the shareholders as dividends. This is a payment made of, say, 10p per share.

2.41 Note here that the value attached to the share in the marketplace has no effect on the bundle of rights itself. The fact the rights are worth more now than a year ago does not mean the rights have grown or altered in any way. For example suppose that two years ago I bought ten shares in a company at £1 a share and a year later I bought ten more at

£5 a share. The company then declared a dividend of 10p a share. I have 20 shares and so will receive £2 as dividends. The fact I paid five times as much for half my shares does not affect the rights I paid for. So I don't get paid five times the dividend of the £1 shares or get five times the votes. It is the same with most appreciating assets. One example is if you bought a house for £100,000 two years ago and it is now worth £120,000. The rights you enjoy over the property have not increased by 20 per cent. Your enjoyment of living in the house has not increased by 20 per cent (OK maybe you enjoy it 10 per cent more because you just made £20,000 in two years). The point is that the rights attached to the property have not increased at all even though the market value of those rights has.

Close companies

2.42 Small one- or two-person companies can also cause confusion here. As with Mr Macaura, if there is only one shareholder then he owns all the control rights in the company and therefore entirely controls the assets of the company. If he entirely controls the assets of the company does he not own the company and its assets? Aren't the shareholders generally considered the owners of the company?

2.43 Here we have to rely on your understanding of corporate personality. The separate personality that is the company is controlled by its constitutional organs, the board or general meeting and not by individual board or individual general meeting members. While the board has the day-to-day control function, the organ that elects the board is the general meeting. The general meeting however acts collectively, so even though there is only one shareholder he or she makes decisions to elect the board through the general meeting. Thus Mr X the sole shareholder in X Ltd exercises his votes at a general meeting of the company in favour of his chosen directors. It is not however Mr X who appoints the directors, it is deemed that they were appointed by the general meeting.

2.44 Throughout company law you will find an emphasis on the exercise of collective shareholders' rights and a reluctance (it does sometimes recognise that the shareholder collective needs tempering) to acknowledge anything other than the shareholder collective. For example the board owe a duty to promote the success of the company (CA 2006, s 172), meaning broadly the members in general meeting. They do not owe the duty to the majority shareholder but rather to the shareholders as a whole (see Chapter 14). This focus on the company acting through its constitutional organs can, as we explained in Chapter 1, have detrimental effects for minority shareholders. Another example you may remember from your study of Tort is the decision in *Caparo v Dickman* (1990) that individual shareholders who rely on the audited accounts to buy more shares in the company cannot recover for loss based on this reliance if the accounts turn out to be incorrect (these are the audited accounts that are sent to every shareholder). Only the company can get damages from the auditor for such a negligent act. In traditional company law theory the focus of the company's activities is the shareholders as a collective (see Chapter 15 for an overview of corporate theory).

2.45 While there are advantages to the primacy of the shareholder collective such as encouraging risk capital, clarity of focus, and authority, increasingly other groups have begun to make strong claims to inclusion. Dissenting minority shareholders often have legitimate claims to ease oppression (see Chapters 10 and 11). Additionally employees, creditors, and the environment can be drastically affected by decisions of the company. These claims to inclusion in the focus of company law have over the recent decades become part of what is known as the 'stakeholder' debate (see Grantham (1998) on the tensions between the traditional doctrinal position and stakeholder theory). While we deal with this development in detail in Chapters 15 and 16, for now you should be aware that stakeholder theory has increasingly gained legitimacy in company law reform circles, culminating in some 'stakeholder lite' provisions being included in the CLRSG's *Final Report* (see Annex C: Statement of Director's Duties) and the Company Law Reform Bill, Part 10, Chapter 2. These changes to the formulation of directors' duties were introduced into the Companies Act 2006 by way of s 172. This section maintains the focus of directors' duties firmly on the shareholders but allows 'enlightened' boards of directors to consider other 'stakeholder' concerns if they wish. The importance of this provision lies more in legitimising 'stakeholder' theory generally in the business world than in any concrete effects the provision will have on displacing shareholders as the main focus of corporate activity (see further Chapter 16).

FURTHER READING

This chapter links with the materials in Chapter 3 of **Hicks and Goo's Cases and Materials on Company Law** (Oxford, OUP, 2011, xl +649p).

Freedman and Finch, 'Limited Liability Partnerships: Have Accountants Sewn up the "Deep Pockets" Debate?' [1997] *JBL* 387.

Grantham, 'The Doctrinal Basis of the Rights of Company Shareholders' [1998] *CLJ* 554.

Ireland et al, 'The Conceptual Foundations of Modern Company Law' [1987] *JLS* 149.

Pettit, 'Limited Liability—A Principle for the 21st Century' [1995] *CLP* 124.

SELF-TEST QUESTIONS

1   Explain how the separate personality of the company facilitates limited liability.

2   Why is *Salomon* an important case?

3   Was justice done in the *Macaura* case?

4   Do shareholders own the company?

5   What determines the market price of a share?

3 Lifting the veil

SUMMARY

Introduction
Statutory examples
Veil lifting by the courts
Classical veil lifting, 1897–1966
The interventionist years, 1966–1989
Back to basics, 1989–present
Tortious liability
Parent company personal injury tortious liability
Commercial tort
The costs/benefits of limited liability

Introduction

3.1 You may not unnaturally wonder at this point what the phrase 'lifting the veil' is about. It refers to the situations where the judiciary or the legislature have decided that the separate personality of the company is not to be maintained and will be wholly or partly disregarded. The veil of incorporation is thus said to be lifted. The judiciary in particular seem to love using unhelpful metaphors to describe this process. In the course of reading cases in this area you will find the process variously described as 'lifting', 'peeping', 'penetrating', 'piercing', or 'parting' the veil of incorporation. In a nutshell, having spent the whole of the last chapter emphasising the separateness of corporate personality, we now turn to those situations where for various reasons that separateness is not maintained.

3.2 While some of the examples of veil lifting involve straightforward shareholder limitation of liability issues, many of the examples involve corporate group structures. As businesses became more adept at using the corporate form, group structures began to emerge. For example Z Ltd (the parent or holding company) owns all the issued share capital in three other companies—A Ltd, B Ltd, and C Ltd. These companies are known as wholly owned subsidiaries (see CA 2006, s 1159(2)). Z Ltd controls all three subsidiaries. In economic reality there is just one business but it is organised through four separate legal personalities. In effect this structure allows the legal personality of the parent company to avail itself of the advantages of limited liability. Thus if the parent conducts its more risky or liability-prone activities through A Ltd and things go wrong the assets of Z Ltd, because it is a shareholder of A Ltd with limited liability, in theory cannot be touched. In certain situations the legislature and the courts will not allow this to happen.

Statutory examples

3.3 The taxation authorities in the UK have been acutely aware of the potential for group structures to avoid taxation by moving assets and liabilities around the group. Thus, there are numerous examples of taxation legislation directed at ignoring the separate entities in the group. The Companies Act also recognises that group structures need to be treated differently for disclosure and financial reporting purposes in order to get a proper overview of the group financial position. The CA 2006, s 399 therefore provides that parent companies have a duty to produce group accounts. Section 409 also requires the parent to provide details of the subsidiaries' names, country of activity, and the shares it holds in the subsidiary.

3.4 The Employment Rights Act 1996 also protects employees' statutory rights when transferred from one company to another within a group, treating it as a continuous period of employment. Additionally, many of the situations where 'lifting the veil' is at issue involve corporate insolvency; the Insolvency Act 1986 has some key veil-lifting provisions. While we deal with these provisions in detail in Chapter 17, we briefly consider them here.

3.5 The Companies Acts have long recognised that the corporate form could be used for fraudulent purposes. Indeed, one of the reactions of Parliament to the *Salomon* decision was to introduce an offence of 'fraudulent trading'. This offence was continued in the 1948 Companies Act which contained both civil and criminal sanctions for fraudulent trading. While the CA 2006 still contains a criminal offence in s 993 for fraudulent trading, the civil provisions are now contained in ss 213–215 of the Insolvency Act 1986. It is these civil sanctions that operate to lift the corporate veil. Section 213 states:

> (1) *If in the course of the winding up of a company it appears that any business of the company has been carried on with intent to defraud creditors of the company or creditors of any other person, or for any fraudulent purpose, the following has effect.*

> (2) *The court, on the application of the liquidator may declare that any persons who were knowingly parties to the carrying on of the business in the manner abovementioned are to be liable to make such contributions (if any) to the company's assets as the court thinks proper.*

3.6 This section and its predecessor in the 1948 Act consistently proved difficult to operate in practice (see *Re Bank of Credit and Commerce International SA (No 14)* (2003)). The main difficulty was that there was the possibility of a criminal charge also arising. The courts therefore set the standard for intent fairly high. As the court explained in *Re Patrick and Lyon Ltd* (1933), this involved proving 'actual dishonesty, involving, according to current notions of fair trading among commercial men, real moral blame'. Reaching this standard was difficult and eventually a new provision was introduced in s 214 of the Insolvency Act 1986 to deal with what is known as 'wrongful trading'.

3.7 Section 214 was introduced to deal with situations where negligence rather than fraud is combined with a misuse of corporate personality and limited liability. In other words there was no need to prove dishonesty. This is known as 'wrongful trading'. Section 214 states:

> (1) ... if in the course of the winding up of a company it appears that subsection (2) of this section applies in relation to a person who is or has been a director of the company, the court, on the application of the liquidator, may declare that that person is to be liable to make such contribution (if any) to the company's assets as the court thinks proper.
>
> (2) This subsection applies in relation to a person if—
>
> > (a) the company has gone into insolvent liquidation,
> >
> > (b) at some time before the commencement of the winding up of the company, that person knew or ought to have concluded that there was no reasonable prospect that the company would avoid going into insolvent liquidation, and
> >
> > (c) that person was a director of the company at that time.

3.8 The idea behind the operation of the section is that at some time towards the end of the company's trading history there was a point of no return. That is, things were so bad the company could no longer trade out of the situation. A reasonable director should have recognised this and stopped trading at this point. If a director continued to trade after this point he risked having to contribute to the debts of the company. The case of *Re Produce Marketing Consortium Ltd (No 2)* (1989) is a good example of the way the section operates. Over a period of seven years the company had slowly drifted into insolvency. There was no suggestion of wrongdoing on the part of the two directors involved; it was just that they did not put the company into liquidation in time and thus they had to contribute £75,000 to the debts of the company (see also *Re Rod Gunner Organisation Ltd* (2004)).

3.9 While s 213 covers anyone involved in the carrying on of the business, thus qualifying the limitation of liability of members, s 214 is aimed specifically at directors. In small companies directors are often also the members of the company and so their limitation of liability is indirectly affected. Parent companies may also have their limited liability affected if they have acted as a shadow director. A shadow director is not a formally appointed director but rather anyone other than a professional adviser in accordance with whose directions or instructions the formally appointed directors of the company are accustomed to act (CA 2006, s 251 and SBEEA 2015, ss 89–91, see Chapter 13). A parent company might be in this position if it was exerting direct control over the board of its subsidiaries.

Veil lifting by the courts

3.10 Since the *Salomon* decision the courts have often been called upon to apply the principle of separate legal personality in what might be called difficult situations. In some cases they have upheld the principle and in others they have not. Over this time various attempts have been made at providing explanations for when the courts will lift the veil of incorporation; none however are really satisfactory. Some texts attempt to explain veil lifting by categories: where the company is an agent of another, where there is fraud, or tax issues, or employment issues, or a group of companies exists the courts will lift the veil. While it is possible to find examples of veil lifting in all these categories it is also possible to find examples of the courts upholding the separateness of companies in these categories. Others have attempted to categorise veil lifting by analysing the ways the judiciary have lifted the veil. Thus Ottolenghi (1990) offers categorisations such as: 'peeping', where the veil is lifted to get member information; 'penetrating', where the veil is disregarded and liability is attributed to the members; 'extending', where a group of companies is treated as one legal entity and; 'ignoring', where the company is not recognised at all. While these categorisations are interesting and useful for understanding how veil lifting has sometimes operated in the past they in no way offer a guide to how the courts will behave in a given situation in the future. The most accurate statement about this that can be made is that sometimes the courts lift the veil and sometimes they refuse to. It may be frustrating and unsatisfactory but that is the reality. Having said that, there have been periods where the courts were more inclined to uphold the veil of incorporation than not. Indeed in recent years both the Court of Appeal and the Supreme Court have reached new levels of obfuscation regarding veil lifting. By way of our own explanation we offer the following timeline which is intended as a general guide.

Classical veil lifting, 1897–1966

3.11 During this period the House of Lords decision in *Salomon* dominated. As we explained in Chapter 2, the House of Lords could not overrule itself during this period and this operated as a significant restraint on veil lifting. However, veil lifting did occur in exceptional circumstances during this period. The court for example in *Daimler Co Ltd v Continental Tyre and Rubber Co (Great Britain) Ltd* (1916) lifted the veil to determine whether the company was an 'enemy' during the First World War. As the shareholders were German, the court determined that the company was indeed an 'enemy'.

3.12 In *Gilford Motor Co Ltd v Horne* (1933) a former employee who was bound by a covenant not to solicit customers from his former employers set up a company to do so. The court found that the company was but a front for Mr Horne and issued an injunction. In *Jones v Lipman* (1962) Mr Lipman had entered into a contract with Mr Jones for the sale of land. Mr Lipman then changed his mind and did not want to complete the sale. He formed a company in order to avoid the transaction and conveyed the land to it instead. He then claimed he no longer owned the land and could not comply with the contract. The judge again found the company was but a façade and granted an order for specific performance. In *Re Bugle Press* (1961) majority shareholders in a company set up a second company in order to force a compulsory purchase of a minority shareholder's shares. The second company then made an offer for the shares in the first company and the majority share-holders accepted. As this meant that over 90 per cent of the shareholders had accepted, it therefore triggered a compulsory purchase of the minority shareholder's shares under the Companies Acts (see Chapter 5). The minority shareholder objected and the court prevented the transaction again as the second company was but a mere façade for the majority shareholders.

The interventionist years, 1966–1989

3.13 By the 1960s the courts were increasingly demonstrating a tendency to free themselves from old precedence they saw as increasingly unjust. In 1966 this tendency led the House of Lords to change the rules under which it had operated and allow it to change its mind and overrule itself. By 1969 Lord Denning seemed to be on a crusade to encourage veil lifting. In *Littlewoods Mail Order Stores v IRC* (1969) he stated:

> [t]he doctrine laid down in Salomon's *case has to be watched very carefully. It has often been supposed to cast a veil over the personality of a limited company through which the courts cannot see. But that is not true. The courts can, and often do, pull off the mask. They look to see what really lies behind. The legislature has shown the way with group accounts and the rest. And the courts should follow suit.*

3.14 In *DHN Food Distributors Ltd v Tower Hamlets* (1976) Denning argued that a group of companies was in reality a single economic entity and should be treated as one. Two years later the House of Lords in *Woolfson v Strathclyde Regional Council* (1978) specifically disapproved of Denning's views on group structures in finding that the veil of incorp-oration would be upheld unless it was a façade. However, Denning's views on the lifting of the corporate veil still had considerable effect. In *Re a Company* (1985) the Court of Appeal stated:

> [i]n our view the cases before and after Wallersteiner v Moir *[1974] 1 WLR 991 [another Lord Denning case]* show that the court will use its power to pierce the corporate veil if it is necessary to achieve justice irrespective of the legal efficacy of the corporate structure under consideration.

This represented probably the high point of the interventionist period where the courts seemed to treat the separate personality of the company as an initial negotiating position which could be overturned in the interests of justice.

3.15   There was however a growing disquiet about the uncertainty this brought to the concept of corporate personality and limited liability. As Lowry (1993) concluded:

> [t]he problem that can naturally arise from this approach is the uncertainty which it casts over the safety of incorporation. The use of the policy to erode established legal principle is not necessarily to be welcomed.

Similarly Gallagher and Ziegler (1990) in an examination of when the courts will lift the veil of incorporation at common law concluded that the lifting of the veil can have negative impacts on other aspects of the law such as directors' duty to the company as a whole, individual taxation principles, and the rule in *Foss v Harbottle* (1843). However, by the late 1980s the Court of Appeal in *National Dock Labour Board v Pinn and Wheeler Ltd* (1989) had moved firmly against a more interventionist approach at least where group structures were concerned. This was a foretaste of what was to come in the following decade.

Back to basics, 1989–present

3.16   In *Adams v Cape Industries Plc* (1990) the Court of Appeal took the opportunity to examine at great length the way the courts have lifted the veil of incorporation in the past and narrowed significantly the way in which the courts could do so in the future. The facts of the case were extremely complex and what follows is but a very simple version. The case concerned the enforcement of a foreign judgment in England. The key issue for the court was whether Cape Industries could be regarded as falling under the jurisdiction of a US court and therefore be subject to its judgment. This could only occur if Cape was present within the US jurisdiction or had submitted to such jurisdiction.

3.17   Until 1979, Cape, an English company, mined and marketed asbestos. Its worldwide marketing subsidiary was another English company, named Capasco. It also had a US marketing subsidiary incorporated in Illinois, named NAAC. In 1974, some 462 people sued Cape, Capasco, NAAC, and others in Texas, for personal injuries arising from the installation of asbestos in a factory. Cape protested at the time that the Texas court had no jurisdiction over it but in the end it settled the action. In 1978, NAAC was closed down by Cape and other subsidiaries were formed with the express purpose of reorganising the business in the USA to minimise Cape's presence there for taxation and other liability issues.

3.18 Between 1978 and 1979, a further 206 similar actions were commenced and default judgments were entered against Cape and Capasco (who again denied they were subject to the jurisdiction of the court but this time did not settle). In 1979 Cape sold its asbestos mining and marketing business and therefore had no assets in the USA. The claimants thus sought to enforce the judgments in England where Cape had most of its assets. At issue in the case was whether Cape was present in the US jurisdiction by virtue of its US subsidiaries. The only way that could be the case in the court's view was if it lifted the veil of incorporation, either treating the Cape group as one single entity, or finding the subsidiaries were a mere façade or that the subsidiaries were agents for Cape. The court exhaustively examined each possibility.

3.19 The court first examined the major 'single economic unit' cases where group structures were treated as being a single entity. It found that the cases all involved the interpretation of a statute or a document. They reached this conclusion even though the Denning judgment (which the Court of Appeal examined) in *DHN Food Distributors Ltd v Tower Hamlets* (1976) is clearly not based upon interpreting a statute or document. The court therefore rejected the argument that the Cape group should be treated as one, stating:

> save in cases which turn on the wording of particular statutes or contracts, the court is not free to disregard the principle of Salomon v A Salomon & Co Ltd [1897] AC 22 merely because it considers that justice so requires. Our law, for better or worse, recognises the creation of subsidiary companies, which though in one sense the creatures of their parent companies, will nevertheless under the general law fall to be treated as separate legal entities with all the rights and liabilities which would normally attach to separate legal entities.

3.20 The court then turned to what they termed the 'corporate veil' point. This category of veil lifting is exemplified by the case of *Jones v Lipman* (1962, see para **3.12**) and was, in the court's view, a well-recognised veil-lifting category. The Court of Appeal quoted with approval the words of Lord Keith in *Woolfson v Strathclyde Regional Council* (1978) where he described this exception as 'the principle that it is appropriate to pierce the corporate veil only where special circumstances exist indicating that it is a mere façade concealing the true facts'. In these special circumstances the motives of those behind the alleged façade could be very important. The court looked at the motives of Cape in structuring its US business through its various subsidiaries. It found that although Cape's motive was to try to minimise its presence in the USA for tax and other liabilities there was nothing wrong with this. The court concluded:

> [w]hether or not such a course deserves moral approval, there was nothing illegal as such in Cape arranging its affairs (whether by the use of subsidiaries or otherwise) so as to attract the minimum publicity to its involvement in the sale of Cape asbestos in

*the United States of America . . . we do not accept as a matter of law that the court is
entitled to lift the corporate veil as against a defendant company which is the member of
a corporate group merely because the corporate structure has been used so as to ensure
that the legal liability (if any) in respect of particular future activities of the group (and
correspondingly the risk of enforcement of that liability) will fall on another member of
the group rather than the defendant company. Whether or not this is desirable, the right
to use a corporate structure in this manner is inherent in our corporate law.*

3.21 The court then considered the 'agency' argument. This was a straightforward application
of agency principle. If it could be established that the subsidiary was Cape's agent and
acting within its actual or apparent authority then the actions of the subsidiary would
bind the parent. However, if there is no express agency agreement between the subsidiary
and the parent, establishing such an agency from their conduct is very hard to achieve. The
court found that the subsidiaries were independent businesses free from the day-to-day
control of the parent with no general power to bind the parent. Thus as none of the three
veil-lifting categories applied Cape was not present in the USA through its subsidiaries.

3.22 The judgment of the Court of Appeal in *Adams* leaves only three circumstances in which
the veil of incorporation can be lifted. The first is if the court is interpreting a statute or
document. This exception to maintaining corporate personality is qualified by the fact
that there has first to be some lack of clarity about a statute or document which would
allow the court to treat a group as a single entity. Some judges will be more enthusiastic
about finding such lack of clarity than others. Although the court is somewhat vague in
Adams on what they mean by this exception, the Court of Appeal in *Samengo-Turner v
J&H Marsh & McLennan (Services) Ltd* (2008) treated a group of companies as a single
legal entity on the basis of their single economic interest in interpreting the application of
an EU Regulation. Similarly in *Beckett Investment Management Group Ltd v Hall* (2007)
in interpreting a clause in an employment contract in the context of a group of companies
that formed a single economic entity the Court of Appeal considered that it was inappropriate to be inhibited by considerations of corporate personality.

3.23 Second, where 'special circumstances exist indicating that it is a mere façade concealing
the true facts' the courts may lift the veil of incorporation. In general, one can describe
these cases as the 'you know it when you see it' cases. These are decisions where there
is some injustice involved in maintaining the veil of incorporation, which was placed
there deliberately to facilitate the injustice complained of. *Jones v Lipman* (1962) is the
classic example. There Mr Lipman's sole motive in creating the company was to avoid the
transaction. We all know it would be morally wrong to maintain the separate personality
of Mr Lipman and the company. The judiciary have thus constructed the exception as 'a
mere façade concealing the true facts'. In determining that exception the motives of those
behind the alleged façade may be relevant. Cape however is confusing in the way the court
applied this exception. The court, although giving the example of *Jones v Lipman* (1962)
when examining Cape's motives, seems to recognise the moral culpability of Cape's
motive in creating the subsidiaries to minimise its liability in the USA when they state,

'[w]hether or not such a course deserves moral approval, there was nothing illegal as such in Cape arranging its affairs'. This seems a strange and confusing point for the court to make as Mr Lipman also did nothing illegal yet the exception applied there. Unfortunately the Court of Appeal offered no other guidance as to when this exception might apply.

3.24 The third exception is not really an exception to the *Salomon* principle but rather a straightforward application of agency principle. Therefore the question is just the same as it would be for two human beings—'have they entered into an express agency agreement or could an agency be implied from their conduct?' Parent companies and their subsidiaries are unlikely to have express agency agreements. They are even less likely to have express agreements if avoidance of liability was the reason for setting the subsidiary up in the first place, as it was in *Adams*. Proving an implied agency will also be very difficult as *Adams* sets the bar very high. An implied agency would need evidence that day-to-day control was being exercised over the subsidiary by the parent. Again, this is unlikely to be the case where liability limitation was one of the motives for forming the subsidiary. (For an interesting example of where a high level of control did attribute liability to a parent company, see *Millam v The Print Factory (London) 1991 Ltd* (2008).)

3.25 As you can see from this discussion, *Adams* significantly narrowed the ability of the courts to lift the veil of incorporation. Gone are the wild and crazy days when the Court of Appeal would lift the veil 'to achieve justice irrespective of the legal efficacy of the corporate structure' as it did in *Re a Company* (1985). The rest of the 1990s contained similar examples of the restrictive approach of *Adams* (for example, see *Yukong Lines Ltd of Korea v Rensburg Investments Corpn of Liberia* (1998)). However, there were also interesting aberrations one of which we now turn to examine.

Creasey v Breachwood Motors Ltd (1993)

3.26 The case concerned two companies Breachwood Welwyn Ltd and Breachwood Motors Ltd. The two companies had directors and shareholders in common. Mr Creasy had been dismissed from his post of general manager by Breachwood Welwyn Ltd and had issued a writ against Welwyn alleging wrongful dismissal. Shortly after this happened Welwyn ceased trading and its assets were transferred to Breachwood Motors Ltd. Breachwood Motors Ltd then took over and carried on the business of Breachwood Welwyn Ltd. In doing this they paid off Breachwood Welwyn Ltd's creditors but did not maintain or return assets to Breachwood Welwyn Ltd to enable it to meet its judgment debt to Mr Creasy. The wrongful dismissal action was not defended by Breachwood Welwyn Ltd and judgment was entered in default in favour of Mr Creasy and an order for £53,835 made against Breachwood Welwyn Ltd. A year later the company was struck off the companies register and dissolved. Mr Creasy successfully applied to have Breachwood Motors Ltd substituted as the defendant in order to enforce the judgment. Breachwood Motors Ltd appealed.

3.27 The judge in the case, Mr Richard Southwell QC, ignored the restrictive approach in *Adams* in finding that the central issue was that, with the benefit of solicitors' advice, the directors of

Breachwood Motors Ltd (who were also directors of Welwyn) had deliberately ignored the separate legal personalities of the two companies. They had transferred Breachwood Welwyn Ltd's assets and business to Breachwood Motors Ltd without regard to their duties as directors and shareholders. The court was justified therefore in lifting the corporate veil and treating Breachwood Motors Ltd as liable for Breachwood Welwyn Ltd's liability to Mr Creasy.

3.28 The case has caused considerable comment because of its maverick status and the novel nature of the rationale. The judge seems to suggest that when determining the façade exception it is not only the motives of those behind the alleged façade that may be relevant but also whether they have breached their duties as directors. Indeed, from the judgment it seems that the motives of the directors were irrelevant and that just the fact of a breach of duty was sufficient to justify lifting the veil. However, the Court of Appeal soon took the opportunity to overrule it.

Ord v Belhaven Pubs Ltd (1998)

3.29 Ord and Belhaven Pubs Ltd were engaged in a legal action about a lease. During the course of the action the group structure of which Belhaven Pubs Ltd was a part was reorganised because of a financial crisis within the group. As a result of the reorganisation Belhaven Pubs Ltd had no assets or liabilities and would therefore have nothing with which to pay any judgment against it. As the litigation regarding the lease was still continuing Ord applied to have the parent company of Belhaven Pubs Ltd substituted. The High Court judge who first heard the case allowed the substitution. The Court of Appeal however took the view that the reorganisation of the group was legitimate and not merely a façade to conceal the true facts. The assets were transferred at full value and the motive appeared to be the group's financial crisis rather than any ulterior motive. The court also took the opportunity to specifically overrule the judgment in *Creasey v Breachwood Motors Ltd* (1993).

3.30 Both the *Creasey* and *Ord* cases are illustrations of a classic veil-lifting issue, that of whether the reorganisation of the company was a legitimate business transaction or the motive was to avoid liability. If the motive was to avoid liability then according to the façade exception there was the possibility of lifting the veil. If the court takes the view that the veil should be lifted (and this is by no means certain as *Adams* takes a very strict view of the types of motives needed) then liability can flow to the parent company. Indeed, in *Kensington International Ltd v Congo* (2006) the court did hold that a dishonest transaction involving transfers between related companies was designed to avoid existing liabilities and was therefore a sham. The court then went on to lift the veil of incorporation.

Trustor AB v Smallbone (No 2) (2001)

3.31 During Smallbone's period as Trustor's managing director various sums of money had been transferred in breach of fiduciary duty from Trustor to another company owned and controlled by Smallbone. Trustor applied to the court to pierce the corporate veil so as to treat receipt by the second company as receipt by Smallbone on the grounds that:

the company had been a sham created to facilitate the transfer of the money in breach of duty; the company had been involved in the improper acts; and the interests of justice demanded such a result.

3.32 The court in an interesting judgment recognised the tension between some of the earlier cases and the *Adams* judgment but concluded that *Adams* was the greater authority. In deciding to lift the veil on the basis of the façade exception the Vice-Chancellor concluded:

> [c]ompanies are often involved in improprieties. Indeed there was some suggestion to that effect in Salomon v Salomon & Co Ltd [1897] AC 22. But it would make undue inroads into the principle of Salomon v Salomon & Co Ltd if an impropriety not linked to the use of the company structure to avoid or conceal liability for that impropriety was enough. In my judgment the court is entitled to 'pierce the corporate veil' and recognise the receipt of the company as that of the individual(s) in control of it if the company was used as a device or facade to conceal the true facts thereby avoiding or concealing any liability of those individual(s).

Here the Vice-Chancellor was faced with a clear case of an improper motive but in deciding to lift the veil he emphasises the connection between the impropriety and the use of the corporate structure. Just as in *Jones v Lipman* (1962) the corporation must be the 'device' through which the impropriety is conducted, impropriety alone will not suffice (see *R v K* (2006)). The type of action and remedy sought may also make a difference as to the court's willingness to lift the veil (see *Re Instant Access Properties Ltd; Secretary of State for Business, Innovation and Skills v Gifford* (2011)).

3.33 Png (1999) makes the point that these cases offer the judiciary the possibility of an interesting development in the façade exception. While *Jones v Lipman* (1962) makes it clear that forming a company as a mere façade will engage a lifting of the veil, there may also be the possibility that a company which was formed for legitimate purposes initially, but which subsequently becomes a façade, will also engage a lifting of the veil. In *Raja v Van Hoogstraten* (2006) the court, faced with a façade claim to lift the veil, emphasised that the dishonest construction of a group of companies to conceal ownership of assets and minimise liability could give rise to a lifting of the corporate veil. Interestingly, the court in *Raja* explicitly moves away from what it calls a 'narrow' reading of *Adams* to adopt an expansive approach which partly encompasses Png's point in finding that the dishonest construction of a group of companies might give rise to a court lifting the veil of incorporation even in relation to liabilities not envisioned by the creator of the sham companies.

3.34 In a number of more recent cases the courts tentatively suggest that a more 'realistic' view of group liability, akin to Lord Denning's original concept of single economic entity, may be appropriate rather than the Court of Appeal's view in *Adams*. In *Beckett Investment Management Group Ltd v Hall* (2007), for example, Maurice Kay LJ rejected what he called a 'purist' interpretation of corporate personality and went on to support Lord Denning's view of a single economic entity. As usual in this area things are rarely straightforward and so while the *Beckett* case indicates change from the strict propositions of the *Adams* era, we have also observed cases on similar issues emphasising the 'purist' approach. For example in *Millam v The Print Factory* (2008) control by a parent company did not justify veil lifting. Similarly in both *Ben Hashem v Ali Shayif* (2008) and *Linsen International Ltd v Humpuss Sea Transport Pte Ltd* (2011) the court specifically attacked the very idea of a single economic unit attributing liability. We seem to have moved back to some uncertainty in this important area (see also *Re Instant Access Properties Ltd; Secretary of State for Business, Innovation and Skills v Gifford* (2011) and *VTB Capital plc v Nutriteck International Corp* (2013)). As we will observe later, developments in the area of group tortuous liability are also moving in a Denning-esque direction with the decision in *Chandler v Cape Plc* (2012) to attribute tortious liability to a parent company, even though, as we will also note, the court claims it is not engaged in lifting or piercing the corporate veil.

3.35 Indeed, confusion hidden behind apparent clarity has become a feature of major decisions in the area over the past several years. None more notable than the Supreme Court decision in *Prest v Petrodel Resources Ltd* (2013). The case concerned ancillary financial relief following divorce proceedings. The central question in the case was whether Michael Prest was entitled to eight residential properties (one was the matrimonial home) owned by two companies in which he held effective controlling shareholdings. A Supreme Court, unusually made up of seven judges, unanimously concluded that the veil of incorporation could not be pierced in this circumstance given the absence of impropriety. The placing of the properties in the companies was unconnected with the breakdown of the marriage. Instead, they held that the properties of the companies should be transferred to Mrs Prest because they were held by the companies on a resulting trust for Mr Prest. The court or rather two of the judges in particular (Lords Sumption and Neuberger) went on to consider that there were very limited circumstances in which piercing the corporate veil will be an appropriate action:

> there is a limited principle of English law which applies when a person is under an existing legal obligation or liability or subject to an existing legal restriction which he deliberately evades or whose enforcement he deliberately frustrates by interposing a company under his control. The court may then pierce the corporate veil for the purpose, and only for the purpose, of depriving the company or its controller of the advantage that they would otherwise have obtained by the company's separate legal personality.

However, even between Lords Sumption and Neuberger there was uncertainty as to what exactly the principle or principles they were operating under amounted to. Additionally the other judges in *Prest* were not so sure as to the extent of its limiting effect or principles and so as the Court of Appeal in *Gramsci Shipping Corp v Lembergs* (2013) noted:

> As to further development of the law, doing so by classical common law techniques may not be easy. In Prest's case Lord Sumption (at [28]) identified two underlying principles which he called 'the concealment principle' and 'the evasion principle'. But Lord Neuberger was of the view (at [75] that there is a 'lack of any coherent principle in the

application of the doctrine of "piercing the corporate veil"', and Lord Walker's view (at
[106]) was that it is not a doctrine in the sense of a coherent principle or rule of law but
a label. Lady Hale (at [92]) was 'not sure whether it is possible to classify all of the cases
in which the courts have been or should be prepared to disregard the separate legal
personality of a company neatly into cases of either concealment or evasion'. Absent a
principle, further development of the law will be difficult for the courts because devel-
opment of common law and equity is incremental and often by analogical reasoning.

In keeping with the sentiment in *Gramsci Shipping* the evasion and concealment principles have subsequently been applied in *Pennyfeathers Ltd v Pennyfeathers Property Co
Ltd* (2013) and in *R v Sale* (2013), while in *Akzo Nobel NV v Competition Commission*
(2013) the court made the point in refusing to restrict its considerations to evasion and
concealment that only two of the judges in *Prest* seemed to agree with. The controversial status of Lord Sumption's principles are evident in the difference between the High
Court and the Court of Appeal decisions in *Rossendale BC v Hurstwood Properties (A) Ltd*
(2019). In the High Court Judge Hodge considered:

*In my judgment, the Claimant does have an arguable case on this particular ground.
The doctrine of piercing the corporate veil is a developing area of jurisprudence. I am not
satisfied that Lord Sumption's judgment was intended as an exhaustive statement of the
circumstances in which the court might disregard the corporate veil.*

In the Court of Appeal Lord Justice Richards recognized the different views of the
Supreme Court Judges in *Prest* and that other disregard categories were possible, albeit in
his view rare, but still declined to disregard the corporate form. As Allan commented '[i]
t seems that the radical approach taken in *Prest* has neither introduced doctrinal coherence nor checked the profligate use of metaphors to justify ignoring the corporate veil'.
That doctrinal incoherence may be resolved in the near future as the Supreme Court will
make the final decision in *Rossendale BC v Hurstwood Properties (A) Ltd* (2019) over the
course of 2021.

In effect it seems broadly that veil lifting is a limited exceptional action but we are not
really sure why. The *Prest* case is on the one hand a significant case in setting out the
limited circumstances in which veil lifting/piercing may occur in future; on the other
hand however, reading the judgments of Lords Neuberger and Sumption one enters a
world where apparently veil lifting/piercing has never occurred or at least not to their
satisfaction, despite the reality of its presence in the case law over the last century. All
this distracts of course from the central outcome of the *Prest* case, which is that a way
was found through a resulting trust to attribute ownership of the company's property
to its shareholder. In fact the outcome is just as if the veil was lifted/pierced. Indeed,
as we will observe with our discussion of tortious liability below, there has been a recent trend within significant veil-lifting/piercing cases to declare that lifting/piercing
is being emphatically rejected as a solution and then to find some other way to achieve
the same outcome.

Tortious liability

3.36 Many of the recent developments in veil lifting have involved claims of tortious liability. Indeed, tortious liability is one of the fault lines created by limited liability with one study of veil-lifting cases (Dignam and Oh (2019)) showing both that general context and particularly a tortious context matter as to whether a court will lift the veil of not. Normal trade creditors when dealing with a limited liability company have the opportunity to assess the risk of doing business. They can then opt to secure their lending, charge a premium for that risk, or do both. However, employees or members of the public (involuntary creditors) who may be at risk of the company causing them personal injury have no way of effectively mitigating that risk. Therefore, limited liability in cases where tortious liability for personal injury is at issue can allow parent companies to avoid liability without providing any compensation.

3.37 This particular problem was recognised by the CLRSG in its preliminary deliberations (*Modern Company Law for a Competitive Economy: Completing the Structure*, Ch 10). In that chapter the CLRSG took a very cautious and conservative view of the problem and concluded that because of the *Adams* case the UK judiciary would be unwilling to lift the veil for involuntary creditors. They concluded no reforms were needed. The matter of parent liability for personal injury torts of its subsidiaries was then dropped and does not appear anywhere in the CLRSG's *Final Report*. Given that over the course of the CLRSG review of UK company law a number of very high-profile (see paras **3.38–3.48**) examples of this problem passed through the UK courts, the omission is all the more bemusing. As Muchlinski (2002) concluded after reviewing the work of the CLRSG, 'the Steering Group does not appear to have been strongly influenced by concerns such as those of involuntary creditors who have suffered personal injuries at the hands of the overseas subsidiaries of United Kingdom-based Multi-National Enterprises [a corporate group with subsidiaries abroad]. Rather, it was oriented towards the traditional, shareholder-based, model of company law and towards a cost-effective, pro-business approach to regulation.'

Parent company personal injury tortious liability

3.38 In *Connelly v RTZ Corporation Plc* (1998) Mr Connelly had been a uranium miner working in Namibia for a subsidiary of RTZ. He subsequently developed cancer and attempted to sue the parent company in London alleging that RTZ had played a part in the health and safety procedures employed by the subsidiary and that RTZ owed a duty of care to him. RTZ applied to have the action struck out in London arguing that Connelly should sue the subsidiary in Namibia. The issue went to the House of Lords who found that the matter could not be heard in Namibia because of the complexity of the case and the cost. London was therefore the appropriate forum. The decision was not unanimous;

Lord Hoffmann dissented on the basis of the implications for the *Salomon* principle, concluding:

> [t]he defendant is a multinational company, present almost everywhere and certainly present and ready to be sued in Namibia. I would therefore regard the presence of the defendants in the jurisdiction as a neutral factor. If the presence of the defendants, as parent company and local subsidiary of a multinational, can enable them to be sued here, any multinational with its parent company in England will be liable to be sued here in respect of its activities anywhere in the world.

3.39 The case went back to the High Court and the tortious issue was tried. RTZ argued that the subsidiary was Connelly's employer. Therefore any duty of care was owed by the Namibian subsidiary. RTZ also argued that the claim was time barred under the Limitation Act 1980. The court refused to strike out the action on the duty of care point finding that it was arguable that the parent company had responsibility for health and safety at the mine and this would have been such as to create a duty of care to Mr Connelly. However, the claim was time barred under the Limitation Act. Mr Connelly could have brought the case in 1989 but chose not to.

3.40 The case opened up the possibility that actions could be brought against a parent company based in London for the actions of its subsidiary based abroad and that, at least in theory, and depending on the amount of control exerted over the subsidiary, a parent company could owe a duty of care to the workers of the subsidiary.

3.41 The case of *Lubbe v Cape Industries Plc* (2000) continued the pattern of lifting the veil where tortious liability for personal injuries is at issue. The case concerned litigation brought by over 3,000 employees and nearby residents of Cape Industry's wholly owned asbestos-mining subsidiary in South Africa claiming damages from the parent company in London for death and personal injury caused by exposure to asbestos at or near the mining operation in South Africa. The issues were the same as in the *Connelly* case. The House of Lords found that South Africa was the more appropriate place to sue but that the lack of legal representation and the expert evidence required to substantiate the claims in South Africa would amount to a denial of justice. The action could therefore proceed against the parent in London. The case went back to the High Court for trial and in January 2002 Cape settled the action for £21 million.

3.42 In *Chandler v Cape Plc* (2012) the claimant was the employee of a wholly owned subsidiary of Cape who suffered asbestos-related injuries in the course of his employment. The subsidiary no longer existed nor was any insurance in place to cover injuries such as the claimant's. The claimant therefore sought to attribute tortious liability to the parent company because of its control over the subsidiary's health and safety policy. The central question was therefore: was the fact of the parent company's control over health and safety policy, despite the subsidiary company being largely independent and legally separate from the parent, sufficient to confer liability for a breach of duty of care? Both the

High Court and the Court of Appeal found that the assumption of responsibility by the parent company over health and safety policy at the subsidiary created a special relationship between the employee and the parent company which gave rise to a duty of care. On the facts of the case this duty had been breached by the parent company and damages were payable. The judgment is an important one in that it is the first time we are aware of an employee of a subsidiary being successfully owed a duty of care by a parent company. As such it represents one of the most significant veil-lifting cases in decades. However, as we noted earlier, beginning a recent trend in veil/piercing lifting cases both the High Court and the Court of Appeal claimed they were not in fact lifting or piercing the veil in attributing liability to the parent company. As Lady Arden in the Court of Appeal stated:

> I would emphatically reject any suggestion that this court is in any way concerned with what is usually referred to as piercing the corporate veil. A subsidiary and its company are separate entities. There is no imposition or assumption of responsibility by reason only that a company is the parent company of another company . . . The question is simply whether what the parent company did amounted to taking on a direct duty to the subsidiary's employees.

Regardless of the view of the judges in this case, which amount to extreme obfuscation, liability was attributed to the parent company because of its control over a key aspect of the subsidiary company's activity. In other words the connection with the employee is through its control over the subsidiary. The parent company may well have pierced/lifted the veil itself through its control over the subsidiary, and the attribution of liability hence flows from that action, but to pretend that somehow this attribution of liability is not a lifting/piercing action is erroneous and unhelpful.

Commercial tort

3.43 The difference in the treatment of tortious actions for personal injury and other more commercial torts such as negligent misstatement that involve, at least tangentially, veil lifting is striking. In *Williams v Natural Life Health Foods Ltd* (1998) the House of Lords emphasised the *Salomon* principle in the context of a negligent misstatement claim. The managing director of Natural Life Health Foods Ltd (NLHF) was also its majority shareholder. The company's business was selling franchises to run retail health food shops. One such franchise had been sold to the claimant on the basis of a brochure which included detailed financial projections. The managing director had provided much of the information for the brochure. The claimant had not dealt with the managing director but only with an employee of NLHF. The claimant entered into a franchise agreement with NLHF but the franchised shop ceased trading after losing a substantial amount of money. He subsequently brought an action against NLHF for losses suffered as a result of its negligent information contained in the brochure. NLHF subsequently ceased to trade and was dissolved. The claimant then continued the action against the managing director and majority shareholder alone, alleging he had assumed a personal responsibility towards the claimant.

3.44 The reality of this claim was to try to nullify the protection offered by limited liability and as Lowry and Edmunds (1998) have pointed out, the House of Lords was particularly aware of this in reaching its decision. The House of Lords considered that a director or employee of a company could only be personally liable for negligent misstatement if there was reasonable reliance by the claimant on an assumption of personal responsibility by the director so as to create a special relationship (as was present in the *Chandler* case (see para **3.42**)) between them. There was no evidence in the *Williams* case that there had been any personal dealings which could have conveyed to the claimant that the managing director was prepared to assume personal liability for the franchise agreement. However, if the tort is deceit rather than negligence the courts will allow personal liability to flow to a director or employee (see *Daido Asia Japan Co Ltd v Rothen* (2001), *Standard Chartered Bank v Pakistan National Shipping Corpn (Nos 2 and 4)* (2002), and *Barclay Pharmaceuticals Ltd v Waypharm LP* (2012)). An officer of the company may also be personally liable for costs if they pursued an action unreasonably or for an ulterior motive (see *Gemma Ltd v Gimson* (2005)).

3.45 The *Williams* case has subsequently been influential where commercial torts are at issue. For example the High Court in *Noel v Poland* (2001) dismissed a negligent misstatement/ deceit action against the chairman and a director of a liquidated insurance company for inducing Noel to become a Lloyds name (a contractual arrangement where an individual agrees (for a fee) to cover certain insurance losses made by the Lloyds insurance market). The court found that the chairman and director were acting on behalf of the company and that there had not been any assumption of personal responsibility.

3.46 The difficult issue of directors' tortious liability, however, has proved an enduring one. In *MCA Records Inc v Charly Records Ltd (No 5)* (2003) a director had authorised a number of infringing acts under the Copyright, Designs and Patent Act 1988. The Court of Appeal, in a very detailed consideration of the issue of directors' liability in tort, including the *Williams* case, took a more relaxed approach to the possibility of liability. The court concluded:

> *if all that a director is doing is carrying out the duties entrusted to him as such by the company under its constitution, the circumstances in which it would be right to hold him liable as a joint tortfeasor with the company would be rare indeed . . . [however] there is no reason why a person who happens to be a director or controlling shareholder of a company should not be liable with the company as a joint tortfeasor if he is not exercising control through the constitutional organs of the company and the circumstances are such that he would be so liable if he were not a director or controlling shareholder. In other words, if, in relation to the wrongful acts which are the subject of complaint, the liability of the individual as a joint tortfeasor with the company arises from his participation or involvement in ways which go beyond the exercise of constitutional control, then there is no reason why the individual should escape liability because he could have procured those same acts through the exercise of constitutional control.*

On the facts of this case the court found that the director was liable as a joint tortfeasor. (See also *Koninklijke Philips Electronics NV v Princo Digital Disc GmbH* (2004) where a company director was also held personally liable.)

3.47 The difference in treatment of personal injury torts and more commercial torts such as negligent misstatement is somewhat consistent with the voluntary/involuntary nature of their transactions with the company. We say somewhat consistent, as there is an obvious inconsistency. The contrast between the outcomes in the cases of *Adams v Cape Industries Plc* (1990) and *Lubbe v Cape Industries Plc* (2000) or more significantly *Chandler v Cape Plc* (2012) is striking. These cases concern the same underlying claim for personal injury for asbestos contamination from the same company. In *Adams* the claimants were successful in the US courts and sought to enforce the action against the parent in London. The Court of Appeal did not lift the veil in that case. In *Lubbe* the same claim for personal injury was made against the same company but because there was an underdeveloped court system where the subsidiary was operating the House of Lords lifted the veil and allowed the parent to be sued in the UK for the action of the subsidiary. The basis of the decision was that not to do so would amount to a denial of justice. In *Chandler* the facts are very similar to *Adams* save for the basis of the action and the court's interpretation of control.

3.48 It is difficult to see how the decision in the *Adams* case, where the subsidiary was operating in a jurisdiction with a developed court system and where the claimants successfully used that system but needed to enforce it against the parent in London, achieved any measure of justice. Thus a personal injury caused by a UK subsidiary operating in the USA or any developed country will not give rise to any liability on the part of the parent but a personal injury caused by the subsidiary of a UK company in an underdeveloped jurisdiction will. The *Chandler* decision while it serves to illustrate the inconsistency of the range of *Cape* decisions based around similar injuries has subsequently become extremely influential where parent subsidiary liability issues arise. (See for example *HRH Emere Godwin Bebe Okpabi v Royal Dutch Shell plc* (2017) and *Lungowe v Vedanta Resources plc* (2017).) In hindsight, the fact that the CLRSG declined to consider any reform of this area looks a poor decision. The CLRSG's predictions that the UK judiciary would not lift the veil for involuntary creditors proved mistaken or at least more complex than they thought. The CLRSG sadly adopted a much more conservative approach to the issue than the judiciary did, which is a terrible thing to conclude about a law reform body.

The costs/benefits of limited liability

3.49 Limited liability has certain advantages. It obviously encourages investment as the members' risk is minimised. It also encourages risk taking on the part of management who can take risks sure in the knowledge that the members will not lose everything. Limited liability is also said to facilitate a public share market. If liability were unlimited then the value of shares would depend on the wealth of the individual holder. Shares would be worth less to a wealthy shareholder as that shareholder would be more likely to be sued in a liquidation than a poor one. This would hinder the development of a liquid share market as the value of the shares could not be assessed until a buyer was found and his personal assets also assessed.

3.50 For example, if we look at the quoted online share price of a company, that price is based, as we discussed in Chapter 2, on the market's perception of all the publicly available information that affects that limited liability company. It is the price at which anyone can buy the shares. If we moved to a situation where liability was unlimited then the price of a share would not be a standard price: it would vary depending on the wealth of the buyer. In other words, only the combination of the public information on the company plus the private information on the potential shareholder's wealth could determine the price of the share. It would also be likely that potential shareholders would try to negotiate both the price and the terms of their shareholding in the company unlike the present situation where we have a set price and a set bundle of shareholder rights and obligations (see Chapter 8 on the set bundle of shareholder rights). This would not help the development of a liquid market in a company's shares.

3.51 Another advantage of limited liability was identified by Hansmann and Kraakman (2000) who noted that not only does limited liability protect the shareholders from the company's creditors but it can also serve to put the business assets of an individual out of reach of that individual's personal creditors. For example in family law, as we observed earlier in *Prest v Petrodel Resources Ltd* (2013) (see para **3.35**) the partitioning effect of limited liability was argued to have removed the assets from a marriage (see also *Hashem v Shayif & Anor* (2008)). Thus, by forming a company and placing his business assets in the company in return for shares in the company the individual no longer has any legal interest in the assets. This serves to partition the personal assets of the shareholder from his business assets. If the shareholder is insolvent the personal creditors can take the shares but cannot get at the assets of the company.

3.52 Oddly, given that limited liability seems to move the risk of doing business away from the shareholders and on to the creditors, large powerful creditors have also benefited from limited liability. As a result of the movement of risk to the creditors, creditors have been forced to monitor and protect against risk more effectively. Secured lending in the form of fixed and floating charges, risk premiums in terms of interest charged, and board representation have all improved the creditors' monitoring mechanisms.

3.53 These are all undoubted advantages but limited liability does have disadvantages. Risk is moved to the creditors, not all of whom can mitigate their risk. Small trade creditors and involuntary creditors cannot secure their transaction, charge a risk premium, or engage in board-level monitoring. As a result in an insolvent liquidation they have little protection. Indeed, the actions of powerful secured creditors are often detrimental to the most vulnerable creditors as they often have priority in a liquidation. This is still the case with employees as even though they have been given priority above floating charges (see Insolvency Act

1986, s 175 and s 386 and Chapter 17) fixed charges (over the most valuable assets) still have priority. Involuntary creditors have little or no protection if limited liability is upheld.

3.54 Perhaps the most disturbing use of limited liability occurs within group structures. In group structures limited liability's facilitation of asset partitioning allows a very effective double limitation of liability for parent companies and their members. Investors in a parent company can achieve limitation of liability not only for themselves but also for the parent company by structuring its business through a number of subsidiaries. For example Fred, Nancy, Dougal, and Mat are the shareholders in M Ltd, the parent company of wholly owned subsidiaries N Ltd, Y Ltd, and X Ltd. M Ltd has divided its business into three between the subsidiaries. Y Ltd independently buys wine for storage and investment, N Ltd stores the wine Y Ltd buys, and X Ltd markets the sale of the wine once it has been stored for a few years. All the profits of the subsidiaries flow back to M Ltd. Y Ltd entered into a number of complex agreements to buy French wine at a guaranteed price. The French wine harvest was a disaster and the harvest in the rest of the world was excellent. As a result of the poor quality of French wine and a glut of excellent wine from everywhere else Y Ltd ended up with liability running into millions of pounds. It could not meet its obligations to its creditors and was eventually placed into insolvent liquidation. Some months later M Ltd forms another wholly owned subsidiary J Ltd to carry out the wine-buying function. The question remains as to whether the parent company could be liable for the debts of the failed subsidiary. The answer is—probably not.

3.55 It is important to note here that we are not discussing Fred, Nancy, Dougal, and Mat being personally liable for the debts of Y Ltd or M Ltd. The group application of the *Salomon* doctrine means we are just discussing whether the assets of the parent company can be attacked by the claimants in virtue of it being the sole shareholder in Y Ltd. The personal assets of Fred, Nancy, Dougal, and Mat are safe no matter what. The question is whether the parent company gets limited liability as well. Thus just as Hansmann and Kraakman (2000) suggest that asset partitioning allows individuals to put their assets beyond their personal creditors, its most important and far-reaching consequence is that it allows a company also to put its assets beyond the reach of its creditors. The word Ltd or Plc after a parent company name now effectively means the company itself has achieved limited liability.

3.56 Despite the fact that this represents an enormous extension of the *Salomon* principle to cover corporate members, the judiciary have treated it as a straightforward application of the *Salomon* doctrine without questioning whether this is appropriate. Thus the starting point in group structure veil-lifting cases has always been that *Salomon* applies unless there are other reasons for lifting the veil, rather than recognising that allowing asset partitioning to operate for parent companies is a radical and far-reaching extension of the *Salomon* principle and taking the starting point in group veil-lifting cases as asking (as the courts do for example in Germany) whether *Salomon* is an appropriate principle to apply to group structures at all. Indeed, fuelled by concerns about combinations of fraud, money laundering, and terrorism, from October 2016 the practice of using companies as directors to further extend both limited liability and diminish transparency will be prohibited and all directors of UK companies must be natural persons (see SBEEA 2015, s 87). However, sometimes the separateness of a subsidiary can be disadvantageous to a parent company. For example in *Barings Plc (in liquidation) v Coopers & Lybrand (No 4)* (2002) a loss suffered by a parent company as a result of a loss at its subsidiary was not actionable by the parent—the subsidiary was the only proper claimant. (See also *Shaker v Al-Bedrawi* (2003).)

FURTHER READING

This chapter links with the materials in Chapters 3 and 14 of **Hicks and Goo's Cases and Materials on Company Law** (Oxford, OUP, 2011, xl +649p).

Allan 'To Pierce or Not to Pierce? A Doctrinal Reappraisal of Judicial Responses to Improper Exploitation of the Corporate Form' [2018] *JBL* 559.

Capuano, 'The Realistic Guide to Piercing the Veil' (2009) 23(1) *AJCL* 56.

Davies, *Gower and Davies' Principles of Modern Company Law*, 10th edn (London, Sweet & Maxwell, 2016), chs 8 and 9.

Dignam and Oh, 'Disregarding the *Salomon* Principle: An Empirical Analysis, 1885–2014' (2019) 39 *OJLS* 16.

Gallagher and Ziegler, 'Lifting the Corporate Veil in the Pursuit of Justice' [1990] *JBL* 292.*

Hansmann and Kraakman, 'The Essential Role of Organisational Law' [2000] *Yale LJ* 387.

Hare, 'Family Division, 0; Chancery Division, 1: Piercing the Corporate Veil in the Supreme Court (Again)' [2013] *CLJ* 72.

Lightman and Hargreaves, '*Petrodel Resources Ltd v Prest*: Where Are We Now?' (2013) 19(9) *Trusts & Trustees* 877.

Lim, '*Salomon* Reigns' (2013) 129 *LQR* 480.

Lowry, 'Lifting the Corporate Veil' [1993] *JBL* 41.

Lowry and Edmunds, 'Holding the Tension between *Salomon* and the Personal Liability of Directors' [1998] *Can Bar Rev* 467.

Miller, 'Piercing the Corporate Veil Among Affiliated Companies in the European Community and in the U.S.: A Comparative Analysis of U.S., German, and U.K. Veil-Piercing Approaches' (1998) *American Business Law Journal* 73.

Mitchell, 'Lifting the Corporate Veil in the English Courts: An Empirical Study' [1999] 3 *Company Financial and Insolvency L Rev* 15.

Moore, 'A Temple Built on Faulty Foundations' [2006] *JBL* 180.

Muchlinski, 'Holding Multinationals to Account: Recent Developments in English Litigation and the Company Law Review' [2002] *Co Law* 168.

Ottolenghi, 'From Peeping Behind the Corporate Veil to Ignoring it Completely' [1990] *MLR* 338.*

Png, 'Lifting The Veil of Incorporation: *Creasey v Breachwood Motors*: A Right Decision with the Wrong Reasons' [1999] *Co Law* 122.

Ramsay and Noakes, 'Piercing the Corporate Veil in Australia' (2002), http://ssrn.com/abstract=299488.

Rixon, 'Lifting the Veil between Holding and Subsidiary Companies' [1986] *LQR* 415.

Thompson, 'Piercing the Corporate Veil: An Empirical Study' [1991] 76 *Cornell L Rev* 1036.

* Note that the articles above that are marked with an asterisk were written prior to the Court of Appeal decision in *Adams v Cape Industries Plc* (1990) and should be read cautiously with that in mind.

SELF-TEST QUESTIONS

1   What is the difference between separate legal personality and limited liability?

2   Why has the legislature introduced statutory veil-lifting provisions?

3   When will the courts lift the veil of incorporation?

4   Ned, Orin, Dan, and Matilda are the shareholders and directors of Q Ltd, the parent company of wholly owned subsidiaries W Ltd, R Ltd, and X Ltd. Q Ltd has divided its business into three between the subsidiaries specifically to minimise its liability for tax and tortious actions. W Ltd buys and mixes chemicals for the paint industry, R Ltd transports the chemicals, and X Ltd markets the mixed chemicals. All the profits of the subsidiaries flow back to Q Ltd. An accident occurs while R Ltd is transporting hazardous chemicals along the motorway. Fifteen people are badly burned and noxious fumes are released into the air near a town. Additionally, chemicals leak into a major river contaminating the water downstream for hundreds of miles. The projected damages and fines payable by R Ltd come to millions of pounds. R Ltd is capitalised only to the extent it needed to transport chemicals in the two trucks it owns. It has some liability insurance but only to the amount of £1 million. After a few months R Ltd is in insolvent liquidation. In the meantime Q Ltd has set up another wholly owned subsidiary to carry out the group's transport needs. Discuss whether the parent company and/or its members could be liable for the actions of R Ltd. When you have done that critically evaluate the legal outcome.

5   Formulate a single rule (bearing in mind the advantages and disadvantages of limited liability) that would provide the courts with guidance as to when to lift the veil of incorporation.

4 Promoters and pre-incorporation contracts

SUMMARY

Introduction
Defining the term 'promoter'
Promoters as fiduciaries
Pre-incorporation contracts
Section 51 CA 2006: pre-incorporation contracts, deeds, and obligations
Freedom of establishment

Introduction

4.1 As we have observed in Chapters 2 and 3, the motives of those registering a company and conducting a business through it may have an effect on whether the judiciary upholds the separateness of the corporate entity. In this chapter we discuss another area where the motives of those behind the formation of a company ('promoters') are also relevant to the way the law treats certain activities carried out in the company's name. Sometimes the promoter may be using the company to perpetrate a fraud (though given the stringent controls now in place for the marketing of securities (see Chapter 5), much of the case law is now outdated). In other cases the promoter may have entered into contracts for the company before it is formally registered. In such situations, because the company does not exist at the time of the contract, the issue that arises is whether the promoter is personally liable on it. With the rise of the registered company in the mid-to-late 19th century the courts had to find solutions to deal with the promotion problem.

Defining the term 'promoter'

4.2 A 'promoter' is the person responsible for forming a company. Whether or not a person is a promoter is a question of fact to be determined according to the role he played in the creation of the company. Typically, the promotion process involves registering the company with Companies House, negotiating pre-incorporation contracts on behalf of the putative company, and finding the initial directors and shareholders. In the case of public companies the promoter will also be responsible for registering and issuing any prospectus. Although the company's constitution is generally drafted by a professional adviser such as a lawyer or an accountant, such a person will not be deemed to be a promoter merely on that account (*Re Great Wheal Polgooth Co* (1883)). But such professionals may be classified as promoters if they agree to become directors of the company or, indeed, if they undertake to find individuals who will (*Lydney and Wigpool Iron Ore Co v Bird* (1886)).

4.3 The term 'promoter' is not defined in the Companies Act 2006 and the judges have shown little inclination towards formulating an all-embracing definition (indeed, the 2006 Act has little to say about promoters generally beyond requiring the independent valuation of all non-cash assets sold to a public company within two years of its incorporation or re-registration by a person who was a subscriber to its memorandum at the time the company was registered, or was a member at the time it was re-registered as a public company: see ss 598–604 and ss 1077–1078(3)). Notwithstanding this judicial timidity, there are some helpful descriptors in the case law. For example, in *Twycross v Grant* (1877), Cockburn CJ stated that a promoter is 'one who undertakes to form a company with reference to a given project, and to set it going, and who takes the necessary steps to accomplish that purpose'. In *Whaley Bridge Calico Printing Co v Green* (1879) Bowen J explained that: '[T]he term promoter is a term not of law, but of business, usefully summing up in a single word a number of business operations familiar to the commercial world by which a company is generally brought into existence' (see also *Lydney and Wigpool Iron Ore Co v Bird* (above)).

4.4 The reluctance on the part of the legislature and the judges to define the term comprehensively is the result of a spate of 19th-century cases involving fraudulent schemes that were perpetrated against investors. Typically this was done by a person selling to the fledgling company his own property at a grossly inflated price (in return either for cash or for fully paid shares) which bore little relation to the property's true value. The response of the judges, therefore, was to leave the meaning of the term 'promoter' fluid so as to include as many such fraudsters as possible. They also developed a range of specific fiduciary duties aimed at setting exemplary standards of behaviour for promoters.

4.5 As far as public companies are concerned much of the case law surrounding promoters is of little more than historical interest. It is unusual, given modern commercial practice, for a new company to make an immediate public issue of securities and, indeed, as commented earlier, there are stringent rules in place which govern the marketing of securities. In the aftermath of the 2008 financial crisis the regulatory regime contained in the Financial Services and Markets Act 2000 was fundamentally reformed and new and complex requirements were introduced by the Financial Services Act 2012 (which came into force on 1 April 2013). The 2012 Act is aimed at bolstering the UK's financial regulatory structures. It imposes strict controls on the marketing of securities which are now to be overseen by three principal bodies: the Bank of England's Financial Policy Committee, the Prudential Regulation Authority (a subsidiary of the Bank of England), and the Financial Conduct Authority (FCA) which is responsible for the regulation of conduct both in retail and wholesale financial markets together with the infrastructure that supports those markets (see the FCA's Listing Rules; see also the Companies Act 2006, Part 43 which implements Directive 2004/109/EC on the harmonisation of transparency requirements relating to information about issuers whose securities are traded on a regulated market—discussed in Chapter 5).

4.6 In general most private companies metamorphose from some pre-existing business relationship such as a joint venture or a partnership and so relatively few such promotions involve persons with dishonest motives trying to obtain finance from outsiders. For private companies, therefore, the promotion is more likely to be effected by the partners or proprietor of the pre-incorporated business enterprise (as was the case with Mr Salomon, see *Salomon v Salomon & Co* (1897), Chapter 2). Such promoters usually become the first directors and shareholders. Indeed, many if not most public companies start out as private companies which, when in need of additional capital, convert by offering securities to the public at large (termed flotation—see Chapter 5).

Promoters as fiduciaries

4.7 It has long been settled that a promoter is not the agent of the company he is promoting (*Kelner v Baxter* (1866)). Prior to incorporation, the company has no legal existence and so to hold otherwise would result in the legal fiction of an agent acting for a non-existent principal. It has also been held that a promoter is not a trustee of the company he is seeking to bring into existence (*Re Leeds and Hanley Theatres of Varieties Ltd* (1902)). Nevertheless, a promoter, being a person who 'undertakes to act for or on behalf of another in some particular matter or matters', is viewed as a fiduciary (Finn (1977)), and is therefore subject to the rigour of a number of fiduciary duties. These duties are owed to the company and so an action for breach must be brought by the company, not by its members (*Foss v Harbottle* (1843)). Defining the term 'fiduciary' is more difficult than attempting to explain the 'off-side' rule in soccer to someone who has no interest in the sport. It is perhaps best explained by reference to the particular obligations a fiduciary owes to his principal. In essence, as we will see in Chapter 14, fiduciary obligations are duties owed to a third party to act with 'loyalty in dealings which affect that person' (Penner (2016)). As Penner points out, the duty to act with loyalty means more than just acting honestly and fairly but rather the fiduciary 'must act solely in the interests of his principal: the fiduciary must act to secure his principal's best interests, and must not allow his own self-interests, or the interests of others, to govern his behaviour in any way that would conflict with the principal's best interests. Fiduciary law is thus the origin in modern society of the legal notion of 'conflict of interest.'

4.8 The particular position of promoters as opposed to other types of fiduciaries such as trustees and directors was explained by Lord Cairns LC in *Erlanger v New Sombrero Phosphate Co* (1878):

> *They stand, in my opinion, undoubtedly in a fiduciary position. They have in their hands the creation and moulding of the company; they have the power of defining how, and when, and in what shape, and under what supervision, it shall start into existence and begin to act as a trading corporation.*

The fiduciary duties of promoters

4.9 The fiduciary duties applicable to promoters principally arise from the nature of the transactions entered into by them in the course of bringing a company into existence. The core duty of a promoter is not to make a secret profit from his position. The scope for abuse is self-evident where a promoter sells property to the company in which he has a personal interest and so the law therefore requires promoters to make full disclosure of any profit derived therefrom (*Re Lady Forrest (Murchison) Gold Mine Ltd* (1901)). Failure to disclose all material facts surrounding such a contract to an independent board renders the contract voidable at the company's option. In *Erlanger v New Sombrero Phosphate Co*, a syndicate purchased a mine containing phosphates for £55,000. The syndicate then formed a company and through a nominee sold the mine to it for £100,000 without disclosing their interests in the contract. The phosphate operations proved to be a failure and the shareholders removed the original directors. The new board successfully brought an action to have the sale rescinded. Lord Penzance was unequivocal in his condemnation of the promoters' conduct:

> *I invite your Lordships to draw two conclusions: first, that the company never had an opportunity of exercising, through independent directors, a fair and independent judgment upon the subject of this purchase; and, secondly, that this result was brought about by the conduct and contrivance of the vendors themselves . . . Placed in [a] position of unfair advantage over the company which they were about to create, they were, as it seems to me, bound according to the principles constantly acted upon in the Courts of Equity, if they wished to make a valid contract of sale to the company, to nominate independent directors and fully disclose the material facts. The obligation rests upon them to shew they have not made use of the position which they occupied to benefit themselves; but I find no proof in the case that they have discharged that obligation.*

4.10 Subsequently, in *Salomon v Salomon & Co Ltd* (1897) the House of Lords accepted that in the absence of an independent board of directors the disclosure duty will be discharged if full disclosure of all material facts is made to the original shareholders. However, in *Gluckstein v Barnes* (1900) the House of Lords stressed that such disclosure will not be sufficient if the original shareholders are not truly independent and the scheme as a whole is designed to defraud the investing public. These decisions give rise to the anomalous situation, at least at common law, that while the company is treated as non-existent for the purpose of ratifying a pre-incorporation contract (see later), it is viewed as existing for the purpose of imposing fiduciary duties on its promoters.

Remedies

4.11 There is a range of remedies available to the company against a promoter who is in breach of his fiduciary duties. For example, it may bring a restitutionary claim for the benefit the promoter received either in equity on the basis of a constructive trust or by way of a claim for money had and received (see *Sealy and Worthington's Text, Cases, & Materials in Company Law* (2016), pp 431 *et seq*); note the effect of the Supreme Court's decision in *FHR European Ventures LLP v Mankarious (No 2)* (2014) on proprietary claims for breach of fiduciary duties (see para **14.85**). The company may also have a claim for equitable compensation for breach of duty. Such compensation will be measured by reference to the difference between the price paid by the company to the promoter for the asset in which he had an undisclosed interest and its market value (*Re Leeds and Hanley Theatres of Varieties Ltd* (see para **4.7**)). In *Target Holdings Ltd v Redferns* (1996), Lord Browne-Wilkinson noted that if a trustee (on the facts, a solicitor) commits a breach of trust, the beneficiary's remedy against him is a personal one:

> a trustee in breach of trust must restore or pay to the trust estate either the assets which have been lost to the estate by reason of the breach or compensation for such loss. Courts of Equity did not award damages but, acting in personam, ordered the defaulting trustee to restore the trust estate . . . If specific restitution of the trust property is not possible, then the liability of the trustee is to pay sufficient compensation to the trust estate to put it back to what it would have been had the breach not been committed.

(See also *Erlanger v New Sombrero Phosphate Co* (1878), Lord Blackburn; and *Tang Man Sit v Capacious Investments Ltd* (1996).)

4.12 Where a promoter fails to make the requisite disclosure of his interest in a contract with the company, its principal remedies are rescission and an accounting of secret profits. The effect of his breach of duty is to render the contract voidable at the company's option (*Erlanger v New Sombrero Phosphate Co* (1878)). The company therefore has the option either to rescind the contract or to affirm it. There are, however, certain limitations on the right to rescind. If the company by its actions, after it becomes aware of the promoter's breach of duty, shows an intention to affirm the contract, rescission will not be available (*Re Cape Breton Co* (1885)). Similarly, the company's delay in rescinding the contract may also bar its right to the remedy (*Long v Lloyd* (1958); *Leaf v International Galleries* (1950)). The contract being voidable, i.e. valid until rescinded, means that if a third party bona fide without notice and for value acquires rights in the contract's subject matter, those rights are valid as against the company, provided it has not rescinded the contract before that time (*Re Leeds and Hanley Theatres of Varieties Ltd*; see para **4.7**). Finally, for rescission to be available there must be *restitutio in integrum*. That is, it must be possible to restore, at least substantially, the parties to their original position unless, due to the fault of the promoter, this possibility has been lost (*Lagunas Nitrate Co v Lagunas Syndicate* (1899)). In *Erlanger*, Lord Blackburn observed that it has always been the practice of the Court of Equity to grant relief by way of rescission whenever by the exercise of its powers it can do justice by directing accounts, awarding equitable compensation, and making allowances, even though it cannot restore the parties exactly to the position they were in before the contract. Even if the company elects not to re-scind the contract, it may still recover any secret profits from the promoter (*Gluckstein v Barnes* (1900); see para **4.10**).

4.13   Where a promoter has been offered but not yet received a bribe or some other benefit, the company may itself enforce his claim for payment against the promisor, on the ground that the promoter holds the claim as trustee for it (*Whaley Bridge Calico Printing Co v Green* (1879); see para **4.3**). Finally, it should also be noted that the company may have an action against the promoter in the tort of deceit.

Pre-incorporation contracts

4.14   In addition to dealing with the fraudulent activities of promoters, certain other prob-lems confronted the courts relating to the practicalities of promoting the company, par-ticularly with respect to contracts entered into prior to registration. A company comes into existence only when the certificate of incorporation is issued by the Registrar of Companies. Until incorporation a company cannot be bound by contracts entered into in its name or on its behalf: it simply does not exist. However, as part of the pro-cess of creating a company its promoters will generally contract with third parties for such things as a lease of premises, equipment, and connection to utilities so that once incorporation is completed the company can begin trading without delay. The issue which arises in relation to such pre-incorporation contracts is whether the promoter can avoid being held personally liable notwithstanding that the company did not exist at the time such contracts were concluded on its behalf. The response of the common law was to apply principles of contract and agency to the issue, but partial reform was implemented by s 9(2) of the European Communities Act 1972, now re-enacted in s 51 of the Companies Act 2006.

The common law position

4.15   You may recall from the law of contract that it is a fundamental requirement of the prin-ciples of offer and acceptance that a party must be in existence in order for an agreement to crystallise: 'If somebody does not exist they cannot contract' (*Rover International Ltd v Cannon Film Sales Ltd (No 3)* (1987), Harman J). Further, since at the time of a pre-incorporation contract the company does not exist, upon its subsequent creation it is necessarily a stranger to it and the doctrine of privity will operate to prevent rights and liabilities being conferred or imposed on the company (*Kelner v Baxter* (1866)). The Contracts (Rights of Third Parties) Act 1999, which allows enforcement of contracts by third parties if the contract expressly so provides or a term of the contract confers a benefit on the third party, does not apply to pre-incorporation contracts. The Act is based on the recommendations of the Law Commission in its report, *Privity of Contract: Contracts for the Benefit of Third Parties* (Law Commission Report No 242, Cm 3329, 1996). Addressing the issue of pre-incorporation contracts, the Law Commission drew the distinction between a contract on behalf of a third party and a contract for the benefit of a third party. The Commission stated that the former category involves the third party company becoming a party to the contract, and subject to all its rights and obligations, after its incorporation. It is the latter situation which the Law Commission intended the Act to cover: in that case 'the third party is not, and will not become, a party to the contract but will simply acquire a right to sue to enforce provisions of the contract' (Report, para 8.11).

4.16 As far as the law of agency is concerned, a person cannot be an agent of a non-existent principal and so a company cannot acquire rights or obligations under a pre-incorporation contract. These principles came together to form the underlying premise of the decision in *Kelner v Baxter* (1866). The promoters of a hotel company entered into a contract on its behalf for the purchase of wine which the company, when incorporated, ratified. The wine was consumed but before payment was made the company went into liquidation. The promoters, as agents, were sued on the contract. They argued that liability under the contract had passed, by ratification, to the company. Erle CJ, rejecting this argument and holding the promoters personally liable, said that:

> I agree that if [the hotel] had been an existing company at this time, the persons who signed the agreement would have signed as agents of the company. But, as there was no company in existence at the time, the agreement would be wholly inoperative unless it were held to be binding on the defendants personally . . . and a stranger cannot by subsequent ratification relieve [them] from that responsibility. When the company came afterwards into existence it was a totally new creature, having rights and obligations from that time, but no rights or obligations by reason of anything which might have been done before . . . There must be two parties to a contract; and the rights and obligations which it creates cannot be transferred by one of them to a third person who was not in a condition to be bound by it at the time it was made.

4.17 A promoter will avoid personal liability if the company, after incorporation, and the other party substitute the original pre-incorporation contract with a new contract on similar terms (*Natal Land Co & Colonization Ltd v Pauline Colliery and Development Syndicate Ltd* (1904) PC). Novation, as this is called, may also be inferred by the conduct of the parties such as where the terms of the original agreement are changed (*Re Patent Ivory Manufacturing Co, Howard v Patent Ivory Manufacturing Co* (1888)). But novation will not be effective if the company adopts the contract due to the mistaken belief that it is bound by it (*Re Northumberland Avenue Hotel Co Ltd* (1886)). A promoter will not be personally liable on a contract where he signs the agreement merely to confirm the signature of the company because in so doing he has not held himself out as either agent or principal. The signature, and indeed the contractual document, will be a complete nullity because the company was not in existence (*Newborne v Sensolid (Great Britain) Ltd* (1954)). However, the promoter may be liable to the other party for breach of warranty of authority on the principle of *Collen v Wright* (1857), in that he misrepresented his authority by purporting to represent a director of a non-existent company which, lacking legal existence, had no validly appointed officers.

4.18 The common law position has now been affected as a result of the UK's implementation of Art 7 of the First Company Law Directive (68/151)) by CA 2006, s 51 (formerly CA 1985, s 36C). The provision seeks to protect the other party by making promoters personally liable when the company, after incorporation, fails to enter into a new contract on similar terms (i.e. novation, the CA 2006 retains this rule). It is noteworthy, however, that the Companies Act 2006 did not introduce a straightforward ratification procedure for pre-incorporation contracts notwithstanding that it was a principal policy objective of the Company Law Review to modernise and simplify UK company law.

Section 51 CA 2006: pre-incorporation contracts, deeds, and obligations

4.19 Section 51 of the 2006 Act provides that a contract which purports to be made by or on behalf of a company at a time when the company has not been formed has effect, subject to any agreement to the contrary, as one made with the person purporting to act for the company or as agent for it, and he is personally liable on the contract accordingly. In short, promoters contracting on behalf of a putative company will be held personally liable. The meaning and scope of this provision was subjected to considerable scrutiny by the Court of Appeal in *Phonogram Ltd v Lane* (1982). Lord Denning MR, with whom Shaw LJ agreed, took the phrase 'subject to any agreement to the contrary' to mean that in order for a promoter to avoid personal liability the contract must expressly provide for his exclusion. The court also held that it is not necessary for the putative company to be in the process of creation at the time the contract was entered into. Subsequent case law has held that s 51 does not apply to a contract involving a misnamed existing company (*Oshkosh B'Gosh Inc v Dan Marbel Inc Ltd* (1988)); or to a contract involving a company no longer in existence (*Cotronic (UK) Ltd v Dezonie* (1991)). However, in *Hellmuth, Obata & Kassabaum Inc v King* (2000) the judge accepted that for the purposes of s 51 persons purporting to act on behalf of an unformed company could be liable for its quasi-contractual obligations. Lord Denning's reasoning in *Phonogram Ltd v Lane* was applied in *Royal Mail Estates Ltd v Teesdale* (2015). The contract in question concerned the sale of property located in London. It contained a clause which stipulated that: 'The benefit of this contract is personal to the buyer.' The defendants argued that this clause constituted a 'contrary agreement' for the purposes of s 51. The deputy judge reasoned that there was only a contrary agreement if there was found to be an agreement between the parties by which they *intended* to exclude the s 51 effect (emphasis added). The words 'the benefit of this contract is personal to [the company]', construed objectively, did not amount to such a contrary agreement. At the time the contract was concluded neither of the parties was aware that the company had not been incorporated. A further twist on the scope of s 51 came before the Court of Appeal in *Braymist Ltd v Wise Finance Co Ltd* (2002). A firm of solicitors contracted as agents on behalf of a company yet to be incorporated, whereby the putative company agreed to sell land to property developers. Subsequently, the developers changed their minds and the solicitors sought to enforce the contract. The issue was whether a person acting as agent of an unformed company could *enforce* a pre-incorporation contract under s 51. The Court of Appeal, affirming the decision of Etherton J, held that although the terms of the first Directive referred only to liability and not to enforcement, it did not follow that s 51 was similarly limited in scope so as to prevent enforcement of contracts made by persons on behalf of unformed companies. The majority found that the words in the section 'and he is personally liable on the contract accordingly' did not operate to negate this view, but rather the phrase merely served to emphasise the abolition of the common law distinction between agents who incurred personal liability on pre-incorporation contracts and those who did not.

4.20 The provision is thus double-edged so that a party who is personally liable for the contract is also able to enforce it. Latham LJ stated:

> I would accordingly hold that the solicitors are entitled to rely upon section 36C [now s 51] in order to enforce the contract in the present case. In my judgment, this produces a just result in that there is no good reason why the defendant should be entitled to resile from their obligations under the contract as a result of a pure technicality when in truth they wish to do so because it proved a bad bargain.

4.21 In summary, the objective of s 51 is to protect third parties who contracted in the belief that they were dealing with a registered company by making pre-incorporation contracts legally enforceable as personal contracts with promoters unless the personal liability of the latter has been unequivocally excluded.

Freedom of establishment

4.22 Companies are no longer static entities whose operations are confined to the jurisdiction in which they incorporated. Mobility is becoming increasingly common as a means of avoiding regulation and this has come to the fore in relation to freedom of establishment.

In furtherance of the internal market ideal, the EC Treaty sought to create a common market with free movement of goods, persons, services, and capital. EC Treaty, Arts 2, 43, and 48 (see now Arts 49–55 of the TFEU; see also Directive 2004/38/EC), seek to confer a right of establishment on natural persons and companies alike to carry on business in any Member State. The threshold requirement for companies is that they must have been formed according to the law of a Member State and that they have their registered office, or centre of administration, or principal place of business within the European Union (EC Treaty, Art 48; Arts 49 and 54 of the TFEU). A Member State which seeks to impede the right of a company registered in another Member State from carrying on business in its jurisdiction will be held to be acting in breach of its EC Treaty (now TFEU) obligations. For example, in *Centros Ltd v Erhversus- og Selkabssyrelsen* (1999), the ECJ held that Denmark was in breach of EU law in refusing to allow Centros Ltd, a private company registered in England, to establish a branch in Denmark, even though Denmark was in fact its primary operational establishment. The Court rejected the argument of the Danish authorities that the Danish owners of Centros Ltd had chosen the UK as the state of incorporation of its undercapitalised company in order to avoid the minimum capital requirements required under Danish law. The motive of the owners could not be regarded as abusive but was a consequence of their freedom to incorporate a company in one Member State and set up a secondary establishment in another (see also *Überseering BV v Nordic Construction Co Baumanagement GmbH* (2002); *Kamer van Koophandel en Fabrieken voor Amsterdam v Inspire Art Ltd* (2003); and *Kornhaas v Dithmar* (2016); cf *Cartesio Okató és Szolgáltató bt* (2009)). For an example in the context of administration, see the reasoning of Judge Raynor QC in *Re European Directories (DH6) BV* (2010), where the centre of main interests (COMI) of a Dutch registered company was held to be London.

In *Polbud Wykonawstwo sp. Z.o.o., in liquidation* (2017), the ECJ held that freedom of establishment meant that a company registered in and governed by the laws of an EU Member State should be permitted to 'convert' itself into a company governed by the laws of another EU Member State provided it complied with the relevant legal requirements laid down by the destination state. Consequently, EU Member States whose national law does not enable companies to migrate to and from other EU countries will need to comply with this ruling. It remains to be seen whether the UK Government will introduce such provisions prior to the UK's departure from the EU. That said, UK companies that wish to have the option to migrate out to an EU Member State may bring pressure to bear on the Government to introduce such provisions during the transitional period following Brexit.

4.23 It is unclear whether the pan-European business entity, the European Company (Societas Europea (SE)) which became available in October 2004, will address the concerns of those Member States wishing to regulate undercapitalised companies operating within their jurisdictions (an SE is required to have a minimum share capital of €120,000). It can be established only by an existing company (therefore, not by a natural person) in four ways: merger (restricted to public companies), formation of a holding SE, formation of a subsidiary SE, and transformation. The take-up of the European Company has been very limited. For example, there are around three registered SEs in the UK, none of which are operating companies.

FURTHER READING

This chapter links with the materials in Chapter 2 of *Hicks and Goo's Cases and Materials on Company Law* (Oxford, OUP, 2011, xl +649p).

Andenas, 'Free Movement of Companies' [2003] *LQR* 221.

Finn, *Fiduciary Obligations* (Sydney, Law Book Co, 1977).

Green, 'Security of Transaction after *Phonogram*' [1984] *MLR* 671.

Griffiths, 'Agents Without Principals: Pre-incorporation Contracts and Section 36C of the Companies Act 1985' [1993] *LS* 241.

Gross, 'Pre-incorporation Contracts' [1971] *LQR* 367.

Lowry, 'Eliminating Obstacles to Freedom of Establishment: The Competitive Edge of UK Company Law' [2004] *CLJ* 331.

McCrea, 'Disclosure of Promoters' Secret Profits' [1968] *UBCLR* 183.

Micheler, 'The Impact of the *Centros* Case on Europe's Company Laws' [2000] *Co Law* 179.

Mitchell, 'Stewardship of Property and Liability to Account' [2014] *Conv* 215.

Penner, *The Law of Trusts* (Oxford, OUP, 2016), ch 2.

Puri, 'The Promise of Certainty in the Law of Pre-Incorporation Contracts' [2001] *Can Bar Rev* 1051.

Twigg-Flesner, 'Full Circle: Purported Agent's Right of Enforcement under section 36C of the Companies Act 1985' [2001] *Co Law* 274.

Worthington, 'The Proprietary Consequences of Rescission' [2002] *RLR* 28.

SELF-TEST QUESTIONS

1   What is the nature of the relationship between a promoter and the company? What consequences flow from the relationship?

2   What is a pre-incorporation contract?

3   Alex, Bill, and Charlie, who are electricians, form a syndicate. They operate the business from premises which Alex bought for £5,000. The business is successful and they have secured a contract to re-wire six hospitals. They decide to form a company. Alex sells the business premises to the company for £10,000. Bill buys several vans for £12,000 each. He sells them to the company for £12,000 but keeps one for his own company which also operates in the same line of business.

Charlie orders computer equipment costing £30,000 from Hightech Ltd together with a servicing agreement for five years costing £120 per month. He tells Hightech Ltd that the company, when incorporated, will assume liability and pay the bill. Charlie pays £1,500 deposit for the computers. The company is formed and Alex, Bill, and Charlie are the sole directors. Charlie telephones Hightech Ltd and reminds them to bill the company. The bill remains unpaid.

The company is insolvent and is being wound up.

Advise the liquidator.

5 Raising capital: equity and its consequences

SUMMARY

Introduction
Public and private companies
Methods of raising money from the public
The Financial Conduct Authority and the London Stock Exchange
The regulation of listed companies
The regulation of takeovers
Insider dealing
The regulation of other public offers
Sanctions
The regulatory regime

Introduction

5.1 Companies raise money in a number of ways. They may have it provided by the founder's savings in which case things are relatively straightforward. More usually a company will obtain its capital through a loan from a bank or other institution or from the general public. We will deal with raising capital through a loan in Chapter 6. The focus of this chapter is on raising equity from the general public and its consequences for the operation of the company. What follows in this chapter is a general broad sweep over a very complex area. While professionals dealing in the equity markets, or advising those who deal in those markets, might need to be familiar with the detail of raising equity, thankfully the student of company law need only have a general knowledge of the area to flesh out the context in which larger companies in the UK operate. In covering this topic we start with the basics of raising equity and then move on to the consequences of operating in a public market, covering areas such as takeovers and insider dealing.

Public and private companies

5.2 As we have observed in Chapter 1, the CA 2006 provides for companies to be either private or public. Essentially the distinction in terms of capital raising between the two types of companies is that the law presumes that in private companies the investment is largely provided by the founding members either through their personal savings or from bank loans and that in public companies the intention is to raise large amounts of money from the general public. Private companies can take a number of forms under the CA 2006. They can be limited or unlimited. If they are limited they can be limited either by shares or by guarantee. Crucially, private companies are prohibited from raising capital from the general public (CA 2006, s 755). Public companies have no such prohibition and may freely raise capital from the general public. Sometimes where extremely large amounts of capital are needed a public company will choose to raise capital through listing their shares for sale on a stock exchange such as the London Stock Exchange (LSE). Additionally the Listing Rules of the LSE require that a company be a public company. Listing your shares for sale on a stock exchange, as we will see, engages a further layer of regulation.

5.3 While the majority of this chapter deals exclusively with the capital-raising activities of public companies this does not mean that all private companies are small concerns. Some private companies are very large, often obtaining their capital through lending (see Chapter 6) or private investment firms (e.g. venture capital firms such as 3i or more recently hedge funds such as Blackstone) rather than from the general public. Sir Richard Branson's Virgin Ltd is an example of a large private company. Virgin was formerly a listed company that de-listed because of the enhanced scrutiny a public listing brings to a business from both regulators and institutional investors (these are the largest investors in listed companies, and are made up of insurance companies, pension funds, and investment funds, see further Chapters 15 and 16). Very large private companies are, however, unusual as most business ventures once they reach a certain size move to convert to a public company in order either to access the public funding market for expansion purposes or provide an easy way for its original shareholders to cash out. We will concentrate here on the public company as a capital-raising vehicle.

5.4 Public companies are subject to a more onerous regulatory regime than private companies because of their dealings with the general public and a long history of scandals involving fraudulent or misleading share sales to the general public. In contrast to private companies, a public company can only be formed as a company limited by shares (CA 2006, s 4(2)). Therefore the application for registration of a public company must state it is public and as with private companies the liability of the members is limited, thus the words public limited company (PLC or plc) must come at the end of its name (CA 2006, s 58(1)). While private companies can have a purely nominal share capital, public companies have much larger requirements imposed. Section 763 of the CA 2006 provides that the authorised minimum share capital for public companies is £50,000.

5.5 Public companies are designed to secure investment from the general public and can advertise the fact that they are offering shares to the public. In doing so the company must issue a prospectus giving a detailed and accurate description of the company's plans (see para **5.9**). Because the general public are involved and need to be protected, the initial capital requirements for a public company are more onerous than for a private one. As we have just discussed there is a minimum capital requirement of £50,000 (CA 2006, s 763). However, the capital requirement may be partly paid so the company does not actually have to have £50,000, it just needs one-quarter of that and an ability to call on the members for the remaining amount (CA 2006, s 586). While there is no formal limitation on public companies having restrictions on transfer of shares similar to those that apply to private companies, any restriction would be highly unusual, given that the aim is to raise money from the general public as it would discourage them. In any case, if the public company is listed on the LSE such restrictions on transfer will be prohibited.

The differing regulation of private and public companies

5.6 As we have just noted, because the general public is affected by the capital-raising activities of these companies the state has taken a greater interest in investor protection where public companies are concerned. For example the CLRSG in its consultation document *Completing The Structure* (para 2.73) identified three distinct areas in the Companies Acts where public companies were subject to enhanced regulation. These were:

- *accounting*: there are tighter deadlines for preparing and filing accounts, and no economic size exemptions similar to those available to small private companies;

- *capital*: public companies are subject to a minimum capital requirement, tight rules on subscription for shares, and tighter rules on financial assistance and purchase of own shares;

- *governance*: there are more demanding requirements for the company secretary, a requirement for at least two directors, no written resolution or elective regime procedures, stricter rules on directors' conflicts of interest etc. (There is also the UK Corporate Governance Code and Stewardship Code for listed companies for which see Chapter 16.)

The distinction between public and listed companies

5.7 As we will see in Chapter 15, one of the key developments in company law was the effective separation of ownership from control once the registered company began to tap the stock exchange for funds in the late 19th and early 20th centuries. The operation of these very large public companies became so complex that shareholders could no longer run the company and so appointed managers. These managers did not control the company by virtue of their shareholdings, as they usually only held a tiny fraction of its shares, but wielded enormous power through their technical skills and the power delegated to them by shareholders. They could therefore act in their own self-interest if they were not monitored. Unfortunately, one of the features of this new managerial company that raised money in the public markets was a very large and dispersed shareholding (i.e. millions of shareholders all holding a tiny fraction of the total shares in the company). Thus because shareholders held only a minute stake in the company they were uninterested in monitoring management. This dispersed and huge shareholder population also caused a problem for regulators as very few of these small shareholders had the expertise to investigate fully the activities of public companies before they invested in them. Therefore they were prone to being de-frauded. While we discuss the consequences of the separation of ownership from control at length in Chapters 15 and 16, the problem for regulators of dispersed ownership is relevant here. At first the quality control function for investors was carried out by the stockbrokers and banks who did have the expertise to assess companies. However, the role of the LSE itself in regulating the equity markets has been crucial as it adopted a disclosure regime with the view to encouraging companies to provide investors with the information they needed to make informed investment decisions. Slowly, however, the state became involved in shareholder protection and, as we will see, in providing sanctions for abuse.

5.8 It is important to note that public companies are not necessarily listed on the stock ex-change. A listing on the stock exchange is essentially a private contractual arrangement between a public company and the LSE (itself a listed public company) to gain access to a very sophisticated market for its shares. The public company, once it gains access to the stock market, is then generally known as a 'listed' company but sometimes a 'quoted' com-pany and its shares as 'listed' or 'quoted' shares or securities. The LSE offers the facility of a secondary market, that is, a place where shares can be traded after they have been issued to shareholders. It also functions as a capital market for companies who wish to fund new investments by selling new shares to the general public who can then trade them on the stock exchange or more recently as an anti-capital market for companies who do not wish to invest their cash to easily buy back existing shares which in turn decreases the supply of the company's shares in the market and in theory boosts the price of the remaining shares. Some public companies do however exist outside the stock exchange listing system. For example, Amstrad plc, Lord Sugar's company (you know, the mean bloke from *The Apprentice*) is a very large public company operating without a listing on the LSE. Amstrad was formerly a listed company but de-listed for the same accountability reasons as Virgin Ltd. However, if a company wishes to raise large amounts of money its efforts will be immeasurably aided by a stock exchange listing. This is because investors will have greater confidence in the business if it is within the regulatory ambit of the LSE and investors will be able to sell their shares easily through the LSE secondary market. While there is only one stock exchange the LSE operates two separate equity markets which together list over 2,000 companies. The main market is the official list made up of established large companies. It has existed since 1801. To list on the main market a com-pany can choose a premium listing, a standard listing, or a high growth one. Standard and high growth listings comply with certain minimum EU standards while a premium listing meets the UK's higher standards for listing. The other equity market is the Alternative Investment Market (AIM) which began life in 1980 as the Unlisted Securities Market

(USM) in response to the demand from less established companies for access to a listing on the LSE. In 1995 the USM became AIM. The idea of the AIM is to promote younger, less established companies which, although good companies, might not have the track record necessary for a full listing. In total some of the largest companies from more than 90 countries are listed on the LSE markets with a total market value of over £4 trillion.

Methods of raising money from the public

5.9 The process of gaining a listing on the LSE is complex, costly, and extremely time-consuming involving a large number of financial and legal advisers. However, as well as preparing the company itself for compliance with the regulations of the LSE the company must also manage to sell its shares to the general public. In order to do this a company will need to employ a merchant bank (the issuing house) as well as a stockbroker to decide on the way to issue the company's shares. This can be done in a number of ways, the following being the most relevant here. First, the company could simply offer its shares for subscription itself by issuing a prospectus and advertising in the trade or general press. Second, the more common method is an offer for sale. This is where the company has an agreement with an issuing house whereby it will allot its entire issue of shares to the issuing house. The issuing house will then try to sell the shares to its clients and the general public. The advantage of this type of sale is that the issuing house takes the risk that the shares will not sell (of course it takes this risk in return for a large fee). Third, the shares may not be offered to the general public at all but be 'placed' with the clients of a merchant bank or group of merchant banks.

5.10 Fourth, the company could raise money through a rights issue. This is where new shares are offered to the existing shareholders in proportion to their existing shareholding usually because of shareholders' pre-emption rights. These rights of pre-emption are conferred on shareholders in s 561 of the CA 2006 but some listed companies may have disapplied their pre-emption rights (this is however likely to make such a company unpopular with investors). Once a company is listed further capital raising is more straightforward without the complication of the initial listing process.

The Financial Conduct Authority and the London Stock Exchange

5.11 Until May 2000 the LSE itself carried out the role of the UK's 'competent authority for listing' with responsibility for admitting securities to listing, making the Listing Rules, and policing compliance with them. Following enactment of the Financial Services and Markets Act 2000 (FSMA), which replaced the Financial Services Act 1986, that function passed to the Financial Services Authority (FSA) (FSMA, s 72), which remained the UK Listing Authority until 2013. As a result of the continuing regulatory reforms deemed necessary to deal with the impact of the financial crisis that unfolded from 2007 onwards, in 2013, with the introduction of the Financial Services Act 2012, the FSA was split into two new regulatory bodies: the Prudential Regulatory Authority (PRA) and the Financial Conduct Authority (FCA). The PRA has primary responsibility for banking and insurance and the FCA has responsibility for retail and wholesale financial markets. As such, the FCA is now the UK Listing Authority and works closely with the LSE to ensure the proper functioning of the listed market. In doing so the FCA does this through:

- *monitoring market disclosures* by issuers and others and through enforcing compliance with the FCA Disclosure and Transparency Rules;

- *reviewing and approving of prospectuses* published by issuers and offerors of securities and through enforcing the FCA Prospectus Rules;

- *operating the UK listing regime* which requires listed issuers to comply with the FCA Listing Rules, and which gives investors an accreditation indicating that those issuers adhere to a range of standards on governance and investor protection.

5.12 Reform has also occurred at the EU level because of regulatory failures within EU institutions, with the creation of the European Securities and Markets Authority (ESMA). ESMA is an independent EU Authority tasked with protecting the stability of the European Union's financial system by ensuring the integrity, transparency, efficiency, and orderly functioning of securities markets, as well as enhancing investor protection. To achieve its task it is provided with a range of powers, from issuing guidance to compulsion of individuals and national-level supervisory authorities. As such, the FCA, and in turn the PRA, have a single EU regulatory authority to work with, although what happens with financial services regulation after Brexit remains unclear as we write in summer 2020 (see https://www.esma.europa.eu/about-esma/who-we-are).

5.13 The UK Listing Authority (the FCA) has primary responsibility for granting listed status to companies. To gain a listing a company must comply with the Listing Rules which are made in accordance with Part VI of the FSMA which is in turn based on a number of EU Directives (see the Consolidated Admissions and Reporting Directive (2001/34/EC)). The status of the LSE as a 'Recognised Investment Exchange' (RIE) under the Financial Services Act 1986 was continued in the FSMA. It is thus exempt from the general prohibition against carrying on a 'regulated activity' in the UK without authorisation or having obtained exemption (FSMA, s 19). An activity is 'regulated' if it is of a specified kind which is carried on by way of business or relates to an investment of a specified kind or is a specified activity carried on in relation to property of any kind (s 22; see the FSMA (Regulated Activities) Order 2001 (SI 2001/544)). The phrase 'by way of business' was also contained in the 1986 Act and was construed by Hobhouse J as meaning a business transaction as opposed to 'something personal or casual' (see *Morgan Grenfell v Welwyn Hatfield District Council* (1995) and *Helden v Strathmore Ltd* (2011)).

5.14 The LSE is therefore the principal RIE for trading securities of UK and foreign companies, government stocks, and options to trade company securities. To become an RIE an exchange must satisfy the FCA that it has sufficient financial resources, that it is a fit and proper body, that it can operate an orderly market, and can secure appropriate protection for investors (FSMA, ss 285–290). The LSE's statutory obligation to operate an orderly market also obliges it to monitor listed companies on an ongoing basis. As a result, when a company has obtained a listing by complying with the Listing Rules it can only maintain listed status if it complies with the continuing obligation specified in the Listing Rules and monitored by the LSE. Of course the fact the LSE is itself a listed company subject to the Listing Rules means it is in effect regulating itself. This odd situation has been compounded by the consistent attempts by US and continental European exchanges to take over the LSE by buying its shares. If for example the New York Stock Exchange or Deutsche Börse was successful in taking over the LSE (both have been trying for some time to buy the LSE) in effect UK listed companies will be partly regulated from the USA or Germany.

The regulation of listed companies

Obligations at the time of listing

5.15 The FCA and the LSE cooperate to ensure that companies comply with the listing requirements and the continuing obligations imposed on listed companies. The main substantive rules regulating admission to listing relate to the availability of past accounts, compliance with a minimum market capitalisation, and a minimum 'proportion of the shares in public hands' (25 per cent for a Premium main market listing) requirement. The FSMA, s 80 specifies in considerable detail the information that must be made available to the public by a company when its shares are being listed. These derive from the requirement that the documents issued must 'contain all such information as investors and their professional advisers would reasonably require, and reasonably expect to find there, for the purpose of making an informed assessment of: (a) the assets and liabilities, financial position, profits and losses and prospects of the issuer of the securities; and (b) the rights attaching to those securities'. The duty of disclosure laid down by s 80(1) applies only to information: (a) within the knowledge of any person responsible for the listing particulars; or (b) which it would be reasonable for him/her to obtain by making enquiries (s 80(3)). In determining what information s 80(1) requires to be included in the listing particulars, s 80(4) provides that regard must be had to: (a) the nature of the securities and their issuer; (b) the nature of the persons likely to consider acquiring them; (c) the fact that certain matters may reasonably be expected to be within the knowledge of professional advisers which the prospective investor may reasonably be expected to consult; and (d) any information available to investors or their professional advisers as a result of requirements imposed on the issuer of the securities by an RIE, by Listing Rules, or under any other enactment.

5.16 Exactly what document has to be issued by the company depends on the procedure being adopted. If an application for listing is being made in respect of shares 'to be offered to the public in the UK for the first time', a prospectus (the document issued to the public inviting them to invest in the shares) must be submitted to, and approved by, the FCA (FSMA, ss 84–85, the Listing Rules), and be in accordance with the EU Prospectus Regulations ((EU) 2017/1129 (at para **5.41**)). In the less common situation where the company is merely applying for admission to listing of a class of shares which has already been issued, then listing particulars also have to be submitted to and approved by the FCA (FSMA, s 79 and the Listing Rules). The content of each document is essentially the same For a good guide to the listing process and the issues involved see https://www.nibusinessinfo.co.uk/content/london-stock-exchange-main-market.

Continuing obligations

5.17 Following listing, companies are subject to a range of continuing obligations to disclose information necessary to maintain an orderly market and to protect investors. Section 96 of the FSMA derives from the Consolidated Admissions and Reporting Directive (see para **5.13**) and is expressed in wide terms: it states that 'Listing rules may specify requirements to be complied with by issuers of listed securities and make provision with respect to the action that may be taken by the competent authority in the event of non-compliance.' The continuing obligations are specified in the FCA Listing Rules. In essence depending on the type of listing (Premium, standard, high growth, or AIM) they require listed companies to adhere to additional requirements for the continued issuing of shares, the provision of enhanced information in accounts and reports, as well as provisions for preliminary statements and dividend disclosure. They also contain obligations with regard to the UK Corporate Governance Code (see Chapter 16) and the model code on managerial dealing in shares (these requirements are in addition to the statutory provisions on insider dealing or market abuse (see later)). Directors of listed companies must also produce a 'business review' (CA 2006, s 417) covering the development and performance of the business which identifies the principal risks and uncertainties ahead as well as the effects of the company's operations on its stakeholders (employees, creditors, environment, and local community). See further http://www.icaew.com/index.cfm?route=143857 and Chapter 16 on the corporate governance implications of the business review.

5.18 As a general means of preventing insider dealing (see later on specific means), the Listing Rules 7.2.1A, Principle 6 require a main market Premium listed company to 'communicate information to holders and potential holders of its listed equity shares in such a way as to avoid the creation or continuance of a false market in such listed equity shares'. This is an important principle upon which the LSE operates as it places the onus on listed companies to push information out to shareholders as quickly as possible to avoid a false market. There are however obvious tensions between maintaining commercial confidentiality and speedy disclosure. For example if a company was planning a takeover this would necessarily need to remain confidential until the last minute despite the possibility of a false market being created. In such a case the company could apply to the FCA for an exemption or if the time span was short a company not wishing to disclose the exact nature of price-sensitive information might request temporary suspension of listing until the information can be published.

5.19 On 20 January 2007 a version of the Transparency Directive (2004/109/EC) was implemented for UK listed companies. The aim of the Directive is to increase transparency of information on the issuers of securities listed on a regulated market in the EU. In doing so Part 43 of the CA 2006 amends Part 6 of the FSMA in a number of ways to implement the requirements of the Directive. Thus it requires companies to produce periodic financial reports and specifies the minimum content of those reports. It requires major shareholders to disclose their holdings at certain thresholds. Indeed, one of the controversies in negotiating the Directive was that the UK threshold for compulsory disclosure under the Companies Act 1985 was triggered at 3 per cent rather than the 5 per cent proposal in the draft Directive. In the final Directive the disclosure percentage was set at 5 per cent, 10 per cent, 15 per cent, 20 per cent, 25 per cent, 30 per cent, 50 per cent, and 75 per cent but the threshold for disclosure with regard to UK issuers of securities was retained at 3 per cent. Thus in the UK where a shareholder achieves a 3 per cent shareholding a disclosure must be made to the company who will then make a public disclosure to the market. Additional disclosures must be made for every 1 per cent increase or decrease in that shareholding and in a takeover situation a similar but lower threshold (1 per cent rather than 3 per cent) disclosure regime applies (http://www.thetakeoverpanel.org.uk/disclosure). On the implementation of the Directive, responsibility for the shareholding disclosures was moved from the Department of Trade and Industry (DTI) (now the Department for Business, Energy & Industrial Strategy (BEIS)) to the FSA (now FCA). The Directive also requires that companies disclose information to investors in a fast, non-discriminatory, and pan-European basis. Additionally the transparency regime also provides for criminal and civil penalties for non-compliance. (See also Chapter 9 on the Shareholders Rights Directive.) Again the financial crisis has impacted in this area and at the EU level. Concern that the disclosure requirements of the Transparency Directive may have encouraged short-term behaviour by companies has led the Commission to propose removing the obligation for quarterly financial reports in the Transparency Directive Amending Directive (2013/50/EU). As a result of the Directive and domestic concerns in the Kay Review (see Chapter 16) in November 2014 the FCA amended its rules and no longer requires interim management statements (see http://www.fca.org.uk/your-fca/documents/policy-statements/ps14-15).

The regulation of takeovers

5.20   Once a company is listed on a stock exchange its shares may be freely traded. This creates the possibility that another individual or more likely another company can gain control of a listed company by buying up the shares in the company. In traditional (neo-classical—see Chapter 15 for a fuller explanation) economics this is termed the market for corporate control and is an important restraint on management acting in their own self-interest (directors' duties also act as a restraint, see Chapter 14). In theory, at least, an underperforming management in a listed company will cause shareholders to sell their shares. At some point those shares will be so low that another company will try to take over the underperforming company and either run it more efficiently or sell off its assets for a profit. Management therefore have an incentive to perform because if they do not they risk losing their jobs if the company is taken over. However, it is worth noting that the CLRSG doubted this was an effective control on management (*Developing the Framework*, para 3.164). Of course, there is the risk that management may just underperform and try to frustrate such a bid. As such, the regulation of takeovers is a matter of some concern for shareholders and, in turn, the market regulators if market confidence is to be maintained. Employees who may lose their jobs in a takeover, for example in the 2010 Kraft/Cadbury takeover, do not get much consideration here as the regulatory focus is on the shareholders being treated fairly.

5.21   Takeovers in the UK have a long history of self-regulation but before we discuss the main form of regulation we must first discuss the few general provisions of the CA 2006 that relate to takeovers. Disclosure provisions relating to directors' salaries contained in s 219 may be relevant if a takeover could result (as it usually does) in directors losing their jobs as it requires member disclosure and approval of such payments in a takeover situation. In such a situation this section is useful in calculating the cost of the takeover. Additionally as we noted earlier the Transparency Directive requires anyone acquiring a 3 per cent holding in a company to disclose their interest to the company and again every time their interest increases or decreases by 1 per cent (note the Takeover Panel's disclosure threshold in a takeover situation is 1 per cent—Rule 8.3(a) of the City Code on Takeovers and Mergers). Section 793 of the CA 2006 also confers on a public company the ability to issue a notice requiring a person who it knows, or has reasonable cause to believe, has an interest in its shares (or to have had an interest in the previous three years) to confirm or deny the fact, and, if they confirm the interest to disclose information about the interest, including information about any other person with an interest in the shares. It serves a useful purpose for companies in that it allows them to find out the identity of those with voting rights (direct or indirect) and it also enables companies (and members of the company) to ascertain the underlying beneficial owners of shares. Additionally the section allows a company to follow a chain of disclosure information by requiring information from nominees about the person they are acting for. The company can additionally construct a chain of ownership by requiring in subsection (6) information from past owners as to the person they sold the shares to. The company can also require information on any share acquisition agreements, or any agreement or arrangement as to how the rights attaching to those shares should be exercised (s 825). As we considered in Chapter 1, concerns about complex company ownership discouraging investment and facilitating crime or tax evasion led to the introduction of statutory guidance in 2017 to expand the public shareholder register to ensure that Persons with Significant Influence or Control (PSC) appear on the public register. Originally all listed companies were exempt from the PSC requirements but from 24 July 2017 AIM companies are required to ensure PSCs appear on their register. A PSC includes an individual holding more than 25 per cent of the shares or voting rights of the company, an individual who could appoint or remove a majority of the board, or an individual who could or does exercise significant influence over the company. It also covers an individual behind a trust or firm that if it were an individual would fulfil these criteria. These various transparency provisions are helpful both for the potential acquirer to assess the cost and feasibility of a bid and for the target company to monitor any potential bidders.

5.22 Originally the common law protected the rights of shareholders to retain their shares in a takeover situation because a compulsory purchase would offend natural justice (see *Brown v British Abrasive Wheel* (1919)). Problems with smaller shareholders however soon arose which caused statutory intervention in the area. The Greene Committee (*Company Law Amendment Committee Report 1925 to 1926* (Cmd 2657, 1926)) recommended allowing compulsory purchase of minority shareholders where a takeover had occurred. They explained their reasoning as follows:

> [t]he acquiring company generally desires to obtain the whole of the share capital of the company which is being taken over and in some cases will not entertain the business except on that basis. It has been represented to us that holders of a small number of shares of the company which is being taken over (either from a desire to exact better terms than their fellow shareholders are content to accept or from lack of real interest in the matter) frequently fail to come into an arrangement which commends itself to the vast majority of their fellow shareholders with the result that the transaction fails to materialise.

The Companies Act 1929 implemented the recommendations of the Greene Committee allowing compulsory purchase and those provisions are now contained in CA 2006, s 979.

5.23 The UK statutory scheme was in effect introduced to resolve a conflict of interest between the owners or contingent owners of a newly acquired majority shareholding in a company and the minority shareholders in the same company. The ultimate aim of the legislation was to make it easier to take companies over. The legislation provides a contingent right of the majority shareholder to compulsorily purchase the shares of the minority shareholders. Arguably of course it can also discourage takeovers in a general sense as a bidder needs to have enough funding to buy all the shares rather than just the funds for a majority stake.

5.24 A potential takeover bidder therefore may proceed with a bid broadly in the knowledge that if they gain a 90 per cent controlling stake in the target company they can force the minority to sell their shares at the same price. A minority shareholder may also force the bidder to buy their shares if the bidder does not try to compulsory purchase their shares (CA 2006, s 983). Section 986 also allows a minority shareholder to apply to court to object to a compulsory purchase. This, however, is an extremely difficult action to succeed in, given that 90 per cent of the shareholders will have considered the price fair enough to accept (see *Re Sussex Brick Co Ltd* (1961)).

5.25   It is worth noting here that there are other provisions for companies in crisis (insolvency and reconstruction) which can lead to a virtual takeover, notably CA 2006, Part 26 and ss 110–111 of the Insolvency Act 1986. Part 26 of the CA 2006 allows creditors and shareholders to effect a takeover as part of a statutory scheme of arrangements for a company in crisis and ss 110–111 allow for the transfer of the business of a company in voluntary liquidation to another company in return for shares in the non-liquidated company.

5.26   However, apart from the statutory provisions just noted dealing with matters before and after the takeover the main regulation of the conduct of the takeover in the UK was until 2007 non-statutory in form. In the late 1960s a body was set up by the financial services industry, encouraged by the Bank of England, to produce rules and act as a regulator of takeovers in the UK. This body is called the Panel on Takeovers and Mergers (the Panel). The Panel administers the rules on takeovers called the City Code on Takeovers and Mergers (the Code). The Panel and the Code aim to achieve equality of treatment and opportunity for all shareholders in a takeover bid. The Panel and the Code have been in existence since 1968 when the Governor of the Bank of England and the Chairman of the LSE set up the Panel in reaction to a number of controversial takeovers in which it was felt unfair tactics had been used to the detriment of shareholders. The Panel is generally agreed to have been a great success and has become a well-respected part of the UK's financial services architecture. Since 1968 the Panel has handled more than 10,000 cases.

5.27   Members of the Panel are often drawn from the financial services sector. There can be up to 36 members of the Panel. This can be comprised of up to 22 members appointed by the Panel itself with the rest appointed directly by organisations representing City of London financial institutions. In 2018 there were 29 members, 17 of whom were appointed by the Panel and the other 12 appointed by organisations such as the Institute of Chartered Accountants in England and Wales and the British Bankers' Association. The Panel's remit covers public companies resident in the UK whether they are listed or not. It may also deal with private companies whose shareholdings are widely dispersed. The focus of the Panel's role in any given takeover is to ensure the fair conduct of the takeover bid for the shareholders. It does not have any role in evaluating the financial or commercial merit of the bid, rather it leaves that decision to the companies involved. Any questions on the competitive impact of a takeover or merger will not be dealt with by the Panel but rather by the UK and EU competition authorities.

5.28 In order to fulfil its role the Panel has produced a code of conduct known as the City Code on Takeovers and Mergers. The Code is an evolving document which the Panel stresses is flexible as long as companies keep to the spirit of the Code. The Code therefore emphasises a number of general principles and rules of which the following are the most important:

- When a person or group acquires interests in shares carrying 30 per cent or more of the voting rights of a company, they must make a cash offer to all other shareholders at the highest price paid in the 12 months before the offer was announced (30 per cent of the voting rights of a company is treated by the Code as the level at which effective control is obtained).

- When interests in shares carrying 10 per cent or more of the voting rights of a class have been acquired by an offeror (i.e. a bidder) in the offer period and the previous 12 months, the offer must include a cash alternative for all shareholders of that class at the highest price paid by the offeror in that period. Further, if an offeror acquires for cash any interest in shares during the offer period, a cash alternative must be made available at that price at least.

- If the offeror acquires an interest in shares in an offeree company (i.e. a target) at a price higher than the value of the offer, the offer must be increased accordingly.

- The offeree company must appoint a competent independent adviser whose advice on the offer must be made known to all the shareholders, together with the opinion of the board.

- Favourable deals for selected shareholders are banned.

- All shareholders must be given the same information.

- Those issuing takeover circulars must include statements taking responsibility for the contents.

- Profit forecasts and asset valuations must be made to specified standards and must be reported on by professional advisers.

- Misleading, inaccurate, or unsubstantiated statements made in documents or to the media must be publicly corrected immediately.

- Actions during the course of an offer by the offeree company which might frustrate the offer are generally prohibited unless shareholders approve these plans.

- Stringent requirements are laid down for the disclosure of dealings in relevant securities during an offer.

- Employees of both the offeror and the offeree company and the trustees of the offeree company's pension scheme must be informed about an offer. In addition, the offeree company's employee representatives and pension scheme trustees have the right to have a separate opinion on the effects of the offer on employment appended to the offeree board's circular or published on a website.

The legal status of the Panel

5.29   The Panel has an executive made up of full-time employees and employees on se-
condment from city firms to deal with the day-to-day aspects of overseeing every
takeover, i.e. checking that all documents and announcements issued, and actions
taken, comply with the Code. The executive will also provide advice to those contemplating a bid as to the conduct of that bid. Appeals from the decisions of the executive
are heard by the Hearings Committee of the Panel. There is then a further right of
appeal to the Takeover Appeal Board. The Panel's decisions are also subject to judicial
review because of the public nature of its regulatory role (see *R v Panel on Takeovers
and Mergers, ex p Datafin* (1987)). However, historically the courts would only hear
the review after the takeover is complete, thus eliminating using the courts in a tac-
tical sense during the progress of a takeover bid (see paras **5.32–5.33** on the reform
of the Panel).

5.30   Despite the court's historic recognition of the Panel's public role it was not a statutory
body nor did it exercise any statutory powers until 2007. However, such was the respect
for the Panel within the financial services sector that its rulings were generally complied
with. The self-regulating status of the Panel has now ended as the result of some significant European reforms in the area of takeovers.

The Takeovers Directive (Directive 2004/25/EC of the European Parliament and of the Council of 21 April 2004 on Takeover Bids)

5.31   In 1989 the European Commission put forward a draft directive on European takeovers
with the aim of harmonising takeover provisions within the EU. The measure was actively encouraged by the UK as there was a long-felt resentment that there was a free
market for takeovers in the UK but that defensive measures were permitted in most
other EU states. Thus a German company could easily take over a UK listed company
but a UK company could not take over a large German company. The draft Thirteenth
Directive was largely based on the City Code's provisions and generally prevented the
use of takeover defences and so found favour with the UK Government. However, it did
not find favour in many other EU states, indeed France and Germany were particularly
opposed. Thus for more than a decade little movement occurred at all. By 1999 there
seemed to be a more favourable environment for the Directive and it began to be promoted by Austria as well as the UK and Ireland. Eventually, in 2001 political agreement
was reached on a text of the draft Directive by the Council of Ministers but it was rejected by the European Parliament. In April 2004 a much compromised Directive was
eventually agreed.

5.32   While the Government emphasised that the final form of legislation implementing the
Directive retains the independence of the Panel, the Directive required the establishment of a statutory body which would oversee statutory takeover provisions. The CA

2006, Part 28 in effect converted the self-regulating Panel (CA 2006, s 942) into just such a statutory body to oversee takeovers in the UK on 6 April 2007. This represented a significant departure from its historic and formerly sacred self-regulatory status. The Panel was far from happy with this outcome primarily because it considered that the creation of a statutory body overseeing takeover legislation would lead to increased litigation and inflexibility which would defeat the usefulness of the Panel. Only time will tell if this is the case but since its inception as a statutory body its functioning has not yet been significantly impaired.

5.33 Under the former self-regulatory system the Panel had no formal powers to sanction but was particularly good at alerting shareholders and regulators to bid irregularities. The effect of this influence was that professional bodies operating in the financial services sector would at the request of the Panel sanction a person or company falling within their jurisdiction. Similarly the FCA might suspend or remove a company's listing as a result of the Panel's findings and impose formal sanctions on individuals involved in the bid irregularities. Under the Takeover Directive reforms, the Panel now has its own range of sanctions contained in CA 2006, ss 952–956. Thus the Panel now has formal powers to issue statements of censure, issue directions, refer conduct to other regulatory bodies, order compensation to be paid for breach of the Code, and refer a matter for enforcement by the court. In 2017, the Panel used its powers under the Companies Act 2006 for the first time to compel compliance with a decision of the panel (see http://www.thetakeover appealboard.org.uk/downloads/2017-01.pdf) and has by necessity developed an increasingly formal regulatory role.

Insider dealing

5.34 Once shares become easily bought and sold on a stock exchange the potential for those inside or connected to the company to abuse their knowledge of the company's future plans or announcements arises. Let us take the example of company X planning to take over company Y. There will be a period when company X will be planning its takeover but has taken no action which would alert the market. During this period employees of company X will have very valuable information that the share market does not have. In general an attempted takeover once it is apparent or formally announced will boost the share price of the target company. Thus in this crucial planning phase the employees of X could buy shares in company Y in the knowledge that the attempted takeover announcement will boost company Y's share price and they can then sell those shares and make a quick profit.

5.35 Every country in the world with a major stock exchange has made this practice illegal because of its potential to destroy public confidence in the stock exchange. However, there are those who believe that insider dealing should not be outlawed as it acts as part of the neo-classical market equilibrium mechanism in setting share prices (see McVea (1995), Carlton and Fischel (1982–3), Leland (1992), and Chapter 15 on neo-classical theory). In other words the buying of shares in company Y by executives of company X will alert the market to the potential takeover and remove a false market in those shares. In general, the view that such behaviour is morally reprehensible prevails and the law attempts to deal with this through criminal and civil sanctions (see Campbell (1996) on why insider dealing is outlawed). As we discussed earlier with regard to the continuing obligations of listed companies, the LSE also tries to ensure that opportunities for in-sider dealing are minimised by ensuring that companies disclose any significant infor-mation that might affect share price as quickly as possible.

Criminal sanctions

5.36   Until 2012 s 397 of the FSMA contained a general catch-all criminal provision on false and misleading information which covered insider dealing-type activity. In 2013 with the implementation of the Financial Services Act 2012, s 397 of the FSMA was replaced with ss 89–91 of the Financial Services Act 2012 criminalising the making of false or misleading statements (s 89), creating false or misleading statements (s 90), and making false or misleading statements or creating false or misleading impressions in relation to specified benchmarks (e.g. LIBOR) (s 91). However, Part V of the Criminal Justice Act 1993 contains the main criminal provisions specifically on insider dealing. Section 52(1) states:

> [a]n individual who has information as an insider is guilty of insider dealing if, in the circumstances mentioned in subsection (3) [that is, it is a regulated market and the in-sider deals himself as a professional or through a professional intermediary,] he deals in securities that are price-affected securities in relation to the information.

The insider will also be guilty of an offence if he induces others to deal (whether they know the information is price-sensitive or not) in price-sensitive securities on a regulated market (s 52(2)(a)). It is also an offence just to disclose price-sensitive information to another person in an irregular manner (s 52(2)(a)). If a person is found guilty a fine or imprisonment for up to seven years is possible.

5.37   The criminal insider-dealing provisions had historically not been a great success because of the difficulty in reaching the criminal standard of proof. As Bagge et al (2000) explain:

> [t]he more onerous criminal standard of proof has meant there have been few prosecu-tions and even fewer convictions under these provisions. Between 1995 and 1999 there have been just three insider trading convictions in the UK. This contrasts with 162 civil cases for insider dealing won by the US Securities and Exchange Commission during the same period. The government has therefore decided that the [FSA now FCA], in pursuit of its statutory objective of maintaining confidence in the financial markets,

ought to be able to take administrative action against any market participant who abuses the market.

However the financial crisis that began in autumn 2008 brought a significant change of priority for the FCA in this area and it has been very active and successful in pursuing insider-dealing activities since then (see https://www.fca.org.uk/markets/market-abuse).

The civil sanction regime

5.38 As a result of the historic difficulty in prosecuting individuals under the criminal regime the UK Government introduced a civil offence of 'market abuse' originally contained in s 118 of the FSMA. In 2016 this was replaced by the Market Abuse Regulation (Regulation (EU) No 596/2014). The Market Abuse Regulation had direct effect in the UK from 3 July 2016. While it is broadly similar to the previous regime set out in s 118 of the FSMA in the UK it creates an enhanced range of prohibited activities and extends the type of markets these might apply to. The Regulation is extensive in its consideration of the scope of market abuse but in essence it focuses on insider dealing, market manipulation, and various safe harbour provisions that exempt certain accepted market behaviour.

Article 8(1) states:

For the purposes of this Regulation, insider dealing arises where a person possesses inside information and uses that information by acquiring or disposing of, for its own account or for the account of a third party, directly or indirectly, financial instruments to which that information relates. The use of inside information by cancelling or amending an order concerning a financial instrument to which the information relates where the order was placed before the person concerned possessed the inside information, shall also be considered to be insider dealing. In relation to auctions of emission allowances or other auctioned products based thereon that are held pursuant to Regulation (EU) No 1031/2010, the use of inside information shall also comprise submitting, modifying or withdrawing a bid by a person for its own account or for the account of a third party.

Article 12(1) states:

For the purposes of this Regulation, market manipulation shall comprise the following activities:

(a) entering into a transaction, placing an order to trade or any other behaviour which:

(i) gives, or is likely to give, false or misleading signals as to the supply of, demand for, or price of, a financial instrument, a related spot commodity contract or an auctioned product based on emission allowances; or

(ii) secures, or is likely to secure, the price of one or several financial instruments, a related spot commodity contract or an auctioned product based on emission allowances at an abnormal or artificial level;

unless the person entering into a transaction, placing an order to trade or engaging in any other behaviour establishes that such transaction, order or behaviour have been carried out for legitimate reasons, and conform with an accepted market practice as established in accordance with Article 13;

(b) entering into a transaction, placing an order to trade or any other activity or behaviour which affects or is likely to affect the price of one or several financial instruments, a related spot commodity contract or an auctioned product based on emission allowances, which employs a fictitious device or any other form of deception or contrivance;

(c) disseminating information through the media, including the internet, or by any other means, which gives, or is likely to give, false or misleading signals as to the supply of, demand for, or price of, a financial instrument, a related spot commodity contract or an auctioned product based on emission allowances or secures, or is likely to secure, the price of one or several financial instruments, a related spot commodity contract or an auctioned product based on emission allowances at an abnormal or artificial level, including the dissemination of rumours, where the person who made the dissemination knew, or ought to have known, that the information was false or misleading;

(d) transmitting false or misleading information or providing false or misleading inputs in relation to a benchmark where the person who made the transmission or provided the input knew or ought to have known that it was false or misleading, or any other behaviour which manipulates the calculation of a benchmark.

5.39   As such the Regulation covers a wide range of actions ranging from insider dealing, improper disclosure, misuse of information, manipulative and deceptive trading, to dissemination or non-disclosure of information. For example in 2014, Tesco Plc released information into the market that for a time created a false or misleading impression as to the value of Tesco Plc's shares. The information at issue had been provided by a subsidiary of Tesco Plc and the FCA did not suggest that the board were aware that the information was not correct. In 2017 Tesco Plc was publicly censured by the FCA for its actions but was not fined as it agreed a compensation order to compensate investors for any losses (see https://www.fca.org.uk/publication/final-notices/tesco-2017.pdf). The Regulation is intended to be somewhat flexible in that it takes into account behaviour and industry standards. Article 13 for example allows the FCA to provide guidance as to the sort of conduct which encompasses acceptable practice.

5.40   In order to investigate a suspected market abuse the FCA has wide investigative powers. It also has a number of possible sanctions such as public censure, fines,

injunctions, restitution and compensation orders, and to vary or cancel an investment authorisation. Despite this, activities that fall within the purview of market
abuse are still generally regarded as widespread and this was one of the reasons for
the introduction of the Market Abuse Regulation (2014/596/EU), although as we
noted earlier since the advent of the financial crisis in autumn 2008 the FCA has been
very active in both insider dealing and market abuse (see https://www.fca.org.uk/
markets/market-abuse/regulation and https://www.fca.org.uk/news/press-releases/
two-found-guilty-insider-dealing).

The regulation of other public offers

5.41 Naturally, concerns about investor protection mean that the offering of shares by non-
listed public companies also has to be regulated. However getting the balance right on
facilitating public offers and onerous regulation has proved challenging. Until 2005
such offers by non-listed companies were governed separately from offers by listed
companies, by the Public Offers of Securities Regulations 1995 (SI 1995/1537; hereafter referred to as the POSR), which implemented the first EU Prospectus Directive
(89/298/EEC). Since 2005 and the implementation of further Prospectus Directives
(Directive 2003/71/EC and Directive 2010/73/EU) in the Prospectus Regulations
2005, a single regime was put in place in Part VI of the FSMA regulating the prospectus requirements of listed and non-listed offerings. This regime proved somewhat obstructive and costly and so the EU Prospectus Regulation ((EU) 2017/1129)
was introduced in 2017 to maintain the same overall principles of disclosure and
investor protection but with the intention of simplifying and focusing the regime.
In particular the Regulation widens the exemptions from having to produce a prospectus, e.g. the offer is less than €1 million. It also reduces the extent of the disclosures needed in a prospectus while at the same time focusing the summary disclosures
on key risk factors.

5.42 In certain cases however a full prospectus may not be needed. Section 101(1) and (2)
of the FSMA state that the Part VI rules may authorise the FCA to 'dispense with or
modify' the duty to prepare a prospectus for shares to be listed or listing particulars. In
such cases information equivalent to a prospectus or listing particulars will have been
published in the preceding 12 months. Provided the duty of disclosure contained in
s 80 has been discharged (see para **5.15**), the issuer need only publish an abbreviated
prospectus which identifies the changes that have occurred since the last prospectus
was published.

5.43 If the offer for sale is not a public offer (because of the exemptions), it may still be
regulated by the rules on investment advertisements contained in s 21 of the FSMA.
Subject to certain exceptions, this prevents issuing an advertisement inviting people

to 'engage in investment activity' (broadly an agreement to buy or sell shares or securities or exercise rights in relation to shares or securities already held, without the approval of a person authorised under the Act (s 21(8); SI 2001/1335, art 4 and Sch 1)).

Sanctions

5.44 The final role identified for the state is to ensure that if there is not complete or accurate disclosure by a company, investors have a satisfactory remedy where they have suffered loss and that offences, where they have occurred, do not go unpunished. Just as there are a variety of ways in which public offers of shares are regulated, so there are a variety of remedies and sanctions.

5.45 Failure to comply with provisions of the FSMA has the most serious consequences as breach is often a criminal offence. This is the case in relation to s 21 (para **5.43**). Breach thereof will also affect the enforceability of any agreement entered into after the issue of the advertisement by the party in breach and will entitle the other party 'to recover any money or other property paid or transferred by him under the agreement; and . . . compensation for any loss sustained by him as a result of having parted with it' (s 26).

5.46 Non-compliance with the Part VI Rules will often be dealt with by the UK Listing Authority or the FCA, imposing the sanctions open to it. These include censure, fines, and compensation (although the Act specifically retains any liability at common law or under any other legislation (s 90(6)) depending on the nature of the breach).

Irregularities in relation to public documents might also cause a breach of the provisions of other statutes (for instance, s 19 of the Theft Act 1968). As noted earlier, other civil remedies are also available if there has been a misrepresentation but they will not often provide a better remedy than those in the FSMA, although the measure of damages may be more beneficial to the misrepresentee if there has been fraud (see *Smith New Court Securities Ltd v Scrimgeour Vickers (Asset Management) Ltd* (1996)).

5.47 Finally, as we discussed earlier with regard to insider dealing, the FSMA and the Financial Services Act 2012 confer power on the FCA to prosecute persons making misleading statements, cases of insider dealing, market manipulation, terrorist financing, and breaches of the Money Laundering Regulations (FSMA, ss 401 and 402; Financial Services Act 2012, ss 89–90). Additionally the Financial Services Acts 2010 and 2012 have given the FCA enhanced powers to fine and suspend individuals and firms, issue warnings, void remuneration packages, and impose consumer redress schemes. These provisions are aimed both at specific behaviour and at behaviour that might damage confidence in the public markets.

The regulatory regime

5.48 The regulation of UK industry generally has something of a distinctive flavour. Historically most of the regulatory environment was provided by industry itself with a loose supervision by the Department of Trade and Industry (now BEIS) and the Bank of England. As Wilks (1997) has observed:

> British economic regulation involves a striking combination of continuity in ideas (or traditions) and innovation in organisations. British traditions of public administration have consistently attached importance to the autonomy of the firm. This has rested on a deep-seated respect for property and the freedom to contract, combined with the legacy of a non-interventionist, minimalist state. In practice this has translated into 'arms length' regulation and has produced a regulatory style which is based on accommodation, mutual respect and negotiation.

5.49 As we noted earlier, the Labour Government elected in 1997 did much to move away from this self-regulatory system in recent years. In particular initial centralisation of authority under the FSA, and since then the fragmentation of regulation to various bodies including the FCA, has done much to change the self-regulatory flavour of the financial services sector. However, although there is now a statutory backing for bodies such as the LSE and the Panel on Takeovers and Mergers much of their activity remains free from the scrutiny that would attach to them if they were originally created by primary legislation.

5.50 The continuing reform of the self-regulatory system was one of the major issues considered by the CLRSG. In 'Regulation and Boundaries of the Law' (see para 5.5 in *The Strategic Framework* consultation document, 1999) the CLRSG noted that although there has been considerable centralising of authority under the old FSA it recognised legislation may be required to simplify the arrangements for allocating jurisdiction between regulatory bodies (see further the *Final Report*, paras 3.56–3.66 and ch 5; and vol I of the 2002 White Paper, ch 4).

5.51 The outcome of that consultation exercise was the recommendation of a new 'Regulatory and Institutional Framework for Company Law' (*Completing the Structure*, ch 12). However, it is envisaged that this would not have a direct effect on the mode of regulating listed companies. In the view of the CLRSG:

> [t]o operate successfully the bodies responsible for company law would need to work effectively alongside other parts of the wider regulatory framework and, in particular, the FSA, both as securities market regulator and as Listing Authority, and the Takeovers Panel.
>
> We recognise the importance of close co-operation between the bodies proposed for company law, and those responsible for these related areas. But we do not see any strong arguments for recommending that any of these functions should be combined with those

of the company law regulatory bodies. Nor do we see any need for any more extensive redrawing of the regulatory 'map'. (Paras 12.112–12.113)

The White Paper and the Consultative Document of March 2005 broadly endorsed this approach (see ch 5 of the White Paper and para 6.2 of the Consultative Document) and the CA 2006 made little change to the overall regulatory structure.

5.52 The financial crisis that unfolded in autumn 2008 however brought significant criticism of the shared regulatory arrangements in the UK, as failures at the FSA, the Bank of England, and the Treasury played a role in the crisis. As UK Government financial commitment to the banking sector as a result of the financial crisis reached over 60 per cent of GDP in late 2009, the biggest bailout of any Western nation, Mervyn King, the Governor of the Bank of England remarked:

> *To paraphrase a great wartime leader, never in the field of financial endeavour has so much money been owed by so few to so many. And, one might add, so far with little real reform.*

Eventually, as we noted earlier in this chapter, extensive EU and UK institutional reform has occurred with the domestic break-up of the FSA and creation of the Prudential Regulatory Authority (PRA), the Financial Conduct Authority (FCA), and the Financial Policy Committee (FPC) tasked with large-scale industry oversight. At the EU level the de Larosière Report (https://ec.europa.eu/info/business-economy-euro/banking-and-finance/financial-supervision-and-risk-management/european-system-financial-supervision_en) reviewing financial supervision in the EU led to the creation of three new EU supervisory bodies: the European Banking Authority, the European Insurance and Occupational Pensions Authority, and the European Securities and Markets Authority. In all, Brexit will mean a significant change from the current EU system of powerful but fragmented regulators coordinating across Member States. (See the Prospectus (Amendment etc) (EU Exit) Regulations 2019.)

FURTHER READING

This chapter links with the materials in Chapters 4, 17, and 18 of *Hicks and Goo's Cases and Materials on Company Law* (Oxford, OUP, 2011, xl +649p).

Bagge, Evans, Wade, and Lewis, 'Market Abuse: Proposals for the New Regime' [2000] X1(9) *PLC* 35.

Carlton and Fischel, 'The Regulation of Insider Dealing' (1982–1983) 35 *Stan L Rev* 857.

Clarke, 'European Union Articles 9 and 11 of the Takeover Directive (2004/25) and the Market for Corporate Control' [2006] *JBL* 355.

Company Law Reform (Cm 6456, 2005) (Consultative Document, March 2005), para 3.6 and para 6.2, http://webarchive.nationalarchives.gov.uk/+/http:/www.dti.gov.uk/cld/WhitePaper .pdf.

Davies, *Gower and Davies' Principles of Modern Company Law*, 10th edn (London, Sweet & Maxwell, 2016), chs 24–26 and 28–30.

Dignam, 'Lamenting Reform? The Changing Nature of Common Law Corporate Governance Regulation' [2007] *Company and Securities LJ* 283.

Ferran, 'The Break-Up of the Financial Services Authority', University of Cambridge Faculty of Law Research Paper Series No. 10/04 (11 October 2010), http://ssrn.com/abstract=1690523.

Financial Services in the UK; A New Framework for Investor Protection (Cmnd 9430, 1983).

Leland, 'Insider Trading: Should It Be Prohibited?' (1992) 100 *Journal of Political Economy* 859.

Lord Alexander of Weedon QC, 'Takeovers: The Regulatory Scene' [1990] *JBL* 203.

Marsh, 'Disciplinary Proceedings Against Authorised Firms and Approved Persons Under The Financial Services and Markets Act 2000' in de Lacy (ed) *The Reform of United Kingdom Company Law* (London, Cavendish, 2002).

Morse, 'The City Code on Takeovers and Mergers—Self Regulation or Self Protection?' [1991] *JBL* 509.

SELF-TEST QUESTIONS

1   What is the difference between a public and a private company?

2   Describe the role of the FCA in regulating listed companies.

3   What is the primary function of the LSE?

4   What does the Panel on Takeovers and Mergers do?

5   What is insider dealing?

6 Raising capital: debentures: fixed and floating charges

Introduction

6.1 It is beyond the scope of this book to provide a detailed analysis of the different types of loan capital provided by financial institutions. This chapter therefore focuses on corporate borrowing where this is done by debentures or debenture stock. It also examines the types of charge that companies can issue to creditors, i.e. floating and fixed charges. The priority of secured creditors is considered, together with an examination of the registration requirements for charges. The related matter of the rules and procedures governing competing corporate creditors in insolvency proceedings is dealt with in Chapter 17.

6.2 By way of preliminary, we should note some important distinctions between the ability of small and large companies to raise loan capital. The most accessible form of external finance for most small to medium-sized companies is a loan from a financial institution. Larger companies with greater loan capital needs can also tap the loan capital markets for funds. The loan capital markets represent an important feature on the corporate finance landscape. Loan capital is an extremely flexible way of raising capital as it can be listed, i.e. issued via a stock market, or unlisted. Investment in loan capital is therefore similar in a number of key respects to investment in shares. Both are 'securities' but the nature of the risk and the returns on the investment will be different. However, it should be noted that the key distinction between shareholders and investment creditors is that the former has rights *in* the company whereas the latter acquires rights *against* the company (for example, as a general rule creditors do not have a right to vote at general meetings: the extent to which they can exercise control over the company depends upon the terms of the debt contract). As we discussed briefly in Chapter 2, if creditors secure their lending they will also have rights in the company's property. In the event of insolvency the claims of a loan creditor must be paid before the shareholders. From the perspective of the debtor company, loan capital, as opposed to share capital, is a more flexible means of raising finance. Loan capital can be issued at a discount (*Moseley v Koffyfontein Mines Ltd* (1904)), interest can be paid out of capital and, importantly, is not subject to the capital maintenance regime (see Chapter 7).

Types of loan capital

Debentures

6.3 The indebtedness of a company to a creditor is generally acknowledged by way of a debenture. A good example from the case law is *Salomon v Salomon & Co* (1897) where, upon incorporation, Mr Salomon changed from being a sole trader to a debenture holder and shareholder. While we provided a brief description of a debenture in Chapter 2, it is not possible to provide a comprehensive definition of the term: the word originates from Latin meaning 'money owed to me'. The Companies Act is of little help in defining the term beyond stating that '"debenture" includes debenture stock, bonds and any other securities of a company, whether constituting a charge on the assets of the company or not' (s 738). This definition is also adopted for the purposes of s 29(2) of the Insolvency Act 1986. An obvious example of a debenture which falls within the statutory definition is a mortgage of freehold land by a company (whereby the lender (mortgagee) takes a legal charge over the property), it being a security of a company and a charge on its assets (see *Knightsbridge Estates Trust Ltd v Byrne* (1940), Lord Romer). The judges have long attempted to formulate definitions of the term. For example, in *Levy v Abercorris Slate and Slab Co* (1887), Chitty J stated that 'a debenture means a document which either creates a debt or acknowledges it, and any document which fulfils either of these conditions is a "debenture"'. The problem with this definition is that it is drawn too wide. For example, it encompasses documents such as a bank statement where the account in question stands in credit (because it is an acknowledgement that the bank effectively owes its client the amount of the credit balance). Nevertheless, Chitty J's definition has been endorsed in a number of cases: see, for example, *Lemon v Austin Friars Investment Trust Ltd* (1926) and *Fons HF v Corporal Ltd* (2014), in which the Court of Appeal found that a loan agreement even if undrawn, is an instrument which evidences or acknowledges debt and is consequently a debenture (the decision corrects what was the widely held view amongst financiers that loan agreements do not of themselves create or acknowledge debt because they merely provide the framework for lending—this view is now untenable). Pragmatic guidance was provided by Lindley J in *British India Steam Navigation Co v IRC* (1881):

> *Now, what the correct meaning of 'debenture' is I do not know. I do not find anywhere any precise definition of it. We know that there are various kinds of instruments commonly called debentures. You may have mortgage debentures, which are charges of some kind on property. You may have debentures which are bonds; and, if this instrument were under seal, it would be a debenture of that kind. You may have a debenture which is nothing more than an acknowledgement of indebtedness. And you may have [as on the facts] . . . a statement by two directors that the company will pay a certain sum of money on a given day, and will also pay interest half-yearly at certain times and at a certain place, upon production of certain coupons by the holder of the instrument. I think any of these things which I have referred to may be debentures within the Act.*

Notwithstanding the breadth of these definitions, the commercial world generally adopts a fairly restrictive view of the term, viewing 'debentures' as referring to secured loans (see *Fons HF (in Liquidation) v Corporal Ltd* (2013)).

Debentures can be categorised as either irredeemable or redeemable. Irredeemable debentures are permitted by the Companies Act notwithstanding equity's prohibition of 'clogs' or fetters on the equity of redemption. Section 739 provides that a condition contained in debentures, or in a deed for securing debentures, is not invalid by reason only that the debentures are thereby made irredeemable or redeemable only on the happening of a contingency (however remote), or on the expiration of a period (however long), any rule of equity notwithstanding (see *Knightsbridge Estates Trust Ltd v Byrne* (1940)). Redeemable debentures are generally expressed to be payable either on demand or on a fixed date. Once redeemed a debenture can be reissued by the company unless there is an express or implied prohibition contained in the articles (s 194).

Debenture stock

6.4 Debenture stock is money borrowed from a number of different lenders all on the same terms. In effect the lenders become a 'class' of creditors and their rights are usually set out in a trust deed whereby trustees are appointed (usually a financial institution) to represent the interests of the creditors, as a class, with the company. The modern practice is that all the loans are aggregated and advanced to the company by the trustees. The contractual relationship here is between the trustees and the company. Individual creditors (or 'investors') then subscribe for debenture stock in the fund (see *Sealy and Worthington's Text, Cases, & Materials in Company Law* (2016), p 620). Where the trustees do not take a charge (i.e. do not secure their lending, see para **6.5**) on the company's property the debenture stock is generally termed 'unsecured loan stock'. Whereas a single debenture cannot be transferred other than as a single unit, debenture stock is transferable in whole or in some fractional part much like a shareholding, although the trust deed may set a minimum amount. Further, debenture stock, as with debentures, may be issued in bearer form as negotiable instruments so that title will pass by mere delivery (*Bechuanaland Exploration Co v London Trading Bank* (1898)).

6.5 The trust deed will list the obligations of the company to the trustees, the central undertaking being to pay to the debenture holders the principal sum with interest. It will specify the security for the loan (if any) namely, a fixed or floating charge or both, together with a legal mortgage by demise of specified real property belonging to the company. The deed will list the events which will trigger the enforceability of the security, for example the company defaulting in payment to the debenture holders. It will also contain provisions relating to meetings of debenture holders, the transfer of debenture stock, and the power of trustees to appoint a receiver in the event of a security becoming enforceable.

Secured borrowing: company charges

6.6 Corporate borrowing is frequently secured, that is to say the debtor company is required to provide some form of security to the lender for the sum borrowed. In the event of the company being in breach of the loan contract, the lender can then take steps to enforce its security interest. For example, a loan can be secured over the company's land and in the event of the company defaulting on its repayments, the creditor can enforce its security interest immediately. Thus, the principal purpose of security is to enable the lender to recover from the company in the event of its default which, in practice, often occurs as a result of impending insolvency. Goode (2008) has described the nature of a security interest as an agreement between the creditor and debtor by which a specified asset or class of assets is appropriated to the satisfaction of the loan. Title does not pass but rather an encumbrance on the property is created. In *National Provincial Bank v Charnley* (1924) Atkin LJ noted that the principal feature of a charge is that the creditor acquired a *present* right to have the charged property made available as security:

> I think there can be no doubt that where in a transaction for value both parties evince an intention that property, existing or future, shall be made available as security for the payment of a debt, and that the creditor shall have a present right to have it made available, there is a charge, even though the present legal right which is contemplated can only be enforced at some future date, and though the creditor gets no legal right of property, either absolute or special, or any legal right to possession, but only gets a right to have the security made available by an order of the Court.

6.7 The concern of lenders when requiring security is to ensure priority in the repayment of their loans notwithstanding the claims of the general body of creditors who are therefore frequently left in the vulnerable position of picking over the few crumbs (if any) remaining of the corporate cake after satisfaction of secured and preferential creditors (preferential creditors primarily consist of employees for arrears of wages and accrued holiday pay etc, all within certain limits. In the autumn 2018 budget the Government announced its intention to restore HMRC as a preferred creditor from April 2020 in respect of PAYE, VAT, and NIC employee contributions (a status it possessed before the Enterprise Act 2002): see further, Chapter 17).

In the context of company borrowing, the most common form of charges encountered as security interests is the fixed charge and the floating charge.

Fixed and floating charges

6.8 Charges may be either fixed (or specific), the effect of which is that the chargee's rights (i.e. the lender's) attach immediately to the property in question, or floating whereby the chargee's rights attach to a 'shifting fund of assets' (*Re Cimex Tissues Ltd* (1994); *Gray v G-T-P Group Ltd* (2010)), such as receivables, stock in trade etc. A fixed charge (or specific charge) is akin to a mortgage and therefore restricts the debtor company's power to deal with the charged asset without first obtaining the creditor's permission.

6.9 The peculiar feature of a floating charge which distinguishes it from a fixed charge is that the company can continue to deal with the assets in the ordinary course of business without the need to obtain the consent of the creditor (it is estimated that some £3 billion of lending to SME is secured by floating charges). This is the very essence of the floating charge and it is, therefore, a commercially convenient way of raising secured borrowing. Refining the point further, Millett LJ in *Re Cosslett (Contractors) Ltd* (1997) commented that '[T]he question is not whether the chargor has complete freedom to carry on his business as he chooses, but whether the chargee is in control of the charged assets'.

Once an event occurs, for example a repayment default, which causes a floating charge to 'crystallise' it becomes a fixed charge over the assets within its scope and the freedom of the company to deal with those assets ceases. The crystallising event, such as default in making payment of the principal or interest, is usually stated in the debenture document although crystallisation will occur by operation of law if the company ceases to carry on business.

6.10 The distinction between fixed and floating charges and the nature of the respective security interests they confer has given rise to considerable academic debate. It is settled that a fixed charge gives rise to an equitable proprietary interest brought into being by a contract supported by consideration; and once a floating charge crystallises into a fixed charge, it is obvious that the chargee enjoys the same interest. However, there is a dispute as to whether or not the holder of a floating charge has an equitable proprietary interest prior to its crystallisation. On this question various views seeking to explain the theoretical basis of the floating charge have been propounded. For example, it has been argued that the floating charge confers an equitable interest in favour of the chargee from the time of its creation (albeit something less than the interest of a fixed chargee), coupled with a *licence* in favour of the company to deal with the assets in the ordinary course of business (see, for example, Ferran (1988 and 2008)). The fact that the holder of a floating charge acquires an immediate equity was recognised by the Court of Appeal in *Evans v Rival Granite Quarries Ltd* (1910). Buckley LJ stressed that a floating charge is not a future security but rather 'it is a present security which presently affects all the assets of the company expressed to be included in it'. The judge went on to note that:

> it is not a specific security; the holder cannot affirm that the assets are specifically mort-
> gaged to him. The assets are mortgaged in such a way that the mortgagor can deal
> with them without the concurrence of the mortgagee. A floating security is not a specific
> mortgage of the assets, plus a licence to the mortgagor to dispose of them in the course of
> his business, but is a floating mortgage applying to every item comprised in the security,
> but not specifically affecting any item until some event occurs or some act on the part of
> the mortgagee is done which causes it to crystallise into a fixed security.

Summarising Buckley LJ's formulation, Slade J in *Re Bond Worth Ltd* (1980), added that a floating charge:

> remains unattached to any particular property and leaves the company with a licence
> to deal with, and even sell, the assets falling within its ambit in the ordinary course of
> business, as if the charge had not been given, until . . . it is said to 'crystallise' . . .

6.11 Goode, agreeing with this view, finds that it is now settled that the floating charge 'creates an immediate interest *in rem*' (Goode (2008)). Further, the Privy Council has accepted that a floating charge confers a proprietary interest on its holder (*Re Goldcorp Exchange Ltd* (1994); see also *Cretanor Maritime Co Ltd v Irish Marine Management Ltd* (1978)). An alternative view is that a floating charge only has contractual effect and therefore the holder acquires no equitable proprietary interest until crystallisation (see Gough (1996)). This view is basically founded upon the fact that when a floating charge is created no appropriation of property is made. However, *Sealy and Worthington's Text, Cases, & Materials in Company Law* (2016), p 624 notes, 'that a charge is a security interest created in or over an asset or assets' by the chargor in favour of the chargee 'by which it is agreed that the property shall be appropriated to the discharge of a debt or other obligation' and that 'there is no transfer of title. The chargee's rights are proprietary, but created by contract . . .'. It should be borne in mind that a company is only permitted to deal with property which is subject to a floating charge in the ordinary course of business. A transaction which falls outside this results in the third party taking subject to the equitable interest created by the charge notwithstanding that crystallisation has not occurred (*Julius Harper Ltd v FW Hagedorn & Sons Ltd* (1989)).

6.12 The outcome of the argument assumes critical importance in the context of company liquidations because s 127 of the Insolvency Act 1986 provides that any disposition of the company's property made after the commencement of the winding-up is, unless the court otherwise orders, void. It follows from the majority views noted earlier that the disposition of property takes place when the charge is created and therefore its crystallisation does not constitute a disposition for the purposes of s 127 (see further *Re French's Wine Bar Ltd* (1987)).

6.13   As indicated earlier, property which is typically made subject to a floating charge is, by its nature, constantly changing and includes stock in trade, plant, book debts, and even the whole assets and undertaking for the time being of the company. Book debts, sometimes referred to as 'receivables', are sums owed to a company in respect of goods or services supplied by it. With respect to stock in trade, when an item is sold the charge ceases to attach to it but when something is subsequently added to the company's stock the charge will automatically extend over the new item. In this sense the idea of a charge that floats over changing property (attaching, de-attaching when sold and re-attaching when something new is added) can be more readily understood.

6.14   Characterising the nature of charges has continued to occupy the minds of judges. As has been pointed out by Lord Millett (see extract in this paragraph), the determination of whether a charge is fixed or floating is not merely a question of construction of the document creating it. The parties may have expressed that the charge in question is one or the other but this is not conclusive of the issue, the courts being more concerned with the substance of the matter rather than the description adopted by the parties (*Royal Trust Bank v National Westminster Bank plc* (1996)). In *Agnew v IRC (Re Brumark)* (2001), Lord Millett stressed that:

> *In deciding whether a charge is a fixed or a floating charge, the Court is engaged in a two-stage process. At the first stage it must construe the instrument of charge and seek to gather the intentions of the parties from the language they have used. But the object at this stage of the process is not to discover whether the parties intended to create a fixed or a floating charge. It is to ascertain the nature of the rights and obligations which the parties intended to grant each other in respect of the charged assets. Once these have been ascertained, the Court can then embark on the second stage of the process, which is one of categorisation. This is a matter of law. It does not depend on the intention of the parties. If their intention, properly gathered from the language of the instrument, is to grant the company rights in respect of the charged assets which are inconsistent with the nature of a fixed charge, then the charge cannot be a fixed charge however they may have chosen to describe it.*

The distinction between fixed and floating charges assumes immense significance during receivership and on liquidation of the company because of the relative ranking of chargees amongst the competing claims of all creditors. According to Romer LJ in *Re Yorkshire Woolcombers Association* (1903) if a charge has the following characteristics, it is a floating charge:

(1) if it is a charge on a class of assets of a company present and future;

(2) if that class is one which, in the ordinary course of the business of the company, would be changing from time to time; and

(3) if you find that by the charge it is contemplated that, until some future step is taken by or on behalf of those interested in the charge, the company may carry on its business in the ordinary way as far as concerns the particular class charged.

6.15 On appeal to the House of Lords, Lord Macnaghten expressed the view that distinguishing a floating charge from a fixed or specific charge rarely poses much difficulty. He said that a fixed charge is one which 'fastens on ascertained and definite property' or property that is 'capable of being ascertained and defined'. On the other hand, a floating charge is 'ambulatory and shifting in nature, hovering over and so to speak floating with the property which it is intended to affect' until it crystallises (*Illingworth v Houldsworth* (1904), Lord Macnaghten). In *Agnew* (para **6.14**), Lord Millett, commenting on Romer LJ's formulation, said that 'it is the third characteristic which is the hallmark of a floating charge and serves to distinguish it from a fixed charge'. More recently, in *National Westminster Bank plc v Spectrum Plus Ltd* (2004), Lord Phillips MR explained that:

> *Initially it was not difficult to distinguish between a fixed and a floating charge. A fixed charge arose where the chargor agreed that he would no longer have the right of free disposal of the assets charged, but that they should stand as security for the discharge of obligations owed to the chargee. A floating charge was normally granted by a company which wished to be free to acquire and dispose of assets in the normal course of its business, but nonetheless to make its assets available as security to the chargee in priority to other creditors should it cease to trade. The hallmark of the floating charge was the agreement that the chargor should be free to dispose of his assets in the normal course of business unless and until the chargee intervened. Up to that moment the charge 'floated'.*

6.16 Thus, like Lord Millett, Lord Phillips MR also places particular emphasis on what Romer LJ noted as the third characteristic (see also Lord Scott's speech in *Spectrum* (2005)). The point is illustrated by *Arthur D Little Ltd v Ableco Finance LLC* (2002). The company, Arthur D Little Ltd, guaranteed the liabilities of its two parent companies to Ableco by creating a charge, described as a first fixed charge, over its shareholding in a subsidiary company, CCL. The chargor company retained both its voting and dividend rights with respect to the shares. The company's administrator argued that it was a floating charge. It was held, applying Lord Millett's reasoning in *Agnew*, that whether or not the charge was fixed or floating is a question of law and the particular charge in issue was fixed. It did not float over a body of fluctuating assets and, notwithstanding the company's voting and dividend rights, it could not deal with the asset in the ordinary course of business: the company could not dispose of, or otherwise deal with, the shares. The asset was therefore under the control of the chargee. On the other hand, in *Queens Moat Houses plc v Capita IRG Trustees Ltd* (2005) it was held that the existence of a right unilaterally to require a chargee to release property from a charge did not render what is otherwise a fixed charge a floating charge. In so finding, Lightman J explained that:

> *There is a critical difference between the right of a corporate chargor to deal with and dispose of property free from charge without reference to the chargee and the right of a corporate chargor to require the chargee to release the charged property from the charge. The right of a corporate chargor in the course of its business to deal with or dispose of charged property without reference to the chargee (save in exceptional circumstances) is inconsistent with the existence of a fixed charge. . . . But there is no inconsistency between*

the existence of a fixed charge and a contractual right on the part of the chargor to re-quire the chargee to release property from the charge.

The decision in *Re Cimex Tissues Ltd* (1994) similarly illustrates how fine the distinction between a fixed and a floating charge may be. Here the charge over plant and machinery was held to be a fixed charge notwithstanding that it was contemplated that certain items of the charged machinery might be replaced from time to time due to wear and tear (see also *Re Atlantic Computer Systems plc* (1992), Nichols LJ). However, had the chargor retained the power to sell the charged machinery and buy replacements, the charge would be floating (see further *Sealy & Worthington's Text, Cases, & Materials in Company Law* (2016), p 651).

6.17 In *Re Property Edge Lettings Ltd: Saw (SW) 2010 Ltd v Wilson* (2017), the Court of Appeal held, applying *Re Yorkshire Woolcombers Association* (at para **6.14**) and *Re Spectrum Plus Ltd* (at para **6.15**), that the validity of a floating charge does not depend upon whether at the time of its creation the chargor had uncharged assets, free from any fixed charge. Briggs LJ emphasised that the earlier authorities make it clear that the determination of a charge as floating has to be made at the date of its creation by reference solely to the instrument creating the charge and not by whether there were assets to which the charge might attach. In his reasoning, Briggs LJ also referred to *Re Croftbell Ltd* (1990) in which Vinelott J had noted that a floating charge can be validly created by a newly incorporated company for the purposes of setting itself up in business by borrowing working capital notwithstanding that it lacked significant assets over which the charge can attach. Even where there is a prior fixed charge over all or part of the company's assets, a subsequent floating charge can still attach to the company's equity on redemption in those assets.

Book debts

6.18 The difficulties encountered in distinguishing a fixed charge from a floating charge have come to the fore in relation to charges granted by a company over its book debts. Companies frequently have debts which are paid on a regular basis for goods or services provided but there may be a delay between the time the obligation to pay arises (for example, when an invoice is issued) and the time payment is actually made. In this situation it is possible for a company to use the money owed to it immediately rather than wait for payment. This can be achieved by obtaining a loan that is secured over its outstanding debts. The term 'book debts' has been defined by Lord Esher MR as 'debts arising in a business in which it is the proper and usual course to keep books, and which ought to be entered in such books' (*Official Receiver v Tailby* (1886)).

6.19 The issue of whether or not a fixed charge could be created over a company's book debts arose in *Siebe Gorman & Co Ltd v Barclays Bank Ltd* (1979). The company granted a debenture in favour of Barclays Bank which was expressed to be a 'first fixed charge' over all present and future book debts. The debenture required the company to pay the proceeds of its book debts into an account held with Barclays Bank and it prohibited the company from charging or assigning its book debts without the bank's consent. In finding that a fixed charge had been created, Slade J held that the restrictions placed on the company's power to deal with the proceeds of the debts, including the bank's right to stop the company making withdrawals even when the account was temporarily in credit, gave the bank a degree of control which was inconsistent with a floating charge (see also *Oakdale (Richmond) Ltd v National Westminster Bank plc* (1996)). A stricter approach was taken in *Re Keenan Bros Ltd* (1986). The company was required to pay the proceeds of book debts into a special account over which the bank had an absolute discretion to permit the company to transfer moneys to its working account. The Supreme Court of Ireland held that the bank's control over the special account was such as to deprive the company of the free use of the proceeds. A fixed charge had, therefore, been created.

6.20 On this basis it could be concluded that the court will categorise a charge as floating if the company can continue to use the proceeds of the book debts without the consent of the chargee (see, for example, *Re Brightlife Ltd* (1987)). However, the simplicity of this test as a determinant breaks down in the light of *Re New Bullas Trading Ltd* (1994) (since overruled by the House of Lords, see paras **6.36-6.39**) in which the Court of Appeal recognised that a charge may be divisible, i.e. combined charge. Here a fixed charge was created over uncollected book debts, but as soon as the proceeds were collected and credited to the specified bank account, a floating charge took effect over them. Nourse LJ, delivering the judgment of the court, observed that the parties had unequivocally expressed their intention to create two distinct charges and that: '[U]nless there is some authority or principle of law which prevented them from agreeing what they have agreed, their agreement must prevail'. He concluded:

> An equitable assignment, whether it takes effect as an out-and-out assignment or, as here, by way of charge, is a creature of exceptional versatility, malleable to the intention of its creators, adaptable to the subject-matter assigned. Provided it is in writing, made for value and the intention is clear, it requires no formalities of expression; it may take effect over property real or personal, and over estates or interests legal or equitable, vested or contingent or, as in the case of future book debts, mere expectancies.

6.21 The decision in *Bullas* is confusing and attracted much criticism, both judicial and academic. For example, in *Royal Trust Bank v National Westminster plc* (1996) Millett LJ commented that: 'I do not see how it can be possible to separate a debt or other receivable from the proceeds of its realisation.' He also observed that:

> A contractual right in the chargor to collect the proceeds and pay them into its own bank account for use in the ordinary course of business is a badge of a floating charge and is inconsistent with the existence of a fixed charge.

(See also *Re Brightlife Ltd* (1987), Hoffmann J, and *Re ASRS Establishment Ltd* (2000), Robert Ealker and Otton LJJ. For academic comment see Goode (1994), Worthington (1997), and Gregory and Walton (1999).)

6.22 Not surprisingly, the decision in *Bullas* was criticised by Lord Millett in *Agnew* (1994). The debenture in question was modelled on the instrument in *Bullas*. The Privy Council, severely curtailing the circumstances in which a charge over uncollected book debts could be categorised as a fixed rather than a floating charge, declared the *Bullas* 'approach to be fundamentally mistaken'. The fact underlying the opinion of the Privy Council was that the debtor company was free to remove the charged assets from the scope of the chargee's security. In other words, the chargor was free to deal with the assets in the ordinary course of business. Lord Millett stated:

> If the chargor is free to deal with the charged assets and so withdraw them from the ambit of the charge without the consent of the chargee, then the charge is a floating charge. But the test can equally well be expressed from the chargee's point of view. If the charged assets are not under its control so that it can prevent their dissipation without its consent, then the charge cannot be a fixed charge.

6.23 Technically, of course, *Bullas* was not overruled by the Privy Council's decision. Indeed, the Court of Appeal in *National Westminster Bank plc v Spectrum Plus Ltd* (2004) felt compelled to follow it. Here, the chargor, Spectrum, granted a fixed (specific) charge to the bank over its book debts to secure an overdraft of £250,000. The debenture stated that the security was a specific charge over all present and future book debts and other debts. It also prohibited Spectrum from charging or assigning debts and the company was required to pay the proceeds of collection into an account held with the bank. The debenture did not specify any restrictions on the company's operation of the account.

6.24 Spectrum's account was always overdrawn and the proceeds from its book debts were paid into the account which Spectrum drew on as and when necessary. When Spectrum went into liquidation the bank sought a declaration that the debenture created a fixed charge over the company's book debts and their proceeds. The Crown, however, argued that the debenture merely created a floating charge so that its claims in respect of tax owed by the company took priority over the bank. The trial judge held, applying *Agnew* and declining to follow *Bullas*, that given the charge permitted Spectrum to use the proceeds of the debts in the normal course of business it must be construed as a floating charge. In so holding the Vice-Chancellor also declined to follow *Siebe Gorman*.

6.25 The bank successfully appealed to the Court of Appeal. Lord Phillips MR, delivering the leading judgment (Jonathan Parker and Jacob LJJ concurred), took the view that where a chargor is prohibited from disposing of its receivables before they are collected and is required to pay the proceeds into an account with the chargee bank, the charge is to be construed as fixed. He explained that it was not, as a matter of precedent, open to the Court of Appeal to hold that *Bullas* was wrongly decided even though the Privy Council had, in *Agnew*, expressed the view that the decision was mistaken. Further, *Siebe Gorman* was correctly decided given that the debenture in that case clearly restricted the company's ability to draw on the bank account into which the proceeds of its book debts were paid. The Court of Appeal noted that the form of debenture used in *Siebe Gorman* had been followed for some 25 years and thus it was inclined to hold that it had, by customary usage, acquired meaning. Lord Phillips observed that in *Siebe Gorman*:

> *Slade J could properly have held the charge on book debts created by the debenture to be a fixed charge simply because of the requirements (i) that the book debts should not be disposed of prior to collection and (ii) that, on collection, the proceeds should be paid to the Bank itself. It follows that he was certainly entitled to hold that the debenture, imposing as he found restrictions on the use of the proceeds of book debts, created a fixed charge over book debts.*

6.26 A seven-member House of Lords, as expected, overturned the decision of the Court of Appeal and overruled *Siebe Gorman* and *Bullas*. Following the line of reasoning adopted by the Privy Council in *Agnew*, it held that although it is possible to create a fixed charge over book debts and their proceeds (*Tailby v Official Receiver* (1888)), the charge in the present case was a floating charge. Lord Scott delivered the leading speech. He stressed that the ability of the chargor to continue to deal with the charged assets characterised it as floating. For a fixed charge to be created over book debts, the proceeds must, therefore, be paid into a 'blocked' account (see *Re Keenan* (see para **6.19**)). Lord Scott reasoned that:

> *The bank's debenture placed no restrictions on the use that Spectrum could make of the balance on the account available to be drawn by Spectrum. Slade J in [Siebe Gorman] thought that it might make a difference whether the account were in credit or in debit. I must respectfully disagree. The critical question, in my opinion, is whether the chargor can draw on the account. If the chargor's bank account were in debit and the chargor had no right to draw on it, the account would have become, and would remain until the drawing rights were restored, a blocked account. The situation would be as it was in Re Keeton Bros Ltd [above]. But so long as the chargor can draw on the account, and whether the account is in credit or debit, the money paid in is not being appropriated to the repayment of the debt owing to the debenture holder but is being made available for drawings on the account by the chargor.*

Although the House of Lords had jurisdiction in an exceptional case to hold that its decision should not operate retrospectively or should otherwise be limited, it nevertheless held that in the present case there was no good reason for postponing the effect of overruling *Siebe Gorman*.

The reasoning of Lord Scott was applied in *Re Harmony Care Homes Ltd* (2010). The issue before the court was whether proceeds collected during receivership were subject to a fixed charge under a debenture or, alternatively, were merely floating charge assets which preferential creditors would enjoy priority over. The debenture in this case purported to create a fixed charge over all present and future book and other debts, including any credit balances on designated accounts. The debenture contained restrictions on disposals of the proceeds of the debts and obliged the debtor to pay the monies received in respect of debts into a separate designated account. The debenture holder argued that it held a valid fixed charge over the book debts by virtue of it having the right to fully control the proceeds of those book debts and, moreover, had actively exercised this right in practice. The debenture holder adduced extensive evidence which demonstrated the level of control it had imposed over the proceeds of books debts over a significant period of time. In addition, the signatories on the designated accounts were the debenture holder's representatives. The court held that the security granted to the debenture holder was a fixed charge as it had sufficient control over the book debts collected by the debtor. Citing the *Agnew* and *Spectrum* decisions, the court found that the case turned on ascertaining the nature and the rights and obligations which the parties intended to grant each other in respect of the book debt proceeds and the company's ability to deal with them at the time when the debenture was granted. On the facts, it was held that the debtor could not make and did not make any use of the monies paid into the account without [the debenture holder's] written instructions to the bank. Accordingly, it was found that all book debts collected in by the debtor from the grant of the debenture were subject to the debenture holder's control and that, unlike the position in *Spectrum*, from the outset, the status of the debenture holder's security over the book debts was specific and ascertained. (See also, the judgment of Briggs J in *Re Lehman Brothers International (Europe) (in administration)* (2012).)

6.27 It is noteworthy that the critical importance of a 'blocked account' into which the proceeds of book debts are paid to a finding that a fixed charge was created from the outset, came to the fore in *Re Beam Tube Products Ltd* (2006). Blackburne J held that the subsequent creation of a blocked account (some four months after the execution of the debenture) did not have the effect of converting what was, as a matter of construction, a floating charge at the time of its creation into a fixed charge.

Crystallisation

6.28 As we discussed briefly earlier, crystallisation converts the floating charge into an equitable fixed charge over the assets of the company owned by it at that time. This will also include future acquired assets if within the scope of the charge (*NW Robbie & Co Ltd v Witney Warehouse Co Ltd* (1963)). Upon crystallisation the chargor loses the right to deal with the assets in the ordinary course of business. Since a charge is created by contract, the events which will trigger crystallisation can be agreed by the parties. Understandably, anxieties arise over the extent to which the parties are free to agree upon the events giving rise to automatic crystallisation. The concern here lies with the potential this carries for subverting the policy of the insolvency rules which gives priority to fixed chargees over preferential creditors and the competing claims of floating chargees in a winding-up (see Chapter 17).

6.29 Unless expressly excluded by the terms of the charge, crystallisation occurs in the event of winding-up irrespective of whether the company is wound up by the court or as a result of a resolution by its members, or whether the winding-up is for the purpose of reconstruction (*NW Robbie & Co Ltd v Witney Warehouse Co Ltd* (1963)). A floating charge will also crystallise when a debenture holder or the trustees take possession or appoint a receiver to realise the security as a result of the occurrence of an event specified in the debenture, for example default in the repayment of principal or payment of interest (*Re Panama, New Zealand and Australian Royal Mail Co* (1870)). It is now settled that cessation of business as a going concern will also cause a floating charge to crystallise (*Re Woodroffes (Musical Instruments) Ltd* (1986)). However, merely instituting an action for the appointment of a receiver, or the fact of default in payment by the company, or making a demand for payment, are not crystallising events unless specified as such in the charge (*Evans v Rival Granite Quarries Ltd* (1910)).

6.30 Given the contractual basis of the relationship between the chargor and the chargee, the parties are free to agree between themselves what acts or events should give rise to crystallisation upon service of notice on the company. It therefore follows that the 'implied events' just stated can be excluded or limited by them or, indeed, additional events may be specified (*Re Brightlife Ltd* (1987), Hoffmann J).

Provisions for automatic crystallisation

6.31 Automatic crystallisation occurs where the active intervention of the chargee, which would normally take the form of serving notice or appointing a receiver, is not required. Consequently, the debenture may provide that on the occurrence of a specified event, such as the creation of a second mortgage, the floating charge automatically converts into a fixed charge (see further *Re Property Edge Lettings Ltd* (see para **6.17**)). Considerable debate has taken place in the past over the desirability of permitting the parties to agree to automatic crystallisation given that such clauses are not required to be registered (see paras **6.36–6.39** on registration). This puts other company creditors in a particularly vulnerable position when seeking to prove their claims in liquidation proceedings (see, for example, the *Report of the Review Committee on Insolvency Law and Practice* (the Cork Committee) (Cmnd 8558, 1982)). Nevertheless, following New Zealand authority (*Re Manurewa Transport Ltd* (1971)), Hoffmann J in *Re Brightlife Ltd* (1987) recognised the validity of automatic crystallisation clauses as a necessary incident of the freedom of parties to contract. He said that the policy objections to such clauses were matters to be addressed by Parliament:

> I do not think that it is open to the courts to restrict the contractual freedom of parties to a floating charge . . . The public interest requires a balancing of the advantages to the economy of facilitating the borrowing of money against the possibility of injustice to unsecured creditors. [The] arguments for and against the floating charge are matters for Parliament rather than the courts . . .

See also *Griffiths v Yorkshire Bank plc* (1994).

6.32 The Cork Committee concluded that there was no place for automatic crystallisation clauses 'in modern insolvency law' and it recommended that the events giving rise to crystallisation should be defined exclusively by statute (*Report of the Review Committee on Insolvency Law and Practice* (Cork Committee Report, Cmnd 8558, 1982)). This particular recommendation has not been taken up. However, s 251 of the Insolvency Act 1986 defines 'floating charge' as meaning 'a charge which, *as created*, was a floating charge' (emphasis added). This certainly undermines automatic crystallisation and if the facts of *Re Brightlife* (the liquidation in this case commenced before the 1986 Act came into force) were to come before the courts again the decision might be different because the statutory definition appears to frustrate automatic crystallisation.

Priority of charges

6.33 The governing principle is that security interests rank according to the order of their creation: *qui prior est tempore, potior est jure*. This is subject to a number of exceptions. A legal mortgage will take priority over a prior equitable security if it is purchased without notice of the prior equitable interest and for value (*Coleman v London County and Westminster Bank Ltd* (1916)). Registration of the charge under the Land Charges Act 1972 constitutes actual notice and registration at Companies House (see paras **6.41–6.42**) constitutes constructive notice.

6.34 We have seen that the peculiar feature of the floating charge is that the company can continue to deal with the assets in the ordinary course of business. Thus, a company can create a fixed charge, legal or equitable, which will rank in priority over an earlier floating charge (*Re Castell and Brown Ltd* (1898)). To protect themselves against this risk it is now common for floating chargees to insert a so-called 'negative pledge' clause in the charge. Such a restriction is not incompatible with the nature of a floating charge (*Re Brightlife* (1987)). The effect of a negative pledge clause is to prohibit the company creating a subsequent mortgage or charge ranking equally with (*pari passu*) or in priority to the earlier floating charge (see, for example, *Re Property Edge Lettings Ltd* (see para **6.17**)). As is commented later at para **6.39**, since a negative pledge clause forms part of the registrable particulars of a charge (see now CA 2006, s 859D(2)(c)) any subsequent debenture holder will have constructive notice not only of the earlier floating charge but also of any restrictions it may contain, and so will not, therefore, take priority.

6.35 As between competing floating charges, the general rule is that the first in time prevails. However, a first floating charge will be postponed to a second floating charge created over a part of the assets, for example book debts, provided the first charge does not restrict the power of the company to create a subsequent floating charge which ranks prior to or *pari passu* with the first (*Re Automatic Bottle Makers Ltd* (1926), see para **6.34**). It is, in any case, open to the parties to a first floating charge to agree that the company can create subsequent floating charges which take priority (*Re Benjamin Cope & Sons Ltd* (1914)). Curiously, in *Griffiths v Yorkshire Bank plc* (1994), it was held that where a subsequent floating charge crystallises into a fixed charge, it will take priority over an earlier floating charge even after that has itself crystallised. This clearly infringes the rule that equitable interests take priority in the order of their creation (see *Re Household Products Co Ltd and Federal Business Development Bank* (1981)).

Registration of charges

6.36 Creditors considering lending money to a company will want to determine the extent to which the prospective debtor has incurred secured debt. Merely looking to corporate assets will not give an accurate impression because, as we have seen in relation to floating charges, the debtor can secure a loan on a non-possessory basis thereby facilitating the continued use of the asset. Recognising the need for creditors to be able to assess the true financial position of a company before lending to it, the requirement to maintain a publicly available register of charges was introduced as far back as the Companies Act 1900, ss 14–18. The current requirements are now laid down in Part 25 of the 2006 Act, as amended by the Companies Act 2006 (Amendment of Part 25) Regulations 2013 (SI 2013/600), which came into force on 6 April 2013, inserting Chapter A1 and Chapter 2 into Part 25. Prior to the 2013 reforms, only the prescribed particulars of certain categories of charges created by a company, together with the instrument creating the charge, had to be registered at Companies House. In other words, certain charges, for example fixed charges over shares, were outside the registration scheme, although all floating charges fell within it. To address the uncertainty over which charges fell within the prescribed list, the 2013 Regulations adopt an exemptions-based approach. Instead of a prescribed list of registrable charges, registration of all charges created by a UK-registered company over any of its property, wherever situated is required (see s 859A; there are certain limited exceptions listed in s 859A(6)). Similar provision is made for where a company creates a series of debentures containing a charge (see s 859B).

6.37 The period for delivery to the Registrar of Companies for registration of a charge remains 21 days, although the Regulations clarify how this period is to be calculated: it begins 'with the day after the date of creation of the charge' (see ss 859A(4) and 859E, though by virtue of s 859F, the court has a discretion to extend the time for registration). Failure to deliver the particulars to the Registrar within the 21-day period renders the charge void as against a liquidator or administrator and any creditor of the company (CA 2006, s 858H). It is noteworthy that it is the security which is void under the section, not the loan, and so in the event of insolvency it will rank as an unsecured debt. In this regard, s 859H(3) goes on to provide that when a charge becomes void under the section, the money secured by it immediately becomes payable. The criminal sanction for failure to register a charge is abolished. Registration may be effected by the company or the charge holder or on the application of any person interested in it (s 859A(2)). Where a company acquires property which is subject to a charge which would be registrable under s 859A if it had been created by the company, it must be registered within 21 days after the date on which the acquisition is completed (s 859C).

6.38 Once the charge is duly registered it is valid as from its creation. This results in a 21-day time lag which has been termed the '21-day invisibility problem' by the CLRSG (*Registration of Company Charges*, Consultation Document, October 2000 (URN 00/1213), para 3.79). An intending creditor searching the register cannot assume that all charges have been duly recorded because there may be a charge for which the 21-day period has not expired. Finally, it should be noted that in order to alleviate administrative burdens on businesses, companies are no longer required to maintain a register of charges, although copies of any charges and any amendments to them must be available for inspection (CA 2006, s 859Q). In fact the requirement to maintain such a register had very little practical effect in any case given that neither the validity of the charge nor its priority was affected by a company's breach.

Particulars of charge

6.39 The particulars relating to a charge created by a company which must be delivered to the Registrar are listed in s 859D, and include, amongst other things, matters such as the date of its creation; whether the instrument is expressed to contain a floating charge, and, if so, whether it is expressed to cover all the property and undertaking of the company; and whether any of the terms of the charge prohibit or restrict the company from creating further security that will rank equally with or ahead of the charge. This latter requirement is new and, as commented earlier, the consequence is that anyone dealing with the company will now be treated as having constructive notice of the 'particulars of a charge' held by the Registrar (thus including a negative pledge clause). This settles a controversy which came to the fore following the decision in *Siebe Gorman & Co Ltd v Barclays Bank Ltd* (1979) in which it was held that the constructive notice doctrine only applies to the particulars of a charge which the then applicable statute required to be registered and therefore did not extend to negative pledge clauses because they fell outwith the mandatory requirements (see also *Wilson v Kelland* (1910) and *G & T Earle Ltd v Hemsworth RDC* (1928)). On the question of whether or not to abolish the doctrine of constructive notice as it applies to the register of charges, the Department for Business, Innovation and Skills (BIS), now the Department for Business, Energy & Industrial Strategy (BEIS), took the view that its removal could have wider legal effects and therefore reserved its position pending further consultation (see the Explanatory Notes accompanying the Companies Act 2006 (Amendment of Part 25) Regulations 2013, at https://www.gov.uk/government/uploads/system/uploads/attachment_data/file/208936/bis-13-973-companies-act-2006-part-25-registration-company-charges-explanatory-notes.pdf).

6.40 As indicated earlier (para **6.36**), the purpose of the registration requirements is to enable creditors to assess the creditworthiness of a company. It is the means by which unsecured creditors are able to ascertain what assets are free and available to meet liabilities in the event of insolvency. Secured creditors can also check whether the asset in question is already charged, although with respect to both unsecured and secured creditors the '21-day invisibility problem' means that the information is not necessarily watertight. The information is also material to those considering investing in a company. In line with the Government's policy objective of increasing transparency and the quality of the information in the public domain, the Companies Act 2006 (Amendment of Part 25) Regulations 2013 also introduced new provisions for placing on the register a statement that a debt secured by a charge has been paid or satisfied in whole, or in part, or all or some of the property or undertaking charged has been released from the charge (s 859L(5)).

Effects of registration

6.41 Section 859I(3) of the CA 2006 provides that the Registrar shall give a certificate of registration to the person who delivered the statement of particulars of the charge. The certificate is 'conclusive evidence that the documents required by the section were delivered to the registrar before the end of the relevant period allowed for delivery' (s 859I(6)). Under the pre-2013 regime, once the charge had been registered it could not be set aside even if the particulars were defective, for example they omitted to state accurately the amount secured (*Re Mechanisations (Eaglescliffe) Ltd* (1966)); or the date the charge was created (*Re Eric Holmes (Property) Ltd* (1965); *Re CL Nye Ltd* (1971)). Consequently, those who searched the register and were misled by the particulars of the charge could not challenge the certificate. The drafting of s 858I(6) appears to address the anomalies which resulted from these decisions insofar as the certificate is no longer conclusive evidence of the statement of particulars filed. Registration is a perfection requirement, it is not determinative of priority. Provided registration has been effected within the 21-day period as required under s 859A(4), priority is to be determined by the order of creation of competing charges and not by the order of their registration.

Late registration and rectification

6.42 Section 859F permits the court to extend the 21-day registration period in circumstances where it is satisfied that the failure to register within the prescribed time period was accidental, or due to inadvertence or to some other sufficient cause, or is not of a nature to prejudice the position of creditors or shareholders of the company, or that on other grounds it is just and equitable to grant relief. In practice, leave to register out of time is invariably granted by the court subject to the rights of intervening secured creditors and provided the company is not in liquidation and winding-up is not imminent (*Re Ashpurton Estates Ltd* (1983)). In similar terms s 859M grants the court discretion to allow the register to be rectified where there has been an omission or mis-statement and s 859N grants the court discretion to replace the instrument or debenture where there has been an omission, mistake, or the copy is defective.

6.43 Since registration is a perfection issue, a creditor who obtains relief under s 859F would obtain priority over subsequent charges effected prior to the late registration. To avoid the prejudice which this anomaly can cause, it is usual for the court order to contain the proviso that the late registration is to be without prejudice to the rights of parties acquired prior to the time when the charge is actually registered (*Re IC Johnson & Co Ltd* (1902); *Barclays Bank plc v Stuart Landon Ltd* (2001); and *Confiance Ltd v Timespan Images Ltd* (2005)).

Avoidance of floating charges

6.44 Section 245 of the Insolvency Act 1986 invalidates a floating charge created within 12 months (termed 'the relevant time') prior to the onset of insolvency unless it was created in consideration for money paid, or goods or services supplied, at the same time as or subsequent to the creation of the charge. The term 'money paid' has been held to include cheques which have been met by a bank on behalf of the company (*Re Yeovil Glove Co Ltd* (1965)). The 'relevant time' is extended to two years where the charge is created in favour of a connected person. However, s 245(4) provides that a floating charge created in favour of a non-connected person within the 'relevant time' (i.e. 12 months) will not be invalidated if the company was able to pay its debts at the time the charge was created and did not become unable to do so as a result of creating the charge. It should be noted that this provision does not extend to charges created in favour of connected persons. The term 'connected person' is defined by s 249 as a director or shadow director of the company; an associate of a director or shadow director of the company; and an associate of the company. The object of s 245 is to prevent an unsecured creditor obtaining a floating charge to secure his existing loan at the expense of other unsecured creditors. In *Unidare plc v Cohen* (2005), the Companies Court held that a shareholder who holds the shares as a bare trustee under which he is required to vote in accordance with the directions of the beneficial owner does not in any real sense have voting power and he is not, therefore, a 'connected person' for the purposes of s 245.

Reform

6.45 The question of reform of security interests has attracted considerable scrutiny over the last 30 years or so. In March 1986 the DTI commissioned Professor Diamond to undertake a study of security interests in property other than land. The Diamond Report, which was published in 1989 (*A Review of Security Interests in Property* (HMSO, 1989)), set out a scheme for a comprehensive register of security interests drawing upon Article 9 of the United States Uniform Commercial Code. It also recommended changes to the existing system of company charges registration. Part IV of the Companies Act 1989 contained provisions broadly based on the Diamond Report recommendations for restructuring the registration system and reducing the scope of the conclusive certificate issued by the Registrar. In 1991 the Government announced that Part IV of the 1989 Act would not be implemented. One of the principal reasons for its non-implementation was the proposal to replace the Registrar's conclusive certificate with a certificate which was conclusive only as to the date on which the particulars were lodged with the Registrar. The sanction of invalidity was to be operative in respect of any breach of the registration requirements. This proposal was severely criticised by users and it was envisaged that problems would arise with respect to the interaction between Part IV of the Act and the land registration system. The conclusive certificate under s 869(6)(b) of the Companies Act 2006 assures the Land Registry that a charge is not void. Had Part IV of the 1989 Act been implemented, the certificate would have given no guarantee that the particulars were accurate, and therefore the charge might be wholly or partially void on the basis that the requirements as to the particulars to be filed had not been satisfied. The Land Registry was concerned that the rights created under the land registration system could be rendered invalid because of some failure to satisfy the Companies Act requirements.

6.46 Following the decision not to implement the relevant provisions in the 1989 Act the DTI issued another consultation document in November 1994 (*Company Law Review: Proposals for Reform of Part XII of the Companies Act 1985* (URN 94/635)). Among its various proposals for reform, the consensus of opinion favoured retention of the main procedural provisions, including the Registrar's conclusive certificate, along with the incorporation of certain of the 1989 Act improvements including the updating of the list of registrable charges and new provisions for overseas companies. This proposal was labelled 'Option B'. A more wide-ranging proposal, 'Option C', involved the replacement of the present 'transaction' filing system (registration only after a charge has been created) with a 'notice' filing system (with registration before or after creation of the charge).

6.47 As part of the fundamental review of company law, a further consultation document on registration of company charges was issued in October 2000 by the CLRSG. Significantly, the Steering Group returned to 'Option C' of the 1994 consultation exercise whereby registration would no longer be 'a mere perfection requirement but would become a priority point'. Under this proposal, which is based upon Article 9 of the United States Uniform Commercial Code, all that is filed is a notice (financing statement) giving particulars of the property over which the filer has taken or intends to take security, and certain other details, including the name and address of the creditor from whom a person searching the register can obtain further information (Consultation Document, para 2.6). The 21-day registration rule would be abandoned as would the requirement that the charge instrument be presented with the application for registration. Detailed rules are set out which would form the basis for a system under which the priority of registered charges would be determined by their dates of registration at Companies House. The period between creation and registration would cease to be relevant as there would be no period of invisibility; and so registration ceases to be a perfection requirement but becomes a priority point (Consultation Document, para 2.8, Rule 2).

6.48 Other proposals considered by the CLRSG included implementation of a number of key 1989 Act provisions. For example, it noted that under the 1985 Act registration ensures that a charge is not invalidated against the liquidator and secured creditors. Section 95 of the 1989 Act would, in effect, have extended this so that, in addition to the liquidator, an unregistered charge would also have been invalidated against 'any person who for value acquires an interest in or right over property subject to the charge'. It noted that under the 1989 Act, but not the 1985 Act, want of registration invalidates the charge in the event of the company selling or disposing of an interest (including a security interest) in the charged property. Further, s 99 of the 1989 Act would also have provided that a charge would not be void 'against a person acquiring an interest in or right over property where the acquisition is expressly subject to the charge'. The CLRSG endorsed those provisions (para 3.7).

6.49 The Steering Group also returned to the issue of the conclusive certificate. The Consultation Document questions whether the Registrar should be placed in the position of verifying the content of information registered. The Diamond Report had commented that the burden of compliance with the registration requirements should fall upon the presenters of the documentation because they were better placed to determine whether what they deliver satisfies the legislative requirements and any liability for inaccuracy in the record should lie with them. Accordingly, the Registrar's certificate should be conclusive only as far as it is practicable for it to be so. To achieve this objective several options were explored, the most radical of which was to dispense with the requirement that the document creating the charge should be delivered to the Registrar. In its place, the requirement was to be that the company only submits particulars of the charge, and these would include the date of its creation. Companies House would simply verify that the required particulars had been filed on time. The presenters would be fully responsible for the information appearing on the public record.

6.50 Finally, other significant proposals included those for widening the range of the categories of charges to be registered. It is argued that the concept of 'book debts' could be broadened by dropping the reference to 'book' and retaining the concept of 'debt' thereby encompassing a wider category of money obligation. All charges on insurance policies would be made registrable irrespective of whether or not other contingent debts should be registrable. Further, in order to enhance the value of floating charges it was proposed that the parties should be permitted to register negative pledge clauses if they so wish. This would provide for constructive notice of the pledge either from the date the charge was created or from the date of its registration.

6.51 The consultation period for the Steering Group's proposals closed on 5 January 2001. In its *Final Report* the Steering Group stated that insufficient time had been given to consult on its proposals and it therefore invited the DTI to consult with the Lord Chancellor's Department with the object of referring the matter to the Law Commission (see also the White Paper, paras 6.18–6.19). The *Final Report* recommended that: (a) the current scheme for the registration of company charges under Part XII of the Companies Act 1985 should be replaced by a system of 'notice filing'; (b) the new system should encompass functionally equivalent legal devices (commonly termed 'quasi-security' devices) such as hire-purchase and sales on retention of title terms; and (c) consideration should be given to whether or not any new system should be extended to charges created by individuals and unincorporated businesses (which was, of course, outside its terms of reference).

6.52 On 2 July 2002 the Law Commission published a consultation paper, *Registration of Security Interests: Company Charges and Property other than Land* (No 164). The LCCP states that a registration scheme should perform two functions: (1) to provide information to persons who are contemplating extending secured lending, credit rating agencies, and potential investors about the extent to which assets that may appear to be owned by the company are in fact subject to security interests in favour of other parties; and (2) to determine the priority of securities (para 12). The LCCP, endorsing the views of the Steering Group, therefore provisionally proposed the introduction of an electronic notice-filing system based on the US model (see para **6.47**; similar schemes also operate in Canada and New Zealand) to replace the current registration scheme for company charges. Further, the new scheme would extend to a seller who takes 'purchase-money security' over the particular asset purchased with the finance provided. Such a seller would have priority over all other creditors. Failing to register a 'financing statement' will result in loss of priority over a charge that is subsequently registered. It is also proposed that a security that has not been registered will be invalid against a liquidator and an administrator and that notice filing should be extended to cover certain quasi-security interests, i.e. transactions that secure payment or performance of an obligation. Hire-purchase agreements, conditional sales, and retention of title clauses would thereby become registrable (LCCP, paras 12.80–12.81). The Law Commission proposals would make registration more straightforward and the priority rules would be more coherent, albeit with some loss of information.

6.53 In August 2004 the Law Commission followed up its earlier work with the publication of a consultative report (CR), *Company Security Interests*. The Commission continues to recommend notice filing on the basis that its proposals provide 'significant improvements and cost-savings in secured finance for companies. The use of technology can make the registration of company charges much easier, cheaper and quicker' (Law Commission, Press Release, 16 August 2004). To replace the paper-based registration scheme which has been in existence for over 100 years, it is stressed that notice filing could be carried out by a secured party online. The CR sets out a range of advantages that notice filing has. These include its speed and efficiency, the fact that advance filing is permissible so that a lender's priority could be protected while negotiations continue (the proposed system is based on the principle that the first to file has priority), and that the floating charge would, in practice, disappear and be superseded by a single type of security interest having all of the advantages of a floating charge but fewer disadvantages to the lender.

6.54 Notice filing has not, however, escaped criticism. It has been pointed out that the proposed scheme could lead to misleading information being on file. For example, a lender searching the register has no way of determining whether a particular registration relates to an

actual transaction or to a proposed transaction that may have been aborted because negotiations broke down. Further, fewer details are available than is the case under transaction
filing (Calnan (2004)). The Law Commission counters this argument with the observation
that the current system 'requires only two additional items; the amount secured by the
charge and the date it was created' (para 2.47). It is stated that the statement of the amount
secured is of little use since, 'unless the charge is for a fixed amount, it is most unlikely to
be accurate by the time anyone searches the register'. With respect to the date of creation,
the CR notes that providing such a date is not possible in a system 'that has the advantage
of allowing filing before the charge has been agreed or has attached' (para 2.47).

6.55   In August 2005 the Law Commission published its final report, *Company Security Interests*
(Report No 296, 2005). Its principal proposals include:

   i.   *A new system of electronic notice filing for registering charges.*

   ii.   *Removal of the 21-day time limit, thus removing the 'invisibility' period (see iv, below).*

   iii.   *Extending the list of registrable charges so that all charges are registrable unless specifically exempted. The principal exemptions will be for some charges over registered
land and over financial collateral.*

   iv.   *Clearer priority rules. Priority between competing charges will be by date of filing
unless otherwise agreed between the parties involved (this will also remove the current 21-day period of invisibility). The distinction between fixed and floating charges
will be preserved. For floating charges it will no longer be necessary to rely on a
'negative pledge clause' to prevent subsequent charges gaining priority. It will also
be unnecessary to rely on 'automatic crystallisation clauses'.*

   v.   *If a charge over registered land is registered in the Land Registry, it will not need to
be registered in the Company Security Register. Instead, the Land Registry will automatically forward to Companies House its information about companies' charges.*

   vi.   *Sales of receivables will be brought within the scheme (e.g. factoring and discounting
agreements' currently a factor will only obtain priority if it gives notice to each
account debtor).*

   vii.   *The rules on charges over investment securities and other forms of financial collateral are to be clarified.*

The report also contains draft Company Security Regulations 2006 prepared by the Law
Commission for adoption by the Department for Trade and Industry (DTI, now BEIS),
under powers conferred by the Companies Act 2006.

6.56   In July 2005 the DTI initiated its own consultation exercise aimed at seeking views on
the economic impact of the Law Commission's proposals in relation to company charges.
This was followed by a Ministerial statement in November 2005 to the effect that there
was no clear consensus of support in favour of the Law Commission's proposals and as
a consequence the Companies Bill (as it then was) would not include a specific power to

implement the recommended changes. However, it was stated that the Bill would include a new general power to introduce company law reform orders and this would provide the mechanism for introducing changes in relation to company charges (Hansard, HL, col WS27 (3 November 2006)). In fact this power was dropped from the Bill during its passage through Parliament. Instead, a new power was enacted by virtue of s 894 permitting the Secretary of State to amend Part 25 of the Act by regulations. Lord Sainsbury, commenting on Part 25 on behalf of the Government, admitted that: 'while there has been an element of restructuring, no substantive changes have been made other than to ensure compatibility with the Bill . . . The approach to restatement of the existing provisions [in CA 1985] means that the new provisions retain the imperfections of the existing system' (*Hansard*, HL Vol 686, col 480 (2 November 2006, https://publications.parliament.uk/pa/ld200506/ldhansard/vo051103/text/51103-27.htm)).

6.57 Yet another consultation exercise on the registration of company charges was launched by the Government on 12 March 2010 (*Registration of Charges Created by Companies and Limited Liability Partnerships: Proposals to amend the current scheme and relating to specialist registers* (URN 10/697)). The consultation sought views on proposed changes to the scheme for registration of company charges set out in Part 25 of the Companies Act 2006 (which, as commented earlier, basically replicated Part XII of the CA 1985) based on the 2001 recommendations of the CLR and the subsequent proposals put forward by the Law Commission. The issues included what charges should be registered, time limits, consequences of registration and of the failure to register a charge, procedures, electronic registration, and the availability of information about company charges (a summary of the responses to the consultation were published by BIS in October 2010, https://www.gov.uk/government/uploads/system/uploads/attachment_data/file/31494/10-1230-summary-responses-consultation-registration-of-charges.pdf). Next, following the publication on 22 December 2010 of the results of an evaluation of the Companies Act 2006, the Government outlined its future priorities with respect to company law including proposals to modernise and simplify the current system for the registration of company charges. The outcome is, as seen earlier, the relatively modest reforms contained in the Companies Act 2006 (Amendment of Part 25) Regulations 2013. The new scheme also applies to limited liability partnerships (see the Limited Liability Partnerships (Application of Companies Act 2006) (Amendment) Regulations 2013 (SI 2013/618)). With respect to the procedure for registration, it is now possible to register charges electronically. The fee for paper filing is currently £13 while for electronic filing it is £10. Further, the 2013 Regulations permit certain information, such as personal information relating to an individual, signatures, and account numbers, to be redacted from the certified copy delivered to Companies House. The requirement for registered overseas companies to file with Companies House charges on property located in the UK (see the Overseas Companies (Execution of Documents and Registration of Charges) Regulations 2009) was repealed on 1 October 2011.

6.58 In January 2012 the Department for Business, Energy & Industrial Strategy (as it is now called) announced that it was continuing its work on reforming how companies register use of their assets to raise finance (*Company Law: Providing a flexible framework which allows companies to compete and grow discussion paper* (Ref: 12/560)). While it is recognised that the current system is antiquated and not fit for purpose, delays in agreeing the necessary reforms risks the position London enjoys as a global financial centre. It is to be hoped that the electronic notice-filing system based on the Uniform Commercial Code (see para **6.47**) will again return to the agenda for serious consideration as a way forward for the UK.

FURTHER READING

This chapter links with the materials in Chapter 15 of **Hicks and Goo's Cases and Materials on Company Law** (Oxford, OUP, 2011, xl +649p).

Atherton and Mokal, 'Charges over Chattels: Issues in the Fixed/Floating Jurisprudence' [2005] *Co Law* 163.

Beale, 'Reform of the Law of Security Interests over Personal Property' in Lowry and Mistelis (eds) *Commercial Law: Perspectives and Practice* (London, LexisNexis Butterworths, 2006).

Berg, 'The Cuckoo in the Nest of Corporate Insolvency: Some Aspects of the Spectrum Case' [2006] *JBL* 22.

Capper, 'Fixed Charges Over Book Debts—Back to Basics but how Far Back?' [2002] *LMCLQ* 246.

Calnan, 'The Reform of the Law of Security' [2004] *Butterworths J of International Banking and Financial Law* 88.

Ferran, 'Floating Charges—The Nature of the Security' [1988] *CLJ* 213.

Ferran, *Principles of Corporate Finance Law* (Oxford, OUP, 2008).

Goode, 'Charges over Book Debts: A Missed Opportunity' [1994] *LQR* 592.

Goode, 'The Case for the Abolition of the Floating Charge' in Getzler and Payne (eds) *Company Charges: Spectrum and Beyond* (Oxford, OUP, 2006).

Gregory and Walton, 'Book Debt Charges—The Saga Goes On' [1999] *LQR* 14.

Gregory and Walton, 'Fixed and Floating Charges—A Revelation' [2001] *LMCLQ* 123.

Law Commission Consultation Paper No 164, *Registration of Security Interests* and the Consultative Report, *Company Security Interests* (2004).

McCormack, 'The Priority of Secured Credit: An Anglo-American Perspective' [2003] *JBL* 389.

McCormack, 'The Law Commission's Consultative Report on Company Security Interests: An Irreverent Riposte' [2005] *MLR* 286.

Pennington, 'The Genesis of the Floating Charge' [1960] *MLR* 630.

Worthington, 'Fixed Charges Over Book Debts and Other Receivables' [1997] *LQR* 562.

Worthington, 'An "Unsatisfactory Area of the Law"—Fixed and Floating Charges Yet Again' [2004] *International Corporate Rescue* 175.

SELF-TEST QUESTIONS

1   How might a fixed charge be created over a company's book debts?

2   Apple Bank Ltd lends £20,000 to Debtor Ltd on the security of a floating charge to be created by Debtor Ltd over the whole of its assets.

Advise Apple Bank Ltd: (i) as to the steps it should take to ensure that the charge will be valid; and (ii) as to the circumstances in which it will become enforceable.

3   On 1 March A Ltd created a floating charge over its assets in favour of Lendit Bank as security for a loan of £70,000. The charge was not registered. On 1 April A Ltd created a second floating charge in favour of Credit Bank as security for an existing overdraft facility of £15,000. The charge contained a term prohibiting A Ltd from creating subsequent charges which would rank in priority to Credit Bank's. Credit Bank's charge is duly registered. On 1 May A Ltd purchased computer equipment from Hightech Ltd at a price of £75,000. A Ltd paid £10,000 in cash and created a fixed charge over its book debts in favour of Hightech Ltd to secure the balance of the purchase price. This charge was duly registered. Discuss.

4   '[W]hat you do require to make a specific security is that the security whenever it has come into existence, and been identified and appropriated as a security, shall never thereafter at the will of the mortgagor cease to be a security' (*Re Yorkshire Woolcombers Association* Ltd (1903), Vaughan Williams LJ). Discuss.

PART II
Behind the Corporate Veil

7

Share capital

SUMMARY

Introduction
Receiving proper value on issue of shares
Returning funds to shareholders: dividends
Returning funds to shareholders: reduction of share capital
Returning funds to shareholders: redemption or purchase by a company of its own shares
Financial assistance for the acquisition of shares in a public company
The prohibition and the exceptions

Introduction

7.1 In this chapter we consider the means by which company law seeks to ensure that a company's share capital is 'maintained' in the company's possession and therefore gives an accurate picture of the company's finances. A principal anxiety of the law is that shareholders should actually pay the price of their shares in money or money's worth and that this sum is not directly or indirectly returned to them except in accordance with the provisions of the Companies Act (see, for example, the Companies Act 2006, ss 641ff, ss 684ff, and ss 829ff, discussed later). The policy here is directed towards protecting creditors who, because of the *Salomon* doctrine and the principle of limited liability, cannot look directly towards shareholders to meet their claims (see *Guinness v Land Corpn of Ireland* (1882), Cotton LJ). Obviously, capital is used to further the commercial activities of the company and in this respect it can, of course, be lost as a result of poor business decisions: that is a legitimate risk which both shareholders and creditors run (*Trevor v Whitworth* (1887) HL). But, from the creditors' perspective, a company's capital gives some measure of its creditworthiness and, if creditors are unsecured, they will look to the capital fund as well as to its unsecured assets as a means of payment should the company be wound up (see Chapter 17). This is not to say that an unsecured creditor is guaranteed payment by virtue of a company's capital. Indeed, many large successful companies have rather low issued capital funds but significant assets perhaps in the way of properties: for example, a hotel chain may have an issued share capital of only £100 but own substantial properties in prime locations throughout the UK that are worth millions of pounds. As with share capital, corporate assets may also be lost or depleted through poor management decisions and no principle of company law in a free enterprise economy can protect investors or creditors against such assets being squandered by underperforming management. As is pointed out by the CLRSG in *The Strategic Framework*, consultation document (DTI, 1999) (para 5.42):

> The principle of capital maintenance is at least as old as the limited liability company. The law gave the shareholder the privilege of limiting his liability, so that once he had paid, or promised to pay on call [in the case of partly paid shares], an amount equal to the nominal value of the shares he took up he had no further responsibility for the debts of the company. In order to protect members and creditors, however, a body of rules was erected; such rules were designed to prevent the capital so provided from being extracted or otherwise eroded, save as a result of trading or other business events.

7.2   As commented earlier, in considering the principles governing share capital it should be borne in mind that the law was, and it may reasonably be concluded still is, notoriously complex. Indeed, the regime governing distributions and capital maintenance attracted considerable scrutiny by the CLRSG and the ensuing White Papers of 2002 (Cm 5553) and 2005 (Cm 6456). In this respect, the 2005 White Paper states that while 'it is obviously important to protect the interests of a company's creditors, the current provisions give rise to some of the most complex and technically challenging provisions of the 1985 Act—94 sections of detailed rules in total' (*Company Law Reform*, para 4.8; see also *Company Law. Flexibility and Accessibility: A Consultative Document* (DTI, 2004)). The result is that the 2006 Act seeks to deregulate the 'old' law by removing the need for private companies to comply with measures that are 'unnecessarily burdensome'. However, as far as public companies are concerned, much of the law is restated. As such it continues to pose a trap for the unwary and is a fertile source of fee income for corporate law practitioners.

7.3   As seen in Chapters 1 and 5, a shareholder subscribes for shares by paying or agreeing to pay the 'price' for the shares to be issued to him. Generally the price paid is made up of two elements. First, there is the par or nominal value of the shares (see s 542 of the CA 2006, which provides that shares in a limited company must each have a fixed nominal value): for example a company's share capital may be £100 made up of one hundred £1 shares, here £1 is the nominal value. Second, a premium for the shares may be attached to the price: thus each £1 share may be sold for £1.25 or more. In practice, a company's existing shareholders would have cause for complaint if a new issue of shares were to be made at par because that would have the effect of reducing the value of their holdings, which may have increased above their par value by the time of the new issue. Where shares are sold at a premium, the amount of the premium is kept separate in the company's accounts by entering it under the heading 'share premium account' (CA 2006, s 610). However, the Companies Act treats such sums as paid-up capital which cannot be returned to members unless by way of a formal reduction of capital (see later). As we have seen in relation to the notion of limited liability (Chapter 2), the share capital contributed by a shareholder represents the extent of his liability should the company become insolvent. The holder of fully paid shares has no further liability to contribute to the company's capital, while the liability of a holder of partly paid shares (a rare species nowadays) is limited to the amount which remains un-paid, i.e. the difference between the sum actually paid and the nominal value of the shares plus any agreed premium (Insolvency Act 1986, s 74(2)(d)). As we will see in Chapter 17, when a company goes into liquidation, its shareholders will not collect any return of their capital while creditors remain unpaid. Of course, while the company is a going concern and enjoying profitability its shareholders can share in those profits (via dividends); but if losses are incurred, no return can be given on their investment until the company has sufficient funds to meet its indebtedness at least equal to the share capital.

7.4 It is important to bear in mind that the regime governing maintenance of share capital is a mixture of substantive legal principles and accounting rules. A company's share capital is not ring-fenced in some separate bank account to be used only in the event of liquidation to pay creditors. Rather, it is a book-keeping entry and before any returns can be paid to shareholders the accounts must show that the value of a company's assets exceeds its share capital. In essence, therefore, share capital operates as a yardstick of profitability.

7.5 There are various ways in which shareholders might legally receive funds ('distributions') from the company. Many shareholders invest not just in the hope of seeing the value of their shares increase as the company prospers so that they make a profit on resale, but also in the expectation of receiving an income by way of a dividend: a share of the company's profits in proportion to the number of shares held. The right to receive a dividend may differ according to the class of shares held (see Chapter 9). However, the law also regulates other types of distributions, whether in cash or in kind, and we now turn to consider the rules that are directed towards maintaining a company's share capital. It should be noted that the regime differentiates between private and public companies.

Receiving proper value on issue of shares

No discount

7.6 One incident of the doctrine of capital maintenance is that shares may not be issued at a discount to their nominal value. This was clearly laid down in *Ooregum Gold Mining Co of India v Roper* (1892) in which the company wished to issue shares with a nominal value of £1 on the basis that they be credited with 75p, meaning each holder had a liability to pay only 25p, because the market value of the shares was then less than their nominal value. In rejecting the power of the company to do this, Lord Halsbury LC stated:

> the Act of 1862 . . . makes [it] one of the conditions of the limitation of liability that the memorandum shall contain the amount of the capital with which the company proposes to be registered, divided into shares of a certain fixed amount. It seems to me that the system thus created by which the shareholder's liability is to be limited by the amount

*unpaid upon his shares, renders it impossible for the company to depart from that re-
quirement, and by any expedient to arrange with their shareholders that they shall not
be liable for the amount unpaid on their shares.*

7.7   This rule is now contained in CA 2006, s 552; and if shares are issued at a discount the allottee is liable to pay the difference with interest. As an anti-avoidance measure, payments
of commissions and brokerage are also prohibited except in very limited circumstances
(see s 553 which permits the payment of commissions (and discounts) up to 10 per cent
of the price at which the shares are issued). The prohibition does not mean that the share
has actually to be paid for in full when it is issued, since payment may be deferred: as we
have seen, there can be paid-up and un-paid-up capital. In the latter case, the shareholder
remains liable to contribute. What it does mean is that the company may not charge less
than the nominal value of the share. Thus, an outsider can be sure that the company has
received (or at least has enforceable claims for) its issued share capital.

7.8   There is a further issue that needs explaining. It is possible for a company to issue shares
fully paid up so that the recipient has no obligation to make any payment at all: it might
do so, for instance, if it wanted to award shares as a bonus to its employees. In order to
do this, the company itself must pay up the share by nominally transferring funds from
its profit account to its share capital account. By thus increasing the nominal value of its
share capital, it protects creditors in the same way as if the shares had been issued fully
paid to an outsider.

Payment in kind

7.9   If the consideration for the shares is in kind (i.e. in goods, property, or services rather than
in cash) there is clearly the opportunity to avoid the no discount rule and a danger that
the shares may be undervalued. This is what the liquidator in *Re Wragg Ltd* (1897) alleged.
In that case Messrs Wragg and Martin sold their omnibus and livery-stable business to
the company they had incorporated for £46,300, paid for by the company by the issue
of debentures and fully paid shares. The liquidator alleged that the value of the business
had been overstated by £18,000 and he claimed to be able to treat shares representing
this amount as unpaid. However the court held that the good faith judgement of the
directors that the benefit received in return for the shares was worth their nominal value
was not open to challenge. Lindley LJ remarked that: 'Provided a limited company does
so honestly and not colourably, and provided that it has not been so imposed upon as to
be entitled to be relieved from its bargain, it appears to be settled . . . that agreements by
limited companies to pay for property or services in paid-up shares are valid and binding
on the companies and their creditors' (see also *Salomon v A Salomon & Co Ltd* (1897),
discussed in Chapter 2; and *Henry Head & Co Ltd v Ropner Holdings Ltd* (1952)).

7.10   Lindley LJ's formulation continues to apply to private companies. However, for public
companies there are various statutory provisions governing this scenario (see CA 2006,

ss 584–587 and ss 593–609). For example, s 585(1) prohibits a public company from accepting an undertaking to do work or perform services in payment of its shares. However, a private company may accept such an undertaking (thus in *Re Theatrical Trust Ltd, Chapman's Case* (1895), payment took the form of an agreement to become manager for five years). Of particular significance is CA 2006, s 593 which requires an independent valuation of non-cash consideration; the rules are even stricter in relation to subscribers to the memorandum (see s 584 and ss 598–599). Failure to comply with the statutory procedure can have significant consequences for the allottee and subsequent holders of the shares (see ss 588, 593(3), and 605, CA 2006). The allottee is required to pay to the company the nominal value of the shares together with any premium, and interest, irrespective of any benefit that the company may have received. In effect, therefore, the allottee is liable to pay for the shares twice. A subsequent holder of the shares is jointly and severally liable with the allottee to pay the same amount, unless he is (or derived title through) a bona fide purchaser for value without actual notice. Given the severity of these provisions, the court does, however, have the power to grant relief from liability, in whole or in part (ss 589 and 606). For example, in *Re Bradford Investments plc (No 2)* (1991) the members of a partnership converted a dormant private company into a public company. Without having first obtained a valuation of the partnership business in accordance with s 103, they sold it to the public company in return for 1,059,000 fully paid £1 shares. Subsequently, the company, being under new management, claimed £1,059,000 from the former partners as the issue price of the shares. They applied to the court under s 113 of the CA 1985 (now CA 2006, s 606) to be relieved from liability to pay this sum. It was held, denying them relief, that the provision puts the onus of proving that value was given on the applicants and they had failed to satisfy the court that the partnership business had any net value at the time it was sold to the company. It should also be noted that criminal penalties are imposed on the company and its officers for contravening the statutory rules (CA 2006, s 590). Further, any such transaction, whilst enforceable by the company against the allottee, is void as against the company (CA 2006, s 591).

Relevance of nominal value

7.11 We have seen that a company may issue shares at above the nominal value (the difference being called a share premium). The combination of this possibility and that of paying for shares in non-cash consideration means that in many cases the price received by the company is not the nominal value. In any event, it will be sheer coincidence if the nominal and market value of a share are the same at any time after issue. The question has therefore been rightly asked whether there is in fact any point in ascribing a nominal value to shares, particularly when the yardstick used for the capital maintenance rules corresponds to the total consideration payable on shares issued and not just the nominal price received. In *The Strategic Framework* consultation document the CLRSG states that 'the requirement that shares should have a nominal value has become an anachronism' and that it would favour the end of the practice (while recognising that because of EU rules (the Second Company Law Directive (77/91/EC), reformulated in 2012, see EU

Directive 2012/30; see also the Consolidated Directive 2017/1132) this would be difficult for public companies). If the requirement were to be removed, it would allow shares to be issued for whatever price the company chose. The actual value received would then be the 'capital' which has to be maintained under the doctrine. Indeed, the creation of no par value shares is permitted in many jurisdictions (for example, the USA).

7.12   That said, because public companies are required to have a nominal value for their shares the CLRSG's consultation process revealed a strong resistance to forcing private companies to have shares with no nominal value; and since it was thought an optional regime would require a commitment of effort and resources 'out of all proportion to the likely benefit' (see para 7.3 of *Completing the Structure* (November 2000)), the CA 2006 essentially restates the law in this respect. The concept of nominal value is thus retained by s 542(1) of the 2006 Act. This is reinforced by s 542(2) which states that an allotment of a share that does not have a fixed nominal value is void. With respect to the question of authorised share capital, the 2005 White Paper states that the requirement is to be removed on the basis that it is invariably set at a level higher than the company will need and so it serves no useful practice. This is implemented by the 2006 Act, although a statement of capital must be registered on formation (see s 10; however, any provision in a company's memorandum of association specifying the company's authorised share capital that was in force immediately before 1 October 2009 is deemed to be a provision in the company's articles. Such a provision continues to operate as a limit on the maximum amount of shares that may be allotted and is alterable by ordinary resolution: see the Companies Act 2006 (Commencement No 8, Transitional Provisions and Savings) Order 2008 (SI 2008/2860)). In November 2009, the Department for Business, Innovation and Skills (now BEIS) launched a consultation exercise aimed at considering three principal questions: what elements of financial information should be included in the statement of capital, the ease with which companies can provide information, and the value of such information to third parties searching the capital of a company. In May 2011 BIS announced that:

> The Government has considered the scope to simplify the financial information requirements in Companies Act statements of capital which were the subject of the consultation. We have also considered concerns, raised by stakeholders but not covered by the consultation, that the requirements to set out the prescribed particulars of the rights attached to shares in statements of capital are particularly costly and duplicative.
>
>   The Government believes that there is a good case to simplify the financial information requirements for all companies, in all statements of capital, except those required on formation and in the Annual Return, to require the following information:
>
> - the total number of shares of the company;
> - the aggregate nominal value of those shares;
> - the aggregate amount unpaid on those shares (whether on account of nominal value of the shares or by way of premium);
> - the total number of shares in each class;

- *the aggregate nominal value of shares in each class;*
- *the aggregate amount unpaid on shares in each class (whether on account of nominal value of the shares or by way of premium).*

At the same time we believe there is scope to simplify the information requirements on the rights attached to shares to address the issues companies have raised.

For many of the 15 instances where a statement of capital is required, including the Annual Return, the Companies Act 2006 contains a power for the Secretary of State to amend the requirements by statutory instrument. But for a number of others there is no such power. After carefully weighing the arguments, we have concluded that the changes to statements of capital should be introduced simultaneously to minimise further confusion for companies. The Government will therefore bring forward detailed proposals as soon as a suitable legislative vehicle is available.

We had previously considered making earlier changes to the requirements in the statement of capital in the Annual Return. However, a further assessment has shown that, in order to reduce burdens and complexity for companies in a way which is cost effective for Companies House and for businesses providing web-filling and software filing services, changes to requirements in statements of capital should be made simultaneously, and apply across the board to all instances in which such statements are required.

(See http://webarchive.nationalarchives.gov.uk/+/http://www.bis.gov.uk/Consultations/companies-act-2006-statements-of-capital-consultation?cat=closedawaitingresponse).

It is, however, still possible to increase share capital by ordinary resolution (s 617). While the concept of authorised share capital is now virtually redundant, s 763 of the CA 2006 nevertheless requires public limited companies to have an allotted share capital of a minimum of £50,000 (the 'authorised minimum') or prescribed euro equivalent (which has been fixed by regulations at €65,000); and, as was the case before the 2006 Act, no minimum capital is prescribed for private companies. A public company that does not meet this minimum requirement will not be issued with a trading certificate by the Registrar (see s 761).

Returning funds to shareholders: dividends

The general rule

7.13 A profitable company may want to pay dividends to its shareholders or instead to reinvest the profits back in the business in order, for example, to expand its operations. The capital maintenance doctrine requires that the overall position must be assessed in deciding whether dividends may be paid, not just whether profits have been made in a particular year, because there may have been losses reducing the value of the company's assets below its share capital in previous years. The detailed rules (see CA 2006, Part 23 (which essentially restate the provisions of the CA 1985)) provide that a company may pay dividends only out of 'distributable profits' (s 830(1)). The underlying policy is to ensure that, while profits can be distributed to the company's shareholders, the share capital and reserves remain available to settle creditors' claims (for a detailed review of the law, see the judgment of Zacaroli J in *Burnden Holdings (UK) Ltd v Fielding* (2019)).

Section 836(1) goes on to provide that 'Whether a distribution may be made by a company . . . is determined by reference to the following items as stated in the relevant accounts – (a) profits, losses, assets and liabilities . . .' The court in *Burnden Holdings (UK) Ltd v Fielding* concluded that this is a 'passive' requirement and so it does not require directors to 'actively reach a determination as to the amount of realizable profits'. Nor is there a requirement to hold a formal board meeting to approve the accounts or to approve a distribution—provided all the directors approve the distribution.

To summarise, the company may pay dividends only out of its accumulated, realised profits (s 830(2), and, in the case of public companies, not insofar as the effect would be to reduce the company's net assets below the value of its called-up share capital (s 831)). Breach of these rules makes a payment unlawful and ultra vires (for recent consideration of the consequences following the declaration of an unlawful dividend, see *Toone v Robbins* (2018)). A director who knew (or ought to have known) that the payment amounted to a breach is liable to repay the dividends (*Bairstow v Queens Moat Houses plc* (2001)). In *Re Exchange Banking Co, Flitcroft's Case* (1882) the liquidator of the bank issued a summons against five of its former directors who had between 1873 and 1878 been concerned in paying half-yearly dividends at a time when they knew that some items in the accounts were bad debts and irrecoverable and that the company had no distributable profits. The directors were held jointly and severally liable for the amount of the dividends. Sir George Jessel MR concluded:

> It follows then that if directors who are quasi trustees for the company improperly pay away the assets to the shareholders, they are liable to replace them. It is no answer to say that the shareholders could not compel them to do so. I am of opinion that the company could in its corporate capacity compel them to do so, even if there were no winding-up.

7.14   In *Bairstow v Queens Moat Houses plc* (above), the directors, acting on the company's 1991 accounts that incorrectly showed inflated profits, unlawfully paid dividends that exceeded the available distributable reserves. The Court of Appeal held that the directors' liability was not limited to the difference between the unlawful dividends and the dividends that could have been lawfully paid, since although they were not strictly speaking trustees, they were in an analogous position because of the fiduciary duties which they owed to the company, and they had trustee-like responsibilities arising out of their power and duty to manage the company's business in the interests of all its members. They were thus liable for deliberately and, in relation to the 1991 accounts, dishonestly paying unlawful dividends out of the company's funds which were in their control. The defendants were therefore ordered to pay the company over £78 million (see also *Commissioners of Inland Revenue v Richmond* (2003)).

Whether or not liability is strict or, on the other hand, depends upon knowledge or fault on the part of the directors has received mixed responses by the courts. In *Progress Property Co Ltd v Moore* (2011), Lord Walker, with whom other members of the Supreme Court agreed, took the view that knowledge that the distribution was unlawful was a necessary ingredient of liability. However, Lord Hope, by way of obiter in *Revenue and Customs Commissioners v Holland, In Re Paycheck Services 3 Ltd* (2010), thought that in the case of an unlawful payment of a dividend, a director who causes the payment to be made is under a strict liability to make good such misapplication of the company's property, subject only to relief from liability if he establishes that he acted honestly and reasonably (see also the judgment of Rimer LJ in the Court of Appeal (2010)). On the other hand, in *Madoff Securities International Ltd v Raven* (2013), Popplewell J, by way of obiter, felt inclined towards the view that liability is fault based. In *Burnden Holdings (UK) Ltd v Fielding* (above), Zacaroli J, having given detailed consideration of the case law, confirmed that if directors were unaware of the facts which rendered a dividend unlawful, then provided they had taken reasonable care in the preparation of the accounts which showed that a dividend could be declared, they would not be personally liable if it turned out that there were in fact insufficient profits lawfully to declare a dividend.

7.15 With respect to the recipient's liability, on the other hand, s 847(1) and (2) of the CA 2006 provide that where a distribution is made in contravention of the Act and, at the time of the distribution, the member knows or has reasonable grounds for believing that it is so made, he is liable to repay it to the company. If only part of a distribution is in contravention of the Act, the member's liability extends only to that part. Similarly, under s 847 a member who, with knowledge of the facts, receives an improper dividend payment, may be held liable to repay it as a constructive trustee (*Precision Dippings Ltd v Precision Dippings Marketing Ltd* (1986); although this may no longer be the case following the decision of the House of Lords in *Westdeutsche Landesbank Girozentrale v Islington LBC* (1996)). In *It's a Wrap (UK) Ltd v Gula* (2006) the liquidator sought repayment of dividends paid to the defendants who were the sole shareholders and directors of the company. During a two-year period in which there were no profits available for distribution, the company's accounts showed that dividends had nevertheless been paid to the defendants. When the company went into insolvent liquidation, the liquidator claimed that the dividends had been paid in contravention of s 263(1) (CA 2006, s 830(1)) and were therefore recoverable under s 277 (now CA 2006, s 847). The defendants argued that the sums in question were paid to them as remuneration and only appeared in the accounts as 'dividends' because they had been advised that this was tax efficient. The trial court dismissed the liquidator's claim on the basis that it was clear that the defendants had sought to gain a proper tax advantage and had not deliberately set out to contravene the Act. The judge found that the phrase 'is so made' contained in s 277(1) of the CA 1985 required that the defendants knew or had reasonable grounds to believe not just the facts giving rise to the contravention but also the legal result of the contravention. Perhaps not surprisingly, the Court of Appeal reversed the judge's decision and held that the defendants' ignorance of the law was no defence. Arden LJ stated that s 277 had to be interpreted in a manner consistent with Art 16 of the Second Company Law Harmonisation Directive which it is designed to implement. On this particular issue she concluded that:

> Section 277 [now s 847] must be interpreted as meaning that the shareholder cannot claim that he is not liable to return a distribution because he did not know of the restrictions in the Act on the making of distributions. He will be liable if he knew or ought reasonably to have known of the facts which mean that the distribution contravened the requirements of the Act.

(See also *Re Snelling House Ltd* (2012); and *Global Corporate Ltd v Hale* (2018), where the Court of Appeal confirmed that for the purposes of s 830, the lawfulness of a dividend is to be assessed at the time it is made, so that re-characterising it later as remuneration is not possible. See also *Toone v Robbins* (2018).)

Directors owe fiduciary duties to the company (see Chapter 14). They have trustee-like responsibilities based on their duty to manage the company in the interests of all its members (for present purposes, see CA 2006, s 172 (paras **14.26-14.41**)). It is settled that where the company is insolvent, or near to insolvency, the interests of members give way to the interests of creditors (s 172(3)). In *BTI 2014 LLC v Sequana SA* (2019), the Court of Appeal took the opportunity to consider a number of issues in this respect. It held that the duty to have regard to creditors' interests arises when directors know or should know that the company is, or is likely to become, insolvent (see s 172(3)), so that the payment of a dividend in these circumstances could be challenged as a transaction defrauding creditors and could be considered to be an attempt to put assets beyond their reach—and thus set aside under s 423 of the Insolvency Act 1986, which allows the court to avoid any transaction designed to defeat the claims of company creditors (see Chapter 17; and see further, *Burnden Holdings (UK) Ltd v Fielding* (above)).

Disguised distributions

7.16 In some rather less obvious cases than those relating to the payment of cash dividends the courts have also been willing to find that there has been a disguised return of capital to shareholders, so that the capital maintenance principle has been breached. For example, in *Re Halt Garage (1964) Ltd* (1982) the court held that although there is no rule that directors' remuneration can only be paid out of distributable profits, when the directors are also shareholders it may be possible to categorise remuneration as a 'disguised gift out of capital'. The issue in this case was relatively straightforward because the director receiving the remuneration (the wife of the majority shareholder) had not actually provided any services for several years due to ill health and the company had gone into insolvent liquidation. Oliver J held that only £10 out of the £30 per week that had been paid to her while she was ill was genuine remuneration. She had to repay the balance. In *Progress Property Co Ltd v Moorgarth Group Ltd* (2011) (see para **7.19**), Lord Mance referred to the decision of the New Zealand Court of Appeal in *Jenkins v Harbour View Courts Ltd* (1966) where Turner J said that:

>   the question which the Court must ask itself is—is this transaction in essence one in which
>   the company divests itself of part of its undertaking in favour of a shareholder otherwise
>   than in the course of a bona fide transaction entered into as a matter of contract, and
>   not as a company-shareholder transaction? If this is the essence of the transaction, then
>   it is in my opinion a return of capital.

(See also *Clearwell International Ltd v MSL Group Holdings Ltd* (2012).)

7.17 The facts of *Re Halt Garage* do not represent the only type of situation where a court has
been prepared to re-categorise a transaction as a return of capital. In *Aveling Barford Ltd v
Perion Ltd* (1989) AB Ltd and P Ltd were both owned and controlled by Lee. AB Ltd, while
not insolvent, did not have any distributable reserves but it owned a sports ground for
which planning permission for residential redevelopment had been granted. In October
1986 its directors resolved to sell the sports ground, valued at £650,000, to P Ltd for only
£350,000. In February 1987 the property was sold to P Ltd for this price. In August of
that year P Ltd resold it for £1.52 million. AB Ltd went into liquidation and the liquidator
successfully sued to have P Ltd declared a constructive trustee of the proceeds of sale on
the basis, inter alia, that the transaction was an unauthorised return of capital by AB Ltd
to Lee, its sole shareholder, via P Ltd.

7.18 The decision in *Aveling Barford* is significant because it had an unwelcome impact on the
way companies in a group who want to transfer assets to each other have to structure the
arrangement (i.e. intra-group transfers). It attracted the particular scrutiny of the CLRSG.
The problem is explained in the June 2000 document, *Capital Maintenance: Other Issues*:

>   The case did not decide anything about the situation where a company has positive dis-
>   tributable reserves. But there is a body of opinion, prompted by the decision, that an intra-
>   group sale of an asset may constitute a distribution for the purposes of section 263 [see now
>   s 830 CA 2006] if the asset concerned is sold for an amount equal to its book value, where
>   this is less than its market value, even where the company has distributable reserves.
>   The result of Aveling Barford and the debate it has engendered have cast doubt on
>   the validity of intra-group asset transfers conducted by reference to book value rather
>   than by reference to market value. It is understood that such transactions are often car-
>   ried out by reference to book value rather than market value for a variety of business,
>   administrative or tax reasons. Because of this doubt such transactions are therefore often
>   carried out in a more complicated way . . . or do not proceed at all.

7.19 Sections 845 to 846 of the CA 2006 are designed to address the uncertainties that arose in
the wake of *Aveling Barford*. Intra-group transfers are permitted provided the company
has sufficient distributable profits to justify a distribution. This is calculated on the basis
of the book value (the value as it appears in the company's accounts) of the asset in question. Thus, the book value rather than the market value is used to assess the amount of
the distribution. Put simply, the effect of these provisions is that where a company with
sufficient distributable profits transfers an asset at its book value, the amount of the distribution is deemed to be zero (s 845). If, on the other hand, the asset is transferred at a value

less than its book value, the difference is deemed to be a distribution. The 2006 Act does not, therefore, change the position where, as in *Aveling Barford*, the company does not have distributable profits. Finally, an important result of the 2006 modifications is that companies can carry out such transfers without the need for revaluations of the asset in question thereby reducing costs that might otherwise be payable to professional advisers.

In *Progress Property Co Ltd v Moorgarth Group Ltd* (2011), a case brought before the enactment of s 845, the Supreme Court held that a mere arithmetical difference between the consideration given for the assets and the figures which they were in subsequent proceedings valued retrospectively would not of itself mean there had been a distribution. In determining the adequacy of the consideration, a margin of appreciation should be properly allowed. The directors should not be held liable unless the payments were made with actual knowledge that the funds of the company were being misappropriated. It was stressed that whether a transaction infringed the common law rule preventing a return of capital was a matter of substance rather than its form or the labels the parties attached to it.

Returning funds to shareholders: reduction of share capital

7.20 It is normal commercial practice to review capital requirements and every year thousands of companies reduce their share capital. A company may wish to do this for one of the following reasons: (i) where the share capital is much greater than the actual net assets, because, for example, of business losses. In such a case a company may seek a formal reduction in share capital so that it corresponds more closely to its actual net assets. This will mean that it is able to resume dividend payments; (ii) the company may wish to reduce share capital and at the same time return some money to shareholders. It might do this where it has more cash than it can use because, for example, it has sold part of its undertaking. But the procedures that were laid down in the 1985 Act were extremely complex and expensive.

7.21 It will be recalled that the 2005 White Paper was particularly critical of the capital maintenance regime (see para **7.2**). In this respect, it is noteworthy that the Government went on to state that relevant provisions contained in the 1985 Act:

> are capable of catching a number of potentially beneficial or at least innocuous transactions and as a result companies, and their advisors, can spend disproportionate amounts of time and money ensuring that they do not inadvertently fall foul of the rules.
>
> Capital maintenance is largely irrelevant to the vast majority of private companies and their creditors. This is recognised by the [1985] Act, which carves out a number of exceptions to the capital maintenance rules for private companies only (para 4.8); see also Company Formation and Capital Maintenance (October 1999); Completing The Framework (November 2000); and the Final Report (2001).

7.22 The 2006 Act therefore contains a range of deregulatory measures that target requirements that were considered unnecessary and burdensome for private companies. However, as far as public companies are concerned, the provisions generally restate the CA 1985 requirements (see in particular CA 2006, ss 642–644).

7.23 Under the CA 2006 companies no longer need authority in the articles of association which permit a reduction of capital although they are able to restrict or prohibit the power if they wish (s 641(6)). Section 641(1) states the general rule that a *private* limited company may reduce its capital by special resolution supported by a solvency statement; but that *any* limited company may reduce its capital by special resolution if confirmed by the court. In other words, a private company is not compelled to follow the new simplified procedure but can opt instead to go through the rather convoluted and expensive step of obtaining the court's confirmation as was required under the 1985 Act and which is preserved for public companies.

(i) Private companies: reduction of capital supported by a solvency statement

7.24 The simplified procedure for private companies is detailed in ss 642–644 of the 2006 Act. The solvency statement, as required for private companies under s 641, must be made by all of the directors not more than 15 days before the date on which the special resolution is passed (s 642(1)). If one or more of the directors is not able or is not willing to make the statement, the company will not be able to use the solvency statement procedure to effect a reduction of capital unless the dissenting director or directors resign (in which case the solvency statement must be made by all of the remaining directors). Where the special resolution is passed as a *written* resolution, a copy of the directors' solvency statement must be sent or submitted to every eligible member at or before the time at which the proposed resolution is sent or submitted to him or her (s 642(2)); if the resolution is passed at a general meeting, a copy of the solvency statement must be made available for inspection by members throughout the meeting (s 642(3)). However, the validity of the resolution is not affected by a failure to comply with these requirements (s 642(4)).

7.25 Section 643 provides that the solvency statement must state that each of the directors has formed the opinion, taking into account all of the company's liabilities (including any contingent or prospective liabilities), that:

(a) as regards the company's situation at the date of the statement, that there is no ground on which the company could then be found to be unable to pay its debts; and

(b) if it intended to commence the winding-up of the company within 12 months of that date, that the company will be able to pay its debts in full within 12 months of the winding-up or, in any other case, that the company will be able to pay its debts as they fall due during the year immediately following that date.

Section 644 lays down the filing requirements in respect of a reduction of capital. Within 15 days after the special resolution is passed, the company must file with the Registrar a copy of the solvency statement together with a statement of capital and a statement of compliance. The special resolution itself must also be filed in accordance with s 30 of the CA 2006. The resolution does not take effect until these documents are registered (s 644(4)).

7.26   If the directors make a solvency statement without having reasonable grounds for the opinions expressed in it, and that statement is subsequently delivered to the Registrar, every director who is in default commits an offence (see s 643(4)); the penalties, which may include imprisonment, are set out in s 643(5). In *LRH Services Ltd (In liquidation) v Trew* (2018), it was held that the solvency statement made by the directors was invalid on the basis that the opinion of solvency had not been properly formed by one director. Upon examining the facts of the case that led to the opinion of solvency being formed, it transpired one of the directors was relying on LRH's parent company to discharge the company's liabilities, without a binding agreement to that effect, in order to support the opinion that the company was solvent. It was further held that in making this assumption, the directors failed to make any enquiry or give any consideration to the company's actual liabilities as is required by s 643. The result was that the solvency statement was found to be invalid and the capital reduction made on the basis of it was therefore unlawful. Each director was personally liable to the company for the £21 million dividend paid out in consequence (see further *BTI 2014 LLC v Sequana SA* (above)).

(ii) Public companies: reduction of capital confirmed by the court

7.27   As we have seen, public companies are required to have the special resolution for the reduction of capital confirmed by the court. The policy here is aimed at safeguarding the interests of creditors. Sections 645 and 646 (which restate s 136 of the 1985 Act) specify the procedure for making such an application for an order confirming the reduction including the creditors' right to object. The court will settle a list of creditors with a view to ensuring that each one of them has consented to the reduction. If a creditor does not consent the court may, in its discretion, dispense with that creditor's consent where the company secures the debt or claim (s 646(4)). If, on such an application, an officer of the company intentionally or recklessly conceals a creditor or misrepresents the nature or amount of a debt owed by the company, or is knowingly concerned in any such concealment or misrepresentation, he or she commits an offence (s 647).

7.28   The court may make an order confirming the reduction of capital on such terms and conditions as it thinks fit (s 648(1)). However, it will not confirm the reduction unless it is satisfied, with respect to every creditor of the company entitled to object, that either his consent to the reduction has been obtained, or his debt or claim has been discharged or secured (s 648(2)). The reduction will take effect on registration of the court order confirming the reduction (and statement of capital) by the Registrar (s 649(5)).

7.29 Where there is a reduction of capital, certain shares will be cancelled or reduced in nominal value. In this regard, the main issue the court has to consider when deciding whether or not to exercise its discretion to approve the reduction is whether the proposal strikes a fair balance between the interests of the different classes of shareholders. It has long been established that the rule most likely to achieve fairness is that money should be repaid in the order in which the classes of shares would rank, as regards repayment of capital, on a winding-up, though if the proposed reduction varies or abrogates class rights it may be possible to disapply this prima facie approach. In *Re Chatterley-Whitfield Collieries Ltd* (1948) the company's coal-mining business had been nationalised and it proposed to carry on operations on a reduced scale for which it would need less capital. It therefore decided to reduce its capital by paying off preference capital but keeping its ordinary shareholders. The court confirmed the reduction as fair because it was carried out in accordance with the rights of the two classes of shareholders in a winding-up. The observations of Lord Greene MR afford a good insight into the judicial approach to reductions of capital:

> A company which has issued preference shares carrying a high rate of dividend and finds its business so curtailed that it has capital surplus to its requirements and sees the likelihood, or at any rate the possibility, that its preference capital will not, if I may use the expression, 'earn its keep', would be guilty of financial ineptitude if it did not take steps to reduce its capital by paying off preference capital so far as the law allowed it to do so ... The position of the company itself as an economic entity must be considered, and nothing can be more destructive of a company's financial equilibrium than to have to carry the burden of capital which it does not need bearing a high rate of dividend which it cannot earn.

(See also *Re Saltdean Estate Co Ltd* (1968); and *Re Holders Investment Trust Ltd* (1971), considered in Chapter 9, Variation of class rights.)

7.30 If the reduction of a public company's capital has the effect of bringing the nominal value of its allotted share capital below the authorised minimum (see para **7.12**), the registrar must not register the court order confirming the reduction unless either the court so directs, or the company is first re-registered as a private company (s 650). Section 651 provides for an expedited procedure for re-registration as a private company.

Returning funds to shareholders: redemption or purchase by a company of its own shares

7.31 There are other means of achieving the effect of a reduction of share capital without having to obtain the court's approval. Although the common law prohibited a company acquiring its own shares because of the risk to creditors (*Trevor v Whitworth* (1887); see now s 658(1) of the 2006 Act), s 684(1) expressly permits a limited company to issue shares that are to be redeemed at the option of the company or the shareholder. A public company must be authorised by its articles to issue redeemable shares (s 684(3)), but for private companies no such authorisation is required, although the articles may exclude or restrict their issue (s 684(2)). Section 690(1) confers on limited companies the power to purchase their own shares, although this is subject to any restriction or prohibition in the articles of association. The difference between a redemption and a purchase of shares in this context is that for the former, the shares will have been issued on the basis that they are redeemable and so the holders will have been aware of the terms of the redemption from the outset; with respect to the latter, the parties will need to agree the terms of the repurchase at the time the company seeks to exercise the power.

(i) Effecting a redemption of shares

7.32 For both public and private companies, the directors may determine the terms, conditions, and manner of the redemption if so authorised by the articles of association or by a resolution of the company (s 685(1)). An ordinary resolution is required notwithstanding that its effect is to amend the articles (s 685(2)). Shares may not be redeemed unless they are fully paid and the terms of the redemption may provide that the amount payable on redemption may, by agreement between the company and the shareholder concerned, be paid on a date later than the redemption date (s 686(1) and (2)). Where the directors are authorised to determine the terms, conditions, and manner of redemption, they must do so before the shares are allotted and such details must be specified in any statement of capital which the company is required to file (s 685(3)). When a company redeems any redeemable shares it must within one month give notice to the Registrar specifying the shares redeemed together with a statement of capital which details the company's shares immediately following the redemption (s 689). If default is made in complying with the notice requirements, an offence is committed by the company and every officer of the company who is in default (s 689(4)).

(ii) Effecting a purchase by a company of its own shares

7.33 As noted earlier, s 690(1) authorises a limited company to purchase its own shares including any redeemable shares, subject to any restriction or prohibition in the company's articles. Further, a company may not purchase its own shares if as a result there would no longer be any issued shares other than redeemable shares (s 690(2)). Only fully paid shares can be purchased and they must be paid for on purchase (s 691). Payment by instalments is not, in general permissible (see *Peña v Dale* (2004); *Kinlan v Crimmin* (2006)). However, the Companies Act 2006 (Amendment of Part 18) Regulations 2013 (SI 2013/999), which came into force on 30 April 2013, amend s 691 so that a private company can pay for its own shares by instalments with respect to purchases relating to an employee share scheme (s 691(3)). A company cannot subscribe for its own shares but is restricted to purchasing them from existing members (see *Re VGM Holdings Ltd* (1942)).

7.34 With respect to financing the purchase, a public company must use distributable profits or the proceeds of a fresh share issue made for the purpose of financing the purchase (s 692(2)). However, a private company may, as under the 1985 Act, purchase its own shares out of capital (s 692(1) and s 709) and, since 30 April 2013, with cash (see later). The main difference introduced by the 2006 Act for a private company is that the power to purchase need no longer be contained in the articles, although its articles may, however, restrict or prohibit the exercise of this statutory power. Where a private company purchases its own shares out of capital the directors are required to make a statement specifying the amount of the permissible capital payment for the shares in question. Section 714 provides that this statement must also confirm that the directors have made a full enquiry into the affairs and prospects of the company and that they have formed the opinion:

(a)   as regards the company's situation immediately after the date on which the payment out of capital is made, there will be no grounds on which the company could then be found unable to pay its debts; and

(b)   as regards the company's prospects for the year immediately following that date, the company will be able to continue to carry on business as a going concern and be able to pay its debts as they fall due in the year immediately following the date on which the payment out of capital is made.

In forming their opinion on the company's solvency and prospects, the directors must take into account all of the company's liabilities (including contingent and prospective liabilities). Directors who make this statement without reasonable grounds for their opinion commit an offence (s 715). As an additional safeguard, s 714(6) provides that the directors' statement must have annexed to it a report by the company's auditor confirming its accuracy. Further, the payment out of capital must be approved by a special resolution of the company which must be passed on, or within the week immediately following, the date of the directors' statement (s 716). The holders of the shares in question are barred from voting on the resolution (s 717). Within the week immediately following the date of the s 716 resolution the company must give public notice in the *Gazette* and in an appropriate national newspaper of the proposed payment which must also state that any creditor may apply to court under s 721 within five weeks of the resolution for an order preventing the payment (s 719). Following the purchase, the company must give notice to the Registrar; such notice must include a statement of capital (s 708). The 2013 Regulations (see para **7.33**) amend s 691(1) so that a private company may purchase its owns shares with cash (if authorised by the articles) up to the value of £15,000 or 5 per cent of its share capital in any financial year (s 692(1)(b)).

7.35 In certain circumstances a company which purchases its own shares need not cancel them but can, instead, hold them 'in treasury' from where they can be either sold or transferred, for example to an employee share scheme. This relaxation, which took effect on 1 December 2003, was introduced by the Companies (Acquisition of Own Shares) (Treasury Shares) Regulations 2003 (SI 2003/1116). The regulations inserted ss 162A–162G into the 1985 Act which were re-enacted in ss 724–732 of the CA 2006. Prior to 30 April 2013, for 'qualifying shares', as defined in s 724(2), to become treasury shares the requirement was that they had to have been purchased by the company out of distributable profits. The 2013 Regulations, however, relax this requirement so that a limited liability company can hold its own shares in treasury where the purchase is made either out of distributable profits or with cash under s 692(1)(b). There are a number of restrictions on the rights attaching to treasury shares. For example, s 726(2) states that the company may not exercise any right in respect of treasury shares. Any purported exercise of such a right is void. Further, no dividend or other distribution may be paid to the company (s 726(3)).

Financial assistance for the acquisition of shares in a public company

Relationship to capital maintenance doctrine

7.36 The term 'financial assistance' refers to a company providing financial assistance for the purchase of its own shares. This could be by way of a gift to a third party on the understanding that the money would be used to buy the donor company's shares or, for instance, through guaranteeing a potential purchaser's borrowing (for more examples, see s 677 of the CA 2006, at para **7.43**). While there are good reasons for prohibiting such practices (for instance, a listed company could give money to people to buy its shares and thus increase its share price, thereby creating a false indication of the true value of its shares), it is not immediately obvious why such provision infringes the capital maintenance doctrine. The financial assistance prohibition was first introduced by the Companies Act 1929, s 45 and, until the CA 2006, applied both to public and private companies, although with respect to the latter there was relaxation (referred to as the 'whitewash' procedure (see CA 1985, ss 151 and 155–158)). A consequence of the repeal of the prohibition for private companies is that financial assistance transactions or arrangements in relation to the shares of a private company are no longer unlawful. However, other general company law principles continue to apply. For example, the transaction or arrangement must be in the best interests of the company (see CA 2006, s 172; see also Chapter 14). Further, the transaction or arrangement must not breach the rules on distributions or otherwise constitute an illegal reduction of capital (see paras **7.13–7.35**).

The general prohibition against financial assistance was enacted as a result of the recommendations of the Greene Committee (Cmnd 2657, 1926), which described the particular mischief to be addressed by it in the following terms:

> A practice has made its appearance in recent years which we consider to be highly improper. A syndicate appears to purchase from the existing shareholders sufficient shares to control a company, the purchase money is provided by a temporary loan from a bank for a day or two, the syndicate's nominees are appointed directors in place of the old board and immediately proceed to lend to the syndicate out of the company's funds . . .

> *the money required to pay off the bank . . . Thus in effect the company provides money for the purchase of its own shares. (Para 30)*

The modern terminology to describe such arrangements is 'leveraged buyouts' which gives a clear indication that the acquisition is financed by debt.

7.37 The Jenkins Committee, *Report of the Company Law Committee* (1962) put the matter bluntly:

> *If people who cannot provide the funds necessary to acquire control of a company from their own resources, or by borrowing on their own credit, gain control of a company with large assets on the understanding that they will use funds of the company to pay for their shares, it seems to us all too likely that in many cases the company will be made to part with its funds either on inadequate security or for an illusory consideration.*

The Committee took the view that the rationale underlying the prohibition was not the need to maintain capital, but rather the potential dangers which indebted acquirers pose to creditors.

7.38 A clear explanation of the mischief to which the prohibition is directed is provided by Arden LJ in *Chaston v SWP Group plc* (2002):

> *[It] is derived from section 45 of the Companies Act 1929 which was enacted as a result of the previously common practice of purchasing the shares of a company having a substantial cash balance or easily realisable assets and so arranging matters that the purchase money was lent by the company to the purchaser . . . The general mischief . . . remains the same, namely that the resources of the target company and its subsidiaries should not be used directly or indirectly to assist the purchaser financially to make the acquisition. This may prejudice the interests of the creditors of the target or its group, and the interests of any shareholders who do not accept the offer to acquire their shares or to whom the offer is not made.*

7.39 More recently, Toulson LJ explained in *Anglo-Petroleum Ltd v TFB (Mortgages) Ltd* (2007), that the prohibition is aimed at preventing the resources of a target company (and its subsidiaries) being enlisted, directly or indirectly, to assist the purchaser financially in his acquisition.

Commenting on the rationale for the rule, Professor Armour (2000) notes that:

> *The ambit of the financial assistance provisions is broader than is necessary to ensure capital is not returned to shareholders. The basic prohibitions apply to any assistance which depletes the company's net assets, regardless of whether it has distributable profits, and even to some transactions, such as loans, which may not deplete its assets at all.*

7.40 With respect to Armour's example relating to loans, it should be noted that the reason why they do not deplete a company's net assets is because although funds leave the company, their loss is matched in the company's accounts by the debt that is thereby created. Thus, it can be seen that the prohibition on financial assistance is wider than that which would be required if the only policy in operation was to maintain the company's share capital. But, as stressed by Arden LJ (see para **7.38**), it recognises the need to protect shareholders and outsiders from misuse by the company of its own assets to finance the purchase of its own shares, even if the capital maintenance doctrine is not thereby infringed (in this regard, see also *Wallersteiner v Moir* (1974), in which Scarman LJ noted that the prohibition is designed 'to protect company funds and the interests of shareholders as well as creditors').

7.41 The 2005 White Paper, in line with the *Final Report* of the CLRSG, states that private companies should no longer be prevented from providing financial assistance for the purchase of their own shares. It endorses the view expressed by the Steering Group that creditors have other safeguards, such as the wrongful trading provision in the Insolvency Act 1986 (see Chapter 17), which render the 'elaborate safeguards specifically directed at financial assistance' superfluous. Thus, a major change introduced by the 2006 Act, and one described by BIS 'as one of the key benefits of the Act for private companies' (see 'Companies Act 2006: Major Business Benefits') is that private companies are no longer prohibited from giving financial assistance for the purpose of acquiring their own shares or those of their private company parent. In terms of transaction costs, it has been esti-mated that this freedom will save private companies some £20 million per year (see the Regulatory Impact Assessment; see also *The Strategic Framework* (1999)). However, the prohibition continues to apply to public companies because of the need to comply with the Second Company Law Directive (see para **7.11**).

The prohibition and the exceptions

The general prohibition

7.42 The statutory provisions are complex. The prohibition against public companies pro-viding financial assistance is laid down by s 678(1) of the 2006 Act (implementing the Second EC Company Law Directive (EEC 77/91), Art 23) which provides:

> Where a person is acquiring or proposing to acquire shares in a public company, it is not lawful for that company, or a company that is a subsidiary of that company, to give financial assistance directly or indirectly for the purpose of the acquisition before or at the same time as the acquisition takes place.

It is noteworthy that s 678(1) makes no reference to proof of improper intention. In this respect, breach is determined objectively from the surrounding circumstances. Section 678(3) broadens the prohibition so as to cover situations where assistance is provided by a private company in order to discharge a liability incurred by a purchaser for the purpose of acquiring shares, but which at the time the post-acquisition assistance is given, has re-registered as a public company. Section 678(1) is bolstered by s 679(1) which extends the prohibition so as to cover financial assistance (directly or indirectly) provided by a public company which is a subsidiary of a private company for the purpose of acquiring shares in that private company before or at the same as the acquisition takes place; and s 679(3) extends the prohibition to cover after the event financial assistance given by a public company to its private holding company.

7.43 Section 677 (together with s 683(1) and (2)) seeks to limit the scope of the meaning of 'financial assistance' by listing certain forms or ways in which it can arise. Examples include: the giving of a guarantee, security, or indemnity, other than an indemnity in respect of the indemnifier's own neglect or default, or by way of release or waiver, or by way of loan. The giving of a security in this context is illustrated by the facts of *Heald v O'Connor* (1971). Mr and Mrs Heald sold all of the shares in DE Heald (Stoke on Trent) Ltd to O'Connor. The price was £35,000 but they lent him £25,000 in order to enable him to complete the purchase. The company thereby granted the vendors a floating charge over all of its assets by way of security for the loan. Thus, if O'Connor defaulted, the security would be enforceable against the company. This was therefore held to be illegal.

7.44 A residual category falls within s 677(1)(d) which adds the following proscription: 'any other financial assistance given by a company where the net assets of the company are reduced to a material extent by the giving of the assistance, or the company has no net assets'. Therefore, even if a public company were in a position to return funds to shareholders because it had distributable profits, it would not be able to provide any sort of financial assistance for the acquisition of its own shares which materially depleted its net assets. In this regard, s 677(2) and (3) state that in determining the company's 'net assets' it is the actual value of the assets and liabilities, as opposed to their book value, that is to be applied (see *Parlett v Guppy's (Bridport) Ltd* (1996); and *Grant v Lapid Developments Ltd* (1996)).

The exceptions

7.45 Section 681 contains a wide list of 'unconditional' exceptions. Those in subsection (2) are unexceptional: they mainly relate to procedures which are specifically authorised elsewhere in the Act: for example, to effect a redemption of shares or a reduction of capital. So-called 'conditional exceptions' are listed in s 682. They therefore only apply if the company has net assets and either: (a) those assets are not reduced by the giving of the financial assistance, or (b) to the extent that those assets are so reduced, the assistance is provided out of distributable profits. An example of a 'conditional exception' is where the provision by the company of financial assistance is for the purposes of an employee share scheme provided it is made in good faith in the interests of the company or its holding company (s 682(2)(b)); or which assists in the promotion of a policy objective such as facilitating the acquisition of the shares by an employee share scheme or by spouses or civil partners, widows, widowers, or surviving civil partners, or children of employees (see s 682(2)(c)).

7.46 Section 678(2) and (3), however, also contain the 'principal purpose' and 'incidental part of a larger purpose' defences which are carried over from the 1985 Act. In essence, financial assistance is *not* prohibited:

- if the principal purpose of the assistance is not to give it for the purpose of an acquisition of shares, or where this assistance is incidental to some other larger purpose of the company; and

- in either case, where the financial assistance is given in good faith in the interests of the company.

7.47 The exceptions are designed to ensure that the prohibition in s 678(1) does not also catch genuine commercial transactions which are in the interests of the company. However attempting to assess a person's 'purpose' is necessarily difficult (for instance, the need to distinguish purpose from effect) because the court will need to determine whether the giving of assistance for *the purpose* of an acquisition of shares is an incidental part of *some larger purpose*. Something is a 'purpose' of a transaction between A and B if it is understood by both of them that it will enable B to bring about the desired result (*Re Hill and Tyler Ltd* (2005); and *Dyment v Boyden* (2005)). The difficulties of assessing 'purpose' came to the fore in *Brady v Brady* (1989).

Brady v Brady

7.48 The scheme in issue in this case basically involved a company's business being divided between two brothers, Jack (J) and Bob (B) who were the controlling shareholders. They were not on speaking terms and the deadlock between them threatened the survival of the company and its subsidiaries. It was decided that J should take the haulage business and B the soft drinks business. However, the haulage business was worth more than the soft drinks business and so to make the division fair and equal, extra assets had to be transferred from the haulage business to the drinks business. In essence this involved the principal company, Brady, transferring assets to a new company controlled by B. It was conceded that s 151 of the CA 1985 (now CA 2006, s 678(1)) had been breached because the transfer involved Brady providing financial assistance towards discharging the liability of its holding company, M, for the price of shares which M had purchased in Brady. When J sought specific performance of the agreement, B contended that it was an illegal transaction. J argued, however, that the financial assistance was an incidental part of a larger purpose of the company, i.e. the removal of deadlock between the two brothers which had threatened to result in the liquidation of the business.

Construing the phrase 'larger purpose' (now re-enacted in s 678(2)(b)), Lord Oliver observed:

> *My Lords, 'purpose' is, in some contexts, a word of wide content but in construing it in the context of the fasciculus of sections regulating the provision of finance by a company in connection with the purchase of its own shares there has always to be borne in mind the mischief against which section 151 is aimed. In particular, if the section is not, effectively, to be deprived of any useful application, it is important to distinguish between a purpose and the reason why a purpose is formed. The ultimate reason for forming the purpose of financing an acquisition may, and in most cases probably will, be more important to those making the decision than the immediate transaction itself. But 'larger' is not the same thing as 'more important' nor is 'reason' the same as 'purpose'. If one postulates the case of a bidder for control of a public company financing his bid from the company's own funds, the obvious mischief at which the section is aimed, the immediate purpose which it is sought to achieve is that of completing the purchase and vesting control of the company in the bidder. The reasons why that course is considered desirable may be many and varied. The company may have fallen on hard times so that a change of management is considered necessary to avert disaster. It may merely be thought, and no doubt would be thought by the purchaser and the directors whom he nominates once he has control, that the business of the company will be more profitable under his management than it was heretofore. These may be excellent reasons but they cannot, in my judgment, constitute a 'larger purpose' of which the provision of assistance is merely an incident. The purpose and the only purpose of the financial assistance is and remains that of enabling the shares to be acquired and the financial or commercial advantages flowing from the acquisition, whilst they may form the reason for forming the purpose of providing assistance, are a byproduct of it rather than an independent purpose of which the assistance can properly be considered to be an incident.*

7.49 The House of Lords held that the purpose of the transaction was to assist in financing the acquisition of the shares: the essence of the reorganisation was for J to acquire B Ltd's shares and therefore the acquisition of those shares was not incidental to the reorganisation. As Lord Oliver concluded, the acquisition 'was not a mere incident of the scheme devised to break the deadlock. It was the essence of the scheme itself and the object which the scheme set out to achieve.' (It should be borne in mind, that if the facts of *Brady* were to arise today, it would not be caught by the prohibition because the case was concerned with a private company.)

7.50 This interpretation of the 'purpose exceptions' has been much criticised in that it appears to restrict unduly the width of the defence and, indeed, it makes it very hard to ascertain exactly what sort of situations would fall within its scope (see *Dyment v Boyden (Liquidator of Pathways Residential and Training Centres Ltd)* (2005)).

7.51 An interesting case on the meaning of financial assistance is *Chaston v SWP Group plc* (2002) (see para **7.38**), in which Arden LJ subjected *Brady* to considerable analysis and came out in support of the reasoning of the House of Lords notwithstanding the strength of criticism the decision has generated. C was a director of DRC, a company which formed part of a group of which DRCH was the parent. SWP, a listed company, wished to take over the DRC group by acquiring the shares in DRCH and, as part of its due diligence exercise, it needed a long form report on the DRC group for informational purposes. Deloitte and Touche (D & T) prepared the report and C agreed that D & T should invoice DRC for their fees. Invoices for fees of nearly £20,000 were submitted and the acquisition was completed. SWP later claimed damages against C for breach of fiduciary duty in having procured or connived in the grant by DRC of financial assistance for the purpose of the acquisition by SWP of the shares in DRCH. The alleged financial assistance was DRC incurring liability to D & T for payment of their professional fees. The Court of Appeal held that this was a breach of s 151. Arden LJ, noting that the term 'financial assistance' was not defined by the 1985 Act, thought that it was clear from the authorities that what matters is the 'commercial substance' of the transaction (citing *Charterhouse v Tempest Diesels* (1986), in which Hoffmann J said that when determining whether the prohibition has been breached: 'One must examine the commercial realities of the transaction and decide whether it can properly be described as the giving of financial assistance by the company, bearing in mind that the section is a penal one and should not be strained to cover transactions which are not fairly within it.' Lord Hoffmann's approach to the determination of financial assistance has been approved by the Court of Appeal in *Barclays Bank plc v British and Commonwealth Holdings plc* (1996)). Arden LJ therefore took the view that as a matter of commercial substance financial assistance was given on the facts of the case. D & T received payment for their professional services and both SWP, the purchasers, and the vendors, DRCH, were relieved of any obligation to pay for those services themselves: 'as a matter of commercial reality, the fees in question smoothed the path to the acquisition of shares'. She concluded:

> Section 151 makes it clear that a transaction can fall within section 151 even if only one of the purposes for which it was carried out was to assist the acquisition of shares. Here the liability to pay the fees of D & T was clearly incurred for the purpose of the acquisition by SWP of DRCH's shares. Brady v Brady also makes it clear that an unlawful purpose is not removed by the fact that, as the judge found here, the directors were motivated by the best interests of the company. Their motivation was only a reason for their acts, not a purpose in itself

(See *Brady v Brady*, (1989) discussed at para **7.48**.)

Finally, the transaction did not fall within the 'larger purpose' exception as there was no corporate purpose other than the acquisition of the shares in the parent company (see also, *Paros plc v Worldink Group plc* (2012)).

7.52   Ascertaining whether or not the prohibition has been breached is necessarily a fact-intensive exercise and previous decisions provide little guidance in predicting an outcome. However, the focus on 'commercial realities' has enabled the modern courts to narrow the scope of the prohibition. For example, in *MT Realisations Ltd v Digital Equipment Co Ltd* (2003), the issue in the case arose out of a subsidiary company (MTR) paying sums owed under a secured loan to its parent company. These sums were used by the parent company to discharge its liability incurred in acquiring its shares in the subsidiary. In fact, MTR paid the sums directly to the vendor of the shares. In structuring the arrangement this way, there was an appearance of MTR's funds being used to pay liabilities arising on the acquisition of its shares. An action was brought on the basis that this amounted to financial assistance. Mummery LJ, delivering the principal judgment, reasoned that on the commercial realities of the transaction, financial assistance had not been given by MTR 'for the purpose of' reducing or discharging a liability incurred for the purpose of the acquisition of its shares. The parent company did not receive anything beyond what it was legally entitled to as secured creditor and structuring the arrangement so that the sums in question were paid directly to the vendor was done merely for commercial convenience. The judge concluded:

> each case is a matter of applying the commercial concepts expressed in nontechnical language to the particular facts. The authorities provide useful illustrations of the variety of fact situations in which the issue can arise; but it is rare to find an authority on s 151 which requires a particular result to be reached on different facts.

More recently, in *Corporate Development Partners LLC v E-Relationship Marketing Ltd* (2009), it was held that as a matter of commercial reality the payment of an introduction fee by a company to an agent who introduced the company to the buyer of its shares did not constitute financial assistance. The agent had played no part in the negotiation of the acquisition. Further, the payment of the fee was not a condition of the acquisition nor did it serve to reduce the purchaser's acquisition obligations and it was neither intended to, nor did it, smooth the path towards the acquisition. Although the payment was made because the agent had introduced a party which had acquired the company, it was not 'for the purpose' of the acquisition.

7.53 An advantage of the emphasis now being placed upon the commercial substance or realities of a particular transaction or arrangement is that it facilitates an open-textured approach towards the determination of the purpose of an acquisition. Thus, the court can examine, for example, whether or not the prohibition is being enlisted expediently by a party with the aim of avoiding a transaction freely entered into on the ground of illegality. In *Dyment v Boyden* (2005) the applicant and the two respondents were partners in a residential nursing home, the freehold of which was owned by each in equal shares. The home was run through a company of which the partners were directors. When one of the respondents was charged with assault the local authority cancelled the nursing home's registration under the Registered Homes Act 1984. As a result, the partnership was dissolved by agreement whereby the respondents transferred their shares in the company to the applicant in return for which she transferred her interest in the freehold to the respondents. They then granted a lease of the property to the company at a rent considerably in excess of its market value. The applicant, clearly unhappy with the excessive rent she was paying, argued that to the extent the rent exceeded the market value, the difference represented financial assistance since it resulted in the company's net assets being reduced. Further, because that assistance had been given to facilitate the acquisition by the applicant of the respondents' shares it had been given either 'directly or indirectly' for the purposes of that acquisition. The Court of Appeal held that the trial judge was right in finding that the company's entry into the lease was 'in connection with' the acquisition by the appellant of the shares but was not 'for the purpose of' that acquisition. His finding that the entry into the lease was for the purpose of acquiring the premises rather than the shares was a finding of fact with which the Court of Appeal should not interfere.

7.54 It is apparent from the decisions in *Charterhouse v Tempest Diesels*, *MT Realisations Ltd*, and *Dyment* that the modern courts are adopting a pragmatic approach towards the prohibition by looking at the 'commercial realities' surrounding a financial assistance claim (see also *Anglo Petroleum Ltd v TFB (Mortgages) Ltd* (2007) and *Cox v Cox* (2006)). This seems to point to the welcome development that there is a judicial consensus emerging around the question of limiting the scope of the prohibition.

7.55 In terms of the geographical limits of the prohibition, the drafting of s 678(1) gives the decision of Millett J in *Arab Bank plc v Mercantile Holdings Ltd* (1994) statutory effect. Here it was held that the prohibition in s 151 of the CA 1985 on a company giving financial assistance for the purpose of acquiring its own shares or shares in its holding company did not extend to the giving of assistance by a subsidiary incorporated in an overseas jurisdiction. The judge, having reviewed the statutory history of the prohibition, applied the presumption that, in the absence of a contrary intention, s 151 could not have extra-territorial effect. Section 151 of the 1985 Act had applied the prohibition 'to the company or any of its subsidiaries'; the term 'subsidiary' being defined as including foreign companies. However, s 678 is more narrowly framed (see para **7.42**): it restricts the prohibition to UK public companies and their UK subsidiaries. This comes about because s 1(1) of the 2006 Act defines 'company' as meaning a company formed and registered under the Act or under previous UK Companies Acts. Further, the Court of Appeal confirmed in *AMG Global Nominees (Private) Ltd v Africa Resources Ltd* (2008), that where an English parent company arranges for a wholly owned foreign subsidiary to provide financial assistance out of the subsidiary's assets for the purpose of acquiring shares in its English parent company, this does not amount to the giving of financial assistance. It did not involve either an asset leaving the parent or an assumption of liability by the parent company.

The sanctions

7.56 Section 680 makes breach of the prohibition a criminal offence with the company being liable to a fine 'and every officer of it who is in default liable to imprisonment or a fine or both'. The effect of this is to make the transaction unlawful which can affect the enforceability of the underlying agreement. The following conclusions can be derived from the cases (see *Gower and Davies* (2016), Chapter 13):

> 1 If the financial assistance has not yet been given and its giving would be unlawful, the agreement to give it cannot be specifically enforced (*Brady v Brady* (1989)).

2 If unlawful financial assistance has been given by the company, that transaction is void. This means that if it consists of an agreement (for instance, a guarantee or a mortgage) the recipient of the financial assistance cannot enforce it (*Heald v O'Connor* (1971); see further *Re Hill and Tyler Ltd (in administration)* (2004); and *Anglo Petroleum Ltd v TFB (Mortgages) Ltd* (2007)). If the assistance took the form of a payment by the company (i.e. it was a gift or a loan) the company will have to sue to recover it. The basis of the claim will depend on who was the recipient: a director might be sued for misfeasance; a third party as constructive trustee (see *Selangor Rubber Estates Ltd v Craddock (No 3)* (1968); and *Re In a Flap Envelope Co Ltd* (2004); see further *Belmont Finance Corpn Ltd v Williams Furniture Ltd* (1979)).

3 If the share acquisition agreement itself forms part of a composite transaction with the agreement to provide financial assistance, it will only be enforceable if it can be severed from the terms relating to the assistance. An inability to sever could lead to unfortunate results: for instance, the prospective purchaser might be able to keep the financial assistance without having to buy the shares.

Carney v Herbert (1985) is a complex case where the court had to decide if the vendors of shares in A Ltd could sue the purchaser (or the guarantor thereof) for the purchase price when a subsidiary of A Ltd had provided illegal financial assistance in relation to the purchaser's acquisition (by charging land owned by it as security for the purchaser's promise to pay for the shares). If the agreement could not have been severed, the purchaser would have been able to keep the shares without any payment being made for them. Lord Brightman, delivering the decision of the Privy Council, stated:

> as a general rule, where parties enter into a lawful contract of, for example, sale and purchase, and there is an ancillary provision which is illegal but exists for the exclusive benefit of the plaintiff, the court may and probably will, if the justice of the case so requires, and there is no public policy objection, permit the plaintiff, if he so wishes, to enforce the contract without the illegal provision.

Applying this, the Privy Council severed the illegal charges and allowed the vendors to sue for the purchase price.

7.57 In their approach to civil sanctions the courts have striven to give effect to the policy of protecting a company's creditors and shareholders. An alternative route for achieving such protection lies within the realm of fiduciary duties (see Chapter 14). In *MacPherson v European Strategic Bureau Ltd* (2002), the Court of Appeal held that an agreement for the distribution by an insolvent company of funds to shareholders amounted to an informal winding-up. As such, it failed to make proper provision for creditors. While it was acknowledged that an effect of the agreement was that the company provided financial assistance for the purpose of an acquisition of its shares, liability was couched in terms of breach of fiduciary duty so that it was not necessary to enlist the statutory provisions (see also Lord Oliver's remarks in *Brady* to the effect that the words '"good faith in the interests of the company" form, I think, a single composite expression and postulate a requirement that those responsible for procuring the company to provide the assistance act in the genuine belief that it is being done in the company's interest'). Sidestepping the Act by recourse to the fiduciary obligations of directors gives rise to the question whether the statutory provisions serve any useful purpose beyond ensuring compliance with the Second Company Law Directive. Although the requirements of the Directive have been the subject of limited relaxation following the report of the High Level Group of Company Law Experts in 2002 (see Directive 2006/68/EC), the UK has not assimilated the reforms into the 2006 Act given the complexity of the procedural requirements which were introduced. The DTI took the view that the procedures for a shareholders' resolution authorising the board to engage in financial assistance were far too onerous to be of practical benefit to UK companies, especially those with widely dispersed memberships.

From the perspective of company creditors, it can be argued that there are alternative common law remedies which offer adequate protection. The requirements covering unlawful dividends, reductions of capital, and the provisions in the insolvency legislation relating to transactions at preference are effective responses to the policy considerations underlying the prohibition, particularly the need to protect corporate assets for their benefit.

FURTHER READING

This chapter links with the materials in Chapters 9 and 10 of **Hicks and Goo's Cases and Materials on Company Law** (Oxford, OUP, 2011, xl +649p).

Armour, 'Share Capital and Creditor Protection: Efficient Rules for a Modern Company Law' [2000] *MLR* 355.

Cabrielli, 'In Dire Need of Assistance? Sections 151–158 of the Companies Act 1985 Revisited' [2002] *JBL* 272.

Clementelli, '(Under)valuing the Rules on Capital Maintenance' [2012] *ICCLR* 191.

Ferran, 'Corporate Transactions and Financial Assistance: Shifting Policy Perceptions but Static Law' [2004] *CLJ* 225.

Ferran, 'Simplification of European Company Law on Financial Assistance' [2005] *European Business Organization L R* 93.

Lowry, 'The Prohibition Against Financial Assistance: Constructing an Alternative Response' in Prentice and Reisberg (eds) *Corporate Finance Law: UK and EU Perspectives* (Oxford, OUP, 2011).

Luxton, 'Financial Assistance by a Company for the Purchase of its Own Shares—The Principal or Larger Purpose Exception' [1991] *Co Law* 18.

Micheler, 'Disguised Returns of Capital—An Arm's Length Approach' [2010] *CLJ* 151.

Payne, 'Unjust Enrichment, Trusts and Recipient Liability for Unlawful Dividends' [2003] *LQR* 583.

SELF-TEST QUESTIONS

1   Why is the amount of a company's share capital important to its creditors?

2   Why is it thought that the interpretation of the statutory provisions on financial assistance by the House of Lords in *Brady* could undermine the policy that those provisions should not invalidate genuine commercial transactions?

3   Bella and Milo, who are directors of Tweenies plc, had agreed to sell their shares in the company to Fizz, the other director. For tax reasons, at Fizz's request, the actual sale was to Doodles plc, a company in which Fizz was a controlling shareholder. To protect themselves Bella and Milo had obtained a guarantee of the purchase price from Fizz herself and a charge on the property of Max Ltd, a wholly owned subsidiary of Tweenies plc. The purchase price was paid by a cheque from Tweenies plc which was dishonoured.

Consider:

(a)   which of these transactions amounted to financial assistance;

(b)   whether any of the statutory exceptions apply;

(c)   if there has been illegal financial assistance, whether Bella and Milo can enforce the guarantee against Fizz.

8 The constitution of the company: dealing with insiders

Introduction

8.1 In Chapter 1 we briefly discussed the constitution of the company. In this chapter we cover the constitution of the company in greater detail focusing particularly on the articles of association, as they form the basis for much of the way the directors, the shareholders, and the company interact. A word of warning however: while the beginning of this chapter outlining the operation of the memorandum and the articles is straightforward, the law surrounding the operation of the s 33 contract is complex, confusing, contradictory, and frustrating. This is not for the usual reason that it is a complex area and it takes some time to absorb. It is rather because the law on s 33 is dominated by layer upon layer of contradictory case law. The CLRSG and the Consultative Document, March 2005 did recognise this problem and recommended some long-needed reforms. However, as we will see, the final reforms in the Companies Act 2006 were somewhat disappointing. We discuss those reforms as they arise in the general course of the chapter.

A company's constitution

8.2 As we noted in Chapter 1 in order to form a company the Registrar of Companies must be provided with the constitution of the company (this contains the internal rules of the company called the articles of association and any objects clause limiting the power of the company the company may have, see later), a memorandum of association stating that the subscribers intend to form a company and become members and an application for registration containing the company name, its share capital, the address of its registered office, whether it's a private or public company, that the liability of its members is limited, a statement of the company's directors names and addresses (this can be the address of the company's registered office, CA 2006, s 165), and a statement of compliance with the CA 2006. The subscribers to the memorandum are those who agree to take some shares or share in the company. If the application to the Registrar is successful the subscribers become the first members of the company.

8.3 Choosing a name for a company is not as straightforward as one might assume. There are restrictions on the name a company can be given. As we discussed in Chapter 1, private companies must have 'Ltd' after their name and public companies 'plc' (CA 2006, ss 58–59). The Registrar of Companies also keeps a list of company names and will not register a company which has the same name as one already on the register. The name of the company must also appear outside the registered office and appear on all correspondence (CA 2006, s 82).

8.4 There are also further restrictions that can be imposed by the Secretary of State, usually the Minister at the Department of Business, Energy & Industrial Strategy (BEIS) (formerly the Department of Business, Innovation and Skills (BIS)). It is not possible to register a company with a name which in the opinion of the Secretary of State would constitute a criminal offence or be offensive (see CA 2006, s 53). Examples are a name which is blasphemous, treasonous, or likely to incite racial hatred, or which contains the name of a proscribed organisation (e.g. IRA Ltd would not be acceptable). The Secretary of State's approval is specifically needed for a name which would give the impression that the company was connected with the Government or any local authority (CA 2006, s 54). There is also a specified list of words which need approval. For example an application to form a company with any of the following in the name, Police, Wales, Queen, or Great Britain would need the approval of the Secretary of State (CA 2006, ss 54–56). During the life of the company the members may only change the name of the company by special resolution (CA 2006, s 77).

8.5 Succeeding in registering a company name will not, however, guarantee that the name of your company is not in use by another business. If two businesses have the same or similar names the issue is usually decided by the common law action of 'passing off'. At common law a business cannot use a name so similar to the name used by an existing business as to be likely to mislead the general public into confusing the two concerns. It involves, in essence, an allegation that company B is trying to pass itself off as company A by using the same or a similar name and in effect trade on the reputation of company A. For example in *Exxon Corpn v Exxon Insurance Consultants International Ltd* (1982) the court granted an injunction to an oil company (Exxon Corporation) restraining an insurance company (Exxon Insurance Consultants International Ltd) from using the word Exxon in its name. It may not be immediately obvious that an insurance company could trade off an oil company's name but many large companies have extremely wide business interests which go beyond their core business.

8.6 Under s 9 the application sent to the Registrar must contain a statement of capital and initial shareholdings. Again as we noted in Chapter 1, it is common for the share capital to be subdivided into small amounts. For example, the share capital of X company is £1 million divided into 1 million shares of £1 each. Therefore, each share is allocated a 'par' or 'nominal' value which represents the minimum amount for which the shares can be issued. In our example £1 is the nominal value of the shares but the company could, if it wished, issue them for £5 each. Note though, it could not issue them for 75p. The shares can therefore be issued for more than their nominal value but not for less. During the life of the company the share capital can be increased if the company wishes to do so (CA 2006, s 617). The application for registration also states the company's registered office. In keeping with the public nature of the application documents this is the address to which all correspondence can be addressed or notices served (CA 2006, s 86). If the address changes the Registrar must be informed (CA 2006, s 87).

8.7 As we will discuss at length in Chapter 12, under the previous principal Companies Acts companies were required to specify their objects (what they were empowered to do, e.g. run a sweet shop etc) in the memorandum of association. In Chapter 2 we covered the origins of companies. Initially companies were formed by charters or grants from the Crown and Parliament. At first they were granted specifically to organisations like the Church or local authorities whose main function was to serve the public interest. As time went by corporate status was conferred on private concerns that were exploiting a particular invention through a patent grant or which had been granted trade rights or rights to build a railway or canal. These were still essentially grants of corporate status to promote private businesses that were deemed to be carrying out important public-related works.

8.8 These charter or statute companies were formed with specific constitutions designed for the particular venture. In those constitutions the purpose or object of the company was stated, i.e. to exploit trade in the East Indies or to build and operate a railway between London and Manchester. Their objects were very specific and the powers granted by the charter or statute had to be used to promote that object. When the state introduced a general incorporation statute which allowed company formations through simple registration, the objects clause requirement remained but was drafted by the individuals forming the company.

8.9 To take an example, if a company was formed to carry on a coal-supply business the objects clause in the memorandum of association would state something like, 'to carry on the business of supplying coal and to carry out all such other activities as are necessary to the attainment of that object'. However, the objects clause also set the limits of the company's power, in that a company formed as a coal-supply business could not enter into transactions to breed racehorses. It would simply have no legal capacity to do anything other than supply coal and carry out transactions related to that object, e.g. buy a truck to transport the coal etc. The coal-supply company could not suddenly transact to breed racehorses—it has no legal capacity to do so and so all such transactions are ultra vires (beyond its powers) and void.

8.10 The ultra vires issue became a problem because unlike public authorities from whom the ultra vires principle was drawn, companies tended to take business opportunities where they were profitable. So as companies increasingly moved away from their original objects, objects clauses in response grew in size as they were drafted to include every type of business imaginable. This meant the company could in effect move into any business listed in its objects. Problems still remained and eventually the Companies Act 1989 introduced provisions to reform ultra vires issues with regard to objects clauses (see Chapter 12). To eliminate any remaining problems the CLRSG in the *Final Report* (July 2001, para 9.10) and the Consultative Document, March 2005 (ch 5) proposed that companies be formed with unlimited capacity. The CA 2006 partly implements the recommended approach (see Chapter 12). As such, new companies registered under the 2006 Act have unrestricted objects unless a company chooses to have an objects clause restricting what it is empowered to do (CA 2006, s 31). A company might do this if it had particular values it wished to enshrine, e.g. an organic or fair-trade business. If a new company does choose to have an objects clause and for companies formed under the previous Principal Acts (the vast majority of existing companies) with an objects clause (unless these older companies have removed their objects clause as they can do if they wish, see CA 2006, s 31(2)) the objects clause forms part of the articles of association (CA 2006, s 28, see further Chapter 12).

Some elements of corporate theory

8.11 This may be a good point to introduce some elements of corporate theory as the articles of association offer some good examples of particular issues in this area (for a more detailed overview, see Chapter 15). The original charter and statutory companies were in no sense general trading companies and they are best described in terms of what is known as the concession or fiction theory (hereafter, concession or fiction). This theory describes incorporation as a concession granted or legal fiction created by the state because of the public good being carried out by the business. The state is central to its existence and the company therefore only exists and is legitimised because it serves the public good. This theory makes it relatively easy to justify the imposition of corporate regulations aimed at promoting the public interest.

8.12   With the advent of the registered company in the mid-19th century it became increasingly difficult to fit registered companies into the concession category. There was no specific charter or statute to form and regulate the company and they were not special business ventures pursuing the public interest. Rather they were easily registrable entities formed to pursue the entirely private concerns of their members. Concession theory had real resonance when the state was deeply involved in the incorporation process of a specific charter company. The advent of general incorporation through a simple registration process changed that, as incorporation became available to all rather than just those deemed worthy by the state. The state provided the general framework for incorporation but was no longer involved in the detail of each corporate venture. Significantly it gave up the ability to set the objectives of a corporation. This was now done by those setting up the company and framed in terms of their own private needs in the objects clause.

8.13   A second theory called the corporate realism theory (hereafter, corporate realism) was at least partly better suited to the registered company. It argued that the company was no fiction but had a real existence. It did not therefore depend on its members or the state for its continued existence. The strength of corporate realism is that it can best explain the separate existence of the corporation and therefore justify departure from a shareholder-oriented focus for the corporation. However, the theory was somewhat malleable. Some who advocated corporate realism argued that as a real person it could be subject to regulation by the state to promote the public good but confusingly others argued that as a real person it was an essentially private entity free from state control. In time however both concession and corporate realism lost ground to the aggregate theory (hereafter, aggregate). That theory describes the company as the central institution formed by the aggregation of private contracting individuals. That is, the members come together to pool their investment on terms they all agree. The state therefore has little to do with the corporation as a nexus of private contracting individuals. Posner (1986) therefore describes the company as 'a method of solving problems encountered in raising substantial amounts of capital. As such it is a kind of standard form contract.' As a result aggregate theory is also sometimes referred to as contractarian theory, particularly where the interaction of law and economics is concerned.

8.14   As with all theories there is something in concession, corporate realism, and aggregate theory that informs and explains aspects of company law—otherwise we would not be discussing them here. It is difficult to deny that the state still has a large role in creating and regulating corporations because they do not occur in nature and run free. Therefore concession theory still has something to offer in trying to understand company law. Corporate realism, while it has particular resonance when dealing with corporate personality (see Chapter 2 on corporate personality) or justifying manager-dominated companies (see Chapter 15 on corporate governance), has diminished as a major influence. Aggregate theory however has come to dominate and the company is largely but not wholly (remember annoyingly for aggregate/contractarian theorists, the state still does have a crucial role in creating the company) seen as a private institution.

8.15 The theories matter because if the company is viewed as a public creation then justifying state regulation of corporate affairs is relatively easy. If it is viewed as a private concern then the state interfering in its activities becomes more difficult to justify and the methods by which it is acceptable to do so become more restrictive. Mandatory rules which override any private agreements between contracting parties sit easier with concession theory. Default rules which apply in the absence of any agreement to the contrary and enabling rules which provide a framework for private parties to carry out certain functions, for example registering the company, sit easier with aggregate theory. As we will see, company law is a mix of all three types of rules. However the articles of association represent a good example of aggregate theory default rules.

The articles of association

8.16 The articles of association are a set of rules governing the running of the company. A model set of articles (historically called Table A but now called the model articles under the CA 2006, s 19 and the Companies (Model Articles) Regulations 2008 (SI 2008/3229)) has been provided by every principal Companies Act as a default set of rules for those setting up a company (note the resonance with aggregate theory). Those setting up the company are free to draft their own set of articles (rules) but if they do not provide such a set, then the model articles will apply. In practice the model articles are generally adopted with some slight amendments because this is both cost-effective and contains a great amount of legal certainty. As a result, even though the model articles are only a default set of rules their almost universal adoption has meant that they form the core organisational structure of the UK registered company—the board of directors (the management committee or organ) and the general meeting (the members' committee or organ) and allocate the powers of each one. Over time, as we will see, the common law and the Companies Acts have added supplementary provisions to flesh out the operation and application of the articles of association. For example in *Cream Holdings Ltd v Davenport* (2011) the court implied a term of cooperation and reasonableness into a set of articles. (See also *Trump International Golf Club Scotland Ltd v Scottish Ministers* (2016).)

8.17 While previous Companies Acts have provided a single set of articles for private and public companies, under the CA 2006 and the Companies (Model Articles) Regulations 2008 (SI 2008/3229), as a response to criticism of this one-size-fits-all approach, public and private companies now have separate articles of association. The articles of association, as we noted in Chapter 1, deal with many of the practicalities of running a business. Primarily, the articles provide for the operation of two organs or committees to operate the company—those being the general meeting and the board of directors. To take some examples with regard to the general meeting, the model articles regulate the organisation of meetings (arts 37–41 private; arts 28–33 public) and voting at the meeting (arts 42–47 private; arts 34–40 public). Similarly the model articles provide, with regard to the board of directors, for the allocation of management power to the board (arts 3–6 private and public), directors' appointment (arts 17–20 private; arts 20–24 public) and decision making by directors (arts 7–16 private; arts 7–19 public). It is important to note here that the articles do not provide for the general removal of directors except in the case of incapacity or resignation (arts 18 private and 22 public). Director removal is covered by CA 2006, s 168 which gives members the right by simple majority (more than 50 per cent of those who vote, vote for the resolution) to remove a director for any reason whatsoever. This is by far the greatest power of the general meeting.

8.18 The most important function of the articles of association is to allocate the power of the company between the board and the general meeting. Historically, this made the old Table A art 70 the most important article as it provided:

> [s]ubject to the provisions of the [CA 1985], the memorandum and the articles and to any directions given by special resolution, the business of the company shall be managed by the directors who may exercise all the powers of the company.

This delegation of power is now found in arts 3 and 4 of the model articles (public and private) and states:

Directors' general authority
3. Subject to the articles, the directors are responsible for the management of the company's business, for which purpose they may exercise all the powers of the company.

Shareholders' (Members) reserve power
4.(1) The shareholders (Members) may, by special resolution, direct the directors to take, or refrain from taking, specified action.

(2) No such special resolution invalidates anything which the directors have done before the passing of the resolution.

These articles provide the board of directors with the power to run the business. Although that power is subject to qualifications (the articles of the company and any special resolutions) it is important to note that the board is as a result of art 3 the primary power-wielding organ of the company.

8.19 The extent of this delegation of power to the directors has been the subject of much judicial deliberation. The key question is whether the delegation of power to run the company to the board creates a substantially independent discretion for the directors. In simple terms, could the directors take a decision which the majority of the members disagreed with? In *Howard Smith Ltd v Ampol Petroleum Ltd* (1974) Lord Wilberforce summed up the position:

> [t]he constitution of a limited company normally provides for directors, with powers of management, and shareholders, with defined voting powers having power to appoint the directors, and to take, in general meeting, by majority vote, decisions on matters not

reserved for management . . . it is established that directors, within their management powers, may take decisions against the wishes of the majority of shareholders, and indeed that the majority of shareholders cannot control them in the exercise of these powers while they remain in office.

This discretion is of course tempered by the fact that s 168 of the CA 2006 allows the majority of the members to remove the board. Nonetheless, it is clear from the judicial consideration of the predecessor of arts 3 and 4 (Table A, art 70) that the board has a substantially independent discretion to run the company as it sees fit (see further Chapter 13).

8.20 The board is also given, by virtue of art 30 (private) and art 70 (public) the power to decide whether to distribute any surplus profits to the shareholders in the form of dividends. Although technically the general meeting declares the dividend it cannot do so unless the board recommends a dividend. This may not seem like a significant power but it is another very important independent management power exercised by the board. The model articles default rule thus recognises that the board needs a significant amount of discretion as to how to allocate any surplus profit generated by the company's activities. The shareholders may want the profits to be distributed to them as dividends but the directors may wish to reinvest the profits to develop the long-term future of the business. The directors are given that discretion in the articles. As we will see in Chapters 13 and 14 maintaining the directors' discretion is a significant feature of UK company law. However, it is worth noting again that if the board consistently acts against the shareholders' wishes the shareholders can remove it and elect a more amenable board.

8.21 While the CA 2006, s 336 means that private companies are no longer required to hold an annual general meeting, it is important to note that it is in theory designed to fulfil an important supervisory function for public companies. The general meeting is in effect the residual power organ which meets once a year (CA 2006, s 336) (or sooner if there is an extraordinary meeting) to exercise its continued supervision over the board. Remember, the art 3 delegation of power to the board is subject to the members' art 4 residual control by special resolution. Additionally, the general meeting has certain other powers. For example its most important power is the power to elect and remove directors (art 20 (public) gives both the shareholders and the board the power to elect directors but the CA 2006, s 168 provides that only shareholders may remove directors). It may also issue shares (art 43 (public), although this is commonly altered to give the board that power). The CA 2006, s 437 requires that the annual accounts and reports be put before the AGM of a public company (there is however no requirement for a vote on these reports but it is common practice for larger companies to require a vote). The Directors Remuneration Report Regulations 2002 (SI 2002/1986, and CA 2006, s 420) and ss 79–82 of the Enterprise and Regulatory Reform Act 2013 also require that the general meeting play a role in setting board pay (see Chapters 13 and 16). The general meeting is also empowered by CA 2006, s 21 to alter the articles if three-quarters of the members (by a special resolution) vote in favour of the resolution. Thus in effect the members can alter the internal rules by which the company's power is allocated.

8.22 The reason the general meeting of public companies has a more important accountability function is because of the large number of shareholders these companies have. This in itself causes a problem because the apathy of the vast majority of shareholders, who tend not to exercise their votes, has effectively caused the AGM to cease operating as a supervisory organ. The CLRSG attempted to solve this problem by providing better information for shareholders (*Final Report*, ch 8) and making institutional investors who have historically held the vast majority of shares (insurance companies, pension funds, and investment trusts, see Chapters 15 and 16) disclose their voting record (*Final Report*, ch 6, paras 6.22–6.40). The financial crisis that unfolded over the course of 2007 and 2008 provided further impetus to address issues with institutional investors who either don't vote or vote with the directors after privately discussing important issues with them behind the scenes. Institutional investors now need, as part of the Stewardship Code introduced in 2010 (see Chapter 16), to have a clear policy on voting and the disclosure of votes. The CLRSG also recommended that public companies could also dispense with AGMs if all the shareholders agree (*Final Report*, para 7.6). The White Paper that followed in 2002 (vol I, paras 2.6–2.48) adopted all the procedural recommendations of the CLRSG regarding the general meeting, except the recommendation to force institutional investors to disclose their votes (para 2.47). In the Consultative Document, March 2005 (para 4.2) the Government changed its mind as to the need for public companies to hold an AGM and the CA 2006 was implemented with the requirement for public companies to hold an AGM still intact.

The contract of membership

8.23 Under the previous principal Companies Acts the constitution of the company (at that time meaning the memorandum and the articles) bound the members of the company and the company, thereby creating a statutory contract between the members themselves and between each member and the company. Under the CA 1985, s 14 it was stated that:

> [s]ubject to the provisions of this Act, the memorandum and articles, when registered, bind the company and its members to the same extent as if they respectively had been signed and sealed by each member, and contained covenants on the part of each member to observe all the provisions of the memorandum and of the articles.

Its replacement in CA 2006, s 33(1) similarly but perhaps more tidily states:

> The provisions of a company's constitution bind the company and its members to the same extent as if there were covenants on the part of the company and of each member to observe those provisions.

The first thing to notice here is that it is an odd sort of contract. It can be constantly varied by the members as the members may alter the articles by special resolution if three-quarters of the members vote in favour of the resolution (s 21). This means one might buy shares in a company because certain rights were conferred in its articles but after joining, a special resolution was passed despite your voting against the special resolution, which altered those rights and which bound you because of s 33 to observe the new provisions. It also binds parties who were not privy to it, for example future shareholders in the company. The reason such an unusual contract was created was as an attempt to bridge the changeover between the deed of settlement company (see Chapter 2) and the new registered company formed under the Joint Stock Companies Act 1844. The practical problem for the legislature at the time was that, while the old deed of settlement created a contractual relationship between the members who sealed it, the new constitutional default documents would not. The answer was to create an artificial contract which would automatically bind all the members of the company. The strength of the section, apart from binding the members and the company together, is that it allows shares to be freely transferable by removing the need for each member to formally agree the constitution each time shares are traded. This avoids the difficulties of having to renegotiate the contract each time shares change hands. However, as we will see, there is much uncertainty as to how exactly this artificial contract operates.

A contract between the company and the members

8.24 The original wording in the Act of 1844 that provided for a statutory contract has evolved through the 1856 Act; the Companies Act 1862, s 16; the Companies Act 1948, s 20(1); and the Companies Act 1985, s 14 finally to reside almost unchanged in terms of its effect in the Companies Act 2006, s 33. The framers of the original section unfortunately did not take account of the company's status as a separate entity. As one can see from s 14 earlier, the words of that section allowed for the constitution to be 'signed and sealed by each member'. It makes no mention of the company signing and sealing. Despite this the judiciary consistently held that the company is a party to the contract. The classic case on this point is *Hickman v Kent or Romney Marsh Sheep-Breeders' Association* (1915). In that case the enforceability of an article of association which allowed for arbitration proceedings where there was a dispute between the members and the company was at issue. Astbury J examined all the authorities on the matter and considered that 'articles regulating the rights and obligations of the members generally as such do create rights and obligations between them and the company respectively'. The article was, therefore, contractually binding between the members and the company. Despite the judiciary clarifying this issue the opportunity was taken when drafting CA 2006, s 33 to formally remedy this omission and the company has now been happily added to the parties that are bound to abide by the constitution of the company.

A contract between the members?

8.25 One of the questions that arose from the s 33(1) contract is whether it binds the members 'inter se'. That is, while we know from what has just been discussed that it binds the members and the company together, does it also mean each member has a binding enforceable contract with every other? This can be an important issue for shareholders who find that they wish to enforce a particular provision of the articles against another shareholder. For example pre-emption rights (the right to buy the shares of a member who wishes to leave the company) contained in the articles may drastically affect the shareholding of a member if they are not complied with. If the member can enforce the rights directly by virtue of s 33(1) it makes the rights easier to enforce. If the company is the only one who can enforce such rights then enforcement becomes more complex and the shareholder may be at risk of the majority shareholders taking advantage of the constitution to do nothing. The question as to the enforceability of the contract between members is one which has caused some difficulty and there has been much judicial debate as to whether a member can enforce a right contained in the articles directly against another member or whether the company is the proper claimant in such an action.

8.26 The following examples should provide some taste of the back and forth nature of the judicial debate. In *Wood v Odessa Waterworks Co* (1889) Stirling J considered that '[t]he articles of association constitute a contract not merely between the shareholders and the company, but between each individual shareholder and every other'. Lord Herschell, in *Welton v Saffery* (1897) stated:

> [i]t is quite true that the articles constitute a contract between each member and the company, and that there is no contract between the individual members of the company, but the articles do not any less, in my opinion, regulate their rights inter se. Such rights can only be enforced by or against a member through the company, or through the liquidators representing the company, but I think that no member has, as between himself and another member, any rights beyond that which the contract with the company gives.

In *Salmon v Quin & Axtens Ltd* (1909) Farwell LJ considered Stirling J's words in *Wood v Odessa* and stated, 'I think that is accurate subject to this observation, that it may well be that the Court would not enforce this covenant as between the individual shareholders in most cases.'

8.27 In *Rayfield v Hands* (1960) Vaisey J considered all the conflicting authorities (in particular he focused on Lord Herschell's statement in *Welton v Saffery*) on the issue and concluded that there was a contract *inter se* which was directly enforceable by one member against another. Vaisey J did not however think that his view was of general application, rather he emphasised the quasi-partnership nature of the company he was dealing with.

8.28 There is still confusion as to whether the contract is enforceable between members. Barc and Bowen (1988) argue that Lord Herschell's dicta, with the quasi-partnership exception provided by Vaisey J, represents the correct position. Thus in their view a member cannot enforce the articles of association of a company directly against another member unless the company is a quasi-partnership. The proper claimant in such a situation is the company itself. However, Davies (2008) considers that a 'direct action between the shareholders concerned is here possible; and for the law to insist on action through the company would merely be to promote multiplicity of actions and involve the company in unnecessary litigation'. The CLRSG in their *Final Report* recommend 'the clarification of the nature of the company's constitution (currently laid down by the outmoded and inadequate s 14), including increased certainty as to what rights are enjoyed and may be pursued by members personally under the constitution' (para 2.26). The solution they recommended was to allow all rights in the constitution to be enforced against the company and the other members unless the constitution provides otherwise. This also seemed to be reflected in the Government's Consultative Document, March 2005 (para 5.1) although it is not entirely clear what the Government intended. This lack of clarity continues in the CA 2006 as the guidance notes to the Act state:

> A company's articles are rules, chosen by the company's members, which govern a company's internal affairs. They form a statutory contract between the company and its members, and between each of the members, and are an integral part of a company's constitution. (The Articles of Association, Note 67, General)

This appears to indicate that the uncertainties about enforceability are resolved but the wording of CA 2006, s 33 in terms of its central contract which replaced s 14 is almost unchanged (see para **8.23**). This is a shame given that during the Grand Committee stage of the Bill in the House of Lords, Lord Wedderburn tabled an amendment to s 33 (at the time numbered as clause 34) which would have clarified the relationship between the company and the members. The Government rejected the amendment stating 'notwithstanding the valuable work of the Company Law Review in this area, we have yet to be convinced that there is anything better and clearer'. As a result we are left somewhat strangely with a 'new' section governing the relationship between the members and the company which is almost exactly the same as its predecessor which the CLRSG described as 'the outmoded and inadequate s 14'.

Who can sue?

8.29 One of the key questions that arises with the s 33 contract is, who is entitled to sue to enforce it? While we have seen in this chapter that members may be able to enforce it against each other, a more complex situation occurs where the members wish to enforce it against the company. The question becomes whether the wrong complained of is a wrong done to the company or to the member. As we will see in Chapter 10, the company operates through its constitutional organs. Either the board of directors agrees to take an action or the general meeting does so. As a general rule individual shareholders are not empowered to initiate proceedings for a wrong to the company. This is known as the rule in *Foss v Harbottle* (1843) (see CA 2006, ss 260–264). This can lead to situations where the majority abuse their power to commit fraud on the minority. If this is the case there are a number of common law and statutory provisions to deal with the minority complaint. The situation with regard to who can sue to enforce the s 33 contract is similar. A majority of the members may vote to do something which breaches the constitution.

The minority shareholders may wish to sue to enforce the s 33 contract. Whether they can do so depends on how the breach of the constitution is perceived.

8.30   If the breach in question is a wrong to the company then only the company can sue. However, if it is classified as a personal right of the shareholder then the individual shareholder can sue. In *Mozley v Alston* (1847) the directors failed to retire by rotation as provided by the articles. They were treated as having committed a wrong to the company rather than breaching individual members' rights regarding re-election. The company was therefore the only one who could complain. In *MacDougall v Gardiner* (1875) the court similarly refused to recognise an individual shareholder's right to a poll. The court considered that rights given in the constitution may not be enforceable if the breach complained of could be ratified by a majority resolution. On the other hand, in *Pender v Lushington* (1877) a shareholder's votes were refused at a general meeting. The member obtained an injunction stopping the directors acting on the resolution passed at the meeting. Jessel MR considered that the shareholder 'is entitled to have his vote recorded—an individual right in respect of which he has the right to sue. That has nothing to do with the question raised in *Foss v Harbottle* (1843) and that line of cases.' Similarly in *Edwards v Halliwell* (1950) the rules concerning voting at a union meeting were broken. Two individual members obtained a declaration invalidating a resolution. Jenkins LJ stated:

> the personal and individual rights of the membership of each of them have been invaded by a purported, but invalid, alteration . . . In those circumstances, it seems to me that the rule in Foss v Harbottle has not application at all, for the individual members who are suing sue, not in the right of the union, but in their own right to protect from invasion their own individual rights as members.

8.31   We can conclude from this that some rights are personal and others not. How can one tell if it is a personal right? Lord Wedderburn (1957) in an article on *Foss v Harbottle* (1843) set out a list of rights the courts have in the past considered personal in nature. These included voting rights, share transfer rights, a right to protect class rights, pre-emption rights, the right to be registered as a shareholder and obtain a share certificate, to enforce a dividend that has been declared and to enforce the procedure for declaring the dividend, the right to have directors appointed in accordance with the articles, and other procedural rights such as notices of meetings. While this list provides some guidance the matter is still less than clear. The root of the difficulty in separating out general membership rights from personal membership rights is that many breaches of membership rights contained in the articles can be interpreted either way, as pure internal irregularities which only the company can put right, or as personal rights which allow the shareholders to sue. The two cases of *MacDougall* and *Pender* (discussed in para **8.30**) are entirely at odds with one another and many of the cases that follow after them emphasise one or the other depending on the individual judge's view. Some judges hold strongly to the view that the courts should not interfere in the internal affairs of the company. In essence they view it as a private arrangement in which they should not interfere except in exceptional circumstances. Other judges prefer to emphasise the contractual nature of the company's constitution and enforce it where they can. The issue of categorising the rights as personal and general is further clouded by the practice of companies adding 'outsider' rights to the articles.

Outsider rights

8.32 Another complication has been added to the s 33 debate by the fact that while there is deemed to be a binding contract between the members and the company, that contract only binds the members in their capacity as members. Where outsider rights are at issue the s 33 contract does not apply. For example in *Eley v Positive Government Security Life Assurance Co* (1876) the articles contained a clause which ensured that a particular member of the company was appointed as the company's solicitor. The member was not appointed as the company's solicitor and sued for breach of contract. The court found that he could not rely on breach of that clause in the articles as the cause of his action as there was no contractual relationship between the member as 'solicitor' and the company. *Eley* does not directly address the s 33 point yet has been the basis of a number of other judgments on the issue. In *Browne v La Trinidad* (1887) a shareholder who had a right to be a director conferred in the articles was removed by a valid resolution of the general meeting. The court placed great emphasis on *Eley* in concluding that 'it would be remarkable that, upon the shares being allotted to him, a contract between him and the company, as to a matter not connected with the holding of shares, should arise'. He therefore could not enforce a right to be a director. By 1915 the court in *Hickman v Kent or Romney Marsh Sheep-Breeders' Association* (1915) considered the matter settled and stated:

> this much is clear, first, that no article can constitute a contract between the company and a third person; secondly, that no right merely purporting to be given by an article to a person, whether a member or not, in a capacity other than that of a member, as for instance, as solicitor, promoter, director, can be enforced against the company; and, thirdly, that articles regulating the rights and obligations of the members generally as such do create rights and obligations between them and the company respectively.

In *Globalink Telecommunications Ltd v Wilmbury Ltd* (2003) the court considered the validity of a directors' indemnity provision that had been placed in the company's articles. The court found that such a provision would not be binding because the articles do not constitute a contract between the company and its officers. It will only bind the company if the provision is contained in a separate contract between the company and the officer.

8.33 However, as you may have noticed by now s 33 matters are rarely straightforward. In *Beattie v E & F Beattie Ltd* (1938) the company was engaged in an action against a director for the return of money it claimed was irregularly paid to him. The articles of association contained a clause which referred any member disputes to arbitration. The director who was also a member attempted to have the article enforced and have his dispute referred to arbitration. The Court of Appeal relying heavily on *Hickman* held that he could not do so as the dispute related to his status as a director. The Master of the Rolls in his judgment saw the issue as being framed as a director-member action in which the enforcement of the director's outsider rights were central rather than tangential. He suggested that had the action been framed as a member-director action in which the central issue was a member suing to enforce the articles which had the tangential effect of enforcing an outsider right it might have been successful. This view has echoes of the earlier decision of the House of Lords in *Salmon v Quin & Axtens Ltd* (1909) which ultimately the Court of Appeal in *Beattie* chose to ignore by placing the emphasis on the *Hickman* decision.

8.34 In *Salmon* the articles of association provided that the consent of both managing directors was needed for certain decisions. Mr Salmon was a managing director and member of the company and he dissented from a decision to buy and let some property. The general meeting then passed a resolution authorising the purchase and letting of the property. Mr Salmon sued as a member to enforce the article requiring his consent as managing director to the transactions. In this situation the House of Lords accepted a general personal right of members to sue to enforce the articles by allowing a member to obtain an injunction to stop the completion of the transactions entered into in breach of the articles. Here the court viewed the issue in terms of enforcing a member right which tangentially affects his right as a director rather than in the *Beattie* case where they viewed it as a director right which has a tangential effect on the membership.

8.35 The ignoring of the *Salmon* case by the judiciary has become somewhat of a cause célèbre for reform-minded academics. Lord Wedderburn (1957), as we have already discussed briefly, in an article on *Foss v Harbottle* (1843) made the important point that in cases such as *Salmon* and *Beattie* the courts have recognised a general personal right to have the articles enforced and that this was in fact the correct way to deal with the matter. This is the case even though it would indirectly enforce an outsider right. Others such as Goldberg (1972 and 1985), Prentice (1980), Gregory (1981), and Drury (1989) have broadly agreed while adding their own particular flourish.

Reform

8.36 Not unnaturally given the complexity of the area the CLRSG gave considerable time to the issue of rights in the articles over the course of its deliberations. In *Developing the Framework* (March 2000) they considered that the present position 'does nothing to resolve the critical question of what rights are personal to the shareholder' (see paras 4.72–4.99). They then went on to recommend a number of reforms. However, after the consultation period they dropped most of these reforms and opted for a catch-all solution whereby all the articles would be enforceable by the members against the company and each other unless the contrary was provided (*Completing the Structure* (November 2000), paras 5.64–5.74). This was also to be accompanied by a power for the courts to strike out trivial actions. The CLRSG's *Final Report* (July 2001, paras 7.34–7.40) maintained this position even though concerns were raised in the consultation period that exclusionary articles would become the norm. The CLRSG considered this a possibility but they considered it outweighed by the benefits of certainty. It did seem however likely that automatically excluding all articles from enforcement by members would be a very likely outcome. While this proposal may have had the benefit of certainty the practical effect of the recommendation would be to remove personal rights completely. The Government's Consultative Document of March 2005 (para 5.1) followed the same logic as the CLRSG in recommending general enforcement and the allowance of exclusionary articles. However, as we noted earlier in para **8.28** the Government in the CA 2006 did not implement this reform, preferring instead to maintain the current unsatisfactory position.

Shareholder agreements and statutory effects

8.37 The articles of association may not be the final word on how the rights and obligations of the members and the company are allocated. Agreements between shareholders have become an increasingly common feature of company law as a result of the uncertainty surrounding s 33. Shareholders' agreements are agreements between shareholders themselves (that is all the shareholders or just between some of them) or between the company and the shareholders (that is all of them or just between some of them). As we discussed in Chapter 2 a share is a bundle of rights that can be bought and sold. A shareholder, as a result of his ownership of a share, can also agree to exercise the rights attached to the share in a particular way. Thus shareholder A can agree with shareholder B that he will exercise his votes in favour of shareholder B if B stands for election to the board. Or, shareholder A could agree to sell his shares to shareholder B only, should he decide to sell them. The shareholders' agreement has the advantage that compared to altering and enforcing the articles it is a relatively easy way to achieve agreement and enforcement. It also has the advantage that it is private and you can easily identify who you wish to transact with, e.g. a large shareholder, and transact only with him. A shareholder can therefore secretly contract to control the majority voting rights in a company without owning a majority of the shares. The disadvantage of a shareholders' agreement is that it does not bind the new owner of the shares. Once a party to a shareholders' agreement sells them on, the new owner has no obligations under the shareholders' agreement. Note here this is in contrast to the way the s 33 contract operates to bind future shareholders to the company's constitution.

8.38 Shareholder agreements purely between shareholders present little difficulty for the parties involved. They can agree the matters they wish and as long as they all agree, they can also alter their agreement formally or informally (on the validity of unanimous informal alterations see *Euro Brokers Holdings Ltd v Monecor (London) Ltd* (2003)). The courts have also been willing to enforce such agreements. For example, in *Puddephatt v Leith* (1916) the court compelled a shareholder to vote as was agreed in a shareholders' agreement. However, agreements purely between the shareholders can only attempt to regulate the rights and obligations belonging to those shareholders. As those rights and obligations largely concern the operation of a company it often makes sense to make the company a party to the agreement. This adds an extra element of security to the agreement as the company will still be bound by the agreement even if some of the parties to the agreement sell their shares and the new shareholders do not join the agreement. Here in practice we are probably talking about small to medium-sized companies where there is little or no separation of ownership from control. Therefore the shareholders and directors will often be the same people and getting the company to join the agreement is easily achieved.

8.39 Adding the company to the agreement, however, also adds an additional problem. That is, if the subject matter of the agreement affects a statutory obligation of the company it may not be enforceable. As we discussed earlier, CA 2006, s 21 allows the company to alter its articles by special resolution if three-quarters of the members vote in favour of the resolution. In *Punt v Symons & Co Ltd* (1903) the court held that a company could not contract out of the right to alter its articles. This means in effect that a provision of a shareholders' agreement which binds the company not to alter its articles will not be enforceable. The company would be in breach of contract if it does so but it is free to alter its constitution (see also *Russell v Northern Bank Development Corpn* (1992)). However, in all situations where aspects of a shareholders' agreement might affect board duties the courts will not imply terms into a shareholders' agreement that override the articles of association (see *Dear and Griffith v Jackson* (2013)).

8.40 However, the courts once again have not been entirely consistent when dealing with the question of the ability of the company to contract out of statutory provisions. In *Bushell v Faith* (1970) the articles contained a provision whereby in the event of a resolution to remove a director that director's shares in the company would be multiplied by three. This in effect entrenched the director on the board of directors as the other shareholders could never outvote him. In effect the article attempted to remove the ability of the members conferred by CA 2006, s 168 (in 1970 it was s 184 of the CA 1948) to remove a director for any reason whatsoever. The House of Lords in a very interesting judgment held that the article in question was not inconsistent with the statutory power. The statute only specified the type of resolution needed to remove a director but was completely silent on the matter of how the company allocated voting rights for such resolutions. In essence the House of Lords treated the issue as no different from a complaint from a 49 per cent shareholder that a shareholder with 51 per cent of the shares in the company could not be removed. It's not that they cannot be removed, it's simply that the other shareholder has not enough votes to remove the 51 per cent shareholder. The same is true where weighted voting rights are concerned (see also *Amalgamated Pest Control Ltd v McCarron* (1995)).

8.41 The issue was reconsidered in the context of a shareholders' agreement in *Russell v Northern Bank Development Corpn* (1992). Here the House of Lords considered a shareholders' agreement where the company agreed not to increase the share capital of the company without the agreement of all the parties to the shareholders' agreement. The company did attempt to increase the share capital of the company and one of the shareholders who was a party to the shareholders' agreement objected and attempted to enforce the agreement. The statutory conflict here was between the agreement and CA 1985, s 121 which allowed companies to increase their share capital if their articles contain an authority. The article of the company did provide such an authorisation. The House of Lords found that the company's agreement not to increase its share capital was contrary to the statutory provision and, therefore, unenforceable. However, the court did not declare the whole shareholders' agreement invalid, just the company's agreement not to increase the share capital. This meant that the shareholder who objected could not enforce it against the company but could enforce it against the other members. As all the members of the company were party to the shareholders' agreement this has the same effect as if the company was bound. The shareholders could not vote to increase the share capital.

8.42 It is important to note here that this judgment greatly enhances the ability of shareholders' agreements to contract out of statutory provisions. If the shareholders place a provision in the articles that purports to contract out of a statutory provision it will probably be invalid, however if they place the same provision outside the articles in a shareholders' agreement and either all the shareholders or a large majority of them are party to it, the provision will be effective. It represents only a private agreement between the shareholders as to how they will exercise their voting rights. Tangentially this has an effect on lenders' ability to protect themselves by placing restrictions on the company's ability to change the articles of association as a condition of their continued lending. A lender has no way of knowing of or restricting shareholders' private agreements which affect the operation of the articles. The recommendation of the CLRSG *Final Report* (July 2001, para 9.8) and the Government's Consultative Document of March 2005 (para 5.1) all agreed that allowing certain provisions of the articles to be entrenched by allowing them to be changed only by unanimity would potentially offer a solution to the problem and the CA 2006, s 22 makes this possible.

Altering the constitution

8.43 The alteration of the articles, as we have also observed in this chapter, is allowed by CA 2006, s 21. This is normally effected by a special resolution (75 per cent) at the general meeting. However, sometimes the courts have allowed more informal resolutions to stand.

In *Re Duomatic* (1969) the court allowed a decision not made at the general meeting but which clearly had the backing of all the shareholders to stand. As we have also seen the alterations to the articles must not conflict with any statutory provisions. However, there is one additional check on the members' ability to alter the articles which has an effect. That is, the members must exercise their power to alter the articles in good faith. This power to alter the articles has been famously expressed by Lindley MR in *Allen v Gold Reefs Co of West Africa* (1900) as being:

> exercised subject to those general principles of law and equity which are applicable to all powers conferred on majorities enabling them to bind minorities. It must be exercised, not only in the manner required by law, but also bona fide for the benefit of the company as a whole, and it must not be exceeded. These conditions are always implied, and are seldom, if ever, expressed.

8.44 The exercise of a member's votes generally may also be subject to a bona fides qualification. In *Clemens v Clemens Bros Ltd* (1976) Foster J declined to recognise the ability of a majority shareholder to authorise an allotment of shares, the motive behind the share allotment being to dilute the voting power of the minority shareholder claimant. Foster J considered that the majority shareholder was 'not entitled to exercise her vote in any way she pleases'. He based his decision on what he termed 'equitable considerations' and thus the mala fides element of the allotment precluded it from ratification (see also *Menier v Hooper's Telegraph Works* (1874) and *Greenhalgh v Arderne Cinemas Ltd* (1951); and see Chapter 11).

8.45 Therefore, a special resolution passed altering the articles or even a resolution exercising powers conferred in the articles may theoretically be challenged for a lack of bona fides (see *Redwood Master Fund Ltd v TD Bank Europe Ltd* (2006)). It must be said, however, that the courts are extremely reluctant to overturn a decision of the general meeting on the grounds of a lack of bona fides, doing so in only a small number of cases (see *Brown v British Abrasive Wheel Co Ltd* (1919) and *Dafen Tinplate Co Ltd v Llanelly Steel* (1920)). One can conclude that the courts in general view the alteration of the articles as a matter of upholding the principle of majority rule. As a result many of the challenges to majority power fall under the remit of minority protection and will be further discussed in Chapters 10 and 11.

8.46 The CLRSG in its *Final Report* (July 2001, paras 7.52–7.62) considered the bona fides issue but after an interesting discussion recommended little change. They did, however, recommend that the new constitution of the company be alterable by special resolution and that certain provisions of the articles could be entrenched by requiring a unanimous resolution to change them (para 9.8). As we have noted both those recommendations are now contained in the CA 2006, ss 21 and 22.

FURTHER READING

This chapter links with the materials in Chapters 6 and 7 of **Hicks and Goo's Cases and Materials on Company Law** (Oxford, OUP, 2011, xl +649p).

Shiraz, 'To What Extent Does the S.33 Contract Differ from an Orthodox Contract?' [2013] *Co Lawr* 36.

Companies (Model Articles) Regulations 2008 (SI 2008/3229), http://www.companieshouse.gov.uk/about/modelArticles/modelArticles.shtml.

Company Law Reform (Cm 6456, 2005) (Consultative Document, March), paras 4.2, 4.3, and 5.1, http://webarchive.nationalarchives.gov.uk/+/http://www.dti.gov.uk/cld/WhitePaper.pdf.

Company Law Reform Bill 2005, HL Bill, http://www.publications.parliament.uk/pa/ld200506/ldbills/034/2006034.htm.

Davies, *Gower and Davies' Principles of Modern Company Law*, 10th edn (London, Sweet & Maxwell, 2016), ch 3.

Ferran, 'The Decision of the House of Lords in *Russell v Northern Bank Development Corporation Limited*' [1994] *CLJ* 343.

Wedderburn, 'Shareholders' Rights and the Rule in *Foss v Harbottle*' [1957] *CLJ* 194.

SELF-TEST QUESTIONS

1   What is the constitution of the company supposed to achieve?

2   Is there a statutory contract created by CA 2006, s 33?

3   Who does the statutory contract bind and in what capacity?

4   Why would a shareholder wish to use a shareholders' agreement?

5   Are shareholders free to exercise their votes as they wish?

6   Hero, Roger, and Kathy hold one-third of the shares each in Grit Ltd. They all sit on the board of directors. The articles of association allow for the removal of a board member if two-thirds of the board vote for their removal. Hero and Roger also have a shareholders' agreement to which Grit Ltd is also a party. The shareholders' agreement has a clause that requires Roger to always vote his shares and board vote as instructed by Hero. Hero has instructed Roger to vote with Hero to remove Kathy from the board. Roger has refused on the basis that to do so would be a breach of his statutory director's duties and s 168 of the Companies Act (shareholder removal by ordinary resolution).

Advise Hero if she can enforce the shareholders agreement against Roger and the company.

9 Classes of shares and variation of class rights

SUMMARY

Introduction
The legal nature of a share
Class rights
Variation of class rights
Enhancing transparency and shareholder engagement

Introduction

9.1 Unlike partnerships where the assets of the business are jointly owned by the partners, shareholders do not have a proprietary interest in the property of the company. Rather the relationship of a shareholder lies with the company as a separate and distinct entity. A paradigm case is the House of Lords' decision in *Macaura v Northern Assurance Co Ltd* (1925) which we considered in Chapter 2. You will recall that the insured, Macaura, was an unsecured creditor and the only shareholder in a limited company which owned a substantial quantity of timber, much of which was stored on his land. Two weeks after effecting insurance policies with several companies in his own name, the timber was destroyed by fire. A claim brought by Macaura on the policies was disallowed on the ground that he lacked insurable interest in the timber. Lord Sumner, proceeding on the basis that neither the company's debt to the insured nor his shares were exposed to fire, observed: 'the fact that he was virtually the company's only creditor, while the timber is its only asset, seems to me to make no difference . . . he was directly prejudiced by the paucity of the company's assets, not by the fire'. His Lordship stated that the insured 'stood in no "legal or equitable relation to" the timber at all. He had no "concern in" the subject insured. His relation was to the company, not to its goods.'

9.2 The guiding principle here is, of course, pivoted upon the separate legal personality accorded to companies. It was the company that owned the timber and therefore had a proprietary interest in it, not its shareholder. The fact that the timber was in his possession did not give him a proprietary interest. He merely had a factual expectation of loss.

9.3 *Sealy and Worthington's Text, Cases, & Materials in Company Law* (2016) at p 512, attribute three principal functions to the concept of a share. First, it denotes the quantification of a shareholder's financial stake in the company and it fixes his liability to contribute to the company's funding. Second, it is a measure of the shareholder's interest in the company 'as an association' and his right to become a member and to exercise all rights incidental to membership. Third, and this is perhaps conceptually the most difficult of the three functions: it is a 'species of property', a chose in action (and therefore not personality) which can be bought, sold, and charged (see further, *Borland's Trustee v Steel Bros & Co Ltd* (1901), discussed at para **9.5**).

9.4 A shareholder will thus have rights and liabilities which are the incidents of the general nature of a share. Additionally, he may also have particular rights and liabilities by virtue of owning a particular type or class of share. Such class rights may, subject to certain conditions, be varied or abrogated by the company. In this chapter we will examine, first, the legal nature of a shareholding, second, the various types of share capital and typical class rights which attach thereto, and, finally, the statutory procedure which a company must go through in order to effect a variation of shareholders' class rights.

The legal nature of a share

9.5 As we discussed in Chapter 2, the primary characteristic of a share which serves to distinguish it from other types of security issued by companies is that a shareholder acquires rights *in* the company not simply *against* it as is the case with debenture holders (see Chapter 6). For example, a shareholder will have financial rights, such as sharing in dividend distributions (if a dividend is declared by the board of directors) and any return of capital on a winding-up, and participative rights, such as voting at general meetings. A share therefore has various legal attributes which confer both property and contractual rights on its holder. The Companies Act 2006 is silent on the nature of a share except for declaring that 'shares or other interest of a member in a company are personal property and are not in the nature of real estate' (s 541). However, the courts have not been so reticent in this regard. For example, in *Borland's Trustee v Steel Bros & Co Ltd* (1901), the articles of association provided that the shares of a member could be compulsorily purchased by particular persons on the occurrence of certain events, including bankruptcy, at a fair price not exceeding the par value. Borland, who held 73 £1.00 shares, was declared bankrupt and the company served notice requiring the trustee in bankruptcy to transfer the shares. The trustee contended that the relevant provision in the articles was void on the basis that it was repugnant to absolute ownership or alternatively, contrary to the rule against perpetuity. Farwell J said that:

> A share is the interest of a shareholder in the company measured by a sum of money, for the purposes of liability in the first place, and of interest in the second, but also consisting of a series of mutual covenants entered into by all the shareholders inter se in accordance with section 16 of the Companies Act 1862 [now the Companies Act 2006, s 33]. The

> contract contained in the articles of association is one of the original incidents of the
> share. A share . . . is an interest measured by a sum of money and made up of the various
> rights contained in the contract.

(See also the judgment of Campbell J in *White v Shortall* (2006).)

9.6 According to Farwell J, a share therefore represents a bundle of contractual rights conferred by the Companies Act 2006 and the company's constitution. In respect of the latter,
as seen in Chapter 8, such rights make up the statutory contract between the members
inter se and the company (see also the speech delivered by Lord Walker in *Grays Timber
Products Ltd v HM Revenue and Customs* (2010)). In *Short v Treasury Commissioners*
(1948), the legal nature of a share and its monetary valuation was subjected to considerable scrutiny by the court. In this case, the government of the day purchased all of the
shares in the company valuing them on the basis of the quoted share price. The shareholders argued that because the whole of the issued shares were being acquired then the
entire undertaking should be valued and the price apportioned between them. It was
held, however, that where a purchaser is buying control but none of the sellers holds a
controlling interest, the higher price that 'control' demands can be ignored. The Treasury
was therefore able to purchase the company for a price considerably less than its asset
value. Although shares are frequently described as 'property', we have seen that they do
not comprise any proprietary interest in the company's assets. Quite simply, a shareholder
pays a sum of money by way of investment from which he hopes to earn a return.

Class rights

9.7 The CA 2006 does not define 'class rights' beyond stating that 'shares are of one class if the
rights attached to them are in all respects uniform' (s 629(1)). As between shareholders
in a company there is a presumption of equality so that they will enjoy equal rights in
respect of voting and dividends when the company is a going concern and a right to participate in any surplus assets in the event of it being wound up (collectively termed class
rights: see *Birch v Cropper* (1889); and *Cumbrian Newspapers Group Ltd v Cumberland &
Westmoreland Herald Newspapers & Printing Co Ltd* (1987), considered later at para **9.18**).
However, this presumption is rebutted if the company issues shares carrying different class
rights. For example, preference shares generally carry preferential dividend rights and priority to a return of capital in a winding-up. It should be noted that a company's right to
issue shares divided into different classes is generally contained in its constitution.

9.8 Where shares are issued with express provisions relating to class rights, such statements
are deemed to be exhaustive. This principle, which in essence is a rule of construction,
was stated by Sarjant J in *Re National Telephone Co* (1914): 'the attachment of preferential
rights to preference shares, on their creation, is, *prima facie*, a definition of the whole

of their rights in that respect, and negatives any further or other right to which, but for the specified rights, they would have been entitled'. The decision in *Will v United Lankat Plantations Co Ltd* (1914) illustrates the point. Preference shares were issued which carried an entitlement to a cumulative preferential dividend at the rate of 10 per cent per annum on the amount for the time being paid up on such shares. The issue before the House of Lords was whether the preference shareholders were also entitled to share in any surplus profits after the ordinary shareholders had also received 10 per cent. It was held that they were not. Viscount Haldane LC said that shares are not issued in the abstract and any priorities and rights attached to them as regards dividends are to be ascertained in the terms of the issue. The court cannot look beyond those express terms in order to imply additional preferential rights (see also *Scottish Insurance Corpn Ltd v Wilsons and Clyde Coal Co Ltd* (1949), Lord Simons).

9.9 There are myriad reasons for the plurality of share classes. The company's original subscribers of ordinary shares may be reluctant to issue further ordinary shares to outsiders as a means of raising additional capital because that would have the effect of diluting or destroying their control of the business. This danger arises because ordinary shares generally carry the majority of the voting rights at meetings and also entitle their holders to the lion's share of any declared dividend. A solution, other than issuing debentures (see Chapter 6), is to issue preference shares. The attraction of this option is that it affords a company an accessible means of raising additional capital without conferring voting rights equal to those of ordinary shareholders. Although the company will undertake to pay a preferential cumulative dividend generally fixed at a pre-determined rate, this may, in appropriate circumstances, be considered a relatively small price to pay for a much needed injection of capital from which trading profits can grow.

Examples of classes of shares

9.10 Provided a company is authorised by its constitution to issue shares with different class rights, it can divide its share capital into as many different classes as it wishes. The rights attaching to each class should be clearly stated either in the company's constitution, or in the resolution authorising the share issue as well as in the prospectus because, as seen earlier, it is a rule of construction that any statement of class rights is presumed to be exhaustive.

Ordinary shares

9.11 Ordinary shares, commonly referred to as equities, are the default category of shares. Holders of this class participate in the company's distributable profits after payment has been made of any fixed level of dividend to preference shareholders. Where the company is enjoying handsome profits ordinary shareholders are not restricted to a pre-determined return on their investment. Ordinary shareholders' rights to a return of capital are commonly deferred to preference shareholders, but as regards participation in any surplus in a solvent winding-up, they will be able to claim after other shareholders have had their capital returned.

In terms of voting, ordinary shareholders control the general meeting on the basis of one vote per share. Non-voting ordinary shares are rare nowadays and in any case do not carry the approval of the Stock Exchange, although it is possible to obtain listing of a company having such shares.

Preference shares

9.12   As the name suggests, preferential rights attach to preference shares. Generally, a fixed preferential cumulative dividend will be paid to the holders in any year in which the company has distributable profits. For example, they may receive a fixed rate of say 10 per cent on the nominal value of the shares in priority to any dividend paid to ordinary shareholders. The cumulative element means that arrears become payable in respect of those years in which a dividend was not declared; and it is presumed that preference shares are cumulative (*Webb v Earle* (1875)). Where preference shares are expressed to be participating as to dividend, the holders have the right to a further dividend payment, after the ordinary shareholders have received a distribution, equivalent to their initial fixed rate. Preference shareholders are also generally entitled to a return of capital on a winding-up in priority to the ordinary shareholders, but unless they have an express right of participation, they do not have a claim to any surplus assets (*Scottish Insurance Corpn Ltd v Wilson and Clyde Coal Co Ltd* (1949)). Preference shares generally have restricted voting rights so that they cannot vote in general meetings unless, for example, their dividends are in arrears.

9.13   The position of preference shareholders is in some ways analogous to that of creditors. Fixed rates for determining dividend entitlement are not dissimilar to fixed rates of interest payable to lenders. Further, as with creditors, preference shareholders enjoy priority over other classes of shareholders to a return of capital in a winding-up although, of course, this priority does not extend over unsecured or secured creditors.

Convertible shares

9.14   A company may, for example, issue preference shares which are capable of being converted into ordinary shares either on a fixed date or at the option of the shareholders themselves or, subject to certain conditions, at the option of the company.

Redeemable shares

9.15   In brief, s 684 of the Companies Act 2006 provides that a company having a share capital may issue shares which are to be redeemed or are liable to be redeemed at the option of the company or the shareholder (see Chapter 7), subject to the following: first, the articles of a private limited company may exclude or restrict the issue of redeemable shares and, second, in the case of a public company, its articles authorise it to issue such shares (s 684(2) and (3)). But a company must always have some non-redeemable issued shares (s 684(4)). Redeemable shares may not be redeemed unless they are fully paid; and the terms of redemption must provide for payment on redemption (s 689(1)). Private companies may redeem shares out of capital (s 687(1)) but public companies may only redeem redeemable shares out of distributable profits or from the proceeds of a new issue of shares which is made for the purpose of redemption (s 687(2)).

Employees' shares

9.16 Successive governments have encouraged companies to give employees a 'stake' in the business by issuing shares to them. Such shares enjoy certain tax advantages. This is generally effected through an 'employees' share scheme' which is defined as being a scheme for facilitating the holding of shares or debentures in a company by or for the benefit of: (a) bona fide employees or former employees of the company, including its subsidiary or holding company; or (b) their spouses, civil partners, surviving spouses, surviving civil partners, or minor children or stepchildren (s 1166). Employees' shares are normally issued as ordinary shares or preference shares and are typically subject to restrictions relating to their disposal.

Variation of class rights

9.17 Section 630 of the Companies Act 2006 (which implements part of the Second EC Company Law Directive) lays down the procedure for effecting a variation of class rights in companies with a share capital. The objective of the statutory requirements is to protect the 'class rights' of shareholders so that they cannot be varied or abrogated by the simple expedient of altering the company's constitution or the shareholders' resolution in which they are contained.

Before examining the statutory procedure it is useful to consider two fundamental issues: (a) how the parameters of class rights are determined; and (b) whether a course of action does, in fact, amount to a variation or abrogation of class rights.

The parameters of class rights

9.18 Although the Companies Act 2006 offers little guidance on the definition of the term 'class right', inevitably the courts have been confronted with determining both the meaning of what is a 'class of shares' and what may amount to a 'class right'. In *Cumbrian Newspapers Group Ltd v Cumberland & Westmoreland Herald Newspapers & Printing Co Ltd* (1987), Scott J took the opportunity to subject these questions to detailed consideration. The claimant company had acquired over 10 per cent of the ordinary shares in the defendant company. The object was to concentrate the local newspaper business under a single title and to deter an outsider from acquiring a controlling interest in the paper. The articles of association of the defendant company were altered so as to confer on the claimant: (1) pre-emption rights over the ordinary shares; (2) rights in relation to unissued shares; and (3) the right to appoint a director, provided it continued to hold at least 10 per cent of the shares. The claimant sought a declaration, among other things, that its rights contained in the articles were class rights for the purposes of s 630. Scott J took the view that rights or benefits conferred by a company's articles of association can be classified into three distinct categories. First are those rights or benefits which are annexed to particular shares. Classic examples are dividend rights and rights to participate in surplus assets on a winding-up. Scott J observed that '[i]f articles provide that particular shares carry particular rights not enjoyed by the holders of other shares, it is easy to conclude that the rights are attached to a class of shares, for the purpose of . . . section 630'. Second are rights or benefits which, although contained in the articles, are conferred on individuals not qua members or shareholders but, for ulterior reasons, are connected with the administration of the company's affairs. Scott J gave the example of *Eley v Positive Government Security Life Assurance Co Ltd* (1876) (see para **8.32**), where the articles included a provision that the claimant should be the company solicitor. Rights or benefits in this category cannot be regarded as class rights. The third and final category comprises rights or benefits that, although not attached to any particular shares, are conferred on the beneficiary in his capacity as member or shareholder in the company. On the facts of the case, it was held that provisions in the company's articles which gave the claimant a pre-emptive right over the transfer of shares in the defendant company, together with the right to nominate a director to its board so long as it held 10 per cent of the ordinary shares in the company, were class rights. Scott J cited by way of example the House of Lords' decision in *Bushell v Faith* (1970) where the articles gave a director weighted voting rights on a resolution to remove any director from office. The judge noted that in this case the right in question was 'conferred on the director/beneficiaries in their capacity as shareholders. The article created, in effect, two classes of shareholders—namely, shareholders who were for the time being directors, on the one hand, and shareholders who were not for the time being directors, on the other hand.'

9.19 The significance of the distinction drawn by Scott J lies in the protection afforded to the beneficiaries of class rights because, as we shall see, such rights can only be varied with their consent. Any other provision contained in the articles which cannot properly be classified as a class right can be altered by special resolution under s 21 of the 2006 Act. The result of the decision in *Cumbrian Newspapers* is that taking s 630 together with s 994 of the Companies Act 2006 (the principal minority shareholder protection provision, see Chapter 11), the rights of shareholders are afforded wide-ranging protection (see *Re Smiths of Smithfield Ltd* (2003), discussed in para **11.27**).

Determining whether there is a variation or abrogation of class rights

9.20 Whether or not a company has varied a shareholder's class rights is not always immediately apparent. In this respect the Companies Act 2006 is far from helpful. Section
630 lays down the procedure to be followed for a variation of class rights but is silent
on the nature and scope of a 'class right'. The case law does, however, provide some
guidelines. It should be noted that the courts have generally adopted a restrictive
approach and have sought to distinguish corporate conduct which impacts upon the
substance of a shareholder's class right (which would amount to a variation), from
conduct which merely affects its exercise or enjoyment. In *White v Bristol Aeroplane
Co Ltd* (1953), the company's articles (art 68) provided that the rights attached to
any class of shares may be 'affected, modified, varied, dealt with, or abrogated in
any manner' with the approval of an extraordinary resolution passed at a separate
meeting of the members of that class. The preference shareholders claimed that
an issue of additional shares, both preference and ordinary, 'affected' their voting
rights and therefore fell within art 68. The company argued that the proposal did not
amount to a variation of class rights but rather it was the effectiveness of the exercise
of those rights which had been affected and that therefore a separate meeting of the
preference shareholders was not required. The Court of Appeal agreed with the company's view. Romer LJ stated:

> [I]n my opinion it cannot be said that the rights of ordinary shareholders would be af-
> fected by the issue of further ordinary capital; their rights would remain just as they were
> before, and the only result would be that the class of persons entitled to exercise those
> rights would be enlarged; and for my part I cannot help thinking that a certain amount
> of confusion has crept into this case between rights on the one hand, and the result of
> exercising those rights on the other hand.

(See also *Greenhalgh v Arderne Cinemas Ltd* (1946); and *Re John Smith's Tadcaster
Brewery* (1953).)

9.21 In order to prove that a proposed course of action constitutes a variation of class rights,
a shareholder will have to show that it will result in some substantive right guaranteed in
the company's constitution being modified or abrogated altogether. For example, a resolution proposing to reduce the fixed preferential cumulative dividend to which a company's preference shareholders are entitled will, of course, amount to a variation of class
rights. Similarly, a proposal to change the voting rights attaching to a particular class of
share would also amount to a variation of their rights.

9.22 A successful claim was brought in *Re Old Silkstone Collieries Ltd* (1954). As a result of
nationalisation, the company's colliery was taken into public ownership by the National
Coal Board. Pending the final settlement of compensation, the company had twice

reduced its capital by returning part of the preference shareholders' capital investment. On both occasions the company had promised them that they would not be bought out entirely but would remain as members so that they could participate in the compensation scheme to be introduced under the nationalisation legislation. Subsequently, it was proposed to reduce the company's capital for a third time by returning all outstanding capital to the preference shareholders. The effect of this would be to cancel the class completely and they would no longer qualify for compensation. The Court of Appeal, refusing to sanction the reduction, held that the proposal amounted to an unfair variation of class rights insofar as the preference shareholders had been promised that they would be able to participate in the compensation scheme.

9.23 In general, however, a cancellation of a class of shares on a reduction of capital will not be held to constitute a variation of class rights because such a course of action must be viewed as consistent with the terms of issue of the particular shares in question (*House of Fraser plc v ACGE Investments Ltd* (1987)). Thus in *Re Saltdean Estate Co Ltd* (1968), Buckley J said:

> [I]t is said that the proposed cancellation of the preferred shares will constitute an abrogation of all the rights attached to those shares which cannot validly be effected without an extraordinary resolution of a class meeting of preferred shareholders under article 8 of the company's articles. In my judgment, that article has no application to a cancellation of shares on a reduction of capital which is in accord with the rights attached to the shares of the company. Unless this reduction can be shown to be unfair to the preferred shareholders on other grounds, it is in accordance with the right and liability to prior repayment of capital attached to their shares.

Buckley J went on to stress that the liability to prior repayment on a reduction of capital corresponds with the right to prior return of capital in a winding-up. Accordingly, the shareholders could not complain of an abrogation of class rights because prior repayment on a reduction of capital was 'part of the bargain between the shareholders and forms an integral part of the definition or delimitation of the bundle of rights which make up a preferred share. Giving effect to it does not involve the variation or abrogation of any right attached to such a share.' However, where a company's articles of association provide that a reduction of capital is to be deemed a variation of class rights, a separate class meeting will have to be held (*Re Northern Engineering Industries plc* (1994)).

The statutory procedure for effecting a variation of class rights

9.24 A company proposing to vary the rights attaching to a class of shares must comply with the procedure laid down in s 630 of the CA 2006. The provision simplifies its predecessor (CA 1985, s 125) which had laid down different procedures for variation of class rights depending upon whether they were attached by the articles or the memorandum of association. Now, of course, the principal constitutional document is the articles of association and class rights can no longer be attached by the memorandum. Section 630 provides that class rights may only be varied:

(a) in accordance with the relevant provisions in the company's articles; or

(b) if no such provision is made in the articles, if the holders of three-quarters in value of the shares of that class consent either in writing or by special resolution (passed at a separate meeting of the holders of such shares).

The company must then notify the Registrar of any variation of class rights within one month from the date on which the variation is made (ss 637 and 640).

9.25 Although the CLRSG had recommended that the consent of 75 per cent of the holders of the class affected should be a statutory minimum notwithstanding any less onerous procedure contained in the company's articles, this was removed from the Companies Bill at a fairly late stage. As a consequence, the company's articles may specify either less or more demanding requirements for variation of class rights than the default provisions laid down in the Act (see s 630(3)). This has two important effects. First, if and to the extent that the company has adopted a more onerous regime in its articles for the variation of class rights, for example requiring a higher percentage than the statutory minimum, the company must comply with the more onerous regime. Second, if and to the extent that the company has protected class rights by making provision for the entrenchment of those rights in its articles (see CA 2006, s 22), that protection cannot be circumvented by changing the class rights under s 630.

The common law requirements

9.26 The statutory procedure is supplemented by the common law requirement that the shareholders voting at a class meeting must have regard to the interests of the class as a whole. The principle here was explained by Viscount Haldane in *British America Nickel Corpn v MJ O'Brien Ltd* (1927). Drawing the analogy between shareholders voting for a special resolution to alter the articles of association and voting on a resolution to vary class rights, he said:

> There is, however, a restriction of such powers, when conferred on a majority of a special class in order to enable that majority to bind a minority. They must be exercised subject to a general principle, which is applicable to all authorities conferred on majorities of classes enabling them to bind minorities; namely, that the power given must be exercised for the purpose of benefiting the class as a whole, and not merely individual members only.

(See also *Re Holders Investment Trust* (1971), Megarry J; see also, *Assénagon Asset Management SA v IBRC (formerly Anglo Irish Bank)* (2012), which concerned voting by classes of creditors (noteholders). Briggs J held that it was not lawful for the majority to support the coercion of a minority by voting in favour of a resolution which expropriated the minority's rights under their notes.) *Sealy and Worthington's Text, Cases, & Materials in Company Law* (2016) at p 588 note that if taken to its logical conclusion, this rule would have what must be the unintended consequence of not permitting 'a class to subordinate its own interests to those of the company as a whole [so that] class rights could never be varied except to the holders' advantage'. It is regrettable that the framers of the 2006 Act did not take the opportunity to address this anomaly.

Right to object to a variation

9.27   Section 633 gives the holders of not less than 15 per cent of the issued shares of the class in question, the right to apply to the court to have the variation cancelled. The application must be made within 21 days after the date on which the consent was given or the resolution was passed (s 633(4)). If such an application is made, the variation has no effect unless and until it is confirmed by the court (s 633(3)). The court may, if satisfied having regard to all the circumstances of the case that the variation would unfairly prejudice the shareholders of the class in question, disallow the variation, but if not so satisfied, confirm it. The decision of the court in this regard is final (s 633(5)).

Enhancing transparency and shareholder engagement

9.28   In May 2005 the European Commission began a consultation exercise, *Fostering an Appropriate Regime for Shareholders' Rights*, on the minimum standards that should apply to shareholders' rights in listed companies. This is the second exercise in the field and is linked to the Commission's wider Action Plan, announced in May 2003, *Modernising Company Law and Enhancing Corporate Governance in the European Union*. The exercise is aimed at removing certain legal and practical hurdles that impede the exercise of shareholders' rights, particularly voting rights, in a cross-border context. Of particular concern to the Commission are the voting rights of non-resident shareholders. In some of the largest markets in the EU, for example the UK (still a Member State at the time of writing), France, Germany, Spain, and Italy, more than 30 per cent of the shares of listed companies are held by non-resident shareholders. Such shares are generally held through intermediaries, who exercise the voting rights, so the investors (termed 'ultimate investors') are not classed as shareholders at all and do not have voting rights. Those who responded to the initial consultation on the issue supported the proposal for an EU-wide principle that a person running the financial risk of an investment should have the right to direct how the votes are exercised.

9.29   This project culminated in the Shareholders Rights Directive (2007/36), which is aimed at improving shareholder participation and information rights (see now Directive 2017/828, below). It applies to traded companies, defined as those with voting shares admitted to trading on an EEA regulated market, such as the UK Official List. Following a consultation exercise carried out by BERR (now the Department for Business, Energy & Industrial Strategy), the Companies (Shareholders' Rights) Regulations 2009 (SI 2009/1632) came into force on 3 August 2009. Although the Directive applies only to members of traded companies, the UK Regulations introduce a number of changes which are of general application. In essence, new voting procedures, including changes to returning proxy forms, have been introduced, resulting in amendments to the relevant provisions of the CA 2006. For example, a new s 360C permits the use of electronic voting for shareholders in any company. For listed companies, changes have been made to the notice periods for meetings (see ss 360C and 307A) and private companies with traded shares are required to hold AGMs (see s 336(1A)). Other changes include a new requirement to put information on the company's website. A directive amending the Shareholder Rights Directive was published in the EU *Official Journal* in May 2017 (Directive 2017/828). It contains a number of measures aimed at improving transparency and encouraging long-term shareholder engagement in companies whose shares are traded on an EU regulated market. The Directive must be implemented by EU Member States by 10 June 2019. As far as the UK is concerned, implementation will depend on the terms of the Brexit deal, though the UK is likely to embrace these initiatives given the Government's current thinking on enhancing shareholder engagement (see Chapter 13). In relation to shareholder rights, intermediaries are required to facilitate the exercise of shareholder rights, including rights to participate and vote in general meetings.

Register of persons having significant control

9.30 Reforms have been implemented in the wake of the 2013 'Transparency and Trust' initiative announced by the then Coalition Government (this followed the 2013 G8 summit which put transparency about the ownership and control of companies at the core of the agenda). The Small Business, Enterprise and Employment Act 2015, s 81 (and Sch 3), introduces a new Part 21A into the CA 2006 which requires companies to maintain a register of persons having significant control (PSC) over the company. A PSC is someone who meets one or more of the following four conditions in relation to a company: (1) those who control directly or indirectly 25 per cent of the shares; (2) those who directly or indirectly hold more than 25 per cent of the voting rights; (3) those who directly or indirectly hold the right to appoint or remove the majority of directors; and (4) otherwise has the right to exercise, or actually exercises, significant influence or control: see CA 2006, Sch 1A. The objective is to provide greater transparency of corporate ownership and control by making it easier to identify those individuals who do not appear on share registers but who nevertheless hold beneficial interests in shares and are therefore able to control companies from the shadows. As from 6 April 2016 all UK incorporated companies (and limited liability partnerships (LLPs)) are required to keep and maintain a PSC register and from 30 June 2016, companies and LLPs are required to file this information at Companies House, creating a publicly accessible central registry of beneficial ownership information. In June 2017 the PSC regime was amended by the Information about People with Significant Control (Amendment) Regulations 2017 (2017/693), in order to implement the Fourth Money Laundering Directive (4MLD) (EU 2015/849) which requires EU Member States to maintain a central register of beneficial owner-ship information for legal entities (amended by the Fifth Money Laundering Directive (5MLD) (EU 2018/843)). The principal requirement is that the PSC register must be updated to reflect a change in PSC information within 14 days of the change and that Companies House must be notified of that change within 14 days of the register being updated (prior to the amendment, companies were only required to notify Companies House of PSC information on an annual basis, as part of the confirmation statement).

FURTHER READING

This chapter links with the materials in Chapter 9 of *Hicks and Goo's Cases and Materials on Company Law* (Oxford, OUP, 2011, xl +649p).

Grantham, 'The Doctrinal Basis of the Rights of Company Shareholders' [1998] *CLJ* 554.

Ireland, 'Company Law and the Myth of Shareholder Ownership' [1999] *MLR* 32.

MacNeil, 'Shareholders' Pre-emptive Rights' [2002] *JBL* 78.

Pennington, 'Can Shares in Companies be Defined?' [1989] *Co Law* 140.

Polack, 'Company Law—Class Rights' [1986] *CLJ* 399.

Reynolds, 'Shareholders' Class Rights: A New Approach' [1996] *JBL* 554.

Rixon, 'Competing Interests and Conflicting Principles: An Examination of the Power of Alteration of Articles of Association' [1986] *MLR* 446.

Worthington, 'Shares and Shareholders: Property, Power and Entitlement (Part I)' [2001] *Co Law* 258.

SELF-TEST QUESTIONS

1   What is meant by the term 'class right'?

2   Can the distinction between class rights and their enjoyment be justified?

3   What is the purpose of the procedural rules governing the variation of class rights?

4   Alex is a shareholder in X Ltd. He holds 10 per cent of the preference shares and 15 per cent of the ordinary shares. The articles of X Ltd provide: 'Alex, for so long as he remains a share-holder of the company, shall be entitled (i) to a pre-emption right over all shares issued by the company, and (ii) to nominate a director to the board of the company'. The directors call a general meeting of the company at which the following resolutions will be proposed:

    (a) to cancel Alex's pre-emption right;

    (b) to cancel Alex's preference shares in the company by way of a reduction of share capital;

    (c) to rescind Alex's right to nominate a director to the board.

    Discuss.

10

Derivative claims

Introduction

10.1 We have come across the principle of majority rule in Chapter 1 in the context of private companies and when discussing the s 33 contract in Chapter 8. It is not overstating the matter to observe that the majority rule principle pervades much of company law as it touches on the key issue of who owns and controls the company. However, before embarking upon an examination of the majority rule principle and the remedies available to shareholders when it is abused in this and Chapter 11, it is useful to consider briefly the landscape against which the relevant legal principles have developed.

10.2 As we observed in Chapter 2, one of the consequences of the doctrine of separate personality is that a company can sue and be sued in its own name. The company as a legal entity can therefore sue to enforce its legal rights and can be sued for breach of its legal duties. It is not generally open to individual shareholders to initiate an action on the company's behalf. That decision must be left to the appropriate organ of the company (which is normally the board of directors). In *John Shaw & Sons (Salford) Ltd v Shaw* (1935), Greer LJ explained that:

> *If powers of management are vested in the directors, they and they alone can exercise those powers. The only way in which the general body of the shareholders can control*

the exercise of the powers vested by the articles in the directors is by altering the articles or . . . by refusing to re-elect the directors of whose powers they disapprove. They cannot themselves usurp the powers by which the articles are vested in the directors any more than the directors can usurp the powers vested by the articles in the general body of shareholders.

(See also *Breckland Group Holdings Ltd v London & Suffolk Properties Ltd* (1989).)

If the law were to allow minority shareholders unfettered standing to sue, there would be a real risk of multiplicity of suits and vexatious litigation. As we will see, practical difficulties arise where the alleged wrongdoers are members of the board and are therefore in a position to prevent action being taken by the company to obtain redress for their wrongdoing.

10.3 In Chapter 8 we saw that by virtue of s 33 of the CA 2006 every member of a company is contractually bound by the terms of its constitution to the company and to the company's other shareholders. The statutory contract therefore lays down the basis of the legal relationship between the company, its members, and the members *inter se*. In consequence, a member agrees to be bound by the decisions of the majority taken at a general meeting of the company. Of course a member may express his dissent from any decision by voting against the resolution in question. But once a resolution is passed by the appropriate majority of members, a dissenting member will nevertheless be bound by it. At its root, this, of course, stems from the 'majority rule' principle. Allied to this point is the fact that the judiciary has long been reluctant to interfere in the internal management of companies. The orthodoxy here is that the management of companies is best left to the judgement of their directors who are assumed to be more commercially aware than judges and are, in any case, elected by the majority of members. This non-interventionist policy (the internal management rule) was explained by Lord Eldon LC in *Carlen v Drury* (1812), who said:

> This Court is not required on every Occasion to take the Management of every Playhouse and Brewhouse in the Kingdom.

(See also the judgment of Russell LJ in *Bamford v Bamford* (1970).)

10.4 At first sight, it would appear that minority shareholders are in a particularly weak position within the company's matrix. The effect of the principle of majority rule (taken together with the judiciary's reluctance to interfere with management decisions) is that considerable power is given to the board of directors and to those who control the general meeting. Where shares in a company are widely dispersed even those with less than an absolute majority in percentage terms (*de facto* control) are nevertheless able to exercise disproportionate power by virtue of the concentration of shares and consequent voting rights which they hold. In effect smaller shareholders will not bother voting, which leaves larger but not majority shareholders in a position to control the company.

If no shareholder has legal or *de facto* control the directors will have virtually unlimited decision-making power. This will be the case where there are no larger shareholders, just dispersed small shareholders (see further Chapter 15 on the emergence of the managerial corporation).

The anxiety of the law is to strike the optimum balance between the principle of majority rule on the one hand, and safeguarding minority shareholders against abuses of power, on the other. If the pendulum were to swing too far in favour of the minority, such share-holders could become the oppressors of the majority insofar as they could impede the carrying on of the proper business of the company.

The rule in *Foss v Harbottle*: the proper claimant principle

10.5 The rule in *Foss v Harbottle* (1843) translates the doctrine of separate legal person-ality, the statutory contract, the 'internal management principle', and the principle of majority rule into a rule of procedure governing *locus standi* (i.e. who has standing to sue). As explained by Jenkins LJ in *Edwards v Halliwell* (1950) there are two limbs to the rule:

(i) The proper claimant in an action in respect of a wrong done to a company is prima facie the company itself.

(ii) Where the alleged wrong is a transaction which might be made binding on the company and all its members by a simple majority of the members, no individual member of the company is allowed to maintain an action in respect of that matter 'for the simple reason that, if a mere majority of the members of the company . . . is in favour of what has been done, then *cadit quaestio*' (in other words, the majority rule).

A particularly clear formulation of the rule in which it was placed in its wider context was delivered by Lord Davey in *Burland v Earle* (1902):

> It is an elementary principle of the law relating to joint stock companies that the Court will not interfere with the internal management of companies acting within their powers, and in fact has no jurisdiction to do so. Again, it is clear law that, in order to redress a wrong done to the company or to recover money or damages alleged to be due to the company, the action should prima facie be brought by the company itself.

10.6 In *Foss v Harbottle* (1843) two members of the Victoria Park Co brought an action against the company's five directors and promoters alleging that they had misapplied company assets and had improperly mortgaged its property. The action sought to compel the de-fendants to make good the losses sustained by the company and also sought the appoint-ment of a receiver. It was held that the injury in question was not suffered by the claimants exclusively, but was an injury against the whole company. Further, given that it was open to the majority in general meeting to approve the defendants' conduct, the claimants' action must fail: to allow the minority to bring an action in these circumstances would risk frustrating the wishes of the majority. Wigram V-C observed:

> [I]t is only necessary to refer to the clauses of the Act to show that, whilst the supreme governing body, the proprietors at a special general meeting assembled, retain the power of exercising the functions conferred upon them by the Act of Incorporation, it cannot be competent to individual corporators to sue in the manner proposed by the plaintiffs on the present record . . . The very fact that the governing body of proprietors assembled at the special meeting may so bind even a reluctant minority is decisive to show that the frame of this suit cannot be sustained whilst that body retains its functions.

This point was again considered in *MacDougall v Gardiner* (1875). The chairman of Emma Silver Mining Co had adjourned a general meeting of the company without putting the question of adjournment to a vote as requested by a shareholder, MacDougall. The shareholder brought an action seeking a declaration that the chairman's conduct was improper, and also an injunction to prohibit the directors from taking further action. The Court of Appeal held that the issue was one of internal management for the majority members to decide. Mellish LJ stressed the futility of allowing an action to proceed where the conduct complained of is capable of ratification by the majority in general meeting. The judge went on to note that:

> [I]f the majority are abusing their powers, and are depriving the minority of their rights, that is an entirely different thing, and there the minority are entitled to come before this court to maintain their rights; but if what is complained of is simply that something which the majority are entitled to do has been done or undone irregularly, then I think it is quite right that nobody should have a right to set that aside, or institute a suit in Chancery about it, except the company itself.

(See also the comments of Lord Cottenham LC in *Mozley v Alston* (1847); and Lord Bingham in *Johnson v Gore Wood & Co* (2002).)

The types of shareholder actions

10.7 The rule in *Foss v Harbottle* (1843) is not an absolute bar to individual shareholders bringing an action in respect of an alleged wrong. The various means by which legal proceedings may be brought are outlined in the following paragraphs. In broad terms we can categorise such actions into two types. The first type is where a claim is brought to vindicate a wrong done to the company. As we saw in Chapter 2, one consequence of the *Salomon* principle is that the company, as a legal entity, can sue in order to obtain redress for a wrong committed against it. A practical difficulty arises, however, where the wrongdoers, for example the directors, control the company and prevent it from bringing an action. There are, therefore, a limited range of principles, both common law and statutory, which are directed towards solving this problem and, in this regard, the emphasis of this chapter lies with considering the circumstances when individual shareholders may bring a derivative claim on behalf of the company. This form of action has now been put on a statutory footing by virtue of the Companies Act 2006, Part 11. The second type of action arises where a shareholder complains that a wrong has been done to him or her personally (as opposed to the company). Here the appropriate course of action is to bring a personal or representative action (the reforms introduced by Part 11 of the 2006 Act do not apply to personal claims). Additionally, a shareholder may also be granted standing by specific provisions contained in the CA 2006. For example, we saw in Chapter 9 that s 633 of the CA 2006 gives the holders of not less than 15 per cent of the issued shares of the class in question, the right to apply to the court to have a variation of class rights cancelled. Further, s 994 provides for a minority shareholder to apply to the court by petition to remedy unfairly prejudicial conduct on the part of the majority (see Chapter 11).

Personal claims

10.8 It is evident from the judgment of Mellish LJ in *MacDougall v Gardiner* (1875), para **10.6**, that where a right of a shareholder has been infringed by the majority he can sue. Here the injury or wrong in question is not suffered by the company as such, but by the shareholder and, therefore, the anxiety underlying *Foss v Harbottle* (1843) does not arise. Shareholders' rights can arise by virtue of a contract (for example, as we discussed in Chapter 8, under the company's constitution or a shareholders' agreement): thus, where a dividend is declared but not paid, then a shareholder can sue for payment by way of a legal debt (see, generally, *Wood v Odessa Waterworks Co* (1889); *Bond v Barrow Haematite Steel Co* (1902); and *Lee v Sheard* (1956)).

Personal claims for reflective loss

10.9 It should be noted that where the wrong results in a loss to the company and the only loss alleged to have been suffered by the shareholder is reflected in the loss sustained by the company the courts will not permit a personal claim. The principle was succinctly stated by the Court of Appeal in *Prudential Assurance Co Ltd v Newman Industries Ltd (No 2)* (1982):

> But what [a shareholder] cannot do is to recover damages merely because the company in which he is interested has suffered damage. He cannot recover a sum equal to the diminution in the market value of his shares, or equal to the likely diminution in dividend, because such a 'loss' is merely a reflection of the loss suffered by the company. The

> *shareholder does not suffer any personal loss. His only 'loss' is through the company, in*
> *the diminution in the value of the net assets of the company.*

10.10 In *Stein v Blake (No 2)* (1998), Millett LJ unhesitatingly rejected a claim alleging wrongful misappropriation of the company's assets which resulted in a diminution of shareholding value on the basis that the company was the *only* proper claimant. The particular claimant's loss merely reflected that sustained by the company (for examples where the claimant's action has been denied on the no reflective loss principle, see *Rushmer v Mervyn Smith* (2009); *Rawnsley v Weatherall Green & Smith* (2009); and *Gaetano Ltd v Obertor Ltd* (2009)). The principal difficulty facing a shareholder in a company which has suffered loss as the result of the conduct of a third party, where, as in *Stein v Blake*, he too claims to have suffered loss from that conduct, is that of establishing causation (*Gerber Garment Technology Inc v Lectra Systems Ltd* (1997)). A major hurdle, as will be seen in Chapter 14, is the principle that directors owe their duties not to individual shareholders but to the company (see, for example, CA 2006, s 170; *Percival v Wright* (1902) and *Peskin v Anderson* (2001)—thus, the company itself must sue for breach). But where the shareholder can establish that the defendant's conduct constituted a breach of some legal duty owed to him personally (for example, under the law of contract, torts or, as in *Walker v Stones* (2001), trusts), and the court is satisfied that such breach of duty caused him personal loss, separate and distinct from that suffered by the company, he will be permitted to bring a personal action (see *Foss v Harbottle* (1843); *Prudential Assurance Co Ltd v Newman Industries Ltd (No 2)* (1982); *Walker v Stones* (2001); and *Johnson v Gore Wood & Co* (2002), Lord Millett). In the *Johnson* case the claimant, a majority shareholder in a company, sued a firm of solicitors in negligence on the ground that their conduct had caused him loss personally. Parallel proceedings brought by the company against the solicitors had been settled. The defendants argued that the shareholder's action brought on the same facts was an abuse of process and amounted to a claim for reflective loss. Lord Bingham summarised the authorities as supporting three propositions:

> *(1) Where a company suffers loss caused by a breach of duty owed to it, only the company may sue in respect of that loss. No action lies at the suit of a shareholder suing in that capacity and no other to make good a diminution in the value of the shareholder's shareholding where that merely reflects the loss suffered by the company. A claim will not lie by a shareholder to make good a loss which would be made good if the company's assets were replenished through action against the party responsible for the loss, even if the company, acting through its constitutional organs, has declined or failed to make good that loss . . . (2) Where a company suffers loss but has no cause of action to sue to recover that loss, the shareholder in the company may sue in respect of it (if the shareholder has a cause of action to do so), even though the loss is a diminution in the value of the shareholding . . . (3) Where a company suffers loss caused by a breach of duty to it, and a shareholder suffers a loss separate and distinct from that suffered by the company caused by breach of a duty independently owed to the shareholder, each may sue to*

recover the loss caused to it by breach of the duty owed to it but neither may recover loss
caused to the other by breach of the duty owed to that other.

Lord Millett, with whom Lord Goff agreed, stressed that the policy reasons underlying the bar on personal claims for reflective loss are based upon the need to protect creditors. He explained that the bar on such claims extends beyond allegations of diminution in share value so as to include claims for loss of dividend (see also *Day v Cook* (2003)). Lord Bingham's first proposition reflects the policy rationale of *Foss v Harbottle* (see further Evans-Lombe J's judgment in *Barings v Coopers & Lybrand (No 1)* (2002)). The second proposition is illustrated by the facts of *George Fisher (GB) Ltd v Multi-Construction Ltd* (1995), where the shareholder, a parent company, entered into a contract for plant on behalf of a subsidiary. The subsidiary, not being a party to the contract, could not sue for the losses it suffered as a result of the plant's defective installation. On the evidence it was clear that an equivalent loss would be suffered by the parent company and the Court of Appeal therefore awarded it damages. The third proposition requires the shareholder to demonstrate that he suffered a distinct loss; one that is separate and independent from that suffered by the company. This is by no means an easy task given that the courts disfavour personal claims because of the need to protect the interests of creditors.

10.11 As is apparent from the foregoing, the no reflective loss principle has generated a significant body of litigation in which its contours have been subjected to considerable judicial scrutiny (for a succinct summary see the judgment of Morgan J in *Sukhoruchkin v Van Bekestein* (2013)). In *Ellis v Property Leeds (UK) Ltd* (2002), the Court of Appeal held that the bar on such claims applies equally where the claimant is suing qua director as to when he sues qua shareholder. It will also trigger to prevent a claim brought qua creditor or employee, and the fact that a company is in administrative receivership does not prevent it from pursuing any claim for wrongdoing (see *Gardner v Parker* (2004), in which the Court of Appeal also stressed that the bar is an obvious consequence of the rule against double recovery). More recently, in *Sevilleja Garcia v Marex Financial Ltd* (2018) the issue was whether the rule against reflective loss bars creditors of a company from claiming directly against a third party for asset-stripping the business. The Court of Appeal held that the reflective loss rule extends to include non-shareholder creditors of the company. It reasoned that because the rule applied to shareholder-creditors, there is no logical reason why it should not also apply to a non-shareholder creditor. The creditor would be barred from bringing a claim belonging to the company. The decision has been appealed to the Supreme Court (SC). It is noteworthy that the SC granted the All-Party Parliamentary Group (APPG) on Fair Business Banking permission to intervene in the hearing. This is unprecedented. The APPG put forward the public policy arguments concerning the obstructive nature of the no reflective loss rule for the personal claims of directors and shareholders of insolvent companies.

Nevertheless, as noted, the prohibition can be circumvented where the shareholder is able to bring a claim qua beneficiary of a trust of shares of which the wrongdoer is trustee (see *Walker v Stones* (2001); and *Shaker v Al-Bedrawi* (2003)). These decisions suggest that the need to ensure proper trusteeship is the overriding policy consideration so that the no reflective loss principle must give way in such circumstances.

10.12 Notwithstanding the formidable array of hurdles ranged against claims for reflective loss, it is possible for a shareholder to circumvent them where the particular facts allow. For example, in *Giles v Rhind* (2003), the company was insolvent due to a former director's breach of certain duties (not to compete or misuse confidential information). Both duties were also express terms in a shareholders' agreement to which the defendant and claimant were parties. Although the company had initiated an action against its former director, the administrative receivers discontinued it when the defendant director applied for a security of costs order. In effect, the defendant had, by his breach of duty, rendered the company incapable of seeking legal redress against him. The claimant sought to recover losses to the value of his shareholding, loss of remuneration, and loss of the value of loan stock. The Court of Appeal, in placing considerable emphasis on the fact that the defendant's own wrongdoing had, in effect, disabled the company from suing him for damages, found that this situation had not confronted the House of Lords in *Johnson v Gore Wood & Co* (2002). Given that the duties in question were expressly provided for in the shareholders' agreement, it was held that the claimant could pursue his claim for breach of the agreement including his losses in respect of the value of his shareholding. The claims for loss of remuneration and losses of capital and interest in respect of loans made by him to the company did not, in any case, fall within reflective losses. Thus, in *Giles v Rhind (No 2)* (2003), the court awarded a substantial sum by way of damages (see also *Webster v Sandersons Solicitors* (2009)). The decision in *Giles* has not escaped judicial criticism. In the decision of the Hong Kong Court of Final Appeal in *Waddington v Chan Chun Hoo* (2008), Lord Millett took the view that no such exception existed and that *Giles* had, therefore, been wrongly decided. He concluded that to permit such an action would 'allow the plaintiff to obtain by a judgment of the court the very extraction of value from the company at the expense of its creditors that it alleged the defendant had obtained by fraud'. It is noteworthy, however, that the court in *Atlasview Ltd v Brightview Ltd* (2004) dismissed the argument that claims for reflective loss fell outwith s 994 petitions. Should the UK Supreme Court follow the position taken by Lord Millett, actions falling within the *Giles v Rhind* exception may, therefore, have to be brought under the unfair prejudice provision (see Chapter 11).

(For further consideration of the 'no reflective loss' principle and the exceptions see, *Malhotra v Malhotra* (2014), Blair J.)

Representative actions (group litigation)

10.13 Where a representative action is brought, the claimant is suing on behalf of himself and other members who have the same right which, it is alleged, has been abused or infringed (it is more common for a whole class of shareholders as opposed to any particular individual to be adversely affected by the conduct which is called into question). In such a case an individual may bring an action in a representative form. Civil Procedure Rule

(CPR), r 19.6, replacing Order 15, r 12(1) of the Rules of the Supreme Court (RSC), now governs representative actions. CPR, r 19.6(1) provides that where more than one person has the same interest in a claim: (a) the claim may be begun; or (b) the court may order that the claim be continued, by or against one or more of the persons who have the same interest as representatives of any other persons who have that interest. CPR, r 19.6(4) goes on to add that unless the court otherwise directs, any judgment or order given in a claim in which a party is acting as a representative under this rule is binding on all persons represented in the claim; but may only be enforced by or against a person who is not a party to the claim with the permission of the court. The danger of multiplicity of suits is therefore avoided (see, for example, *Quin & Axtens Ltd v Salmon* (1909)).

Derivative claims: the statutory procedure and the shadow of the common law

10.14   Derivative claims are defined by s 260(1) of the CA 2006 as proceedings brought by a member of a company in respect of a cause of action vested in the company and seeking relief on behalf of the company. Section 260(5)(c) defines a member of a company as including 'a person who is not a member but to whom shares in the company have been transferred or transmitted by operation of law'. As will be seen, this definition has not escaped judicial criticism. The statutory provisions setting out the procedural requirements do not replace the rule in *Foss v Harbottle* with a substantive rule but rather seek to implement the recommendations of the Law Commission (see LCCP No 142 (1996) and the ensuing Report No 246 (Cm 3769, 1997)) that there should be 'a new derivative procedure with more modern, flexible and accessible criteria'. The Law Commission's Report endorsed the proper claimant principle as sound, but criticised the rule in *Foss v Harbottle* as 'complicated and unwieldy'. More particularly, the Report concludes that the procedural complexities were such that establishing *locus standi* to bring a derivative action results in a mini-trial which increases the length and cost of litigation. Because of amendments introduced at a fairly late stage as the Companies Bill was proceeding through Parliament, the common law exceptions to the rule in *Foss v Harbottle* are, sadly, still material because the conditions laid down for obtaining the courts' permission to continue the claim are rooted in the common law requirements. Consequently, we cannot jettison the case law entirely given that the decisions offer some insight into the issues relevant to the exercise of the discretion conferred on the court by ss 261–264 of the 2006 Act (discussed at paras **10.33** *et seq*). Further, the common law rules continue to be directly applicable to 'multiple' derivative claims.

Multiple derivative claims

10.15   Such actions arise in relation to groups of companies. As the Law Commission's consultation paper notes, an action by a shareholder of a parent company on behalf of a subsidiary is a 'double' derivative action and, if on behalf of a 'second tier' subsidiary, it is a 'triple' derivative suit: collectively these are commonly termed multiple derivative claims (see the judgment of Lord Millett in *Waddington Ltd v Chan Ho Thomas*

(2009)). In *Universal Project Management Services Ltd v Fort Gilkicker Ltd* (2013), it was held that the 'multiple' derivative claim does not fall within the statutory procedure but continues to be subject to the common law. Although Briggs J was clearly reluctant to reach that decision, he nevertheless felt compelled to do so in the light of the statutory language:

> There is, on the face of it, no persuasive reason why Parliament should have wished to provide a statutory scheme for doing justice where a company is in wrongdoer control, but none where its holding company is in the same wrongdoer control . . . It might have been tempting to construe 'member of a company' in s 260(1) as including member of its holding company, but the express and inadequately narrow widening of the ordinary meaning of member in [s 260(5)(c), above] makes that impossible.

Although the decision must be correct given the drafting of s 260, it is unfortunate, not least because it frustrates the hopes of the CLRSG that multiple derivative claims would be included in the statutory procedure. The reasoning of Briggs J was followed in *Abouraya v Sigmund* (2013) by David Richards J who also made it clear that in the absence of fraud or an ultra vires act, a common law derivative claim cannot be brought for breaches of fiduciary duty unless the derivative claimant can demonstrate that the wrongdoers directly benefited from the breach of duty: 'The significance of this requirement is that their breach of duty cannot be ratified by a majority vote which depends on the votes of the wrongdoers' (see paras **10.24** *et seq*).

(Accepting that a double derivative claim was outwith Part 11 of the CA 2006, permission to continue a double derivative claim at common law was granted in *Bhullar v Bhullar* (2015) by Morgan J, applying *Iesini v Westrip Holdings Ltd* (see para **10.34**). The judge refused a pre-emptive costs order but granted a three-month stay so as to encourage mediation between the parties.)

Exceptions to the rule in *Foss v Harbottle*

10.16 Having restated the rule, Jenkins LJ in *Edwards v Halliwell* (1950) (para **10.5**) considered the circumstances in which it will not operate to prevent a shareholder from suing. In essence, he stated that there were four exceptions to the rule in *Foss v Harbottle* (1843):

(i) where the act complained of is illegal or is wholly ultra vires the company;

(ii) where the matter in issue requires the sanction of a special majority, or there has been non-compliance with a special procedure;

(iii) where a member's personal rights have been infringed;

(iv) where a fraud has been perpetrated on the minority and the wrongdoers are in control.

One question that is much debated is whether these are, in fact, really exceptions to the rule or whether they are rights of action which exist in spheres untouched by the rule.

(i) Illegality and ultra vires acts

10.17 In *Prudential Assurance Co Ltd v Newman Industries Ltd (No 2)* (1982), the Court of Appeal explained that where the wrongful act in issue is ultra vires the company, the rule does not operate because the majority of members cannot ratify the transaction. *Smith v Croft (No 2)* (1988) exemplifies the point. The act in question related to the giving of financial assistance to facilitate the acquisition of shares in the company contrary to the requirements of the Companies Act 1981: it was illegal and therefore ultra vires the company. It was held that an individual shareholder could bring a personal action to restrain the company from so acting because it infringed his personal right as an investor to have the business conducted in accordance with the memorandum and the articles of association. However, where the shareholder is seeking damages for the loss suffered by the company as a result of a transaction actually entered into, the action will fail if he does not satisfy the requirement of wrongdoer control: see paras **10.24** *et seq.* (*Taylor v National Union of Mineworkers (Derbyshire Area)* (1985)). This is because the wrong is done to the company directly, and so the company is the proper claimant.

10.18 With respect to 'pure' ultra vires acts, as distinct from illegality, the position is now qualified by s 40(4) of the 2006 Act which provides that a member may not bring proceedings in respect of an ultra vires act if it is to be done in fulfilment of a legal obligation arising from a previous act of the company (see further Chapter 12).

(ii) Where the matter in issue requires the sanction of a special majority, or there has been non-compliance with a special procedure

10.19 An individual shareholder will have *locus standi* to sue where the act complained of is one which requires the approval of a special majority of members and such a resolution has not been obtained. In *Edwards v Halliwell* (1950) two members of a trade union obtained a declaration that a resolution increasing members' subscriptions was invalid because the required two-thirds majority for such a resolution had not been obtained. Jenkins LJ said that:

> [T]he reason for [the] exception is clear, because otherwise, if the rule were applied in its full rigour, a company which, by its directors, had broken its own regulations by doing something without a special resolution which could only be done validly by a special resolution could assert that it alone was the proper plaintiff in any consequent action and the effect would be to allow a company acting in breach of its articles to do de facto by ordinary resolution that which according to its own regulations could only be done by special resolution. That exception exactly fits the present case.

In other words, this is not a true exception to the rule in *Foss v Harbottle* (1843) because it is the company that has done something wrong, rather than being the victim of a wrong.

10.20 This exception also overlaps with the next insofar as a shareholder has a personal right to have the articles of association observed. Thus, where the conduct in question is an attempt to alter the s 33 contract by not following a procedure requiring a special resolution, the court may grant an injunction to an individual member prohibiting the majority from acting in breach of the article in question (*Quin & Axtens Ltd v Salmon* (1909)). The decision in *Edwards v Halliwell* (1950) itself can be explained on the basis that the two members in question had a personal right not to have their subscriptions increased without the proper procedure being followed.

(iii) Where a member's personal rights have been infringed

10.21 In these circumstances a member does not have an absolute right to sue. In seeking to bring an action under this exception to the rule in *Foss v Harbottle* (1843) there are two hurdles which must be overcome: first, the bar on enforcing so-called 'outsider' rights conferred on a member by the articles of association; and, second, the difficulty in predicting when the court will hold that the breach of a provision in the company's constitution is a mere 'internal irregularity' of procedure, and therefore a wrong to the company, as opposed to a constitutional infringement (a matter of substance) for which a member can sue. The distinction between these two types of irregularity can be obscure.

10.22 The first hurdle just referred to encompasses the difficulties surrounding the enforceability of rights purportedly conferred on a member by the articles of association and, more particularly, the distinction between insider rights, which are enforceable by virtue of the statutory contract, and outsider rights which, traditionally at least, are viewed as not enforceable (see Chapter 8).

10.23 With respect to the second hurdle, in *MacDougall v Gardiner* (1875) the Court of Appeal reasoned that if every irregularity could be litigated by a member 'then if there happens to be one cantankerous member, or one member who loves litigation, everything of this kind [as on the facts] will be litigated' (see also *Bamford v Bamford* (1970), Harman LJ). On the other hand, in *Pender v Lushington* (1877) Jessel MR held that a member has a personal right to have his vote counted and could sue in the company's name and in his own name to enforce that right. It is noteworthy that the judge placed emphasis on the fact that at issue was a question of property rights. Attempts at reconciling the case law can be a frustrating exercise. *Sealy and Worthington's Text, Cases, & Materials in Company Law* (2016) at p 703, note that where the infringement relates to a constitutional right which also carries an element of property, such as the right to vote and be counted, or not to have one's union dues increased without proper procedure (see *Edwards v Halliwell* (para **10.5**), or to have a declared dividend paid in accordance with the articles—then the courts recognise the right of an individual member to sue. But mere irregularities which can be waived by a majority vote or, indeed, acquiesced in by the majority will not support a member's action (see *MacDougall v Gardiner* (1875) and *Mozley v Alston* (1847), earlier; and *Devlin v Slough Estates Ltd* (1983) in which, curiously, the court held that a member could not sue personally, or bring a derivative action, for breach of a statutory duty relating to the form and distribution of the company's accounts).

(iv) A fraud has been perpetrated against the company and the wrongdoers are in control–the true exception to *Foss v Harbottle*

10.24 It has been long settled that the one true exception to the rule in *Foss v Harbottle* (1843) is where a fraud has been perpetrated against the company by those who 'hold and control the majority of shares in the company and will not permit an action to be brought in the name of the company' (*Burland v Earle* (1902), Lord Davey).

10.25 The effect of the fraud here is to render any resolution purporting to ratify the conduct voidable (*Brown v British Abrasive Wheel Co* (1919), Astbury J). Before the introduction of the statutory procedure by the Companies Act 2006, the exception operated as a procedural device whereby a shareholder could bring a derivative action to enforce the company's rights. It was common in the early case law to refer to this exception as being a 'fraud on the minority', however, nothing turns on this—any fraud has, in truth, been perpetuated against the company and the award will be in the company's name. This distinction should be carefully observed.

Meaning of 'fraud'

10.26 The judges have not set precise limits on the meaning of fraud in this context although it has been acknowledged that it is plainly wider than fraud at common law. In *Estmanco (Kilner House) Ltd v Greater London Council* (1982), Megarry V-C said that 'the essence of the matter seems to be an abuse or misuse of power' and that the term carried its wider equitable meaning. It therefore covers conduct that is plainly improper but not necessarily deceitful. Templeman J in *Daniels v Daniels* (1978) took the view that the exception would permit a minority to sue even in the absence of fraud where directors have abused their powers, 'intentionally or unintentionally, fraudulently or negligently, in a manner which benefits themselves at the expense of the company'. The judge concluded that fraud should extend to cases of self-serving negligence which is tantamount to misappropriation of company assets. This accords with the view expressed by Lord Davey in *Burland v Earle* (1902) who gave the following examples of fraudulent conduct:

> [W]hen the majority are endeavouring directly or indirectly to appropriate to themselves money, property or advantages which belong to the company or in which the other shareholders are entitled to participate.

On the other hand, in *Pavlides v Jensen* (1956) Danckwerts J accepted that the forbearance of shareholders should extend to directors who are 'an amiable set of lunatics'. Although the directors were negligent, they did not derive any benefit. Further, in *Prudential*

Assurance Co Ltd v Newman Industries Co Ltd (No 2) (1982) Vinelott J stated that the requirement of 'fraud' would be satisfied where the interested shareholders use their voting power to stultify any proceedings being taken against them.

10.27 As we have seen, it has long been held that the expropriation of company property is obviously fraudulent conduct. *Cook v Deeks* (1916) is a clear example. Three directors controlling a private company appropriated to themselves a contract in breach of duty and then purported to ratify their breach of duty. The Privy Council held that the directors held the benefit of the contract on constructive trust for the company. Lord Buckmaster took the view that if:

> [T]he contract in question was entered into under such circumstances that the directors could not retain the benefit of it for themselves, then it belonged in equity to the company and ought to have been dealt with as an asset of the company. Even supposing it be not ultra vires of a company to make a present to its directors, it appears quite certain that directors holding a majority of votes would not be permitted to make a present to themselves. This would be to allow a majority to oppress the minority.

(See also *Menier v Hooper's Telegraph Works* (1874).)

Meaning of 'wrongdoer control'

10.28 The second element of the exception requires proof that the alleged wrongdoers (for example, the self-dealing directors) exercised sufficient control so as to prevent legal proceedings being brought in the name of the company. There has been some debate over whether *de facto* control is sufficient for this purpose, or whether *de jure* control must be established (as in *Pavlides v Jensen* (1956)). In other words, do they actually have to own or control the majority of the company's shares or do they just have to be able to exercise sufficient control as to prevent the proceedings, e.g. through the exercise of directorial power? In *Prudential Assurance Co Ltd v Newman Industries Co Ltd (No 2)* (1982) Vinelott J was prepared to sanction the action even though the two directors whose conduct was impugned did not hold the majority of the shares. The judge held that the 'control' element is satisfied where the question of civil proceedings is not put before the shareholders in a way which would enable them to consider the issue properly. The Court of Appeal also took a realistic view of the meaning of 'control' noting that it should not necessarily be limited to *de jure* control, but that it could encompass the situation where the majority vote is made up of those votes 'cast by the delinquent himself plus those voting with him as a result of influence or apathy'.

10.29 Some tempering of this dilution of the control requirement was undertaken by Knox J in *Smith v Croft (No 2)* (1988). He stated that if the majority of the remaining shareholders who were independent of the wrongdoers (termed 'the majority inside the minority') did not desire the proceedings for 'disinterested reasons', the single member seeking to sue would be denied *locus standi*. Indeed, on the facts of the case, the action did not proceed for this reason. In determining the independence of the shareholders, Knox J was of the view that their:

> *votes should be disregarded if, but only if, the court is satisfied either that the vote or its equivalent is actually cast with a view to supporting the defendants rather than securing benefit to the company, or that the situation of the person whose vote is considered is such that there is a substantial risk of that happening. The court should not substitute its own opinion but can, and in my view should, assess whether the decision making process is vitiated by being or being likely to be directed to an improper purpose.*

10.30 Davies has observed that this development represents a significant tightening of the *locus standi* conditions to be met by an individual shareholder who wishes to sue in order to vindicate a wrong to the company (whether it be by way of a fraud (for example, expropriating an asset belonging to the company) or, as on the facts of *Smith v Croft* (1986) itself, illegality and ultra vires). If a majority of the minority decide not to support the action, the individual shareholder will not be able to initiate proceedings notwithstanding that he satisfies the requirements of *Foss v Harbottle* (1843). The views of Knox J therefore went to the root of the derivative action in that the ratifiability of the wrongful act in question by the majority in general meeting was no longer decisive. Indeed, even if the wrong was not ratifiable by the company in general meeting, if the 'majority inside the minority' of independent shareholders decided against legal proceedings the individual shareholder would not be permitted to enforce the company's rights. Davies concludes that this development, together with the antipathy shown towards individual shareholders who initiate actions (see, for example, the Court of Appeal's refusal to endorse the public spirit of the claimants in bringing the action in *Prudential Assurance*), highlights how the derivative action came to be seen not as an integral part of the 'enforcement apparatus of the law' but as 'a weapon of last resort' (Davies (2003: 463)). It was such criticisms that gave impetus to the calls for a simplified statutory derivative action which was embraced by the Law Commission and endorsed by the CLRSG.

10.31 Before turning to consider the new statutory procedure, it should be noted that in the cases following *Smith v Croft (No 2)*, the courts continued to develop strict conditions for shareholder-claimants to meet. Thus, the view was taken that since the origins of the derivative action are rooted in equity, its availability was a matter within the discretion of the court, and in exercising its discretion the court would have regard to all circumstances, including the claimant's conduct (i.e. the 'clean hands' maxim), his motives in seeking to sue, and the availability of alternative remedies. For example, in *Barrett v Duckett* (1995), Mrs Barrett (B) and Mr Duckett (D) each owned 50 per cent of the shares in the company, Travel Ltd. B initiated a derivative claim against the company and another company (X Ltd) controlled by D and his wife. B claimed that D and his wife had set up X Ltd for the purpose of diverting business away from Travel Ltd to it. She also claimed that D and his wife had profited from various breaches of fiduciary duty and had paid themselves excessive remuneration. The defendants presented a claim for the winding-up of the company on the basis of the company's insolvency and, alternatively, the just and equitable ground on the basis of deadlock, and applied to have B's action struck out. The Court of Appeal held that the winding-up petition, which was lodged before B's action was commenced and, indeed, before B had intimated that she was considering bringing a derivative suit, was an alternative remedy and therefore the derivative action ought to be struck out. The court was also mindful of the fact that B was motivated not by the company's interests, but by personal reasons following the divorce of her daughter from D (see further, *Nurcombe v Nurcombe* (1985)).

10.32 The judgment of Peter Gibson LJ in *Barrett v Duckett* was considered at length and applied in *Portfolios of Distinction Ltd v Laird* (2004). Launcelot Henderson QC, sitting as a Deputy High Court Judge, stressed that in determining whether to permit a derivative action to continue 'the shareholder must establish a positive case for being allowed to sue on behalf of the company, and that the shareholder will be allowed to do so only if two conditions are satisfied, namely that he is bringing the action bona fide for the benefit of the company, and that no other adequate remedy is available'.

The statutory procedure: CA 2006, Part 11

10.33 As we saw earlier, s 260(1) of the CA 2006 defines derivative claims as proceedings brought by a member of a company in respect of a cause of action vested in the company and seeking relief on behalf of the company. The grounds for bringing a derivative claim are laid down by s 260(3) which provides that such a claim may be brought *only* in respect of a cause of action arising from an actual or proposed act or omission involving negligence, default, breach of duty, or breach of trust by a director of the company (the term 'director' is broadly defined and includes former directors and shadow directors (as to which, see Chapter 13)). The provision has some significant facets. It is clear that claims against directors for breach of their duties owed to the company (now restated in Part 10 of the 2006 Act (see Chapter 14)) fall within its scope and in this respect s 260(3) is wider than the common law action it replaces insofar as it permits a derivative claim in cases involving breach of the duty to exercise reasonable care, skill, and diligence (see CA 2006, s 174). Significantly, under the statutory procedure there is no need to demonstrate 'fraud on the minority' and 'wrongdoer control', so that even where the defendant director has acted in good faith and has not gained personally, a claim can nevertheless be brought (cf *Pavlides v Jensen* (see para **10.26**)). Section 260(3) also makes it clear that a derivative claim may be brought, for example, against a third party who dishonestly assists a director's breach of fiduciary duty or one who knowingly receives property in breach of a fiduciary duty (see further Chapter 14). Further, it is immaterial whether the cause of action arose before or after the person seeking to bring or continue the derivative claim became a member of the company (s 260(4)).

The application for permission to continue a derivative claim: the two-stage process.

10.34 The procedural rules are contained in CPR, rr 19.9, 19.9A–19.9F, and Practice Direction 19C. Section 261(1) states that once a derivative claim has been brought, the member must apply to the court for permission to continue it (see also CPR, r 19.9(4)). This is the first step in a two-stage process. It is designed to enable the court to make a decision quickly as to whether the permission application should be permitted to proceed in the absence of the company's involvement. A paper hearing will take place where the court considers the member's evidence. The onus is on the member to establish that he or she has a prima facie case for permission to continue the derivative claim. If this is not demonstrated the court will dismiss the application. If the application is dismissed at this stage, the applicant may request the court to reconsider its decision at an oral hearing, although no new evidence will be permitted at this hearing from either the member or the company. Practice Direction 19C, Derivative Claims, which amends Part 19 of the CPR, provides that this stage of the application will normally be decided without submissions from the company. If the court does not dismiss the application at this stage, the application will then proceed to the full permission hearing and the court may order the company to provide evidence at this stage. In *Iesini v Westrip Holdings Ltd* (2009), the court, commenting on the first stage of the permission process, said:

> The Act now provides for a two-stage procedure where it is the member himself who brings the proceedings. At the first stage, the applicant is required to make a prima facie case for permission to continue a derivative claim, and the court considers the question on the basis of the evidence filed by the applicant only, without requiring evidence from the defendant company. The court must dismiss the application if the applicant cannot establish a prima facie case. The prima facie case to which s 261(1) refers is a prima facie case 'for giving permission.' This necessarily entails a decision that there is a prima facie case both that the company has a good cause of action and that the cause of action arises out of a director's default, breach of duty (etc). This is precisely the decision that the Court of Appeal required in Prudential.

Accordingly, the threshold test at the first stage for permission is relatively low. The role of the court is to filter out cases that stand little or no chance of success such that they should not be permitted to proceed to the second stage. In practice, the parties have been able to bypass the first stage where the defendants concede that there is a prima facie case (see, for example, *Franbar Holdings Ltd v Patel* (2008)); or where the court is prepared to hear the first and second stages for permission together (see, for example, *Stimpson v Southern Landlords Association* (2010), where the court rejected the defendant's objection to combining the two stages). Lord Reed observed in *Wishart v Castlecroft Securities Ltd* (2010) that 'In practice, the parties may agree to telescope this procedure by dealing with the application in its entirety at a single hearing.' Such conflation of the two-stage process has the advantage of saving costs. However, this practice was severely criticised by the court in *Re Seven Holdings, Langley Ward Ltd v Trevor* (2011). The judge said:

> My experience in this case . . . suggests that applications of this sort are set fair to become another time-consuming and expensive staple in the industry of satellite litigation. In the present case, the court was presented with three lever-arch files of pleadings, statements and documents in addition to detailed skeleton arguments and extensive lists of authorities. The argument before me was contained within a day, but only as the result of extensive (and underestimated) pre-reading by the court. . . .
>
> The inclusion in the Companies Act of an ex parte stage provides a hurdle and filter which in my view should not be dispensed with. As with any ex parte application the matter should be presented and explained transparently and fairly so that the court can make a properly informed decision whether it is right to put the company (and the potential defendant) to the expense and inconvenience of considering and contesting the application. This can only be achieved if the applicant sets out clearly and coherently the nature and basis of each claim. . . .
>
> [T]hose standards were not met in the present case. If they had been, the task of the court would have been greatly simplified, even though the case did not in the event pass through the [second] filter stage. Moreover, if that stage had been observed, it seems to me likely that at least a large number of claims, and perhaps all of them, would have been eliminated then. Either way the cost and time expended by the parties and court in this matter would have been significantly reduced. . . .

(See *Re Singh Brothers Contractors (North West) Ltd* (2014); see further the comments of Pilkington J in *Saggart Motors Ltd v NG Motors Ltd* (2019), emphasising the need for litigants to adhere strictly to court procedures when commencing a derivative action.) In a highly unusual case, *Wilton UK Ltd v Shuttleworth* (2017), HHJ Davis-White QC was called upon to consider whether the court has the power retrospectively to validate service of a claim form and particulars of claim where the claimant was in breach of the statutory requirement under s 261 to obtain the court's permission to continue the derivative claim and where a new claim would have been time-barred. In holding that the failure to obtain permission did not invalidate steps which had thereafter been taken, the judge noted that:

> I do not regard the need for permission to be one that can be ignored in the sense that all steps taken without permission will be valid unless and until set aside by the court. In my judgment, that would give insufficient weight to the need to seek permission and not sufficiently protect the company or the other defendants to the proceedings. On the other hand, I see no reason at all why, exercising its discretion, the court should not have power to validate with retrospective effect steps taken in the proceedings without permission. Such power would be entirely consistent with the policy underlying the filtering role of the court. It would enable (e.g.) the company . . . to adopt proceedings where it wanted to in circumstances where (e.g.) a claim form and the limitation period had expired prior to its adoption and where service of the claim form (without permission) had otherwise

been served within the time limits concerned. . . . It also has to be recognised that the need to seek permission could arise at a later stage of the proceedings than immediately post issue. If, for example, permission were only granted up to a certain stage of the proceedings, further permission would thereafter be needed. There could easily be a (forgivable or not very serious) mistake to obtain the same. It would be odd if subsequent steps were necessarily and irretrievably void for want of such permission.

The judge adjourned the applications for further argument as to whether he should exercise the discretion which he found he had.

10.35 For the second stage, s 263(2) sets out the criteria which the court must take into account when determining whether to grant permission to a member to continue a derivative claim. It directs that permission must be refused if the court is satisfied that:

(a) a person acting in accordance with s 172 (duty to promote the success of the company) would not seek to continue the claim; or

(b) where the claim arises from an act or omission that is yet to occur, that the act or omission has been authorised by the company; or

(c) where the complaint arises from an act or omission that has already occurred, that act or omission was authorised before it occurred, or has been ratified since it occurred.

Accordingly, these factors represent a total bar to a derivative claim proceeding. The requirement that the court should take into account the importance that a director acting in accordance with the duty to promote the success of the company would attach to the claim appears to dispense with the old common law prerequisite of 'wrongdoer control'. The list of factors to be taken into account for determining the refusal of permission is supplemented by s 263(3) which sets out the factors which the court must, in particular, take into account when exercising its discretion to grant permission to continue a derivative claim:

(a) whether the member is acting in good faith;

(b) the importance that a person acting in accordance with s 172 (duty to promote the success of the company) would attach to pursuing the action;

(c) whether prior authorisation or subsequent ratification of the act or omission would be likely to occur;

(d) whether the company has decided not to pursue the claim; and

(e) whether the shareholder could pursue the action in his own right.

(See *Zavahir v Shankleman* (2016).) In *Saatchi v Gajjar* (2019), Briggs J gave a comprehensive review of the statutory procedure and the applicable case law, noting that while individual claims of wrongdoing by a director may not carry the same weight, when viewed cumulatively they may well merit the court concluding that a derivative action ought to proceed on the basis 'that a person acting in accordance with section 172 of the Act would attach significant importance to the [cumulative] claims' such 'that they are not merely speculative. There is something more to them than a prima facie case.'

Section 263(4) goes on to add the requirement, as laid down in the much criticised decision in *Smith v Croft (No 2)* (see paras **10.29-10.31**), that the court 'shall have particular regard' to any evidence before it as to the views of members who have no personal interest in the derivative claim. There will need to be a factual enquiry into whether or not the breach is likely to be ratified. In practice the courts will probably adjourn the permission hearing in order for the question of ratification to be put to the company.

10.36 Provision is also made for an alternative member of the company to apply to the court to continue a derivative claim originally brought by another member but which is being poorly conducted by him or her. Section 264 provides that the court may grant permission to continue the claim where the manner in which the proceedings have been commenced or continued by the original claimant amounts to an abuse of the process of the court, the claimant has failed to prosecute the claim diligently, and it is appropriate for the applicant to continue the claim as a derivative claim. Similarly, by virtue of s 262, where a company has initiated proceedings and the cause of action could be pursued as a derivative claim, a member may apply to the court to continue the action as a derivative claim on the same grounds listed in s 264. This addresses the situation where directors fearing a derivative claim by a member seek to block it by causing the company to sue but with no genuine intention of pursuing the action diligently.

10.37 If we compare the language of ss 261–264 with the common law rules they replace, it is apparent that there is little or no change of emphasis in terms of formulation. The focus of the rule laid down in *Foss v Harbottle* and its jurisprudence was on prohibiting claims unless one of the exceptions to the rule was satisfied. The statutory language similarly proceeds from the rather negative standpoint that the court *must dismiss* the application or claim in the circumstances specified in ss 261(2), 262(3), 263(2)–(3), and 264(3). It is noteworthy that during the course of the parliamentary debates on the Bill, the point was made that the new statutory procedure carried the risk of increased litigation against directors which could impede the efficient management of companies (in this regard, it should be recalled that the derivative claim has been expanded to include claims against directors for negligence). One particular solution thought to offer some safeguard against this risk was introduced in the House of Lords, by way of amendment, in the form of the additional procedural requirement contained in 263(4) (see para **10.35**).

10.38 Without doubt, the new procedural requirements, as was the case before their introduction, represent significant hurdles to be overcome and the early case law decided under Part 11 of the Act shows that the courts are adopting a cautious approach when called upon to exercise their discretion under ss 261–264. In *Mission Capital plc v Sinclair* (2008), two directors of Mission Capital were dismissed from the board and their service contracts were terminated. The company later brought an action against them. They counterclaimed seeking reinstatement. Further, the former directors, who also held shares in the company, launched a derivative claim against the continuing directors. In denying the permission application, the High Court considered the discretionary factors to be taken into account and decided that a notional director acting in accordance with his s 172 duty to promote the success of the company would give little weight to continuing the claim. Further, as shareholders, they could pursue their claims under the unfair prejudice provision.

10.39 In *Franbar Holdings v Patel* (2008), the claimant was a shareholder of the corporate defendants and the other defendants were directors. Disagreements arose about the way the business was being managed and about the proper operation of a shareholders' agreement. The claimant brought an action for breach of the shareholders' agreement, an unfair prejudice petition, and a derivative claim against the directors. In relation to the derivative claim, the court found that the mandatory factors under s 263(2) were not made out. With respect to the discretionary factors under s 263(3), the court found that a notional director would not attach particular importance to the continuation of the derivative claim because the matters complained of were also covered by the action based on the shareholders' agreement and the s 994 petition. However, in appropriate circumstances the discretion may be exercised the other way so that the fact that there are extant s 994 proceedings will not necessarily result in permission to continue a derivative claim being denied, and the court may hear both proceedings together (*Phillips v Fryer* (2012)). Permission was refused in *Stimpson v Southern Landlords Association* (2010), where the applicant's motives were a deciding factor in not granting leave. HHJ Pelling QC found that a hypothetical director acting in accordance with the s 172 duty would not seek to continue the claim under s 263(2)(a). On the issue of good faith, the judge found that the claimant had brought the action in order to retain control of the company and because he did not want it to lose its identity through a merger. Whether this motive demonstrated a lack of good faith was not strictly material, but it was certainly a relevant factor to the application. The judge noted that the list of factors contained in s 263(3) were not exhaustive, and it was open to the courts to take account of other factors and the applicant's motive was a negative factor. Section 263(3)(d) required consideration to be given to whether the matters complained of could be ratified and it was now unlikely that ratification could be obtained. Although common law prerequisites such as 'wrongdoer control' are not specified in the 2006 Act, this did not mean they were no longer relevant (though it should be stressed that wrongdoer control is not an absolute condition for a derivative claim under Part 11 (see para **10.35**; and see Roth J's judgment in *Bamford v Harvey* (2012)). HHJ Pelling QC concluded by noting that it was open to the applicant to requisition an extraordinary general meeting, put in place a replacement board, and that board could, if it judged it appropriate, in accordance with the s 172 duty, authorise the proceedings. This factor was material and negatived the granting of permission and could be overwhelming although the court would have refused permission irrespective of this last point.

10.40 It is apparent that the approach taken in these cases where permission was sought under the statutory procedure continues to reflect in part the stance established by the case law predating the 2006 Act. For example, in *Mumbray v Lapper* (2005) the availability of alternative remedies, for instance s 994 (see Chapter 11), and the fact that the derivative action would not have been in the interests of the company, were factors taken into account in deciding to refuse leave. Similarly, in *Jafari-Fini v Skillglass* (2005) the Court of Appeal upheld the judge's refusal to allow the derivative claim to continue. Chadwick LJ explained that the company itself would not benefit from the action and the claimant shareholder had alternative avenues open to him, in particular, a personal claim (see also, *Harley Street Capital Ltd v Tchigirinsky* (2006), and *Barrett v Duckett* (1995) (see para **10.31**).

However, in *Kiani v Cooper* (2010), limited permission to continue the claim down to disclosure in the action was granted. The application by K, a director and shareholder of the company, related to allegations of breaches of fiduciary duty by C, the other director and shareholder in the company. It also extended to applications restraining the presentation of winding-up petitions threatened by C and the third defendant, DPM Property Services Ltd (DPM), a company in which C was both a director and the majority shareholder. On the facts, Proudman J, having reviewed s 263(3), identified as crucial factors the requirement of good faith, the availability of an alternative remedy, and, in particular, the attitude of a person acting in accordance with the duties imposed by s 172 of the CA 2006. In her reasoning, the judge drew upon Lewison J's detailed and insightful analysis of the statutory procedure in *Iesini v Westrip Holdings Ltd* (2009), where it was held that the directors had not breached their duties so that there were no grounds for launching a derivative claim. Reviewing the first of the two-stage procedure introduced by s 263(2) and (3), Lewison J had noted that the applicant is required to make a prima facie case for permission to continue a derivative claim. As noted in para **10.34**, this is considered on the basis of the evidence filed by the applicant only, without requiring evidence from the defendant or the company. Thus, in determining whether to grant permission, the court must be convinced 'that there is a *prima facie* case both that the company has a good cause of action and that the cause of action arises out of a directors' default, breach of duty (etc)'. Lewison J went on to state that the second stage is not simply a matter of establishing a prima facie case that the claim arises from an act or omission involving default or breach of duty as was the case under the old law, because that forms the first stage of the procedure:

> At the second stage something more must be needed. In Fanmailuk.com v Cooper (2008) Mr Robert Englehart QC said that on an application under section 261 it would be 'quite wrong ... to embark on anything like a mini-trial of the action.' No doubt that is correct; but on the other hand not only is something more than a prima facie case required, but the court will have to form a view on the strength of the claim in order properly to consider the requirements of section 263(2)(a) and 263(3)(b). Of course any view can only be provisional where the action has yet to be tried; but the court must, I think, do the best it can on the material before it.

With respect to s 263(2)(a), Lewison J observed that there is a range of factors that a director, acting in accordance with s 172, would consider in reaching his decision. They would include:

> the size of the claim; . . . the costs of the proceedings; the company's ability to fund the proceedings; the ability of the potential defendants to satisfy a judgment; the impact on the company if it lost the claim and had to pay not only its own costs but the defendants as well; any disruption to the company's activities while the claim is pursued; whether the prosecution of the claim would damage the company in other ways . . . and so on. The weighting of these considerations is essentially a commercial decision, which the court is ill-equipped to take, except in a clear case.
>
> In my judgment therefore . . . section 263(2)(a) will apply only where the court is satisfied that no director acting in accordance with section 172 would seek to continue the claim.

Following Lewison J's reasoning, Proudman J, stressing the very many factual disputes between the parties, found that in the circumstances K was acting in good faith and that a notional director acting in accordance with his duties under s 172 would pursue the action given the strength of the evidence in favour of the case advanced by K. With respect to the availability of an alternative remedy (it was argued that an unfair prejudice petition under s 994 of the CA 2006 was the proper remedy available to K), the judge took the view that this was merely one of the factors to be taken into account and it was no means determinative (see further, *Phillips v Fryer* (2012) (see para **10.39**)). Similarly, in *Stainer v Lee* (2010), the court granted limited permission to continue a derivative action, subject to various conditions, including one relating to costs. The permission granted was limited to the conclusion of disclosure on the basis that by that stage, the facts and strength of the case would be much clearer. With respect to s 263 the judge observed that:

> I consider that section 263(3) and (4) do not prescribe a particular standard of proof that has to be satisfied but rather require consideration of a range of factors to reach an overall view. In particular, under section 263(3)(b), as regards the hypothetical director acting in accordance with the section 172 duty, if the case seems very strong, it may be appropriate to continue it even if the likely level of recovery is not so large, since such a claim stands a good chance of provoking an early settlement or may indeed qualify for summary judgment. On the other hand, it may be in the interests of the Company to continue even a less strong case if the amount of potential recovery is very large.

(See also, *Kleanthous v Paphitus* (2011); and *Re Charles Parry Group, Parry v Bartlett* (2011).)

10.41   In *Cinematic Finance Ltd v Ryder* (2010), permission was refused by the court. Cinematic Finance ('CF') Ltd granted loans to several investment companies. When these loans were not repaid, CF Ltd became the sole and majority shareholder of those companies. It sought permission to pursue a derivative action against the former directors of the investment companies for alleged breaches of their fiduciary duties. At the time, CF Ltd was having difficulties gaining access to the companies' books and records, but had not disclosed to the court that it was the sole and majority shareholder. It claimed that there were exceptional circumstances that made its derivative claim appropriate where it is likely that the debtor companies were or would become insolvent. The court held that as the sole and majority shareholder of the investment companies, CF Ltd had complete control over them and so a derivative action was neither necessary nor appropriate. Although the court did not go so far as to say that permission would never be granted to a majority shareholder, it confirmed that permission would only be granted in exceptional circumstances. The circumstances before it were not viewed as exceptional. The court concluded that one of the principal reasons for the use of the derivative claim procedure was to save the cost of pursuing the remedy through the insolvency regime. That was not a sufficient reason to allow a derivative action to proceed. Roth J reasoned that since the companies were insolvent, 'The controlling shareholder should not seek to circumvent the insolvency regime by starting a derivative claim.'

The cases discussed above have done much to establish the parameters of the permission stage in derivative claims and against this backdrop the outcome in the next two decisions is hardly surprising. In *Cullen Investments Ltd v Brown* (2015), permission was granted to proceed to trial. The claim alleged that a director had usurped a corporate opportunity for his own benefit. The court rejected the contention that no director acting in pursuance of his duty under s 172 of the CA 2006 would have supported the claim. Further, the shareholder had assumed all of the financial risks of the litigation. On the other hand, in *Bridge v Daley* (2015), permission to proceed with a derivative claim was refused. Most of the allegations were unsubstantiated, though the judge accepted that the claimant was acting in good faith. The overwhelming majority of shareholders did not support the claim nor did the independent board members. The judge took the view that it would be more appropriate to test the complaints in question via a s 994 petition (see Chapter 11). Costs were awarded against the claimant.

10.42   An obvious deterrent against speculative claims is, of course, costs (see para **10.43**). Although CPR, r 19.9E enables the court to order the company to indemnify the member, in practice such an order will rarely be granted where permission is denied. Finally, it is also noteworthy that the law on ratification has been tightened insofar as the votes of the 'wrongdoers' will no longer be counted on such ordinary resolutions (although such members may be counted towards the quorum and may participate in the proceedings; see further, CA 2006, ss 175 and 239, considered in Chapter 14). The courts may, therefore, view the process, for the purposes of denying permission, as carrying greater integrity than was formerly the case.

The proceedings, costs, and remedies

10.43   If permission is granted to continue the claim the member will bring the action on the company's behalf. The Civil Procedure (Amendment) Rules 2007 (SI 2007/2204), r 7 and Sch 1 substitute CPR, r 19.9 and inserts new CPR, rr 19.9A–19.9F. The company for whose benefit a remedy is sought must be made a defendant in the proceedings in order formally to be a party to the action and be bound by any judgment. If permission is granted to continue the claim the member will bring the action on the company's behalf. Unless otherwise permitted or required by r 19.9A or r 19.9C, the claimant may take no further action in the proceedings without the permission of the court. A practical hurdle which confronts a shareholder litigant, and one which acts as a major disincentive to launching a derivative action, is the cost of a proposed action. Rule 19.9E covers costs. The court may order the company to indemnify the claimant against any liability in respect of costs incurred in the claim or in the permission application, or both. An application for costs made at the time of applying for permission to continue the claim is commonly called a pre-emptive costs order. It derives from the decision in *Wallersteiner v Moir (No 2)* (1975), where Buckley LJ observed that the shareholder who initiates the derivative claim may be entitled to be indemnified by the company at the end of the trial for his costs provided he acted reasonably in bringing the action (for an example where a '*Wallersteiner* order' was refused, see *Halle v Trax BW Ltd* (2000)). The position in the event of the action failing was also addressed by the court. Lord Denning MR said:

> But what if the action fails? Assuming that the minority shareholder had reasonable grounds for bringing the action—that it was a reasonable and prudent course to take in the interests of the company—he should not himself be liable to pay the costs of the other side, but the company itself should be liable, because he was acting for it and not for himself. In addition, he should himself be indemnified by the company in respect of his own costs even if the action fails. It is a well-known maxim of the law that he who would take the benefit of a venture if it succeeds ought also to bear the burden if it fails . . . In order to be entitled to this indemnity, the minority shareholder soon after issuing his writ should apply for the sanction of the court in somewhat the same way as a trustee does.

In *Smith v Croft* (1986), decided under the old Rules of the Supreme Court, Walton J held that the shareholder's personal means to finance the action was a relevant factor to be taken into account by the court in determining the need for an indemnity. The judge also added that even where the shareholder is impecunious, he should still be required to meet a share of the costs as an incentive to proceed with the action with due diligence.

10.44   In *Kiani v Cooper* (2012) (see para **10.40**), Proudman J was prepared to make an order that K's costs should be borne by the company, but she was not prepared to grant her an indemnity in respect of any adverse costs order in favour of C and DPM. The judge concluded that: 'It seems to me that she should be required to assume part of the risk of the litigation.' And in *Stainer v Lee* (2010), Roth J said:

> The applicant seeks an indemnity for his costs, relying on Wallersteiner v Moir (No 2) . . . I think that is clear authority that a shareholder who receives the sanction of the court to proceed with a derivative action should normally be indemnified as to his reasonable costs by the company for the benefit of which the action would accrue. But where the amount of likely recovery is presently uncertain, there is concern that his costs could become

disproportionate. Accordingly, I place a ceiling on the costs for which I grant an indemnity for the future . . . There will be liberty to apply to extend the scope of that indemnity.

10.45 Legal aid has never been available to those seeking to bring a derivative action and so in *Wallersteiner v Moir (No 2)* Lord Denning MR expressed the minority view that contingency fees could be used to fund such an action. Buckley and Scarman LJJ, however, held that contingency fee arrangements were unlawful and therefore not available for derivative actions. By virtue of ss 58 and 58A of the Courts and Legal Services Act 1990 and SI 1998/1860, conditional fee arrangements are, subject to certain limited exceptions, now lawful in all proceedings. Thus a solicitor may take on a case on the basis that they will only get paid if they win the case.

10.46 The CA 2006 makes no specific provision for the remedies available in a derivative claim. However, given that such claims are based upon breaches of directors' duties (see s 260(3)), s 178 CA 2006 no doubt applies. This provides that the consequences of breach or threatened breach of the duties owed by directors to the company are the same as would apply if the corresponding common law rule or equitable principle applied (see Chapter 14).

Section 996(2)(c) Companies Act 2006

10.47 Where a minority shareholder has been unfairly prejudiced he may petition the court which, under s 996, is empowered to make such order as it thinks fit in the circumstances (see Chapter 11). More specifically, s 996(2)(c) goes on to grant the court the power to authorise civil proceedings to be brought in the name and on behalf of the company by the prejudiced minority. Put simply, the court may direct the petitioner to bring a derivative claim. This possibility is reinforced by s 260(2)(b) which states that the only alternative to bringing a derivative claim under Part 11, Chapter 1 of the Act is where it is brought in pursuance of a court order under the unfair prejudice remedy. Given the array of remedies available to the court under s 996, it is unlikely that this power will be used in a s 994 unfair prejudice petition. In this respect it is noteworthy that in *Barrett v Duckett* (1995) the Court of Appeal refused to allow the shareholder to bring a derivative action when she could have sought a share purchase order under the unfair prejudice provision. It is evident from the paucity of case law on the point that relief under s 996(2)(c) has rarely been ordered in practice. Such a remedy can be a lengthy and potentially expensive procedure as the petitioner is required to prove his entire case under s 994 before an action on behalf of the company can be commenced. In circumstances where a wrong is done to the company and corporate relief is sought by a petitioner, it is difficult to see why the cost and inconvenience of two sets of proceedings should be preferable to the court simply awarding corporate relief directly under s 996 (see *Re a Company (No 005287 of 1985)* (1986)). Moreover, the chances of a petitioning shareholder wishing to undertake a second piece of litigation are also extremely unlikely given the fact that in most circumstances they are seeking to exit the company by obtaining a buy-out order (see Chapter 11). There may, however, be circumstances that will nevertheless warrant a petitioner seeking a s 996(2)(c) order. As pointed out by Lewison J in *Iesini v Westrip Holdings Ltd* (2009), 'where the petitioner's complaint is that [he has been unfairly prejudiced because] the company has failed to assert a good claim against a third party' the court has the power under the provision to make an order 'requiring the company to assert that claim'. In such circumstances 'the directors would not need to be parties to the subsequent claim against the third party', and 'the width of the jurisdiction under s 996 enables the joinder of third parties to the petition itself, at least where relief is claimed against them'.

Bars to a derivative action

A company in liquidation

10.48   Where a company goes into liquidation the court will not allow a derivative action to be brought or continued because the liquidator then has the statutory power to litigate in the company's name (Insolvency Act 1986, s 165(3), s 167(1) and Sch 4, para 4). The position was succinctly stated by Walton J in *Fargro Ltd v Godfroy* (1986):

> But once the company goes into liquidation the situation is completely changed, because one no longer has a board, or indeed a shareholders' meeting, which is in any sense in control of the activities of the company of any description, let alone its litigation. Here, what has happened is that the liquidator is now the person in whom that right is vested.

(See also *Cinematic Finance Ltd v Ryder* (para **10.41**); *Montgold Capital LLP v Ilska* (2018); and *Re Core VCT plc* (2019).)

The rationale for this is clear. Once a company goes into liquidation the liquidator takes control of the company's affairs. If the liquidator refuses to initiate litigation a shareholder may apply to the court for an order directing the liquidator to sue, or an order permitting the shareholder to bring proceedings in the name of the company (*Fargro Ltd v Godfroy* (1986)). Before granting such an order the court must be convinced either that the liquidator exercised his discretion mala fides (for example, he was a participant in the wrongdoing), or that he came to a decision to which no reasonable liquidator would have come (*Leon v York-O-Matic Ltd* (1966)).

Liability insurance and qualifying third party indemnity provisions

10.49   The Companies Act 2006 incorporates the amendments introduced by the Companies (Audit, Investigations and Community Enterprise) Act 2004 into the CA 1985. Section 232 of the CA 2006 renders void any provisions in the articles or in any contract with the company (e.g. a service contract) that purport to exempt a director from, or indemnifying him against, any liability that would otherwise attach to him in connection with any negligence, default, breach of duty, or breach of trust in relation to the company. Indemnification by an associated company is also prohibited (companies are treated as associated if they are in the same group). However, ss 232(2)–233 allow companies to purchase and maintain insurance cover against such liability (so-called D & O liability cover). Similarly, by s 234, the prohibition against provisions indemnifying directors laid down by s 232(2) does not apply to 'qualifying third party indemnity provisions' (QTPIPs). For example, a provision will qualify if it indemnifies directors against liabilities (damages, costs, and interest), in a civil action by a person other than the company (i.e. a third party) or an associated company, and against the costs of their defence, even if judgment is given against the directors or the litigation is settled out of court or otherwise comes to an end without judgment being obtained. Companies can also indemnify directors against costs incurred in connection with applications for relief from liability made under, for example, s 1157 (see Chapter 14). However, it must not cover any fine in criminal proceedings or any penalty imposed by a regulator, or defence costs where the director is convicted. The directors' report in the company's annual report and accounts must disclose the existence of a QTPIP (s 236).

10.50 These provisions were introduced in the light of the findings of the Higgs Review (see Chapter 16) together with the DTI's (now BEIS) own consultation exercise that revealed two major difficulties affecting the recruitment and behaviour of directors: first, an increase in litigation against directors and, second, the cost of defending lengthy proceedings which can result in financial ruin. As a consequence, it was thought that companies should be able to assist their directors financially while litigation or other proceedings are in progress, and to indemnify their directors against certain liabilities to third parties even if the directors themselves are at fault.

Conclusion

10.51 There is a consensus of opinion amongst academic commentators that the procedural complexities ranged against a minority shareholder who sought to bring a derivative action under the common law rules acted as a major deterrent against enforcing company rights (although the task of impeaching directorial/majority conduct in small private companies was made considerably easier by s 459 of the 1985 Act (now s 994 CA 2006, see Chapter 11; see also the comments of Lord Coulsfield in *Anderson v Hogg* (2001)). The effectiveness of the one true exception to the rule in *Foss v Harbottle* (1843) as a safeguard against wrongdoing was clearly dependent upon the vigilance of shareholders in detecting fraudulent conduct on the part of the controllers. It was evident that shareholders were ill-suited to perform the task of policing directorial wrongdoing particularly in large public companies, given that as a body they are generally diffuse with limited access to material information. More generally, it was difficult to understand why a shareholder would wish to bring a derivative action. Apart from the procedural hurdles and the issue of costs, the remedy was, and is, the company's. Thus, a shareholder contemplating such an action must do so for altruistic reasons since he will not benefit directly from any award. The introduction of the statutory procedure in Part 11 of the Companies Act 2006 represents a lost opportunity to address many of these concerns. Certainly the CLR's objectives of minimising complexity and maximising accessibility seem to have been lost somewhere along the way. As a consequence, the effectiveness of the derivative claim as a tool for ensuring good corporate governance remains highly questionable. Further, the fear that the new statutory procedure would open the floodgates of litigation against directors has not come to pass (see, in particular, *Mission Capital plc v Sinclair* (2008); *Franbar Holdings v Patel* (2008); and *Stimpson v Southern Landlords* (2010)).

FURTHER READING

This chapter links with the materials in Chapter 13 of *Hicks and Goo's Cases and Materials on Company Law* (Oxford, OUP, 2011, xl +649p).

Armour, 'Derivative Actions : A Framework for Decisions' [2019] *LQR* 412.

Baxter, 'The Role of the Judge in Enforcing Shareholder Rights' [1983] *CLJ* 96.

Ferran, 'Litigation by Shareholders and Reflective Loss' [2001] *CLJ* 245.

Keay and Loughrey, 'Derivative Proceedings in a Brave New World for Company Management and Shareholders' [2010] *JBL* 151.

Law Commission Consultation Paper No 142, *Shareholder Remedies* (1996).

Law Commission Report No 246, *Shareholder Remedies* (Cm 3769, 1997).

Lightman, 'The Role of the Company at the Permission Stage of the Statutory Derivative Claim' [2010] *CJQ* 23.

Lowry, 'Self-Dealing Directors—Constructing A Regime of Accountability' [1997] *NILQ* 211.

Mitchell, 'Shareholders' Claims for Reflective Loss' [2004] *LQR* 457.

Prentice, 'Shareholder Actions: the Rule in *Foss v Harbottle*' [1988] *LQR* 341.

Reisberg, *Derivative Actions and Corporate Governance: Theory & Operation* (Oxford, OUP, 2007).

Reisberg, 'Derivative Claims under the Companies Act 2006: Much Ado About Nothing?' in Armour and Payne (eds) *Rationality in Company Law: Essays in Honour of DD Prentice* (Oxford, Hart Publishing, 2008).

Sealy, 'Problems of Standing, Pleading and Proof in Corporate Litigation' [1987] *Current Legal Problems: Company Law in Change* 1.

Sullivan, 'Restating the Scope of the Derivative Action' [1985] *CLJ* 236.

Wedderburn, 'Shareholders' Rights and the Rule in *Foss v Harbottle*' [1957] *CLJ* 154 and [1958] *CLJ* 219.

SELF-TEST QUESTIONS

1   What are a personal claim, a representative claim, and a derivative claim?

2   'The spectre of increased derivative claims is now a distinct probability in the light of the 2006 reforms.' Discuss.

3   Will the statutory procedure empower shareholders in large companies? Will it alter their position in small companies?

4   Should judges adopt a more interventionist role in corporate affairs? If so, at what price?

11 Statutory shareholder remedies

SUMMARY

Just and equitable winding-up
Unfairly prejudicial conduct: CA 2006, Part 30 (ss 994–996)
Other specific statutory minority rights
The Law Commission's proposals for reforming the unfair prejudice provision

Just and equitable winding-up

11.1 As we saw in Chapter 10, given the procedural obstacles posed by the rule in *Foss v Harbottle* (1843) and the judicial timidity in interpreting the oppression remedy (CA 1948, s 210, the precursor of today's main minority shareholder remedy in CA 2006, s 994, see later) aggrieved minority shareholders in small private companies historically either suffered their lot or sought relief through a winding-up order on the just and equitable ground (now contained in s 122(1)(g) of the Insolvency Act 1986 ('the 1986 Act')). That is, they asked the court to end the life of the company and distribute the remaining assets to the shareholders. This remedy originates from the law of partnership in which the equity courts retained jurisdiction to dissolve a partnership where the relationship between its members had broken down.

Following the introduction of the 'unfair prejudice remedy' by the Companies Act 1980, this avenue of redress has come to the fore so that the just and equitable winding-up remedy occupies a less prominent position in the minority shareholder's armoury, although it is by no means redundant (see *Re Phoneer Ltd* (2002), see para **11.27**). The pre-eminence which s 994 now enjoys must also be viewed against the CPR whereby the courts take a proactive role in case management (see, for example, *Re Rotadata Ltd* (2000) in which Neuberger J stressed that the CPR encouraged the court to take an active part in case management and this also included encouraging the parties to cooperate with each other in the conduct of the proceedings; see further para **11.50**).

11.2 Section 122(1)(g) of the 1986 Act provides that 'a company may be wound up by the court if the court is of the opinion that it is just and equitable that the company should be wound up'. Since just and equitable winding-up is necessarily draconian (in effect, ending the company and distributing the assets to the shareholders) in nature it is obvious that there will have to be strong grounds to convince the court to grant the remedy. In this respect the dire consequences for a prosperous company which the presentation of a petition for winding-up carries are compounded by s 127 of the 1986 Act which, in effect, renders the company incapable of carrying on business freely. Section 127 provides 'that any disposition of the company's property, and any transfer of shares, or alteration in the status of the company's members, made after the commencement of the winding up is, unless the court otherwise orders, void' (see further Chapter 17). Accordingly, any disposition of company property after a petition has been brought requires the court's consent. Further, any payments made out of the company's bank account after the presentation of the petition can be set aside by the liquidator once the company has been wound up. Banks therefore freeze company bank accounts as soon as they receive notice of the presentation of the petition (*Re XYZ Ltd* (1987)).

Grounds for petition

11.3 The classic case on the remedy is *Ebrahimi v Westbourne Galleries Ltd* (1973) in which the scope of the court's jurisdiction under the just and equitable ground was subjected to considerable scrutiny by the House of Lords. The company was established in 1958 to take over the oriental rug business which the respondent (Nazar) and the petitioner (Ebrahimi) had run in partnership for over a decade. Initially, the two were equal shareholders and the only directors. Eventually, Nazar's son joined the company as director and shareholder. The effect of this was that Ebrahimi now became a minority both within the board and at the general meeting where he could be outvoted by the combined shareholding of Nazar and his son. Friction developed between the parties and Ebrahimi was voted off the board using the power conferred by s 303. After this, he was not consulted on the running of the business and neither did he continue to share in its profits. No dividends were paid to him because all profits were distributed by way of directors' remuneration. In consequence, Ebrahimi failed to obtain any further return on his investment and he petitioned the court for a winding-up order under s 122(1)(g) of the 1986 Act, and alternatively for relief under the 'oppression' remedy contained in the Companies Act 1948 (the predecessor of the unfair prejudice remedy).

11.4 The House of Lords took the view that notwithstanding that Ebrahimi had been removed by Nazar and his son in accordance with the Companies Act and the articles of association, the just and equitable ground conferred on the court the jurisdiction to subject the exercise of legal rights to equitable considerations. It was held that because the petitioner had agreed to the formation of the company on the basis that the essence of their business relationship would remain the same as with their prior partnership, his exclusion from the company's management was clearly in breach of that understanding, and it was therefore just and equitable to wind up the company. Lord Wilberforce, who delivered the leading speech, stressed that the remedy conferred a wide discretionary jurisdiction on the court. He said: 'there has been a tendency to create categories or headings under which cases must be brought if the clause is to apply. This is wrong. Illustrations may be used, but general words should remain general and not be reduced to the sum of particular instances.'

The following are illustrations of the grounds which will support a petition under s 122(1)(g) of the 1986 Act.

(i) Substratum has failed

11.5 This is arguably the narrowest of the grounds for just and equitable winding-up. The petitioner will need to establish that the commercial object for which the company was formed has failed or has been fulfilled. In *Re German Date Coffee Co* (1882) the company was registered with the object of acquiring a German patent for manufacturing a coffee substitute from dates. The German patent was not granted but a Swedish one was. Notwithstanding that the company had built a factory at Hamburg and was doing a prosperous trade in the commodity, the Court of Appeal made a winding-up order on the basis that the whole substratum of the company was gone. Jessel MR stated that the minority shareholders could maintain that they 'did not enter into partnership on these terms . . . It was not a general partnership to make a substitute for coffee from dates, but to work a particular patent, and as that particular patent does not exist, and cannot now exist, they are entitled to say the company ought to be wound up.' The courts approach the issue on the basis that a member subscribes to a company on the understanding that it will engage in a particular business venture, so that if it fails to do this, the member is entitled to recover his investment (see also *Virdi v Abbey Leisure Ltd* (1990) (para **11.16**); and *Re Perfectair Holdings Ltd* (1990)).

11.6 This ground is now of much less importance especially in the light of s 31(1) of the CA 2006 which has reformed the law governing a company's objects clause. This provides that 'Unless a company's articles specifically restrict the objects of the company, its objects are unrestricted' (see further Chapter 12).

(ii) Fraud

11.7 Where a company is formed to perpetrate a fraud and winding up represents the best means for its shareholders for recovering money invested by them from its promoters, the court may grant a winding-up order on the just and equitable ground. In *Re Thomas Edward Brinsmead & Sons* (1897) three men who were named Brinsmead, and who were former employees of John Brinsmead & Sons, a renowned piano-manufacturing company, formed Thomas Brinsmead & Sons to make pianos which were to be passed off as manufactured by John Brinsmead & Sons. Following a fraudulent promotion the public had subscribed for shares worth some £35,000 in the new company. It was held to be just and equitable to wind up the company.

(iii) Deadlock

11.8 In practice it is rare for there to be total deadlock in the management of a company because the chair of a meeting will generally have a casting vote. However, where deadlock does occur, whether it be total or practical deadlock, the court may order the company to be wound up. In *Re Yenidje Tobacco Co Ltd* (1916), two tobacco manufacturers formed the company in order to merge their businesses. They were equal shareholders (with equal voting rights) and the only directors. Relations between the two became acrimonious and they refused to communicate with each other except through the company secretary. Although the company was enjoying substantial profitability the court ordered it to be wound up. Lord Cozens-Hardy MR, who took as his starting point the law of partnership, said that had this been a partnership where the relationship between the partners had degenerated into a state of animosity with no hope of reconciliation, the court would order a dissolution:

> All that is necessary is to satisfy the Court that it is impossible for the partners to place their confidence in each other which each has a right to expect, and that such impossibility has not been caused by the person seeking to take advantage of it.

There is a clear and obvious overlap between this ground and the next.

(iv) Justifiable loss of confidence in the company's management

11.9 The court may order a company to be wound up where there is a lack of confidence in the competence or probity of its management provided the company is, in essence, a quasi-partnership (see *Ebrahimi*, paras **11.3–11.4**). In *Loch v John Blackwood Ltd* (1924) the majority shareholder dominated the board of directors. He regarded the business as his own and, in order to induce the minority shareholders to sell their shares at an undervalue, refused to declare dividends. Further, general meetings were not called and accounts were not published. The Privy Council ordered the company to be wound up. Lord Shaw said:

> It is undoubtedly true that at the foundation of applications for winding-up, on the 'just and equitable' rule, there must lie a justifiable lack of confidence in the conduct and management of the company's affairs. But this lack of confidence must be grounded on conduct of the directors, not in regard to their private life or affairs, but in regard to the company's business. Furthermore the lack of confidence must spring not from dissatisfaction at being outvoted on the business affairs or on what is called the domestic policy of the company. On the other hand, wherever the lack of confidence is rested on a lack of probity in the conduct of the company's affairs then the former is justified by the latter, and it is under the statute just and equitable that the company be wound up.

(v) Exclusion from participation in a small private company where there was a relationship based on mutual confidence

11.10 Typically in this situation the action is brought by the petitioner on the basis that there was a fundamental understanding between the 'partners' to the effect that he would be permitted to participate in management and this has been broken. Unless the petitioner brought this state of affairs about through his own fault (see *Re Quiet Moments Ltd* (2013)), the court will generally make a winding-up order. The classic example here is *Ebrahimi v Westbourne Galleries* (1973) (paras **11.3-11.4**), in which Lord Wilberforce listed the typical elements in petitions brought under this ground:

(i) the basis of the business association was a personal relationship and mutual confidence (generally found where a pre-existing partnership has converted into a limited company);

(ii) an understanding that all or certain shareholders (excluding 'sleeping' partners) will participate in management;

(iii) a restriction on the transfer of members' interests preventing the petitioner leaving.

Where these elements are present, such companies are generally termed 'quasi-partnerships' so as to reflect the personal relationships between the protagonists within the company.

It is worth recalling that Lord Wilberforce, in noting that Ebrahimi's removal had been effected in accordance with the Companies Act, nevertheless stressed that the court was entitled to superimpose equitable constraints upon the exercise of rights set out in the articles of association or the Act. He went on to say that the words 'just and equitable':

> are a recognition of the fact that a limited company is more than a mere legal entity, with a personality in law of its own: that there is room in company law for recognition of the fact that behind it, or amongst it, there are individuals, with rights, expectations and obligations inter se *which are not necessarily submerged in the company structure . . .* The just and equitable' provision does not . . . entitle one party to disregard the obligation he assumes by entering the company, nor the court to dispense him from it. It does, as equity always does, enable the court to subject the exercise of legal rights to equitable considerations . . . which may make it unjust, or inequitable, to insist on legal rights, or to exercise them in a particular way.

This approach has coloured the jurisprudence on s 459 of the CA 1985, which is now restated in s 994 of the 2006 Act (see later), in determining unfairly prejudicial conduct: see, for example, *Re Noble & Sons (Clothing) Ltd* (1983) and the House of Lords' decision in *O'Neill v Phillips* (1999), considered later in this chapter.

11.11 Taking the typical elements just listed, Lord Wilberforce concluded that the just and equitable ground for winding-up will assist the petitioner if:

> he can point to, and prove, some special underlying obligation of his fellow member(s) in good faith, or confidence, that so long as the business continues he shall be entitled to management participation, an obligation so basic that, if broken, the conclusion must be that the association must be dissolved.

It should be noted that not every bona fide exercise of majority power will be subject to equitable constraints. The overriding factors are the three typical elements which were listed by Lord Wilberforce.

11.12 The decision in *Re A and BC Chewing Gum Ltd* (1975) is, arguably, a curious application of the *Ebrahimi* principles. By virtue of a shareholders' agreement the petitioner, a US public corporation which had provided one-third of the company's share capital, was entitled to appoint a director to the board but the majority shareholders refused to give effect to the proposed appointment. Applying Lord Wilberforce's approach, a winding-up order was made on the basis of the petitioner's exclusion from management in breach of the fundamental understanding from the outset that it would participate in management. This decision has been criticised on the basis that an injunction to enforce the shareholders' agreement was the more appropriate remedy and would have avoided the dire consequences of a winding-up order (see Womack (1975)). A more straightforward illustration of the application of *Ebrahimi* is the decision in *Re Zinotty Properties Ltd* (1984) in which the court considered that it was just and equitable to wind up the company despite the fact that it was in voluntary liquidation. The petitioner's allegation was based on breach of trust and confidence on the grounds that he had not been appointed as a director as he had expected; the company, a property business, had not been dissolved when a site development was completed, as he had assumed it would be, but rather interest-free unsecured loans had been made to other businesses in which he had no interest; and the company had not maintained proper accounts or called general meetings.

Extending the shadow of *Ebrahimi* beyond s 122

11.13 The question has arisen whether the principles promulgated by Lord Wilberforce extend beyond the statutory context of just and equitable winding-up. The issue arose in *Clemens v Clemens Bros Ltd* (1976). The claimant owned 45 per cent and her aunt, Miss Clemens, owned 55 per cent of the shares in the company. The articles of association contained a pre-emption clause and so the niece expected to gain total control of the company upon her aunt's departure. In the meantime she exerted negative control, having the power to block a special resolution. The board of directors, which was made up of the aunt and four non-shareholders, decided to increase the company's share capital by issuing new shares to the directors and to an employees' trust. The appropriate general meeting resolution was passed by virtue of the aunt's votes. The effect of this was to reduce the claimant's shareholding to below 25 per cent. Foster J, setting the resolutions aside and adopting the terminology of Lord Wilberforce, stated that the general voting rights of majority share-holders 'were subject . . . to equitable considerations . . . which may make it unjust . . . to exercise [them] in a particular way'. The judge concluded that:

> I do not doubt that Miss Clemens is in favour of the resolutions and knows and under-stands their purport and effect; nor do I doubt that she genuinely would like to see the other directors have shares in the company and to see a trust set up for long service em-ployees. But I cannot escape the conclusion that the resolutions have been framed so as to put into the hands of Miss Clemens and her fellow directors complete control of the com-pany and to deprive the plaintiff of her existing rights as a shareholder . . . [the resolutions were] specifically and carefully designed to ensure not only that the plaintiff can never get control of the company but to deprive her of what has been called her negative control.

Foster J's reasoning dovetails with that of the House of Lords' decision in *O'Neill v Phillips* (1999), considered later. The view expressed by Plowman J in *Bentley Stevens v Jones* (1974) to the effect that the *Ebrahimi* principles should be confined to their statu-tory context must now be doubted (for a critique of Foster J's reasoning, see *Sealy and Worthington's Text, Cases, & Materials in Company Law* (2016), pp 227–8).

The right to petition

11.14 Section 124(1) of the 1986 Act provides that an application to the court for a winding-up order may be made by a contributory. 'Contributory' is defined as every person liable to contribute to the assets of a company in the event of it being wound up, and the term also encompasses every present and past member (s 74(1) and s 79(1)). Section 250 provides that 'a person who is not a member of a company but to whom shares in the company have been transferred, or transmitted by operation of law, is to be regarded as a member of the company'. In *Re CMB Holdings Ltd* (2016) it was held that trustees in bankruptcy therefore had standing to present a winding-up petition of the bankrupt's company (and a s 994 petition, see later) and were to be regarded as registered members from the date the bankrupt's shares vested in them. This was so despite the fact that the shares, which had vested in them upon their appointment, had not been registered in their name for the six-month period as required by s 124(2)(b).

For a fully paid-up member to have standing he/she must show a tangible interest in the company by proving, on a balance of probabilities, that there will be a surplus divisible among the shareholders after payment of the company's debts, liabilities, and the expenses of the liquidation (*Re Rica Gold Washing Co* (1879), Jessel MR; and *Re Expanded Plugs Ltd* (1966)). More recently, however, a broader approach has been taken to the meaning of 'tangible interest'. In *Re Chesterfield Catering Co* (1977) Oliver J did not limit its meaning to the need to prove surplus assets but held that:

> In order to establish his locus standi to petition a fully paid shareholder must . . . show that he will, as a member of the company, achieve some advantage, or avoid or minimise

some disadvantage, which would accrue to him by virtue of his membership of the company. For instance, a member of a company might have a strong interest in terminating its life because he was engaged in a competing business or because he was engaged in litigation with the company . . .

By way of limited exception, Hoffmann J held in *Re Commercial and Industrial Insulations Ltd* (1986) that if the petitioner cannot prove his tangible interest because of the company's 'default in providing him with information to which as a member he is entitled' he will not be required to establish the existence of surplus assets.

Relationship with other remedies

11.15   Section 125(2) of the 1986 Act provides that the court will not grant a winding-up order if it is of the opinion 'both that some other remedy is available to the petitioners and that they are acting unreasonably in seeking to have the company wound up instead of pursuing that other remedy'. The fact that a wider range of relief is available under s 994 of the CA 2006 will not, of itself, make it unreasonable to seek a winding-up order. In *Re Copeland & Craddock Ltd* (1997), Dillon LJ commented that:

> *If it is reasonable for the petitioner to pursue the petition for the purposes of obtaining an order under s 459 [now s 994]—that he be put in control of the company by the opposing shareholders being ordered to sell their shares to him—I do not feel that it is right, at any rate at this juncture, to hold that it must inevitably be unreasonable for him to ask in the alternative that the company be wound up with the consequence that, on a sale of its business as a going concern in the open market, the petitioner will have an opportunity to bid for it.*

11.16   However, in general the received wisdom is that the winding-up remedy should be viewed as a matter of last resort and that the availability of alternative relief such as that under s 994 will normally result in the winding-up petition being struck out (*Re a Company (No 004415 of 1996)* (1997); *Re Woven Rugs Ltd* (2008)). This is clearly the case where the petitioner has an appropriate alternative remedy available to him. For example, the articles of association may lay down a procedure whereby a shareholder who is dissatisfied with the way in which the company is being managed can sell his shares at a fair price and without discount. Typically in such a case the court will strike out the petition on the basis that the petitioner is acting unreasonably in seeking a winding-up order. In *Re a Company (No 002567 of 1982)* (1983), which involved a breakdown of confidence, Vinelott J held that since the petitioner had indicated from the start that he would be prepared to sell his shares if a fair price was offered, and having encouraged the respondents to continue managing the company in the expectation that a fair valuation procedure would be agreed, and having been offered a price for his shares which was negotiated in accordance with the agreed procedure which provided for a valuation by an independent expert without discount to reflect his minority shareholding, he could not now have the company wound up (see also, *Maresca v Brookfield Development & Construction Ltd* (2013)). On the other hand, in *Virdi v Abbey Leisure Ltd* (1990) the company had been formed for a single venture, that of acquiring and running a particular nightclub, the Pavilion. The controlling shareholders having sold the Pavilion intended to reinvest the proceeds in another club. A winding-up petition was brought by V who held 40 per cent of the shares. The company's articles contained a provision whereby a member wishing to sell his shares was required to offer them to other members. The articles also laid down that the valuation of such shares would be carried out by an accountant. The Court of Appeal held that V was not acting unreasonably in refusing to sell his shares pursuant to the articles of association. An accountant valuing V's shares might apply a discount to reflect his minority holding whereas in a winding-up the liquidator would be in a better position to ensure that the price paid to V was similar to that paid to another shareholder for a similar stake. Balcombe LJ stressed that the company's assets consisted almost entirely of cash which made it unreasonable for V to accept the risk of his interest being discounted. It is noteworthy that in *Hawkes v Cuddy (No 2)* (2009), Stanley Burnton LJ (delivering the principal judgment of the Court of Appeal), having reviewed the relevant case law on the point, reached the conclusion that facts which were sufficient to justify a winding-up on the just and equitable ground were not necessarily sufficient to give the court jurisdiction to award relief under the unfair prejudice provision because the two jurisdictions were parallel but not coterminous and a winding-up could be ordered under s 122(1)(g) where no unfair conduct was alleged. Placing particular reliance on Lord Hoffmann's views expressed in *O'Neill v Phillips* (1999), to similar effect, the judge stated:

> Deadlock and the inability of a company to conduct its business as initially contemplated when the parties trusted and had confidence in each other may be inherent in the breakdown of that trust and confidence, but in my judgment do not without more satisfy the requirements of ss 994 and 996.

Stanley Burnton LJ did, however, acknowledge that in many cases one party will be able to point to unfairness in the other party's reaction to the deadlock.

Relevance of petitioner's own conduct

11.17 As has been seen, a failure to act in accordance with quasi-partnership duties and understandings may justify the making of a winding-up order. But if the petitioner, by his own conduct, has brought about the breakdown, his conduct will be a relevant factor when the court determines whether or not to grant the application. In *Ebrahimi*, Lord Cross (with whom Lord Salmon agreed) said: 'A petitioner who relies on the "just and equitable" clause must come to court with clean hands, and if the breakdown in confidence between him and the other parties to the dispute appears to have been due to his misconduct he cannot insist on the company being wound up if they wish it to continue.' However, there is authority which suggests that if the petitioner is substantially at fault for the breakdown in relations with his co-venturer he may be denied relief under s 994 yet, paradoxically, succeed in a petition for just and equitable winding-up. In *Re Noble & Sons (Clothing) Ltd* (1983) Nourse J held that the circumstances of the case justified a winding-up order on the basis of a breakdown in mutual confidence between the company's two founding members (equal shareholders) but not relief under the unfair prejudice provision. The petitioner by his lack of interest in the management of the business had brought about his own exclusion from it by the other member (see also *Badyal v Badyal* (2018), where the court agreed with the respondents' argument that the petitioner's removal from the board was justified given that he had assisted his son to establish a rival business, had provided it with funds, and had solicited company employees).

Unfairly prejudicial conduct: CA 2006, Part 30 (ss 994–996)

Introduction

11.18 A minority shareholder who feels aggrieved by virtue of unfairly prejudicial conduct on the part of the majority has a powerful avenue for redress in the form of a petition brought under s 994(1). This provides that:

> A member of a company may apply to the court by petition for an order . . . on the ground
>
> (a) that the company's affairs are being or have been conducted in a manner which is unfairly prejudicial to the interests of its members generally or of some part of its members (including at least himself), or
>
> (b) that any actual or proposed act or omission of the company (including an act or omission on its behalf) is or would be so prejudicial.

11.19 To appreciate the breadth of the modern unfair prejudice remedy it is useful to consider briefly its antecedents and to outline the role which its architects had in mind when framing the remedy well over 50 years ago. The genesis of the provision can be traced to the Cohen Committee, *Report of The Committee on Company Law Amendment* (Cmnd 6659, 1945) the terms of reference of which encompassed shareholder remedies. The Committee, which took the rule in *Foss v Harbottle* (1843) as the background for its deliberations, found that shareholders frequently considered themselves impotent when seeking to institute an action challenging the conduct of the majority. The only real means of outflanking the rule was to petition the court for a winding-up order. Yet, as far as the petitioner was concerned, the deterrent value of this course of action was inherent in its very nature for, '[i]n many cases . . . the winding up of the company will not benefit the minority shareholders, since the break-up value of the assets may be small, or the only available purchaser may be that very majority whose oppression has driven the minority to seek redress'. The Committee therefore went on to recommend that the court should be given unfettered discretion to impose upon the parties to a dispute whatever settlement it considers just and equitable. This was translated into the so-called 'oppression' remedy contained in s 210 of the Companies Act 1948. It provided a discretionary remedy but which, by virtue of its drafting, was expressly stated to be only available where the facts of the case justified a winding-up order.

11.20 However, due to the inadequacies of its drafting and the restrictive approach adopted by the judges towards its interpretation, only two cases were successfully brought under s 210 in its 32-year history (*SCWS Ltd v Meyer* (1959) and *Re HR Harmer* (1959)). The difficulty underlying s 210 was that the term 'oppression' was very narrowly construed. For example, in *SCWS Ltd v Meyer* (1959) Lord Simonds stated that it was restricted to conduct on the part of the majority which was 'burdensome, harsh and wrongful'. This was compounded by the view expressed in *Re HR Harmer Ltd* (1959) that the conduct in question had to be of a continuous nature. Unfairness was, of itself, therefore insufficient to found a claim under the oppression remedy. Consequently, petitions brought on the grounds of directors awarding themselves excessive remuneration (*Re Jermyn Street Turkish Baths Ltd* (1971)) and mismanagement (*Re Five Minute Car Wash Service Ltd* (1966)) were unsuccessful.

11.21 Given the failure of the section to provide adequate relief the Jenkins Committee (*Report of the Company Law Committee* (Cmnd 1749, 1962)), which reviewed the operation of the remedy, identified a number of defects which it felt should be addressed if it was 'to afford effective protection to minorities in circumstances such as those with which it is intended to deal' (para 201). The Committee felt that the section 'must extend to cases in which the acts complained of fall short of actual illegality' (para 203). It therefore recommended its amendment to cover complaints that the affairs of the company were being conducted in a manner *unfairly prejudicial to the interests of the petitioner* (at para 204, emphasis added). Somewhat belatedly, this was put into effect by the Companies Act 1980, s 75; it was re-enacted in Part XVII of the Companies Act 1985, s 459 (as amended by the Companies Act 1989); and now it now appears in restructured form in s 994 of the Companies Act 2006.

11.22 An initial problem, resulting from judicial timidity in interpreting the provision as originally drafted, was that s 75 and later, s 459, stated that a petition could only be brought where the company's affairs were being conducted in a manner which is unfairly prejudicial to the interests of 'some part' of the members. This was construed to mean that a petitioner had to show discrimination. Thus in *Re Carrington Viyella plc* (1983) it was held that a breach of directors' duties could not form the basis of a s 459 petition since this, *ipso facto*, affects all shareholders; and in *Re a Company (No 00370 of 1987)* (1988) Harman J held that the board's failure to declare a dividend was not discriminatory between shareholders given that all members were affected equally. Section 459 was therefore amended by the Companies Act 1989 which, by inserting the words 'of its members generally', reversed the requirement of discrimination. This wording has been retained by the 2006 Act (see para **11.18**). Since s 994 restates s 459 of the CA 1985 without any substantive changes, the jurisprudence (and academic literature) surrounding the remedy continues to be relevant.

The constituent elements of CA 2006, s 994

(i) Conduct of the company's affairs

11.23 Section 994(1) states that a petitioner must establish unfairly prejudicial conduct arising from some corporate act or omission, including any act or omission on the company's behalf. Unlike the old oppression remedy it is not necessary to show a continuing course of conduct, or indeed, unfairly prejudicial conduct subsisting at the date of the petition. An isolated act or omission may, depending upon the circumstances of the particular case, be sufficient (*Re Norvabron Pty Ltd (No 2)* (1987)). An interesting case is *Lloyd v Casey* (2001) because the court permitted the petitioner to include allegations relating to conduct which took place before he became a registered shareholder in the company on the basis that the section states that 'the company's affairs are being or *have been conducted in an unfairly prejudicial manner*'. It therefore follows that where, as in *Odutola v Hart* (2018), the behaviour complained about has yet to take place, it cannot be said to be acts of the company.

11.24 The meaning of 'conduct of the company's affairs' was considered in *Re Legal Costs Negotiators Ltd* (1999). The company had been incorporated by four individuals who were equal shareholders; they were also its directors and employees. Relations broke down with the fourth individual and he was dismissed as an employee and he resigned from the board just before it was resolved to remove him. However, he remained as a shareholder and refused to sell his shares to the other three. The majority petitioned under s 459 seeking an order that he should transfer his shares to them. The Court of Appeal rejected the petition on the basis that as majority shareholders they could prevent any prejudice being inflicted by him on the company. Simply remaining as a shareholder was not conduct relating to the company's affairs. The court stressed that the conduct complained of must: relate to the affairs of the company; be acts done by the company, i.e. by those authorised to act as its organs; and it should not be referable to the conduct of an individual shareholder acting in his private capacity. In *Re Coroin Ltd, McKillen v Misland (Cyprus) Investments Ltd* (2012), David Richards J emphasised that the complaint must centre on how the affairs of the company have been managed so that personal disputes *per se* between shareholders generally fall outside the scope of s 994:

> [Section 994] is not directed to the activities of shareholders amongst themselves, unless those activities translate into acts or omissions of the company or the conduct of its affairs. Relations between shareholders inter se are adequately governed by the law of contract and tort, including where appropriate the ability to enforce personal rights conferred by a company's articles of association.

Yet, set against the strict distinction drawn by David Richards J, is the wide approach taken in *Re Home & Office Fire Extinguishers Ltd* (2012) towards 'conduct of a company's affairs' which suggests that there can be an overlap between the requirement and a personal dispute between the parties if it is such as to make it impossible for them to continue working together as directors/shareholders. The facts are particularly colourful. Two brothers, S and

G, were directors and equal shareholders in the company. S attacked G with a hammer at the company's premises following G's refusal to make a salary advance. G had refused because the company was in a poor financial state. S was charged with grievous bodily harm but was acquitted. The judge held that S's conduct related to the affairs of the company because it was a breach of the implied understanding that he and G would act properly and in good faith towards each other. It was a single event which made it impossible for them to continue their association as directors/shareholders in the company. He therefore ordered S to sell his shares to G (see paras **11.68-11.73**). The question of what constitutes the company's affairs for the purposes of s 994(1) was returned to by the Court of Appeal in *Re Charterbridge Capital Ltd* (2015) where the Chancellor of the High Court, Sir Terence Etherton, noted that:

> The expression 'the company's affairs' . . . is of wide ambit and plainly covers all matters decided by the board of directors. Equally plainly, it does not extend to matters which are neither effected by the company nor on its behalf but, for example, concern activities of shareholders solely in that personal capacity and as between themselves. Accordingly, actions or omissions in compliance or contravention of the articles of association of a company may or may not constitute the conduct of the company's affairs within section 994(1) depending on the precise facts . . .
>
> A member of a company will not normally be entitled to complain that the conduct of the company's affairs is unfair if it is consistent with the agreement between the shareholders as to the way in which those affairs would be conducted as reflected in the articles of association and any related agreements between the shareholders. . . .

The Court of Appeal held that the amendment of a company's articles of association to permit the shares of a minority shareholder to be compulsorily acquired under a takeover offer was consistent with the terms of a shareholder's agreement and did not involve any unfairly prejudicial conduct. The shareholders' agreement had provided that its terms prevailed over any inconsistent provision in the articles of association.

11.25 A further question that arises is whether, notwithstanding the *Salomon* doctrine, the actions of a parent company can be regarded as falling within its subsidiary company's affairs. In *Nicholas v Soundcraft Electronics Ltd* (1993), the Court of Appeal held that the failure of a parent company (Electronics) to pay debts due to its subsidiary (in which the petitioner was a minority shareholder) constituted acts done in the conduct of the affairs of the company. Fox LJ said:

> It seems to me that Electronics, when it withheld payments from the [subsidiary] company, was doing so as part of the general control of the financial affairs of the company. It exercised that general control by deciding how much the company should receive (by withholding sums due to the company) and restricting the company's ability to spend money (by the signature requirements on cheques drawn by the company). In my view Electronics, when it withheld from the company payments which were due to the company, was conducting the affairs of the company.

11.26 Conversely, in *Re City Branch Group Ltd, Gross v Rackind* (2005), the issue was whether conduct within a subsidiary could be regarded as falling within the affairs of the holding company. Judge Weeks, citing *Nicholas v Soundcraft Electronics Ltd*, took the view that 'in the right circumstances acts in the conduct of a subsidiary's affairs can also be acts in the conduct of the holding company's affairs'. He could 'see no logical reason for protecting shareholders of a trading company by s 459 [s 994] but not shareholders in a holding company'. The facts were that the shares in the holding company, Citybranch Group Ltd, were held in equal shares by the Gross and Rackind families. The holding company had been incorporated in 2001 in order to acquire two companies, Citybranch Ltd and Blaneland Ltd. The shares in these companies had been held by two families. The relationship between the families broke down and Mr Rackind (R), a director and shareholder of the holding company, decided to wind it up. The Gross family petitioned under s 994 on the basis that R was in breach of fiduciary duty to Blaneland Ltd and had misappropriated funds belonging to Citybranch Ltd. They argued that R's conduct with respect to the subsidiaries amounted to conduct in relation to the affairs of the parent company. Sir Martin Nourse, who delivered the only reasoned judgment of the Court of Appeal, endorsed the views of the trial judge that conduct taking place in relation to a subsidiary could fall within the affairs of the holding company. He agreed that the decision in *Nicholas* could support such a conclusion on the basis that it is in line with the views expressed by Phillimore J in *R v Board of Trade, ex p St Martins Preserving Co Ltd* (1965):

> The observations of Phillimore J demonstrate that the expression 'the affairs of the company' is one of the widest import which can include the affairs of a subsidiary. Equally, I would hold that the affairs of a subsidiary can also be the affairs of its holding company, especially where, as here, the directors of the holding company, which necessarily controls the affairs of the subsidiary, also represent a majority of the directors of the subsidiary. (In the case of Blaneland they are identical.)

(See also *Brown v Bray and Sharp* (2019).)

11.27 Although there are first instance decisions (not considered by Sir Martin Nourse) which take a contrary view (see, for example, *Re Leeds United Holdings plc* (1996) and *Reiner v Gershinson* (2004)), the Court of Appeal's approach is in line with the flexibility being advocated in relation to corporate conduct in other decisions. Thus, it has been held that where a petitioner withdraws from the management of the company in breach of an undertaking given by him to his co-shareholder/director, while not strictly speaking an act of the company, did amount to him breaching an agreement 'as to the conduct of the company's affairs . . . [and] that, as such, was an act of the company or conduct of the company's affairs' (*Re Phoneer Ltd* (2002), Roger Kaye QC sitting as a deputy judge in the High Court). However, as noted by David Richards J in *Re Coroin Ltd* (2012) (para **11.24**), a strict line is drawn where the conduct in question is that of a shareholder or director in his private capacity (though note the fine distinction drawn in *Re Home & Office Fire Extinguishers Ltd* (2012) (para **11.24**)). The action of the board of directors is clearly conduct of the company, but disputes between shareholders relating to dealings with their shares is not (*Re Unisoft Group Ltd (No 3)* (1994); and *Re Legal Costs Negotiators Ltd* (see para **11.24**)). On the other hand, a special resolution to amend the articles to exclude pre-emption rights in a company could amount to unfairly prejudicial conduct (*Re Smiths of Smithfield Ltd* (2003)).

11.28 If the reasoning in *Re City Branch Group Ltd* is accepted as correct, some questions remain unanswered. For example, must the subsidiary company be wholly owned in order for its affairs to fall within those of the parent company? Must the subsidiary company's directors also be directors of the parent company? Deploying s 994 to address problems arising within corporate groups will often involve a difficult choice between the consequences of preserving the separate legal identity of group companies and acceding to the call for enhanced protection of (minority) shareholders (see Goddard and Hirt (2005)).

The decision of Sales J in *Oak Investment Partners XII, Limited Partnership v Boughtwood* (2009), also offers interesting insights into the determination of what constitutes the carrying on of the company's affairs. Adopting a purposive interpretation of s 994(1), the judge stressed that the provision was concerned with the practical reality which obtained on the ground in relation to the conduct of a company's affairs, 'and there is no sound reason to exclude the possibility that what someone does in exercising or purporting to exercise managerial powers as a director or senior employee should not in principle qualify as conduct of the affairs of a company for the purposes of that provision'. The judge took the view that such an interpretation accorded with the broad equitable jurisdiction which s 994 was intended to confer on the court, 'which was required to take account of all the myriad different ways in which the affairs of a company might be carried on'. Sales J concluded the point by noting that the precise distribution of management decision-making authority in any particular company may be a matter of chance. In some companies, the board may take a larger role in routine management decisions than in others, where greater scope is left to the directors or managers acting alone. He questioned why the application of s 994 should turn upon such fortuitous matters: 'the jurisdiction under that provision is above all a jurisdiction concerned with substance rather than form'. Accordingly, the conduct of a significant shareholder or director who improperly asserts control over the management of the affairs of the company may be acting in an unfairly prejudicial manner. This conduct need not be as a director. Acting as a senior manager may, therefore, attract relief under the provision. In such situations the court may order the shareholder who has caused the unfair prejudice to sell his shares to the petitioner.

(See also *F&C Alternative Investments (Holdings) Ltd v Barthelemy* (2011).)

(ii) Interests qua member

11.29 The petitioner must prove that his interests qua member have been unfairly prejudiced as a result of conduct on the part of the company. These requirements are interdependent so that, for example, the determination of prejudice cannot be taken in isolation from the question of what a member's interests are and this, in turn, will set the parameters for deciding the critical issue of whether or not a member's interests have been *unfairly* prejudiced. The point was succinctly made by Peter Gibson J in *Re a Company (No 005685 of 1988), ex p Schwarcz (No 2)* (1989) that the conduct complained of must be: 'both prejudicial (in the sense of causing prejudice or harm) to the relevant interests and also unfairly so: conduct may be unfair without being prejudicial or prejudicial without being unfair and in neither case would the section be satisfied' (see also *Rock Nominees Ltd v RCO (Holdings) plc* (2004); and *Sikorski v Sikorski* (2012)). We now turn to consider each of these requirements in turn.

11.30 Early case law on s 994 took a narrow view of the term 'interests' by placing emphasis on the need to show that the interests of the petitioner qua member had been unfairly prejudiced. More recent case law, however, points to a wider view being taken towards the scope of a member's interests and the House of Lords in *O'Neill v Phillips* (1999) stressed that the qua member requirement should not be 'too narrowly or technically construed'. An unusual illustration of this approach is afforded by *Gamblestaden Fastigheter AB v Baltic Partner Ltd* (2007), where a member had provided a loan to the company in order to inject working capital. The issue was whether the member's petition should be struck out in circumstances where the company was insolvent and the relief sought (payment of compensation by the directors to the company) would confer no financial benefit on the petitioner qua member. The Privy Council took the view that 'interests' may extend to cover those of a member qua creditor where, in the circumstances, the distinction becomes artificial. A full explanation of the qua member requirement was provided by Hoffmann J (as he then was) in *Re a Company (No 00477 of 1986)* (1986):

> In principle I accept [the] proposition [that the section must be limited to conduct which is unfairly prejudicial to the interest of the members as members. It cannot extend to conduct which is prejudicial to other interests of persons who happen to be members] . . . but its application must take into account that the interests of a member are not necessarily limited to his strict legal rights under the constitution of the company. The use of the word 'unfairly' in section 459 [of the 1985 Act, now s 994], like the use of the words just and equitable' in [s 122(1)(g)], enables the court to have regard to wider equitable considerations . . . Thus in the case of a managing director of a large public company who is also the owner of a small holding in the company's shares, it is easy to see the distinction between his interests as a managing director employed under a service contract and his interests as a member. In the case of a small private company in which two or three members have invested their capital by subscribing for shares on the footing that dividends are unlikely but that each will earn his living by working for the company as a director, the distinction may be more elusive. The member's interests as a member who has ventured his capital in the company's business may include a legitimate expectation that he will continue to be employed as a director and his dismissal from that office and exclusion from the management of the company may therefore be unfairly prejudicial to his interests as a member.

(See also *Re Phoenix Contracts (Leicester) Ltd* (2010); *Re Woven Rugs Ltd* (2010); and *Wootliff v Rushton-Turner* (2018), where the judge held that in the case of a quasi-partnership, exclusion from management and breach of employment rights could be grounds for unfair prejudice.)

11.31 One particular feature of the wording of the provision is that the use of the term 'interests' is designed to be expansive in effect, thereby effectively avoiding the straitjacket which terminology based on the notion of legal rights would impose on the scope of the provision. This is manifest in Peter Gibson J's judgment in *Re Sam Weller & Sons Ltd* (1990) in which the judge observed that: '[t]he word "interests" is wider than a term such as "rights", and its presence as part of the test . . . to my mind suggests that Parliament recognised that members may have different interests, even if their rights as members are the same'.

11.32 Obviously, the interests of a member can be discerned by reference to the company's constitution which, by virtue of s 17, includes the articles of association together with any resolutions of the company and any shareholders' agreements. It has also been held that a member will have an interest in the value of his or her shares. Thus, in *Re Bovey Hotel Ventures Ltd* (1981) Slade J formulated the following test for determining the issue:

> Without prejudice to the generality of the wording of the section, which may cover many other situations, a member of a company will be able to bring himself within the section if he can show that the value of his shareholding in the company has been seriously jeopardised by reason of a course of conduct on the part of those persons who have had de facto control of the company, which has been unfair to the member concerned.

(See also *Re City Branch Group Ltd* (2005).)

Legitimate expectations

11.33 An important question arising from the case law surrounding the provision is the extent to which the courts will recognise a member's so-called legitimate expectations as falling within interests which may be unfairly prejudiced. In this regard it will be recalled that in *Ebrahimi* Lord Wilberforce observed that behind the corporate veil there are individuals with 'rights, expectations and obligations *inter se* which are not necessarily submerged in the company structure' (see para **11.10**). In small private companies it is often unrealistic to sever the various roles played by a petitioner for in such companies, termed quasi-partnerships, a petitioner will not only be a shareholder but frequently a director and an employee of the business as well. However, and as has been seen, in *Ebrahimi* Lord Wilberforce stressed that although in most companies the member's rights under the articles of association and the Companies Act provide an exhaustive statement of his interests, there are three typical cases in which equitable considerations may be superimposed upon the strict legal rights of members. It will be recalled that the three categories Lord Wilberforce listed were as follows:

    (i)   the basis of the business association was a personal relationship and mutual confidence (generally found where a pre-existing partnership has converted into a limited company);

     (ii) an understanding that all or certain shareholders (excluding 'sleeping' partners) will participate in management;

     (iii) a restriction on the transfer of members' interests preventing the petitioner leaving.

11.34 In examining the scope of shareholders' obligations in these three categories the court will look beyond the articles of the particular company. For example, even if the parties have not expressly agreed that the petitioner will participate in the management of the company, the court may imply such an undertaking from the conduct of the parties. In *Re Fildes Bros Ltd* (1970) Megarry J stated that:

> It cannot be just and equitable to allow one party to come to the court and require the court to make an order which disregards his contractual obligations. The same, I think, must apply to a settled and accepted course of conduct between the parties, whether or not cast into the mould of a contract.

11.35 Although Lord Wilberforce's reasoning in *Ebrahimi* was based on the just and equitable winding-up remedy, nevertheless it has fundamentally shaped the development of the s 994 jurisprudence which has grown up around small owner-managed companies. In *Re a Company (No 4377 of 1986)* (1986) Hoffmann J considered that the language of s 994 facilitated the exercise by the court of its residual equitable jurisdiction. He observed that the interests of a member are not necessarily limited to the strict legal rights conferred by the constitution of a company. Accordingly, a member's interests can encompass the *legitimate expectation* that he will continue to participate in management as a director and his dismissal from that office and consequent exclusion from the company's management may be unfairly prejudicial to his interests as a member. The rationale for this departure from the rigidity of the capacity-based approach which had so thwarted the development of the old oppression remedy was explained by Lord Grantchester QC in *Re a Company (No 004475 of 1982)* (1983) in the following terms:

> It is obvious that in a small private company it is legalistic to segregate the separate capacities of the same individual as shareholder, director or employee. His dismissal from the board or from employment by the company will inevitably affect the real value of his interest in the company expressed by his shareholding.

In *Re a Company (No 003160 of 1986)* (1986), Hoffmann J, again echoing Lord Wilberforce's reasoning, said that the court's jurisdiction under s 994 enables it 'to protect not only the rights of members under the constitution of the company but also the "rights, expectations and obligations" of the individual shareholders *inter se*. In the typical case of the corporate quasi-partnership, these will include the expectations that the member will be able to participate in the management of the company.'

11.36 However, the House of Lords in *O'Neill v Phillips* (1999) expressed doubt over whether the use of the term 'legitimate expectations' was entirely appropriate. The term had been imported from the realms of public law as a label for the 'correlative right' not to have a power conferred by the articles exercised in a manner unfairly prejudicial to a particular member. Lord Hoffmann said its adoption was probably a mistake and that it is more accurate to speak of *equitable restraints* which may make it unfair for a party to exercise rights under the articles. He concluded that the notion of 'legitimate expectation' is 'a consequence, not a cause, of the equitable restraint . . . [i]t should not be allowed to lead a life of its own, capable of giving rise to equitable restraints in circumstances to which the traditional equitable principles have no application'.

The limits of equitable restraints

11.37   In *Ebrahimi* Lord Wilberforce recognised that where, in a commercial enterprise, the relationship between the members is governed by comprehensively drafted articles of association—to this, shareholder agreements and service contracts should be added (*Re Ringtower Holding plc* (1988))—then the superimposition of equitable considerations would require 'something more'. It follows that the scope for the courts to find legitimate expectations which go beyond strict contractual rights under the company's constitution, yet which nevertheless fall within the protection of s 994, is subject to strict limitation. In *Re a Company (No 004377 of 1986)* (1987) the majority, including the petitioner, voted for a special resolution to amend the company's articles so as to provide that a member, on ceasing to be an employee or director of the company, would be required to transfer his or her shares to the company. To remedy a situation of management deadlock, the petitioner was dismissed as director and was offered £900 per share. When he declined this offer his shares were valued by the company's auditors in accordance with the pre-emption clauses. He petitioned the court under s 459 (now s 994) to restrain the compulsory acquisition of his shares, arguing that he had a legitimate expectation that he would continue to participate in the management of the company which, he argued, was in essence a quasi-partnership. Hoffmann J held that there could be no expectation on the part of the petitioner that should relations break down the article would not be followed, '[t]o hold to the contrary would not be to "superimpose equitable considerations" on his rights under the articles but to relieve him from the bargain he made'.

(See further the comments of Hildyard J in *Re LCM Wealth Management Ltd* (2013).)

11.38   It therefore seems that in applying equitable restraints to the exercise of a power by the majority, the courts will seek to strike a balance between recognising the supremacy of a company's constitution on the one hand (i.e. the statutory contract, see Chapter 8), and a member's extraneous expectations on the other. At its crux the issue lies with the proper determination of at which point a member's interests or expectations are totally subsumed in the company's constitution. It is not possible to glean a clear answer to this question from Hoffmann J's judgment but it can be argued that if a petitioner expressly consents to a particular provision in the articles, as by voting for it, it will be impossible for him to avoid the consequences which flow from his consent. Further guidance on the limits of 'equitable restraints' has emerged in more recent case law. For example, the point was made in *Brett v Migration Solutions Holdings Ltd* (2016) that the scope for the application of 'equitable considerations' is severely limited where the parties have entered into their relationship through arms' length commercial negotiations.

11.39 The scope for finding expectations which are supplementary to a member's strict legal rights is obviously greater in small quasi-partnership types of private limited companies where joint venturers enter into business on the basis of certain fundamental understandings about management participation, than it is in public limited companies (see *Strahan v Wilcock* (2006) CA). The point received emphasis in *Re Coroin Ltd* (2012) (para **11.24**), where David Richards J observed:

> . . . *Equitable considerations, affecting the manner in which legal rights can be exercised, will arise only in those cases where there exist considerations of a personal character between the shareholders which makes it unjust or inequitable to insist on legal rights or to exercise them in a particular way. Typically that will be in the case of a company formed by a small number of individuals on the basis of participation by all or some of them in the management of the company.*

(See also the observations of Mann J in *Re Migration Solutions Holdings Ltd* (2016). It is noteworthy that in *Re Edwardian Group Ltd; Estera Trust (Jersey) Ltd v Singh* (2018) it was held that even if the company could be described as a quasi-partnership when it was first formed, it was superseded by a subsequent shareholders' agreement—the point is that contract overrides equitable considerations, cf *Sudicka v Morgan* (2019).)

In *Re Blue Arrow plc* (1987) the petitioner complained that her removal from the office of permanent non-executive president of the company constituted unfairly prejudicial conduct in that she had the legitimate expectation of being consulted on company policy on a continuing basis. Vinelott J, however, emphatically disagreed with this line of argument:

> *it must be borne in mind that this is a public company, a listed company, and a large one, and that the constitution was adopted at the time when the company was first floated on the Unlisted Securities Market. Outside investors were entitled to assume that the whole of the constitution was contained in the articles, read, of course, together with the Companies Acts. There is in these circumstances no room for any legitimate expectation founded on some agreement or arrangement made between the directors and kept up their sleeves and not disclosed to those placing the shares with the public . . .*

In *Re Posgate & Denby (Agencies) Ltd* (1987) Vinelott J stated, in a similar vein, that s 994 'enables the court to give full effect to the terms and understandings on which the members of the company became associated but not to rewrite them'.

11.40 That the scope for applying equitable restraints is significantly restricted in listed public companies was again emphasised by the Court of Appeal in *Re Saul D Harrison & Sons plc* (1995). The petitioner complained that the prospects for the company's business had for a number of years been so poor that any reasonable board would have put it into voluntary liquidation and distributed its considerable assets to the shareholders. The essence of the petition was that the directors, in allowing the company to continue trading, dissipated its assets so as to preserve their inflated salaries and perquisites. The Court of Appeal recognised that the personal relationship between a petitioner and the controlling members may be such that a legitimate expectation may be inferred which will effectively estop the exercise of a legal power by the majority. However, Hoffmann LJ stressed that in the absence of 'something more', there can be no basis for finding a legitimate expectation which goes beyond the articles. On the facts of the case, it was found that the petitioner's rights were exhaustively laid down in the articles of association. Consequently, her legitimate expectations did not extend beyond the expectation that the board would manage the company in accordance with their fiduciary duties, the Companies Act, and the articles.

11.41   It is apparent from the Court of Appeal's approach that the judges are anxious to temper the ambit of the concept of legitimate expectations lest it drive a coach and horses through the contractual undertakings of members as contained in the articles of association. In Hoffmann LJ's analysis, if the conduct complained of is in accordance with the company's constitution it cannot, as a general rule, be viewed as unfair since 'there is no basis for a legitimate expectation that the board and the company . . . will not exercise whatever powers they are given by the articles of association'. The rationale underlying this concern was previously expressed by Hoffmann J in *Re a Company (No 007623 of 1986)* (1987) in which he observed that while s 459 was a long-overdue reform 'the very width of the jurisdiction means that unless carefully controlled it can become a means of oppression' (see also *Re a Company (No 004377 of 1986)* (1987)). It is noteworthy that the shares in *Saul D Harrison* were inherited by the petitioner. In such a situation, the scope for finding legitimate expectations is severely limited. For example, in *Jackman v Jackets Enterprises Ltd* (1977) the petitioner's claim that her exclusion from participating in the company's management constituted oppression was dismissed. The court, in finding no such expectation on her part, had regard to the fact that she had acquired her shares by way of gift.

11.42   However, and as has been seen, there are two established categories of cases where the courts are prepared to look beyond a company's constitution on the basis that it may not necessarily be conclusive on the question of shareholder expectations: first, where the petitioner can demonstrate that a personal relationship exists with the controlling members of the company which has given rise to a legitimate expectation that a constitutional power will not be exercised; and, second, where a power contained in the articles is exercised for an improper purpose. In these situations it will be just and equitable for the court to grant a remedy.

(iii) Unfair prejudice

11.43   The notion of unfairness was considered by the Jenkins Committee to be 'a visible departure from the standards of fair dealing and a violation of the conditions of fair play on which every shareholder who entrusts his money to a company is entitled to rely' (at para 204—adopting the view expressed by Lord Cooper in *Elder v Elder & Watson Ltd* (1952)). With respect to s 994, the courts have been striving to find an appropriate definition and set of guidelines for the determination of when majority conduct will be considered 'unfairly prejudicial' to the interests of the minority. In *Re Coroin Ltd* (2012), David Richards J took the opportunity to provide further guidance on the determination of 'prejudice':

> Prejudice will certainly encompass damage to the financial position of a member. The prejudice may be damage to the value of his shares but may also extend to other financial damage which in the circumstances of the case is bound up with his position as a member. So, for example, removal from participation in the management of a company and the resulting loss of income or profits from the company in the form of remuneration will constitute prejudice in those cases where the members have rights recognised in equity if not at law, to participate in that way. Similarly, damage to the financial position of a member in relation to a debt due to him from the company can in the appropriate circumstances amount to prejudice. The prejudice must be to the petitioner in his capacity as a member but this is not to be strictly confined to damage to the value of his shareholding. Moreover, prejudice need not be financial in character. A disregard of the rights of a member as such, without any financial consequences, may amount to prejudice falling within the section.

Initial judicial thinking tended towards objective assessment as the governing criterion but, as is apparent from recent judicial pronouncements, doubt has been cast on the correctness of this approach.

An objective concept?

11.44 Although s 994 does not define unfairly prejudicial conduct, early case law took the view that unfair prejudice should be objectively determined. In *Re Bovey Hotel Ventures Ltd* (1981) Slade J formulated the test in the following terms:

> The test of unfairness must, I think, be an objective, not a subjective, one. . . . the test, I think, is whether a reasonable bystander observing the consequences of their conduct, would regard it as having unfairly prejudiced the petitioner's interests.

Prentice (1988), citing this passage, has noted that: '[t]he focal point of the court's enquiry in determining whether conduct has been unfairly prejudicial is its impact and not its nature'. This can be seen in *Re RA Noble & Sons (Clothing) Ltd* (1983) (para **11.17**). Nourse J, applying the objective test, held that a reasonable man might well have thought that the conduct complained of was prejudicial but would not have regarded it as unfair, for the petitioner, by his indifference, had partly brought it upon himself. Similarly, in *Waldron v Waldron* (2019) it was held that the petitioners 'manifestly improper' behaviour had made what was a breach of their legitimate expectations nevertheless fair.

(The objective approach to the determination of unfair prejudice has been endorsed by Peter Gibson J in *Re Sam Weller* (1990); and by Arden J in *Re Macro (Ipswich) Ltd* (1994).)

The move towards a more open-textured assessment of unfair prejudice

11.45   The opportunity to re-examine the objective concept of unfair prejudice was taken by the Court of Appeal in *Re Saul D Harrison & Sons plc* (1995). While Hoffmann LJ recognised that the court has always determined the issue of unfairness objectively for the purposes of s 994 petitions, he questioned whether such an approach is necessarily 'the most illuminating way of putting the matter', and doubted whether objective assessment is the most appropriate test in the circumstances:

> For one thing, the standard of fairness must necessarily be laid down by the court. In explaining how the court sets about deciding what is fair in the context of company management, I do not think that it helps a great deal to add the reasonable company watcher to the already substantial cast of imaginary characters which the law uses to personify its standards of justice in different situations. An appeal to the views of an imaginary third party makes the concept seem more vague than it really is.

Hoffmann LJ went on to lay down guidelines for determining unfairness, and in so doing, reaffirmed the sanctity of the statutory contract. He stressed that fairness for the purposes of s 994 must be viewed in the context of a commercial relationship and that the articles of association are the contractual terms which govern the relationship of shareholders with the company and *inter se*. He said:

> Since keeping promises and honouring agreements is probably the most important element of commercial fairness, the starting point in any case under s 459 [now s 994] will be to ask whether the conduct of which the shareholder complains was in accordance with the articles of association.

This approach was carried further in his pronouncement on the issue in *O'Neill v Phillips* (1999), the first appeal under s 994 to reach the House of Lords, in which Lord Hoffmann noted that fairness was to be determined by reference to 'traditional' or 'general' equitable principles.

11.46   In *O'Neill v Phillips* (1999) the respondent, P, originally held all of the issued share capital in the company and was its sole director. The petitioner, O, was employed by the company in 1983 as a manual worker. P was favourably impressed by O's ability and he received rapid promotion. In early 1985 O received 25 per cent of the company's shares and he was made a director. In May 1985 O was informed by P that he, O, would eventually take over the running of the company's business and at that time he would receive 50 per cent of the profits. In December 1985 P retired from the board and O became sole director and effectively the company's managing director. For a while the business enjoyed good profitability. However, its fortunes declined and in August 1991, disillusioned with O's management of the business, P used his majority voting rights to appoint himself managing director and he took over the management of the company. O was informed that he would no longer receive 50 per cent of the profits but his entitlement would be limited to his salary and dividends on his 25 per cent shareholding. Earlier discussions about further share incentives when certain targets were met were aborted. O thereupon issued a petition alleging unfairly prejudicial conduct on the part of P.

11.47 The trial judge dismissed the petition on the ground, inter alia, that the alleged unfairly prejudicial conduct affected O qua employee not qua member. O's appeal to the Court of Appeal was successful on the basis that as from 1985 O had the legitimate expectation that he would receive 50 per cent of the profits, and that as from 1991 he had the legitimate expectation that he would receive 50 per cent of the voting shares. P appealed to the House of Lords. The central issue was whether P's conduct was unfairly prejudicial. It was held that P's conduct would have been unfair had he used his majority voting power to exclude O from the business. This he had not done, but had simply revised the terms of O's remuneration. P's refusal to allot additional shares as part of the proposed incentive scheme was not unfair because the negotiations between them were not completed and no contractual undertaking had been entered into by the parties. Nor was P's decision to revise O's profit-sharing arrangement unfair conduct. O's entitlement to 50 per cent of the company's profits was never formalised and it was, in any case, conditional upon O running the business. That condition was no longer fulfilled because P had to assume control over the running of the company. Although O argued that he had lost trust in P, that alone could not form the basis for a petition under the unfairly prejudicial conduct provision. The House of Lords took the view that to hold otherwise would be to confer on a minority shareholder a unilateral right to withdraw his capital. O therefore failed to prove that P's conduct was both unfair and prejudicial. Lord Hoffmann, in a closely reasoned speech, stressed that the concept of 'fairness' will depend upon the context in which it is being used and also its background. He explained that in the case of s 994, the background has two features:

> First, a company is an association of persons for an economic purpose, usually entered into with legal advice and some degree of formality. The terms of the association are contained in the articles of association and sometimes in collateral agreements between the shareholders. Thus the manner in which the affairs of the company may be conducted is closely regulated by rules to which the shareholders have agreed. Secondly, company law has developed seamlessly from the law of partnership, which was treated by equity, like the Roman societas, as a contract of good faith. One of the traditional roles of equity, as a separate jurisdiction, was to restrain the exercise of strict legal rights in certain relationships in which it considered that this would be contrary to good faith. These principles have, with appropriate modification, been carried over into company law.
>
> The first of these two features leads to the conclusion that a member of a company will not ordinarily be entitled to complain of unfairness unless there has been some

breach of the terms on which he agreed that the affairs of the company should be con-
ducted. But the second leads to the conclusion that there will be cases in which equitable
considerations make it unfair for those conducting the affairs of the company to rely
upon their strict legal powers. Thus unfairness may consist in a breach of the rules or in
using the rules in a manner which equity would regard as contrary to good faith.

11.48 Taking the decisions in *Saul D Harrison* and *O'Neill v Phillips* together, the position appears to be that in order to establish unfair prejudice, a petitioner must prove either a
breach of contract (referable to the articles or a shareholders' agreement), or a breach
of some fundamental understanding in which case equity will intervene to preclude the
majority from repudiating such an obligation despite the fact that it lacks contractual
force. In s 994 petitions, the court will begin by looking at whether or not the conduct
complained about is in accordance with the articles. If it is not, the court will next consider the scope of any fundamental understandings between the parties. Unfairness is
not to be tested by reference to subjective notions of fairness but is to be determined
by applying settled equitable principles to see whether the majority had acted or was
proposing to act in a manner which equity would regard as contrary to good faith (*Re
Guidezone Ltd* (2000)). In *Saul D Harrison* Hoffmann LJ stressed that unlawful conduct
will not necessarily be unfairly prejudicial, and so trivial or technical infringements of the
articles may not give rise to s 994 petitions. To succeed in such cases a petitioner will need
to demonstrate either that he relied on some pre-association understanding, or a post-
association agreement that was either legally binding or specifically relied on by him. For
example, in *Sikorski v Sikorski* (2012), two brothers who were shareholders agreed that
one of them (the petitioner, who was the minority shareholder) would receive payment
via an index-linked dividend funded by a company's rental income paid by an associated
company. The majority shareholder then procured for his own benefit a reduction in the
rental payments so no dividend could be paid to his brother. Briggs J held that the company had engaged in unfairly prejudicial conduct. It had departed from an agreement
by decreasing the amount of funds available and rendering itself unable to pay the petitioner the dividends due under the agreement. On the other hand, Jonathan Parker J in
Re Guidezone Ltd (2000), and Auld and Jonathan Parker LJJ in *Phoenix Office Supplies Ltd
v Larvin* (2003), stressed that a petitioner cannot enlist s 994 to force a right of exit from
the company that does not exist under the company's constitution. But the failure on the
part of the majority shareholders to hold meetings and to otherwise conduct the affairs
of the company as a going concern will be held to be unfairly prejudicial to the interests
of the minority (*Fisher v Cadman* (2005)).

In a cogent summary of the jurisprudence, Arden LJ in *Re Tobian Properties Ltd* (2012),
said:

The key phrase in section 994(1), 'unfairly prejudicial', comprises two elements, unfair-
ness and prejudice but both of these must be understood in the context of company law.
The concept of fairness inherent in this phrase is flexible and open-textured but it is not
unbounded. The courts must act on a principled basis even though the concept is to be

approached flexibly. They cannot decide whether to grant or refuse relief from unfair prejudice on the basis of palm-tree justice.

Examples of unfairly prejudicial conduct

(i) Exclusion from management

11.49 The majority of petitions presented under the unfair prejudice provision allege exclusion from management (see, for example, *Re BC & G Care Homes Ltd; Crowley v Bessell* (2015); *Wootliff v Rushton-Turner* (at para **11.30**); and *Sprint Electric Ltd v Buyer's Dream Ltd* (2018)). We have seen that in a small quasi-partnership type of company a member may, on the basis of a fundamental understanding between the parties, expect to participate in the management of the business notwithstanding that strictly speaking every director can be removed from office by an appropriate resolution of the company in general meeting (although, of course, a dismissed director may have a good cause of action for breach of contract). In companies with outside investors it will be rare for a petition alleging exclusion from management to be successful because the expectations of such members rarely go beyond the hope of obtaining a return on their investment (see *Re Blue Arrow plc* (1987) and *Re Posgate & Denby Agencies Ltd* (1987)). Thus, in *Re Tottenham Hotspur plc* (1994) Terry Venables, the chief executive of the 'Spurs' football club, a quoted public company, was dismissed from office. He brought a petition claiming unfair prejudice, but it was held that he could have no legitimate expectation of remaining in control of the company. The Vice-Chancellor took the view that nothing had been disclosed to the company's other shareholders which would suggest that the appointment of Mr Venables would be regulated by anything other than the company's constitution and the formal legal documents.

11.50 With respect to claims originating from the more typical private company, early case law suggests that in such claims the court would engage in a fact-intensive exercise as a means of apportioning fault for the purposes of determining whether or not a petitioner's exclusion from management was unfairly prejudicial. The decision in *Re RA Noble & Sons (Clothing) Ltd* (1983) was taken as authority for the proposition that if the petitioner was partly to blame for bringing about the deadlock in relations which resulted in his exclusion from management, no unfair prejudice could be made out although, of course, the facts could justify a winding-up order under the just and equitable ground. More recent authority, however, points to the court's reluctance to become immersed in a quagmire of evidence relating to fault. In *Re XYZ Ltd (No 004377 of 1986)* (1987) Hoffmann J drew the analogy between s 994 petitions and old-style divorce cases, and alluded to the difficulties experienced by judges when called upon to attribute fault. Indeed, it does not follow that simply because the petitioner is innocent, the respondent is presumed to have been guilty of the relevant culpable conduct. The judge remarked that:

> *There are many cases in which it becomes in practice impossible for two people to work together without obvious fault on either side. They may have come together with a*

confident expectation of being able to co-operate but found that insurmountable dif-
ferences in personality made it impossible. In those circumstances the only solution is
for them to part company. If one of them asks the other to leave the business, I cannot
accept that the former must automatically be regarded as having acted in a manner
unfairly prejudicial to the interests of the latter.

In *Re Sprintroom Ltd; Prescott v Potamianos* (2019) the petitioner's (P) breach of fiduciary duties did not automatically mean his exclusion from management was fair. The Court of Appeal found that P had engaged in an open and bona fide dispute, noting that 'there is no rule of law that every breach of fiduciary duty will necessarily render exclusion from management fair: it is always a question of fact and degree'. The court found that the case law relied upon to justify the exclusion included secretive and/or dishonest conduct (i.e. serious breaches of duty). This was not the case here.

11.51 This move away from a fault-based approach is also evident in the way in which the courts now favour the view that a valuation of a petitioner's shares should normally be made without any discount being applied to reflect his or her minority shareholding (see later). However, it was made clear by Lord Hoffmann in *O'Neill v Phillips* (1999) that the shift from the fault-based approach stops short of permitting a shareholder to withdraw unilaterally from a company and demand that the majority should buy him out (see, for example, *Phoenix Office Supplies Ltd v Larvin* (2003) (para **11.48**)). Similarly, the Law Commission did not favour the introduction of 'no fault divorce' which would permit a shareholder to exit at will (Law Com No 246, para 3.66). In its view there are sound economic reasons against allowing such a remedy and, as a matter of principle, it would fundamentally contravene the statutory contract. In *Phoenix Office Supplies Ltd v Larvin* (above) the petitioner, who held one-third of the shares in the company, wished to terminate his association with the business for personal reasons. He resigned his employment and gave notice of his intent to resign his directorship once the sale of his shares at their full value and without discount to reflect his minority shareholding had been agreed. He alleged that the remaining two directors (holding between them two-thirds of its issued share capital) had wrongfully excluded him from his entitlement as director to access financial information thereby preventing him from protecting his interest as a shareholder. The Court of Appeal, reversing the trial judge, held that the conduct of the majority did not amount to unfairly prejudicial conduct. Jonathan Parker LJ observed:

Thus the issue which lies at the heart of this appeal, as I see it, is whether section 459 [CA 1985] extends to affording a member of a quasi-partnership company who wishes, for entirely his own reasons, to sever his connection with the company—and who de facto has done so—an opportunity to 'put' his shareholding onto the other members at its full, undiscounted, value when he has no contractual right to do so. I can for my part see no basis for concluding that section 459 can have such a Draconian effect.

(See also *Parkinson v Eurofinance Group Ltd* (2001).)

(ii) Mismanagement

11.52 The scope for finding that managerial incompetence falls within the ambit of s 994 is necessarily limited and on a number of occasions the courts have stressed that ordinarily they would be very reluctant to find that management decisions could amount to unfair conduct. In *Re Elgindata Ltd* (1991) Warner J observed that the risk of poor management is an incident of share ownership given that managerial competence will generally determine the value of the shareholder's investment in the company. Further, it has long been settled that the courts will not interfere with a bona fide business decision made by a company's board or its majority shareholders (the internal management rule), except where there is a clear conflict of interests (*Nicholas v Soundcraft Electronics Ltd* (1993)). In *Re Elgindata Ltd* (1991) it was alleged, inter alia, that the controlling director had managed the company incompetently. Warner J refused to grant relief, stressing that: '[s]hort of a breach by a director of his duty of skill and care . . . there is prima facie no unfairness to a shareholder in the quality of the management turning out to be poor'. It is noteworthy from this passage that proving breach of the common law duties of prudence is, as a general rule, the decisive factor, so that 'cases where there is a disagreement between petitioners and respondents as to whether a particular managerial decision was, as a matter of commercial judgement, the right one to make, or as to whether a particular proposal relating to the conduct of the company's business is commercially sound' do not fall within s 994.

11.53 In *Re Macro (Ipswich) Ltd* (1994) an allegation of mismanagement resulting in economic loss to the company was found to amount to unfairly prejudicial conduct. The evidence of the events giving rise to the claim spanned a period of some 40 years. Central to the mismanagement allegations was the complaint that the sole director of the two associated companies in question neglected his management responsibilities and this was exploited by dishonest employees who stole commissions earned by the estate agency arm of the business. It was successfully argued by the petitioners that substantial financial losses were suffered by the companies which unfairly prejudiced them. In granting relief, Arden J noted that the facts before the court were analogous to the example formulated by Warner J in *Re Elgindata Ltd* (1991) to the effect that absent breach by a director of his duty of care and skill, the court might nonetheless find that there was unfair prejudice to minority shareholders where the majority, for reasons of their own, persisted in retaining in charge of the management of the company a family member who was demonstrably incompetent. In *Re Saul D Harrison* the Court of Appeal stressed that for an allegation of mismanagement to succeed it would need to be proved that the directors had abused their powers or exercised them for some ulterior purpose so as to step outside the bargain between the shareholders and the company. Thus, in *Oak Investment Partners XII, Limited Partnership v Boughtwood* (para **11.28**), Sales J, having reviewed the case law, observed that 'the court will be astute not to "second guess" legitimate management decisions taken upon reasonable grounds at the time, albeit as events transpired they may not have been the best decisions. . . .'

(iii) Breach of directors' fiduciary duties

11.54 There have been a number of successful petitions where the allegation has centred on directors acting in breach of their fiduciary duties (see Chapter 14). For example, in *Re London School of Electronics Ltd* (1986) the allegation was that those in control of the company had misappropriated its assets by diverting them to another business owned by them. It was held that this conduct was unfairly prejudicial to the interests of the petitioner as a member of the company. In *Re Elgindata Ltd* (1991) Warner J pointed to the misapplication of company assets by the respondent for his personal benefit and for the benefit of his family and friends as being the decisive factor in the court's finding that his conduct was unfairly prejudicial to the interests of minority shareholders. A further illustration is afforded by *Re Little Olympian Each-Ways Ltd (No 3)* (1995), in which the directors sold the company's business at a substantial undervalue, some £2 million, to another company as part of a wider transaction from which they derived significant personal benefits. The court did not hesitate in finding such conduct of the company's affairs to be unfairly prejudicial to the petitioner's interests. In *Dalby v Bodilly* (2005), Blackburne J held that the respondent's conduct, as the only director, in allotting himself an additional 900 shares was a clear breach of fiduciary duty in that he was plainly putting his own interests before those of his fellow shareholder, the petitioner. The allotment could not, in any sense, be justified as being in the interests of the company as a whole. It was, without doubt, unfairly prejudicial conduct and the respondent had no real prospect of successfully arguing otherwise at trial. By his conduct, he had forfeited the petitioner's confidence in his ability to conduct the company's affairs in a proper way.

11.55 The case law therefore reveals that s 994 may be used to obtain a personal remedy despite the proper claimant rule (see Chapter 10). In this respect, other examples of successful s 994 petitions brought for breach of fiduciary duties include allegations that directors have made secret profits (*Re a Company (No 005287 of 1985)* (1986); *O'Donnell v Shanahan* (2009); and *Re Baumler (UK) Ltd* (2005)); have exercised their powers to issue and allot shares for an improper purpose, for example to reduce the petitioner's shareholding (*Re Cumana Ltd* (1986); *Dalby v Bodilly* (2005)); have diverted a corporate opportunity (*Re Baumler (UK) Ltd* (2005); *Gerrard v Koby* (2004); *Re Edwardian Group Ltd* (2018)); and have abused their powers by recommending shareholders to accept the lower of two offers for the shares of the company without disclosing that they were the promoters of the company making the lower offer (*Re a Company (No 008699 of 1985)* (1986)).

11.56 While loss of trust is not sufficient per se to found a petition under s 994 (*Re Jayflex Construction Ltd* (2003)), the point was made in *Re Baumler (UK) Ltd* (2005), by George Bompas QC (sitting as a deputy judge of the High Court) that in the case of a quasi-partnership company, a breach of duty by one participant may lead to such a loss of confidence on the part of the innocent participant and breakdown in relations that the innocent participant is entitled to relief under s 996 of the CA 2006 (see later). The judge noted that, in effect, the unfairness lies in compelling the innocent participant to remain a member of the company.

(iv) Excessive remuneration and the failure to pay dividends

11.57 A company's articles of association will generally provide that directors' remuneration shall be determined by the general meeting. In practice, however, the power to determine remuneration for directors is delegated to the board. Such provisions, it will be recalled, form part of the statutory contract between the shareholders and the company. In general, the court will be disinclined to interfere with the business judgement of the board, and so provided it has honestly and genuinely determined the level of remuneration the court will not enquire whether the award was reasonable (*Re Halt Garages (1964) Ltd* (1982)).

11.58 That there is ample scope for abuse of this power by the board was recognised by both the Cohen and the Jenkins Committees which considered the problem of directors awarding themselves excessive remuneration, thereby leaving little or no surplus profits for distribution by way of dividends to shareholders. In extreme cases the court will be prepared to hold that the failure to pay dividends and/or excessive remuneration or fees amounts to unfairly prejudicial conduct (for examples, see *Rahman v Malik* (2008); *Re McCarthy Surfacing Ltd* (2008); *Croly v Good* (2010); *VB Football Assets v Blackpool FC* (2017) where the extraction of large sums of money from the company by the respondent amounted to disguised dividends; *Re CF Booth Ltd* (2017); *Re Edwardian Group Ltd* (para **11.55**); *Routledge v Skerritt* (2019); and *Sikorski v Sikorski* (para **11.48**); cf *West Coast Capital (Lios) Ltd* (2008), discussed at para **14.23**). Prior to the 1989 amendment of the unfair prejudice provision (see para **11.22**), claims under this head would fail on the basis that the conduct complained of was not discriminatory between shareholders, although it could give rise to a just and equitable winding-up order (*Re a Company (No 00370 of 1987), ex p Glossop* (1988)). However, in *Re Sam Weller & Sons Ltd* (1990) Peter Gibson J refused to strike out a petition alleging that the refusal of the majority shareholders to increase the dividend yield which had remained the same for 37 years despite the company's positive performance in the years leading up to the petition, while they continued to draw directors' remuneration and accumulating cash reserves, amounted to unfairly prejudicial conduct.

11.59 In *Re a Company (No 004415 of 1996)* (1997) the Vice-Chancellor observed that if remuneration and dividend levels cannot be justified by 'objective commercial criteria' it would seem to follow that the affairs of the company have been managed in a way unfairly prejudicial to the interests of the shareholders who are not directors. In *Re Cumana Ltd* (1986) it was held that the payment of some £356,000 to the respondent over a 14-month period was excessive and was unfairly prejudicial to the petitioner. Vinelott J said that the remuneration was 'plainly in excess of anything the [respondent] had earned'. On the other hand, in *Re Saul D Harrison* the same judge struck out a petition in which the allegations included a claim that the directors had awarded themselves excessive remuneration. He noted that the sums involved did not exceed those which other comparable companies paid their executive directors. In *Anderson v Hogg* (2002), a Scottish decision of the Inner House, the payment by a director to himself of an unauthorised and excessive sum as a redundancy payment was held to be unfairly prejudicial to the petitioner's interests.

The decision again illustrates the trend towards bypassing the proper claimant rule (see Chapter 10) given that the remedy sought was an order for payment to the company. Lord Prosser, dissenting, took the view that the petitioner should have caused the company to initiate proceedings.

Whether or not shareholders are under a duty to read their company's accounts in order to monitor the remuneration levels of directors as a pre-condition to bringing a petition was addressed by the Court of Appeal in *Re Tobian Properties Ltd* (2012). The petitioner, M, claimed that the company's majority shareholder and sole director, A, had awarded himself excessive remuneration. The petition failed at first instance chiefly on the basis that A's remuneration was disclosed in the company's accounts and had gone unchallenged by M. Allowing the appeal, Arden LJ said; '[t]he judge's approach means that minority shareholders are at risk of losing their rights if they do not read their company's filed accounts. This approach imposes a requirement for diligence that has no basis in the statutory provisions or in principle or authority.'

Locus standi and procedural aspects of s 994

11.60 Section 994(1) states that a 'member of a company' may petition for an order under the provision. Section 112 defines 'a member' as a subscriber to the company's memorandum and '[e]very other person who agrees to become a member of the company and whose name is entered in its register of members'. The section is satisfied whenever a person assents to become a member without the necessity of a contract in the strict sense (*Re Nuneaton Borough Association Football Club Ltd* (1989)). In *Harris v Jones* (2011), Morgan J took the view that the right to petition under s 994 extended to a person to whom shares have been transferred but who had not been registered as a member. In *Blunt v Jackson* (2013), Roth J, having noted that the court had the power to amend the register of members retrospectively, found that the petitioner, who had agreed to become a 50 per cent shareholder and had worked for the company on low wages in the belief that he was in fact a shareholder though he was not registered as such, had been unfairly prejudiced by virtue of his exclusion from management. Further, by virtue of s 994(2), those to whom shares in the company have been 'transferred or transmitted by operation of law' have standing, and so, for example, the personal representatives of a deceased or bankrupt member may bring a petition (see *Re CMB Holdings Ltd* (para **11.14**)). On the other hand, a beneficial owner whose shares are held by a nominee will not qualify (*Re Quickdome Ltd* (1988)); while in *Re Brightview Ltd* (2004), the court was of the view that a nominee shareholder would have standing to petition. It is noteworthy that in *John Reid & Sons (Strucsteel) Ltd* (2003), the petition was dismissed because it principally concerned conduct related to the petitioner's future status as an employee of the company as opposed to his position as shareholder. In *Baker v Potter* (2005), David Richards J held that where the petitioner is seeking financial relief but has agreed to sell his share to the respondent, who, on the facts, was the company's sole director and owned one share in it, such agreement converted the petitioner's interest in the company into a right to receive the purchase price. Accordingly, if there had been a misappropriation of corporate assets, for example by the respondent prior to the sale agreement, there might be a case for financial relief. But financial relief is not appropriate where the alleged unfairly prejudicial conduct occurs after the parties have concluded the agreement, provided the petitioner was paid the agreed price, because he would not have suffered prejudice.

The issue has arisen whether an arbitration clause in a company membership agreement, for example the Football Association rules, will operate to exclude the statutory right of access to the courts under s 994. In *Fulham Football Club (1987) Ltd v Richards* (2011), the trial judge, faced with conflicting authorities namely, *Re Vocam Europe Ltd* (1998) and *Exeter City Association Football Club Ltd v Football Conference Ltd* (2004), granted an application under s 9 of the Arbitration Act 1996 to stay a petition brought under s 994, in circumstances where rules had been agreed under which disputes would be referred to and resolved by arbitration. On appeal it was argued that the petition should not have been stayed and that the trial judge should have followed *Exeter City* in which HHJ Weeks QC held that the shareholder's right to petition for relief under s 994 was inalienable and could not be 'diminished or removed by contract or otherwise'. The Court of Appeal, rejecting this argument, upheld the trial judge's decision to stay the petition. Patten LJ, delivering the leading judgment, stated that *Exeter City* had been wrongly decided and observed that s 994 gave shareholders 'an optional right to invoke the assistance of the court in cases of unfair prejudice . . . there is nothing in the scheme of these provisions which . . . makes the resolution of the underlying dispute inherently unsuitable for determination by arbitration on grounds of public policy'.

11.61 There is no procedural requirement that a petitioner must satisfy the court that he has an arguable case as is the situation with derivative actions. But a respondent can apply to the court to have a summary judgment or to have a petition struck out. The CPR (r 3.4(2)) empowers the court, as was the case under the old rules, to strike out statements of case which disclose no reasonable grounds for bringing or defending the claim, or which are an abuse of the court's process or likely to obstruct the just disposal of the proceedings. Thus, if the action is brought in order to achieve some collateral purpose, for example to obtain repayment of a loan to the petitioner, the court may strike out the petition as an abuse of process (*Re Bellador Silk Ltd* (1965)). When considering a strike-out application the court will look at the realities of the petitioner's case and a petition will not be allowed to proceed if the likelihood of the claimed relief being granted 'is so remote that the case can be described as perfectly hopeless' (*Re Legal Costs Negotiators Ltd* (see para **11.24**), Peter Gibson LJ).

11.62 Further, the CPR, Part 24 allows the court to enter summary judgment without the delay and expense of a trial. Summary judgment may be entered where the petition or defence has no realistic prospect of success. There is an overlap between Part 24 and r 3.4 (see earlier) and in many cases applications are combined under both provisions. A typical example of where a respondent might apply for striking-out or summary judgment is where the petitioner seeks an order to have his shares purchased, and he has refused a reasonable offer for his shares. Similarly, such an application might be made by a respondent where the articles of association or a shareholders' agreement contain a pre-emption clause (whereby in the event of a shareholder wishing to sell his shares to an outsider, the other members shall have the option to buy him out at a fair value to be fixed by the auditors). Thus, if the petition is being brought as a means of evading the contractual obligation, the court will not permit the action to proceed unless the petitioner can point to equitable considerations which render the enforcement of the obligation unfairly prejudicial (*O'Neill v Phillips* (1999); see also Hoffmann's J's judgment in *Re a Company (No 007623 of 1986)* (1986)). In *Re Belfield Furnishings Ltd* (2006), the parties had agreed both the circumstances in which a shareholder would be compelled to transfer his shares and the valuation procedure that would be followed. The applicants unsuccessfully sought to strike out the action on the basis that it was an abuse of process. While recognising that in the 'usual case' where there is no question of any wrongdoing by the majority it will normally be an abuse of process for a petition to proceed where an offer has been made to purchase the shares at a fair value, or where the petitioner is contractually bound to sell his stake in given circumstances and has agreed a fair valuation method, the judge went on to state that the continuation of a petition will not, however, amount to an abuse of process if:

(a) there is evidence to suggest that substantial assets of the company have been misapplied as a result of the conduct of the majority; or

(b) the agreed valuer is not in a position to exercise independent judgement on the question of value (as in *Re Boswell & Co (Steels) Ltd* (1989) or *Re Benfield Greig Group plc* (2000)).

11.63 Although disputes involving allegations of unfairly prejudicial conduct typically arise between factions of shareholders, the company should always be joined as a nominal party to the proceedings so that a court order is enforceable against it (*Re Little Olympian Each-Ways Ltd (No 3)* (1995)). In petitions involving quasi-partnership types of companies, generally all existing shareholders irrespective of whether or not any wrongdoing is alleged, should be joined as respondents (*Re a Company (No 007281 of 1986)* (1987)). This is because a share purchase order will normally be made against the current shareholders of the company. A past member of a company may also be joined as a party if relief is sought against him (*Re a Company (No 005287 of 1985)* (1986)).

Remedies

11.64 If the petitioner establishes unfairly prejudicial conduct, s 996(1) of the Companies Act 2006 provides that the court 'may make such order as it thinks fit for giving relief in respect of the matters complained of'. More particularly, s 996(2) goes on to add that:

Without prejudice to the generality of subsection (1), the court's order may—

(a) regulate the conduct of the company's affairs in the future;

    (b) *require the company—*

        (i) *to refrain from doing or continuing an act complained of, or*

        (ii) *to do an act which the petitioner has complained it has omitted to do,*

    (c) *authorise civil proceedings to be brought in the name and on behalf of the company by such person or persons and on such terms as the court may direct;*

    (d) *require the company not to make any, or specified, alterations in its articles without the leave of the court;*

    (e) *provide for the purchase of the shares of any members of the company by other members or by the company itself and, in the case of a purchase by the company itself, the reduction of the company's capital accordingly.*

Unlike winding-up on the just and equitable ground, it is clear that the court has an extremely wide discretion as to what type of relief should be granted, and even as to whether relief should be granted at all (see, for example, the judgment of Briggs LJ in *Thomas v Dawson* (2015)). Indeed, s 996 allows the court to construct a remedy according to the nature of the wrong done. In this regard, it was observed by Mummery J in *Re a Company (No 00314 of 1989), ex p Estate Acquisition and Development Ltd* (1991) that:

> *Under sections 459–461 [now ss 994–996] the court is not, therefore, faced with a death sentence decision dependent on establishing just and equitable grounds. The court is more in the position of a medical practitioner presented with a patient who is alleged to be suffering from one or more ailments which can be treated by an appropriate remedy applied during the course of the continuing life of the company.*

Further, the breadth of the courts' powers may extend to an award of damages for reflective loss (see *Re Brightview Ltd* (2004), and Chapter 10); see also *Apex Global Management Ltd v FI Call Ltd* (2015) in which Hildyard J noted that s 996 could be used to award equitable compensation; see further *Rembert v Daniel* (2018)). In *Re Phoneer Ltd* (2002), the petitioner sought a winding-up order on the just and equitable ground and the respondent cross-petitioned for winding-up under s 994. Roger Kaye QC, granting a winding-up order since both parties obviously desired it, noted that 'section 996 enables, but does not compel, the court to make an order under that section'. Although the respondent held 70 per cent of the shares, the judge felt that on the facts of the case 'justice is served by ordering the winding-up of the company . . . on the basis of a 50/50 split'.

11.65 Section 994 is so drafted as to permit a member to bring a petition in respect of any proposed act or omission of the company, and s 996(2)(b) enables the court to order a company to refrain from a course of conduct, whether actual or proposed, which is unfairly prejudicial to the interests of the shareholders. In *Whyte Petitioner* (1984) the court issued an injunction to prevent the majority shareholders removing a director from the board and in *Re a Company (002612 of 1984)* (1985) the court issued an interlocutory injunction to prohibit a proposed allotment of shares which would have had the effect of diluting the petitioner's shareholding (see also *Re Last Lion Holdings Ltd* (2018)).

11.66   Section 996(2)(c) empowers the court to authorise a petitioner who successfully establishes unfairly prejudicial conduct, for instance by way of a director's breach of duty, to bring an action in the name of the company. There is little case law on this provision although such an order was granted in *Re Cyplon Developments Ltd* (1982). One advantage to the petitioner lies in the fact that he can avoid the procedural complexity of a derivative action (see Chapter 10). However, a petitioner seeking such an order would face the prospect of two actions: he would have to prove his case under s 994 before bringing an action in the name of the company. However, with respect to costs it was suggested by Hoffmann J in *Re Sherborne Park Residents Co Ltd* (1987) that a petitioner bringing a derivative action under this provision would be entitled to an indemnity by way of a *Wallersteiner v Moir (No 2)* (1975) order. We return to this issue later (see para **11.74**).

11.67   The most common form of relief granted by the court is an order for the purchase of the petitioner's shares by the company or another shareholder (s 996(2)(e)). Indeed, in *Grace v Biagioli* (2006), the Court of Appeal affirmed the view that there is a presumption in favour of a buy-out order for successful unfair prejudice petitions. The remedy is usually sought by shareholders in private or unlisted companies who do not have the option of leaving the company by selling their shares on the open market. Nourse J stressed in *Re Bird Precision Bellows Ltd* (1984) that in valuing the petitioner's shares the guiding principle is to fix a price that is fair in all the circumstances. A range of factors are taken into account by the court, including the conduct and culpability of the parties. On this point, Nourse J said that '[a] shareholder who deserves his exclusion has, if you like, made a constructive election to sever his connection with the company and thus sell his shares' (see also *Richardson v Blackmore* (2005)). We now turn to consider the various factors which may inform share valuations in this context. In framing an appropriate remedy under the provision the objective is achieving fairness and in *Rahman v Malik* (2008), the court not only ordered the wrongdoer to purchase the petitioner's shares, but took into account dividends which had not been paid to him and the under-declaration of profits (see also *Re McCarthy Surfacing Ltd* (2008)).

Valuation of shares on a buy-out

11.68   For quoted companies valuing shares is a fairly straightforward exercise because reference can be made to their market price. But for unquoted companies, and the vast majority of s 994 petitions fall within this category, the valuation exercise is a far more difficult undertaking (see, for example, the reasoning of David Richards LJ in *Wann v Birkinshaw* (2017)). The court has a wide discretion to do what is fair and equitable in all the circumstances of the case and under the CPR the court is expected to adopt a vigorous approach towards share valuation (*North Holdings Ltd v Southern Tropics Ltd* (1999)).

11.69 Generally, of course, it will be the majority who are ordered to purchase the petitioner's shares, however there are rare examples where the converse has been ordered, albeit subject to conditions. An order that the minority purchase the majority's shares would be particularly appropriate where the majority are incompetent to manage the company's affairs (cf *Re Five Minute Car Wash Service Ltd* (1966)). Further, such an order was made by Harman J in *Re Nuneaton Borough Association Football Club Ltd* (1989) in which he found that the majority shareholder was clearly at fault and had shown himself unfit to exercise control of the company. Since the respondent had made substantial interest-free loans to the company the judge found that 'it would not . . . be proper equitable relief to compel the transfer of the controlling shares without arranging for the repayment of the advances'. Another example is *Oak Investment Partners XII, Limited Partnership v Boughtwood* (para **11.28**), where, as commented earlier, the court ordered the significant shareholder to sell his shares to the petitioner. The significant shareholder's appeal against the buy-out order was dismissed by the Court of Appeal on the basis that the conduct in question made such an order inevitable and unchallengeable (see *Boughtwood v Oak Investment Partners XII Ltd Partnership* (2010)).

11.70 Where the court in its determination of the value of the petitioner's minority shareholding takes into account that he has limited voting power and therefore little control over the company's management, it is said that the shares are valued on a 'discounted' basis. Where, on the other hand, in the interests of arriving at a fair and equitable result no discount is applied, the shares are said to be valued on a pro rata basis (i.e. according to the value of all the issued share capital). As far as it is possible to distil any general principle from the case law, it can be said that normally no discount is applied by the courts to reflect a petitioner's minority shareholding where the company in question is a small quasi-partnership in the *Ebrahimi* sense (*Virdi v Abbey Leisure Ltd* (1990); cf *Re McCarthy Surfacing Ltd* (2008)). Conversely, in *Irvine v Irvine* (2006), the court decided that for the purposes of a buy-out order following a successful petition, a shareholding of 49.96 per cent was to be valued as any other minority holding, so that no premium should be attached to the shares simply because the buyer was the majority shareholder who would gain control of the whole of the issued share capital.

11.71 Nourse J in *Re Bird Precision Bellows Ltd* (1984) subjected the valuation process to exhaustive examination. He noted that as far as petitioners in quasi-partnership companies are concerned, the sale is, in effect, being forced upon them as a result of the unfairly prejudicial conduct and it would normally be most unfair to impose a discounted price for their shares in such circumstances. The Court of Appeal agreed. This approach was endorsed by the Privy Council in *CVC/Opportunity Equity Partners Ltd v Almeida* (2002), on the basis that where the petitioner was an unwilling seller the shares should normally be valued as a rateable proportion of the value of the company as a going concern without any discount for a minority holding (see also *Re Annacott Holdings Ltd* (2013)). In *Re Blue Index Ltd* (2014), the issue was whether a discount should be applied to the purchase of the petitioner's 3 per cent shareholding. On the particular facts, it was held that it would be inappropriate to apply a discount. Rather, in valuing the shares the price could be increased to take account of the excessive remuneration that had been paid to the respondent directors. Valuation without discount now appears to be generally applied in s 994 cases (see *Strahan v Wilcock* (2006) CA; *Re BC & G Care Homes Ltd* (2015); and *Re AMT Coffee Ltd; McCallum-Toppin v McCullum-Toppin* (2019)). Although where petitioners acquire their shares by way of investment and therefore without any legitimate expectation of participating in management, they would have paid a discounted price initially anyway to reflect the value of the minority holding acquired. In such cases it would be normally fair and appropriate for the court to arrive at a discounted valuation (*Re DR Chemicals Ltd* (1988)). In *Crabtree v Ng* (2012), Lewison J considered the principles that should apply to the valuation of the shares of a petitioner who was to be bought out by the other 50 per cent shareholder. The valuation was to be based on the value to the co-owner rather than on an open market value and, subject to that, the petitioner's interest was to be fixed at one half of the valuation of the company as determined through its statutory accounts.

In *Birdi v Specsavers Optical Group Ltd* (2015), Nugee J noted that 'where the value is to be determined by a valuer and the Court has no expert evidence, the Court is unlikely to be in a good position to determine what adjustment should be made to the price'. He went on to explain that where a valuer is valuing the shares, it is for the valuer to determine what adjustment should be made and the initial order only required the court to decide whether the matters required an adjustment to be made, not the amount of any such adjustment. The judge also observed that the question of what adjustment should be made 'is not just a question of looking at whether the particular matters concerned had a continuing effect on the value of the shares as at the date of valuation . . . the price payable for a petitioner's shareholding should include a sum to make good the prejudice which has been unfairly suffered by the petitioner'. Thus, it appears that in accordance with the principle of achieving a fair valuation, there is a difference between the value of the shares and the price payable for them (see also *Shah v Shah* (2011)).

11.72 A critical factor in the valuation process is the date at which the shares are to be valued. Obviously the value of the shares may have fluctuated considerably between the launch of the petition and the date of the trial. The length and expense of typical s 994 proceedings can cause the value of the company's shares to decline sharply. The anxiety of the court in determining the relevant date at which the valuation is to be fixed is, as we have seen, directed towards achieving fairness. In *Abbington Hotel Ltd* (2011), the court stated that 'The starting point for the date of valuation of shares for a buy-out order under s.996 is the date of judgment, but the court is free to choose such date as is most appropriate and just in the circumstances of the case. In particular, the date should be that which best remedies the unfair prejudice held to be established.' (See also *Re Sprintroom Ltd; Prescott v Potamianos* (2019).)

Subject then to the overriding requirement of achieving fairness by remedying the unfair prejudice suffered by the petitioner, the starting point is that 'prima facie an interest in a going concern ought to be valued at the date on which it is ordered to be purchased' (*Re*

London School of Electronics (1986), Nourse J, approved by Robert Walker LJ in *Profinance Trust SA v Gladstone* (2002)). However, as commented earlier, in seeking to achieve a fair valuation, the court may opt for a date that predates the unfairly prejudicial conduct in question (*Re a Company (No 003843 of 1986)* (1987)). In *Croly v Good* (2010) it was found that following the petitioner's exclusion from the management of the business the fortunes of the company had declined to the point where it had entered insolvency. Although there was no evidence of impropriety, the circumstances gave rise to suspicion which could not be dispelled because the respondent had not made available relevant financial information. Since there was a substantial risk that a valuation of the petitioner's shares at a date after his expulsion would be unfair to him, his shares should be valued as at the date of his expulsion from the management of the company. Similarly, in *Re Phoenix Contracts (Leicester) Ltd* (2010), the court found that the petitioner, S, had been unfairly excluded from the management of the company and ordered the respondent, W, to purchase the petitioner's shares. At the relevant time, the company operated as a quasi-partnership with S and W being the only shareholders and executive directors. Proudman J held that S had been unfairly excluded from the management of the company when W suspended him as a director (after he had made a protected disclosure about the company being involved in anti-competitive practices) when W had no right to do so. Since the date of S's exclusion, the value of the company, PC(L) Ltd, had declined. This was partly due to the general fall in the market but had also occurred whilst PC(L) Ltd was under the sole control of W. Although W had made various offers to purchase the petitioner's shares, these could not be regarded as 'fair offers'. By the time of the hearing PC(L) Ltd had been placed into administration by way of a pre-pack sale (allegedly at an undervalue), to a new company controlled by senior employees of PC(L) Ltd. W had known about this; S did not. These were all factors which led the court to conclude that the correct date for valuation of the petitioner's shares was the date of his exclusion, rather than the date of the order. The factors which were relevant to the court's conclusion that the offers by W to purchase S's shares were not 'fair' included the fact that there was no equality of arms between the two parties. At the time of the offer, S was still suspended, was denied access to the company's management accounts and the minutes and papers of management meetings, and a bonus which had been allocated to him had remained unpaid. The court found that it was unfair to expect S to take the risk of a valuation at current values without knowledge of what had happened whilst he had been suspended. Other relevant factors which led the court to conclude that the offers by W to purchase S's shares were unfair, included the fact that no provision had been made for costs and no provision had been made for the payment of the bonus owing to S, and the fact that under the terms of the offer, W reserved the right to reject the independent valuer's valuation and place the company into liquidation instead. The court therefore held that it would not strike out the proceedings on the basis that these offers had not been accepted by S. (See also the reasoning of Newey J in *Re Scitec Group Ltd* (2010); see further *Re KR Hardy Estates Ltd* (2014).)

On the other hand, in *Re London School of Electronics Ltd* (1986) Nourse J took the date on which the petition was presented as the appropriate valuation date. On the facts of the case the court was of the opinion that the petitioner's conduct was such that it would be unfair for him to benefit from the respondents' management of the company after his departure because since that time they had increased the company's profitability. Similarly, in *Re Regional Airports Ltd* (1999) Hart J preferred taking the most up-to-date valuation available because 'to do otherwise risked the possibility that the petitioners might unfairly benefit from my shutting my eyes to a foreseeable "post balance sheet" event'. In *Profinance Trust SA v Gladstone* the Court of Appeal held, on the particular facts, that the fairest course would be to take the agreed value, determined by expert accountants, as at the time of the first-instance hearing (£215,000) rather than the agreed value taken at the time when the petition was presented (£80,000).

11.73 In *O'Neill v Phillips* (1999) Lord Hoffmann observed that if a respondent has made a reasonable offer to buy out the petitioner (i.e. the valuation is to be carried out by a competent expert without discount being applied and the petitioner is to have equal access to all relevant information) 'the exclusion as such will not be unfairly prejudicial and [the respondent] will be entitled to have the petition struck out' (cf *Re Belfield Furnishings Ltd*; and *Harborne Road Nominees Ltd v Karvaski* (2011)). Strategically, respondents are well advised to make a fair offer for the petitioner's shares, one which is based on Lord Hoffmann's guidelines, before applying for striking-out. Should the expert valuer not be independent, the petitioner may have an arguable case of unfair prejudice. In *Re Benfield Greig Group plc* (2002) the articles provided that on the death of a member the shares held by the executors would become subject to compulsory transfer and that the valuation would be carried out by the company's auditors who were required to be independent. The petitioners, the deceased's executors, sought to challenge the auditors' valuation on the basis that, having previously advised the company immediately following the member's death on how to achieve a low valuation for the purposes of the Inland Revenue, their independence was compromised. The Court of Appeal held that the evidence disclosed a case that had a real prospect of success.

Costs

11.74 It will be recalled that it is possible to petition under s 994 for breach of fiduciary duties notwithstanding that such conduct is technically a wrong to the company (see *Re London School of Electronics Ltd*; and *Re Little Olympian Each-Ways Ltd (No 3)*). It was seen in Chapter 10 that in *Wallersteiner v Moir (No 2)* (1975), Buckley LJ stated that the shareholder who initiates a derivative action may be entitled to be indemnified by the company at the end of the trial for his costs provided he acted reasonably in bringing the action. CPR, r 19.9(7) covers costs. It states that the court may order the company to indemnify the claimant against any liability in respect of costs incurred in the claim. An application under CPR, r 19.9(7) may be made at the time of applying for permission to continue the claim.

11.75 Given that s 994 is a personal remedy, the courts have resisted claims by petitioners that companies should pay their costs. This has been the case even where the substance of the allegation is that directors had used their powers for an improper purpose by issuing shares to alter the constitutional make-up of the company (i.e. in breach of their fiduciary duties (see *Re a Company* (1987); see further Chapter 14). Although, as we commented earlier, where the court authorises a petitioner to bring an action in the name of the company under s 996(2)(c), such a petitioner may be entitled to a *Wallersteiner* order (*Re Sherborne Park Residents Co Ltd* (1987)). In *Clark v Cutland* (2003) the issue of funding a s 994 petition came to the fore where the conduct complained of related to a director misappropriating substantial sums of money from the company without the knowledge of Mr Clark, an equal shareholder and co-director. This clearly constituted a breach of fiduciary duty and the petitioner brought a derivative action on behalf of the company which was later consolidated with a petition under s 994. Arden LJ took the provisional view that although a remedy was claimed under s 996 of the CA 2006 this was essentially for the benefit of the company so that, therefore, the petitioner could seek an order against the company for payment to him of costs unless, of course, costs were recovered from the respondent, Mr Cutland. It therefore seems that if the company benefits from the remedy sought, it may be ordered to pay the petitioner's costs. The point was also made that, when considering the range of remedies available under s 996, the court can have recourse to those available on a derivative action which may include those which are proprietary in nature.

More generally on the issue of s 994 costs, in *Re Southern Counties Fresh Foods Ltd* (2011) Warren J took the view that costs flowing from an unfair prejudice petition did not attract any special principles: the starting point was the general rule in CPR, r 44.3(2)(a) that the unsuccessful party will be ordered to pay the costs of the successful party. However, an unsuccessful party did not bear an onus to demonstrate that adopting the general rule would be unjust because it was for the court to consider what departures from the general rule were appropriate in light of all the circumstances of the case. In the case before him, the costs order had to reflect the fact that although C was successful in obtaining the relief sought, its success was qualified as it had failed to establish many of its allegations of unfair prejudice. There was no way of sensibly apportioning the overall costs between general costs and costs of specific issues without engaging in a disproportionate detailed analysis of the transcripts or expending a great deal of time and expense. Accordingly, it was necessary to do the best one could do on the material available (see also *Ashdown v Griffin* (2018)).

Relationship with the winding-up remedy

11.76 As indicated earlier (see paras **11.15-11.16**), claims for just and equitable winding-up in petitions which principally seek relief under s 994 are discouraged by the courts—the more so in the light of the CPR and the case management powers of judges. However, s 122(1)(g) of the 1986 Act is commonly pleaded in the alternative to s 994 for three main reasons. First, as we have seen, facts which satisfy the threshold tests under s 994 may not necessarily satisfy the test under s 122(1)(g) and vice versa (see *Hawkes v Cuddy (No 2)* (2009), para **11.16**). Second, winding-up is not available as a remedy under ss 994–996.

Pleading the two in the alternative therefore gives the court more flexibility to deal with the case. Third, historically, the tactic of pleading a winding-up petition as an alternative to s 994, even where this was not an appropriate remedy, allowed the petitioner to put the maximum pressure possible on the respondents to settle the case as soon as possible. However, the policy against adding winding-up as a matter of course in a petition for unfairly prejudicial conduct is manifest from the following practice direction, the CPR Practice Direction, Part 49B, para 9(1) (replacing Chancery 1/90 (Practice Direction)):

> *Attention is drawn to the undesirability of asking as a matter of course for a winding-up order as an alternative to an order under s. 459 of the Companies Act 1985 [now s 994]. The petition should not ask for a winding-up order unless that is the relief which the petitioner prefers or it is thought that it may be the only relief to which he is entitled.*

In *Fulham Football Club (1987) Ltd v Richards* (2011) the court held that s 994 will usually provide the source of a satisfactory alternative remedy such as a buy-out order so that winding-up under s 122(1)(g) is therefore a last resort and an exceptional remedy to grant in the context of disputes between shareholders. The court stated that this is confirmed by the terms of the current Practice Direction 49B which draws attention to the undesirability of asking, as a matter of course, for a winding-up order as an alternative to an order under s 994.

(See also *Dineshkumar Jeshang Shah v Mahendra Jeshang Shah* (2010).)

11.77 Thus, in *Re a Company (No 004415 of 1996)* (1997) allegations concerning remuneration and dividends were held to constitute a prima facie case of unfairly prejudicial conduct and the court struck out the petition for winding-up on the just and equitable ground (see also *Re Copeland & Craddock Ltd*). The point is reinforced by the Law Commission's Report No 246, *Shareholder Remedies* (1997), which recommended that winding-up should be specifically added to the remedies available under s 996, subject to the petitioner being required to obtain the leave of the court before seeking a winding-up order (para **4.44**). As the language of s 996 makes clear, this recommendation was not adopted. However, winding-up may be an appropriate remedy for the court to at least consider when determining the price to be paid for the petitioner's shares under s 996. As explained in *Re Sunrise Radio Ltd* (2010):

> *A winding-up, though producing a rateable proportion of the assets for all shareholders, will often be at break-up value, and therefore not necessarily advantageous to the shareholders. Nevertheless, in the case of a solvent company, I do not see why the court should not direct the liquidator to carry on business in an appropriate case, if necessary appointing a special manager to assist him, thus preserving the value of the business which can be realised on a going concern basis. Given that possible alternative, the court should not in general put a shareholder in a worse position than would be the case in a winding-up, if the facts would otherwise justify invocation of the 'just and equitable' jurisdiction. That does not mean, however, that winding-up should routinely be sought*

as an alternative in s 994 cases. Rather, the potential availability of relief through the winding-up process should in an appropriate case be taken into account in fashioning the remedy, including the determination of the price, under s 996.

Finally, it is noteworthy that in *Amin v Amin* (2009) Warren J, finding that the petitioners' allegations of unfair prejudice were unfounded, nevertheless recognised that the circumstances may well have supported a successful petition for just and equitable winding-up, although the petitioners had not sought this. The judge went on to observe that:

If the facts are such that a winding up petition on the 'just and equitable' ground would succeed but the majority refuse to agree to a winding-up out of court, that conduct might amount to unfair prejudice, the unfairness being to compel the minority to continue to participate in the company when the court would, on this hypothesis, wind it up.

Relevance of the petitioner's conduct

11.78 It was settled by the House of Lords in *O'Neill v Philips* (1999) that in determining the issue of unfair prejudice, the equitable principles laid down in *Ebrahimi* will necessarily come to the fore where the company in question is a small quasi-partnership. Accordingly, where a petitioner seeks to rely on equity his conduct becomes a relevant factor in the court's determination. It is also apparent from the case law that regard will be had to the petitioner's conduct when determining the question of whether or not the respondent's behaviour was unfair. It will be recalled that in *Re RA Noble Ltd* it was held that the petitioner by his own 'disinterest' was to blame for his exclusion from management and so the respondent's conduct, although prejudicial, was not unfair (see also *Jesner v Jarrad Properties Ltd* (1993); see further the Court of Appeal's decision in *Richardson v Blackmore* (2005); and *Badyal v Badyal* (para **11.17**)). It has also been seen that the petitioner's conduct may be material to the court in framing its remedy, particularly in relation to fixing the appropriate valuation date for the purposes of s 996(2)(e) (*Re London School of Electronics Ltd* (1986)). However, Peter Gibson LJ has observed that 'the conduct of a member of his own affairs, for example by requesting a general meeting of the company or seeking answers to an excessive number of questions, is irrelevant' (*Re Legal Costs Negotiators Ltd* (1999)).

11.79 While the courts take a dim view of petitioners who delay in presenting their petition, they are mindful that to strike out a petition on this ground may be unduly harsh. In *Hateley v Morris* (2004), the petition was presented some two years after the events complained of. It then took another three years for it to reach the court. Mann J criticised the delay but felt there were compelling reasons for excusing it, including fault on the part of the respondents in failing to expedite the proceedings (see also *Rahman v Malik* (2008)). On the other hand, in *Re Grandactual Ltd* (2006), the petition was struck out where the allegation of unfairly prejudicial conduct related to conduct in which the petitioners had participated without complaint some nine years before the claim was presented. The judge explained that while s 994 was not subject to any period of limitation, relief under the provision was discretionary. He emphatically stated that a court should not countenance proceedings such as those before him where the petition was presented nearly ten years after the events complained of.

Other specific statutory minority rights

Introduction

11.80 Thus far we have examined the principal substantive remedies available to aggrieved minority shareholders. Additionally, the Companies Act contains a number of provisions which grant rights to minority shareholders who dissent from certain decisions taken by the company or who wish to require it to perform certain statutory duties. For instance, the Act lays down specific procedures for the alteration of a company's constitution which are aimed at preventing changes being effected unless supported by 75 per cent of the general meeting. Other specific statutory provisions include the right of shareholders to requisition an extraordinary general meeting; demand a poll; and remove a director by a simple majority of votes.

Alterations to the company's constitution

11.81 Minority shareholders are protected against alterations to the articles of association of the company being carried by a simple majority of the general meeting. Subject to ss 631–633 of the CA 2006, s 21 empowers a company to alter its articles by special resolution. As we discussed in Chapter 8, this, of course, gives rise to the curious result that, in contrast to the general law of contract, the statutory contract found in s 33 can be changed without the unanimous consent of the parties. However, an existing member is not bound by an alteration to the articles which increases his liability to contribute capital unless he agrees in writing either before or after the alteration is made (s 25). By way of an additional safeguard, it is possible to prevent provisions in the company's articles of association from being altered by special resolution by including a so-called 'provision for entrenchment' to the effect that specified provisions 'may be amended or repealed only if conditions are met, or procedures are complied with, that are more restrictive than those applicable in the case of a special resolution' (s 22(1); see further Chapter 8). But a company cannot restrict the right to alter its articles by a declaration in the articles themselves, nor can it contract not to alter its articles. Thus, in *Walker v London Tramways Co* (1879) the court held that a clause in the company's articles which declared that certain articles were essential and unalterable was ineffective and Jessel MR placed considerable emphasis on the fact that no company could contract itself out of its right to exercise the powers conferred by statute (see further *Punt v Symons & Co Ltd* (1903)). While it seems settled that a company cannot bind itself not to exercise a statutory right, an agreement outside the articles between the shareholders *inter se* as to how they will exercise their voting rights on a resolution to alter the articles may be enforceable as between themselves (*Russell v Northern Bank Development Corpn Ltd* (1992)). In this way shareholders' rights may be indirectly entrenched insofar as the court will enforce such an agreement as between the members who were parties to it although it will not be binding on their transferees or non-assenting shareholders (*Welton v Saffery* (1897); see Chapter 8).

The right to requisition an extraordinary general meeting

11.82 Section 303 provides that shareholders may require the directors to convene a general meeting of the company. The requisition, which must be supported by holders of not less than 5 per cent of the voting paid-up capital or, in the case of a company with no share capital, by members representing not less than 10 per cent of the total voting rights in the company, must state the objects of the meeting. If the directors fail to convene a meeting within 21 days from the date of the requisition, the requisitionists may do so themselves. Finally, it is provided that the meeting convened by the directors must take place within 28 days after the date of the notice convening it (s 304).

The right to demand a poll

11.83 The practice in general meetings is for voting to take place on a show of hands, a poll is taken only if a valid demand is made. On a show of hands each member will have one vote irrespective of the number of shares held and normally a proxy cannot vote at all. Where a poll is taken all members can cast their votes according to the number of shares held and this therefore gives a more accurate picture of the opinion of the shareholders. Uncontroversial resolutions are normally voted on by a show of hands only but where an issue is disputed, a member can demand that a poll be taken. Section 321 provides that notwithstanding anything in the articles to the contrary, other than on a resolution to elect a chair or to adjourn the meeting, a poll must be taken if demanded by any of the following: not less than five members having a right to vote at the meeting; members holding not less than 10 per cent of all voting rights that could be cast at the meeting; members holding shares conferring a right to vote at the meeting on which the aggregate sum paid up equals not less than 10 per cent of the total sum paid up on all such shares.

The Law Commission's proposals for reforming the unfair prejudice provision

11.84 The Law Commission's Consultation Paper No 142 (1996) and its ensuing Report, No 246 (Cm 3769, 1997), which were considered in Chapter 10 in relation to reforming the derivative action, also encompassed statutory shareholder remedies.

Procedural reform

11.85 The principal concern of the Law Commission was not directed towards the substantive remedy itself but rather towards the length and cost of typical unfair prejudice actions and the destructive effect such proceedings had on small private companies. The Consultation Paper gave a number of examples to highlight this problem. For instance, it found that the trial in *Re Elgindata Ltd* spanned some 43 days with costs of £320,000 while the shares in the company, originally purchased for £40,000, fell in value to £24,600. In *Re Macro (Ipswich) Ltd* the hearing of the petition and a related action lasted 27 days and the costs claimed came to some £725,000. This did not include appeal costs. The Law Commission, taking the Woolf Civil Justice Reforms as its backdrop (*Access to Justice, The Final Report to the Lord Chancellor on the Civil Justice System in England and Wales* (1996)), therefore recommends that the difficulties of length, cost, and complexity of s 459 (now s 994) proceedings should be addressed by active case management by the courts. More particularly, the Commission took the view that the courts should make greater use of the power to direct that preliminary issues be heard, or that some issues be tried before others; to impose costs sanctions; and to have the power to dismiss any claim or part of a claim or defence thereto which, in the opinion of the court, has no realistic prospect of success at full trial.

It is noteworthy that the length and costs of such proceedings are not the only problems of which the courts and prospective parties to such proceedings need to be aware. As Vinelott J observed in *Re a Company, ex p Burr*, there is also '[t]he damaging effect which the presentation of the petition may have on the business of a company, even if it is not advertised'.

Substantive reform

11.86 The Commission noted from its statistical survey that the majority of petitions were brought by minority shareholders in small private companies seeking to have their shares purchased on the basis of exclusion from management. In order to attain the objectives of providing such petitioners with a speedy and economical exit route, the Law Commission recommends that the unfair prejudice provision should be amended so as to raise rebuttable presumptions that where a shareholder has been excluded from participating in management:

(a) the affairs of the company will be presumed to have been conducted in a manner which is unfairly prejudicial to the petitioner; and

(b) if the presumption is not rebutted and the court is satisfied that it ought to order a buy-out of the petitioner's shares, it should do so on a pro rata basis.

The presumption would only apply where the company is a private limited company in which the petitioner held shares in his sole name giving him not less than 10 per cent of the rights to vote at general meetings, and all, or substantially all, of the members of the company were directors. The petitioner must have been removed as a director or prevented from carrying out all or substantially all of his functions as a director.

Winding-up as an alternative remedy

11.87   While noting that the remedies available under s 461 (now s 996) are very wide, the Law Commission recommends that shareholder remedies would be streamlined if winding-up was added to the array of orders available to the court under the provision. To avoid the risk of reputational damage and loss of confidence among its customers and suppliers which a company may suffer in the event of an unjust claim for winding-up, a petitioner who seeks such an order will first have to obtain the court's leave to do so. Further, a petitioner who seeks a winding-up order under s 122(1)(g) of the 1986 Act in conjunction with an application under s 459 (s 994) would also be required to obtain the leave of the court before making such an application.

Exit articles

11.88   It also recommended that the model articles of association should be amended so as to include an exit provision whereby shareholders would be encouraged from the outset to provide for what is to happen in the event of a dispute. An exit article would enable a shareholder to leave a company without necessarily having to resort to proceedings. The Law Commission states that the exit regulation would be conferred by an ordinary resolution and that every shareholder who is to have or be subject to exit rights must be named in the resolution and must consent to it. The resolution must set out the events in which exit rights are to be exercisable and the shareholder entitled to the right may require other shareholders named in the resolution to buy his shares at a 'fair price'. Such shares must be shares he held when the resolution was passed or shares acquired in right of them, for example on a bonus issue. The company will not be permitted to amend the resolution or the exit article without the consent of the named shareholders. Further, the resolution must state how the 'fair price' is to be calculated and, if the shares are to be valued, how the valuer is to be appointed. The purchase will need to be completed within three months.

The Law Commission concludes that at the minimum the exit provision would at least prompt registration agents to advise their clients to consider entering into a shareholders' agreement as an alternative means of providing for dispute resolution. The effect of which would be that the current burgeoning case load would be significantly reduced.

11.89   The CLRSG's proposals were broadly based on the principles put forward by the Law Commission but differed in several key respects as a result of its consultation exercise. It is particularly noteworthy that the November 2000 Consultation Paper, *Completing* *the Structure*, states that s 459 should be retained in its present form 'and subject to the focus laid down' in the House of Lords' decision in *O'Neill v Phillips* (para 5.108; see also the *Final Report*, para 7.41). Thus, as we saw earlier, s 994 restates s 459of the CA 1985. The CLRSG came down against including winding-up to the array of remedies available under the provision (*Final Report*, paras 7.41–7.45), thus s 996 restates s 461 of the CA 1985, albeit in restructured form.

FURTHER READING

This chapter links with the materials in Chapter 13 of **Hicks and Goo's Cases and Materials on Company Law** (Oxford, OUP, 2011, xl +649p).

Company Financial and Insolvency Law Review. Special issue, Autumn 1997.

Company Law Review Steering Group, *Modern Company Law For a Competitive Economy: Completing the Structure* (DTI, November 2000), http://www.bis.gov.uk/policies/business-law/company-and-partnership-law/company-law/publications-archive.

Company Lawyer. Special issue [1997] 18(8).

Goddard and Hirt, 'Section 459 and Corporate Groups' [2005] *JBL* 247.

Hannigan, 'Drawing Boundaries between Derivative Claims and Unfairly Prejudicial Conduct' [2009] *JBL* 606.

Law Commission Consultation Paper No 142, *Shareholder Remedies* (1996).

Law Commission Report No 246, *Shareholder Remedies* (Cm 3769, 1997).

Lowry, 'Mapping the Boundaries of Unfair Prejudice' in de Lacy (ed) *The Reform of United Kingdom Company Law* (London, Cavendish, 2002).

Payne, 'Shareholders' Remedies Reassessed' [2004] *MLR* 500.

Prentice, 'The Theory of the Firm: Minority Shareholder Oppression: Sections 459–461 of the Companies Act 1985' (1988) 8 *OJLS* 55.

Reisberg, 'Indemnity Costs Orders Under s 459 Petitions' [2004] *Co Law* 116.

Riley, 'Implicit Dimensions of Contract and the Oppression of Minority Shareholders' in Campbell et al (eds) *Implicit Dimensions of Contract* (Oxford, Hart Publishing, 2003).

SELF-TEST QUESTIONS

1   What factors would influence a petitioner's choice in deciding whether to pursue a remedy under the just and equitable' winding-up provision or s 994 of the CA 2006?

2   What is a quasi-partnership company?

3   The most common remedy sought by petitioners under s 994 is a share purchase order. How do the courts value shares for the purpose of an order under s 996(2)(e)?

4   Rodney and Dell run a successful wholesaling partnership, specialising in high-quality organic foods. Wishing to expand the business they invite Tracey to invest £50,000 in a joint venture with them. A new company, Grubber Ltd, is formed, with the issued shares taken in three equal parts by Rodney, Dell, and Tracey respectively. The understanding between the parties is that the new company will take over and expand the wholesaling business; that Rodney and Dell will work full-time in the business; that all three will be members of the board of directors; and that the company's profits will be distributed in three equal shares as directors' remuneration. Grubber Ltd is run in accordance with this understanding for five years. The company is profitable, but not on the scale anticipated by Rodney and Dell. They decide, without consulting Tracey, that the company should acquire a number of retail outlets in shopping malls from which to operate shops. The scheme involved a large capital expenditure. Tracey is informed that for an indefinite period the company, because of the debt-servicing burden that the expansion scheme involves, will only be able to pay a fixed salary to Rodney and Dell in return for their full-time services and that Tracey must forego profit in favour of capital growth of her investment. Tracey asks to be bought out. Rodney and Dell refuse, informing her that all company resources are needed for the expansion.

Advise Tracey.

PART III

Issues of Corporate Authority

12 The constitution of the company: dealing with outsiders

SUMMARY

Introduction
The ultra vires doctrine
The reform of ultra vires
Agency
Statutory authority

Introduction

12.1 The artificial nature of the company creates one very specific problem—it does not physically exist. If the organs of the company (the general meeting or the board of directors) make a decision we can say that that decision is an act of the company. However, most of the time dealings with outsiders (to buy, sell etc) occur through individual officers (e.g. the managing director), agents (a simple example is a travel agent), or employees (a stationery manager who buys stationery) of the company. This chapter is concerned with how the law determines whether those transactions with those outside the company (called outsiders or third parties) are legitimate and will be binding on the company.

12.2 As we observed briefly in Chapter 8 and we will explore further in this chapter, historically the company's total power to do something was determined by its objects clause (i.e. what business it was empowered by Parliament to carry out, e.g. to run a sweet shop). After an extensive reform process, unless a company chooses to have an objects clause which sets out the limit of its power, CA 2006, s 31 now provides that companies have unrestricted objects, i.e. they are empowered by Parliament to take part in any business they wish. It is worth noting however that most companies were incorporated under previous Companies Acts which required an objects clause and so will still be operating (unless they remove that objects clause, see para **12.20**) within the power conferred by Parliament in that objects clause. A large part of that limited or unlimited power (but note not all of it, see para **8.18**) is then delegated in the articles to the board who may exercise it itself or may delegate part of the power to the company's agents or employees. Those agents and employees may then contract with outsiders in the exercise of that delegated power. The power of the company in effect gets narrower as it moves away from the original source. Thus, a stationery manager when he transacts to buy stationery is exercising a minute part of the total power of the company.

12.3   Historically, where there was some doubt as to whether a transaction was authorised two questions arose. First, was the act within the power of the company? If the answer was yes then we moved to the second question. If the answer was no, the transaction was void and unenforceable—this could have very serious consequences as we will see. Second, if the act was within the power of the company was the individual who contracted on the company's behalf authorised to do so? If they were, the transaction was valid but if not it was voidable at the instance of the company. As a result the area was full of uncertainty and danger for people dealing with companies. However, over time some judicial intervention and a largely successful reform process have combined to protect those dealing with the company.

The ultra vires doctrine

12.4   As we discussed briefly in Chapter 8, the 19th-century companies legislation created registered incorporated companies with a requirement that the memorandum of association specify the objects of the company. This was a hangover from the period when companies were formed by charters or grants from the Crown and Parliament. Organisations like the Church or local authorities whose main function was to serve the public interest were among the first to exploit corporate status. Over time this practice expanded to encompass trading companies formed to exploit trade, transport, or technology rights (for example, the East India Company, the Great Western Railway, and the British Indian Submarine Telegraph Company (now Cable and Wireless plc)). In theory these grants of corporate status to private businesses were still granted primarily because of the public interest in promoting a specific business venture. However, the registered company was somewhat different because those forming the company set out its objects rather than Parliament itself which, in most cases, would have no public interest element at all.

12.5   Legal theory at the time the registered companies appeared was dominated, as we observed in Chapter 8, by concession theory. Legal theorists considered that companies were similar to public bodies. A public body is conferred with certain power by Parliament and cannot go beyond that power (termed an ultra vires act). If it did act ultra vires that act was void. For public bodies to be subject to such restrictions was necessary in order to safeguard democracy because if a public body takes more power than the elected representatives of the people have given it, an act in furtherance of that excessive power has no legitimacy. There was another reason why the ultra vires doctrine was deemed to apply to a registered company, it was thought to protect the shareholders and the creditors. If the company was restricted to one function, the members and the creditors were protected because the directors were restricted in their choice of business to that which the share-holders and the creditors had initially provided money to fund.

12.6 However, as we will see historically three particular issues combined to make ultra vires a very tricky problem for the courts. First, initially the objects clause was unalterable and then only alterable in limited circumstances until 1989. Second, unlike public bodies whose functions are relatively fixed (for example, BEIS is unlikely to decide to become the Department of Education) registered companies often did change the central nature of their business. This can happen relatively easily, for example X Ltd is a coal-mining business with simple objects stating it is to mine coal. It decides to move into coal delivery and ultimately finds that transporting goods generally is more profitable than mining coal. In order to buy more trucks it gets a large loan from a bank. The delivery business is successful for a while but the company goes into insolvent liquidation within three years. The liquidator then notices that the objects clause is to mine coal and declares all the contracts of the creditors of the company (including the bank) void and unenforceable. On a classical interpretation of the ultra vires rule the liquidator is correct.

12.7 Third, the doctrine of constructive notice could combine with the ultra vires rule to leave unwary third parties with unenforceable contracts. The doctrine applies to public documents (remember the documents required to form a registered company, including the memorandum and the articles, are public documents) and deems anyone dealing with registered companies to have notice of the contents of its public documents. Therefore, anyone dealing contractually with a company was deemed to have knowledge of its objects clause and was presumed to enter into the void transaction with that knowledge. The doctrine makes it impossible for someone dealing with the company to argue that they did not know that the company lacked capacity to enter the transaction.

The classic rule

12.8 As a result of the moveable nature of business, constructive notice and the fact that the memorandum was unalterable for much of the 19th and 20th centuries, the courts at first had some difficulty applying the ultra vires principle strictly to registered companies. In *Riche v Ashbury Railway Carriage & Iron Co* (1874) the trial court adopted a flexible approach to the concept by allowing the company to do anything not prohibited in its constitution. However, the judge's relatively simple solution to the problem did not ultimately find favour when the case reached the House of Lords. In *Ashbury Carriage Company v Riche* (1875) the House of Lords took the opportunity to state clearly that the ultra vires doctrine did apply to registered companies. Thus, if a company incorporated by or under statute acted beyond the scope of the objects stated in the statute or in its memorandum of association such acts were void as beyond the company's capacity even if ratified by all the members. This is a useful reminder that in this period the judiciary still largely viewed the registered company as a part of the state and applied a concession theory approach to its regulation.

12.9   However, the courts quickly began to recognise the difficulty with treating registered companies as if they were public bodies and started to erode that statement of high principle by applying a certain ingenuity to avoid the ultra vires doctrine. For example, in *A-G v Great Eastern Rly* (1880) the House of Lords outlined a very important broad interpretation of the powers that could be exercised in the pursuit of its objects. They considered a company could enter into transactions which were fairly regarded as incidental or consequential to its objects. This provided companies with some room to manoeuvre.

12.10 While this represented some progress with the issue it still left problems where the object could not strictly be achieved. For example, in *Re German Date Coffee Co* (1882) the company's object was to acquire and exploit a German patent for producing coffee from dates. The company failed to get the German patent but obtained a Swedish one instead. Despite the fact the company had a thriving date coffee business it was wound up by the court because it could not achieve its stated object. As a result of the dangers posed to companies by this rule much legal ingenuity went into framing objects clauses to minimise the impact of the ultra vires rule. Some objects clauses listed a large number of activities the company could carry on. This was sometimes successful but at other times the courts interpreted anything following the main object as being only a power that must be exercised in furtherance of the main object. In response companies then drafted objects clauses which stated that each object or power was to be treated as independent and in no way attached to the main object. In *Cotman v Brougham* (1918) the House of Lords reluctantly accepted an objects clause that was very widely drafted with a clause at the end stating that any of the objects listed could be carried on as the company's main object.

12.11 By the 1960s companies had objects clauses which stated their objects widely, generally concluding with the following statement:

> to carry on any other trade or business whatsoever which can, in the opinion of the board of directors, be advantageously carried on by the company in connection with or as ancillary to any of the above businesses or the general business of the company.

This clause was accepted as a valid one in *Bell Houses Ltd v City Wall Properties Ltd* (1966). By the 1980s objects clauses had continued to grow in breadth. For example:

> to carry on business as bankers, capitalists, financiers, concessionaires and merchants ... and generally to undertake and carry out all such obligations and transactions as an individual capitalist may lawfully undertake and carry out.

This clause was accepted in *Newstead v Frost* (1980) as allowing the company to enter into a partnership in order to avoid a tax liability. It is worth noting here that this acceptance of the wide objects clause also emphasises the private nature of the company and represents a move firmly away from the concession theory upon which the application of the public law concept of ultra vires was based.

12.12 As a result of the judicial acceptance of these wide clauses the courts were not faced with objects issues as frequently as they once had been. However, the problem did not go away and occasionally the courts would be presented with an objects issue which no amount of flexibility could solve. In *Re Jon Beauforte (London) Ltd* (1953) the company's objects stated it was to carry on a business as gown makers but the business had evolved into making veneered panels. No change had been made to the objects clause to reflect this change. A coal merchant had supplied coal to the company which was ordered on company notepaper headed with a reference to the company being a veneered panel maker. The coal merchant was deemed because of constructive notice to know of the original objects clause and because of the headed notepaper to have actual notice of the change in the business. As a result the transaction was ultra vires and void. Another clear example of this is *Re Introductions Ltd v National Provincial Bank* (1970). This case concerned a company incorporated in 1951 around the time of the Festival of Britain with the object of providing foreign visitors with accommodation and entertainment. After the Festival was over the company diversified and eventually devoted itself solely to pig breeding which the original framers of the objects had not considered (naturally enough). The company had granted National Provincial Bank a debenture to secure a substantial overdraft which had accumulated prior to its eventual insolvent liquidation. The company was held to have acted ultra vires and therefore the transaction was void and the bank could not enforce the debenture or even claim as a normal creditor in the liquidation (see Chapter 17 on the statutory liquidation procedure).

Ultra vires and the benefit of the company

12.13 Certain decisions of the company which have no immediate tangible benefit to the company have also fallen foul of the ultra vires doctrine. During their lifetime companies often make charitable donations, political donations, and gratuitous payments to employees (e.g. granting pensions or retirement gifts). All of this is generally deemed to be of benefit to the company while it is a going concern. However, once the company ceases to do business such payments become problematic. In *Hutton v West Cork Rly Co* (1883) the court held that a railway company, whose undertaking had been transferred to another company and whose affairs were being wound up, could not pay gratuitous compensation to its former employees or to its directors for loss of employment. This was so despite the fact that they had never been paid during the life of the company. The company was in liquidation and could not benefit from the gift to the directors, any such transaction being ultra vires and void. This introduced a new formulation into the objects debate to the effect that not only did the act of the company have to be within the objects clause but the company's power had to be exercised bona fides for the benefit of the company.

12.14 Similarly in *Parke v Daily News Ltd* (1962) the same issue arose out of the sale of the newspaper, the *News Chronicle and Star*. The Cadbury family, who controlled the selling company, wished to distribute the proceeds of the sale amongst the employees who would be made redundant by the sale. A shareholder sued to restrain them from doing so and was successful on the basis that the company would receive no benefit from the action so it was, therefore, ultra vires. The introduction of the benefit of the company criterion was clearly problematic for companies and eventually led to a raft of legislation to allow payments to be made to employees both generally and specifically in a liquidation (CA 1985, s 309 now contained in CA 2006, ss 172 and 247, and s 187 of the Insolvency Act 1986). (Political donations engage a higher level of regulation and need shareholder approval, CA 2006, Part 14.)

12.15 There was however something odd about the addition of the benefit of the company criterion to the ultra vires issue; clearly in the *Parke* case the act (paying employees) was within the objects clause yet was found to be ultra vires. The courts eventually decided (see *Rolled Steel Ltd v British Steel Corpn* (1986) and *Brady v Brady* (1988)) that these decisions are in fact not ultra vires cases at all but are rather cases where the issue was whether directors exceeded their powers (as opposed to the company's power) or a question of whether they exercised their power properly (see the Agency and Statutory Authority sections, paras **12.21** and **12.28** respectively). Corporate capacity questions were solely to be determined by the construction of the objects clause. The question of whether the power was exercised for the benefit of the company had nothing to do with whether the company had capacity to do the act in question.

The reform of ultra vires

12.16 The slow liberalisation of the judicial concession approach was accompanied by occasional recommendations for reform of the area. In 1945 the Cohen Committee (Cmnd 6659) recommended doing away with the ultra vires concept where third parties were involved. However, nothing came of this recommendation and it was not until the UK was forced to act as part of its obligations on joining the European Community that legislation reforming ultra vires was introduced in s 9(1) of the European Communities Act 1972. The domestication of the First European Community Company Law Harmonisation Directive a version of which remains in what is now CA 2006, s 39 (formerly contained in CA 1985, s 35) removed the doctrine of constructive notice where it concerned the memorandum and articles of association. It also contained a saving provision for ultra vires transactions where the transaction was dealt with by the directors and the third party was acting in good faith (now CA 2006, s 40). While this reform narrowed the extent of the ultra vires rule it still left the potential for problems to arise. In 1986 the DTI (now BEIS) produced a report (the Prentice Report) recommending much deeper reforms. The Prentice Report formed the basis of a number of provisions introduced in the CA 1989 amending the CA 1985 with respect to its ultra vires sections.

12.17 The reforms had a dual approach. First, it made it easier for companies to arrange their constitution to avoid ultra vires issues. Thus, s 110 of the CA 1989 introduced a new s 4 into the CA 1985 which allowed the memorandum to be changed by special resolution (now CA 2006, s 21). This had the effect of allowing companies who wished to diversify, to change the objects clause with relative ease. The same section of the CA 1989 also introduced a new s 3A into the CA 1985 which allowed companies to have an objects clause which stated that it was to carry on business as a general commercial company. This allowed the company to carry on any trade or business whatsoever and the company had the power to do all such things as were incidental or conducive to the carrying on of any trade or business.

12.18 Second, it dealt directly with ultra vires transactions by repealing the old s 35 and introducing new ss 35, 35A, and 35B in the CA 1985. Section 35 stated:

> (1) *The validity of an act done by a company shall not be called into question on the ground of lack of capacity by reason of anything in the company's memorandum.*

As a result of this section a transaction which was technically ultra vires the company was still valid and enforceable. The question became rather whether those representing the company had the authority to enter into the contract. As both statutory reforms introduced in ss 35A and 35B of the CA 1985 and subsumed into the CA 2006 plus common law developments primarily dealt with this question of internal authority we will deal with this issue in the sections on Agency and Statutory Authority later in this chapter.

12.19 As we observed in Chapter 8, the memorandum and the articles form a statutory contract between the company and the members and therefore if the company entered into an ultra vires act it was bound to the outsider because of s 35 but the same act would also breach the contract with the members for which the directors were potentially liable. The amendments to the CA 1985 in 1989 dealt with this issue in two ways. The 1989 amendments introduced a new s 35(2) whereby if a member was aware of an imminent ultra vires act he could bring proceedings to restrain the doing of that act. Second, s 35(3) was also introduced to emphasise that the directors had a duty to observe any internal restrictions on their powers flowing from the memorandum. However, an ultra vires transaction could be ratified by a special resolution of the general meeting but this would not affect the liability of the directors for breach, thus a separate special resolution passed by the members was the only way the directors could be relieved from liability for an ultra vires act.

12.20 While the 1989 amendments were on the whole largely successful there was general agreement that the way this was achieved was unnecessarily complex. The CLRSG in their *Final Report* (July 2001) (para 9.10) recommend simplifying this and that any company formed under a new Companies Act have unlimited capacity whether or not it chooses to have an objects clause. The White Paper (2002) (Vol I, paras 2.2 and 6.2) and the Government's Consultative Document of March 2005 (para 5.1) also broadly followed these recommendations. As a result the CA 2006 attempted yet again to reform this area. As we have already observed in Chapters 1 and 8 under the CA 2006 a company's constitution means only the articles of association and associated resolutions of the general meeting (CA 2006, s 17). The memorandum still exists but it is not part of the constitution and acts purely as a statement by the founders of the company that they wish to form the company and become members of it (CA 2006, s 8). Everything else that was formerly in the memorandum now forms part of the articles of association or the application for registration (CA 2006, s 9 and s 28). Under the CA 2006 all companies are deemed to have unrestricted objects unless the company's articles specifically restrict the objects of the company (CA 2006, s 31). As most companies currently in existence were formed under principal Companies Acts that required an objects clause, this change will only really affect companies newly incorporated under the CA 2006. For companies already in existence with an objects clause, that clause still operates to restrict them, and will now become part of their articles of association (CA 2006, s 28). Companies with such an objects clause could if they wished choose to remove it but it is doubtful whether there would be any particular advantage in doing this for companies with a general objects clause—again the vast majority. In recognition of the fact that a large number of companies will still have an objects clause s 35 of the CA 1985 has been replaced by an almost exact replica in s 39 which states:

> (1) The validity of an act done by a company shall not be called into question on the ground of lack of capacity by reason of anything in the company's constitution.

It is worth noting that the shareholder injunctive provisions and the director's duty to observe internal restrictions which were in the CA 1985, s 35(2) and (3) are not similarly repeated in the CA 2006. The Explanatory Notes to the CA 2006 offer this explanation:

> The section does not contain provision corresponding to section 35(2) and (3) of the 1985 Act. It is considered that the combination of the fact that under the Act a company may have unrestricted objects (and where it has restricted objects the directors' powers are correspondingly restricted), and the fact that a specific duty on directors to abide by the company's constitution is provided for in section 171, makes these provisions unnecessary.

However, given that the reason for replicating s 35 in the new s 39 was to cover companies that retain a restrictive objects clause and thus to protect against the problems that have historically been evident with restrictive objects, this seems an odd omission.

Agency

12.21 As we discussed briefly earlier, a company presents certain unique challenges to the traditional interpretation of agency principles. Unlike humans it cannot operate itself, it acts only through agents. Either it directly appoints an outsider as an agent (for example, a travel agent) or it authorises a director or employee to be its agent. Therefore whenever we wish to attribute responsibility for a contract to the company we must use agency principles. An agent is someone appointed by a principal to act on their behalf. Thus, in our travel agent example, the company or more usually its employee agent appoints an external travel agent to make its travel arrangements. The company is the principal and first party, the travel agent is obviously the agent and second party, and the third party being the person or company on the other side of the contact (for example, an airline). The contract will be between the principal (the company) and the third party (airline) even though it is the agent who has signed the contract. This is one of the features of agency that the agent has the legal authority to enter into contracts on behalf of the principal as if the principal had signed the contract personally. The agent has no part in the contract other than to represent the principal.

12.22   However, companies are complex organisations. While the articles of association create a simple organisational structure (general meeting and board of directors) this often only represents the root of the organisational structure of the company. The articles delegate power to the board but the board will by necessity have to delegate the day-to-day running of the company to managers who will in turn delegate tasks to other staff, who will in turn delegate and so on. Each layer down in the organisational structure represents transference of authority from one agent to another. Sometimes as we will see that transference of authority is not entirely clear and questions may arise as to whether certain decisions or acts taken or done can be attributed to the company.

12.23   The normal general principles of agency will then apply in order to determine whether the company is bound by a particular transaction. A principal will be bound by a contract entered into on his behalf by his agent if that agent acted within either the actual scope of the authority given by the principal before the contract or the apparent or ostensible scope of his authority. The principal may also ratify a contract entered into without authority. While specific authority is conferred on the board to run the company, once the authority goes below board level actual authority in the context of a corporation or any other complex organisation is somewhat misleading as specific authority to carry out some functions may not be conferred.

12.24   A manager can be given a specific job description by the board but often much of the actual authority is implied by the position held and by the custom in the company or industry. For example Mike is a purchasing manager who used to work for X Ltd as head of its purchasing department. Mike has just started working with Y Ltd in the same role and has found that although in his previous job the human resources department did all the hiring, Y Ltd has only a small HR department and thus it is the practice in Y Ltd that all staffing issues are the responsibility of individual department heads. Here Mike has actual authority to hire employees even though his job description contains no such reference, it is purely implied from the internal practice in Y Ltd.

12.25   Apparent or ostensible authority arises where, rather than any actual authority being given, the board of directors or the general meeting allows someone to hold themselves out as having such authority or allowing someone to hold themselves out as having a position in the company that would have such authority. For example in *Freeman & Lockyer v Buckhurst Park Properties Ltd* (1964) a firm of architects were engaged by a person acting as Buckhurst's managing director. Buckhurst would not pay the fees as it claimed he was not the managing director as he had never been appointed managing director. The Court of Appeal upheld the architect's claim, finding that the board had held out the person as the managing director and that he therefore had ostensible authority to bind the company. However, sometimes the line between actual authority that is implied and ostensible authority is very fine. In *Hely-Hutchinson v Brayhead Ltd and Richards* (1968) the Court of Appeal found that Richards who had acted as managing director but had never been formally appointed had implied actual authority to bind the company rather than ostensible authority. (See *MCI WorldCom International Inc v Primus Telecommunications Inc* (2004) and *Quinn v CC Automotive Group Ltd t/a Carcraft* (2010) for examples of how complex ostensible authority can be.)

12.26   Another problem for agency arose where the company's constitution sets out a certain procedure before a transaction can be carried out by the company. Here the doctrine of constructive notice, as we briefly discussed earlier, had a potentially drastic effect on outsiders as they were deemed to know about any internal procedures in the constitution as it is a public document. So sometimes, even though an action is within the capacity of the company, it may be outside the powers of the individual representing the company because an internal procedure was not complied with. For example in *Knopp v Thane Investments Ltd* (2003) the court found that the director's failure to observe the articles rendered a contract contrary to the articles unenforceable. If the doctrine of constructive notice was applied strictly the outsider could not complain about the lack of authority as they were deemed to know that there was a limit on the actual authority of the company's agent. However, the courts were often keen to mitigate the effect of constructive notice. In *Royal British Bank v Turquand* (1856) an action was brought for the return of money borrowed by the company. The company argued that it was not required to pay back the money because the manager who negotiated the loan should have been authorised by a resolution of the general meeting to borrow but he had no such authorisation. As a result of the doctrine of constructive notice the bank was deemed to know this. The court held that the public documents only revealed that a resolution was required not whether the resolution had been passed. The bank had no knowledge that the resolution had not been passed and thus it did not appear on the face of the public documents that the borrowing was invalid. Outsiders are therefore entitled to assume that the internal procedures have been complied with. This is often called the indoor management rule. The rule only applies to those acting in good faith or who have no actual notice of the irregularity (see *Rolled Steel Ltd v British Steel Corpn* (1986)). It also has no application where the third party is an insider, for example a director who enters into a contract with the company (see *Morris v Kanssen* (1946)).

12.27   As we will see in the following paragraphs there have been a number of statutory provisions aimed at protecting the third party when dealing with the board or those authorised by it. These statutory provisions are important but it should be noted that general agency principles are still significant. In particular the rule in *Turquand* is still important where the third party has not dealt directly with the board or a question of whether the agent was authorised by the board arises.

Statutory authority

12.28 As we have noted, the CA 1989 introduced further reform provisions to deal with situations where internal irregularities might upset outsider rights. Section 35A of the Companies Act 1985 was the result of these reforms and stated:

(1) *[i]n favour of a person dealing with a company in good faith, the power of the board of directors to bind the company, or authorise others to do so, shall be deemed to be free of any limitation under the company's constitution.*

(2) *[f]or this purpose—*

(a) *a person 'deals with' a company if he is a party to any transaction or other act to which the company is a party;*

(b) *a person shall not be regarded as acting in bad faith by reason only of his knowing that an act is beyond the powers of the directors under the company's constitution; and*

(c) *a person shall be presumed to have acted in good faith unless the contrary is proved.*

(3) *The references above to limitations on the directors' powers under the company's constitution include limitations deriving—*

(a) *from a resolution of the company in general meeting or a meeting of any class of shareholders, or*

(b) *from any agreement between the members of the company or of any class of shareholders.*

(4) *Subsection (1) does not affect any right of a member of the company to bring proceedings to restrain the doing of an act which is beyond the powers of the directors; but no such proceedings shall lie in respect of an act to be done in fulfilment of a legal obligation arising from a previous act of the company.*

(5) *Nor does that subsection affect any liability incurred by the directors, or any other person, by reason of the directors' exceeding their powers.*

12.29 As we can see from this the protection offered to the outsider by s 35A not only covered the board but also recognised that the board often delegated some of its functions to others. In particular it seems to be weighted heavily in favour of the third party. Not only did it cover directors' and agents' actions but it set the standard of bad faith fairly high as subsection 2(b) specifically allowed third parties to have knowledge that the transaction was irregular. This suggested that perhaps active dishonesty might have been required in order to qualify as bad faith (see *EIC Services Ltd v Phipps* (2004)). In any case subsection 2(c) set a presumption of good faith.

12.30   Section 35A also covered insiders, which the rule in *Turquand* does not. However insiders may have more difficulty with the good faith requirement (see *Smith v Henniker-Major & Co* (2002) for an interesting attempt by an insider to use s 35A). For example, breach of duty by the insider will mean that the protections of s 35A may not apply (see *Cooperative Rabobank Vechten Plassengebied BA v Minderhoud* (1998) and *International Sales and Agencies Ltd v Marcus* (1982)). Section 322A of the CA 1985 was also introduced by the CA 1989 and s 35A was subject to it. The section provides that a transaction between the company and a director or a person connected to him (family etc) which exceeds the powers of the board would be voidable at the instance of the company.

12.31   Section 35A(3) went on to provide a wide definition of 'limitation' under the constitution as including the memorandum, articles, and shareholders' resolutions and agreements. This was a recognition that the delegation of the company's powers to the board in the articles was subject to change by the general meeting and that it could be affected by a shareholders' agreement. Subsections (4)–(5) contained similar provisions to s 35(2)–(4) (para **12.19**) whereby members were able to bring a pre-emptive action to restrain a breach and the subsection also emphasised the directors' duty to observe the internal limits on their powers. Unlike s 35, there were no ratification provisions specified for exceeding internal limitations on authority, thus an ordinary resolution would suffice to ratify and forgive directors where an internal limitation was at issue.

12.32   Additionally the CA 1989 introduced two further sections into the 1985 Act to deal with constructive notice. Section 35B of the CA 1985 stated:

> [a] party to a transaction with the company is not bound to enquire as to whether it is permitted by the company's memorandum or as to any limitation on the powers of the board of directors to bind the company or authorise others to do so.

This was supposed to be reinforced by CA 1985, s 711A which was to abolish the concept of constructive notice for corporations. However, s 711A has never been implemented and so only s 35B dealt with constructive notice.

Statutory authority and the CA 2006 reforms

12.33   The CLRSG in its *Final Report* (July 2001, para 9.10), recommended that provisions be introduced clarifying the law on when directors were deemed to have authority to bind the company or authorise others to do so. The White Paper (2002, Vol I, para 6.2) followed the CLRSG recommendations and provided in clause 17 of its Draft Bill a broad catch-all saving provision whereby the board was deemed for the purposes of outsider transactions to exercise all the powers of the company and to authorise others to do so. Insiders and connected persons were specifically excluded from the saving provision. The CA 2006 did not follow this formulation, instead preferring a more limited reform of essentially tidying up and replicating the provisions of ss 35A and 35B in one new section (CA 2006, s 40) which reads:

40 Power of directors to bind the company

(1) In favour of a person dealing with a company in good faith, the power of the directors to bind the company, or authorise others to do so, is deemed to be free of any limitation under the company's constitution.

(2) For this purpose—

(a) a person 'deals with' a company if he is a party to any transaction or other act to which the company is a party,

(b) a person dealing with a company—

(i) is not bound to enquire as to any limitation on the powers of the directors to bind the company or authorise others to do so,

(ii) is presumed to have acted in good faith unless the contrary is proved, and

(iii) is not to be regarded as acting in bad faith by reason only of his knowing that an act is beyond the powers of the directors under the company's constitution.

(3) The references above to limitations on the directors' powers under the company's constitution include limitations deriving—

(a) from a resolution of the company or of any class of shareholders, or

(b) from any agreement between the members of the company or of any class of shareholders.

(4) This section does not affect any right of a member of the company to bring proceedings to restrain the doing of an action that is beyond the powers of the directors. But no such proceedings lie in respect of an act to be done in fulfilment of a legal obligation arising from a previous act of the company.

(5) This section does not affect any liability incurred by the directors, or any other person, by reason of the directors' exceeding their powers.

(6) This section has effect subject to—section 41 (transactions with directors or their associates), and section 42 (companies that are charities).

Additionally CA 1985, s 322A (connected persons) was also essentially tidied up and replicated in a new section (CA 2006, s 41).

12.34 To sum up, the effect of the 1989 amendments was to negate questionable corporate capacity and board or board-delegated authority issues for outsiders. Constructive notice
still operated, but the fact that knowledge of the irregularity would not affect the outsider's good faith combined with no duty to enquire meant the outsider in most cases was
in a position to enforce an unauthorised act of the board or someone authorised by it.
Where it was a question of the internal authority of an agent and the outsider did not deal
with the board or it was unclear if the board authorised the agent to deal with the outsider the common law rules would then impact to provide a safety net. Thus as we have
observed while the impact of these reforms was to mostly negate corporate and agent
capacity issues for outsiders, it did so in a complicated way. The reform process leading
to the 2006 Act had tried to tackle this complexity but the CA 2006 oddly did not follow
the recommendations of the CLRSG on this. Instead we now have a two-tiered system—
newly incorporated companies with unlimited capacity and companies incorporated
under previous Companies Acts with objects clauses for whom the previous complex
1985 Act regime has been largely reincarnated in ss 39 and 40 of the CA 2006.

Other attribution issues

12.35 Agency, however, does not cover all situations where attribution is at issue. Tort presented
one such problem which the courts originally had great difficulty with in the corporate
context. At first it was considered that a tort was an ultra vires act in that a company
could never be authorised by its objects clause to commit a tort. However, in *Campbell v
Paddington* (1911) the court accepted that companies could commit torts and the courts
have subsequently applied the principle of vicarious liability to the company as employer.
Thus the company as principal can be vicariously liable in tort for acts of its employees
even though they may not be specifically authorised but are nevertheless acting within
the scope of their employment. In general vicarious liability will not attribute criminal
liability for the act of an employee. Attribution in the context of a tort involves no fault
on the part of the company, it is just legally responsible for the acts of another. Where a
fault qualification or intention is required by law attribution of liability becomes more
complex. In these cases the courts began to develop what is known as the alter ego or
organic theory of the company.

12.36 In *Lennard's Carrying Co Ltd v Asiatic Petroleum Co Ltd* (1915) the fault requirement
arose in relation to a particular section of the Merchant Shipping Act 1894. Viscount
Haldane LC set out an organic theory of the corporation in order to deal with the fault
issue. He considered that:

> [a] corporation is an abstraction. It has no mind or will of its own any more than it has a
> body of its own; its active and directing will must consequently be sought in the person
> of somebody who for some purposes may be called an agent but who is really the dir-
> ecting mind and will of the corporation, the very ego and centre of the personality of the
> corporation . . . somebody who is not merely an agent or servant for whom the company

*is liable upon the footing respondeat superior, but somebody for whom the company is
liable because his action is the very action of the company itself.*

As a result, if one individual can be identified who can be said to be essentially the company's alter ego and that individual has the required fault, then the fault of that individual will be attributed to the company. It is important to note here that attribution is not as with tort because the company is responsible for the actions of another. Here the individual's fault is attributed to the company because the law treats the individual and the company as the same person. You might not unnaturally wonder how this is compatible with the *Salomon* principle which emphasises the separateness of the company from its members and officers. The answer is that it is not compatible with it and the theory has probably caused more problems than it solved.

12.37 This, however, did not stop the profusion of metaphors when attempts were made to apply the concept. In *Bolton (Engineering) Co Ltd v Graham & Sons* (1957) Lord Denning offered his particular view of the organic theory:

> *[a] company may in many ways be likened to a human body. It has a brain and nerve centre which controls what it does. It also has hands which hold the tools and act in accordance with directions from the centre. Some of the people in the company are mere servants and agents who are nothing more than hands . . . and cannot be said to represent the mind and will of the company and control what it does. The state of mind of these managers is the state of mind of the company and is treated in law as such.*

The difficulty with this attribution theory was that it required the identification of a single individual in what was often a complex corporate organisational structure. This was often not possible. In particular the criminal law has had the greatest difficulty with the organic theory when attempting to determine the company's *mens rea* or guilty mind.

12.38 In *Tesco Supermarkets Ltd v Nattrass* (1971) Tesco was charged with an offence under the Trade Descriptions Act 1968. Tesco had advertised goods at a reduced price but sold them at a higher price. In order to avoid conviction Tesco had to show that they had put in place a proper control system. Tesco argued that they had and that the manager of the store had been at fault. The court considered whether the manager was acting as an organ of the company. Lord Reid found that:

> *[a] living person has a mind which can have knowledge or intention or be negligent and he has hands to carry out his intentions. A corporation has none of these; it must act through living persons, though not always one or the same person. Then the person who acts is not speaking or acting for the company. He is acting as the company and his mind which directs his acts is the mind of the company. There is no question of the company being vicariously liable. He is not acting as a servant, representative, agent or delegate. He is an embodiment of the company or, one could say, he hears and speaks through the persona of the company, within his appropriate sphere, and his mind is the mind of the company.*

In this case the manager who was at fault was not the guiding mind and therefore Tesco could not be liable for his action. The application of the organic theory acted effectively as an immunity from criminal prosecution for large complex corporate organisations.

12.39 In the Privy Council decision in *Meridian Global Funds Management Asia Ltd v Securities Commission* (1995) Lord Hoffmann considered that organic theory provided a misleading analysis. The real issue was who were the controllers of the company for the purposes of attribution. This was compatible with the maintenance of the *Salomon* principle and had the advantage of being able to attribute liability to the company for the actions of individuals lower down the organisational structure. In the *Meridian* case the controllers were found to be two senior managers. Lord Hoffmann's approach was applied with some success in *McNicholas Construction Co Ltd v Customs and Excise Comrs* (2000). The case concerned the operation of a VAT fraud and the knowledge of the company's site managers was enough to attribute liability to the company for the fraud. (See also *Crown Dilmun v Sutton* (2004), *Morris v Bank of India* (2005), and on the complexities of attribution *Safeway Stores Ltd v Twigger* (2010).) Despite this the idea of an alter ego or directing mind and will of a company still appears in the case law from time to time. In *Stone & Rolls Ltd v Moore Stephens* (2009) attribution through the use of the company's alter ego was crucial to the attribution of liability. Similarly in *R v St Regis Paper Co Ltd* (2011) the lack of a directing mind and will of the company proved fatal to the attribution of an offence. The Law Commission in its 2011 consultation suggests that when the courts are dealing with this issue they do not start with the identification doctrine as a default but rather look to the underlying purpose of a relevant statutory scheme. (See http://www.lawcom.gov.uk/project/criminal-liability-in-regulatory-contexts/). This has not helped enormously as the judiciary still find the complexity of corporate attribution to be problematic. In 2015 the Supreme Court for example in *Jetivia SA and another v Bilta (UK) Ltd (in liquidation) and others* (2015) found that the wrongdoing of the directors could not be attributed to the company and also seemed to limit the scope of *Stone & Rolls Ltd v Moore Stephens*. However, they also confusingly left the door open to revisit the issue. They did so again in *Singularis Holdings Ltd (in liquidation) v Daiwa Capital Markets Europe Ltd* (2019) where again, admittedly in unusual circumstances, they found the wrongdoing of a director could not be attributed to the company.

12.40 The application of the organic theory where crimes of violence are at issue still remains a problem. These crimes happen mainly in the workplace but occasionally enter the public domain through major transport disasters like the Zeebrugge ferry tragedy. Larger, more complex corporate organisations can never be attributed with the required *mens rea* as identification of an alter ego is impossible in such complex delegated structures (see *Jenkins v P & O European Ferries Ltd* (1990)). In response to a number of high-profile disasters and the growing problem of workplace deaths, the Government proposed the creation of a specific offence of corporate manslaughter (*Reforming the Law on Involuntary Manslaughter: The Government's Proposals* (May 2000)). An offence of corporate manslaughter was introduced in the Corporate Manslaughter and Corporate Homicide Act 2007 which came into force on 6 April 2008. The offence of corporate manslaughter is based around 'management failure' of the company or its parent, leading to the cause of death. Thus if the way the company is managed fails to protect the health and safety of those employed in or affected by the company's activities and the manner in which its management fails is far below the standards that would be reasonably expected of a company in such circumstances it will be guilty of the offence. In *R v Cotswold Geotechnical Holdings Ltd* (2012) a company was convicted of the first ever manslaughter prosecution under the 2007 Act and fined £385,000. Since then prosecutions have become a regular occurrence, see http://www.hse.gov.uk/corpmanslaughter/about.htm (For an overview of the issues, see http://www.youtube.com/watch?v=l0iuTZ0iyGw).

FURTHER READING

This chapter links with the materials in Chapters 3 and 5 of *Hicks and Goo's Cases and Materials on Company Law* (Oxford, OUP, 2011, xl +649p).

Company Law Reform (Cm 6456, 2005) (Consultative Document, March 2005), para 5.1, http://webarchive.nationalarchives.gov.uk/+/http://www.dti.gov.uk/cld/WhitePaper.pdf.

Ferran, 'The Reform of the Law On Corporate Capacity and Directors' and Officers' Authority Parts 1 and 2' [1992] *Co Law* 124 and 177.

Gobert, 'The Corporate Manslaughter and Corporate Homicide Act 2007—Thirteen Years in the Making But was it Worth the Wait?' [2008] *MLR* 413.

Hannigan, 'Contracting with Individual Directors' in Rider (ed) *The Corporate Dimension* (Bristol, Jordan Publishing, 1998).

Munoz Slaughter, 'Corporate Social Responsibility: A New Perspective' [1997] *Co Law* 313.

Nyombi, 'The Gradual Erosion of the Ultra Vires Doctrine in English Company Law' (2014) 56(5) *International J of Law and Management* 347, https://doi.org/10.1108/IJLMA-08-2012-0027.

Poole, 'Abolition of the Ultra Vires Doctrine and Agency Problems' [1991] *Co Law* 43.

Prentice, 'The Enforcement of Outsider Rights' (1980) 1 *Co Law* 179.

Sullivan, 'Corporate Killing—Some Government Proposals' [2001] *Crim LR* 31.

SELF-TEST QUESTIONS

1 Explain how you would decide if a particular transaction was outside the company's objects clause.

2 Explain the difference between actual and ostensible authority.

3 If a transaction within the company's capacity but outside an agent's authority is entered into will it bind the company?

4 Do you think that s 40 of the CA 2006 is more effective than ss 35A and 35B of the CA 1985?

5   Can an ordinary employee of the company attribute liability to the company?

6   The objects clause of Bottle Ltd provides that:

'a)   The business of the company shall be the construction of hotels and all other forms of accommodation.

b)   The company may make whatever borrowings and charge whatever of its assets as the board of directors consider desirable.'

Although never formally appointed managing director, Tim, to the knowledge and with the full agreement of his co-directors, Bernice and Camilla, carries out the day-to-day management of Bottle Ltd. Tim, acting on behalf of Bottle Ltd, agreed that the company would manufacture and supply 5,000 deckchairs for the Briton Local Authority beachfront. To finance this operation he borrowed £50,000 from Z Bank PLC to enable Bottle to purchase the machinery to carry out this agreement. The loan was signed on Bottle's behalf by Tim and Bernice.

Camilla has just discovered this and seeks your advice as to the legal issues that arise here.

13

Corporate management

SUMMARY

Introduction

The emergence of the professional managerial organ

The relationship between directors and the general meeting

Appointment of directors

The fiduciary nature of the office

Directors' remuneration

Vacation and removal from office

Disqualification of directors

Introduction

13.1 As we discussed in Chapter 12, because artificial legal entities can only function through the medium of human organs they invariably have a variety of decision-makers ranging from shop-floor supervisors to top executives. In small private companies individuals will often perform several roles: worker, supervisor, shareholder, and director. In large public companies, however, the boundaries between these roles are more clearly defined. The focus of this chapter is on those individuals who are responsible for making key strategic decisions.

13.2 Corporate decision making is carried out by those officers who stand at the company's helm, namely the members of its board of directors. Given the strategic importance of directors in relation to corporate management it is curious that the Companies Act is silent in several key respects on prescribing their role. More fundamentally, the Act does not provide an exhaustive definition of the term 'director' beyond stating in s 250 of the CA 2006 that the term 'includes any person occupying the position of director, by whatever name called'. Thus, whatever term the articles use to describe the members of the company's board (for example, governors, administrators, trustees), as far as the law is concerned they are directors. Section 154 lays down the minimum number of directors which companies must have (for public companies it is two and for private companies the minimum is one). Although a company can be appointed a director, s 155(1) of the CA 2006 now requires that every company must have at least one director who is a natural person (see para **13.14**). Beyond laying down these basic requirements, the Act does not attribute specific functions to company directors nor does it lay down the structure and form of corporate management more generally. This is left to the articles of association (see later).

13.3   The approach of UK company law legislation in failing to prescribe the structure and functions of the board of directors stands in marked contrast to the company law regimes found in the Member States of the EU, most notably Germany and the Netherlands. While UK company law, at least as it applies to listed companies, is wedded to a governance system based upon a unitary board of directors in which the market acts as the supreme control device, corporate governance in Germany is founded upon internal monitoring via a two-tier board: the supervisory board which includes employee directors, and the management board. In the majority of German public companies, the shareholders elect two-thirds of the members of the supervisory board and one-third is elected by the company's employees. The EC Draft Fifth Directive [1972] OJ C131/49, which has undergone various revisions since it was first published, was intended to bring the boards of UK public companies broadly in line with this model. Nevertheless, reform initiatives in this regard have continued. On 29 November 2016, BEIS published a Green Paper, 'Corporate Governance Reform', which introduced a consultation exercise on the reform of corporate governance. BEIS published its response document to the Green Paper on 29 August 2017: this had been preceded by the report of the House of Commons Business, Energy and Industrial Strategy Select Committee inquiry into corporate governance and directors' remuneration (5 April 2017); note also EU Directive 2017/828. Notwithstanding the promises made by Theresa May both during her candidacy for the leadership of the Conservative Party and again shortly after she became Prime Minister to reform the structure of UK boards along the lines of Germany so as to include employee representation, the Green Paper and the subsequent response document do not take this proposal further.

The spectacular corporate collapses of the 1980s (for example, Blue Arrow, BCCI, Barlow Clowes, Polly Peck, and Maxwell) heralded a significant shift in UK corporate governance culture. One particular consequence of this is the recognition of the potential of non-executive directors (NEDs) to perform a monitoring role over executive directors albeit on a self-regulatory basis and within the structure of a single-tier board (see Chapters 15 and 16). The role of NEDs has been increased in the light of the Green Paper and the response document following the recommendation to have a particular non-executive director tasked with representing the interests of one or more groups of stakeholders in board-level discussions (see now the UK Corporate Governance Code 2018, Provisions 5 and 6 (Chapter 16)). Also, as will be seen, shareholders were given increased influence over the levels of directors' pay and their service contracts by the Enterprise and Regulatory Reform Act 2013, and the 2016 Green Paper and the response document contain a number of recommendations for enhancing shareholder and other stakeholders' engagement with the board by strengthening the reporting requirements. In the light of this, the Financial

Reporting Council (FRC), at the Government's invitation, launched a consultation on a new UK Corporate Governance Code in December 2017 (see paras **13.38-13.41**), which culminated in an updated set of Principles in the 2018 Code (note also the new Stewardship Code published by the FRC in November 2019 (see Chapter 16)).

The emergence of the professional managerial organ

13.4 The role and position of directors within the corporate management matrix is coloured by the fact that company law is rooted in the law of partnership which is based upon agency principles. In partnership law each partner is an agent of his fellow partners. The 19th-century view of the role of company directors was that they were merely the agents of the company's shareholders. As we have seen in previous chapters, there are two primary collective corporate organs: the board of directors and the shareholders (or company) in general meeting. Historically, the company in general meeting had constitutional supremacy insofar as the directors, as its agents, had to act strictly in accordance with its decisions (*Isle of Wight Rly Co v Tahourdin* (1883)). This thinking was also reflected in the legislation of the day: s 90 of the Companies Clauses Consolidation Act 1845 provided that the authority of directors to manage the affairs of the company was subject to the relevant legislation then in force and 'to the control and regulation' of the general meeting.

The separation of ownership and control

13.5 This view of the pre-eminence of the company in general meeting was steadily eroded over the course of the 20th century not by specific law reform but by changing practice and social phenomena which judges were quick to recognise. In listed companies share ownership is now more widespread and the attention of shareholders, both private and institutional, is, by and large, focused upon investment returns rather than upon monitoring directorial conduct. The general meeting in large public companies, particularly through the use of proxy voting (where shareholders do not attend the meeting but instead send in a written vote or, more usually, assign their votes to the board to exercise as it wishes) often becomes little more than a forum for rubber-stamping boardroom decisions. This shift of power from those who own the company to those who control it was identified by Berle and Means in their pioneering empirical study conducted between 1929 and 1930 of the 200 largest US non-financial corporations (Berle and Means (1932)) (see Chapter 15). They argued that one of the consequences of the separation of ownership from control, taken together with the dispersion of share ownership, was that shareholders could no longer control the direction of the company. It was found that although the directors in the companies surveyed had functional control, they had relatively small personal shareholdings. A large dispersed shareholding in turn had neither the means nor the incentive to monitor these new powerful managers. In other words, ownership was now separate from control. Berle and Means therefore argued that:

> *Economic power in terms of control over physical assets, is apparently responding to a centripetal force, tending more and more to concentrate in the hands of a few corporate managements. At the same time, beneficial ownership is centrifugal tending to divide and subdivide, to split into even smaller units and to pass freely from hand to hand. In other words, ownership continually becomes more dispersed: the power formerly joined to it becomes increasingly concentrated.*

13.6 The practical effect of this shift in power is that the principal concern of shareholders in large public companies is their investment returns, while the focus of directors is centred on their power over the enterprise. If the shareholders disagree with the directors' management of the company, the only realistic option open to them is to sell their shares and leave. The ground-breaking work of Berle and Means has had an immense influence over the form and approach of modern corporate governance regulation (see Chapter 15).

The recognition of directorial autonomy

13.7 The judicial break with the traditional view of equating shareholders with 'the company' and treating directors as their agents is discernible in the Court of Appeal's decision in *Automatic Self-Cleansing Filter Syndicate Co Ltd v Cunninghame* (1906). The issue in this case was whether or not the directors were bound to give effect to a resolution of the company in general meeting. Collins MR, having reviewed the authority given to the directors by the company's articles of association, observed that 'unless the other powers given by the memorandum were invoked by a special resolution, it was impossible for a mere majority at a meeting to override the views of the directors'. This line of reasoning was adopted by Buckley LJ in *Gramophone and Typewriter Ltd v Stanley* (1908) who said:

> *The directors are not servants to obey directions given by the shareholders as individuals; they are not agents appointed by and bound to serve the shareholders as their principals. They are persons who may by the regulations be entrusted with the control of the business, and if so entrusted they can be dispossessed from that control only by the statutory majority which can alter the articles. Directors are not, I think, bound to comply with the directions even of all the corporators acting as individuals.*

The board of directors therefore occupies a pre-eminent position in the management of companies (see also *Towcester Racecourse Co Ltd v Racecourse Association Ltd* (2002), Patten J). The position is that directors, who are subject to being removed by the general meeting in accordance with the provisions laid down by the Act (CA 2006, s 168) and by any relevant regulation in the articles, cannot be controlled by the shareholders in general meeting as if they were delegates or agents. In other words, directors are free within certain boundaries to take a different course of action from that desired by the shareholders. As we discussed in Chapter 8, the company's articles of association will give the power of management to the directors while reserving for shareholders defined voting powers with respect to appointments to the board together with the power to take, in general meeting, decisions on matters not reserved for management. At its base level, this is what Berle and Means (1932) identified as the separation of ownership and control. However, it should be borne in mind that in the majority of private companies the directors are also generally the shareholders and so in such enterprises there is no strict separation between these corporate roles.

The relationship between directors and the general meeting

13.8 The Companies Act is generally silent on the issue of the distribution of power between shareholders and directors apart from reserving to the exclusive province of the company in general meeting authority over certain key matters, such as the right to alter the articles (s 21); alter share capital (ss 617 and 641); and to delegate authority to allot shares (see ss 550–551). In general, therefore, it is the articles which prescribe the scope of the management powers of directors and so the relationship between the board and the company in general meeting is based upon the statutory contract. That shareholders lack executive authority can be seen by reference to Table A, art 70 (Companies (Tables A to F) Regulations 1985 (SI 1985/805), now replaced by the 2008 model articles (below) which provides:

> Subject to the provisions of the Act, the memorandum and the articles and to any directions given by special resolution, the business of the company shall be managed by the directors who may exercise all the powers of the company . . .

Section 19 of the CA 2006 confers on the Secretary of State for Business, Energy & Industrial Strategy the power to prescribe model articles, and in this regard the Companies (Model Articles) Regulations 2008 (SI 2008/3229) were published on 23 December 2008. The Regulations set out model articles of association for private companies limited by shares (Sch 1); private companies limited by guarantee (Sch 2); and public companies (Sch 3). These articles replace those set out in the Companies (Tables A to F) Regulations 1985 although these (and their predecessors under earlier companies legislation) continue to apply to companies incorporated before 1 October 2009 (although such companies can choose to adopt all or some of the new model articles (see s 19(3)). Table A has been amended insofar as it conflicts with the CA 2006 and in practice it is likely to continue as the principal constitutional model for many companies.

The equivalent of Table A, art 70 is set out in the 2008 model articles for private companies limited by shares (Sch 1), hereafter pcls, and public companies (Sch 3), hereafter plcs, in arts 3 and 4. Article 3 for both pcls and plcs states, in simpler terms than its Table A counterpart, that: 'Subject to the articles, the directors are responsible for the management of the company's business, for which purpose they may exercise all the powers of the company.' Article 3 thus confirms the power base of the board. Article 4 for both pcls and plcs states:

> (1) The shareholders may, by special resolution, direct the directors to take, or refrain from taking, specified action.

> (2) No such special resolution invalidates anything which the directors have done before the passing of the resolution.

13.9 We have seen that the courts have taken the view that shareholders do not have general supervisory powers over directors. This stance is reflected in the wording of the model art 70 of the 1985 Table A, and arts 3 and 4 of the 2008 model articles for pcls and plcs (see para **13.8**), which reserve to shareholders only very limited means for intervening in management affairs: a special resolution must be carried by three-quarters of the votes of the members entitled to vote and voting whether in person or by proxy (s 283, CA 2006). Directors therefore enjoy wide-ranging management powers and, provided they act within their powers, they may take decisions against the wishes of the majority of shareholders (see *Gramophone and Typewriter Ltd v Stanley* (1908), Buckley LJ and *Howard Smith Ltd v Ampol Petroleum Ltd* (1974), Lord Wilberforce (discussed in Chapter 14)). The practical effects of the board's autonomy were explained by Greer LJ in *John Shaw & Sons (Salford) Ltd v Shaw* (1935):

> If powers of management are vested in the directors, they and they alone can exercise these powers. The only way in which the general body of the shareholders can control the exercise of the powers vested by the articles in the directors is by altering their articles, or, if opportunity arises under the articles, by refusing to re-elect the directors of whose actions they disapprove. They cannot themselves usurp the powers which by the articles are vested in the directors.

Shareholders do not have executive authority and so the general meeting lacks managerial power unless, exceptionally, there is sufficient support to secure the passage of a *special resolution* (see the judgment of the High Court of Ireland in *Petroceltic International plc v Worldwide Capital Management SA* (2015)). Such a resolution may be passed in order to give specific directions to the directors in relation to a particular matter, or to change their mandate on a more fundamental basis by altering the articles of association (s 21). The ultimate sanction which shareholders can exercise to express their disapproval of a director's managerial conduct is, of course, to remove him from office (s 168, see later).

13.10 However, executive power will revert to the members in general meeting where, for example, the board is incapable of acting as such, or has fallen below the required minimum number, or has become deadlocked. In the absence of an effective board the general meeting has a residual authority to use the company's powers (*Alexander Ward & Co Ltd v Samyang Navigation Co Ltd* (1975)). In *Barron v Potter* (1914) the company's two directors were not on speaking terms and so effective board meetings could not be held.

The claimant had requisitioned a shareholders' meeting at which additional directors had been appointed to the board but the defendant objected on the ground that under the articles only the directors could make such appointments. It was held that in the light of the deadlock, the power to appoint additional directors reverted to the general meeting and so the appointments were valid. Warrington J observed:

> in ordinary cases where there is a board ready and willing to act it would [not] be competent for the company to override the power conferred on the directors by the articles except by way of special resolution for the purpose of altering the articles. But the case which I have to deal with is a different one. For practical purposes there is no board of directors at all ... The directors in the present case being unwilling to appoint additional directors under the power conferred on them by the articles, in my opinion, the company in general meeting has power to make the appointment.

13.11 As we saw in Chapter 10, an issue which has given rise to considerable judicial debate has been the question of which organ, the board or the general meeting, has the power to bring legal proceedings in the name of the company. The basic principle is that where a wrong has been done against a company, the proper claimant is the company itself (*Foss v Harbottle* (1843), see CA 2006, s 260). If the company has adopted art 70 of the 1985 Table A, or some such similar article, or arts 3 of the 2008 model articles for pcls or plcs, the power to sue is treated no differently from any other executive power and is thus vested in the board (*Breckland Group Holdings Ltd v London & Suffolk Properties Ltd* (1989)). Should the board decide to bring proceedings the members in general meeting cannot intervene to direct that they be discontinued. Conversely, a decision not to sue, it being a management matter, cannot be challenged by the shareholders. If, however, the wrongdoing directors hold the majority of shares themselves so that they are in control and thus refuse to initiate litigation on the company's behalf, the minority shareholders may bring a derivative action by way of exception to the proper claimant rule (see further Chapter 10).

Appointment of directors

General

13.12 The 2006 Act, like its predecessors, is far from prescriptive in relation to the appointment of directors. Section 9, which deals with registration requirements, states that an application for registration must contain a statement of the company's proposed officers, and this must give the required particulars of the person who is, or persons who are, to be the first director or directors of the company (s 12(1)(a)). We have seen that s 154 stipulates the minimum number of directors for companies. Section 157 introduces a minimum age of 16 for appointment as a company director. However, an appointment can be made below the minimum age provided it does not take effect until the person attains the age of 16 (s 157(2)). Section 160 provides that for public companies the appointment of directors shall be voted on individually unless a block resolution is unanimously agreed. A resolution moved in contravention of this provision is void. Beyond these particular statutory provisions the Companies Act is silent on boardroom appointments, leaving the issue to the articles of association.

13.13 While the first directors are appointed in accordance with s 9 of the CA 2006, their successors are elected by the shareholders in general meeting. Article 73 of the 1985 Table A for public companies provides that at the first AGM all the directors shall retire from office, and at every subsequent AGM one-third of the directors who are subject to retirement by rotation (or if less than three or a multiple of three, the number nearest to one-third) shall retire from office. If there is only one director who is subject to retirement by rotation, he shall retire. Article 21 of the 2008 model articles for plcs provides:

> (1) *At the first annual general meeting all the directors must retire from office.*
>
> (2) *At every subsequent annual general meeting any directors—*
>
>> (a) *who have been appointed by the directors since the last annual general meeting, or*
>>
>> (b) *who were not appointed or reappointed at one of the preceding two annual general meetings, must retire from office and may offer themselves for reappointment by the members.*

The 2008 model articles for pcls do not provide for retirement by rotation, the assumption being that this is not required in most private companies.

The power of the majority to appoint directors must 'be exercised for the benefit of the company as a whole and not to secure some ulterior advantage' (*Re HR Harmer Ltd* (1959)). Casual vacancies arising before the next AGM may be filled by the directors (art 79 of the 1985 Table A; art 20 of the 2008 model articles for plcs; art 17(1) for pcls). In any case, a company in general meeting retains an inherent power to fill board vacancies (*Worcester Corsetry Ltd v Witting* (1936)). In small private owner-managed companies the articles will often provide for the permanent appointment of directors.

When a director is appointed by a company it must make a statement of truth that the appointee has consented to become a director. Companies House then notifies every newly appointed director that they can object if they did not consent to the appointment. Under the Registrar of Companies and Applications for Striking Off (Amendment) Regulations 2016 (SI 2016/441) (which result from s 102 of the Small Business, Enterprise and Employment Act 2015 (SBEEA 2015), amending s 1095 of the Companies Act 2006), where a person who has purportedly been appointed as a director applies to have his appointment removed from the Companies House register, Companies House will act on that application unless the company in question provides evidence that that person did consent to act.

13.14 It was long settled that a company or other corporation could be appointed a director (*Re Bulawayo Market and Offices Co Ltd* (1907)). Although the CLRSG recommended the abolition of corporate directors, the Government of the day concluded that an 'outright ban might harm those companies who make use of the current flexibilities' (*Company Law Reform* (DTI, 2005, para 3.3)). By way of compromise, s 155 required that at least one director be a natural person. However, as part of the Government's recent drive for transparency in corporate management and control, this position has now been changed as a result of s 87 of the SBEEA 2015. The anxiety is that a lack of transparency and accountability of those controlling a company can facilitate illicit activity and erode trust and so, subject to exceptions which are to be introduced by regulations (now delayed, see below), the appointment of new corporate directors will be prohibited (see ss 156A and 156B, CA 2006), and the appointments of existing corporate directors will automatically cease after a 12-month period of grace (s 156C). Although the Government had originally decided that these provisions would come into force in October 2015, the exceptions to the general prohibition have proved difficult to finalise. It therefore delayed implementation of the provisions for an additional 12-month period to allow time for further consultation. Initially it appeared that the exceptions might centre upon the size of the company and whether or not it was listed. But the Government decided that a more 'principles-based' approach is needed. Announcing the postponement of the prohibition, Companies House stated: 'The detail of these exceptions are still under development. Any further information including a date for implementation will be provided on GOV.UK as soon as it's available.'

In summary, ss 154–167 govern the appointment and registration of directors. The principal requirements for appointment are:

(i) every private company is to have at least one director, and every public company to have at least two (s 154);

(ii) 16 is set as the minimum age (as in Scotland) for a director to be appointed (s 157) and the maximum age limit of 70 for directors of public companies is abolished;

(iii) the appointment of a director of a public company is to be voted on individually, unless there is unanimous consent to a block resolution (s 160);

(iv) the acts of a person acting as a director are valid notwithstanding that it is afterwards discovered that there was a defect in his appointment, that he was disqualified from holding office, that he has ceased to hold office, or that he was not entitled to vote on the matter in question (s 161, replacing s 285 of the CA 1985. See the construction given to the provision in *Morris v Kanssen* (1946), where Lord Simonds drew the distinction between a defective appointment and no appointment at all);

(v) subject to certain exceptions, directors must be natural persons.

In addition to holding the office of director, a director may be employed by the company under a service contract (see later). In *Ranson v Customer Systems plc* (2012) the Court of Appeal noted that:

The appointment of a person as a company director does not make that person an employee of the company. A director is the holder of an office. Nor does appointment as a company director of itself bring into existence any contract between the director and the company. Many directors will have contracts of service running in parallel with their status as officers of the company. But they are distinct legal relationships.

(See also *Hutton v West Cork Railway* (1883).)

Categories of directors

Executive and non-executive directors

13.15 While the Companies Act 2006 does not categorise directors into executive and non-executive directors, modern corporate practice, particularly in the light of corporate governance reforms, recognises the division between the two types (see further Chapter 16). Executive directors are generally full-time officers of the company who carry out the management of the company's business. As we have seen, the articles typically give extensive management powers to them and they will usually have separate service contracts with the company. The articles will also usually provide for the appointment of a managing director, often referred to as chief executive, who has overall responsibility for the running of the company.

13.16 Non-executive directors are normally appointed to the boards of larger companies to act as monitors of the executive management. They are typically part-time appointments. The corporate governance committees (the Cadbury Committee, the Greenbury Study Group, the Hampel Committee, the Higgs Review, and the Walker Report) view non-executive directors as holding the potential to perform a monitoring role over their executive brethren, ensuring that they act strictly in the interests of the company (see now the UK Corporate Governance Code (FRC, 2016); see further, Chapters 15 and 16).

De facto *directors*

13.17 A *de facto* director is one who has not been formally appointed as such (and therefore is not a *de jure* director) but has nevertheless acted as a director insofar as he has openly undertaken a directorial role in the conduct of the company's affairs (*Re Kaytech International plc* (1999) CA). The notion of *de facto* directorship was considered in *Re Canadian Land Reclaiming and Colonising Co* (1880). The liquidator brought a misfeasance action against two individuals who had acted as directors of the company in question despite not holding the requisite number of qualifying shares. Jessel MR observed:

No doubt they were not properly elected and were, therefore, not de jure directors of the company; but that they were de facto directors of the company is equally beyond all question. The point I have to consider is whether the person who acts as de facto director is a director within the meaning of [s 165 CA 1862 (misfeasance)], or whether he can afterwards be allowed to deny that he was a director within the meaning of this section.

> *I think he cannot. We are familiar in the law with a great number of cases in which a man who assumes a position cannot be allowed to deny in a Court of Justice that he really was entitled to occupy that position. The most familiar instance is that of executor de son tort. In like manner, it seems to me, in an application under this section, the* de facto *director is a director for the purposes of this section.*

(See also *Murray v Bush* (1872), Lord Hatherley.)

As can be seen from Jessel MR's judgment, the question of whether or not an individual is a *de facto* director generally arises in relation to the imposition of liability (see also, for example, *Statek Corp v Alford* (2008), involving breach of fiduciary duties; and *Re Snelling House Ltd (in liquidation); Alford v Barton* (2012), involving liability for misfeasance) and more particularly in the context of disqualification orders under the Company Directors Disqualification Act 1986 (see later). The difficulty which has faced the courts has been to devise a satisfactory test for determining whether or not an individual's conduct in relation to the company's affairs is such as to render him a *de facto* director.

13.18 In *Re Hydrodam (Corby) Ltd* (1994) Millett J, defining a *de facto* director, stressed the necessity of the person in question being 'held out' as a director by the company. He went on to state that:

> *To establish that a person was a* de facto *director of a company it is necessary to plead and prove that he undertook functions in relation to the company which could properly be discharged only by a director. It is not sufficient to show that he was concerned in the management of the company's affairs or undertook tasks in relation to its business which can properly be performed by a manager below board level.*

The requirement of 'holding out' was criticised by Lloyd J in *Re Richborough Furniture Ltd* (1996). He preferred the latter part of Millett J's formulation whereby emphasis was given to the functions performed by the individual concerned (see also *Smithton Ltd v Naggar* (2013); and *Secretary of State for Business, Innovation and Skills v Chohan* (2013)). Lloyd J added that where it is unclear whether the acts of the individual were referable to an assumed directorship or to some other capacity, such as a shareholder or (as on the facts of the case) a consultant, the person in question is to be given the benefit of the doubt. It is noteworthy that in *Secretary for State for Trade and Industry v Jones* (1999), a management consultant was disqualified as a *de facto* director of a company. He had signed a letter to the client's auditors to confirm their appointment on the headed notepaper of the client, describing himself as 'joint managing director'. He had also become a signatory on the company's bank account, dealt directly with the company's creditors, and agreed prices with suppliers of the company. Jonathan Parker J warned that if a substantial shareholder in a small company took an active part in running the company's affairs in order to protect his investment, he will run the risk of being found to be a *de facto* director and therefore subject to disqualification under the 1986 Act (see, for example, *Secretary of State for Business, Enterprise and Regulatory Reform v Poulter* (2009)).

13.19 The tests formulated in *Re Hydrodam* and *Re Richborough* were reviewed by Jacob J in *Secretary of State for Trade and Industry v Tjolle* (1998) in which the judge acknowledged the difficulties in framing a decisive test. He stressed that the nature of the exercise was necessarily fact-intensive and was a question of degree. Although Jacob J doubted whether holding out in itself was decisive, it would certainly be a factor in the court's determination and could raise a rebuttable presumption of a *de facto* directorship. Other factors to be taken into account include whether the person in question was in a position to commit the company to major obligations on the basis of access to management accounts, whether he used the title of director, and whether or not he took part in management decisions at boardroom level albeit, as is the case with most boards of directors, he may have lacked equal power. Jacob J concluded by noting that 'one asks "was this individual part of the corporate governing structure?", answering it as a kind of jury question'. Jacob J's approach was approved by the Court of Appeal in *Re Kaytech International plc* (1999).

13.20 In *Secretary of State for Trade and Industry v Hollier* (2006) Etherton J, having made the point that no one can simultaneously be a *de facto* and a shadow director (see later), went on to state that although various tests have been laid down for determining who may be a *de facto* director there is no single touchstone. The key test is whether someone is part of the governing structure of a company in that he participates in, or is entitled to participate in, collective decisions on corporate policy and strategy and its implementation. He drew a distinction between those who make decisions without being accountable to others, and those who advise or otherwise act on behalf of a company. Etherton J's approach can be seen to have influenced the court's reasoning in *Gemma Ltd v Davies* (2008). An action was brought against a husband and wife for misfeasance in the management of a company that had entered into a creditors' voluntary winding-up. An issue was whether the wife, who was company secretary but not appointed a director, was nevertheless a *de facto* director who could also be liable for misfeasance under s 212 of the Insolvency Act 1986 (see para **17.74**). Holding that the husband was liable, the judge reasoned that to establish that the wife was a *de facto* director it was necessary to demonstrate that she performed functions which could properly be discharged only by a director. For this it would have to be shown that she exercised real influence in the governance of the company on an equal footing with her husband. Holding her out was at best slight evidence of her having acted as a director. She merely performed clerical tasks under the direction of her husband and exercised no real decision-making powers. Accordingly, she was not a *de facto* director and was not liable for misfeasance. Reviewing the modern case law, the judge derived the following propositions as being material to the facts of the case:

> (1) *To establish that a person was a* de facto *director of a company, it is necessary to plead and prove that he undertook functions in relation to the company which could properly be discharged only by a director: per Millett J in* Re Hydrodam (Corby) Ltd *[1994] 2 BCLC 180 at 183.*
>
> (2) *It is not a necessary characteristic of a* de facto *director that he is held out as a director; such 'holding out' may, however, be important evidence in support of the conclusion*

that a person acted as a director in fact: per Etherton J in Secretary of State for Trade and Industry v Hollier *[2006] EWHC 1804 (Ch), [2007] Bus LR 352 at [66].*

(3) *Holding out is not a sufficient condition either. What matters is not what he called himself but what he did: per Lewison J in* Re Mea Corp Ltd *[2007] 1 BCLC 618.*

(4) *It is necessary for the person alleged to be a* de facto *director to have participated in directing the affairs of the company on an equal footing with the other director(s) and not in a subordinate role: per Etherton J in* Secretary of State for Trade and Industry v Hollier *[2006] EWHC 1804 (Ch), [2007] Bus LR 352 at [68] and [69] explaining dicta of Timothy Lloyd QC in* Re Richborough Furniture Ltd *[1996] 1 BCLC 507 at 524.*

(5) *The person in question must be shown to have assumed the status and functions of a company director and to have exercised 'real influence' in the corporate governance of the company: per Robert Walker LJ in* Re Kaytech International plc *[1999] 2 BCLC 351 at 424.*

(6) *If it is unclear whether the acts of the person in question are referable to an assumed directorship or to some other capacity, the person in question is entitled to the benefit of the doubt (per Timothy Lloyd QC in* Re Richborough Furniture Ltd *[1996] 1 BCLC 507 at 524), but the court must be careful not to strain the facts in deference to this observation: per Robert Walker LJ in* Re Kaytech International plc *[1999] 2 BCLC 351 at 423.*

The decision of the Supreme Court in *The Commissioners for HM Revenue and Customs v Holland* (2010) is of particular significance because the highest UK court was at long last afforded the opportunity to review the case law on the vexed issue of *de facto* directorships. The question in the case was whether Mr Holland (H), who was a *de jure* director of a corporate director, was a *de facto* director of its subject companies, and therefore subject to the fiduciary duties which would be owed to them. For Lord Collins this gave rise to both question of law and a question of principle. Having considered the case law, he took the view that the basis of liability for a *de facto* director is an assumption of liability together with his being a part of a company's governance structure. As long as the relevant acts were done by H entirely within the scope of his duties and responsibilities as a director of the corporate director, it was in that capacity that his acts had to be attributed. It had not been shown that H was acting as a *de facto* director of the subject companies so as to make him responsible for the misuse of their assets. In *Smithton Ltd v Naggar* (2014) Arden LJ, drawing on Lord Collins' speech, noted a number of points that are applicable to the determination of who is a *de facto* director—she said:

> Lord Collins sensibly held that there was no one definitive test for a de facto director. The question is whether he was part of the corporate governance system of the company and whether he assumed the status and function of a director so as to make himself responsible as if he were a director. However, a number of points arise out of Holland and the previous cases which are of general practical importance in determining who is a de facto director. I note these points in the following paragraphs.
>
> The concepts of shadow director and de facto are different but there is some overlap.
>
> A person may be de facto director even if there was no invalid appointment. The question is whether he has assumed responsibility to act as a director.

> *To answer that question, the court may have to determine in what capacity the director was acting (as in* Holland).
>
> *The court will in general also have to determine the corporate governance structure of the company so as to decide in relation to the company's business whether the defendant's acts were directorial in nature.*
>
> *The court is required to look at what the director actually did and not any job title actually given to him.*
>
> *A defendant does not avoid liability if he shows that he in good faith thought he was not acting as a director. The question whether or not he acted as a director is to be determined objectively and irrespective of the defendant's motivation or belief.*
>
> *The court must look at the cumulative effect of the activities relied on. The court should look at all the circumstances 'in the round' (per Jonathan Parker J in* Secretary of State v Jones *(above).*
>
> *It is also important to look at the acts in their context. A single act might lead to liability in an exceptional case.*
>
> *Relevant factors include:*
>
> i)   *whether the company considered him to be a director and held him out as such;*
>
> ii) *whether third parties considered that he was a director;*
>
> *The fact that a person is consulted about directorial decisions or his approval does not in general make him a director because he is not making the decision.*
>
> *Acts outside the period when he is said to have been a* de facto *director may throw light on whether he was a* de facto *director in the relevant period.*

(See also *Re Snelling House Ltd (In Liquidation)* (2012); note the fact-sensitivity of the cases, for example in *Re Sports Management Group Ltd; Green v Marston* (2016), the court concluded that a consultant could properly be viewed as a *de facto* director because he was part of the corporate governance structure; cf *Elsworth Ethanol Co Ltd v Hartley* (2015); see further *Popely v Popely* (2019) where the issue arose in the context of D & O insurance; and *Instant Access Properties Ltd v Bradley Rosser* (2018).)

Shadow directors

13.21 Sometimes a shareholder may deliberately try to avoid the legal duties borne by directors by exercising influence over the board but without being formally appointed as a director. So-called 'shadow directors' will be subject to the obligations and liabilities imposed by the Companies Act 2006, the Company Directors Disqualification Act 1986 (CDDA 1986), and the Insolvency Act 1986 (IA 1986), a position now made clearer as a result of ss 89–91 of the SBEEA 2015 (see Chapter 14). With respect to the IA 1986, ss 214 and 214(7) provide that a shadow director may be liable to contribute to the company's assets if it goes into insolvent liquidation and it is proved that at some time before the liquidation he knew or ought to have known that there was no reasonable prospect of avoiding insolvent liquidation. Shadow directors will also be subject to the fiduciary duties owed by directors generally (s 89(1) of the SBEEA 2015, substituting s 170(5) of the CA 2006; see further Chapter 14).

13.22 As the term 'shadow directors' suggests, they are distinguishable from *de facto* and *de jure* directors by virtue of the fact they seek to evade the duties and liabilities of directors by remaining in the background, instructing and directing the actions of the board members, while taking care to avoid directorial appointment, whether on a *de jure* or *de facto* basis. Section 251(1) of the CA 2006 defines a shadow director as a person in accordance with whose directions or instructions the directors are accustomed to act. The provision expressly excludes from its definition those who provide professional advice (s 251(2)). However, it has been held that if the conduct of an adviser is such that it goes beyond the normal scope of his professional capacity and is tantamount to effectively controlling the company's affairs, he will be held to be a shadow director (*Re Tasbian Ltd (No 3)* (1993) in which an accountant controlled the company's banking so as to decide which of the company's creditors should be paid and in which order). The definition of a shadow director in s 251(1) of the CA 2006 has been made clearer by s 90 of the SBEEA 2015 to make it clear that acting in accordance with directions or guidance given by a person exercising a function conferred by or under legislation does not constitute the person exercising the function of a shadow director. Further, acting on any advice or guidance issued by a Minister of the Crown does not constitute the Minister of the Crown a shadow director (s 90 also refines the definition of shadow director in s 251 of the IA 1986 and s 22(5) of the CDDA 1986).

13.23 In *Re Hydrodam (Corby) Ltd* (para **13.18**), the issue was whether two directors of the parent company could be deemed to be shadow directors of its subsidiary company and therefore liable under s 214 of the Insolvency Act 1986. It was held that their actions were not such as to render them shadow directors. Being members of the parent company's board was not of itself sufficient. It would have to be shown that they personally instructed and directed the subsidiary's board. Millett J, considering the definition contained in s 251(1), took the view that there are four indices. First, the *de jure* and *de facto* directors of the company must be identifiable. Second, the person in question must have directed those directors on how to act in relation to the company's affairs or must have been one of the persons who did. Third, the directors must have acted in accordance with his instructions. Finally, they must have been accustomed so to act. The judge concluded that a pattern of behaviour must be shown 'in which the board did not exercise any discretion or judgement of its own but acted in accordance with the directions of others'. With respect to the fourth requirement, a course of conduct must be shown on the part of the board in acting on the instructions of a shadow director. Controlling shareholders are perhaps the most obvious category of persons vulnerable to a finding of being shadow directors. But merely controlling one director will not render the controller a shadow director; he must exercise control over the whole board or at least a governing majority of it (see also *Re Lo-line Electric Motors Ltd* (1988); *Re Unisoft Group Ltd (No 2)* (1993); and the judgment of Morgan J in *Instant Access Properties Ltd v Bradley Rosser* (2018)).

In *Secretary of Trade for Trade and Industry v Deverell* (1999) the Court of Appeal held that the definition of a 'shadow director' for the purposes of the Company Directors Disqualification Act 1986, s 22(5), included anyone, other than professional advisers, with real influence in the corporate affairs of the company. On the facts, both respondents were described as consultants and the company's board was accustomed to act in accordance with their directions and 'suggestions'. They were, therefore, shadow directors. In *Ultraframe (UK) Ltd v Fielding* (2005), Lewison J, having noted that a governing majority of the board must be accustomed to act in accordance with the directions of the alleged shadow director, went on to consider the nature and scope of the duties of such directors. He observed that from the time that it can be established that a person is a shadow director, he will owe certain statutory duties and prohibitions to the company (see, for example, s 170(5), which states that the general duties apply to shadow directors where, and to the extent that, the corresponding common law rules or equitable principles so apply: note the clarification to the law introduced by s 89(1) of the SBEEA 2015, below; see Chapter 14). Applying *Paragon Finance plc v DB Thakerar & Co* (1999) and *Dubai Aluminium Co Ltd v Salaam* (2002), the judge concluded that shadow directors would not usually owe fiduciary duties to a company because they do not deal directly with corporate assets (see CA 2006, Part 10; Chapter 14). However, a shadow director will be required to declare his interest in any contract with the company at a board meeting (see s 177) and obtain members' approval in relation to substantial property transactions (see s 190). On the other hand, in *Vivendi SA v Richards* (2013), Newey J went much further by holding that 'shadow directors commonly owe fiduciary duties to at least some degree'. The judge reasoned that in giving directions to *de jure* directors, a shadow director assumed responsibility for a company's affairs. He concluded that public policy pointed towards the imposition of fiduciary duties on shadow directors. On this view, all those involved in directing a company, whether as a *de jure* or *de facto* director or as an individual who controls him or her, are subject to the same duties (see now, s 89(1) of the SBEEA 2015, amending s 170(5) of the CA 2006), which puts the matter beyond doubt by extending the general duties in Part 10 to shadow directors, thus giving statutory effect to the decision in *Vivendi*).

Alternate directors

13.24   The office of director is personal in character and so a director cannot appoint a delegate to act in his place should he be prevented from attending board meetings unless the company's constitution permits this. Table A, arts 65–69 provide that a director may appoint any other director or any other person approved by the board to be his alternate (alternate directors are more commonly found in public rather than private companies). Article 25 of the 2008 model articles for public companies is drafted in similar terms. An alternate director is entitled to receive notice of all meetings of the board and its committees of which the appointing director is a member and to attend and vote at all such meetings from which the appointing director is absent. However, an alternate director is not entitled to remuneration from the company for his services and he will cease to hold office if the appointing director ceases to be a director. Subject to anything in the articles to the contrary, an alternate director is not deemed to be the agent of the director appointing him, but is deemed for all purposes to be a director (and therefore subject to the duties and liabilities of directors) and shall alone be responsible for his own acts and defaults (art 26 of the 2008 model articles for public companies).

The fiduciary nature of the office

13.25 Directors stand in a fiduciary relationship with the company. While we deal with the statutory codification of the equitable and common law obligations of directors that arise from this fiduciary relationship in Chapter 14, the nature of this relationship is worth exploring further here before we continue to the next section on directors' remuneration. The early case law on fiduciary duties owed by directors described them in terms of trustee status. This relates specifically to the origins of companies themselves. Companies, prior to the Joint Stock Companies Act 1844, were unincorporated and the constitutional document was a deed of settlement vesting the assets of the company in trustees. This practice of describing directors as trustees continued even after the advent of the registered company had done away with the need for a deed of settlement (see, for example, *A-G v Belfast Corpn* (1855) and *Grimes v Harrison* (1859)).

13.26 However by the mid-1840s, around the time when the registered company first appeared, the term fiduciary began to be used by the judiciary to describe the relationship between the directors and the company. By the 1920s there was still some confusion as to whether directors were trustees. Romer J in *Re City Equitable Fire Insurance Co* (1925) sought to clarify the issue. He stated:

> [i]t is sometimes said that directors are trustees. If this means no more than that directors in the performance of their duties stand in a fiduciary relationship with the company, the statement is true enough. But if the statement is meant to be an indication by way of analogy of what those duties are, it appears to me to be wholly misleading. I can see but little resemblance between the duties of a director and the duties of a trustee of a will or of a marriage settlement. It is indeed impossible to describe the duty of a director in general terms, whether by way of analogy or otherwise.

Directors are not, therefore, trustees as such. Rather their fiduciary relationship arises from their appointment and empowerment by the general meeting, in other words from their status as a species of agent. For example, in *Lindgren v L & P Estates Ltd* (1968) an argument that 'directors-elect' have a fiduciary relationship with the company was rejected. The fiduciary relationship and thus the fiduciary duties begin once the appointment takes place.

Directors' remuneration

General

13.27 A director is not entitled as of right to be paid for his services unless the articles of association or a service contract between him and the company provide otherwise (*Re George Newman & Co* (1895); *Guinness plc v Saunders* (1990); *Toone v Robbins* (2018); *Yusuf v*

Yusuf (2019)). This is a legacy from the law of trusts whereby a trustee is not entitled to remuneration unless the trust instrument so provides—a director, being a fiduciary, is therefore deemed to be in a similar position to a trustee. This is because, in effect, the trustee would be applying trust funds for his own benefit and not the benefit of the beneficiaries. The orthodox view taken towards directors' remuneration was stated by Bowen LJ in *Hutton v West Cork Rly Co* (1883) who said that a 'director is not a servant; he is a person doing business for the company, but not upon ordinary terms. It is not implied from the mere fact that he is a director that he is to be paid for it.' However, the articles of association invariably provide for directors' remuneration.

13.28 Article 82 of the 1985 Table A model articles (the relevant provisions in the 2008 model articles are considered below) provides that directors shall be entitled to such remuneration as the company may by ordinary resolution determine. A formal resolution is not required if all the members entitled to vote on the matter give their informal assent (*Re Duomatic Ltd* (1969)). For the *Duomatic* principle to apply, the consent must be unanimous (see *Extrasure Travel Insurances Ltd v Scattergood* (2003), discussed in Chapter 14; and *Reiner v Gershinson* (2004)). Further, members can only assent where they have full knowledge of the facts (*EIC Services Ltd v Phipps* (2003)). While the question of remuneration is a constitutional matter, it is nevertheless subject to certain statutory restrictions (in particular, ss 188–189 and ss 227–230 (service contracts); considered later). Further, Table A, art 83 requires the company to pay all travelling, hotel, and other expenses properly incurred by directors in connection with their attendance at meetings of directors or committees of directors or general meetings or separate meetings of the holders of any class of shares or of debentures of the company or otherwise in connection with the discharge of their duties (see also art 20 for pcls; art 24 for plcs of the 2008 model articles). It is noteworthy that arts 19 and 23 of the 2008 model articles for pcls and plcs respectively, provide that directors are entitled to such remuneration as the directors determine for their services (cf Table A, art 82 requiring shareholder approval). Vesting this power in the directors gives rise to an obvious conflict of interest. In public companies this is dealt with by delegating the determination of remuneration to a remuneration committee as required by the UK Corporate Governance Code (2018), Provisions 32 and 33 (see paras **13.37-13.38** and Chapter 16). For listed companies there are also disclosure requirements in relation to directors' remuneration (see paras **13.39-13.41**). Moreover, the Enterprise and Regulatory Reform Act 2013, the Large and Medium-sized Companies and Groups (Accounts and Reports) (Amendment) Regulations 2013 (SI 2013/1981), the Companies (Miscellaneous Reporting) Regulations 2018 (SI 2018/860), together with changes introduced in June 2019 in order to implement the Shareholder Rights Directive II (EU/2017/828) (SRD II), see para **13.31**, have put in place additional legal requirements in relation to the disclosure of directors remuneration (see para **13.41**).

13.29 The power to set the level of a director's remuneration will, of course, depend upon the proper construction of the articles where it is contained. *Guinness plc v Saunders* (1990) concerned the claim by a director, W, to remuneration for his services in successfully negotiating a takeover by Guinness for Distillers Co plc. The House of Lords, having found that W was not entitled to remuneration under the terms of the company's articles, also refused to grant him in the alternative any form of allowance for the work he had undertaken for the company. This aspect of the decision is particularly harsh given that Guinness benefited from the advice and services provided by W for free. Taking W's claim for a *quantum meruit* first, he sought to rely inter alia on *Craven-Ellis v Canons Ltd* (1936). In this case the claimant was awarded a *quantum meruit* for work done as the managing director of a company although he had failed to obtain the necessary qualification shares within two months of his appointment as required by the company's articles of association. Lord Templeman concluded that because the claimant in *Craven-Ellis* was not a director:

> there was no conflict between his claim to remuneration and the equitable doctrine which debars a director from profiting from his fiduciary duty, and there was no obstacle to the implication of a contract between the company and the plaintiff entitling the plaintiff to claim reasonable remuneration as of right by an action in law.

The anxiety of the House of Lords in refusing to grant W a *quantum meruit* was that to do so would run counter to the no-profit rule that lies at the root of the fiduciary duties applicable to directors.

W's claim to an equitable allowance was similarly rejected. Lord Goff, mindful that the exercise of this discretion could constitute interference in company affairs, doubted whether it would ever be exercised in favour of a company director. Lord Templeman stated that he could not envisage circumstances 'in which a court of equity would exercise a power to award remuneration to a director when the relevant articles of association confided that power to the board of directors'.

Service contracts

13.30   A director's service contract with a company is defined as a contract whereby: (a) a director undertakes personally to perform services for the company; or (b) services (as a director or otherwise) that he undertakes personally to perform are made available by a third party to the company, or to a subsidiary of the company (CA 2006, s 227). It is common practice for executive directors to have a service contract with the company which sets the level of remuneration. The articles of association commonly provide for the terms of such service contracts to be set by the board of directors or a committee of the board. In the exercise of this power they must act bona fide in the interests of the company (*UK Safety Group Ltd v Heane* (1998)). However, beyond the requirement that there must be a genuine exercise of the power, the courts have shown little inclination to intervene in matters concerning directors' remuneration particularly in relation to the amount awarded which is viewed as a matter of company management (*Re Halt Garage (1964) Ltd* (1982), Oliver J). However, where directors award excessive salaries that the company can ill-afford, this may be taken as evidencing their 'unfitness' and lead to disqualification proceedings (see paras **13.61–13.68**).

13.31 As commented earlier, the Companies Act 2006, as amended by the Enterprise and Regulatory Reform Act 2013 (ERRA 2013), the Large and Medium-sized Companies and Groups (Accounts and Reports) (Amendment) Regulations 2013 (SI 2013/1981), the Companies (Miscellaneous Reporting) Regulations 2018 (SI 2018/860), together with the implementation of SRD II in June 2019, impose a number of controls on directors' service contracts and salaries by prescribing certain disclosure obligations—and under SRD II shareholders must be given the right to vote on the company's remuneration policy and on the remuneration report at a company's annual general meeting (see later). To prevent directors entrenching themselves by long-term service contracts which would attract significant compensation packages (so-called 'golden parachute' payments), ss 188–189 require shareholder approval of any service contract which may run for more than two years (under the 1985 Companies Act the period was five years). Failure to obtain such approval renders the relevant terms void and the contract is deemed to contain a term entitling the company to terminate it at any time by the giving of reasonable notice. The requirement applies to both contracts of service and contracts for services (s 227) and also applies to shadow directors. The ERRA 2013 introduces a new s 226C into the CA 2006 which adds further requirements in relation to loss of office payments (see para **13.49**).

13.32 Where the service contract is between the director and a subsidiary of the company of which he is a director, both companies must pass resolutions. Approval is by an ordinary resolution (s 218(3)), although the articles of association may impose a stricter requirement. For private companies, approval may be by written resolution (s 188(5)(a)).

13.33 Section 412 of the CA 2006 requires disclosure in the annual accounts of the aggregate amount of directors' emoluments, including present and past directors' pensions and compensation for loss of office. Further, ss 228–230 provide that the terms of a director's service contract must be made available for inspection by the members. A shadow director is treated as a director for the purposes of these provisions (s 230). Breach of this requirement may result in a fine on conviction and the court can order an inspection (s 229(4) and (5)).

The Greenbury Committee

13.34 The wider issues arising from the corporate governance debate and the reports of the committees established in the first half of the 1990s, namely Cadbury (December 1992) and Hampel (January 1998) which, together with the Greenbury Study Group on directors' remuneration (July 1995), culminated in the adoption by the London Stock Exchange of the *Principles of Good Governance* and the *Code of Best Practice* (now the UK Corporate Governance Code (2018), see para **13.37**) (see also the Higgs Report which was published in January 2003 (see Chapter 16)). One particular aspect of corporate governance which became a major cause of public and shareholder concern in the late 1980s and early 1990s was the high levels of remuneration being awarded to directors particularly in the then newly privatised utilities (the controversy over boardroom remuneration re-ignited following the 2007/8 global financial crisis). The anxiety, which also found support in Parliament and much of the media, centred on the apparent lack of any link between boardroom remuneration and performance, and the lack of procedural transparency in the determination of directors' remuneration. As a reaction to these concerns the Greenbury Committee was established in January 1995 by the Confederation of British Industry (CBI). It was charged with reporting on best practice in determining directors' remuneration and drafting a code of practice for use by public companies. Its report and *Code of Best Practice* were published in July 1995 (*Directors' Remuneration, Report of the Study Group chaired by Sir Richard Greenbury*).

13.35 Before Greenbury, the Cadbury Committee (the Committee on the Financial Aspects of Corporate Governance, chaired by Sir Adrian Cadbury (1992)) had recommended that quoted companies should adopt a committee system as a means of improving the effectiveness of the board structure and enhancing the strength and influence of non-executive directors. As part of this system, a remuneration committee was proposed, dominated in its membership by non-executive directors, to advise the board on the remuneration (in all its various forms) of executive directors. The aim here was to address the perception of directors effectively determining their own pay. Greenbury noted in 1995 that most quoted companies had established remuneration committees.

13.36 The Greenbury Report concluded that 'accountability, transparency and linkage to performance' should be the axioms underlying the determination of directors' remuneration. To this end its *Code of Best Practice* stated:

  • to avoid potential conflicts of interest, boards of directors should set up remuneration committees of non-executive directors to determine on their behalf, and on behalf of the shareholders, within agreed terms of reference, the company's policy on executive remuneration and specific remuneration packages for each of the executive directors, including pension rights and any compensation payments;

  • remuneration committee chairmen should account directly to the shareholders for the decisions their committees reach;

  • remuneration committees should consist exclusively of non-executive directors with no personal financial interest other than as shareholders in the matter to be decided, no potential conflicts of interest arising from cross-directorships and no day-to-day involvement in running the business;

  • remuneration committees should consult the company Chairman and/or Chief Executive about their proposals and have access to professional advice inside and outside the company.

Directors' remuneration: principle and policy

13.37 The Combined Code (published in 2008), laid down the principle that companies should establish a formal and transparent procedure for developing policy on executive remuneration and that that principle governed the setting of remuneration packages of individual directors. It also stated that no director should be involved in deciding his own remuneration (Principle B.2 (Principle Q of the 2018 Code)). The Code required boards of directors to set up remuneration committees of independent non-executive directors. While the Listing Rules themselves do not require companies to set up a remuneration committee they did, however, require companies to state whether or not they complied with the Code, and to give reasons for any non-compliance.

Following a review of the Combined Code by the Financial Reporting Council in 2009 (in the aftermath of the financial crisis) and consultation on a revised Code that ended in March 2010, the FRC published the 'UK Corporate Governance Code' in May 2010 (which replaced the Combined Code). Revisions were made in September 2012, September 2014, April 2016, and July 2018 (together with revised Guidance on Board Effectiveness which supplements the 2018 Code by suggesting good practice to assist companies in applying the 2018 Code's Principles and reporting on their application). The change in name to the Combined Code in 2010 was designed to make it clearer to foreign investors and to foreign companies listed in the UK that, as a result of changes to the FCA's Listing Regime, they now needed to report on how they have applied the UK Corporate Governance Code if they have a Premium Listing of equity shares. In tandem with these initiatives, the government of the day established the Wates Group (January 2018), chaired by James Wates CBE, in order to develop a set of corporate governance principles for large privately-owned businesses. The FRC published the Wates Corporate Governance Principles for Large Private Companies at the end of 2018. There are six Principles that cover: (i) purpose and leadership; (ii) board composition; (iii) director responsibilities; (iv) opportunity and risk; (v) remuneration; and (vi) stakeholder relationships and engagement. The Principles adopt an 'apply and explain' approach. Companies are expected to apply the Principles and, for each one, provide a supporting statement that gives an understanding of how their corporate governance processes operate and achieve the desired outcomes. The Principles provide very large private companies with a framework when complying with the corporate governance reporting requirements in the Companies (Miscellaneous Reporting) Regulation 2018 (see earlier), which apply to accounting periods beginning on or after 1 January 2019.

The UK Corporate Governance Code (FRC, July 2018)

13.38 The Code is discussed in Chapter 16 and so our examination at this point is restricted to the requirements set out in Section 5 relating to directors' remuneration. The relevant provisions of the Code are complex and it is not practicable to set them out in full here. Rather, we consider briefly the principles and include references to the Code provisions. Section 5 comprises three Principles and ten Provisions covering both the remit of the remuneration committee and the structure of remuneration schemes. The FRC states that the 2018 Code should be non-prescriptive on the structure of remuneration schemes and should avoid encouraging companies, either explicitly or by implication, to adopt one form of scheme over another. It therefore removed language that might be perceived as encouraging long-term incentive plans. The key points are:

- Principle P states, inter alia, that remuneration policies 'should be designed to support [the company's] strategy and promote long-term sustainable success'.

- Principle Q gives emphasis to the need for a formal and transparent procedure for developing policy on executive remuneration and emphasises that 'no director should be involved in deciding their own remuneration outcome'.

- Principle R makes it clear that directors 'should exercise independent judgement and discretion when authorising remuneration outcomes . . .' Provision 37 reinforces the point, explaining that remuneration policies 'should enable the use of discretion to override formulaic outcomes'. The FRC states in its Feedback Statement that it expects remuneration committees to consider annually, as a normal part of the process to determine remuneration outcomes, whether there are circumstances which warrant the exercise of discretion.

The principal policy objective of Section 5 is to align executive remuneration and workforce policies with the company's strategy and values. Further, the 2018 Code introduces new provisions which carry forward the emphasis on increased disclosure by expanding the information to be included in the remuneration committee's report (Provision 41).

Disclosure of remuneration: the directors' remuneration report

13.39 A remuneration report was made mandatory in 2002 for all quoted companies for financial years ending on or after 31 December 2002 by statutory instrument (the Directors' Remuneration Report Regulations 2002 (SI 2002/1986)), which came into force on 1 August 2002. This was incorporated into the Companies Act 2006 by s 420. By virtue of s 421, the Secretary of State in 2008 laid regulations determining how the remuneration report should be presented and which parts of the report were to be subject to audit. Following a consultation exercise which began in March 2012 on how to increase shareholder voting rights on directors' pay policies and on exit payments, major reforms were introduced by the Large and Medium-sized Companies and Groups (Accounts and Reports) (Amendment) Regulations 2013 (SI 2013/1981) (amending the 2008 regulations; amended again in 2019 so as to implement SRD II, see later). As a result, for listed companies a more comprehensive directors' remuneration reporting regime was introduced for accounting periods ending on or after 30 September 2013. Relevant amendments to the CA 2006 were made by the Enterprise and Regulatory Reform Act 2013. In terms of structure, the reforms required the directors' remuneration report (DRR) to be in three parts:

(i) a statement from the chair of the remuneration committee summarising major decisions on directors' remuneration, any substantial changes made to directors' remuneration during the year, and the context in which those changes and decisions occurred or were made;

(ii) the company's policy on directors' remuneration (the remuneration policy). This applies to all remuneration and loss of office payments so that such payments must comply with the company's approved remuneration policy, or be separately approved by shareholder resolution; and

(iii) an annual report on how the remuneration policy was implemented setting out actual payments made to directors in the last financial year, including a single figure for the total pay directors received that year (the implementation report). Tables must show not only base salary but also taxable benefits, bonus entitlements (including any percentage deferred), cash awards, the value of share and share options awards, pension benefits, and any other items in the nature of remuneration.

Shareholders have a binding vote (by ordinary resolution) to approve the remuneration policy, at least every three years, but if a company wishes to change its remuneration policy in the meantime, it is required to put the new policy to shareholders for their approval at a general meeting (see also CA 2006, s 439A). The policy report must set out the main elements of directors' remuneration and how it supports the company's long-term strategy and performance. It must also state whether, and how, any views expressed by shareholders in relation to remuneration at the previous AGM or otherwise have been taken into account in the formulation of the policy. Shareholders will also have an annual advisory (non-binding) vote on a resolution to approve the implementation report. If the resolution is not passed in a year in which the remuneration policy was not put to a shareholder resolution, the policy will return for a binding vote the following year.

Where the remuneration committee considers that the disclosure of performance measures or targets may be commercially sensitive, such details may be omitted, provided an explanation for the omission is provided and an indication provided as to when, if at all, shareholders will receive that information. The DRR may draw a distinction between executive and non-executive directors (Part 1 of the Regulations), and certain requirements of the regulations may be omitted or modified in relation to non-executive directors where the requirement is not applicable given the nature of the appointment of such directors, though reasons must be provided. The Companies (Miscellaneous Reporting) Regulations 2018 (see earlier), require quoted companies with more than 250 UK employees in their group to include in the DRR the pay ratio of the total remuneration of the CEO compared to UK employees, and explain how it is consistent with UK employee pay policies.

As noted previously, a directive amending the Shareholder Rights Directive (2007/36/EC) seeks to enhance transparency and encourage long-term shareholder engagement in companies whose shares are traded on an EU regulated market (which, in the UK, includes the main market of the London Stock Exchange but not AIM). The amending Directive (SRD II (EU/2017/828)) builds on the requirements of the original Shareholder Rights Directive (which was implemented in the UK through the Companies (Shareholders' Rights) Regulations 2009 (SI 2009/1632)), aimed at giving shareholders minimum rights of access to information about company meetings and participation rights at those meetings. Implementation of SRD II took place on 10 June 2019 (see the Companies

(Directors' Remuneration Policy and Directors' Remuneration Report) Regulations 2019 (SI 2019/970), amending the CA 2006 and the Large and Medium-sized (Accounts and Reports) Regulations 2008). The 2019 Regulations reinforce the right of members to have a say in director remuneration policy by extending the existing UK regime to include unquoted traded companies (i.e. companies which are not 'listed', but which are traded on the London Stock Exchange (as defined in s 360C of the CA 2006)). The company's remuneration policy will require shareholder approval. Further, the remuneration policy and report will now cover any person not on the board of directors but who carries out the functions of a CEO or deputy CEO.

As part of its review of corporate governance, the Business, Energy and Industrial Strategy Committee (BEISC) published its report 'Executive rewards: paying for success' (26 March 2019). The report recommends a stronger link between executive and employee pay particularly through the deployment of profit-sharing schemes. To strengthen this link, the Committee recommends an employee representative on the Remuneration Committee. BEISC also reviewed the Corporate Governance Code requirements to have a director appointed from the workforce; a formal workforce advisory panel; and/or a designated non-executive director for workforce relations. While welcoming these measures, it concluded that they are not an adequate substitute for the permanent engagement achieved by Remuneration Committee membership. The Government addressed each of the Committee's recommendations and stated that it was reluctant to introduce further changes to executive pay reporting until the successful implementation of the recent reforms. More particularly, the Government rejected the BEISC's central recommendation that the remuneration committee should be required to appoint at least one employee representative on the basis that the diversity of UK companies precludes the adoption of just one method of workforce engagement.

13.40 With respect to liability under the regime, any obligation, however arising, to make a payment which would be in contravention of the remuneration policy will have no effect (s 226E(1) of the CA 2006, inserted by the Enterprise and Regulatory Reform Act 2013, ss 80 and 103(3)). If, however, a payment has been made in breach of the policy, it will be held by the recipient on trust for the company or other person making the payment. Further, in the case of a payment by a company, any director who authorised the payment will be jointly and severally liable to indemnify the company for any loss resulting from making the payment (s 226E(2)). By virtue of s 226E(5), a court may relieve the director, either wholly or in part, from liability in any proceedings against the director, if the director shows that he or she has acted honestly and reasonably and the court considers, having regard to all the circumstances, that the director ought to be relieved of liability. The criminal liability laid down by s 422(2) of the CA 2006 is extended by s 422A(5) to apply to the directors' remuneration policy contained in the DRR. Section 422(2) provides that where a directors' remuneration report is approved but it does not comply with the statutory requirements, every director of the company who knew of its non-compliance, or was reckless as to whether it complied, and failed to take reasonable steps to secure compliance or to prevent the report from being approved, commits an offence punishable by fine.

13.41 The effectiveness of the recent initiatives dating from 2002 to increase shareholder engagement with directors' remuneration via the mandatory directors' remuneration report became apparent during the general meeting 'season' following initial implementation starting around April/May 2003. Press and radio reports were filled with details of directors apparently reaping rewards for failure. For example, in late May 2003 a shareholder revolt at GlaxoSmithKline plc culminated in it becoming the first company to have its executive remuneration package rejected by shareholders (it was the so-called 'Shareholder Spring' in 2012, which saw similar shareholder revolts within plcs, that led to the ERRA 2013 reforms). An independent report published by Deloitte and Touche, *Report on the Impact of the Directors' Remuneration Report Regulations* (November 2004), found that the 2002 regulations had had a 'positive impact' insofar as they facilitate the scrutiny by shareholders of directors' remuneration. The new format DRR is the latest development aimed at bolstering such scrutiny. It is also noteworthy that in tandem with this, the FCA has in place a Remuneration Code that applies to over 3,000 firms, including all banks, amongst other financial institutions. With respect to financial institutions, and following the recommendations of the Parliamentary Commission on Banking Standards (June 2013), the FCA introduced a new Remuneration Code for dual-regulated firms, i.e. banks, building societies, and PRA-designated investment firms. Following a consultation exercise in July 2014, the final rules were published in June 2015. The principal aims of the FCA's Remuneration Code are to:

- ensure greater alignment between risk and individual reward;
- discourage excessive risk taking and short-termism;
- encourage more effective risk management; and
- support positive behaviours and a strong and appropriate conduct culture within firms.

The Code states that all applicable firms must make sure their remuneration policies and practices are consistent with and promote sound and effective risk management. This includes the following:

- at least 40 per cent of a bonus must be deferred over a period of at least three years. At least 60 per cent must be deferred for the most senior management, or when an individual's bonus is a particularly high amount;
- at least 50 per cent of a bonus must be made in shares, share-linked instruments, or other equivalent non-cash instruments (or units of shares of the alternative investment fund for firms subject to SYSC 19B). These shares or instruments should be subject to an appropriate retention period;
- ensure guarantees are only given in exceptional circumstances to new hires for the first year of service;
- ensure senior management adopts and periodically reviews the general principles of the remuneration policy and handles its implementation as well as discloses details of their remuneration policies at least annually;

- ensure performance is assessed with respect to financial and non-financial factors and is based on the performance of the individual, business unit concerned, and the overall results of the firm;

- ensure that any variable remuneration, including a deferred portion, is paid or vests only if it is sustainable according to the financial situation of the firm as a whole, and justified on the basis of the performance of the firm, the business unit, and the individual concerned.

The Code was introduced as a measure to address inappropriate remuneration policies which, as stated by the FCA, were a contributory factor behind the banking crisis. It also meets the requirements of the Capital Requirements Directive (2010/76/EU) (CRD3). Finally, it should be noted that the FCA has amended the Listing Rules as a result of the new DRR and recent changes to the narrative reporting requirements so as to ensure that any duplication in relation to directors' remuneration is minimised.

Vacation and removal from office

Retirement, resignation, and vacation

13.42 As commented earlier, arts 73–80 of the 1985 Table A (for public companies) provide for the retirement of all directors at the first AGM and thereafter for the retirement by rotation of one-third of the directors (or such number as may be specified) each year. Retiring directors remain eligible for re-election and will be automatically reappointed should another appointment not be made (Table A, art 75 (public companies; for the position under the 2008 model articles for plcs, art 21, see para **13.13**)).

13.43 A director may also resign his office. The articles of association will normally require notice in writing to the board, the effect of which is that the director is deemed to have vacated his office (art 81(d) of the 1985 Table A for both private and public companies; arts 18(f) and 22(f) of the 2008 model articles for pcls and plcs respectively). Additionally, both Table A and the 2008 model articles go on to list a number of other instances where a director will be deemed to have vacated his office. These include becoming a bankrupt or suffering from a physical disorder such as to render the director incapable of acting as such for more than three months (the Mental Health (Discrimination) Act 2013 amends the model articles by removing the provision which terminated a director's appointment on the grounds of mental health). More generally, the articles of association may include a provision that the office of a director will be vacated if he is requested in writing to resign by all his co-directors. Such a power must be exercised in the best interests of the company (*Lee v Chou Wen Hsien* (1985) PC).

Removal

13.44 Section 168(1) of the Companies Act 2006 provides that a company may by ordinary resolution remove a director before the expiration of his period of office, notwithstanding anything in any agreement between him and the company. Special notice must be given of the resolution, that is to say that at least 28 days' notice must be given before the meeting at which the resolution is to be moved (ss 168(2) and 312). The director concerned is entitled to address the meeting at which it is proposed to remove him (s 169(2)). He may also require the company to circulate to the shareholders his representations in writing provided they are of a reasonable length, unless the court is satisfied that this right is being abused to secure needless publicity for defamatory matter (s 169(3)).

13.45 Although the power contained in s 168 cannot be ousted by the articles, it is possible for a director of a private company to entrench himself by including in the articles a clause entitling him to weighted voting in the event of a resolution to remove him. In *Bushell v Faith* (1970) the articles provided that on a resolution to remove a particular director, his shares would carry the right to three votes per share. The result was that he was able to outvote the other shareholders who held 200 votes between them and so the ordinary resolution could be blocked by him. At first instance, Ungoed-Thomas J held that the article in question was invalid on the basis that it would make a mockery of the law if the courts were to hold that in such a case a director was to be 'irremovable'. However, the Court of Appeal and the House of Lords approved the clause. Lord Upjohn reasoned that: 'Parliament has never sought to fetter the right of the company to issue a share with such rights or restrictions as it may think fit'. He went on to state that, in framing s 303 of the CA 1985 (now CA 2006, s 168), all that Parliament was seeking to do was to make an ordinary resolution sufficient to remove a director and concluded that: 'Had Parliament desired to go further and enact that every share entitled to vote should be deprived of its special rights under the articles it should have said so in plain terms by making the vote on a poll one vote one share.' Nowadays, however, while weighted clauses are commonly encountered in private companies of a quasi-partnership nature, they are expressly prohibited by the Listing Rules.

13.46 A major consideration for companies seeking to remove a director is the amount of damages or compensation which may become payable to him upon his termination. This is because the power conferred by s 168 does not deprive the director of a claim for damages for a breach of his service contract (s 168(5); *Southern Foundries (1926) Ltd v Shirlaw* (1940)). To prevent directors awarding themselves long-term service contracts in order to obtain inflated compensation payments in the event of dismissal, s 188 provides that where a director's service contract or contract for services is for a period in excess of two years and contains a term whereby it cannot be terminated by the company giving notice, or that it can be so terminated but only in specified circumstances, the contract must be approved by the company in general meeting. A term in contravention of this section is void and the contract is deemed to contain a term entitling the company to terminate it at any time by giving reasonable notice (s 189). In *Wright v Atlas Wright (Europe) Ltd* (1999) the Court of Appeal held that the purpose of s 188 was to protect and benefit shareholders and so the requirement of formal approval by the general meeting could be waived where there was informal approval of the service contract by the entire body of shareholders.

13.47 It should be noted that in appropriate circumstances a company which decides to remove a director, particularly if the company is a small quasi-partnership, may face the prospect of a claim for relief by the ousted director under the unfair prejudice provision contained in s 994. In such cases the court has a wide discretion in framing a remedy to suit the particular circumstances (see Chapter 11).

Compensation payments to directors on loss of office

13.48 One of the anxieties which Greenbury sought to address was shareholder and public concern at the size of some compensation payments given to directors on loss of office and what was perceived to be, in many cases, a lack of justification in terms of directorial performance. The Hampel Committee made the point that the notice period required by an employer has become a fiction insofar as neither party expects the notice period in a director's service contract to be worked out; and in this regard it has become merely a device for the payment of money. Hampel concluded that service contracts should make detailed provision at the outset for the payments to which the director would be entitled if at any time he were removed from office, except for misconduct. The UK Corporate Governance Code encompasses these points (see, for example, para D.14).

13.49 Additionally, there are a number of provisions in the Companies Act 2006 which cover compensation for loss of office (ss 215–222). The object of the statutory provisions is to make payments to directors for loss of office or as consideration for or in connection with retirement from office unlawful unless there has been prior disclosure and approval. More particularly, s 217 prohibits a company from making any payment to a director by way of compensation for loss of office without particulars of the proposed payment being disclosed to and approved by the company. Payments made to a person connected with the director, or at the direction of the director, may also be treated as payments to the director, and if regarded as sums paid by way of compensation for loss of office, will also require member approval (s 215(3)). Sections 218–219 extend the prohibition to cover payments made in a takeover situation (see also ss 226A(2) and 226E(4)). The prohibition in s 217 does not apply to payments which the company is legally obliged to make as a result, for example, of a contractual undertaking (s 220; see *Taupo Timber Co Ltd v Rowe* (1978), Lord Wilberforce). Further, s 220(1) excludes from the general prohibition any bona fide payment by way of damages for breach of contract or by way of pension for past services. The new format DRR (considered earlier at para **13.39**) also requires the remuneration policy to set out the company's approach to payments for loss of office. Further, in order for a payment for loss of office to be made to a director of a quoted company, s 226C, inserted into the CA 2006 by the Enterprise and Regulatory Reform Act 2013, requires that: (a) the payment is consistent with the approved directors' remuneration policy; or (b) the payment is approved by resolution of the shareholders (for quoted companies, see ss 227B and 227C, CA 2006). Whenever a director leaves office, companies must publish on their website, as soon as reasonably practicable, a statement detailing the payments the director has received or may receive in the future. Where a payment is made in breach of s 226C, it is held by the recipient on trust for the company or other person making the payment and, in the case of a payment by a company, any director who authorised the payment is jointly and severally liable to indemnify the company for any loss resulting from it (s 226E(2)).

13.50 In addition to the disclosure requirements, the Listing Rules require listed companies to include in the remuneration report details of compensation for loss of office and payments for breach of contract or other termination payments in respect of each director by name. The report should also include details of any director's service contract with a notice period exceeding one year, together with details of any provisions for pre-determined compensation on termination which exceed one year's salary and benefits in kind. Finally, the report should state the unexpired term of any service contract of a director proposed for election or re-election at the next AGM. The Listing Rules also go on to require companies to make copies of each director's service contract available for inspection.

Disqualification of directors

13.51 As we have seen in Chapter 3, the protection afforded by limited liability is open to abuse. A major anxiety of the Cork Committee was the ease with which a director could carry on business through the agency of a limited liability company, allow it to slide into insolvency, form a new company, and carry on in business as before 'leaving behind him a trail of unpaid creditors' (*Report of the Review Committee on Insolvency Law and Practice* (the Cork Committee), Cmnd 8558, para 1813). As a result of the Cork Report recommendations the provisions for the disqualification of directors contained in the Companies Act 1985 and the Insolvency Act 1985 were reinforced and consolidated in the Company Directors Disqualification Act 1986 (CDDA 1986). The policy underlying the disqualification regime was explained by Hoffmann J in *Re Ipcon Fashions Ltd* (1989):

> The public is entitled to be protected not only against the activities of those guilty of the more obvious breaches of commercial morality, but also against someone who has shown in his conduct . . . a failure to appreciate or observe the duties attendant on the privilege of conducting business with the protection of limited liability.

Thus, the CDDA regime, together with provisions contained in the Insolvency Act 1986 (see Chapter 17), is designed to protect the public against abuses of limited liability. Against this, of course, is the need to strike a balance so as not to 'stultify all enterprise' (*Re Douglas Construction Ltd* (1988), Harman J). As will be seen, the judges have long sought to formulate a satisfactory test for determining whether 'commercial morality' has been breached. It is noteworthy that the disqualification regime has recently been bolstered by a series of reforms introduced by the SBEEA 2015 in order to carry forward the Government's objective of increasing trust, transparency, and accountability in companies. The relevant reforms are discussed later.

The effect of a disqualification order

13.52 The CDDA 1986 lays down a regime designed to address the need to protect the general public against abuses of the corporate form. The effect of a disqualification order is that a person shall not, without the leave of the court, 'be a director of a company, or a liquidator or administrator of a company, or be a receiver or manager of a company's property or, in any way, whether directly or indirectly, be concerned or take part in the promotion, formation or management of a company, for a specified period beginning with the date of the order' (s 1(1)). A disqualified person is therefore precluded from acting in any of the alternative capacities listed and so, for example, a disqualified director cannot then participate in the promotion of a new company during the disqualification period (*Official Receiver v Hannan* (1997)). Nor can he be 'concerned' or 'take part in' the management of a company by virtue of acting in some other capacity such as a management consultant (*R v Campbell* (1984)). It is noteworthy that the CDDA 1986 also extends to corporate directors, i.e. companies that hold director positions (*Official Receiver v Brady* (1999)).

The Secretary of State maintains a register of disqualification orders which is open for public inspection at the Companies Houses in London, Cardiff, and Edinburgh, and at the Royal Courts of Justice (s 18). When an order ceases to be in force such entry must be deleted.

Grounds for disqualification

Discretionary orders

Conviction of an offence

13.53 Section 2 of the CDDA 1986 provides that the court may, in its discretion, issue a disqualification order against a person convicted of an indictable offence (whether on indictment or summarily) in connection with the promotion, formation, management, liquidation, or striking-off of a company, or with the receivership or management of a company's property. The offence does not have to relate to the actual management of the company provided it was committed in 'connection' with its management (see, for example, *R v Creggy* (2008)). It has therefore been held to include insider dealing (*R v Goodman* (1994)). The maximum period of disqualification is five years where the order is made by a court of summary jurisdiction and 15 years in any other case (s 2(3)). It will not necessarily amount to an abuse of process for civil proceedings to be brought under s 6 of the CDDA 1986 (disqualification for unfitness, see later) where a director has been disqualified under s 2 given that s 6 is not concerned with criminality but with unfit conduct (*Cedarwood Productions Ltd, Re, Secretary of State for Trade and Industry v Rayna* (2004); cf *Secretary of State for Business, Innovation and Skills v Weston* (2014)).

As commented above, as part of the Government's objective of improving the trust and confidence of those dealing with UK companies, the SBEEA 2015, s 104, inserts a new s 5A into the CDDA 1986 which empowers the Secretary of State to apply for a disqualification order against a director for convictions abroad of a relevant foreign offence. Section 5C defines 'relevant foreign offence' as including certain offences connected with the promotion, formation, or management of a company. Further, rather than applying for a disqualification order on this ground, the Secretary of State can accept a disqualification undertaking instead (see later). These provisions were implemented on 1 October 2015.

Persistent breaches of the companies legislation

13.54 The court may disqualify a person where it appears that he has been 'persistently in default' in relation to provisions of the companies legislation requiring any return, account, or other document to be filed with, delivered or sent, or notice of any matter to be given, to the Registrar (s 3(1)). Persistent default will be presumed by showing that in the five years ending with the date of the application the person in question has been convicted (whether or not on the same occasion) of three or more defaults (s 3(2)). Otherwise, 'persistent' has been construed as meaning some degree of continuance or repetition (see *Re Arctic Engineering Ltd (No 2)* (1986) in which the failure to send 35 required returns to the Registrar was held to be sufficient evidence of persistent default). Section 5 goes on to provide that a disqualification order for persistent default can be made by a magistrates' court (in England and Wales) at the same time as a person is convicted of an offence relating to the filing of returns etc.

Fraud

13.55 The court may make a disqualification order against a person if, in the course of the winding-up of a company, it appears that he:

(a) *has been guilty of an offence for which he is liable (whether he has been convicted or not) under section 993 of the Companies Act 2006 (fraudulent trading), or*

(b) *has otherwise been guilty, while an officer or liquidator of the company or receiver or manager of its property, of any fraud in relation to the company or of any breach of his duty as such officer, liquidator, receiver or manager. (S 4)*

The maximum period for disqualification on this ground is 15 years (s 4(3)). Where a person has been found liable under s 213 or s 214 of the Insolvency Act 1986, respectively the fraudulent trading and wrongful trading provisions (see Chapter 17), the CDDA 1986 gives the court a discretion to disqualify such person for a period of up to ten years.

Disqualification after investigation of the company

13.56 Section 8 provides that if it appears to the Secretary of State from a report following a BIS (now BEIS) investigation that it is expedient in the public interest that a disqualification order should be made against any person who is or has been a director or shadow director of any company, he may apply to the court for a disqualification order. The court can disqualify such person for up to 15 years if it is satisfied that his conduct in relation to the company makes him unfit to be concerned in the management of a company. This power has been used where, following a BIS investigation, it was apparent that a director had abused his power to allot shares in order to retain control of the company (see *Re Looe Fish Ltd* (1993)). In *Secretary of State for Business, Innovation and Skills v Sullman* (2010), the application by the Secretary of State for a disqualification order was brought under s 8 following an investigation of the company. Norris J found the director, S, to be unfit to be concerned in the management of a company. S was culpable in seeking to establish a business by widespread misrepresentation of the nature of the risk which customers ran in buying 'after the event' insurance. The judge noted that disqualification under s 8 was not mandatory (as under s 6, see later), but in the case before him there was no doubt that the need to protect the public and to deter other directors from engaging in similar conduct required a period of disqualification. In *Secretary of State for Business, Innovation and Skills v Pawson* (2015) a company director was disqualified for eight years under s 8 of the 1986 Act. The central complaint against him was that he had run nine companies, which he controlled, for his own financial benefit by overcharging them for professional services. He had virtually exhausted their funds, rendering their objectives unsustainable, and achieved nothing of any value for the shareholders. His conduct rendered him unfit to be a director. It went beyond incompetence, indicating a lack of probity and integrity.

Mandatory disqualification orders for unfitness

13.57 The Insolvency Act 1985 introduced 'unfitness' as a ground for disqualification. This is now contained in s 6(1) of the CDDA 1986 which provides that the court shall make a disqualification order against a person in any case where it is satisfied:

(a) *that he is or has been a director of a company which has at any time become insolvent (whether while he was a director or subsequently), and*

(b) *that his conduct as a director of that company (either taken alone or taken together with his conduct as a director of any other company or companies) makes him unfit to be concerned in the management of a company.*

The minimum period of disqualification is two years and the maximum period is 15 years (s 6(4)). In contrast with the other grounds for disqualification noted earlier, s 6 is restricted to directors or shadow directors, including *de facto* directors. Commenting on the policy underlying s 6, Dillon LJ said in *Re Sevenoaks Stationers (Retail) Ltd* (1991) that its purpose 'is to protect the public, and in particular potential creditors of companies, from losing money through companies becoming insolvent when the directors of those companies are people unfit to be concerned in the management of a company'. The policy of protecting the public is not limited to the British public (*Re Westminster Property Management Ltd (No 2)* (2001)); and cannot be avoided by a controlling director resigning and then running the company as a shareholder without incurring the liabilities of being a *de facto* or shadow director (*Re Windows West Ltd* (2002)).

13.58   An application under s 6 must be brought by the Secretary of State or, if the company is in compulsory liquidation, by the Official Receiver, if it appears to him that it is expedient in the public interest that a disqualification order should be made against any person (s 7(1)). An insolvent company is defined as including a company which goes into liquidation at a time when its assets are insufficient to meet the payment of its debts, liabilities, and liquidation expenses (s 6(2)).

13.59   Disqualification proceedings are civil and consequently the standard of proof is that a director's unfitness must be established on a balance of probabilities. However, because of the serious nature of the allegations made during such proceedings the court will be loath to find unfitness unless the misconduct in question is clearly made out (*Re Verby Print for Advertising Ltd* (1998)). In *Secretary of State for Trade and Industry v Ettinger; Re Swift 736 Ltd* (1993), Hoffmann J viewed s 6 as essentially a penal provision and he observed that the court should give the director the benefit of any doubt when weighing the evidence of his misconduct.

13.60   With respect to the determination of the disqualification period, the Court of Appeal in *Re Sevenoaks Stationers (Retail) Ltd* (see para **13.57**) expressed the view that in general terms there were three levels of prohibition, each of which depended upon the seriousness of the conduct in question. For particularly serious cases the period should be over ten years; a middle level of between six to ten years was set for serious cases; and a minimum level was set for less serious cases (see also *R v Bott-Walters* (2005) CA).

The meaning of 'unfitness'

13.61   Section 6 provides that the court must be satisfied that the director's conduct 'makes him unfit to be concerned in the management of a company'. This has been construed as meaning unfit to manage companies generally rather than unfit to manage a particular company or type of company (*Re Polly Peck International plc (No 2)* (1994)). In *Reynard v Secretary of State for Trade and Industry* (2002) Mummery LJ observed that s 6(2) was so framed as to be wide enough to enable the court to take into account a director's dishonest conduct in giving evidence in disqualification proceedings against him: 'Indeed, it would be surprising if a court had to exclude from consideration of unfitness or length of disqualification serious misconduct by a director defendant in the proceedings; for example, shredding or fabricating documents in the course of the proceedings.' Further, because s 6 is mandatory, the court must disqualify a director if it is established that his conduct renders him unfit, and no regard is to be had to the likelihood of the particular director reforming his past misconduct (*Re Grayan Building Services Ltd* (1999); *Re Migration Services International Ltd* (2000)).

13.62   In determining whether a person's conduct renders him unfit to be a director, the court was required by s 9 (see now s 12C) to take into account the matters listed in Sch 1, although those matters are non-exhaustive. As is discussed below, Sch 1 has now been replaced with an expanded list of factors as a result of the reforms introduced by the

SBEEA 2015. The list in the original Sch 1 is divided into those matters of general application and those applicable only where the company has become insolvent. The first category comprises misfeasance or breach of any fiduciary or other duty by the director (para 1); the degree of the director's culpability in concluding a transaction which is liable to be set aside as a fraud on the creditors (paras 2 and 3); and the extent of the director's responsibility for any failure by the company to comply with the numerous accounting and publicity requirements of the CA 1985 (paras 4 and 5). Those matters to which regard is to be had in cases of insolvent companies are to be found in Part II of the original Sch 1 and include: the extent of the director's responsibility for the causes of the company becoming insolvent (para 6); and the extent of the director's responsibility for any failure by the company to supply any goods or services which have been paid for, in whole or in part (para 7). Section 106 of the SBEEA 2015 amends s 6 of the CDDA 1986, replaces s 9 with s 12C, and substitutes Sch 1 so as to expand the matters a court must have regard to when deciding whether or not to disqualify a director so as to include a person's track record, the nature and extent of any loss or harm caused, and their activities overseas. The court can now, therefore, take into account conduct in relation to overseas companies when it is considering disqualification of a director of an insolvent company and, in considering whether disqualification is expedient in the public interest under the CDDA 1986, the court can take into account a director's conduct in relation to more than one company, including any overseas company. More specifically, in determining the unfitness of a director, the additional factors to be considered in all cases now include:

- the extent to which the person was responsible for the causes of any material contravention by a company (or overseas company) of any applicable legislation or other requirement;

- the extent to which the person was responsible for the causes of a company (or overseas company) becoming insolvent; and

- the nature and extent of any loss or harm which could have been caused by the person's conduct in relation to a company (or overseas company) (Sch 1, implemented 1 October 2015).

13.63 The courts have also provided guidance as to what should render a person unfit to be concerned in the management of a company although the adage that each case depends upon its facts should be borne in mind. For example, in *Re Lo-Line Electric Motors Ltd* (1988) Sir Nicolas Browne-Wilkinson V-C said that while ordinary commercial misjudgement is not in itself sufficient, conduct which displays 'a lack of commercial probity' or conduct which is grossly negligent or displays 'total incompetence' would be sufficient to justify disqualification. On the particular facts of the case, the judge observed that the director:

> has been shown to have behaved in a commercially culpable manner in trading through limited companies when he knew them to be insolvent and in using the unpaid Crown debts to finance such trading.

(See also *Baker v Secretary of State for Trade and Industry* (2001); and *Kappler v Secretary of State for Trade and Industry* (2006).)

In *Secretary of State for Trade and Industry v Lewis* (2003), the Chief Registrar explained that commercial misjudgement does not amount to either dishonesty or incompetence such as to support the Secretary of State's claim that it was in the public interest to disqualify the directors. A stark illustration of dishonest conduct such as to render the director in question unfit to be concerned in the management of a company is afforded by the facts of *Secretary of State for Trade and Industry v Blunt* (2005). The defendant director of a company in insolvent liquidation had removed a substantial amount of stock and attempted to conceal its whereabouts from the liquidator. On the basis that he had eventually admitted the charges brought, the court disqualified him for six years. District Judge Mithani observed that the defendant had deliberately concealed assets belonging to the company in order to benefit personally at the expense of the creditors:

> Misappropriation by a director is always serious. Creditors would legitimately feel aggrieved at others . . . benefiting at their expense . . . It is a very serious allegation in respect of which disqualification is entirely justified. The allegation of concealment is no less serious . . . I have little doubt that where, as in the present case, there has been an attempt by a director to deliberately conceal assets from [the liquidator] or to deliberately mislead him about the affairs of a company with a view to obtaining financial or other benefit, the imposition of a disqualification order will almost always be appropriate.

(See also *Re Vintage Hallmark plc; Secretary of State for Trade and Industry v Grove* (2008); and *Secretary of State for Business, Innovation and Skills v Drummond* (2015).)

13.64 Hoffmann J has observed that there must be some conduct which though not dishonest must fall below standards of 'commercial morality' or at least amounts to gross incompetence (*Re Dawson Print Group Ltd* (1987); see also the comments of the Court of Appeal in *Secretary of State for Trade and Industry v Ettinger; Re Swift 736 Ltd* (1993); and the judgment of Newey J in *Secretary of State for Business, Innovation and Skills v Doffman* (2010)). Allowing a company to continue trading knowing it to be insolvent will not necessarily lead to a finding of unfitness; it must also be shown that the director knew or ought to have known that there was no reasonable prospect of satisfying creditors' claims (*Secretary of State for Trade and Industry v Creegan* (2004) CA; and *Re Uno plc; Secretary of State for Trade and Industry v Gill* (2006)). In *Secretary of State for Trade and Industry v TC Stephenson* (2000), H, who had been a non-executive director of the company for some five years, was signatory to the company's cheque account. In June 1996 the company went into liquidation. Its accounts, which H relied on when assessing the company's financial position, had always been prepared by professional accountants. The Secretary of State applied for an order under s 6 on the basis that H had caused the company to operate a policy of not paying Crown monies and had failed to keep himself properly informed of the company's financial position. The grounds of the application were that beginning in June 1995 the company had ceased making National Insurance Contributions and PAYE payments. Also, the fact that the company was in arrears of VAT was apparent in the management accounts for February and April 1995. It was alleged by the Secretary of State that H either knew the payments were not being made or ought to have realised they were not being paid because he had not been requested to sign any cheques in respect of such payments. Further, H had signed a number of cheques to pay another director's son's school fees thereby allowing that director to breach his fiduciary duties by misusing company funds for his own personal use. H had questioned the propriety of these payments but had been assured by the accountants that they would be treated as part of that director's remuneration and would be properly reflected in the accounts as such. Notwithstanding the accountants' advice H had refused to sign additional cheques for school fees and he had reported these payments to the board.

13.65 Dismissing the application, it was held that merely being a signatory to the company's cheques was not sufficient to make H a person responsible for any policy of not paying Crown monies. He was entitled to rely on the assurances of the accountant that the finances of the company were being properly managed. The Secretary of State's allegation that H had failed to keep himself properly informed of the company's financial health was rejected. The court held, taking into account H's lack of experience in operating corporate finances together with his non-executive status, that he was entitled to rely on the accountants to prepare the accounts and on their assurances that the finances were being properly run. A cheque signatory is not a finance director and is therefore not expected to possess such expertise. With respect to the cheques for school fees, H had acted on the advice of the accountant and had reported the payments to the board. This allegation was therefore also rejected. Similarly, in *Re Dawson Print Ltd* (1987), the director had used monies which represented Crown debts (VAT, NICs, PAYE, and rates) to finance company operations and Hoffmann J was not inclined to find this as being culpable conduct:

> *The fact is that [the tax authorities] have chosen to appoint traders to be tax collectors on their behalf with the attendant risk . . . There is as yet no obligation upon traders to keep such moneys in a separate account as there might be if they were really trust moneys, they are simply a debt owed by the company. I cannot accept that failure to pay the debts is regarded in the commercial world generally as such a breach of commercial morality that it requires in itself a conclusion that the directors concerned are unfit.*

A case which fell on the other side of the line is *Secretary of State for Trade and Industry v Thornbury* (2008), also involving the non-payment of Crown debts (VAT and PAYE/NIC). While it was accepted that the director in question, T, was unaware of the problems over the debts insofar as he did not have actual knowledge, the court accepted the Secretary of State's alternative argument that T ought to have known. He took no steps beyond speaking to his colleagues of ascertaining what the true financial position of the company was. He did not check to see whether the Crown debts, or even any debts, were being paid. His questions were of a general nature merely seeking the verbal assurances of his fellow directors. While directors are entitled to rely on their colleagues, that did not mean they could abdicate all responsibility. T was guilty of a culpable failure to make enquiries, he allowed the company to trade to the detriment of the Crown, and was, therefore, unfit (see also *Secretary of State for Business, Innovation and Skills v Reza* (2013); and *Secretary of State for Business, Innovation and Skills v Hawkes* (2015)). In *Re AG (Manchester) Ltd (in liquidation); Official Receiver v Watson* (2008), the company, AG, went into liquidation with a deficiency of £81.2 million. It was alleged that W, the finance director and CEO, had, with two others, including L a director and widow of the company's founder, usurped the functions of the board to an inner group of directors which made all the strategic and financial decisions, including the decision to authorise dividends amounting to some £11.2 million and the entry into an Employee Benefit Fund for the personal benefit of all of the directors and their families as an offshore vehicle for undisclosed payment of remuneration. It was also alleged that some of the dividends were unlawful given that distributable reserves were insufficient and that he had provided misleading information to the company's auditors by sending them what purported to be a 'full and complete record of all meetings of directors and shareholders' including false minutes of full board meetings apparently approving payment of dividends.

Patten J made the disqualification orders. It was the duty of a finance director to assess a company's ability to pay dividends and other expenses and to inform the board, and through it the shareholders, of any concerns which might exist about the affordability of the proposals. If the shareholders were nevertheless determined to pay themselves dividends at a level which the company could not afford and were prepared to over-rule any objections which the board might have, then the directors had no option but to resign. It was a dereliction of duty to acquiesce in dividend decisions without actively considering the obligation to ensure that the company operated on a solvent basis and in accordance with the Companies Acts. On the evidence it was clear that W was in breach of his standard of care having acquiesced in a system of governance which permitted a trust to be set up and dividends paid which he ought to have realised were illegal. He had allowed his incentive for personal profit to blind him to his obligation to challenge these arrangements. L, like the other directors, was content to leave strategic decisions to the inner group and failed to act independently and in the best interests of the company by ensuring that decisions of the kind in question were brought to the full board on a properly informed basis. Her abdication of responsibility amounted to unfitness and she was disqualified for four years.

It is apparent that the judges in determining unfitness frequently examine directorial behaviour on a subjective basis. In this regard, it is interesting to note that in *Re Dawson Print Ltd*, Hoffmann J observed that having seen the director in the witness box, 'I thought he was a great deal more intelligent than many directors of successful companies that I have come across'. On the other hand, in *Official Receiver v Wild* (2012), the defendant, who had been involved in a number of companies which had become insolvent, was disqualified for nine years. In determining the disqualification period, the judge took into account 'the use of high pressure sales techniques, the failure to give customers what they had bargained for, and the unauthorised use of another's intellectual property, and the fact that the Secretary of State was obliged to step in on two occasions to curtail the companies' activities'.

13.66 In *Re Bradcrown Ltd* (2001), Lawrence Collins J held that a finance director who had exercised no independent judgement on the effect of transactions entered into by the company by which it transferred most of its assets to other companies in the group, leaving it with a burdensome lease and no assets, was unfit to act as a director and was therefore disqualified for two years. Although the finance director had not participated in the decision-making process, he was aware of the scheme but took no steps to satisfy himself that the proposal was in the best interests of the company. He could not rely on the fact that the company's solicitors had failed to alert him to the pitfalls of the scheme. He had abrogated his responsibility throughout the process. (See also *Re Ipcon Fashions Ltd* (1989); *Re Queens Moat Houses plc (No 2)* (2005); and *Re AG (Manchester) Ltd (in liquidation); Official Receiver v Watson* (para **13.65**).)

13.67 An interesting decision is *Secretary of State for Trade and Industry v Swan (No 2)* (2005), in which Etherton J subjected the responsibilities of a non-executive director, against whom an application for disqualification under s 6 had been brought, to detailed consideration. N, a senior non-executive director and deputy chairman of the board and chairman of the audit and remuneration committees of Finelist plc, together with S, the company's CEO, were disqualified for three and four years respectively. N's reaction upon being informed by a whistle-blower of financial irregularities ('cheque kiting') going on within the group was held to be entirely inappropriate. He failed to investigate the allegations properly. Nor did he bring them to the attention of his fellow non-executive directors or to the auditors. The judge held that N's conduct fell below the level of competence to be expected of a director in his position and he was, therefore, 'unfit' to be concerned in the management of a company.

13.68 In summary, it seems that the courts will look for abuses of the privilege of limited liability as evidenced by capricious disregard of creditors' interests or culpable commercial behaviour amounting to gross negligence such as a director's failure to construct effective internal controls over the activities of employees which is found to have led to the harm in question (see *Re Barings plc* (1999); *Secretary of State for Trade and Industry v Lewis* (2003); and *Secretary of State for Business, Innovation and Skills v Dymond* (2014)). Non-executive directors who lack corporate financial experience may rely on the advice and assurances provided by the company's accountants although they should be vigilant and raise objections whenever they have concerns about the financial operation of the company.

Procedure

13.69 Section 108 of the SBEEA 2015 amends s 7(2) of the CDDA 1986 by extending the period within which an application for a disqualification order for unfitness can be made from two years to three years. Further, s 109 of the 2015 Act amends s 8 of the 1986 Act so as to remove the restriction that only information or documents obtained under certain legislative powers may be used to decide whether or not to apply for a disqualification order. For the purposes of disqualification under s 6 (and, in fact, under s 8, discussed earlier) there is no procedure which allows for a guilty plea by the defendant director along the lines of that found in criminal proceedings. Therefore in such applications the case against the director must be made out. However, where the facts are not disputed the so-called *Carecraft* procedure could be used. Under this procedure, which took its name from the decision in which it was first laid down, *Re Carecraft Construction Co Ltd* (1993), cases could be disposed of expeditiously because it avoided the need for a full trial where an agreed statement of facts was placed before the court. No oral evidence was given thereby avoiding the need for cross-examination. The court was informed of the category into which the parties agreed the disqualification should fall and counsel addressed the court on that basis (see *Secretary of State for Trade and Industry v Rogers* (1996), Scott V-C; *Official Receiver v Cooper* (1999), Jonathan Parker J). In *Rogers* the Court of Appeal stressed that the procedure did not operate to remove a judge's discretion to overturn the agreed statement of facts entered into between the Secretary of State and the director, nor did it preclude a judge from fixing another disqualification period.

The *Carecraft* procedure has now been superseded by disqualification undertakings introduced by the Insolvency Act 2000 (see later).

Leave to act

13.70 Notwithstanding that a disqualification order is mandatory if the director's conduct is such as to make him unfit to be concerned in the management of a company, s 17 nevertheless allows a disqualified director to apply to the court for leave to act. In granting leave the court will invariably attach conditions in order to ensure, as far as possible, that the overriding policy of the Act of protecting the general public against miscreant directors continues to be met (*Re Gibson Davies Ltd* (1995)). Typically the court will impose conditions relating to the control of the companies in question and the appointment of additional directors to the board, such as a finance director (see, for example, *Re Lo-Line Electric Motors Ltd* (1988); and *Re Brian Sheridan Cars Ltd, Official Receiver v Sheridan* (1996)). In deciding whether or not to grant leave the court will consider the probability of the director re-offending (*Re Grayan Building Services* (1995)). In *Secretary of State for Trade and Industry v Collins* (1999), Peter Gibson LJ stated that it was highly desirable that a director who was facing a possible disqualification order but who, in the event of such an order being granted, intended to seek leave to act, should apply early enough to enable the same judge to hear both sets of proceedings. He stressed that an application for leave should be supported by clear evidence as to the precise role he would play and up-to-date and adequate information about the company (see *Re Hennelly's Utilities Ltd* (2004)). In *Hease v Secretary of State for Trade and Industry* (2005) the court held that an application under s 17 required it to consider the public interest and to balance such interest against any private interests involved. It should be noted that where the Secretary of State considers that the judge has erred in granting leave, it is open to him to appeal against the decision.

(See also *Harris v Secretary of State for Business, Innovation and Skills* (2013).)

Criminal penalties

13.71   If a person acts in contravention of a disqualification order he is guilty of a criminal offence and is liable to imprisonment or a fine or both (s 13). Further, he will be personally liable for all the relevant debts of the company, i.e. those debts incurred at a time when he was acting in contravention of a disqualification order (s 15). The company is jointly and severally liable with the disqualified director for the debts incurred during the disqualification period (see *Sharma v Yardley* (2005)).

13.72   Personal liability also extends to those persons who act or are willing to act on instructions given without the leave of the court by a person known to be subject to a disqualification order or known to be an undischarged bankrupt (s 15(1)(b)). It is a criminal offence for a person who is an undischarged bankrupt to act as a director of, or directly or indirectly to take part in or be concerned in the promotion, formation, or management of, a company, except with the leave of the court (s 11). Liability is joint and several (s 15(2)). Section 11 is an offence of strict liability and whether the defendant director was concerned in the management of the company is a question of fact for the jury; the fact that he did not realise he was doing acts which constituted management is irrelevant (*R v Brockley* (1994); *R v Doring* (2002)).

Compensation orders

13.73   The liability of directors under the disqualification regime is strengthened further by s 110 of the SBEEA 2015 which inserts ss 15A–15C into the CDDA 1986 so as to empower the Secretary of State to apply to the court for a compensation order against a director who has been disqualified (the Insolvency Service is also empowered to accept a compensation undertaking offered by such a director) where creditors have suffered losses from the director's misconduct. In determining the amount to be paid pursuant to a compensation award or undertaking the court must have regard to the amount of the loss caused, the nature of the director's conduct, and whether the director has made any other financial contribution in recompense for the conduct (s 15B(3)). As explained by ICC Judge Prentis in *Secretary of State for BEIS v Eagling* (2019), the first case brought under the compensation order regime:

> *the intention was to enhance in the public interest the protective aspect of the disqualifi-cation regime by giving monetary redress to creditors financially affected by the miscon-duct, thereby giving the regime as a whole more 'bite', actual and perceived; and also to fill gaps in the exploitation of IA86 remedies, notwithstanding that that would only be in cases where there was a disqualification.*

Here, the company, Noble Vintners Ltd, entered a voluntary creditors' liquidation with an estimated deficiency of £1.7 million. The sole shareholder and director of the company, Eagling, was alleged to have misappropriated some £559,484 of company funds between 2 November 2015 and 18 October 2016. The Secretary of State issued proceedings seeking both Eagling's disqualification under s 6 of the CDDA 1986 and a compensation order totalling £559,484.

The judge disqualified Eagling for the maximum period of 15 years, noting that his 'miscon-duct was of the most serious sort'. The director was ordered to pay compensation in the full amount claimed. On the question of division, the judge found that £460,067 ought to be paid to the Secretary of State for the benefit of 28 named creditors whose debts had accrued after 2 November 2015, and at whose expense the director had benefited himself. The balance, £99,416, was to be paid to the liquidator as a contribution to the company's assets. The judge subjected ss 15A–15C to considerable scrutiny, and noted that:

> *Radically, liability is based not on loss to the relevant company but on loss to its individual creditors. That removes any direct correlation between this regime and the remedies available under the IA 1986. Potentially, it also enables recoveries to be made in cases where there is wrongdoing which causes no loss to the company, or where such loss is problematic. . .*

In his reasoning, the judge also provided valuable insights into the application of the compensation order regime and how it sits with the other remedies provided by the IA 1986. On the issue that ss 15A–15C of the CDDA 1986 effectively gives rise to double liability, ICC Judge Prentis remarked that 'that no statute should be interpreted so as to impose a double liability absent clear words'. The fact that the court has to take into account any financial contribution made by the director or is at risk of having to do so, means that this fact will be 'at the forefront of the court's mind' when compensation orders are sought.

Disqualification undertakings: the Insolvency Act 2000

13.74 The Insolvency Act 2000, which came into force on 2 April 2001, contains provisions which amend the CDDA 1986. The Act introduces a procedure whereby in the circumstances specified in ss 7 and 8 of the 1986 Act, the Secretary of State may accept a disqualification undertaking by any person that, for a period specified in the undertaking, the person will not be a director of a company, or act as a receiver, 'or in any way, whether directly or indir-ectly, be concerned or take part in the promotion, formation or management of a company unless (in each case) he has the leave of the court' (s 6(2) of the 2000 Act, inserting s 1A into the CDDA 1986). The Secretary of State may still require the director to submit a statement of grounds for the undertaking along the lines of those required under the *Carecraft* pro-cedure (*Re Blackspur Group plc* (2001); *Re Blackspur Group plc (No 4)* (2004)).

In determining whether to accept a disqualification undertaking by any person, the Secretary of State may take account of matters other than criminal convictions, notwith-standing that the person may be criminally liable in respect of those matters.

13.75 It is further provided that if it appears to the Secretary of State that the conditions mentioned in s 6(1) are satisfied with respect to any person who has offered to give him a disqualification undertaking, he may accept the undertaking if it appears to him that it is expedient in the public interest that he should do so (instead of applying, or proceeding with an application, for a disqualification order) (s 6(3) of the 2000 Act, inserting s 7(2A) into the CDDA 1986).

13.76 Section 8 of the CDDA 1986 is amended so that where it appears to the Secretary of State from the report of a DTI investigation that, in the case of a person who has offered to give him a disqualification undertaking that: (a) the conduct of the person in relation to a company of which the person is or has been a director or shadow director makes him unfit to be concerned in the management of a company; and (b) it is expedient in the public interest that he should accept the undertaking (instead of applying, or proceeding with an application for a disqualification order), he may accept the undertaking (s 6(4) of the 2000 Act, inserting s 8(2A) into the CDDA 1986).

13.77 Section 8A of the CDDA 1986 provides that the court may, on the application of a person who is subject to a disqualification undertaking: (a) reduce the period for which the undertaking is to be in force; or (b) provide for it to cease to be in force (s 6(5) of the 2000 Act; see, for example, *Re INS Realisations Ltd; Secretary of State for Trade and Industry v Jonkler* (2006)).

13.78 These reforms are designed to save court time so that in the specified circumstances, disquali- fication can be achieved administratively without the need to obtain a court order. The anx- iety of the legislature (and the judges, see the comments of the Court of Appeal in *Secretary of State v Davies* (1998)), is to reduce the burgeoning CDDA case load (see, also, the Explanatory Notes to the Insolvency Bill as brought from the House of Lords, 27 July 2000). The number of disqualification orders over the last eight years or so displays a marked increase as a result of the increase in investigations being undertaken by the Insolvency Service (these account for some 95 per cent of all disqualification orders) into 'failed companies'. Thus, allowing the company to continue trading while insolvent is now the most common reason for a finding of 'unfitness' under s 6 and the average disqualification period is 6.5 years.

13.79 The introduction of disqualification undertakings by the 2000 Act has been a success in terms of reducing the case load. Some 80 per cent of disqualifications are effected through the use of the undertakings procedure. In 2003/4 there were 1,710 disqualifica- tion notices of which 1,278 were undertakings. For 2004/5 there was a fall in the number of disqualification orders. Of 1,320 disqualification notices received by the Registrar, 945 were by way of undertakings.

Disqualifying non-directors

13.80 The scope of the disqualification regime is expanded considerably by virtue of s 105 of the SBEEA 2015, inserting ss 8ZA–8ZE into the CDDA 1986, so that an application for disqualification can be brought against a person who, although not a director or a shadow director, is someone who has exerted the 'requisite influence' over a director who has in fact been disqualified for unfitness. The objective is to increase the accountability of those who seek to control directors for reasons that are not in the interests of the company. The non-director can be disqualified if any of the conduct for which the actual director was disqualified was because he followed his instructions or directions. However, the non-director will not have exercised the requisite influence over the actual director if the instructions or directions were given by him in a professional capacity. Any application must be made by the Secretary of State but such an application must be in the public interest. In an appropriate case a disqualification undertaking may be accepted. The maximum period of disqualification is 15 years.

This new power seeks to address the problem of a non-director not being eligible for disqualification because he falls outwith the definition of a shadow director (see paras **13.21–13.23**) and his instructions or directions were only followed by one director and not by the board.

Competition disqualification orders

13.81 Directors who have breached competition law may also be disqualified by virtue of s 204 of the Enterprise Act 2002 which inserts ss 9A–9E into the CDDA 1986 with effect from June 2003. Section 9A places the court under a duty to make a disqualification order against a director of a company which commits a breach of competition law, provided that the court considers that his conduct as a director makes him unfit to be concerned in the management of a company. The maximum period for disqualification is 15 years. Application for a disqualification order on this ground was made by the Office of Fair Trading (OFT) which is now, as from 1 April 2014, part of the Competition and Markets Authority (CMA) established by the ERRA 2013 which merges the OFT and the Competition Commission into a new unified authority (certain other specified regulators (including, among others, Ofcom, ORR, and Ofgem) can also bring proceedings). The 2002 Act also introduces a parallel scheme for competition disqualification undertakings (CDUs) under s 9B as there is for disqualification undertakings introduced by the Insolvency Act 2000. The CMA or a specified regulator may accept a disqualification undertaking for up to 15 years from a director instead of applying for a court order. Section 9C provides that if the CMA (or specified regulator) has reasonable grounds for suspecting that a breach of competition law has occurred, it may carry out an investigation for the purpose of deciding whether to make an application under s 9A for a disqualification order.

13.82 In May 2003 the OFT published a detailed guide to the new competition disqualification orders (CDOs), *Competition Disqualification Orders—Guidance*. This sets out the powers of what was the OFT and each specified regulator and explains the circumstances which will be taken into account when deciding whether or not to apply for a CDO or accept a disqualification undertaking.

By s 9C the CMA or regulator must give notice to a director before seeking a CDO against him. The notice will explain, inter alia, the consequences of a CDO, the grounds for the application, and the evidence to be relied on. It will explain the director's right to access the file concerning the application and his right to make representations. It will also state that the director may wish to offer a competition disqualification undertaking which, if accepted, will mean that a CDO will not be sought against him.

In August 2009 the OFT announced that it was considering widening its use of CDOs. As seen (para **13.80**), currently, directors are, in practice, only likely to face disqualification for breach of competition law if they are found to have personal responsibility for their companies' breach of the competition rules. The OFT, now the CMA, wanted to improve company and boardroom compliance. It thought that the way in which it had used its powers to seek CDOs thus far had not had the desired deterrent effect. The OFT therefore proposed a new approach by seeking a CDO where a director 'ought to have known of' or 'should have taken steps to prevent' a breach of competition (antitrust) law, even if the director was not personally involved in the breach. In terms of strengthening its powers, the CMA published revised guidance on CDOs in February 2019 (CMA102, 6 February 2019). It aims to simplify the CMA's internal processes for applying CDO/CDUs. The CMA states that it will make greater use of its directors' disqualification power which it views as an important deterrent against anti-competitive conduct. The new guidance sets out a non-exhaustive range of principles (replacing the 2003 list) which the CMA may take into account when deciding to seek a disqualification order. Other changes include:

(i) streamlining the procedure and reducing evidentiary burdens by removing the automatic right of a director to make oral representations, and stating that access to the file is limited to the index of evidence provided;

(ii) removing the limits on the CMA to apply for a CDO before the expiry of the period in which a company may appeal an infringement decision;

(iii) recognising material assistance and cooperation from directors as mitigating factors that may reduce the period of disqualification; and

(iv) taking the early offering of CDUs into account when considering the appropriate length of a CDU disqualification period.

To encourage the early offering of information on cartels, the OFT stated that it would not seek disqualification of first whistle-blowers or in other cases where a company has qualified for the highest levels of leniency. Disqualification undertakings have proved a particularly effective power for the CMA. To date, all director disqualifications (nine directors so far) have been obtained via CDUs by the individuals concerned—and all cases involved cartel conduct.

FURTHER READING

This chapter links with the materials in Chapters 8 and 11 of *Hicks and Goo's Cases and Materials on Company Law* (Oxford, OUP, 2011, xl +649p).

Berle and Means, *The Modern Corporation and Private Property* (New York, Harcourt, 1932; revised edn 1968).

Bradley, 'Enterprise and Entrepreneurship: The Impact of Director Disqualification' [2001] *JCLS* 53.

Corporate Governance Code (2018), https://www.frc.org.uk/getattachment/88bd8c45-50ea-4841-95b0-d2f4f48069a2/2018-UK-Corporate-Governance-Code-FINAL.PDF.

Corporate Governance Reform the Government response to the Green Paper consultation (2017), https://www.gov.uk/government/uploads/system/uploads/attachment_data/file/640631/corporate-governance-reform-government-response.pdf.

FRC consultation on a new UK Corporate Governance Code (2017), https://www.frc.org.uk/consultation-list/2017/consulting-on-a-revised-uk-corporate-governance-co.

Finch, 'Disqualification of Directors: A Plea for Competence' [1990] *MLR* 385.

Hicks, 'Disqualification of Directors—40 Years On' [1988] *JBL* 27.

Lowry, 'The Whistle-Blower and the Non-Executive Director' [2006] *JCLS* 249.

Lowry A.K., 'De Facto Directorships: Multiple Tests Prevail' (2011) 8 *ICR* 194.

Lowry and Edmunds, 'Disqualifying "Unfit" Directors at RBS and HBOS: Political Rhetoric and the Sidelining of the Directors' Disqualification Regime' in Chiu (ed) *The Legal Framework for Corporate Governance in Banks and Financial Institutions in the UK* (Cheltenham, Elgar Publishing, 2015).

Noonan and Watson, 'Examining Company Directors through the Lens of De Facto Directorship' [2008] *JBL* 587.

Sullivan, 'The Relationship Between the Board of Directors and the General Meeting in Limited Companies' (1977) 93 *LQR* 569.

SELF-TEST QUESTIONS

1   The relationship between the board of directors and the general meeting is such that shareholders do not play an active or influential role in company decision making. Discuss.

2   What is the CDDA 1986 (especially s 6) trying to achieve and in whose interests? How effective is it as a mechanism for controlling directors? Is it in need of reform?

3   A major deterrent operating against companies seeking to remove a director from office is the amount of compensation which may be payable. How does the 2006 Act seek to control such payments? Is further reform needed?

4   A director of a company has made suggestions to her boardroom colleagues of measures which could be taken which would help the company trade out of its difficulties. The suggestions were not taken, but the director remained on the board even though it was clear that the company was unlikely to avoid insolvency. Should this director have been disqualified?

   If you think she should not be disqualified, what circumstances might change your views?

5   A director signed cheques in batches on the advice of a financial consultant. The directors relied upon an employee's (an accountant) cash flow projections and continued to trade. There were no management accounts. Adequate accounting records were not kept, so that it was impossible to give a true and fair view of the company's financial position. The directors continued to trade when the company was unlikely to be able to meet the claims of creditors.

   Should the directors be disqualified?

14 Directors' duties

SUMMARY

Introduction
The fiduciary position of directors
To whom do directors owe their duties?
The general duties of directors: CA 2006, Part 10
Remedies
Accessory liability
Relief from liability

Introduction

14.1 In this chapter we consider the duties which a director owes to the company. In Chapter 13 we explained that directors are fiduciaries and so much of the case law on their duties is founded on principles originating from the law of trusts and agency. We also saw that the early part of the 20th century marked a significant shift in the way the judges viewed the office of director. In tandem with this development the courts adopted a stricter approach towards the standard of care and skill expected of directors in the performance of their management roles. A concern of both equity and common law courts was to develop a corpus of rules designed to prevent directors abusing their considerable powers. The policy objective is based on prophylaxis and the result is a formidable body of reported decisions in which the judges have been developing the contours of directors' liabilities. In addition to the work of the courts, legislation has also imposed a range of duties, devised principally as reactive measures against specific abuses by directors, particularly in relation to fraudulent asset stripping. Confronted with this considerable body of law, it came as little surprise that the Company Law Review (CLR), in line with its objectives of maximising clarity and accessibility, recommended that the duties of directors should be codified by way of a statutory restatement. Thus, the 'general duties of directors' now appear in Part 10 of the 2006 Act.

14.2 By way of background, it is noteworthy that the issue of restating directors' duties in statutory form caused considerable controversy and generated widespread debate. It was a question first considered by the Law Commission and the Scottish Law Commission in their joint report, *Company Directors: Regulating Conflicts of Interests and Formulating a Statement of Duties* (Nos 261 and 173, respectively). The Law Commissions' examination of directors' duties was already under way at the time of the Government's announcement in March 1998 of the company law review. As part of this wider project the Law Commissions undertook to place their final report before the Company Law Review Steering Group. The Commissions were charged with the objective of determining whether or not the relevant law could be 'reformed, made more simple or dispensed with altogether' (see the Law Commissions Consultation Paper No 153, para 1.7 (the LCCP)). The Report was lodged with the CLRSG in July 1999 and informed its deliberations in several key respects.

14.3 The Law Commissions examined the case for restating directors' duties in statute. Arguments against this were founded on loss of flexibility, while those in favour saw advantages in terms of certainty and accessibility. The Commissions' conclusion was that the case for legislative restatement was made out and that the issue of inflexibility could be addressed by:

(i) *ensuring the restatement was at a high level of generality by way of a statement of principles; and*

(ii) *providing that it was not exhaustive: i.e. while it would be a comprehensive and binding statement of the law in the field covered, it would not prevent the courts inventing new general principles outside the field.*

Much of the Law Commissions' joint report is devoted, amongst other things, to achieving the principle of efficient disclosure on the part of directors. The hallmark of their approach is the emphasis placed on the wider economic context in which company law, particularly that regulating directors, operates. It is asserted that in regulating the enterprise, the law should operate efficiently, promoting prosperity (para 2.8). More particularly, Part 3 of the LCCP recommended that the law 'should move towards a general principle of meaningful *disclosure*, and that *approval* rules should be seen as the exception' (Law Com Nos 261 and 173, para 3.72).

14.4 The proposals put forward by the Law Commissions were broadly endorsed by the CLR. In its *Final Report* (at Chapter 3), the Steering Group recommended a legislative statement of directors' duties for three principal reasons:

• to provide greater clarity on what is expected of directors and to make the law more accessible. More particularly, it would help to improve standards of governance and provide authoritative guidance and clarification on issues such as 'scope'—i.e. 'in whose interests should companies be run?'—in a way which reflects modern business needs and wider expectations of responsible business behaviour;

• to enable defects in the common law to be corrected in important areas where it no longer corresponds to accepted norms of modern business practice;

• to make development of the law in this area more predictable (but without hindering its development by the courts).

The Government accepted these proposals and it is clear that the approach taken by the Law Commissions and the CLR shaped the framing of Part 10 of the 2006 Act. To aid our understanding of the equitable principles which underpin the statutory provisions, we first consider the nature of the fiduciary relationship that exists between a director and the company.

The fiduciary position of directors

14.5 As we saw in Chapter 13, it has long been settled that directors are viewed as agents of the company and as such they are subject to the full rigour of the fiduciary duties developed by equity to ensure strict compliance with the overriding principle that fiduciaries must not benefit from their position of trust. The classic statement on the position of directors was given by Lord Cranworth LC in *Aberdeen Rly Co v Blaikie Bros* (1854):

> The directors are a body to whom is delegated the duty of managing the general affairs of the company. A corporate body can only act by agents, and it is of course the duty of those agents so to act as best to promote the interests of the corporation whose affairs they are conducting. Such agents have duties to discharge of a fiduciary nature towards their principal.

14.6 One consequence of this fiduciary relationship has been the judicial juxtaposition of the terms fiduciary and trustee when referring to the legal status of company directors. In tracing the origins of the director/trustee concept, Sealy (1967) points to the widely held view 'that the concept had its origin in the fact that, in the earliest companies, the director *was* a trustee in the full technical sense'. Before the modern process of incorporation was introduced most companies were established by a deed of settlement, and the deed almost invariably declared the directors to be trustees of the funds and assets of the business venture (see, for example, *Charitable Corpn v Sutton* (1742)). The courts therefore called directors to account on a trustee basis. In *Re Lands Allotment Co* (1894) Lindley LJ explained that:

> Although directors are not properly speaking trustees, yet they have always been considered and treated as trustees of money which comes to their hands or which is actually under their control; and ever since joint stock companies were invented directors have been held liable to make good moneys which they have misapplied upon the same footing as if they were trustees.

14.7 The earliest cases in which the equitable or fiduciary duties were developed relate to the usual 18th- and 19th-century uses of equity namely, regulating the conduct of trustees of family trusts (see, for example, the leading trust case of *Keech v Sandford* (1726)). Adopting this case law by analogy, the courts used it as the template for framing the fiduciary obligations of directors. However, unlike trustees, directors do not hold the legal title to the property under their control which, as we saw in Chapter 2, belongs to the company as a separate legal person. But, directors are analogous to trustees because they have the duty to manage the company's affairs in the interest of the company (see

Bairstow v Queens Moat Houses plc (2001)). As explained by Mummery LJ in *Towers v Premier Waste Management Ltd* (2011), the fiduciary nature of the office of director can be summed up thus:

> A director of a company is appointed to direct its affairs. In doing so it is his duty to use his position in the company to promote its success and to protect its interests. In accordance with equitable principles the special relationship with the company generated fiduciary duties on the part of a director. His fiduciary commitments to the company took the form of a duty of loyalty and a duty to avoid a conflict between his personal interests and his duty to the company.

(See, also, the judgment of Norris J in *Breitenfeld UK Ltd v Harrison* (2015).)

Given the wealth of case law which spans almost two hundred years the CLRSG's task of restating it cannot be overestimated. Before examining the duties of directors set out in ss 171–177 of the CA 2006 and related provisions, we begin by addressing the key anterior question, one which was identified by the CLRSG as holding the potential to clarify the scope and nature of the duties generally, namely: to whom are the duties owed?

To whom do directors owe their duties?

14.8   Section 170(1) of the CA 2006 provides that the general duties specified in ss 171–177 are owed by a director of a company to the company. The general duties also apply to shadow directors (s 170(5); it should be noted that s 89(1) of the Small Business, Enterprise and Employment Act 2015 substituted the original s 170(5) in order to make it abundantly clear (given the conflicting case law) that the general duties do apply to shadow directors, see Chapter 13). A breach of duty is therefore a wrong done to the company and the proper claimant in proceedings in respect of the breach is the company itself (see the rule in *Foss v Harbottle* (1843) and Part 11. CA 2006; Chapter 10). Section 170(1) gives statutory effect to the decision in *Percival v Wright* (1902). The shareholders accepted an offer for the purchase of their shares by the defendants, the directors of the company. The directors had not disclosed that at the time of the purchase they were negotiating with an outsider for the sale of the company's undertaking at a higher price. The shareholders claimed that the defendants stood in a fiduciary relationship with them and the purchase ought to be set aside for non-disclosure. The court rejected this argument. Swinfen Eady J stressed that to hold otherwise 'would place directors in a most invidious position, as they could not buy or sell shares without disclosing negotiations, a premature disclosure of which might well be against the best interests of the company'. It should be noted, however, that in reaching its decision the court stressed that there was no unfair dealing by the directors. Further, the fact that the shareholders had themselves first approached the directors requesting the share purchase was material to the court's deliberations.

(See also, *Multinational Gas and Petrochemical Co Ltd v Multinational Gas and Petrochemical Services Ltd* (1983), in which Dillon LJ explained, that: 'directors indeed stand in a fiduciary relationship to the company, as they are appointed to manage the affairs of the company and they owe fiduciary duties to the company though not to the creditors, present or future, or to individual shareholders' (with respect to creditors, see now the proviso in s 172(3) and paras **14.36–14.41**)).

It was confirmed by the Court of Appeal in *Hawkes v Cuddy (No 2)* (2009), that the fact that a director was nominated by a shareholder did not, of itself, impose any duty owed to his nominator by the director. A nominee director could take into account the interests of his nominator without being in breach of his duties to the company, provided that his decisions as a director were taken in what he bona fide considered to be in the best interests of the company. (See also *Northampton BC v Cardoza* (2019) reasserting the point that directors of what is, in essence, an incorporated family business owe their duties to the company, not to the family members.)

14.9   To say that directors owe their duties to the 'company' is not particularly illuminating. It leaves the key question central to corporate theory unanswered (see Chapter 15). That is, what are the company's interests? Do the shareholders, as a contractarian analysis would demand, constitute the company's interests, or is a more pluralist approach adopted by realist theory whereby the company's interests are aligned with those of the shareholders, creditors, employees, and the general public, correct? The courts have cleverly fudged the answer. In *Greenhalgh v Arderne Cinemas Ltd* (1951) Evershed MR took the view that: 'the phrase "the company as a whole" does not . . . mean the company as a commercial entity, distinct from the corporators: it means the corporators as a general body'. Thus, he rules out a free-floating corporate interest that corporate realists would advocate and identifies the company's interests with the shareholders as a general body indicating a contractarian bias. However, that has not been the end of the matter. Detailed consideration was given to the meaning of the 'interests of the company' in the Report of the Second Savoy Hotel Investigation (*The Savoy Hotel Ltd, and the Berkeley Hotel Co Ltd, Report of an Investigation under section 165(6) of the Companies Act 1948* (London, HM Stationery Office, 1954)). There, a Board of Trade Inspector was appointed to report on the legality of the directors' actions in trying to remove an asset from the company's control so as to take it beyond the reach of a takeover bidder. The Report considered that it was not enough for directors to act in the short-term interests of the company alone, regard must be taken of the long-term interests of the company. The basis for this is that the duty is not confined to the existing body of shareholders, even future shareholders must be considered (see Grantham (1993)). We return to this issue in relation to s 172 (see para **14.26**).

14.10 Notwithstanding the broad statement of principle by s 170(1) of the CA 2006, there are certain limited circumstances where a special factual relationship can be said to arise between the directors and individual shareholders, for example in takeover situations, where the courts have been prepared to find that 'fiduciary duties . . . carry with them a duty of disclosure' to shareholders. For example, it has been held that directors in recommending that a takeover offer should be accepted owe a duty to the shareholders which includes a duty to be honest and not to mislead (*Gething v Kilner* (1972)). This particular situation can of course mean that the 'future shareholder' element of the company's interests is irrelevant. In this regard Lawton LJ in *Heron International Ltd v Lord Grade* (1983) observed that: '[W]here the directors must only decide between rival bidders, the interests of the company must be the interests of the current shareholders. The future of the company will lie with the successful bidder.'

14.11 In the context of a very close family company situations may arise which place directors in a direct fiduciary relationship with the shareholders. In *Coleman v Myers* (1977) the board recommended to the shareholders a takeover offer by a company owned by one of the directors. The New Zealand Court of Appeal, having stressed that *Percival v Wright* (1902) had been correctly decided, found that in a small private domestic company where the shares were concentrated in the hands of a few family members, a duty of disclosure arose which placed the directors in a direct fiduciary relationship with the shareholders. (See also *Re Chez Nico (Restaurants) Ltd* (1992), Browne-Wilkinson V-C.) In effect in this context the directors were treated as agents of the shareholders and not the company. Commenting on Browne-Wilkinson V-C's observations in the *Re Chez Nico* case and on the decision in *Coleman v Myers* (1977), David Mackie QC (sitting as a deputy judge in the High Court) in *Platt v Platt* (1999) stressed that:

> [t]hese are, however, cases of the highest persuasive authority and . . . plainly right. Accordingly, the fact that the relationship between director and shareholder does not of itself give rise to a fiduciary duty does not prevent such an obligation arising when the circumstances require it. In so far as Percival v Wright (1902) indicates otherwise this is only because of the significance attached to the headnote which . . . is broader than is justified by the underlying decision.

The limits of any such fiduciary relationship between directors and shareholders was explored in *Vald Nielsen Holding A/S v Baldorino* (2019) where it was held that the directors of a company did not owe a fiduciary duty to the company's shareholders when implementing a management buy-out, although the court found, on the facts, that they had committed the tort of deceit. Having reviewed the relevant case law, the court found that the mere fact that a director has more knowledge about a company's affairs than its shareholders does not automatically give rise to a fiduciary duty. Such a duty is less likely still to arise where, as in this case, the shareholders had a degree of access to information about the company and had a 'regular channel of communication' if they had wanted more. The court observed that the majority of cases where directors have been found to have owed a fiduciary duty to shareholders involved closely-held family enterprises. Although a family connection is not a prerequisite to the creation of a fiduciary duty, it is clearly a situation where shareholders will generally place trust in directors.

(See also *Glandon Pty Ltd v Strata Consolidated Pty Ltd* (1993); *Brunninghausen v Glavanics* (1999).) In *Sharp v Blank* (2019), which concerned the 2009 takeover of HBOS plc by

Lloyd's TSB Group, Norris J explained that in recommending a takeover to shareholders, the directors' duty to shareholders to exercise reasonable care and skill was 'consonant' with the statutory duty owed to the company under s 174 (see later). Accordingly, in framing their recommendation, directors must first consider the interests of the company's shareholders from time to time (a long-term view). Second, the directors must honestly believe that the takeover was in the shareholders' best interests, and that belief also had to be one that a reasonable director would hold (a dual-limbed subjective/objective test). Third, the fact that directors act on expert advice, as was the case here, was material in deciding whether the duty was satisfied, but directors still need to reach their own decision. On the evidence, the judge held that a reasonably competent director of a large bank could reasonably have reached the view that the takeover was beneficial to the shareholders.

14.12 It is clear from the case law that where 'directors take it upon themselves to give advice to current shareholders . . . they have a duty to advise in good faith and not fraudulently, and not to mislead whether deliberately or carelessly' (*Dawson International plc v Coats Patons plc* (1989), Lord Cullen). This apart, Lord Cullen stressed that 'directors have but one master, the company'. The resonance of Lord Cullen's view is clearly evident in the approach adopted by Neuberger J in *Peskin v Anderson* (2000), which was affirmed by the Court of Appeal. The dispute arose out of the demutualisation of the Royal Automobile Club (RAC) in which the members at the time of the sale received substantial payments. Former members of the club claimed that the directors were in breach of fiduciary duty in failing to disclose their plans to demutualise. They argued that had they known of the proposal they would have been able to make a properly informed choice as to whether to remain members. The judge, dismissing the claims, held that the directors did not owe any fiduciary duty to the members who had terminated their membership of their own motion when no specific proposal was in contemplation. The judge stated:

> I am satisfied, both as a matter of principle and in light of the state of the authorities, that Percival v Wright *is good law in the sense that a director of a company has no general fiduciary duty to shareholders. However, I am also satisfied that, in appropriate and specific circumstances, a director can be under a fiduciary duty to a shareholder. To hold that he has some sort of general fiduciary duty to shareholders (a) would involve placing an unfair, unrealistic and uncertain burden on a director and (b) would present him frequently with a position where his two competing duties, namely his undoubted fiduciary duty to the company and his alleged fiduciary duty to shareholders, would be in conflict.*

14.13 Apart from restating the common law in s 170(1), the provision goes on to address a range of issues that came to light during the various consultation exercises on whether or not the Act should set out in the form of a restatement the general duties of directors. A point of contention that emerged during both the Law Commissions and the CLR's consultations was whether the statutory statement of duties should be exhaustive. Section 170(3) attempts to settle the matter in two ways. First, it provides that the general duties are based on certain common law rules and equitable principles governing the behaviour of directors. Second, it states that the statutory restatement shall have effect in place of those principles. Indeed, even in current litigation where the events in issue may have occurred before Part 10 of the 2006 Act entered into force, the statutory language will nevertheless influence the approach of the courts. In *Towers v Premier Waste Management Ltd* (2011), Mummery LJ observed that:

> I have described the equitable principles and duties in the past tense because, under the codification measures in Chapter 2 of the Companies Act 2006, a director's general duties to the company are now statutory. The codified duties are expressly derived from common law rules and equitable principles as they apply to directors. The relevant events in this litigation occurred in 2003, well before those provisions of the 2006 Act were brought into force. Although the pre-2006 Act common law rules and equitable principles continue to apply to a pre-2006 Act case, it is unrealistic to ignore the terms in which the general statutory duties have been framed for post-2006 Act cases. They extract and express the essence of the rules and principles which they have replaced.

Section 170(3) has to be read together with s 170(4) which directs the courts to interpret and apply the general duties having regard to the pre-existing case law and thus the significant body of jurisprudence surrounding directors' duties is by no means redundant. In *Eastford Ltd v Gillespie* (2010), Lord Hodge, considering s 170(4), observed that it:

> seeks to address the challenge which the Law Commissions and the Company Law Review had identified, namely of avoiding the danger that a statutory statement of general duties would make the law inflexible and incapable of development by judges to deal with changing commercial circumstances. Parliament has directed the courts not only to treat the general duties in the same way as the pre-existing rules and principles but also to have regard to the continued development of the non-statutory law in relation to the duties of other fiduciaries when interpreting and applying the statutory statements. The interpretation of the statements will therefore be able to evolve.

Taking these two subsections together, some doubt remains over the extent to which the restated duties merely replicate or, indeed, replace the pre-existing duties: for example, it will be seen that the duties of directors encapsulated in ss 175 and 176 (respectively, the no-conflict duty and the prohibition against accepting benefits from third parties) are not framed so as to reflect precisely the applicable equitable principles and terminology found in the case law. Such uncertainty runs counter to the declared objectives of the CLR to provide greater clarity on what is expected of directors and to make the law more accessible. On the other hand, in the interests of clarity, s 170(2) does restate the point that emerges from the case law that the duties encompassed in ss 175 and 176 continue to apply after a person ceases to be a director:

    (a) as regards the exploitation of any property, information, or opportunity of which he became aware at a time when he was a director (duty to avoid conflicts of interests), and

(b) as regards things done or omitted by him before he ceased to be a director (duty not to accept benefits from third parties).

(See *Safetynet Security Ltd v Coppage* (2012) in which the court applied s 170(2) in holding a former director liable for breaches of the no-conflict rule.) Further, whether or not directors' duties survive insolvency was addressed in *Re System Building Services Group Ltd* (2020) where the impugned transaction took place when the company was in liquidation and therefore at a time when the director no longer controlled its affairs. The judge put the issue beyond doubt, holding that 'the [general] duties owed by a director to the company and its creditors survive the company's entry into administration and voluntary liquidation'. No doubt this will also be the case when the company has entered compulsory liquidation.

Finally, it is also noteworthy that s 179 states that, except as otherwise provided, more than one of the general duties may apply in any given case. The duties are thus cumulative. Depending on the particular circumstances, directors may, therefore, be liable under one or more of the provisions contained in Part 10 of the Act.

The general duties of directors: CA 2006, Part 10

(i) Duty to act within powers

14.14 Section 171 of the CA 2006 provides that a director of a company must:

(a) act in accordance with the company's constitution, and

(b) only exercise powers for the purposes for which they are conferred.

Part (a) of s 171 restates the common law principle that directors must act within the limits of the company's constitution which is defined by s 17 as including the company's articles and any shareholder resolutions and agreements (see further Chapter 8). Part (b) restates the so-called 'proper purposes doctrine' formulated by Lord Greene MR in *Re Smith & Fawcett Ltd* (1942), in which he explained that:

> [Directors] must exercise their discretion bona fide in what they consider—not what a court may consider—is in the interests of the company, and not for any collateral purpose.

There are two limbs to Lord Greene's statement of the duty. The first relates to good faith which falls within the scope of s 172 (see later), while the duty not to act for a collateral purpose is encompassed in s 171. The two elements are distinct duties (*Bishopsgate Investment Management Ltd v Maxwell* (1993)), and it is logical that they should be accorded separate provision in the Act.

14.15   The proper purposes doctrine has frequently been applied, although not exclusively, in relation to the power to issue shares; an obvious consequence of which is that the voting rights of an existing majority shareholder may be adversely affected. While a majority shareholder or controlling interest does not have a right of property to prevent a further allotment of shares being made, such a shareholder is entitled to demand that the power be exercised lawfully. Share issues aside, the application of the doctrine arose in *Extrasure Travel Insurances Ltd v Scattergood* (2002) which concerned the power of directors to deal with corporate assets. The directors of Extrasure had transferred company funds, some £200,000, to another company in the group, Citygate Insurance Brokers Ltd (the parent company), to enable it to pay a creditor who had been pressing for payment. One of the arguments put forward by the claimant was that the directors had exercised their powers for an improper purpose.

14.16   There is an overlap between the duty of good faith (now contained in s 172 (see later): duty to promote the success of the company) on the one hand, and the proper purposes doctrine in s 171 on the other, insofar as the latter operates to limit the authority of directors even if their action was carried out in what they bona fide believed to be in the best interests of the company. If a power is exercised primarily for some collateral purpose (which is objectively determined as a matter of construction of the articles), the directors are guilty of an abuse of power and their action can be set aside. Thus, for example, while the directors may believe it is in the best interests of the company to defeat a takeover by allotting shares to shareholders who they trust in order to reject the bid, that will probably be viewed as an improper exercise of the power to allot shares as it was originally conferred to raise capital: not to increase the voting rights of certain shareholders for some collateral purpose. As was pointed out by Wilson J in *Whitehouse v Carlton Hotel Pty* (1987), it is 'no part of the function of directors as such to favour one shareholder or group of shareholders by exercising a fiduciary power to allot shares for the purpose of diluting the voting power attaching to the issued shares held by some other shareholder or group of shareholders'. The interplay between ss 171 and 172 was more recently explained by Mann J in *Eclairs Group Ltd v JKX Oil & Gas plc* (2013), discussed more fully later. The judge said that s 172 is an 'overarching obligation which arises when directors are considering the exercise of powers'. He went on to state that s 172 does not 'trump' s 171:

> In relation to any given power, it is necessary to identify the purposes for which the power is exercised . . . and having identified that purpose one then has to see whether the directors have exercised it for that purpose, and also whether it was exercised so as to 'promote the success of the company.'

14.17   As seen, the duty evolved out of disputes in which it was typically argued that the power to issue shares is conferred on directors in order to raise capital for the company and that a share allotment for any other purpose is necessarily improper. For example, in *Hogg v Cramphorn* (1967) a share allotment was held invalid notwithstanding that the directors had acted in good faith on the basis that their primary motive was to forestall a takeover bid and remain in control. The judge found that while the directors had acted in the interest of the company, the share issue involved 'an improper use by the directors of their discretionary and fiduciary power'. Another clear illustration of self-interest being the principal motivating factor in the exercise of the power to issue shares is afforded by *Piercy v S Mills & Co Ltd* (1920). The directors allotted shares although the company was not in need of additional capital. The court held, setting aside the allotment, that this was done 'simply and solely for the purpose of retaining control in the hands of the existing directors'.

14.18   A thorough analysis of the proper purposes doctrine was undertaken by Lord Wilberforce in the Privy Council decision in *Howard Smith Ltd v Ampol Petroleum Ltd* (1974). Two shareholders, Ampol Ltd and its associated company 'Bulkships', held 55 per cent of the shares in RW Miller (Holdings) Ltd. Ampol and Howard Smith made rival takeover offers for Miller. Preferring the latter's bid because it was more generous than Ampol's, and because they believed that the long-term future of the company would be more secure in its hands, Miller's directors issued shares to Howard Smith which had the effect of diluting Ampol's shareholding from 55 per cent to 36 per cent. Ampol sought a declaration that the share allotment was invalid as being an improper exercise of power. The directors contended that the allotment was made primarily in order to obtain much needed capital for the company. Both at first instance and on appeal it was accepted that the directors were not motivated by self-interest. However, it was held that the share allotment was not made to satisfy Miller's need for further capital but to destroy Ampol's majority shareholding in the company. The share issue was therefore invalid.

14.19   Lord Wilberforce stated that when the exercise of a particular power is challenged, the determination of whether or not it had been exercised for an improper purpose is a twofold process. First, it is necessary to consider the power in question in order to ascertain, 'on a fair view', its nature and the limits within which it may be exercised. Second, the substantial purpose for which the power was exercised should be examined so as to determine whether that particular purpose was proper or not. The court 'will necessarily give credit to the *bona fide* opinion of the directors, if such is found to exist, and will respect their judgement as to matters of management; having done this, the ultimate conclusion has to be as to the side of a fairly broad line on which the case falls'. Although the court will not challenge the commercial judgement of the directors nevertheless in relation to the second stage, i.e. determining the substantial purpose for the particular exercise of a power, Lord Wilberforce stressed that it is entitled to take an objective approach in order to estimate how critical or pressing, or substantial or, per contra, insubstantial an alleged requirement may have been. In this regard, Kirby P explained in *Advance Bank of Australia Ltd v FAI Insurances Australia Ltd* (1987), that:

> statements by directors about their subjective intention, whilst relevant, are not conclusive of the bona fides of the directors or of the purposes for which they acted as they did. In this sense, although the search is for the subjective intentions of the directors, it is a search which must be conducted objectively as the court decides whether to accept or discount the assertions which the directors make about their motives or purposes.

On the facts of *Ampol Petroleum*, the Privy Council concluded that:

> Just as it is established that directors, within their management powers, may take deci-
> sions against the wishes of the majority of shareholders, and indeed that the majority of
> shareholders cannot control them in the exercise of these powers while they remain in
> office (Automatic Self-Cleansing Filter Syndicate Co Ltd v Cunninghame [earlier]), so
> it must be unconstitutional for directors to use their fiduciary powers over the shares in
> the company purely for the purpose of destroying an existing majority, or creating a new
> majority which did not previously exist. To do so is to interfere with that element of the
> company's constitution which is separate from and set against their powers.

Therefore, it is not sufficient for directors to act in what they believe is in the best interests
of the company unless they can also establish that their actions are within the scope of
the powers conferred on them.

More recently, the determination of the proper purposes rule came to the fore in the
Supreme Court decision in *Eclairs Group Ltd v JKX Oil & Gas plc* (2015). The issue here
centred on the power of directors, conferred by ss 793–797 of the CA 2006, to issue a disclosure notice calling for information about persons interested in its shares. In the event
of non-compliance, the company can apply to the court to restrict the exercise of rights
attaching to the shares. Additionally, the articles of JKX Oil and Gas plc (JKX) also included the common provision that the board could treat a response to a disclosure notice
as non-compliant where there was reasonable cause to suspect that the information provided was false or otherwise materially incorrect (art 42). The articles also provided for
the restrictions that the company itself could impose on a shareholder for non-compliance, which included disenfranchising those shares at company general meetings. In
brief, the case involved a 'corporate raid' on JKX which, as noted by the Supreme Court,
was 'an attempt to exploit a minority shareholding in [the] company to obtain effective
management or voting control without paying what other shareholders would regard as
a proper price'. The minority shareholding, some 39 per cent of JKX's shares, was held
by two companies incorporated in the British Virgin Islands which were controlled by
Ukrainian businessmen: Eclairs Group Ltd and Glengary Overseas Ltd. The directors
of JKX suspected these companies of mounting a corporate raid and therefore issued
a number of s 793 notices on Eclairs and Glengary. Believing that the responses to the
notices fell short of the information requested, JKX's directors used their powers under
the constitution to stop Eclairs and Glengary from voting at the 2013 AGM where the two
companies were opposing resolutions proposed by JKX's board.

Eclairs and Glengary challenged this exercise of power. The trial judge, Mann J, held that
their disenfranchisement was invalid on the basis that the JKX board had been motivated
by improper purposes: the purposes of the board's decision included a desire to interfere
with voting control in order to ensure that various AGM resolutions were passed. The
judge reasoned that any restrictions imposed by the directors in response to a failure to
provide information had to be for the purpose of eliciting that information. Accordingly,

the restrictions, being tainted by improper purposes, were invalidated. Taking a purposive view of ss 793–797, the judge said:

> [The directors] took the opportunity of using the power to alter the potential votes at the forthcoming AGM in order to maximise the chances of the resolutions being passed in a manner which they thought was in the best interests of the company. I do not doubt the genuineness or reasonableness of their belief as to what was in the best interests of the company. However, what they did was to use a power given for a limited purpose, related to a failure to give proper information in response to a s 793 notice, and then to apply it for another, namely to stop shareholders voting so that the rights of shareholders could be successfully changed (and directors defended, though as it happened the latter would have happened anyway). That contravenes the basic provision that powers are to be exercised for the purposes for which they are given. The purposes of the majority of the directors had this impermissible purpose as a substantial, if not a principal, purpose of their exercising the power, notwithstanding that they may have had at least half an eye to the obtaining of information. Most of the directors gave far more importance to the advantage per se of getting their resolutions through than they did to the obtaining of the information.

JKX's appeal was successful. The Court of Appeal took the view that provided the board had reasonable grounds to believe that the required information had not been furnished, it could impose the restrictions provided for in the relevant article—and the purpose underlying the imposition was irrelevant. Sir Robin Jacob and Longmore LJ, delivering a joint judgment which sought to identify the legislative intent behind the relevant statutory provisions (Briggs LJ dissenting), observed:

> The 2006 Act does not specify that the sanction of restrictions on voting can only be imposed for any particular purpose. We find it difficult to believe that Parliament intended a detailed inquiry into the minds of the directors of a company to be undertaken before the sanction can be imposed. . . . Section 800(3) of the 2006 Act make clear that, once imposed, the sanction cannot be released except in the circumstances there specified. Absence of dominant purpose of obtaining the information is not there specified. If all (or a majority of directors) have to give evidence of their dominant purpose in imposing the relevant sanction and be prepared to submit to cross-examination, it is difficult to see how s 793 of the 2006 Act can function in what may often be a rapidly changing scene. It is much more likely that Parliament intended that the relevant sanction be imposed (and remain imposed) while no or incorrect information is given.
>
> This construction moreover gives substance to the 2006 Act or an article such as Art 42. For in reality it is precisely the circumstances of this sort of case where the section (or an article such as Art 42) is most likely to be invoked . . . The result is that if the predominant motive test applies the provisions would be unlikely to have any or much application: they would be emasculated.
>
> We think that any other construction of the section (or in this case JKX's Articles) would only be an encouragement to deceitful conduct and not something which English company law should countenance.

The Supreme Court, however, unanimously disagreed. Restoring the decision of Mann J, it held that the proper purposes rule did apply to the exercise of the power by JKX's board, and it had been breached. In its view, there are three purposes underlying the power to restrict the rights of shareholders who fail to comply with a s 793 notice:

(i)   to induce a shareholder to comply with a disclosure notice;

(ii) to protect the company and its shareholders against having to make decisions about their respective interests without having relevant information; and

(iii) as a punitive sanction for failure to comply with a disclosure notice.

As Lord Sumption explained in the clearest of terms, seeking to control the outcome of shareholders' resolutions forms no part of those proper purposes: 'there is in principle a clear line between protecting the company and its shareholders against the consequences of non-provision of the information, and seeking to manipulate the fate of particular shareholders' resolutions or to alter the balance of forces at the company's general meetings. The latter are no part of the purpose of article 42. They are matters for the shareholders, not for the board.'

The members of the Supreme Court expressed different views on the application of the proper purposes rule in cases where directors exercise their powers for mixed purposes (as in *Howard Smith*)—'some good, some bad' (citing *Buckley on Companies*). In the absence of oral or written submissions, Lord Mance stressed that the court should not express any concluded views on points which do not arise for decision in the present appeal. However, he went on to say that he would have welcomed submissions on the scope of s 171(b) in order to clarify its meaning given that the section states that directors may use their powers 'only' for the purposes for which they were conferred. For Lord Mance, this is clear: '[A]ll purposes in mind must be legitimate.' But, he notes, that *Buckley* suggests that it itself involves a primary purpose test as held in *Howard Smith* (noting that by virtue of s 170(4), the common law should inform the construction of s 171(b)), so that where directors exercise a power with mixed motives, the court will seek to determine the principal purpose of their conduct (and if that is found to be improper, the exercise of the power in question will be voidable (see *Bamford v Bamford* (below))). In other words, construing s 171(b) in line with the pre-existing case law means 'that a director must exercise his powers primarily (or substantially) only for the purposes for which they are conferred'.

In the light of this uncertainty over the scope of the statutory duty and the appropriate test to be applied where directors have multiple concurrent purposes for exercising a power in a particular way, Lord Sumption expressed the view (with which Lord Hodge agreed) that a 'but for' test of causation should be applied. In support of this opinion, Lord Sumption relied on *Whitehouse v Carlton* (see para **14.16**), in which High Court of Australia stated:

> As a matter of logic and principle, the preferable view would seem to be that, regardless of whether the impermissible purpose was the dominant one or but one of a number of significantly contributing causes, the allotment will be invalidated if the impermissible

purpose was causative in the sense that, but for its presence, the power would not have been exercised.

Thus, the court would need to determine whether or not the same decision would have been made by the directors if there had not been any improper purpose at play. Lord Mance, in the majority, expressed his sympathy with Lord Sumption's reasoning that 'but for causation offers a single, simple test which it might be possible or even preferable to substitute for references to the principal or primary purpose', but felt that this important question must be left undecided having not heard argument on the point.

14.20 Returning now to other facets of the proper purposes rule that have been addressed by the courts over the years, it was long thought that the effect of an improper exercise of power was to render the director's conduct capable of ratification by the company in general meeting. In *Hogg v Cramphorn*, the Court of Appeal declined to set a disputed allotment aside until a general meeting of the company, as it was before the disputed share issue was made, had had the opportunity to either approve or disapprove of the share issue. In fact the directors' conduct was duly ratified by the company. This was followed in *Bamford v Bamford* (1970). However, in *Re Sherborne Park Residents Co Ltd* (1987) a shareholder petitioned the court under s 459 (now CA 2006, s 994, the unfair prejudice provision, see Chapter 11) in order to restrain an allotment of new shares which would alter the balance of power in the company. The court took the view that the petitioner's complaint was not that a wrong had been done to the company but that his personal rights qua shareholder had been infringed. Although the alleged breach of duty might in theory be a breach of duty owed to the company, Hoffmann J held that in substance it was an infringement of a shareholder's contractual rights under the articles of association. On this analysis the issue of ratification by the general meeting of the directors' conduct does not arise since a member will have a personal cause of action.

14.21 There is clear and obvious merit in Lord Mance's call for a definitive determination of the scope of s 171(b). But pending future judicial resolution of the questions raised by the Supreme Court in *Eclairs Group Ltd* about the test for determining breach of s 171(b), what seems settled for the time being is that *Howard Smith* should not be taken as holding, without more, that directors can only legitimately exercise the power to issue shares in order to raise additional capital. Nor should it be simply construed as laying down an absolute prohibition against directors issuing shares to change the balance of control of the company. In this regard, the High Court of Australia has acknowledged that the power to issue shares may be exercised for reasons other than the raising of capital provided 'those reasons relate to a purpose of benefiting the company as a whole, as distinguished from a purpose, for example, of maintaining control of the company in the hands of the directors themselves or their friends' (*Harlowe's Nominees Pty Ltd v Woodside (Lake Entrance) Oil Co* (1968); see also *Mutual Life Insurance Co of New York v Rank Organisation Ltd* (1985)):

> *If Company A and Company B are in business competition, and Company A acquires a large holding of shares in Company B with the object of running Company B down so as*

> to lessen its competition, I would have thought that the directors of Company B might well come to the honest conclusion that it was contrary to the best interests of Company B to allow Company A to effect its purpose . . . If, then, the directors issue further shares in Company B in order to maintain their control of Company B for the purpose of defeating Company A's plans and continuing Company B in competition with Company A, I cannot see why that should not be a perfectly proper exercise of the fiduciary powers of the directors of Company B. The object is not to retain control as such, but to prevent Company B from being reduced to impotence and beggary, and the only means available to the directors for achieving this purpose is to retain control. This is quite different from directors seeking to retain control because they think that they are better directors than their rivals would be. (Cayne v Global Natural Resources plc *(1984)*, Sir Robert Megarry V-C)

14.22 In *Teck Corpn Ltd v Millar* (1972), noted by Lord Wilberforce in *Howard Smith* as being a decision in line with English and Australian authority, the British Columbia Supreme Court held that an allotment of shares designed to defeat a takeover was proper even though it was made against the wishes of the existing shareholder and deprived him of control. Berger J criticised *Hogg v Cramphorn* as laying down the principle that directors have no right to issue shares in order to defeat a takeover bid even if they consider that in doing so they are acting in the company's best interests. He took the view that this was inconsistent with the law as laid down by Lord Greene MR in *Re Smith & Fawcett Ltd*. Berger J stressed that directors are entitled to consider the reputation, experience, and policies of anyone seeking to take over the company and to use their power to protect the company if they decide, on reasonable grounds, that a takeover will cause substantial damage to the company. Declining to follow *Hogg v Cramphorn*, he reasoned:

> How can it be said that directors have the right to consider the interests of the company, and to exercise their powers accordingly, but there is an exception when it comes to the power to issue shares, and that in the exercise of such power the directors cannot in any circumstances issue shares to defeat an attempt to gain control of the company?

The judge concluded that directors must act in good faith and must have reasonable grounds for their belief. The absence of reasonable grounds will 'justify a finding that the directors were actuated by an improper purpose'. Citing *Australian Metropolitan Life Assurance Co Ltd v Ure* (1923), Berger J said that the onus of proof is on the person challenging an exercise of power. On the particular facts of *Teck* it was held that 'the plaintiff has failed to show that the directors had no reasonable grounds for believing that a takeover by Teck would cause substantial damage to the interests of [the company] and its shareholders'.

14.23 The tests for determining whether or not a power has been exercised for an improper purpose came to the fore in *Extrasure Travel Insurances Ltd v Scattergood* (see para **14.15**). Jonathan Crow QC, sitting as a deputy judge of the High Court, stated that:

> The law relating to proper purposes is clear, and was not in issue. It is unnecessary for a claimant to prove that a director was dishonest, or that he knew he was pursuing a

collateral purpose. In that sense, the test is an objective one. It was suggested by the par-
ties that the court must apply a three-part test, but it may be more convenient to add a
fourth stage. The court must:

1. *identify the power whose exercise is in question;*

2. *identify the proper purpose for which that power was delegated to the directors;*

3. *identify the substantial purpose for which the power was in fact exercised; and*

4. *decide whether that purpose was proper.*

Applying this four-part test to the facts, the judge reasoned that the power in question was the directors' ability to deal with the assets of Extrasure in the course of trading. He noted that the purpose for which that power was conferred on the directors was broadly to protect Extrasure's survival and to promote its commercial interests in accordance with the objects set out in its memorandum. Finding that the defendants' substantial purpose in making the transfer was to enable Citygate to meet its liabilities, not to preserve the survival of Extrasure, the judge concluded that the purpose for which the transfer was made was plainly an improper one. There appears to be nothing in the views expressed by the majority in the Supreme Court in *Eclairs Group* (see para **14.19**) that would challenge the judge's approach here.

The proper purposes doctrine as manifested in the second limb of s 171 was considered in *West Coast Capital (Lios) Ltd* (2008), by the Court of Session. Tesco Holdings Ltd was prevented from obtaining complete control of Dobbies Garden Centres plc, in part, because a rival bidder, West Coast Capital (WCC), purchased shares in the market at above the offer price. Although Tesco achieved a 65 per cent holding, WCC remained a significant minority shareholder. The new board of Dobbies announced that it would not be paying dividends and proposed to raise £150 million by way of an issue of new shares. WCC petitioned under s 994 of the CA 2006 (the unfair prejudice provision, see Chapter 11), on the basis that it was highly unusual for companies to cease to pay dividends when they have not suffered a poor operating performance and so the court should 'infer a sinister intent' in this regard. WCC also argued that the current directors consistently exercised their powers in Tesco's interests to the prejudice of other shareholders, including themselves, rather than for the purposes for which those powers were conferred and the proposed share allotment made no commercial sense. On the evidence, the petition was unsuccessful. However, for our current purposes, the observations of Lord Glennie about s 171 are of particular interest. He noted that the statutory provision did little more than set out the pre-existing law. Citing *Howard Smith Ltd v Ampol Petroleum Ltd*, it was accepted by the court that the test under s 171(b) was subjective and that it was necessary to consider the actual motivation of the directors. The judge concluded the point thus:

The test . . . is essentially one of looking at the purpose or purposes for which the directors were exercising their powers, i.e. their motivation. If an improper motivation can be shown, if only by inference from an objective assessment of all the surrounding circumstances, the basis of [liability] . . . might be established.

14.24 An unusual illustration of improper purposes, at least insofar as Hart J, at first instance, and the Court of Appeal were concerned, arose in relation to so-called 'poison pill' arrangements in *Criterion Properties plc v Stratford UK Properties LLC* (2004). While such arrangements are extremely rare in the UK (indeed, *The Takeover Code* prohibits action by the board of directors of an offeree company which might frustrate a bona fide offer for the company (see General Principle 7, and Rule 21)), they are commonly encountered in North American jurisdictions. In essence a poison pill is a mechanism designed to deter hostile takeovers by making the target company unattractive. Typically a poison pill, also known as a shareholder rights plan, is used to prevent corporate raiders from gaining control by making it prohibitively expensive for the raider to acquire sufficient interest in the target company to gain control over it. This is achieved in numerous ways. Commonly, it is done by diluting the acquiring company's interest in the target company or by allowing target shareholders to buy shares in the acquiring company at bargain prices (for a full examination of poison pills, see Lowry (1992)). In *Criterion Properties plc v Stratford UK Properties LLC*, two companies, Oaktree (O), a US company, and Criterion (C), a UK company, were parties to a joint venture for investment in real property. They entered into a supplementary agreement intended to protect C against takeover and change of management by what is termed a 'poison pill' arrangement. Its effect was to give O the right to have its interest in the joint venture bought out at a very favourable price (i.e. above market valuation) should another party gain control of C or in the event of N or G ceasing to be directors or employees or involved in the management of C. This agreement achieved its objective of deterring a takeover. Subsequently, the parties began negotiations to rescind it. These broke down and C brought an action to have the agreement set aside. The Court of Appeal upheld Hart J's finding that the supplementary agreement was an improper use of the directors' power to bind C because, unlike the authorities we have considered, this agreement:

> involved not the issue of shares, but the gratuitous disposition of the company's assets . . . The buyback provision could be triggered by any takeover, not only by a hostile predator, but even one regarded as wholly beneficial . . . Furthermore, it could be triggered by the departure of N or G, even in circumstances which had nothing to do with a change of control, for example, death or dismissal due to misconduct.

While the Court of Appeal's analysis of the purpose behind the exercise of the power in question is of interest, it should be noted that the House of Lords approached the issue on the basis of directors' authority, i.e. whether the directors had actual, apparent, or ostensible authority to sign the agreement (see further Chapter 12). Since this could not be decided on the evidence available, the case was remitted for trial.

14.25 Directors frequently have an interest as shareholders in the company, and the courts recognise that in promoting the interests of the company they will also necessarily promote their own interests. In this regard a realistic view is taken that does not require 'detached altruism' on the part of directors, so that in determining whether they have acted in the best interests of the company or for some improper purpose, the test is '[W] hat was "the moving cause" of the action of the directors?' (*Mills v Mills* (1938), Latham CJ citing Lord Shaw in *Hindle v*

John Cotton Ltd (1919)). Thus, the fact that a director derives some incidental benefit from the action taken will not in itself mean that the fiduciary duty has been broken (*Madden v Dimond; Rudolf v Macey* (1905), Martin J). The appropriate test in such circumstances seems to be along the lines of the 'but for' test of causation familiar to tort lawyers. In *Mills v Mills* (1938), the court upheld a resolution to distribute bonus shares even though it had the effect of consolidating the majority voting power of the company's managing director. Dixon J said:

> but if, except for some ulterior and illegitimate object, the power would not have been exercised, that which has been attempted as an ostensible exercise of the power will be void, notwithstanding that the directors may incidentally bring about a result which is within the purpose of the power and which they consider desirable.

(See further *Stobart v Tinkler* (2019) where the court reviewed the fiduciary duties of a dissenting director who was also a large shareholder of the company.)

(ii) Duty to promote the success of the company

14.26 The CLR considered whether to retain the traditional understanding that companies should be run for the benefit of shareholders or whether a broader stakeholder approach should be adopted. By way of a limited compromise it proposed that directors should promote 'enlightened shareholder value' (see *Developing the Framework*, paras 2.19–2.22; and *Completing the Structure*, para 3.5). According to this approach, directors, while ultimately required to promote shareholder interests, must take account of a range of factors affecting the company's relationships and performance: 'the objective is to be achieved by the directors successfully managing the complex of relationships and resources which comprise the company's undertaking' (*Developing the Framework*, para 3.51). The CLR therefore recommended that the duty should be so formulated as to remind directors that shareholder value depends on successful management of the company's relationships with other stakeholders. Section 172(1), which generated considerable debate in the House of Lords, is designed to reflect this objective. It provides that 'a director must act in the way he considers, in good faith, would be most likely to promote the success of the company for the benefit of its members as a whole . . .'. The provision therefore aligns the interests of the company (as a metaphysical entity) and its members 'as a whole' (see para **14.9**).

The scope of the provision was explained by Lord Goldsmith in the Lords Grand Committee:

> it is for the directors, by reference to those things we are talking about—the objective of the company—to judge and form a good faith judgment about what is to be regarded as success for the members as a whole . . . the duty is to promote the success for the benefit of the members as a whole—that is, for the members as a collective body—not only to benefit the majority shareholders, or any particular shareholder or section of shareholders, still less the interests of directors who might happen to be shareholders themselves. (6 February 2006 (col 256))

14.27   Looking to the case law upon which s 172 rests, it was long settled that the pivotal duty of a director is to act honestly and in good faith in the best interests of the company and are thus precluded from exercising their powers to further their own interests or the interests of some third party (i.e. it encapsulates the overriding duty of loyalty directors owe to the company). The classic formulation, upon which s 172(1) is based, was made by Lord Greene MR in *Re Smith & Fawcett Ltd* (1942) who said that directors 'must exercise their discretion *bona fide* in what they consider—not what a court may consider—is in the interests of the company'. As is apparent from this statement, and its statutory manifestation, the court will not substitute its own view about which course of action the directors should have taken in place of the board's own judgement—to this extent the duty is subjective. In *Regentcrest plc v Cohen* (2001), Jonathan Parker J explained that:

> The question is not whether, viewed objectively by the court, the particular act or omission which is challenged was in fact in the interests of the company; still less is the question whether the court, had it been in the position of the director at the relevant time, might have acted differently. Rather, the question is whether the director honestly believed that his act or omission was in the interests of the company. The issue is as to the director's state mind.

(See also *Extrasure Travel Insurances Ltd v Scattergood* (2002), discussed later; and *LNOC Ltd v Watford AFC Ltd* (2013).)

14.28   However, objective considerations are hard to avoid in determining compliance. Accordingly, the determination of whether a director has complied with the s 172 duty appears to involve a combined subjective–objective test. The objective element was explained by Pennycuick J in *Charterbridge Corpn Ltd v Lloyd's Bank Ltd* (1970), where the judge stated that the test for determining whether this duty has been discharged 'must be whether an intelligent and honest man in the position of a director of the company concerned, could, in the whole of the existing circumstances, have reasonably believed that the transactions were for the benefit of the company'. The approach that the court should take when evaluating decision making by directors, was explained by Lord Hatherley LC in *The Overend & Gurney Co v Gibb* (1872) where he noted that the court had to ask:

> were [the directors] cognisant of circumstances of such a character, so plain, so manifest, and so simple of appreciation, that no men with any ordinary degree of prudence, acting on their own behalf, would have entered into such a transaction as they entered into?

Thus, if a director embarks on a course of action without considering the interests of the company and there is no basis on which he or she could reasonably have come to the conclusion that it was in the interests of the company, the director will be in breach (see *Bell Group Ltd (in liquidation) v Westpac Banking Corporation (No 9)* (2008), in which court applied a dual-limbed subjective/objective test; see also *Madoff Securities International Ltd (in liquidation) v Raven* (2013)). In *Re Southern Counties Fresh Food Ltd* (2009), Warren J said that 'it is accepted that a breach will have occurred if it is established that the relevant exercise of power is one which could not be considered by any reasonable director to be in the interests of the company'. In *Re CF Booth* (2017) the court held that the long-standing 'no dividend' policy pursued by the directors while at the same time paying themselves excessive remuneration was a breach of s 172. A recent illustration of the test is found in *Antuzis v DJ Houghton Catching Services Ltd* (2019). Mr Antuzis and other Lithuanian nationals were employed by DJ Houghton as chicken catchers. They worked in appalling conditions, received less than the minimum wage, worked extremely long hours, had payments withheld as a form of punishment, did not receive holiday pay, and were subject to other unlawful deductions. The men sought compensation for unpaid wages, distress, personal injuries, and consequential losses as a result of the company's unlawful actions. Finding in favour of the employees, the court held that in directing the company to commit the irregularities, the director and the company secretary had breached s 172 (and s 174 (see later)). They did not honestly believe they were acting properly and so had not been acting in good faith. The court found that in acting to maximise their own profit, the defendants had ruined the reputation and the fortunes of the company, as well as causing it to lose the gangmasters' licence it required to employ the workers.

Further, in *Item Software (UK) Ltd v Fassihi* (2004) the Court of Appeal found that directors are under a fiduciary duty to disclose a breach of duty, and this duty is a facet of the core duty of loyalty. Fassihi was employed as the sales and marketing director of the claimants. He set out to disrupt the claimants' renegotiation of their distribution agreement for software products with Isograph Ltd. He first unsuccessfully attempted to procure the contract for RAMS International Ltd, a company he established for that purpose. Thereafter, he persuaded the claimants to adopt a tough bargaining stance with Isograph. Notwithstanding these breaches of fiduciary duty, Item could not establish any resultant loss. The negotiations with Isograph failed because the claimants had pressed them too hard, not because of Fassihi's influence and Isograph did not contract with RAMS. It was therefore critical to identify a further basis of liability to which Item's loss of the contract might be attributed. At first instance, the trial judge held that Fassihi was owed a 'superadded' duty (both as employee and director) to disclose his misconduct. Had he done so, this would have caused the claimant to accept Isograph's proposed terms. It therefore followed that the claimant was entitled to recover for the particular losses flowing from Isograph's termination. On appeal, the existence in law of a duty to disclose misconduct came to the fore. Arden LJ, rejecting the argument that such a separate and independent duty exists, took the view that the disclosure duty is intrinsic to the overarching duty of loyalty and, therefore, Fassihi was in breach of his duty of loyalty by failing to tell Item that he had set up RAMS and planned to acquire the contract for himself. Summarising the case law on the matter, Hart J in *British Midland Tool Ltd v Midland International Tooling Ltd* (2003) said:

> A director's duty to act so as to promote the best interests of his company prima facie includes a duty to inform the company of any activity, actual or threatened, which damages those interests. The fact that the activity is contemplated by himself is . . . a circumstance which may excuse him from the latter aspect of the duty. But where the activity involves both himself and others, there is nothing in the authorities which excuses him

from it. This applies, in my judgment, whether or not the activity in itself would constitute a breach by anyone of any relevant duty owed to the company. It does not, furthermore, seem to me that the public policy of favouring competitive business activity should lead to a different conclusion. . . . A director who wishes to engage in a competing business and not to disclose his intentions to the company ought, in my judgment, to resign his office as soon as his intention has been irrevocably formed and he has launched himself in the actual taking of preparatory steps.

(See also *Forse v Secarna Ltd* (2019).)

Further, in *Haysport Properties Ltd v Ackerman* (2016), Peter Smith J noted that it is now well established that a director has a continuing duty until he ceases to be a director to disclose his own wrongdoing so that, on the facts, there was no limitation issue arising in relation to his breaches of duty. In *GHLM Trading Ltd v Maroo* (2012), Newey J, considering the directors' duty of good faith, explained that its scope could extend to disclosing any information of interest to the company:

it can be incumbent on a fiduciary to disclose matters other than wrongdoing. The 'single and overriding touchstone' [citing Etherton J in Sheperds Investments Ltd v Walters *(2006)] being the duty of a director to act in what he considers in good faith to be in the best interests of the company . . . there is no reason to restrict the disclosure that can be necessary to misconduct. Were a director subjectively to consider that it was in the company's interests for something other than misconduct to be disclosed, he would, it appears, commit a breach of his duty of good faith if he failed to do so.*

The judge also considered whether a director is under a duty to disclose his misconduct to shareholders. He took the view that if a director subjectively concluded that it was in the company's interest for a matter to be disclosed to a person who is not a director then he must make such disclosure (see also *Odyssey Entertainment Ltd v Kamp* (2012)).

14.29 The overarching nature of the s 172 duty is illustrated by the decision of the Supreme Court of Canada in *Sun Trust Co v Bégin* (1937). The Court stated that self-dealing on the part of directors and giving preference to one shareholder group over and above the shareholders as a whole are types of motivation which could lead a court to conclude that the directors had not acted in good faith for the benefit of the company. An obvious example of a breach of this duty is afforded by *Neptune (Vehicle Washing Equipment) Ltd v Fitzgerald (No 2)* (1995). At a board meeting attended only by the defendant, the company's sole director, and the company's secretary, it was resolved that his service contract should be terminated and that £100,892 be paid to him as compensation. It was held that the defendant was not acting in what he honestly and genuinely considered to be the best interests of the company but rather was acting exclusively to further his own personal interests (see also *JJ Harrison (Properties) Ltd v Harrison* (2002), discussed later). Similarly, a director who borrows money ostensibly for the benefit of company A but then transfers it to benefit company B which was insolvent and in which he held a substantial shareholding is not acting bona fide in the interests of company A (*Knight v Frost* (1998)).

Further, a director exploiting the goodwill of the company's business for his own benefit by registering a trade mark linked to the company's business in his own name is in 'clear breach of his fiduciary duty' (*Ball v Eden Project Ltd* (2002), Laddie J).

14.30   Provided directors act in good faith and in the interests of the company and are not wilfully blind to the company's interests they will not be liable for breach of fiduciary duty if they make a mistake and act unreasonably, but may be liable for breach of their duty of care (*Colin Gwyer & Associates Ltd v London Wharf (Limehouse) Ltd* (2003), Leslie Kosmin QC, sitting as a deputy judge in the High Court).

14.31   A further issue that arises in the context of this duty, and one that serves to show how directors may find themselves placed in an invidious position, concerns groups of companies. Here the question is, in whose interests should the directors act? It will be recalled that in *Extrasure Travel Insurances Ltd v Scattergood* (2002), the directors of Extrasure had transferred company funds, some £200,000, to another company in the group, Citygate Insurance Brokers Ltd (the parent company), to enable it to pay a creditor who had been pressing for payment. It was held that the directors had acted without any honest belief that the transfer was in the interests of the transferor company. The decision serves to illustrate that where a company is one of a number in a group structure, the directors must act bona fide in the interests of that company. This is, after all, a straightforward application of the decision in *Salomon* (see Chapter 2). There may be situations, however, where acting in the interests of the group furthers the interests of the particular company. For example, if a subsidiary company is owed money by its parent company which is in financial difficulty, the failure on the part of the directors to take action to recover its debts may be in the interests of the subsidiary if, on balance, it would be adversely affected by the liquidation of the parent company (see *Nicholas v Soundcraft Electronics Ltd* (1993), considered in Chapter 11). It is noteworthy that in *Extrasure* the judge emphasised that mere incompetence will not constitute a breach of fiduciary duty provided the director honestly believed he was acting in the best interests of the company. As commented earlier, on the facts, however, the payment of a debt owed by the parent company was not in the best interests of the subsidiary company. The directors were therefore ordered to pay equitable compensation.

Enlightened shareholder value

14.32   The CLR's objective that the statutory formulation of the good faith duty (which it termed the 'duty of loyalty') should promote 'enlightened shareholder value' resonates with the approach taken by the Supreme Court of Canada in *People's Department Stores v Wise* (2004), in which the Court stated that acting in the 'best interests of the company required directors to maximise the value of the corporation. This did not mean acting solely in the interests of the shareholders or in any one stakeholder's interest. Rather, as Major and Deschamps JJ explained:

> We accept as an accurate statement of law that in determining whether they are acting with a view to the best interests of the corporation it may be legitimate, given all the circumstances of a given case, for the board of directors to consider, inter alia, the interests

*of the shareholders, employees, suppliers, creditors, consumers, governments and the
environment . . . At all times, directors and officers owe their fiduciary duties to the corporation. The interests of the corporation are not to be confused.*

14.33 Section 172(1) goes on to give content to the notion of enlightened shareholder value by
listing a range of factors which, in the discharge of this duty, directors are to have regard
(amongst other matters) to:

(a) the likely consequences of any decision in the long term,

(b) the interests of the company's employees,

(c) the need to foster the company's business relationships with suppliers, customers, and others,

(d) the impact of the company's operations on the community and the environment,

(e) the desirability of the company maintaining a reputation for high standards of
business conduct, and

(f) the need to act fairly as between members of the company.

The phrase 'have regard to' was explained by Margaret Hodge, then Minister of State for
Industry and the Regions:

> The words 'have regard to' means 'think about'; they are absolutely not about just ticking
> boxes. If 'thinking about' leads to the conclusion, as we believe it will in many cases, that
> the proper course is to act positively to achieve the objects in the [provision], that will be
> what the director's duty is. In other words 'have regard to' means 'give proper consider-
> ation to' . . . (Hansard, HC, vol 450, col 789 (17 October 2006))

The list of factors set out in s 172 is not exhaustive but is indicative of the importance
that the CLR paid to the wider expectations of responsible business behaviour (see the
White Paper (2005), para 3.3). The framing of s 172(1) is intended to place beyond doubt
that the need to have regard to the specified factors is subject to the overriding duty to
act in the way the director considers, in good faith, would be most likely to promote the
success of the company (after all, the duties are owed directly to the company (s 170)).
However, in discharging this duty and, more particularly, in taking account of the factors,
directors are bound to exercise reasonable care, skill, and diligence (see s 174, discussed
later). If challenged on this ground, a director will, therefore, need to demonstrate that
the interests listed informed his or her deliberations. This has led to significant changes to
the way in which directors document and report on their decisions. The requirement for
a strategic report introduced by the Companies Act 2006 (Strategic Report and Directors'
Report) Regulations 2013 (SI 2013/1970) (though not applying to small companies and
is qualified with respect to medium-sized companies) now specifies that the report: 'must
include a statement (a "section 172(1) statement") which describes how the directors
have had regard to the matters set out in section 172(1)(a) to (f) when performing their

duty under section 172' (CA 2006, ss 414C and 414CZA(1), inserted by the Companies (Miscellaneous Reporting) Regulations 2018 (SI 2018/860), reg 1(1) and 4)).

14.34 As noted earlier, this provision attracted significant debate while the Companies Bill was going through Parliament and was the cause of considerable anxiety amongst interested parties. For example, the Law Society thought that s 172 might open the commercial decision making of directors to judicial challenge (see the Law Society's 'Proposed Amendments and Briefing for Parts 10 & 11' (23 January 2006)). To allay the fear that directors would be exposed to increased litigation and to aid understanding of the statutory statement of directors' duties, DBERR (now BEIS) published a compilation of ministerial statements on the meaning of the relevant provisions (June 2007). In the Minister of State's introduction to the document she placed particular emphasis on s 172 explaining that it 'captures a cultural change in the way in which companies conduct their business'. Accordingly, she stated that there was a time when business success in the interests of shareholders was thought to be in conflict with society's aspirations for people who work in the company or supply chain companies, for the long-term well-being of the community and the environment: 'Pursuing the interests of shareholders and embracing wider responsibilities are complementary purposes, not contradictory ones'. The position taken is that businesses 'perform better' when they have regard to a wider group of issues in pursuing success and it concludes by noting that it makes 'good business sense' to have regard to the various factors listed in the provision and thereby embrace 'wider social responsibilities'. Given the anxiety which surrounded the scope of the provision, it is noteworthy that in *Re Southern Counties Fresh Foods Ltd* (2008), the court took the opportunity to compare the statutory formulation of the duty with Lord Greene MR's statement of the duty in *Re Smith & Fawcett Ltd* and concluded that they amounted to the same thing, although the court acknowledged that the statutory provision gave a more readily understood definition of the scope of the duty. Indeed, proof that s 172 will not lead to an opening of the floodgates of litigation against directors is evident from the short shrift given by Mr Justice Sales to the claimant in *R (on the application of People & Planet) v HM Treasury* (2009). The case arose by way of an application for permission to bring judicial review proceedings. People & Planet objected to HM Treasury's policy in relation to the management of the Royal Bank of Scotland (RBS) by UK Financial Investments Ltd (UKFI), the company through which the Government owns RBS. The claimant argued that HM Treasury acted unlawfully in adopting the policy it promulgated relating to how UKFI should manage the investment in RBS. The policy it adopted calls for a commercial approach on the part of UKFI. The claimant objected to this on the basis that UKFI should be promoting a more interventionist approach as a major shareholder in RBS, and seek to persuade or require RBS to change its current commercial lending practices and adopt instead lending policies which did not support ventures or businesses which might be said to be harmful to the environment by reason of their carbon emissions or be said to be insufficiently respectful of human rights. One of the lines of attack made by the claimant was that there was a misdirection of law by HM Treasury as to the effect of s 172. The application was refused. The judge held that in evaluating the policy with reference to the Green Book (which set out guidance for decision making in central government), officials correctly identified the proper way in which social and environmental considerations may be taken into account by the directors of RBS in the context of the duties of those directors under s 172. He noted that the question then was whether HM Treasury should have sought to go further, so as in effect to seek to impose its own policy in relation to combating climate change and promoting human rights on the board of RBS, contrary to the judgement of the directors:

> In my view, that clearly would have a tendency to come into conflict with, and hence would cut across, the duties of the RBS Board as set out in section 172(1). It would also have given rise to a real risk of litigation by minority shareholders seeking to complain that the value of their shares had been detrimentally affected by the Government seeking to impose its policy on RBS, as was identified in the background document which accompanied the Green Book assessment.

Sales J stressed that decisions regarding the management of RBS will be matters for the judgment of the directors of RBS:

> The policy adopted by HM Treasury is that UKFI can properly seek to influence the Board of RBS to have regard to environmental and human rights considerations in accordance with the RBS Board's duty under s 172 . . . It was a legitimate argument against going further than that that there would be a risk of trying to press the RBS Board beyond the limits of their own duties, and in my view that is all that has been said in paragraph 13(e) of the Green Book assessment, read in its proper context as one reason among others. In my view, on a fair reading of that document, it was not being said that there was an absolute legal bar to the introduction of a different policy, but rather that was a good reason for not pressing the RBS Board by means of a more interventionist policy for UKFI.

14.35   Taking account of the interests of employees as required by s 172(1)(b) has long been a statutory requirement. Section 309 of the CA 1985 had provided that 'the matters to which the directors of a company are to have regard in the performance of their functions include the interests of the company's employees in general, as well as the interests of its members'. There were two significant problems with this duty. The first related to its enforceability because it could only be enforced in the same way as any other fiduciary duty owed to a company by its directors (CA 1985, s 309(2)). Either the company had to sue for its breach, or a shareholder had to bring a derivative action (although see *Re Welfab Engineers Ltd* (1990), considered later). Second, it was difficult to identify the precise scope of the duty for the purposes of determining whether it had been discharged or not. Directors were not bound to give the interests of employees priority over those of shareholders. The CLR therefore reached the conclusion that the provision should be repealed on the basis, as we have seen, that directors should consider employees' interests only as an incident of promoting the company's success for the benefit of its members (*The Strategic Framework* (1999), paras 5.1.20–5.1.23). However, s 247 of the CA 2006 does permit directors to make provision for the benefit of employees and former employees of the company or any of its subsidiaries on the cessation or transfer of the whole or part of the undertaking of the company or the subsidiary. Significantly, s 247(2) states that the power can be exercised even if it will not promote the success of the company in accordance with s 172. In terms of reporting, the directors' report must contain a statement summarising (i) how the directors have engaged with employees and (ii) how the directors have had regard to employee interests, and the effect of that regard, including on the principal decisions taken by the company during the financial year (the Large and Medium-sized Companies and Groups (Accounts and Reports) Regulations 2008, as amended (see Chapter 13)). Directors may, however, include this information in the strategic report instead (s 414C(11), CA 2006); for measures aimed at reporting on employee involvement, see Sch 7, para 11(3) of the Accounts Regulations.

Following recent Government initiatives for strengthening stakeholder engagement (see Chapters 13 and 16), the Institute of Chartered Secretaries and Administrators (ICSA) and the Investment Association (IA) published guidance notes, 'The Stakeholder Voice in Board Decision Making' (November 2017) aimed at helping boards of directors understand the views of their employees and other stakeholders and how they should take these into account for the purposes of s 172 when making strategic decisions. Ten core principles are listed:

1. boards should identify, and keep under regular review, who they consider their key stakeholders to be and why;

2. boards should determine which stakeholders they need to engage with directly, as opposed to relying solely on information from management;

3. when evaluating their composition and effectiveness, directors should identify what stakeholder expertise is needed in the boardroom and decide whether they have, or would benefit from, directors with directly relevant experience or understanding;

4. when recruiting any director, the nomination committee should take the stakeholder perspective into account when deciding on the recruitment process and the selection criteria;

5. the chair (supported by the company secretary) should keep under review the adequacy of the training received by all directors on stakeholder-related matters, and the induction received by new directors, particularly those without previous board experience;

6. the chair (supported by the board, management and the company secretary, if applicable) should determine how best to ensure that the board's decision-making processes give sufficient consideration to key stakeholders;

7. boards should ensure that appropriate engagement with key stakeholders is taking place and that this is kept under regular review;

8. in designing engagement mechanisms, companies should consider what would be most effective and convenient for the stakeholders, not just the company;

9.   the board should report to its shareholders on how it has taken the impact on key stakeholders into account when making decisions; and

10. the board should provide feedback to those stakeholders with whom it has engaged, which should be tailored to the different stakeholder groups.

The guidance defines stakeholders as those groups that are likely to be affected by the company's actions, or whose actions can affect the company's operation or business model. Key stakeholders will obviously vary according to a particular company's circumstances, for example its size, nature of business, and location, and so the guidance notes do not provide an exhaustive list.

Finally, it is noteworthy that the directors' report must also contain a statement summarising how the directors have had regard to the need to foster the company's business relationships with suppliers, customers, and others as required by s 172(1)(c). Further, following its annual review of corporate reporting for 2018/19, the FRC published a report on climate-related reporting (November 2019) which sets out guidance for companies for improving their reporting in this regard. Similarly, the FRC has also provided guidance on key s 172 statements, including environmental disclosures (s 172(1)(d)), recommending that companies should report on the direct and indirect effects of climate change on their businesses.

Creditors

14.36   As a separate constituency creditors do not appear in the list of factors contained in s 172(1), although some of the categories listed such as employees, suppliers, and customers may indeed be creditors. However, s 172(3) provides that 'the duty imposed by this section has effect subject to any enactment or rule of law requiring directors, in certain circumstances, to consider or act in the interests of creditors of the company'. In this regard, in *Stone & Rolls Ltd v Moore Stephens* (2009), Lord Mance (dissenting) stressed that:

> Section 172(1) of the Companies Act 2006 now states the duty, in terms expressly based on common law rules and equitable principles (see s 170(3)), as being to 'act in the way he considers, in good faith, would be most likely to promote the success of the company for the benefit of its members as a whole'—a duty made expressly 'subject to any enactment or rule of law requiring directors, in certain circumstances, to consider or act in the interests of creditors of the company' (see s 172(3)).

The reference to 'any enactment' encompasses, for example, the 'wrongful trading' provision in s 214 of the Insolvency Act 1986 (see Chapter 17); while the reference to any 'rule of law' encompasses the case law in which the courts have recognised that where the company is insolvent, or is of doubtful solvency, the interests of creditors supersedes those of the company's members so that the focus of the duty switches accordingly. The concern of creditors in this situation lies with ensuring that company assets, to which they will look for payment of their loans, are not dissipated by the directors.

14.37 There are now significant dicta in a number of English and Antipodean cases in which the judges recognise that directors should have regard to the interests of creditors where the company's fortunes have declined into insolvency. The position was succinctly stated by Street CJ in *Kinsela v Russell Kinsela Pty Ltd* (1986):

> In a solvent company the proprietary interests of the shareholders entitle them as a general body to be regarded as the company when questions of the duty of directors arise ... But where a company is insolvent the interests of the creditors intrude. They become prospectively entitled, through the mechanism of liquidation, to displace the power of the shareholders and directors to deal with the company's assets. It is in a practical sense their assets and not the shareholders' assets that, through the medium of the company, are under the management of the directors pending either liquidation, return to solvency, or the imposition of some alternative administration.

This passage was cited with approval by the Court of Appeal in *West Mercia Safetywear Ltd v Dodd* (1988) which stressed that shareholders do not have the power to absolve directors from a breach of duty to the creditors so as to bar the liquidator's claim. Indeed, in *Winkworth v Edward Baron Development Co Ltd* (1987) Lord Templeman went further by stating that directors owe a duty to the company and to its creditors to ensure that its affairs are properly administered and that its property is not dissipated.

14.38 The parameters of this duty are still being configured by the courts and the Explanatory Notes to the CA 2006 state that s 172(3) will leave the law to develop in this area. It is clear that in contrast to the duty owed directly to the company during solvency, the duty owed to creditors is indirect because their interests are represented through a liquidator. In *Yukong Line Ltd of Korea v Rendsburg Investment Corpn of Liberia (No 2)* (1998), Toulson J held that a director of an insolvent company who breached his fiduciary duty to the company by transferring assets beyond the reach of its creditors owed no corresponding fiduciary duty to an individual creditor of the company. The creditor could not therefore bring an action against the director for breach of duty. The appropriate cause of action would lie with the liquidator under s 212 of the Insolvency Act 1986 (misfeasance proceedings, see Chapter 17). The issue has come to the fore in two decisions of the Companies Court. In *Re Pantone 485 Ltd* (2002) Richard Reid QC, sitting as a deputy judge in the High Court, observed that:

> In my view, where the company is insolvent, the human equivalent of the company for the purposes of the directors' fiduciary duties is the company's creditors as a whole, i.e. its general creditors. It follows that if the directors act consistently with the interests of the general creditors but inconsistently with the interest of a creditor or section of creditors with special rights in a winding-up, they do not act in breach of duty to the company.

14.39 Further, in *Colin Gwyer and Associates Ltd v London Wharf (Limehouse) Ltd* (2003), it was held that a resolution of the board of directors passed without proper consideration being given by certain directors to the interests of creditors would be open to challenge if the company had been insolvent at the date of the resolution. Leslie Kosmin QC, sitting as a deputy judge in the High Court, stated that:

> In relation to an insolvent company, the directors when considering the company's interests must have regard to the interests of the creditors. If they fail to do so, and therefore ignore the relevant question, the [Charterbridge Corpn Ltd v Lloyd's Bank Ltd (1970)] test can be applied with the modification that in considering the interests of the company the honest and intelligent director must have been capable of believing that the decision was for the benefit of the creditors. In my view the Charterbridge Corporation test is of general application.

In *Re HLC Environmental Projects Ltd* (2013), the judge reasoned that while the duties under s 172 were usually subjective (see *Re Regentcrest plc v Cohen* (see para **14.27**)), this is subject to three qualifications in the case of a company of doubtful solvency where an objective assessment becomes more appropriate: (a) in considering whether creditors' interests were 'paramount' (per Leslie Kosmin QC in *Colin Gwyer* (see earlier)); (b) where there was no evidence of actual consideration of the best interests of the company, the test is that as set out in *Charterbridge Corporation*; and (c) where a very material interest, such as that of a large creditor, was overlooked (see also *Hedger v Adams* (2015); *BTI 2014 LLC v Sequana SA* (2019); *Ball v Hughes* (2017); and *Wessely (Joint Liquidator of Laishley Ltd (in liquidation) v White* (2018)).

14.40 In summary, it seems that the obligation in s 172(3) is fiduciary in nature; that, as with members, the duty is not owed to any individual creditor but only to the general body of creditors; and that for insolvent companies (or companies of doubtful solvency) the duty to act in the best interests of the company requires the substitution of the word 'creditors' for the word 'company' in s 172(1). Whether or not creditors need this additional protection is questionable given the fraudulent trading and wrongful trading provisions contained in the Insolvency Act 1986 together with s 212 (misfeasance proceedings) of the 1986 Act (considered in Chapter 17; see Finch (1995)).

14.41 These points aside, while s 172(3) settles the issue that directors of insolvent or prospectively insolvent companies owe duties to creditors, the relevant decisions upon which the provision is based do not lay down any guidance as to when directors should shift their attention away from the company qua body of shareholders towards the interests of its creditors. Clearly this depends upon the company's solvency. But identifying the point in time when a company is insolvent (i.e. when debts cannot be met) is, in practical terms, fraught with difficulty (see the Cork Report (Cmnd 8558, 1982), discussed in Chapter 13). Guidance as to the point in time when the duty triggers was recently provided by the Court of Appeal in *BTI 2014 LLC v Sequana SA* (2019). David Richards LJ reviewed the relevant case law in considerable detail, noting that in all cases the company was insolvent. The judge concluded that 'there are at least four possible answers to the question of when the creditors' interests duty is triggered'. In summary, these are:

(i) when the company is actually insolvent, either on a cash-flow or balance sheet basis;

(ii) when the company 'is on the verge of insolvency' or nearing or approaching insolvency;

(iii) when the company is or is likely to become insolvent (referred to in the case law as being 'of dubious solvency');

(iv) when there is a real as opposed to remote risk of insolvency.

Concluding that 'the duty may be triggered when a company's circumstances fall short of actual, established insolvency', David Richards LJ opted for the third test. He said:

> the duty arises when the directors know or should know that the company is or is likely to become insolvent accurately encapsulates the trigger. In this context, 'likely' means probable. . . .

The court held that payment of a dividend could, therefore, be challenged as a transaction defrauding creditors (see Chapter 17). The Supreme Court has granted permission to appeal the Court of Appeal's decision and the hearing date is scheduled for late March 2020. (See further *Burnden Holdings (UK) Ltd v Fielding* (2019); *Northampton BC v Cardoza* (above); and *LRH Services Ltd v Trew* (2018).) In summary, it is clear that when directors are considering declaring a dividend, it is not sufficient to merely consider whether there are distributable profits available for the purpose (see Chapter 7), but they should also satisfy themselves that the dividend is being paid for proper purposes and, if the dividend would result in the company being, or likely to become, insolvent, they must have regard to the interests of creditors. *BTI* also makes clear that payment of a dividend might constitute a transaction caught by s 423 of the IA 1986.

(iii) Duty to exercise independent judgement

14.42 Section 173(1) provides that a director must exercise independent judgement. This codifies the principle of law whereby directors must not fetter the future exercise of their discretion unless, as laid down in subsection (2), they are acting:

(a) in accordance with an agreement duly entered into by the company that restricts the future exercise of discretion by its directors, or

(b) in a way authorised by the company's constitution.

This is an incident of the overarching duty to promote the success of the company laid down in s 172. The duty operates to prevent directors fettering their discretion by, for example, contracting with a third party as to how a particular discretion conferred by the articles will be exercised (*Kregor v Hollins* (1913); see also *Kuwait Asia Bank EC v National Mutual Life Nominees Ltd* (1990)). In *Boulting v Association of Cinematograph, Television and Allied Technicians* (1963), Lord Denning explained the nature of the duty in typically clear terms:

> It seems to me that no one, who has duties of a fiduciary nature to discharge, can be allowed to enter into an engagement by which he binds himself to disregard those duties or to act inconsistently with them. No stipulation is lawful by which he agrees to carry

out his duties in accordance with the instructions of another rather than on his own con-
scientious judgment; or by which he agrees to subordinate the interests of those whom
he must protect to the interests of someone else.

14.43 But where the board is able to establish that it was in the best interests of the company
to enter into such an agreement, the duty will not be broken. For example, the directors
may be able to point to some commercial benefit accruing to the company as a result
of their undertaking to the third party. In *Fulham Football Club Ltd v Cabra Estates plc*
(1994) four directors of Fulham Football Club agreed with Cabra, the club's landlords,
that they would support Cabra's planning application for the future development of the
club's grounds rather than the plan put forward by the local authority. In return for this
undertaking, Cabra paid the football club a substantial fee. The directors subsequently
sought to renege on this promise and argued that it was an unlawful fetter on their
powers to act in the best interests of the company. The Court of Appeal, rejecting this
argument, stated that:

> It is trite law that directors are under a duty to act bona fide in the interests of their com-
> pany. However, it does not follow from that proposition that directors can never make a
> contract by which they bind themselves to the future exercise of their powers in a par-
> ticular manner, even though the contract taken as a whole is manifestly for the benefit
> of the company. Such a rule could well prevent companies from entering into contracts
> which were commercially beneficial to them.

14.44 Neil LJ endorsed the view of Kitto J in the Australian case *Thorby v Goldberg* (1964) who
had stated that:

> There are many kinds of transaction in which the proper time for the exercise of the dir-
> ectors' discretion is the time of the negotiation of a contract and not the time at which the
> contract is to be performed . . . If at the former time they are bona fide of opinion that it
> is in the interests of the company that the transaction should be entered into and carried
> into effect I see no reason in law why they should not bind themselves.

Further, the duty prohibits directors delegating their powers unless the company's articles
provide otherwise. It has been suggested that s 173 casts doubt on the extent to which a
director can rely on other directors (for example, a managing director or a colleague with
specialist expertise in relation to a matter requiring a decision of the board) or external
consultants (see the Law Society's 'Proposed Amendments and Briefing for Parts 10 and
11 CA 2006' (23 January 2006)). Responding to this anxiety, Lord Goldsmith, in the Lords
Grand Committee (6 February 2006 (col 282)), explained that:

> The duty does not prevent a director from relying on the advice or work of others, but the
> final judgment must be his responsibility. He clearly cannot be expected to do everything
> himself. Indeed, in certain circumstances directors may be in breach of their duty if they
> fail to take appropriate advice—for example, legal advice. As with all advice, slavish

reliance is not acceptable, and the obtaining of outside advice does not absolve directors from exercising their judgment on the basis of such advice.

(See further *Re Westmid Packing Services Ltd* (1998).)

In *Madoff Securities International Ltd v Raven* (2013), Popplewell J explained that in discharging the duty under s 173 it is 'legitimate for there to be division and delegation of responsibility for particular aspects of the management of a company'. However, the judge went on to stress that:

> *Nevertheless each individual director owes inescapable personal responsibilities. He owes duties to the company to inform himself of the company's affairs and join with his fellow directors in supervising them. It is therefore a breach of duty for a director to allow himself to be dominated, bamboozled or manipulated by a dominant fellow director. . . .*

(See further para **14.51**.)

(iv) Duty to exercise reasonable care, skill, and diligence

14.45 Section 174(1) provides that a director of a company must exercise reasonable care, skill, and diligence. Section 174(2) goes on to state that this means the care, skill, and diligence that would be exercised by a reasonably diligent person with—

> (a) *the general knowledge, skill and experience that may reasonably be expected of a person carrying out the functions carried out by the director in relation to the company, and*
>
> (b) *the general knowledge, skill and experience that the director has.*

The pre-existing case law on the common law duty can be divided into two streams. First, those decisions handed down principally during the 19th century when the courts generally had low expectations of the standard of care to be expected of directors and, second, those cases decided after the landmark decision in *Donoghue v Stevenson* (1932).

14.46 To understand the former category, it should be recalled that the early companies frequently appointed a director by virtue of his social standing. They were, therefore, generally symbolic appointments only. For example, in *Re Cardiff Savings Bank, Marquis of Bute's case* (1892), the Marquis had been appointed president of the bank when six months old and had attended only one board meeting in 39 years. It was held that he did not share responsibility for the bank's heavy losses resulting from the irregular conduct of its trustees and managers. Stirling J formulated what has been described as the 'intermittent' theory of directors' duties—namely, that a director must exercise care at the meetings at which he is actually present, but owes no duty to attend any specific meeting, or even any meeting at all.

14.47 The concern of the courts was to frame the standard of care in terms that were appropriate to company directors who, as commercial risk-takers, should not be held to the same performance standards as trustees. In *Re Forest of Dean Coal Mining Co* (1878), Jessel MR stated that directors are 'commercial men' and that an ordinary director who only attends board meetings periodically 'cannot be expected to devote as much time and attention to the business as the sole managing partner of an ordinary partnership, but they are bound to *use fair and reasonable diligence* in the management of their company's affairs, and to act honestly'. Recourse to objective assessment can therefore be seen in Jessel MR's reasoning; a view which seems to have presaged the approach of Neville J in *Re Brazilian Rubber Plantations and Estates Ltd* (1911) in which the judge laid down a semi-subjective standard of care which was to be determined according to the expertise of the particular director:

> He is not, I think, bound to take any definite part in the conduct of the company's business, but so far as he does undertake it he must use reasonable care in its despatch. Such reasonable care must, I think, be measured by the care an ordinary man might be expected to take in the same circumstances on his own behalf. He is clearly, I think, not responsible for damages occasioned by errors of judgment.

14.48 These early decisions were considered by Romer J in *Re City Equitable Fire Insurance Co Ltd* (1925) in which he attempted to formulate criteria for the assessment of whether the duties of care, skill, and diligence have been discharged. In this case the company's managing director, B, had been convicted of fraud and his fellow directors, who had acted honestly, were alleged to have been negligent in leaving the running of the company in B's hands. Romer J, having reviewed the relevant authorities, said:

> In discharging the duties of his position thus ascertained a director must, of course, act honestly; but he must also exercise some degree of both skill and diligence. To the question of what is the particular degree of skill and diligence required of him, the authorities do not, I think, give any very clear answer. It has been laid down that so long as a director acts honestly he cannot be made responsible in damages unless guilty of gross or culpable negligence in a business sense.

To this broad statement Romer J added three guiding principles for the determination of the director's duty of care. First, '[a] director need not exhibit in the performance of his duties a greater degree of skill than may reasonably be expected from a person of his knowledge and experience'. He noted that a director of a life insurance company, for example, does not guarantee that he has the skill of an actuary or of a physician. Second, Romer J stated that a director 'is not bound to give continuous attention to the affairs of his company'. He added that a director's duties are of an 'intermittent nature to be performed at periodical board meetings' and at committees of the board although he 'is not, however, bound to attend all such meetings, though he ought to attend whenever, in the circumstances, he is reasonably able to do so'. Finally, Romer J stated the position with respect to delegation by a director of certain duties: '[I]n respect of all duties that, having regard to the exigencies of business, and the articles of association, may properly be left to some other official, a director is, in the absence of grounds for suspicion, justified in trusting that official to perform such duties honestly.'

14.49 Romer J's judgment was delivered some seven years before the landmark decision in *Donoghue v Stevenson* in which the House of Lords triggered the existence of a general duty of care based upon reasonable foresight. Since 1932 the reach of the law of negligence has ebbed and flowed but it seems certain that directors 'will not be somehow ring-fenced from its reach so that they are deemed to owe different—and, history would suggest—lower duties of care than non-fiduciaries' (Worthington (1997); cf Finch (1992)). Since the decision in *Re City Equitable* the law has of course continued to evolve, a process which gained considerable momentum from the corporate governance debate (see Chapters 15 and 16), and, as restated by s 174, has reached the stage of holding directors accountable along the lines of traditional negligence principles. For example, in *Daniels v Anderson* (1995) the New South Wales Court of Appeal held that directors owe a common law duty to take reasonable care. Clarke and Sheller JJA stated that: 'The law of negligence can accommodate different degrees of duty owed by people with different skills but that does not mean that a director can safely proceed on the basis that ignorance and a failure to inquire are a protection against liability for negligence.'

14.50 Unlike actions for breaches of fiduciary duties, there is a paucity of case law in which directors have been challenged for negligent management (although such allegations are frequently made in cases involving the unfair prejudice remedy, see Chapter 11; now, of course, a derivative claim can be brought against directors for negligence following the reforms introduced by the CA 2006, Part 11, s 260(3), discussed in Chapter 10). However, in two important cases decided by Hoffmann J the standard of care was not measured solely by reference to subjective factors. The approach taken in these decisions clearly informed the drafting of s 174. In *Norman v Theodore Goddard* (1991) Hoffmann J accepted counsel's submission that the appropriate test was accurately stated in s 214(4) of the Insolvency Act 1986, which defines negligent conduct for the purposes of 'wrongful trading':

> the facts which a director of a company ought to know or ascertain, the conclusions which he ought to reach and the steps which he ought to take are those which would be known or ascertained, or reached or taken, by a reasonably diligent person having both: (a) the general knowledge, skill and experience that may reasonably be expected of a person carrying out the same functions as are carried out by that director in relation to the company; and (b) the general knowledge, skill and experience that that director has.

In *Re D'Jan of London Ltd* (1994) Hoffmann LJ, relying on s 214(4) of the 1986 Act, held a director negligent and prima facie liable to the company for losses caused as a result of its insurers repudiating a fire policy for non-disclosure. The director had signed the inaccurate proposal form without first reading it (see later on the issue of relief from liability).

14.51 The effect of s 174(2), which adopts Lord Hoffmann's position and mirrors the wrongful trading provision, is that a director's actions will be measured against the conduct expected of a reasonably diligent person (see *Gregson v HAE Trustees Ltd* (2008), in which the court confirmed that s 174 codifies the pre-existing law). However, subjective considerations will also apply according to the level of any special skills the particular director may possess. In determining whether the s 174 duty has been breached, McCombe LJ in *Weavering Capital (UK) Ltd v Dabhia* (2013), made the point that provided a trial judge had considered and applied the s 174 standard of care, 'it is not necessary to spell out any further what the duty is or the standard of care to be exercised by the particular [defendant] director . . .'

There is a synergy between s 174 and cases brought under the Company Directors Disqualification Act 1986 (CDDA 1986) particularly in relation to Romer J's third proposition relating to delegation. Inactivity on the part of directors is not acceptable so that short shrift is given to any contention to the effect that the director was unaware of a state of affairs because he had trusted others to manage the company (*Re Peppermint Park Ltd* (1998); *Re Park House Properties Ltd* (1998); *Re Brian D Pierson (Contractors) Ltd* (2001); *Re Landhurst Leasing plc* (1999); and *Re Finch (UK) plc* (2015)). Or had relied on professional advice as in *ASIC v Healey* (2011), discussed by Lowry (2012); and *Re Bradcrown Ltd* (2001) (discussed at para **13.66**); but note the comments of HHJ Behrens in *Re Pro4Sport Ltd* (2016): 'relying on professional advice . . . is an important factor in determining if [the director] was in breach of his duty to exercise reasonable care'. In *Re Barings plc (No 5)* (1999), proceedings were brought under the CDDA 1986 for the disqualification of directors of the Barings Bank following the spectacular losses resulting from the unauthorised dealings of a trader, Nick Leeson, who was based in the bank's Singapore office. One of the issues in the case was what level of supervision should be expected of T, the deputy chairman of the Barings Group, chairman of Barings Investment Bank, and chairman of the Barings Investment Bank Managing Committee. T had argued that in view of the size of the bank's operations his role was basically reactive and that he was justified in trusting delegatees until matters came to his attention which required his response. This would appear to accord with Romer J's view of delegation. However, it was held that in determining the period for disqualification, the guiding principle is that directors, collectively and individually, had a duty to acquire and maintain a sufficient knowledge of the company's business so as to enable them to discharge their responsibilities. The power to delegate did not absolve directors from the duty to supervise the way in which delegated functions are carried out. For the duty to be discharged it now seems that proactive monitoring of the operations of delegatees must be demonstrated. The courts will not countenance the argument that the director lacked sufficient time to undertake this task.

14.52 The *Barings* approach can also be seen to have overshadowed the thinking of the Commercial Court in *Equitable Life Assurance Society v Bowley* (2003). It is noteworthy that the action was brought against the insurers' non-executive directors (NEDs). Following the Court of Appeal's decision that the insurer had a real chance of succeeding in negligence against its auditors (see *Equitable Life Assurance Society v Ernst & Young* (2003)), the issue before Langley J was whether the insurer had a real chance of succeeding in negligence against its former NEDs. The background to the case concerned with-profits policies that provided for guaranteed annuity rates (GARs). After 1995 the GARs exceeded current annuity rates and Equitable's board decided to adopt a differential terminal bonus policy which permitted the insurer to reduce terminal bonuses to GAR policy-holders in order to align their annuities with those payable to non-GAR policy-holders. In 2000 the House of Lords held that the directors had no power under the articles to devalue guaranteed rates and that differential bonus rates were contrary to the terms of the guaranteed annuity policies (see *Equitable Life Assurance Society v Hyman* (2000)). This decision was disastrous for the insurer since it was exposed to liabilities of £1.5 billion. In the present case against the NEDs, Equitable was claiming that they were negligent and in breach of fiduciary duty in failing to take professional advice as to the validity of the differential bonus rates paid out between 1996 and 1998 and, having taken legal advice, in failing to reduce bonuses in 1999 and 2000. Langley J explained that the extent to which a NED could rely on executive directors and other professionals to perform their duties was one in which the law was evolving. However, it was reasonable to expect modern NEDs to be more proactive than traditionally had been the case. The negligence claim had a real prospect of success and it should, therefore, go to trial.

Against the background of the modern case law, the decision in *Lexi Holdings plc (in administration) v Luqman* (2009), is unsurprising. The managing director of Lexi, S, dishonestly misappropriated some £59 million of the company's money via three of its bank accounts. More particularly, S had used a fictitious directors' loan account as a vehicle for perpetrating the fraud. The trial judge found that the inactivity of non-executive directors, M and Z, who were S's sisters, had not caused the loss to the company so that they were not liable to it except in relation to misappropriations he paid to them. The company successfully appealed to the Court of Appeal claiming equitable compensation or damages against M and Z. The Chancellor, delivering the principal judgment of the court, explained that:

> *M and Z knew of [S's] convictions. They ought to have known that the directors' loan account as shown in the accounts required convincing explanation. Their duty as directors required them to be on their guard in relation to any explanations from S in response to 'the searching questions' the judge considered that they should have directed to him about the directors' loan account. Had they done their duty S could not have satisfied them that the directors' loan account was genuine.*

It was held that had Z informed the auditors they would not have provided unqualified accounts with the consequence that increased banking facilities would not have been granted and subsequent misappropriations could not have been perpetrated. She was therefore found liable for later misappropriations of nearly £42 million. The misappropriations claimed against M, some £37 million, started three weeks after her appointment and it was held that the loss to that extent was caused by M failing to discharge her duty as director of Lexi. The passivity of the sisters in failing to act thus constituted a breach of duty and substantial liability ensued.

(v) Duty to avoid conflicts of interest; duty not to profit personally; and the duty to declare an interest in a proposed or existing transaction or arrangement

14.53 Section 175 (duty to avoid conflicts of interest) and ss 177 and 182 (duty to declare an interest in proposed or existing transaction or arrangement) are framed to encompass the equitable obligations which are generally described, respectively, as the 'no-conflict' rule, the 'no-profit' rule, and the 'self-dealing' rule. These principles can all be classified as incidents of the core fiduciary duty of loyalty (see *Bristol and West Building Society v Mothew* (1996), Millett LJ, later at para **14.55**). Section 175(1) and (2) conflate the equitable principles relating to the 'no-conflict' rule and the 'no-profit' rules with the result that the provision encompasses the case law on the corporate opportunity doctrine notwithstanding that the reasoning in much of the relevant jurisprudence is concerned with the no-profit rule (see later). With respect to the duty to avoid self-dealing (i.e. the duty to avoid a personal interest in a transaction to which the company is a party), this has been displaced by a more limited duty to disclose an interest to fellow-directors, 'to the exclusion of the no-conflicts and no-profits rules' (see s 175(3) and ss 177 and 182 later).

(a) The no-conflict and no-profit rules

14.54 Section 175(1) provides that a director of a company must avoid a situation in which he has, or can have, a direct or indirect interest that conflicts, or possibly may conflict, with the interests of the company. The provision replaces the equitable obligation to avoid conflicts of interest whereby directors are liable to account for any profit made personally in circumstances where their interests may conflict with their duty owed to the company. As explained by Deane J in *Chan v Zacharia* (1984), the fiduciary in breach of the no-conflict duty: 'must account . . . for any benefit or gain which has been obtained or received in circumstances where a conflict or significant possibility of conflict existed between his fiduciary duty and his personal interest in the pursuit or possible receipt of such a benefit or gain' (see s 178, later). The substance of the rule is strict as is reflected in the language of s 175(1) in that it is framed in terms of the possibility of conflict rather than actual conflicts of interest. This encompasses the significant body of case law spanning over a century or so which the provision restates (see, for example, *Boardman v Phipps* (1967); in *Sharma v Sharma* (2013), Jackson LJ noted that there is 'no material difference between the statutory duties under s 175 . . . and the pre-existing fiduciary duties imposed by equity'). However, the provision significantly alters the equitable rules with respect to the authorisation of, and consent or approval to, conflicts of interest (see s 175(4)(b), (5), and (6), and s 180, later).

14.55 The classic judicial formulation of the no-conflict duty was delivered by Lord Herschell in *Bray v Ford* (1896): 'It is an inflexible rule of a court of equity that a person in a fiduciary position . . . is not . . . entitled to make a profit; he is not allowed to put himself in a position where his interest and duty conflict.' A century later, Millett LJ explained in *Bristol and West Building Society v Mothew* (1998), that:

The distinguishing obligation of a fiduciary is the obligation of loyalty. The principal is entitled to the single-minded loyalty of his beneficiary. This core liability has several facets. A fiduciary must act in good faith; he must not make a profit out of his trust; he must not place himself in a position where his duty and his interest may conflict.

Commenting on the scope of the no-conflict rule, Upjohn LJ in *Boulting v Association of Cinematograph, Television and Allied Technicians* (1963) said that it must be applied realistically to a situation which discloses 'a real conflict of duty and interest' and not to some 'theoretical or rhetorical conflict'. Returning to the point again in his dissenting speech in *Boardman v Phipps* (1967), Lord Upjohn stressed that there must be a 'real sensible possibility of conflict' between his duty and interest. He concluded:

In my view it means that the reasonable man looking at the relevant facts and circumstances of the particular case would think that there was a real sensible possibility of conflict; not that you could imagine some situation arising which might, in some conceivable possibility in events not contemplated as real sensible possibilities by any reasonable person, result in a conflict.

This approach can also be seen in *Chan v Zacharia* (para **14.54**), where Deane J spoke of a 'significant possibility' of conflict. Similarly, in *Hospital Products Ltd v United States Surgical Corp* (1984), Mason J thought that 'a real or substantial possibility of a conflict' had to be demonstrated (see also *Queensland Mines Ltd v Hudson* (1978); and *Burns v The FCA* (2017), discussed at **14.77**).

This position is mirrored in s 175(4)(a) which states that the duty is not infringed if 'the situation cannot reasonably be regarded as likely to give rise to a conflict of interest' (see, for example, *Peso Silver Mines Ltd v Cropper* (para **14.62**)). The provision thus recognises that unexpected situations can arise where a conflict exists but a director will not be in breach until he knows of the conflict and fails 'to do something about it' (Official Report, 6/2/2006; col GC289, Lord Goldsmith).

14.56   The policy underlying this core fiduciary duty is premised upon the notion of prophylaxis and the approach of the common law in terms of how strict it needed to be cast is an issue that has attracted much academic debate (see, by way of examples, Austin (1987); Lowry (1994); Lowry and Edmunds (1998)). Taken at its absolute level, the case law suggests that liability is triggered without enquiry into the circumstances surrounding the breach of duty and irrespective of whether the company itself suffers loss and so no consideration is given by the courts to whether the errant director was acting in good faith. This absolutist application of fiduciary standards is regarded, at least in the orthodox legal canon, to be the minimum necessary to provide an effective deterrent and ensure the highest degree of loyalty. That said, as we shall see, s 175(4) relaxes the duty insofar that a breach can be authorised by directors.

14.57   Section 175(2) reflects the equitable rule that it is immaterial whether the company could take advantage of the property, information, or opportunity which has been diverted away from it by the errant director. The leading company law decision is *Regal (Hastings) Ltd v Gulliver* (1942). The company, Regal, owned a cinema in Hastings and its directors wished to acquire two additional local cinemas in order to facilitate the sale of the whole undertaking as a going concern. They therefore formed a subsidiary company in order to take a lease of the other two cinemas. However, the landlord was not prepared to grant the subsidiary a lease on these two cinemas in the absence of a personal guarantee by the directors unless its paid-up capital was £5,000. The company was unable to inject more than £2,000 in cash for 2,000 shares, and given that the directors did not wish to grant their personal guarantees, the original scheme was changed. It was decided that Regal would subscribe for 2,000 shares and the outstanding 3,000 shares would be taken up by the directors and their associates. Later, the whole undertaking was sold by way of takeover and the directors made a handsome profit. The purchasers of Regal installed a new board of directors and the company brought this action against its former directors claiming that they should account for the profit they had made on the sale of their shares in the subsidiary. The House of Lords found in favour of Regal. Lord Russell of Killowen stated that the opportunity and special knowledge to obtain the shares had come to the directors qua fiduciaries:

> I am of the opinion that the directors standing in a fiduciary relationship to Regal in regard to the exercise of their powers as directors, and having obtained these shares by reason of the fact that they were directors of Regal, and in the course of the execution of that office, are accountable for the profits which they have made out of them.

This was so despite the fact that the directors had acted bona fide throughout the process, had used their own money, and had not denuded Regal of an opportunity because the company itself was financially incapable of purchasing the shares. Consequently, Regal itself did not suffer any actual loss. Lord Russell enunciated the principle of law thus:

> The rule of equity which insists on those, who by use of a fiduciary position make a profit, being liable to account for that profit, in no way depends on fraud, or absence of bona fides; or upon such questions or considerations as whether profit would or should otherwise have gone to the plaintiff, or whether the profiteer was under a duty to obtain the source of the profit for the plaintiff, or whether he took a risk or acted as he did for the benefit of the plaintiff, or whether the plaintiff has in fact been damaged or benefited by his action. The liability arises from the mere fact of a profit having, in the stated circumstances, been made.

14.58 The fact that the company's claim was unjust and that the purchasers had received an 'unexpected windfall' was an issue which was taken up only by Lord Porter, who said that the purchasers of Regal 'receive[d] in one hand part of the sum which ha[d] been paid by the other'. Having identified the obvious lack of merit in the claim, he nevertheless went on to conclude that 'whether it be so or not, the principle that a person occupying a fiduciary relationship shall not make a profit by reason thereof is of such vital importance that the possible consequence in the present case is in fact as it is in law an immaterial consideration'. Equity's inexorable rule was thus applied without regard to the resulting anomalies.

14.59   The no-conflict and no-profit rules have in recent times manifested themselves under the guise of the so-called corporate opportunity doctrine—a term which has been imported from North American jurisprudence. Although the doctrine no doubt has its origins in the no-conflict rule it is, however, distinguishable. As will be seen, the Companies Act and the courts will tolerate directors being interested in transactions with the company provided certain disclosure and approval requirements are satisfied. This tolerance does not extend to directors who usurp a corporate opportunity.

Corporate opportunities

14.60   Professor Prentice (1974) defines the corporate opportunity doctrine as a principle which 'makes it a breach of fiduciary duty by a director to appropriate for his own benefit an economic opportunity which is considered to belong rightly to the company which he serves'. As is made clear by s 175(2), a corporate opportunity is regarded as an asset belonging to the company which may not therefore be misappropriated by the directors. *Cook v Deeks* (1916) is a paradigm case. The Toronto Construction Co had secured a series of contracts with Canadian Pacific (CP) to build various stretches of railway line. Three of the company's directors, the defendants, decided to sever their links with the fourth director, Cook, and proceeded to incorporate another company, the Dominion Construction Co. The defendants informed CP that their new company would be undertaking the work. The Privy Council held that the defendants held the contract on behalf of the Toronto Construction Co. Lord Buckmaster said that the directors:

> while entrusted with the conduct of the affairs of the company [had] deliberately de-
> signed to exclude, and used their influence and position to exclude, the company whose
> interest it was their first duty to protect . . . men who assume the complete control of a
> company's business must remember that they are not at liberty to sacrifice the interests
> which they are bound to protect, and, while ostensibly acting for the company, divert in
> their own favour business which should properly belong to the company they represent.

14.61   The central thrust of equity in relation to corporate opportunities lies in its prophylactic anxiety aimed at preventing directors being unjustly enriched. It is not restricted in scope to only prescribing profits being made at the expense of the company. The prohibition against usurping a corporate opportunity extends to situations where an opportunity is presented to a director personally and not in his capacity as director of the company. In *Industrial Development Consultants Ltd v Cooley* (1972) the defendant, who was managing director of Industrial Development Consultants Ltd (IDC), a design and construction company, failed to obtain for the company a lucrative contract to undertake work for the Eastern Gas Board. The Gas Board subsequently approached Cooley indicating that they wished to deal with him personally and would not, in any case, contract with IDC. Cooley did not disclose the offer to the company, but promptly resigned his office so that he could take up the contract having deceived the company into thinking he was suffering from ill-health. Roskill J held that he was accountable to the company for all of the profits he received under the contract. Information which came to Cooley while he was managing director and which was of concern to the claimants and relevant for the claimants to know, was information which it was his duty to pass on to the claimants. It was irrelevant to the issue of liability that Cooley had been approached in his personal capacity and that the Gas Board would not have contracted with IDC. Roskill J concluded that 'if the defendant is not required to account he will have made a large profit as a result of having deliberately put himself into a position in which his duty to the plaintiffs [claimants] who were employing him and his personal interests conflicted'.

14.62   Compared with the strict approach that characterises English decisions on corporate opportunities, some Commonwealth courts have adopted a less restrictive view towards the issue of liability. In determining whether or not a director has usurped a corporate opportunity, Canadian courts, for example, will have regard to the fides of the director whose conduct has been challenged. In *Peso Silver Mines v Cropper* (1966) Peso's board was offered the opportunity to buy 126 mining claims, some of which were on land which adjoined the company's own mining territories. The board bona fide declined the offer on the basis of the then financial state of the company, and also because there was some doubt over the value of the claims which therefore rendered them a risky proposition. Subsequently, the company's geologist formed a syndicate with the defendant and two other Peso directors to purchase and work the claims. When the company was taken over, the new board brought an action claiming that the defendant held his shares on constructive trust for the company. The action was unsuccessful and the Supreme Court of Canada dismissed the appeal by the company. It was held that the decision of the Peso directors to reject the opportunity had been made in good faith and for sound commercial reasons in the interests of the company. They could therefore exploit the opportunity themselves. In its reasoning, the Court approved the following statement of Lord Greene MR, from his judgment in the Court of Appeal in *Regal Hastings*:

> To say that the Company was entitled to claim the benefit of those shares would involve this proposition: Where a Board of Directors considers an investment which is offered to their company and bona fide comes to the conclusion that it is not an investment which their Company ought to make, any Director, after that Resolution is come to and bona fide come to, who chooses to put up the money for that investment himself must be treated as having done it on behalf of the Company, so that the Company can claim any profit that results to him from it. That is a proposition for which no particle of authority was cited; and goes, as it seems to me, far beyond anything that has ever been suggested as to the duty of directors, agents, or persons in a position of that kind.

14.63   This approach was again picked up by the Canadian Supreme Court in *Canadian Aero Service Ltd v O'Malley* (1973) ('*Canaero*') even though the defendant directors in question were held liable. Two directors resigned their posts with Canaero in order to secure a contract in their own right which the company had been actively seeking. It was, in fact, unlikely that the company would have won the contract in question. Distinguishing the facts before it from those in *Peso*, the Court awarded the company damages based on the profits earned by the two directors. Further, it was held that Canaero did not have to prove that it would have gained the contract or to establish what its profit would have been had it secured the contract. Of particular significance, however, is the approach adopted by Laskin J to the determination of liability. He stated that the Court should give cognisance to all the circumstances surrounding a particular breach including the director's fides:

> The general standards of loyalty, good faith and avoidance of a conflict of duty and self interest . . . must be tested in each case by many factors. . . . Among them are the factor of position or office held, the nature of the corporate opportunity, its ripeness, its specificness and the director's or managerial officer's relation to it, the amount of knowledge possessed, the circumstances in which it was obtained and whether it was special or indeed even private.

14.64 Such an open-textured approach to liability contrasts sharply with the orthodox English position which focuses solely upon the capacity of the individual concerned. Yet, together with the *Peso* line of reasoning, Laskin J's approach seems to underlie the Privy Council decision in *Queensland Mines Ltd v Hudson* (1978). Hudson was the managing director of Queensland Mines which had been negotiating with the Tasmanian Government for mining exploration licences. The company decided not to pursue the opportunity due to a lack of capital and the significant risks involved in the development. Hudson thereupon used his own resources to prove the value of the mineral deposits in his own name. Resigning as Queensland's managing director, Hudson formed his own company and sold the licences to a US company for a significant profit. Queensland Mines sought to make Hudson liable to account. The Privy Council held that he was not liable. The company was fully informed that Hudson was seeking this opportunity, having rejected it itself. In reaching its decision, the Privy Council was mindful that Hudson had also incurred significant potential personal liability in the event that the mineral deposits had proved inadequate.

14.65 Modern English decisions have, however, stressed that the determination of liability for breach of fiduciary duty necessarily requires the court to engage in a fact-intensive exercise in examining the circumstances surrounding a director's alleged breach. For example, in *In Plus Group Ltd v Pyke* (2002), the defendant, Pyke, and Plank were the only two directors and shareholders of the claimant company. A stroke in 1996 resulted in the defendant being unable to work. His absence continued when his working relationship with Plank broke down early in 1997. From that time until the defendant formally resigned, he was effectively excluded from decision making and participation in the management of the claimant company's affairs. In June 1997, during his period of exile, the defendant incorporated his own company, John Pyke Interiors Ltd, through which he procured and discharged a contract worth £200,000 with Constructive Ltd, a customer of Plus Group Ltd. It was alleged, therefore, that this was done in breach of duty to the claimant company. The evidence from the correspondence between Constructive Ltd and the claimants suggested that the relationship between the two had deteriorated to such an extent that it was highly unlikely that further contracts would be placed with the claimants. On a pure application of *Cooley* this, in itself, would not absolve Pyke. Yet the Court of Appeal, by differing routes, exonerated him. First, the court enlisted *Mashonaland Exploration Co Ltd v New Mashonaland Exploration Co Ltd* (1891) (considered later) that has been taken as holding that directors can hold competing directorships. Further, Sedley LJ, while acknowledging that Pyke successfully poached a customer, nevertheless took the view that:

> *Quite exceptionally, the defendant's duty to the claimants had been reduced to vanishing point by the acts (explicable and justifiable as they may have been) of his sole fellow director and fellow shareholder Mr Plank. . . . The defendant's role as a director of the claimants was throughout the relevant period entirely nominal, not in the sense [in] which a non-executive director's position might (probably wrongly) be called nominal but in the concrete sense that that he was entirely excluded from all decision-making and all participation in the claimant company's affairs. For all the influence he had, he might as well have resigned.*

In his reasoning, Brooke LJ called in aid the observation of Lord Upjohn in *Phipps v Boardman* (1967), to the effect that the circumstances of 'each case must be carefully examined to see whether a fiduciary relationship exists in relation to the matter of which complaint is made'. He laid particular emphasis on the fact that following his stroke Pyke had been effectively expelled from the company some six months prior to any of the events in question. Brooke LJ stressed that although the defendant had invested a significant sum of money in the companies of which he was a director and on favourable interest-free terms, he was not permitted to withdraw any of it and he was denied any remuneration. Further, at the time of the contract with Constructive he was not using any of the claimants' property nor was he using any confidential information which came to him qua director of the companies. He therefore concluded that in contracting with Constructive, Mr Pyke was not in breach of fiduciary duty.

14.66 It is curious that the Court of Appeal did not follow the more principled route of finding the director liable but granting him relief under s 1157 of the CA 2006 (discussed later), or, indeed, holding that the appropriate cause of action was for Pyke to petition for relief under s 994 (see Chapter 11). Exclusion from management is, after all, a paradigm illustration of unfairly prejudicial conduct.

14.67 Equity's strict prophylactic view of fiduciary liability where a director has misappropriated a corporate opportunity for his own benefit can be seen in the reasoning of Peter Smith J in *Crown Dilmun v Sutton* (2004). The dispute centred on the £50 million sale of Fulham Football Club's Craven Cottage ground. As managing director of Crown Dilmun, Sutton's primary role was to identify suitable investment opportunities for the claimant company. Acting in this capacity, he first declined the development proposal of Craven Cottage on behalf of the claimant company. Thereafter, he pursued negotiations for a revised development project through the medium of the second defendant company which Sutton established specifically for this purpose. Peter Smith J dismissed Sutton's evidence of his genuine belief that the company would not have been interested in the development opportunity, finding it to be untrue and dishonest. Echoing the reasoning of Roskill J in *IDC v Cooley* (1972) (discussed earlier), he said:

> Given my decision that Mr Sutton had no right to make any decision to take opportunities which came his way whilst he was a director of the claimants, the parties all agree that he came under a duty not to take opportunities which arose that might put him in conflict with his duties to the claimants. As a director of the claimants, he had a duty to exploit every opportunity that he became aware of for the benefit of the claimants. The only exception is if they permit him to take such opportunities after he has made full and frank disclosure and they have given full and informed consent.

(See also *Berryland Books Ltd v BK Books Ltd* (2009); *Don King Productions Inc v Warren* (2000) CA; and *Gencor ACP Ltd v Dalby* (2000).)

14.68 Similarly, the approach adopted by the Court of Appeal in *Bhullar v Bhullar* (2003) resonates clearly with that seen in the classic decisions on liability for usurping corporate opportunities such as *Regal (Hastings)*, *Cook v Deeks*, and *IDC v Cooley*. Silvercrest (S), a company controlled by the two appellants, acquired a property, White Hall Mill, at a time that they, along with other family members who included the respondents, were directors of Bhullar Bros Ltd (B Ltd). The objects of B Ltd included the acquisition of investment property. It already owned property in the vicinity of White Hall Mill; and in evidence the appellants conceded that its acquisition would have been commercially worthwhile. One of them even sought legal advice on the propriety of Silvercrest entering into the transaction. However, before the purchase, B Ltd's board resolved to divide its business, and refrain from making any further property acquisitions. The appellants therefore resisted B Ltd's claim to White Hall Mill because, they argued, its purchase was not related to that company's affairs, nor could it be described as a maturing business opportunity available to it. Counsel for B Ltd countered with a submission based upon *IDC v Cooley*:

> that a director may come under a positive duty to make a business opportunity available to his company if it is in the company's line of business or if the director has been given responsibility to seek out particular opportunities or the company and the opportunity concerned is of such a nature as to fall within the scope of that remit.

As commented above, the approach of the Court of Appeal owes much to the traditional line of authority on fiduciary obligations which also includes *Aberdeen Rly Co v Blaikie Bros* (see earlier) and *Phipps v Boardman* (see earlier). This being so, the court noted that reasonable men looking at the facts would have concluded that the appellants faced a real sensible possibility of conflict of interest. The court's reasoning affirms counsel's preference for a broad, capacity-based approach as articulated by Roskill J in *IDC v Cooley*. It thus seems that any opportunity within the company's line of business is off-limits to the director unless the company's permission to proceed is first obtained. As Jonathan Parker LJ explained:

> *Whether the company could or would have taken that opportunity, had it been made aware of it, is not to the point: the existence of the opportunity was information which it was relevant for the company to know, and it follows that the [directors] were under a duty to communicate it to the company.*

(See also *Quarter Master UK Ltd v Pyke* (2005), and the Court of Appeal's approach in *Wrexham Association Football Club Ltd v Crucial Move Ltd* (2006).)

More recently, the approach seen in *Bhullar* towards the liability of directors who benefit from a corporate opportunity notwithstanding the fact that the company itself could not have benefited from it was also taken by the Court of Appeal in *O'Donnell v Shanahan* (2009), where the action against the directors was brought under the unfair prejudice provision (see Chapter 11). Rimer LJ observed that:

> *the rationale of the 'no conflict' and 'no profit' rules is to underpin the fiduciary's duty of undivided loyalty to his beneficiary. If an opportunity comes to him in his capacity as a fiduciary, his principal is entitled to know about it. The director cannot be left to make the decision as to whether he is allowed to help himself to its benefit.*

(See also *Towers v Premier Waste Management Ltd* (2011).)

The judge (with whom Aikens and Waller LJJ agreed) laid emphasis on the fact that, as explained by Lord Russell in *Regal (Hastings)*, directors are precluded from making use of information concerning an opportunity for their own benefit when that information is obtained in the course of them acting as directors of the company, and the opportunity presented itself to them by reason of the fact that they were directors of the company.

Post-resignation breach of duty

14.69 It will be recalled that s 170(2) provides that a person who ceases to be a director continues to be subject to the duty in s 175 (and s 176, see later). Consequently, resignation does not immunise a director against liability for breach of the no-conflict duty. Looking to the case law, it seems safe to conclude that the statutory formulation of the no-conflict duty does not prevent a director from forming the intention, while still a director, to set up in competition after his directorship has ceased nor does it prevent him from taking *preliminary* steps to investigate or forward that intention provided he did not engage in any actual competitive activity while his directorship continued, provided, of course, any contract of service does not prohibit such activity. Policy considerations underlie the decisions. For example, in *Balston Ltd v Headline Filters Ltd* (1990), Head (H), a director of the plaintiff company, agreed to lease certain commercial premises in order to start up his own business. He then resigned from the company although, unlike Cooley, he had not at that stage decided upon the nature of the business he would enter. However, shortly after his resignation, one of Balston's customers contacted H after being told that the company would be discontinuing its supply to him of a certain type of filter tube. H therefore began manufacturing the filters and supplied them to the customer. Balston sought to hold him liable to account. Falconer J held that it was not a breach of fiduciary duty for a director to start up a business in competition with his former company after his directorship had ceased, even where the intention to commence business was formed prior to the resignation. On the evidence, H had not attempted to divert to himself a maturing business opportunity, an opportunity which was in the contemplation of Balston Ltd. Falconer J explained that:

> In my judgment an intention by a director of a company to set up business in competition with the company after his directorship has ceased is not to be regarded as a conflicting interest within the context of the principle, having regard to the rules of public policy as to restraint of trade, nor is the taking of any preliminary steps to investigate or forward that intention so long as there is no actual competitive activity, such as, for instance, competitive tendering or actual trading, while he remains a director.

Similarly, in *Island Export Finance Ltd v Umunna* (1986), Hutchinson J said:

> It would . . . be surprising to find that directors alone, because of the fiduciary nature of their relationship with the company, were restrained from exploiting after they had ceased to be such any opportunity of which they had acquired knowledge while directors. Directors, no less than employees, acquire a general fund of knowledge and expertise in the course of their work, and it is plainly in the public interest that they should be free to exploit it in a new position.

And again, in *Framlington Group plc v Anderson* (see earlier), Blackburne J reasoned that in the absence of special circumstances, such as a prohibition in a service contract, a director commits no breach of duty merely because, while a director, 'he take steps so that, on ceasing to be a director . . . he can immediately set up business in competition with that company or join a competitor of it. Nor is he obliged to disclose to that company that he is taking those steps'.

(See also *Coleman Taymar Ltd v Oakes* (2001); and *LC Services Ltd v Brown* (2003).)

14.70 Further, a director can utilise confidential information or 'know-how' acquired while working for the company after he departs but not 'trade secrets' (*Dranez Anstalt v Hayek* (2002), Evans-Lombe J; *FSS Travel and Leisure Systems Ltd v Johnson* (1998), Mummery LJ). Typical examples of trade secrets include company databases, customer lists, suppliers' agreements, and business and sales strategy (see *Item Software (UK) Ltd v Fassihi* (2003); and *Quarter Master UK Ltd v Pyke* (2004)).

A cogent summary of the case law was provided by Etherton J in *Shepherds Investments Ltd v Walters* (2006):

> What the cases show . . . is that the precise point at which preparations for the establish-ment of a competing business by a director become unlawful will turn on the actual facts of any particular case. In each case, the touchstone for what, on the one hand, is per-missible, and what, on the other hand, is impermissible unless consent is obtained from the company . . . after full disclosure, is what, in the case of a director, will be in breach of the fiduciary duties to which I have referred. . . . It is obvious, for example, that merely making a decision to set up a competing business at some point in the future and dis-cussing such an idea with friends and family would not of themselves be in conflict with the best interests of the company. . . . The consulting of lawyers and other professionals may, depending on all the circumstances, equally be consistent with a director's fiduciary duties. . . . At the other end of the spectrum, it is plain that soliciting customers of the company . . . or the actual carrying on of trade by a competing business would be in breach of the duties of the director. . . . It is the wide range of activity and decision making between the two ends of the spectrum which will be fact sensitive in every case. . . .

In *Shepherds Investments Ltd*, the directors were found to be in breach of duty because they had formed an irrevocable intention to establish a business which they knew would fairly be regarded as a competitor but continued to take steps to bring it into existence contrary to the best interests of the company. At that point, it was held to be incumbent upon them to inform the company of the relevant activity (see also *Gamatronic (UK) Ltd v Hamilton* (2016)).

14.71 In *Foster Bryant Surveying Ltd v Bryant* (2007), Rix LJ confirmed the need for a nuanced approach to be taken towards allegations of post-resignation breaches. Drawing on Lawrence Collins J's reasoning in *CMS Dolphin Ltd v Simonet* (2001), he gave prominence to the finding that there must be 'some relevant connection or link between the resigna-tion and the obtaining of the business'. In so doing, he placed emphasis upon the need to demonstrate both lack of good faith with which the future exploitation was planned while still a director, and the need to show that the resignation was an integral part of the dishonest plan. These factors are clearly illustrated by *CMS Dolphin Ltd v Simonet* (2001). C, an advertising company, successfully claimed that S, its former managing director, was in breach of fiduciary duty and duty of fidelity by virtue of his employment contract by diverting a maturing business opportunity to a new company established by him fol-lowing his resignation from C. It was argued that S had resigned in order to acquire for himself the opportunity sought by C and that he had diverted parts of C's business, and taken its staff with him, to his new company. Lawrence Collins J held that a director's power to resign from office is not a fiduciary power and a director is entitled to resign even if it might have a disastrous effect on the business or reputation of the company and he was not precluded from using his general fund of skill and knowledge to compete with his former company. However, appropriating a maturing business opportunity belonging to C was a misuse of its property for which S was liable.

14.72 Thus, in cases where liability for post-resignation breach of duty had been found, there was a causal connection between the resignation and the subsequent diversion of the opportunity to the director's new enterprise. On the other hand, in cases such as *Island Export Finance Ltd* (see earlier) and *Balston* (see earlier), the resignations 'were unaccompanied by disloyalty' so that there was no liability. That said, in *Foster Bryant*, Rix LJ recognised the difficulty of accurately summarising the circumstances in which retiring directors may or may not be held to have breached their fiduciary duties given that the issue is 'fact sensitive'.

(See also *Hunter Kane Ltd v Watkins* (2002); *Berryland Books Ltd v BK Books Ltd* (2009); and *Thermascan Ltd v Norman* (2011).)

The pragmatic approach taken by the judges in these modern decisions is manifested in s 175(4)(a) which states, in language that mirrors the limits placed on the scope of duty by, for example, Lord Upjohn (see para **14.55**), that the no-conflict duty is not infringed if the situation cannot reasonably be regarded as likely to give rise to a conflict of interest. The provision thus acknowledges that cases involving breaches of fiduciary duty by a director are indeed 'fact-sensitive'. As Moses LJ in *Foster Bryant* concluded, this tends 'to make one almost nostalgic for the days when there were inflexible rules, inexorably enforced by judges who would have shuddered at the reiteration of the noun-adjective'.

Conflicts of interest and duty and conflicts of duties

14.73 Section 175(7) states that 'any reference in this section to a conflict of interest includes a conflict of interest and duty and a conflict of duties'. This at last injects a long-awaited measure of cohesion into the law and settles a long-running dispute surrounding what was seen to be an anomalous decision of Chitty J in *London and Mashonaland Co Ltd v New Mashonaland Exploration Co Ltd* (1891). The claimant company sought an injunction to prohibit one of its directors, Lord Mayo, from holding such office with the defendant company, a business rival. In April 1891, one month after the claimant company's registration, its directors resolved to appoint Lord Mayo as director and chairman of the board. In July of the same year, the defendant company issued its prospectus which contained Lord Mayo's name at the head of its list of directors. The claimant was unable to prove that any confidential information had been disclosed to the defendant company. Chitty J refused the injunction, reasoning that even if Lord Mayo had been duly appointed to the claimant company's board, its articles did not contain any provision which required him to give 'any part of his time . . . to the business of the company, or which prohibited him from acting as a director of another company; neither was there any contract . . . to give his personal services to the plaintiff company and to another company'. This decision was approved by the House of Lords in *Bell v Lever Bros Ltd* (1932).

14.74 While *Mashonaland* has long been accepted as authority for the proposition that a director is not placed in breach of duty by acting as director for a competing company—double employment nevertheless—on its facts, no actual conflict arose because the defendant company had not commenced business and therefore no damage had been sustained by the claimant. In any case, if *Mashonaland* was authority for permitting double employment, a director of two competing companies would have to walk a fine line to avoid a finding of conflict of duty: '[a]t all times . . . he metaphorically wears both hats and owes duties in both capacities' (*Gwembe Valley Development Co Ltd v Koshy* (1998), Harman J). Further, Millett LJ in *Bristol and West Building Society v Mothew* (1998) placed the 'double employment rule' firmly within the realms of conflicts of interests and in *In Plus Group Ltd v Pyke* (see earlier), Sedley LJ questioned whether *Mashonaland* could still be regarded as good law. Citing, inter alia, Lawrence Collins J's judgment in *CMS Dolphin Ltd v Simonet* (see earlier), he explained that:

> If one bears in mind the high standard of probity which equity demands of fiduciaries, and the reliance which shareholders and creditors are entitled to place upon it, the Mashonaland *principle is a very limited one. If, for example, the two* Mashonaland Exploration *companies had been preparing to tender for the same contract, I doubt whether Lord Mayo's position would have been tenable, at least in the absence of special arrangements to insulate either company from the conflict of his interests and duties, for I see no reason why the law should assume that any directorship is merely cosmetic. A directorship brings with it not only voting rights and emoluments but responsibilities of stewardship and honesty, and those who cannot discharge them should not become or remain directors . . . [T]he fiduciary must not only not place himself in a position [of conflict of interest]; if, even accidentally, he finds himself in such a position he must regularise or abandon it . . . [It is not the case that] a director can cheerfully go to the brink so long as he does not fall over the edge. It means that if he finds himself in a position of conflict he must resolve it openly or extract himself from it.*

In this regard, the remarks of Lord Denning in *Scottish Co-operative Wholesale Society Ltd v Meyer* (1959), a case decided under the old oppression remedy (see Chapter 11), are particularly pertinent. Three directors of a holding company, SCWS, were appointed to the board of its subsidiary, a textile company. Lord Denning observed that:

> So long as the interests of all concerned were in harmony, there was no difficulty . . . But, so soon as the interests of the two companies were in conflict, the nominee directors were placed in an impossible position . . . They put their duty to the co-operative society above their duty to the textile company . . . By subordinating the interests of the textile company to those of the co-operative society, they conducted the affairs of the textile company in a manner oppressive to the other shareholders.

Section 175(7) therefore gives statutory effect to the views expressed by Millett LJ (in *Bristol and West Building Society v Mothew*) and Sedley LJ (in *In Plus Group Ltd v Pyke*) so that such appointments will need to be authorised in accordance with s 175(5) (see later).

Avoiding liability for conflicts of duty: authorisation by the directors

14.75   A major concern expressed by the Company Law Review was that the case law on conflicts of duty holds the potential to 'fetter entrepreneurial and business start-up activity by existing directors' and that 'the statutory statement of duties should only prevent the exploitation of business opportunities where there is a clear case for doing so' (*Completing the Structure*). The 2005 White Paper echoes this concern by stating that it is important that the duties do not impose impractical and onerous requirements which stifle entrepreneurial activity (at para 3.26). Section 175(5)(a) therefore implements the CLRSG's recommendation that conflicts may be authorised by independent directors unless, in the case of a private company, its constitution otherwise provides. For a public company the directors will only be able to authorise such conflicts if its constitution expressly permits (s 175(5)(b)). Further, s 175(6) provides that board authorisation is effective only if the conflicted directors have not participated in the taking of the decision or if the decision would have been valid even without the participation of the conflicted directors; the votes of the conflicted directors in favour of the decision will be ignored and the conflicted directors are not counted in the quorum. If all the directors are or may be conflicted, only shareholder approval will suffice (see para **14.92**).

(b) Self-dealing directors

14.76 The underlying rationale of the self-dealing rule which prohibits a director from being interested in a transaction to which the company was a party was explained by the House of Lords in *Aberdeen Rly Co v Blaikie Bros* (1854). The company had contracted with John Blaikie for the supply of iron chairs. At the time of the contract John Blaikie was both a director of Aberdeen Railway and a partner of Blaikie Bros. Lord Cranworth LC, having stated that 'no-one, having [fiduciary] duties to discharge, shall be allowed to enter into engagements in which he has, or can have, a personal interest conflicting, or which possibly may conflict, with the interests of those whom he is bound to protect', went on to stress that:

> his duty to the company imposed on him the obligation of obtaining these iron chairs at the lowest possible price. His personal interest would lead him in an entirely opposite direction, would induce him to fix the price as high as possible. This is the very evil against which the rule in question is directed.

In a similar vein Megarry V-C observed in *Tito v Waddell (No 2)* (1977):

> The self-dealing rule is (to put it very shortly) that if a trustee sells the trust property to himself, the sale is voidable by any beneficiary ex debito justitiae, however fair the transaction. . . . . [E]quity is astute to prevent a trustee from abusing his position or profiting from his trust: the shepherd must not become a wolf.

(See also the joint judgment of Rich, Dixon, and Evatt JJ in *Furs Ltd v Tomkies* (1936).)

The rule extends to third party interests (for example, a spouse or other relative) where the director obtains a direct or indirect benefit not amounting to a profit. So, although the director may lack a personal interest in the contract itself, the self-dealing rule encompasses the situation where he may nevertheless be conflicted by personal loyalties. For example, in *Breitenfeld UK Ltd v Harrison* (above), the managing director, on behalf of the company, entered into contracts with a company owned by his son and daughter-in-law. In *Newgate Stud Co v Penfold* (2008), David Richards J observed:

> What is however true is that in any such relationship there exists the potential for the exercise of fiduciary duties to be influenced by personal considerations. If a director causes his company to enter into a transaction with a close relation, or a spouse or other partner, there is a significant risk that the director will be compromised by a desire to favour the other party . . .

14.77 The statutory statement of directors' duties modifies the common law position by removing self-dealing from the realms of directors' fiduciary duties and replaces it with a statutory obligation to disclose an interest. Section 175(3) makes it clear that the duty to avoid conflicts of interest contained in s 175(1) 'does not apply to a conflict of interest arising in relation to a transaction or arrangement with the company'. Rather, 'self-dealing' falls within s 177(1) which provides that: '[i]f a director is in any way, directly or indirectly, interested in a proposed transaction or arrangement with the company, he must declare the nature and extent of that interest to the other directors'. In similar terms, s 182 applies to cases where a director has an interest in a transaction after it 'has been entered into by the company'. The provisions do not apply to substantial property transactions, loans, quasi-loans, and credit transactions which require the approval of the company's members (see ss 190–203, later).

The Court of Appeal has recently provided some guidance on the threshold at which an 'interest' is such that it must be declared to the board. In *Burns v The FCA* (2017) the defendant, Ms Burns, was an investment consultant. In 2006 she undertook consulting work for Vanguard, a US asset manager. In 2008 and 2010 Burns became an NED of two mutual societies, Marine and General Mutual Life Assurance Society (MGM) and Teachers Provident Society Limited (Teachers). Her work for MGM and Teachers included acting as chair of their respective investment committees. In 2009 MGM was considering engaging Vanguard to provide investment services for a new asset-based annuity business. In 2010 Teachers was looking into replacing its existing investment manager, and Vanguard was one of the possible replacements. However, without disclosing the full facts to either MGM or Teachers, Burns had been maintaining her contacts with Vanguard. In fact, she had been attempting to get additional work from Vanguard, including becoming an NED of its UK branch. None of these attempts had resulted in any business relationship between Vanguard and Burns. In bringing the action, the FCA's main contention was that Burns (as NED) had a duty to declare her interest in Vanguard to MGM and Teachers under s 177 of the CA 2006. By way of defence, Burns argued that she had no 'interest' in Vanguard, admittedly she had asked for an NED role and remuneration, but did not receive anything—and so there was nothing to declare. She also argued that at the material time, Vanguard's potential role with the MGM and Teachers was remote and speculative.

The issue before the Court of Appeal was whether the fact that Burns was trying to get work from Vanguard was sufficient in itself to place her in a conflict of interest. The court found that it did, observing that for the purposes of s 175 it was enough that there was a 'real sensible possibility of a conflict'. An actual conflict was not necessary:

> She was actively soliciting a remunerative relationship with Vanguard, for her own personal benefit, at the very same time as she owed an undivided duty of loyalty to MGM. . . . In our view there was clearly a sufficient likelihood of a conflict of interest.

With respect to Teachers, the court noted:

> Ms Burns' duty of undivided loyalty to Teachers required that she should have no undisclosed interest in Vanguard, yet . . . she actively sought to bring about a situation where she would have such an interest. In our view the act of solicitation itself, against this background, was sufficient.

14.78 Sections 177 and 182 reflect the common practice that companies (see, for example, art 85 of the 1985 Table A and s 317 of the CA 1985) generally permitted directors to have interests in conflict transactions, provided they were declared to the board. The reason why the common law tolerated such relaxation of the rule was explained by Upjohn LJ in *Boulting v Association of Cinematograph Television and Allied Technicians* (1963):

> It is frequently very much better in the interests of the company . . . that they should be advised by someone on some transaction, although he may be interested on the other side of the fence. Directors . . . may sometimes be placed in such a position that though their interest and duty conflict, they can properly and honestly give their services to both sides and serve two masters to the great advantage of both. If the person entitled to the benefit of the rule is content with that position and understands what are his rights in the matter, there is no reason why he should not relax the rule, and it may commercially be very much to his advantage to do so.

14.79 The principal distinction between the two statutory provisions is that whereas breach of s 177 carries civil consequences (s 178), breach of s 182 results in criminal sanctions (s 183). More particularly, s 178 states that the consequences of breach (or threatened breach) of ss 171–177 are the same as would apply if the corresponding common law rule or equitable principle applied. This is subject to the proviso introduced by s 180(1) that, subject to any provision to the contrary in the company's constitution, if s 177 is complied with, the transaction is not liable to be set aside by virtue of any common law rule or equitable principle requiring the consent of members. We explore this provision further later, but for present purposes it is noteworthy that under s 317 of the CA 1985, the predecessor to both ss 177 and 182, it was settled that a director's breach of the statutory duty of disclosure triggers only the criminal sanctions provided for, and not any civil consequences per se. The contract itself is valid until avoided by the company (*Guinness plc v Saunders* (1990); *Hely-Hutchinson v Brayhead Ltd* (1968)). As a condition of rescission of a voidable contract there must be *restitutio in integrum*: 'the parties must be put in *status quo*; for this purpose a court of equity can do what is practically just, even though it cannot restore the parties precisely to the state they were in before the contract' (*Guinness plc v Saunders*, Lord Goff). In *Craven Textile Engineers Ltd v Batley Football Club Ltd* (2000) the issue was whether H, a former director of the defendant football club, could claim payment of unpaid invoices for goods and work and materials supplied to the club, even though he had failed to disclose his interest as a director and principal shareholder of the claimant company, Craven. The Court of Appeal held that notwithstanding H's failure to disclose his interest in the contracts, the football club should pay the outstanding invoices. Clarke LJ, citing Lord Goff's statement of principle in *Guinness plc v Saunders*, said that '[i]t is important to note that the court does not have a general discretion to do what seems fair and just in all the circumstances. The court will only treat the company as entitled to avoid the contract if it can do what is practically just to restore the parties to the position which existed before.' Finally, commenting on the consequences which flow from a breach of the statutory duty of disclosure, the judge in *Coleman Taymar* (earlier) observed that it does not give the company a separate right of action for damages against the director: '[a]ny right of action arises from the breach of fiduciary duty and not from the section [317 of the CA 1985]'. Now that the self-dealing rule is outwith the no-conflict rule, it would seem that the civil consequences for failing to declare an interest under s 177 are extremely limited.

14.80 An issue which came before the courts under s 317 of the CA 1985 was whether it required disclosure at a formal board meeting in cases where all the directors of a company have informal notice of the conflict-transaction. It was held at first instance in *Guinness plc v Saunders* (1990) that compliance with s 317 requires disclosure to a duly convened and constituted board meeting, a function which cannot be delegated to a sub-committee of the board. The issue was not directly addressed in the House of Lords' decision. Fox LJ in the Court of Appeal opined that even if all the members of the board had known of a contract this would not validate payments made thereunder. Whether or not a director should make formal disclosure of interests which are patently obvious, such as his interest in his own service contract which is generally known to all boardroom colleagues, has been a matter on which the judges have differed. In two 1990s cases it was said that in such circumstances formal disclosure is not required (*Lee Panavision Ltd v Lee Lighting Ltd* (1992); *Runciman v Walter Runciman plc* (1992)). On the other hand, in *Neptune (Vehicle Washing Equipment) Ltd v Fitzgerald* (1995), Lightman J held that strict compliance with the statutory disclosure requirement was necessary even in the case of companies with a sole director. Such a director should make the declaration to himself and record the declaration in the minutes. This was reluctantly applied by the court in *Neptune (Vehicle Washing Equipment) Ltd v Fitzgerald (No 2)* (1995), although the court expressed the view that a better solution would be to require disclosure by a sole director to the members in general meeting. This is a somewhat curious conclusion given the nature of such companies where generally a sole director will also control the majority of the shares. The most recent judicial pronouncement departs from Lightman J's formalistic approach. In *MacPherson v European Strategic Bureau Ltd* (1999) Ferris J emphatically supported the line of reasoning adopted by the court in *Runciman*. On the facts of *MacPherson*, each of the shareholders and the directors knew the precise nature of others' interest so that there was in effect unanimous approval of the agreement. Ferris J thus concluded that '[n]o amount of formal disclosure by each other to the other would have increased the other's relevant knowledge'. But it should be noted that a board's knowledge in general terms that a colleague has engaged in a conflict-transaction will not amount to sufficient disclosure. The board has to be given full and precise information (*Gwembe Valley Development Co Ltd v Koshy* (1999), Harman J; see also the comments of Neuberger J on the disclosure standard in *EIC Services Ltd v Phipps* (earlier)).

14.81 Section 177(6)(b) and s 182(6)(b) seek to solve this problem by providing that a director need not declare an interest 'if, or to the extent that, the other directors are already aware of it (and for this purpose the other directors are treated as aware of anything of which they ought reasonably to be aware)'. As the duty requires disclosure to be made 'to the other directors', no disclosure is required where the company has only one director.

It should be noted that the 2008 model articles prohibit a director who has an interest in an actual or proposed transaction or arrangement with the company from participating in the decision-making process for quorum or voting purposes (art 14(1) for private companies limited by shares; arts 13(3) and 16(1) for public companies). It is expressly provided that the prohibition does not apply if the director's interest cannot reasonably be regarded as likely to give rise to a conflict of interest (see also ss 177(6)(a) and 182(6)(a)). The 2008 model articles also provide for members, by ordinary resolution, disapplying the prohibition on voting.

(vi) Duty not to accept benefits from third parties

14.82 Section 176(1) provides that a director must not accept a benefit from a third party conferred by reason of (a) his being a director, or (b) his doing (or not doing) anything as director. This duty is an element of the wider no-conflict duty laid down in s 175 and it too will not be infringed if acceptance of the benefit cannot reasonably be regarded as likely to give rise to a conflict of interest. As Lord Goldsmith explained in the Lords Grand Committee (Official Report, 9 February 2006 (col GC330)), the provision codifies the 'long-standing rule, prohibiting the exploitation of the position of director for personal benefit'. It should be noted that the duty applies only to benefits conferred because the director is a director of the company or because of something that the director does or does not do as director. The word 'benefit', for the purpose of this section, is not defined by the statute although during the parliamentary debates on the Bill it was made clear that it includes benefits of any description, including non-financial benefits (Official Report, 9 February 2006 (col GC330) (Lord Goldsmith)). Guidance on bribes was given by Andrew Smith J in *Fiona Trust & Holding Corp v Privalov* (2010):

> English law takes a broad view of what constitutes a bribe for the purposes of civil claims. It considers that a bribe (or 'secret commission' or 'surreptitious payment') has been paid where '(i) . . . the person making the payment makes it to the agent of another person with whom he is dealing; (ii) . . . he makes it to that person knowing that that person is

acting as the agent of the other person with whom he is dealing; and (iii) . . . he fails to disclose to the other person with whom he is dealing that he has made that payment to the person he knows to be the other person's agent': Industries & General Mortgage Co Ltd v Lewis *(1949).*

While s 175(5) provides for board authorisation in respect of conflicts of interest, this is not the case with this particular duty. However, the company may authorise the acceptance of benefits by virtue of s 180(4) (see later). Section 176(2) defines a 'third party' as a person other than the company or its holding company or its subsidiaries and thus s 176(3) provides that benefits provided by the company fall outside the prohibition.

If the benefit in question amounts to a bribe, the provisions of the Bribery Act 2010 will apply. A bribe is defined as giving someone a financial or other advantage to encourage that person to perform their functions or activities improperly or to reward that person for having already done so. In *Novoship (UK) Ltd v Mikhaylyuk* (2012), the court explained that it would be a plain breach of the duty of loyalty for a fiduciary to accept a bribe. Such a recipient, together with those who dishonestly assist him, will be liable to account for their profits.

Remedies

14.83   The remedies for breach of directors' duties have not been incorporated into the statutory statement of directors' duties but, as we have seen, s 178(1) of the CA 2006 provides that the consequences of breach (or threatened breach) of ss 171–177 are the same as would apply if the corresponding common law rule or equitable principle applied. With respect to the no-conflict duty, it has long been settled that a director must disgorge any secret profit resulting from his breach of duty unless it was authorised (see s 175(4)(b), CA 2006, earlier). The liability to account arises even where the director acted honestly and where the company could not otherwise have obtained the benefit (*Regal (Hastings) Ltd v Gulliver*; *IDC v Cooley*). In *Murad v Al-Saraj* (2005) Arden LJ explained the policy underlying such liability:

> It may be asked why equity imposes stringent liability of this nature . . . equity imposes stringent liability on a fiduciary as a deterrent—pour encourager les autres. Trust law recognises what in company law is now sometimes called the 'agency' problem. There is a separation of beneficial ownership and control and the shareholders (who may be numerous and only have small numbers of shares) or beneficial owners cannot easily monitor the actions of those who manage their business or property on a day to day basis. Therefore, in the interests of efficiency and to provide an incentive to fiduciaries to resist the temptation to misconduct themselves, the law imposes exacting standards on fiduciaries and an extensive liability to account.

In *Parr v Keystone Healthcare Ltd* (2019) Lewison LJ took the opportunity to explain that the liability to account is neither compensatory nor restitutionary in nature, but rather its aim is to strip the fiduciary of the unauthorised profits made while in a position of conflicting interests. Applying *Regal (Hastings) Ltd v Gulliver*, the judge emphasised that while a claimant must prove causation when claiming equitable compensation for loss resulting from a breach of fiduciary duty, claims for disgorgement of unauthorised profits require nothing more than that the profit was obtained by virtue of the fiduciary position—although there must be a sufficient degree of connection between the breach of duty and the receipt of the secret profit.

In *Coleman Taymar Ltd v Oakes* (2001), Robert Reid QC, sitting as a deputy judge of the High Court, stated that a company is entitled to elect whether to claim damages (equitable compensation) or an account of profits against a director who, by abusing his position, makes a secret profit. Where the director derives no personal financial benefit from the breach of duty, the court may award equitable compensation assessed by reference to any loss suffered by the company (*Breitenfeld UK Ltd v Harrison* (earlier); *Auden McKenzie (Pharma Division) Ltd v Patel* (2019)). Where, on the other hand, the director does derive a personal financial benefit, though the profit may arise out of the use of position as opposed to the use of trust property, the judges typically resort to the language of the 'constructive trust' as the means for fashioning a remedy (*Boardman v Phipps*, although, Lord Guest excepted, all of the judges spoke of the defendant's liability to account). In *A-G for Hong Kong v Reid* (1992), Lord Templeman explained that *Boardman* 'demonstrates the strictness with which equity regards the conduct of a fiduciary and the extent to which equity is willing to impose a constructive trust on property obtained by a fiduciary by virtue of his office' (though some judges and commentators have doubted whether a constructive trust was actually imposed in *Boardman*, see, for example, Lewison J's comments in *Sinclair Investments* (see para **14.85**) and Penner (2016)). And in *Chan v Zacharia I* (1983) Deane J stated in broad terms that 'any benefit or gain is held by the fiduciary as constructive trustee . . . and it is immaterial that there was no absence of good faith or damage [to the company]'.

14.84   In *JJ Harrison (Properties) Ltd v Harrison* (2002) a director usurped a corporate opportunity by acquiring for his own benefit development land owned by the company. At the time of valuation he failed to disclose that planning permission was forthcoming which, once granted, would greatly inflate its value. The company, having unsuccessfully applied for planning permission a couple of years earlier, was unaware that local authority policy in this respect had changed. The director purchased the land from the company in 1985 for £8,400. Having obtained planning permission through, to add insult to injury, use of the company's resources, he then resold part of it for £110,300 in 1988 and the rest in 1992 for £122,500. The director resigned and the company sought to hold him liable as a constructive trustee. Chadwick LJ, citing Millett LJ in *Paragon Finance plc v DB Thakerar & Co* (1999), said:

> It follows . . . from the principle that directors who dispose of the company's property in breach of their fiduciary duties are treated as having committed a breach of trust that, a director who is, himself, the recipient of the property holds it upon a trust for

the company. He, also, is described as a constructive trustee . . . The reason is that a director, on appointment to that office, assumes the duties of a trustee in relation to the company's property. If, thereafter, he takes possession of that property his possession 'is coloured from the first by the trust and confidence by means of which he obtained it'. The true analysis is that his obligations as a trustee in relation to that property predate the transaction by which it was conveyed to him.

Chadwick LJ's reasoning was applied by the Court of Appeal in *First Subsea Ltd v Balltec Ltd* (2018).

14.85 In the *CMS Dolphin* case (see earlier), Lawrence Collins J subjected the issue of remedies for diverting a corporate opportunity to detailed analysis. He held that S was a constructive trustee of the profits referable to exploiting the corporate opportunity and, in general, it made no difference whether the opportunity is first taken up by the wrongdoer or by a 'corporate vehicle' established by him for that purpose: 'I do not consider that the liability of the directors in *Cook v Deeks* would have been in any way different if they had procured their new company to enter the contract directly, rather than (as they did) enter into it themselves and then transfer the benefit of the contract to a new company.' Further, the director is:

accountable for the profits properly attributable to the breach of fiduciary duty taking into account the expenses connected with those profits and a reasonable allowance for overheads (but not necessarily salary for the wrongdoer), together with a sum to take account of other benefits derived from those contracts. For example, other contracts might not have been won, or profits made on them, without (eg) the opportunity or cash flow benefit which flowed from contracts unlawfully obtained. There must, however, be some reasonable connection between the breach of duty and the profits for which the fiduciary is accountable.

The basis of a director's liability in this situation is that, as seen in *Cook v Deeks*, the opportunity in question is treated as if it were an asset of the company in relation to which the director had fiduciary duties. He thus becomes a constructive trustee 'of the fruits of his abuse of the company's property' (per Lawrence Collins J, earlier).

The decision in *Sinclair Investments (UK) Ltd v Versailles Trading Finance Ltd* (2011) is significant because the Court of Appeal has explained the distinction that should be drawn between personal liability to account for unauthorised profit as opposed to the Privy Council's view in *Reid* that liability is proprietary. Lord Neuberger MR, delivering the leading judgment, held that a beneficiary of a fiduciary's duties has no proprietary interest in any money or asset acquired by the fiduciary in breach of his duties, 'unless the asset or money is or has been beneficially the property of the beneficiary or the trustee acquired the asset or money by taking advantage of an opportunity or right which was properly that of the beneficiary', even if the fiduciary could not have acquired the asset had he not been a fiduciary. In finding that the appropriate remedy is an equitable account, the Court of Appeal did not follow the decision in *Attorney-General for Hong Kong v Reid* (1992), preferring its own decision in *Lister & Co v Stubbs* (1890). The Master of the Rolls added that if it is a matter of equitable policy that a fiduciary should not be allowed to profit from his breach of duties, that can be achieved by extending or adjusting the rules relating to equitable compensation rather than those relating to proprietary interests. The judge explained that:

> [I]t seems to me that there is a real case for saying that the decision in Reid . . . is unsound. In cases where a fiduciary takes for himself an asset which, if he chose to take, he was under a duty to take for the beneficiary, it is easy to see why the asset should be treated as the property of the beneficiary. However, a bribe paid to a fiduciary could not possibly be said to be an asset which the fiduciary was under a duty to take for the beneficiary. There can thus be said to be a fundamental distinction between (i) a fiduciary enriching himself by depriving a Claimant of an asset and (ii) a fiduciary enriching himself by doing a wrong to the Claimant.

(See also *Cadogan Petroleum plc v Tolly* (2011).)

As Penner (2019) comments, the decision in *Sinclair* (and in *FHR*, discussed later) 'draw[s] a distinction between those cases in which the asset which constitutes the unauthorised profit would have gone to the [company] but for its interception by the [director], and those cases in which the fiduciary enriches himself in the course of doing a wrong to the [company]'.

The issue addressed in *Sinclair Investments* came before the Court of Appeal again in *FHR European Ventures LLP v Mankarious* (2013). While it acknowledged that it was bound to follow its own decision in *Lister* and *Sinclair Investments*, the court was clearly unhappy with this and urged the Supreme Court to consider whether *Sinclair* was 'right to decide that *Lister* is to be preferred to *Reid*'. With considerable agility it distinguished the facts before it from *Lister* and held that a purchasing agent held a secret commission on constructive trust for its principal. The Court of Appeal's call for final determination by the Supreme Court of the circumstances when a proprietary remedy (a constructive trust) will be imposed rather than a personal remedy (liability to account for a profit or bribe received in breach of duty) was answered in *FHR European Ventures LLP v Mankarious (No 2)* (2014). The Supreme Court took the opportunity to lay the matter to rest by holding that a fiduciary who receives a bribe or secret commission in his capacity as a fiduciary holds the proceeds on constructive trust for his principal. Thus, any benefit which results from a breach of fiduciary duty to the company is held on trust for it. Lord Neuberger PSC expressed the view that this position at least has the advantage of clarity and certainty and is consistent with *Regal (Hastings)* and *Phipps*. It also has the advantage of 'harmonising the development of the common law round the world'. The consequence, as explained by Patten LJ in *First Subsea Ltd v Balltec* (para **14.84**):

> is that a constructive trust will be imposed on fiduciaries in such cases regardless of whether it is possible to treat the benefit or payment received by the agent as derived from property in which the principal had a pre-existing interest.

The imposition of a constructive trust can carry disastrous consequences for innocent third parties in circumstances where the defendant is bankrupt. It is, of course, right to strip a director of a gain made in breach of duty, but should that gain, without more, be regarded as representing trust property belonging to the company from the moment in time he received it? Although Lord Neuberger recognised the force of this argument, he thought it must be 'balanced by the fact that it appears to be just that a principal whose agent has obtained a bribe or secret commission should be able to trace the proceeds of the bribe or secret commission into other assets and to follow them into the hands of knowing recipients (as in *Reid*)'.

14.86 As was commented in Chapter 13, the court, exercising its inherent jurisdiction, has the power to grant an equitable allowance to a fiduciary. In *Phipps v Boardman* (see earlier), the trustees who acted in breach of the no-conflict rule thereby created a handsome profit for the trust. They had acted honestly throughout and, though liable, were awarded an allowance on 'a liberal scale' to take account of their special expertise. Such an allowance may be awarded 'if it was thought that justice between the parties' so demands (*O'Sullivan v Management Agency and Music Ltd* (1985)). However, in the case of directors the scope of this jurisdiction has now been severely limited following Lord Goff's remarks in *Guinness plc v Saunders* (see earlier) to the effect that it should be 'restricted to those cases where it cannot have the effect of encouraging the trustees [or directors] in any way to put themselves in a position where their interests conflict with their duties as trustees [or directors]'. Further, the House of Lords, mindful that the exercise of this discretion could constitute interference in company affairs, doubted whether it would ever be exercised in favour of a company director. Mindful of Lord Goff's speech in *Guinness*, Paul Morgan QC, sitting as a deputy judge of the High Court, in *Quarter Master UK Ltd v Pyke* (2005) stated that:

> I hold on the facts of the present case that the fundamental principle should prevail that a director is not to benefit from his breach of fiduciary duty and that no allowance is to be made.

The judge concluded that the fact that the company would not itself have otherwise received the benefits which flowed from the breach made no difference (see also the remarks of Peter Smith J in *Crown Dilmun v Sutton* (2004)).

Accessory liability

Knowing assistance

14.87 In certain circumstances those who assist a director in the course of a breach of duty will also be held liable for breach of fiduciary duty (see *Barnes v Addy* (1874), Lord Selborne LC). The test for determining dishonesty for the purposes of determining the liability of an accessory to the director's breach of duty (traditionally termed '*knowing assistance*') was formulated by Lord Nicholls in *Royal Brunei Airlines Sdn Bhd v Tan* (1995). He stated that dishonesty should be judged according to whether an honest person in the defendant's position would have acted in the way that the defendant acted. If he had acted in the same way, then the defendant will not be liable (see *Dubai Aluminium Co Ltd v Salaam* (1999); *Grupo Torras SA v Al-Sabah* (2001); and *Bank of Scotland v A Ltd* (2001); see further Lewison J's survey of the case law in *Ultraframe (UK) Ltd v Fielding* (2005)). Lord Nicholls' objective test was considered by the House of Lords in *Twinsectra Ltd v Yardley* (2002). Confirming that the Privy Council's decision was also the law in England and Wales, the majority favoured a test of dishonesty that is neither purely objective nor subjective but one which depends upon what Lord Hutton called the 'combined test'. This asks, first, whether the defendant's conduct was objectively dishonest by reference to the ordinary standards of reasonable people. If the answer is in the affirmative, the second step of the combined test is applied by determining whether there is evidence that the defendant realised that he had behaved dishonestly in the circumstances. Lord Hoffmann explained that the principles require more than simply showing dishonest conduct, '[t]hey require a dishonest state of mind, that is to say, consciousness that one is transgressing ordinary standards of behaviour'.

The observations of Lord Hutton and Lord Hoffmann were considered in *Barlow Clowes International v Eurotrust International* (2005) PC, where the panel included Lord Nicholls and Lord Hoffmann. The Privy Council stated that it was unnecessary for the defendants to have considered what these ordinary standards of honest behaviour were, it was enough that the defendant was conscious of those parts of the transaction which rendered participation in it a breach of ordinary standards of honest behaviour. The Panel also took the view that someone can be held to know or suspect that undertaking an act will render assistance in the misappropriation of funds even if that person is unaware that the funds are held on trust or, indeed, what a trust involves. Further, in response to the academic criticism that *Twinsectra* had changed the law by inviting enquiry not merely into the defendant's mental state about the nature of the transaction in which he was participating but also into his views about generally accepted standards of dishonesty, Lord Hoffmann explained that the principles laid down in *Twinsectra* were 'no different from the principles stated in *Royal Brunei*'. Accordingly, emphasis was given to the objective nature of the test for dishonest assistance. This was confirmed in *Group Seven Ltd v Notable Services LLP* (2019) where the Court of Appeal held that the test for dishonesty is objective, based on what the defendant knows. The court thus followed the approach taken by Lord Nicholls in *Tan*. It also had the benefit of the Supreme Court's reasoning in *Ivey v Genting Casinos UK Ltd* (2017) where it was explained that:

> The fact-finding tribunal must first ascertain (subjectively) the actual state of the individual's knowledge or belief as to the facts. . . . When once his actual state of mind as to the knowledge or belief as to the facts is established, the question whether his conduct was honest or dishonest is to be determined by the fact-finder applying the (objective) standards of ordinary decent people. There is no requirement that the defendant must appreciate that what he has done is, by those standards, dishonest.

The Court of Appeal concluded that 'in the light of *Ivey*' the 'touchstone of accessory liability' for breach of fiduciary duty is dishonesty and that there is no room for the application of the subjective test. However, the court did admit that subjective knowledge is important and 'forms a crucial part of the first stage of the test for dishonesty set out in *Tan*'. It continued:

> But once the relevant facts have been ascertained, including the defendant's state of knowledge or belief as to the facts, the standard of appraisal which must then be applied ... is a purely objective one. The court has to ask itself ... a jury question, namely whether the defendant's conduct was honest or dishonest according to the standards of ordinary decent people.

Knowing receipt

14.88 In broad terms, the governing principle is that to establish liability in knowing receipt, the recipient must have actual knowledge (or the equivalent). Constructive knowledge is not enough (*In Re Montagu's Settlement Trusts* (1987)). The principle that arises in relation to knowing receipt in the context of companies was explained by Buckley LJ in *Belmont Finance Corpn Ltd v Williams Furniture Ltd (No 2)* (1980) in the following terms:

> So, if the directors of a company in breach of their fiduciary duties misapply the funds of their company so that they come into the hands of some stranger to the trust who receives them with knowledge ... of the breach, he cannot conscientiously retain those funds against the company unless he has some better equity. He becomes a constructive trustee for the company of the misapplied funds.

The precise state of mind on the part of the recipient has generated considerable debate. In *BCCI Ltd v Chief Akindele* (2000), Nourse LJ, delivering the principal judgment of the Court of Appeal, held that there should be a single test for *knowing receipt*, namely that the recipient's state of knowledge had to make it *unconscionable* for him to retain the benefit of the receipt. Nourse LJ said:

> [J]ust as there is now a single test of dishonesty for knowing assistance, so ought there to be a single test of knowledge for knowing receipt. The recipient's state of knowledge must be such as to make it unconscionable for him to retain the benefit of the receipt.

(See also *Houghton v Fayers* (2000); and *Charter v City Index Ltd* (2008).)

In *Thanakharn Kasikorn Thai Chamkat (Mahachon) v Akai Holdings Ltd* (2010), Lord Neuberger, sitting as a non-permanent Judge of the Court of Final Appeal of Hong Kong, took the view that the test of unconscionability was identical to irrationality (as in establishing want of authority). For example, the recipient might be irrational in believing that the fiduciary in question possessed apparent authority to commit the principal to hand over the asset, yet not be dishonest in believing or assuming he had that authority. His Lordship said:

> If the recipient's reliance on the alleged agent's apparent authority, when accepting the asset from the alleged agent on behalf of his principal, was dishonest or irrational, it seems to me that it would be unconscionable for the recipient to retain the asset . . . or, to put it another way, the recipient would have the relevant 'actual knowledge (or the equivalent)'.

Lord Neuberger concluded the point by doubting whether negligent reliance would satisfy the unconscionability test. In *Otkritie International Investment Management Ltd v Urumov* (2014), a further attempt at unravelling the meaning of unconscionability was made. Eder J, accepting counsel's submission on the point, said that:

> it is important to note that the test for knowledge in a knowing receipt claim is lower than it is for dishonest assistance: dishonesty is not a prerequisite of liability, and the question is whether the defendant had such knowledge as to render it unconscionable for the defendant to retain the benefit of the receipt . . .

Citing *Snell's Equity*, the judge thought that in certain circumstances a defendant will be liable if he fails to make reasonable enquiries about the circumstances of the receipt: 'in gratuitous transactions, where the defendant has no reasonable justification to rely unquestioningly on the trustee's authority to transfer the property to him, it may be reasonable to impose a duty of inquiry on him. The recipient's knowledge of facts that would put a reasonable person on inquiry might amount to unconscionable knowledge . . .'

It is noteworthy that Penner (2016) criticises the test of 'unconscionability' on the basis that it gives little or no guidance to a court attempting to delineate the appropriate degree of intent for the purposes of establishing liability. It is suggested that a single test for all accessory liability, whether knowing assistance or knowing receipt, in line with that stated in *Twinsectra* at least has the advantage of practicality and certainty.

14.89 A significant case dealing with knowing receipt is *Brown v Bennett* (1999) where the Court of Appeal stressed that, to enforce a constructive trust on this ground, a claimant company had to show both a disposal of its property in breach of fiduciary obligation and beneficial receipt by the defendant of traceable property belonging to the company. Thus, liability for knowing receipt only arises where the property in question is transferred in breach of duty. A past breach of duty in relation to the company's property that has since been transferred does not necessarily render the recipient guilty of any dishonest receipt (see also Hoffmann LJ's judgment in *El Ajou v Dollar Land Holdings plc* (1994)).

14.90 As is apparent from the decisions considered so far, the judges take the view that where a company's asset reaches the hands of an accessory it is impressed with a constructive trust (see, for example, the reasoning of the judge in *Chard Hunt Investments Ltd v Hunt* (2017)).

This is logical where the asset in question is trust property. The issue that arises, however, is what is the appropriate remedy where company property does not reach the hands of a dishonest accessory given that, as Lord Nicholls recognised in *Royal Brunei*, liability as a dishonest assistant 'is not dependent upon receipt of trust property [and] arises even though no trust property has reached the hands of the accessory'. Although in such situations the courts frequently resort to the 'constructive trust', it is suggested that what is meant is that the accessory's liability to account is similar in nature. Indeed, Ungoed-Thomas J in *Selangor United Rubber Estates Ltd v Cradock (No 3)* (1968) was moved to observe that the use of the term 'constructive trustee' in this context is 'nothing more than a formula for equitable relief'. Thus, where no trust property is passed to the accessory, the company's claim is personal not proprietary in nature (see *Houghton v Fayers* (2000), Nourse LJ; *Paragon Finance plc v DB Thakerar & Co* (1999), Millett LJ; *Belmont Finance Corpn Ltd v Williams Furniture Ltd* (1979), Goff LJ; and *Bank of Scotland v A Ltd* (earlier), Lord Woolf CJ. See further Penner (2016: ch 11)).

Finally, it should be noted that the company's claim against any accessory is additional to its claim against the director. This is especially useful where the wrong-doing director has disappeared or is bankrupt.

Relief from liability

14.91 There are three ways in which a director who is in breach of duty may be relieved from liability: (i) by obtaining the 'consent, approval or authorisation' by the members of the company under s 180; (ii) through ratification by the company under s 239; or (iii) by the court under s 1157.

Consent, approval, or authorisation by members

14.92 Section 180 sets out the circumstances in which members of the company may give their consent, approval, or authorisation (and when they are not required to do so), to a breach of a director's general duties. Section 180(1)(a) and (b) provide that if the requirement of authorisation is complied with for the purposes of s 175 (see s 175(4) and (5), discussed earlier), or if the director has declared to the other directors his interest in a proposed transaction with the company under s 177, these processes replace the equitable rule that required the members to consent or authorise such breaches of duty. This is made subject to any enactment (for example, the transactions contained in Chapter 4 of Part 10, see para **14.93**) or any provision in the company's articles of association which requires the authorisation or approval of members (s 180(1) and (3)). Compliance with s 177 (see paras **11.77** *et seq*) does not, therefore, mean that approval under Chapter 4 is dispensed with and vice versa. As Lord Goldsmith explained:

Section 175 permits director authorisation of what would otherwise be impermissible conflicts of interest. Section 177 requires declarations of interest in proposed company transactions. In both those cases, the general duty no longer requires the consent of members.

The common law rules or principles that refer to the failure to have had a conflict of interest approved by the members of a company under certain circumstances need to be set aside. If they are not, although the Act provided that it was all right for there to be an authorisation, it might be suggested that the director should still be capable of being impeached by reference to this common law rule or principle. However, s 180(1) goes on to say: 'This is without prejudice to any enactment, or provision of the company's constitution, requiring such consent or approval'.

Certainly, the company's constitution can reverse the change and can insist on certain steps being taken requiring the consent of the members in certain circumstances. In that event, that provision would have to be given effect to. That is the consequence of the change of approach—and therefore a change of approach to the appropriate consequence of there not being members' approval in particular cases because it would no longer be required. (See Official Report, 9 February 2006 (col GC337)

Section 180(2) goes on to provide that the general duties apply even though the transaction falls within Part 10, Chapter 4, of the CA 2006 (see later), except that there is no need to comply with s 175 or 176 where the approval of members is obtained. Section 180(4) preserves the common law position on *prior* authorisation of conduct that would otherwise be a breach of the general duties (ratification under s 239 necessarily takes place *after* the relevant conduct or omission, discussed later). In line with the case law on the issue, it is settled that the consent of the members must be fully informed (*Kaye v Croydon Tramways Co* (1898)); and members may give their unanimous consent informally (*Re Duomatic Ltd* (1969), see para **14.103**). However, members cannot authorise conduct that would be unlawful, a fraud on the company, or is dishonest (*Madoff Securities International Ltd v Raven* (2011)). Similarly, where the company is insolvent, or of doubtful solvency, members cannot authorise conduct which is prejudicial to the interests of creditors (*West Mercia Safetywear Ltd v Dodd* (see para **14.37**)). As we saw in Chapter 10, where conduct has been previously approved or subsequently ratified, a member will not be permitted to bring a derivative claim against the director in question. This is because the effect of authorisation by the members is that the act in question becomes the act of the company (*Multinational Gas and Petrochemical Co Ltd v Multinational Gas and Petrochemical Services* (1983)). It is noteworthy that interested directors qua members can vote on a resolution to approve a prospective breach of the statutory duties under s 180, but cannot do so to ratify a breach after the event (see s 239(4), later). Finally, s 180(5) provides that subject to the other provisions in s 180, the general duties have effect notwithstanding any enactment or rule of law, except as otherwise provided or the context otherwise requires. This permits directors to make provision for employees under s 247 of the CA 2006 when the company ceases or transfers its business even if this would otherwise be a breach of the s 172 duty to promote the success of the company (see para 320, Explanatory Notes to CA 2006).

14.93 As commented in the previous paragraph, Part 10, Chapter 4 of the CA 2006 lists certain transactions that require the approval of the members of the company. These include long-term service contracts (s 188); substantial property transactions (s 190); loans, quasi-loans, and credit transactions (ss 197–214); and payments for loss of office (ss 215–222) (for the provisions relating to directors' service contracts, see para **13.27**). The policy underlying the requirement of shareholder approval of these specified transactions was explained by Carnwath J in *British Racing Drivers' Club Ltd v Hextall Erskine & Co* (1997), who stressed that the possibility of conflicts of interests in these circumstances is such that there is a danger that the judgement of directors may be distorted and so it ensures that 'the matter will be . . . widely ventilated, and a more objective decision reached'. Section 180 thus sets out, in part, the relationship between the general duties of directors and these more specific provisions contained in Part 10, Chapter 4 of the Act. The requirements for approving long-term service contracts and payments for loss of office were discussed in Chapter 13. Here we outline the provisions dealing with substantial property transactions and loans, quasi-loans, and credit transactions.

Substantial property transactions

14.94 Sections 190–196, which replace ss 320–322 of the CA 1985, require substantial property transactions involving the acquisition or disposal of substantial 'non-cash assets' by directors or connected persons (including shadow directors (s 223(1)(b))) to be approved in advance by the company's members. A 'substantial property transaction' is defined as arising where the market value of the asset exceeds the lower of £100,000 or 10 per cent of the company's net asset value if more than £5,000 (s 191). The principal features of the regime are:

- it permits a company to enter into a contract which is conditional on member approval. This implements a recommendation of the Law Commissions (s 190). The company is not to be liable under the contract if member approval is not forthcoming (s 190(3));

- it provides for the aggregation of non-cash assets forming part of an arrangement or series of arrangements for the purpose of determining whether the financial thresholds have been exceeded so that member approval is required (s 190(5));

- it excludes payments under directors' service contracts and payments for loss of office from the requirements of these clauses (s 190(6)). This implements a recommendation of the Law Commissions;

- it provides an exception for companies in administration or those being wound up (s 193).

Terry v Watchstone Ltd (2018) concerned the sale of the shares in a technology development company. Shortly before the sale was completed, the company granted an indemnity to one of its directors, who was also a shareholder. The indemnity was designed to protect the director against any tax liability he might incur when selling his shares in the company. Following the sale, the company unsuccessfully claimed that the grant of the indemnity was void because it was a 'substantial property transaction' under CA 2006, s 190 and it had not been approved by the company's members. The court held that s 190 requires 'property' that amounts to a non-cash asset. The indemnity was neither property nor an interest in property. Further, there was no acquisition which means that the asset must be in existence at the time the transaction took place. Here the rights under the indemnity were created by the indemnity itself and did not exist prior to the transaction taking place. In any case, the indemnity had been granted to the director qua member. Further, the shareholders had approved the indemnity (although they had not needed to for the reasons given above).

14.95   The purpose of s 190 is to protect the company's members. The requirement of approval by the general meeting may be satisfied informally under the *Duomatic* principle (see later), given that the members of the company make up the class the provision is designed to protect (see *Re Duckwari plc (No 2)* (1998); *Wright v Atlas Wright (Europe) Ltd* (1999); *Re Conegrade Ltd* (2002)). Such informal consent must be unanimous. The remedies for breach are laid down by s 195 which provides that any arrangement or transaction entered into by a company in contravention of s 190 is voidable at the instance of the company (s 195(1)). The company's right to avoid the arrangement or transaction will, however, be lost if restitution is no longer possible, if the company has been indemnified, if rights to the property have been acquired by a bona fide third party for value without notice of the breach of s 190, or if the arrangement has, within a reasonable period, been retrospectively approved by the company (ss 195–196). Irrespective of whether the transaction is or can be avoided, the director or connected person and any other director who authorised the transaction will be liable to account to the company for any profit or loss sustained as a result of the breach of s 190. In *Re Duckwari plc (No 2)* (1998) and *Re Duckwari plc (No 3)* (1999) the Court of Appeal stated that to be recoverable the loss or damage had to result from the arrangement or transaction identified as falling within s 190; and the loss may be measured by reference to any depreciation in value of the asset acquired in contravention of the provision. The court was concerned with a transaction involving the acquisition of property rather than the borrowing or use of monies to finance its acquisition. The indemnity covered the difference between the purchase price and its proceeds of sale taking account of any expenditure incurred in increasing the property's value, but excluding the finance costs of the acquisition.

(See also *Smithton Ltd v Naggar* (2013).)

Loans, quasi-loans, and credit transactions

14.96   The regulation of loans by companies to their directors dates back to the Companies Act 1948 and was severely tightened in the CA 1980 in order to address the growing problem identified in a series of DTI (now BEIS) investigations of directors secretly directing money to themselves under the guise of loans on highly favourable terms from their companies (see the White Paper, *The Conduct of Company Directors* (Cmnd 7037, 1977)).

In contrast to the CA 1985, ss 197–214 of the CA 2006 do not impose an absolute pro-hibition on loans to directors (including shadow directors, (s 223(1)(c))) and connected persons but make such transactions subject to the approval of the company's members by resolution and, in certain circumstances, also subject to the approval by the members of its holding company. Further, there are no criminal sanctions for breach of the pro-visions but rather s 213 provides for civil consequences only and s 214 also provides for subsequent affirmation. The requirement for members' approval of loans apply to all UK-registered companies with the exception of 'wholly-owned' subsidiaries (s 195(7)). The provisions relating to quasi-loans and credit transactions apply only to public companies and associated companies (ss 198–203).

14.97   There are a number of exceptions to the requirement for members' approval which have been consolidated (see ss 204–209). These cover expenditure on company business (s 204); expenditure on defending proceedings etc (s 205); expenditure in connection with regulatory action or investigation (s 206); expenditure for minor and business trans-actions (s 207); expenditure for intra-group transactions (s 208); and expenditure for money-lending companies (s 209).

14.98   The effect of a breach of s 197, 198, 200, 201, or 203 is that the transaction or arrangement is voidable at the instance of the company (s 213(2)). Further, regardless of whether the company has elected to avoid the transaction, an arrangement or transaction entered into in contravention of the provision renders the director (together with any connected person to whom voidable payments were made and any director who authorised the transaction or arrangement) liable to account to the company for any gain he made as well as being liable to indemnify the company for any loss or damage it sustains as a result of the transaction or arrangement (s 213(4)). A director who is liable as a result of the company entering into a transaction with a person connected with him has a defence if he can show that he took all reasonable steps to secure the company's compliance with s 200, 201, or 203.

14.99   The Act does not define 'loan', although s 199 does define the term 'quasi-loan' and related expressions (see s 199). Some guidance was provided in *Champagne Perrier-Jouet SA v HH Finch Ltd* (1982) in which the court explained that a loan is a sum of money lent for a period of time to be returned in money or money's worth. In general, whether or not a payment to a director by the company is a loan for the purposes of s 197 as opposed to remuneration for work done is a fact-intensive exercise. The distinction is not always obvious. In *Currencies Direct Ltd v Ellis* (2002) the defendant, a shareholder and director of the claimant company, received sums in cash or payment by way of expenses incurred by him. When he was excluded from the management of the company it sought repay-ment of £253,000 arguing that the sums were loans. The defendant argued that the money received was remuneration. The trial judge held that the company could only recover £43,117 that the defendant acknowledged was a loan, the balance being remuneration. The company's appeal to the Court of Appeal was dismissed. Mummery LJ stated that it is 'a misconception that a payment can only be properly characterised as remuneration if there is a specific agreement fixing the level or rate of remuneration or defining a formula for ascertaining a definite amount to be paid. The essence of remuneration is that it is consideration for work done or to be done . . . [it] may take different forms. It is not necessarily in the conventional form of a direct payment of a regular wage.' The evidence was plain, particularly the minutes of the board, that the payments were made as remuneration.

Ratification of acts giving rise to liability

14.100 Section 239 puts the process of ratification by members of a breach of duty by directors onto a statutory footing. While broadly based on equitable rules, it imposes stricter requirements and s 239(7) makes it clear that to the extent that the statutory process is more lax, if at all, than the equitable rules and those in any enactment, then those rules prevail so as to supplement or increase the requirements laid down in the provision. Section 239(1) applies to the ratification by a company of conduct by a director 'amounting to negligence, default, breach of duty or breach of trust in relation to the company'. It therefore extends the ratification process to all breaches of the duties set out in the CA 2006, Part 10. It should also be recalled that ratification is also relevant to the court's consideration of whether or not to allow a derivative claim to succeed under s 263 (see Chapter 10).

14.101 The notice convening the members' meeting must state in explicit terms the purpose for which the meeting is being called insofar that it must provide a 'fair, candid, and reasonable explanation' of the business proposed (*Kaye v Croydon Tramways Co* (1898)). Failure to comply with this requirement will result in the resolution, if passed, being held ineffective as against those shareholders who dissented or who were absent from the meeting.

14.102 Section 239(2) provides that the decision of the company to ratify such conduct *must* be made by a resolution of the members. This appears to be based on the equitable rule noted by Lord Russell in *Regal (Hastings) Ltd v Gulliver* (see earlier), that the directors 'could, had they wished, have protected themselves by a resolution . . . of the Regal shareholders in general meeting'. On the other hand, where a director has fraudulently expropriated a company asset, the breach is non-ratifiable (*Cook v Deeks* (see earlier)).

14.103 Section 239(3) and (4) provide that the ratification is effective only if the votes of the director (qua member) in breach (and any member connected with him) are disregarded. This changes the pre-existing law (see, for example, *North-West Transportation Co Ltd v Beatty* (1887)), by disenfranchising the defaulting director. Section 239(6) provides that nothing in the provision affects the law on unanimous consent. This presumably means that the restrictions in s 239(3)–(4) on who may vote on a resolution will not apply when every member (including a director qua shareholder) votes, whether by informal means or otherwise, in favour of the resolution. In this regard it is settled that a breach of duty is ratifiable by obtaining the informal approval of *every* member who has a right to vote on such a resolution (*Re Duomatic Ltd* (1969)). The *Duomatic* rule only applies where unanimous consent can be shown to exist, it will not validate majority decisions made informally (see *Knopp v Thane Investments Ltd* (2002); *Extrasure Travel Insurances Ltd v Scattergood* (earlier); and *Dickinson v NAL Realisations (Staffordshire) Ltd* (2019)). Further, members must have full knowledge of the circumstances surrounding the breach and be aware of the fact that their assent is being sought (*Kaye v Croydon Tramways Co* (1898); and *EIC Services Ltd v Phipps* (2003)). In *Sharma v Sharma* (2013), Jackson LJ, applying *Re Home Treat Ltd* (1991), stressed that if the shareholders with full knowledge of the relevant facts *acquiesce* in the director's proposed conduct, then that may constitute consent (emphasis added).

Relief from liability

14.104 Section 1157 of the CA 2006, which replaces s 727 of the CA 1985, confers on the court the discretion to relieve, in whole or in part, an officer of the company from liability for negligence, default, breach of duty, or breach of trust where it appears to the court that the officer has acted *honestly and reasonably* and that, having regard to all the circumstances of the case, he ought fairly to be excused on such terms as the court thinks fit (s 1157 may also be available to shadow directors, see *Instant Access Properties Ltd v Rosser* (2018)). Although there is relatively little case law where relief has been granted, some guidance on the type of conduct for which relief will be denied has emerged. The courts will not grant relief where directors have abused their position for financial gain. In *Neptune (Vehicle Washing Equipment) Ltd v Fitzgerald (No 2)* (1995), a sole director, in breach of his fiduciary duties, had secured company resolutions in order to obtain the payment to himself of £100,892 for the termination of his service contract. He could not be said to have acted reasonably. Similarly, relief was refused in *Guinness plc v Saunders* (1990), on the basis that it was out of the question to relieve a director who retained £5.2 million paid to him, allegedly by way of remuneration, under a void contract (see also *Toone v Robbins* (2018)). In *Re Duckwari plc (No 2)* (1998), the point was made obiter that a director who intends to profit by way of a direct or indirect personal interest in a substantial property transaction could not be said to have acted reasonably and therefore would be denied relief under s 1157. Further, the discretion to relieve a director from liability will not be exercised merely because of the absence of any finding of bad faith or actual conflict and the absence of quantifiable loss by the company or because of the negligible profit to the defendant director (*Towers v Premier Waste Management Ltd* (2011), Mummery LJ; applied in *McGivney Construction Ltd v Kaminski* (2015), Lord Wollman). In *Burnden Holdings (UK) Ltd v Fielding* (2019), where a number of issues arose including directors' duties and alleged unlawful distributions, Zacaroli J considered the scope of the discretion which s 1157 confers on the court, observing:

> *While I do not accept that the discretion in s 1157 is fettered such that the court can never relieve a director from liability in circumstances where he or she is the recipient of the unlawful dividend, even where the company subsequently goes into liquidation so that the retention of the dividend can be said to be at the expense of creditors, I nevertheless*

accept that the fact that a director received an unlawful dividend at the expense of creditors is a powerful factor against granting relief. Whether that factor is enough to preclude relief being granted will depend upon matters such as the causal link between the dividend and prejudice to creditors, the length of time between the dividend and the action being commenced and whether the director retains the benefit of the dividend.

(Cf *Inn Spirit Ltd v Burns* (2002).)

14.105   The section requires a director seeking relief from liability to prove honesty and reasonableness. In *Re Welfab Engineers Ltd* (1990), the directors of a company which had been trading at a loss sold its principal asset for the lower of two competing bids on the understanding that the company would continue to be run as a going concern. Shortly afterwards the company went into liquidation and the liquidator brought misfeasance proceedings against the directors. It was held that the directors had not acted in breach of duty in accepting the lower offer but, even if they had, it was a case in which relief would be granted under s 1157. Hoffmann J took the view that the directors were motivated by an honest and reasonable desire to save the business and the jobs of the company's employees.

14.106   The requirement of reasonableness contained in s 1157 has presented the judges with the apparent conundrum of finding negligent conduct reasonable. The judicial response appears to suggest a willingness to dilute the objective character of the concept of reasonableness when determining the availability of relief. This is particularly discernible in Hoffmann LJ's judgment in *Re D'Jan of London Ltd* (1994), where he fashioned a solution based upon a subjective consideration of the director's conduct. A straightforward proposal form for property insurance contained numerous factual errors. The insurers subsequently repudiated liability on the policy when the company claimed for fire damage. The controlling director had signed the proposal without reading it. Hoffmann LJ thought that it was the kind of mistake that could be made by any busy man. In granting the director partial relief from liability, the court had regard to the fact that he held 99 of the company's shares (his wife held the other), and therefore the economic reality was that the interests the director had put at risk were those of himself and his wife. The judge observed:

It may seem odd that a person found to have been guilty of negligence, which involves failing to take reasonable care, can ever satisfy the court that he acted reasonably. Nevertheless, the section clearly contemplates that he may do so and it follows that conduct may be reasonable for the purposes of section 727 [now s 1157] despite amounting to lack of reasonable care at common law.

14.107   Similarly, in *Re Brian D Pierson (Contractors) Ltd* (2001), Hazel Williamson QC, sitting as a deputy judge in the High Court, applying *Re D'Jan of London Ltd* observed that "reasonableness" for the purpose of s 1157 must be meant to be capable of being satisfied by something less than compliance with the common law standard of care in negligence' (see also *Re Paycheck Services 3 Ltd* (2009)). The reasoning in these decisions discloses that the court can take into account considerations such as directors favouring corporate stakeholders, and the degree of culpability of his or her conduct when determining whether or not it is reasonable and therefore excusable. In the latter type of case, an honest but negligent director might therefore be relieved from liability provided the negligence in question was not gross but the kind of thing that could happen to any busy person (cf *Dorchester Finance Co Ltd v Stebbing* (1989)). Complete inactivity as a director is clearly unreasonable and cannot, therefore, be enlisted for the purposes of s 1157 to support the contention that the director had acted honestly and reasonably (*Lexi Holdings plc (in administration) v Luqman* (2007); see also *Re Brian D Pierson (Contractors) Ltd* (see earlier)). Subjectivity also significantly and peculiarly coloured the interpretation of s 1157 by the trial judge in *Re Simmon Box (Diamonds) Ltd* (2000). Peter Smith QC, sitting as a deputy judge of the Chancery Division, expressed the view that s 1157 is designed to achieve fairness as between wrongdoers. The judge thought it fair to grant partial relief to a 19-year-old director against the consequences of the actions, which were not caused by any direct fault on his part, but arose from the conduct of his father in whom he reposed too much trust. In the event, relief became irrelevant because the Court of Appeal found that the director was not liable at all (*Cohen v Selby* (2001)). In *Hedger v Adams* (at para **14.39**), the court expressed the view that had the director been found liable for breach of duty it would have relieved him from liability because he had followed professional advice. Having taken professional advice, there was no doubt that the defendant had been acting honestly and reasonably (see also *Re Finch (UK) plc* (at para **14.99**)); but note, claims for relief where it is argued that professional advice had been followed will depend upon whether full disclosure to the professional had been made, see the reasoning of the judge in *Chard Hunt Investments Ltd v Hunt* (at para **14.90**), where the defendant director argued that he had acted on the liquidator's advice.

14.108 However, Lord Hoffmann's subjective approach has been challenged. In *Bairstow v Queens Moat Houses plc* (2001), the directors, acting on the company's 1991 accounts that incorrectly showed inflated profits, unlawfully paid dividends which exceeded the available distributable reserves (see Chapter 7). Robert Walker LJ refuted the notion that reasonableness is capable of being satisfied from an essentially subjective point of view (see also *Re MDA Investment Management Ltd; Whalley v Doney* (2005); *Re Loquitur Ltd; IRC v Richmond* (2003); cf *Inn Spirit Ltd v Burns* (2002)). A similar view was also expressed by the judge in *Coleman Taymar Ltd v Oakes* (2001), although relief was granted in respect of the account of profit arising from a breach of fiduciary duty where, it will be recalled, the director had honestly and reasonably launched another company as a competitor while still technically a director of, but after the termination of his employment with, Coleman Taymar Ltd.

14.109 The issue of relief has also come to the fore in relation to the wrongful trading provision, s 214(1) of the Insolvency Act 1986 (see Chapters 3 and 17). By way of defence to such a claim, s 214(3) provides that the court will not hold a director liable if, once he found himself in a position where he knew or ought to have known that the company was going into insolvent liquidation, he took every step with a view to minimising the potential loss to the company's creditors. The facts which a director ought to know or ascertain for the purposes of s 214(3) are determined predominantly by way of objective assessment (s 214(4) refers to 'a reasonably diligent person' as the principal criterion). In *Re Produce Marketing Consortium Ltd* (1989), Knox J examined the interrelationship between s 1157 and the wrongful trading provision. He took the view that s 214 contains sufficient safeguards for the protection of directors and that the provision could not be easily accommodated with the 'essentially subjective approach that section 1157 . . . requires'. In *Re Brian D Pierson (Contractors) Ltd* (see earlier), the court held that s 1157 did not apply to a wrongful trading claim because Parliament did not intend both s 214 and s 1157 of the several Acts to be operated by the same judge at the same time.

FURTHER READING

This chapter links with the materials in Chapter 12 of *Hicks and Goo's Cases and Materials on Company Law* (Oxford, OUP, 2011, xl +649p).

Birks, 'The Content of Fiduciary Obligation' [2002] *TLI* 34.

Conaglen, 'The Nature and Function of Fiduciary Loyalty' [2005] *LQR* 452.

Curl, 'Remote, Doubtful, Dubious, Probable, Likely: What are the Conclusions from *BTI v Sequanta*?' [2019] *ICR* 333.

Edelman, 'When do Fiduciary Duties Arise?' [2010] *LQR* 302.

Edmunds and Lowry, 'The Continuing Value of Relief for Directors' Breach of Duty' [2003] *MLR* 195.

Elliott and Mitchell, 'Remedies for Dishonest Assistance' [2004] *MLR* 16.

Etherton, 'The Legitimacy of Proprietary Relief' [2014] *Birkbeck LR* 59.

Finch, 'Company Directors: Who Cares about Skill and Care' [1992] *MLR* 179.

Grantham, 'The Unanimous Consent Rule in Company Law' [1993] *CLJ* 245.

Ho, 'Bribes and the Constructive Trust as a Chameleon' [2012] *LQR* 485.

Kershaw, 'Lost in Translation: Corporate Opportunities in Comparative Perspective' (2005) 25 *OJLS* 603.

Lim, 'Directors Fiduciary Duties: A New Analytical Framework' [2013] *LQR* 242.

Lowry, 'Self-Dealing Directors—Constructing A Regime of Accountability' [1997] *NILQ* 211.

Lowry, 'Judicial Pragmatism: Directors' Duties and Post-resignation Conflicts of Duty' [2008] *JBL* 83.

Lowry, 'The Duty of Loyalty of Company Directors: Bridging the Accountability Gap Through Efficient Disclosure' [2009] *CLJ* 607.

Lowry, 'The Irreducible Core of the Duty of Care, Skill and Diligence of Company Directors' [2012] *MLR* 249.

Lowry and Edmunds, 'The Corporate Opportunity Doctrine: The Shifting Boundaries of the Duty and its Remedies' [1998] *MLR* 515.

Lowry and Edmunds, 'Of Resigning Directors: Lessons in Reform' [2013] *HKLJ* 55.

Nolan, 'The Proper Purpose Doctrine and Company Directors' in Rider (ed) *The Realm of Company Law* (London, Kluwer Law International, 1998).

Penner, *The Law of Trusts* (Oxford, OUP, 2019), ch 12.

Prentice, 'The Corporate Opportunity Doctrine' [1974] *MLR* 464.

Riley, 'The Company Director's Duty of Care and Skill: The Case for an Onerous but Subjective Standard' [1999] *MLR* 697.

Sealy, 'The Director As Trustee' [1967] *CLJ* 83.

Smith, 'Conflict, Profit, Bias, Misuse of Power: Dimensions of Governance' in Miller and Harding (eds) *Fiduciaries and Trust: Ethics, Politics, Economics and Law* (Cambridge, CUP, 2020).

Teele Langford, 'The Duty of Directors to Act Bona Fide in the Interests of the Company: A Positive Fiduciary Duty? Australia and the UK Compared' [2011] *JCLS* 215.

Watts, '*Tyrrell v Bank of London*—An Inside Look at an Inside Job' [2013] *LQR* 527.

Worthington, 'Reforming Directors' Duties' [2001] *MLR* 439.

SELF-TEST QUESTIONS

1   When directors exercise their duties on behalf of the company, whose interests are they required to consider?

2   A company is in need of additional capital. The board decides to issue additional shares and makes an allotment to an existing shareholder, X. It does so in preference to another shareholder, Y, who has created difficulties for the board by insisting that the company pursue ethical policies and whose shareholding the board now wishes to dilute.

    Advise Y who wishes to have the allotment set aside.

3   Arthur is the managing director of Apex plc, a large computer technology company. In recent years the company has enjoyed record levels of profitability. It is generally recognised that the company's success is due to Arthur's technical expertise and management skills. The articles of association of Apex plc provide:

   90.   Remuneration of directors. The board shall fix the annual remuneration of the directors provided that without the consent of the company in general meeting such remuneration shall not exceed the sum of £1,000,000 per annum.

   91.   The board may, in addition to the remuneration authorised in article 90, grant special remuneration to any director who serves on any committee of the company.'

In the past 12 months, the following events have occurred:

(i)   Arthur is paid £1 million consultation fee for successfully guiding Apex plc through its takeover of Xon Ltd, a competing business. This payment was agreed by a special committee of the Apex plc board constituted to advise the main board on mergers and acquisitions.

(ii)   Arthur forms a private company, Macro Electronics Ltd, which develops software programs for computers. Arthur places large orders with Macro Electronics Ltd without informing Apex plc of his interest in the company.

(iii) Arthur is approached by Bsquare Corporation, a large US company, with the offer to enter into a joint venture with them in order to develop a revolutionary word processing program. Arthur resigns his post with Apex plc and accepts the offer. He makes a handsome profit. Apex plc has recently been taken over by Ytel plc. The details of the events outlined above have now come to the notice of the board of Ytel plc. They wish to pursue any claims they may have against Arthur.

Advise the board of Ytel plc.

4   Are the duties of directors too stringent?

5   'The statutory statement of directors' duties contained in the CA 2006 does little to clarify or simplify the confused state of the case law.' Discuss.

15 Corporate governance 1: corporate governance and corporate theory

Introduction

15.1 Corporate governance has become almost a subject in its own right over the past decade and university courses on corporate governance now abound. This might give the impression that it is a new topic but that would be misleading. Corporate governance issues are as old as companies themselves. Despite this longevity the phrase 'corporate governance' is somewhat malleable. Almost every article or book on the subject offers us a different view as to what the phrase means or rather, means to the author concerned. At its broadest, it concerns the question of who should own and control the company and at its narrowest, it purely concerns the relationship between the shareholders and the directors. However, it is a vast and growing area and so to make it manageable it is divided here into two chapters. In this chapter we will explore the history and theory associated with corporate governance. In Chapter 16 we will explore the specific UK corporate governance debate and its effects.

A brief history of corporate governance

15.2 The 18th- and 19th-century business landscape was largely filled with unincorporated business associations in which individual owners were also the controllers. This is often referred to as the traditional enterprise model. As we have discussed in earlier chapters some large charter and statutory companies existed and were important in providing a model for the emergence of the registered company but they were by no means the dominant business form. The key corporate governance factor at this time was the fact that owners were also managers of the business. However, the emergence of the registered company provided these traditional enterprises with access to incorporated status and slowly the corporation became the normal means by which businesses operated. Until the end of the 19th century these registered companies remained essentially traditional enterprises utilising the advantages of corporate form. That is, they remained businesses in which the owners were also the controllers.

15.3 At the turn of the 19th century three factors had converged. First, a largely untaxed middle class had amassed a huge amount of wealth over the course of the mid- to late 19th century which needed a home. Second, the registered public company with its ability to facilitate large-scale investment with minimal risk to the investor was easily available. Third, large-scale projects involving the exploitation of transport and communications technology were emerging to tap into the wealth available for investment. The result was the emergence of a corporation where ownership was separated from control. As Chandler (1990) explains:

> [t]he building and operating of the rail and telegraph systems called for the creation of a new type of business enterprise. The massive investment required to construct those systems and the complexities of their operations brought the separation of ownership from management. The enlarged enterprises came to be operated by teams of salaried managers who had little or no equity in the firm. The owners, numerous and scattered, were investors with neither the experience, the information, nor the time to make the myriad decisions needed to maintain a constant flow of goods, passengers, and messages. Thousands of shareholders could not possibly operate a railroad or a telegraph system.

15.4 The arrival of a successful managerial class in these large-scale transport and communications companies who controlled without owning was the catalyst for the opening up of mass markets and further industrial growth to provide for those markets. In essence the success of the managerial class was self-perpetuating. As more markets were opened up by manager-dominated rail and telegraph companies, more managerial companies emerged to exploit those markets and more investment was in turn available to fund those companies. Over the course of the 20th century the managerial corporation became the main economic actor in many of the world's major economies.

15.5 While 19th-century figures such as Adam Smith had made the observation that managers of joint stock companies were separate from the owners, for the first few decades of the 20th century the emergence of the managerial firm went almost unnoticed by academic commentators. However, by the time of the stock market crash in the USA in 1929 and the Great Depression that followed major academic figures were writing about the separation of ownership and control and its associated problems. In 1932 Berle and Means published *The Modern Corporation and Private Property* which was to become the classic work on the separation of ownership and control.

15.6 Berle and Means (1932) made two key observations about the operation of American companies in the 1930s. The first was that shareholders were so numerous (described as dispersed ownership) that no individual shareholder had an interest in attempting to control management. They claimed that 65 per cent of the largest two hundred US companies were controlled entirely by their managers. Second, they expressed concern that managers were not only unaccountable to shareholders but exercised enormous economic power which had the potential to harm society. As Mizruchi (2004) described it:

> Berle and Means' concern about the separation of ownership from control was not only about managers' lack of accountability to investors. It was also a concern about managers' lack of accountability to society in general. Berle and Means thus wrote of a small group, sitting at the head of enormous organisations, with the power to build, and destroy, communities, to generate great productivity and wealth, but also to control the distribution of that wealth, without regard for those who elected them (the stockholders) or those who depended on them (the larger public). This was hardly a cause for celebration, and Berle and Means, in the tradition of Thomas Jefferson, expressed considerable concern about this development.

15.7 These managerial corporations continued to grow and became the dominant business form of the 20th century. However, by the 1970s the legitimacy of the managerial corporation was increasingly questioned and by the 1980s a change was occurring in the way shareholders were behaving. Reform in state pension and healthcare funding had pushed enormous amounts of money into the equity markets through institutional investors (pension funds, investment funds, and insurance companies). At the same time barriers to capital inflows and outflows were removed in many countries, resulting in international investment funds operating in both the London and New York markets. In all, the institutional investor emerged as a dominant force in those markets—holding nearly 80 per cent of the shares in the UK market and 50–60 per cent of the shares in the US market—by the late 1980s.

15.8 While institutional investors preferred to remain largely passive investors for the most part, they did favour market mechanisms in order to promote shareholder wealth maximisation. Thus share options grew as a percentage of managements' total salary as this focused management on share price as a measure of performance and the non-executive director emerged as a monitoring mechanism on management. By the 1990s the excesses of corporate behaviour in the market-oriented 1980s resulted once again in public disquiet about corporate accountability. In particular, in the early 1990s the German economy and its company law system oriented towards the inclusive stakeholder (employees, customers, and the general public) appeared to have triumphed over the recession-bound UK/US system. As a result pressures increased on companies to recognise 'stakeholder' constituencies which continue to the present day, even though the German economy is now deep in recession. More recently, institutional investors have been retreating from shares as they seek better returns elsewhere. This may be an early indication that the Berle and Means corporation is undergoing transformation as the largest shareholders withdraw to be replaced by more activist investment and hedge funds (see Dignam (2013)).

15.9 The emergence of the Berle and Means corporation has not been universal. Indeed it only emerged in the UK in the late 1960s. In most of the rest of the world a managerial class emerged but not accompanied by dispersed ownership. Rather founding families, other companies, the state, and banks held controlling stakes in these companies. Thus, outside the UK and the USA the accountability issue has not formed such a large part of the corporate governance debate. The differences in the corporate governance systems around the world have also (as we will discuss in the section on global corporate governance) become a major area of study based around the preconditions necessary for the emergence of a US/UK corporate governance system. As we will observe in the next section the corporate governance debate in the USA/UK within the general framework of corporate theory was greatly enlivened by the observations of Berle and Means.

Corporate theory

15.10 In this section we attempt something both difficult and dangerous—an overview of the major influences on corporate theory. This is difficult because it involves distilling centuries of thought and numerous complex theories into a few pages. It is dangerous because it may convey the impression that once it is read the reader will know all there is to know about corporate theory. So we start this section with a 'health warning'—while hopefully the following section provides an accessible overview of the progression of corporate theory over the past 200 years it is not complete or simple. Theory is by its nature complex and we make no attempt to make it less so here because to do so would only create a false impression. In order to give it form the section emphasises major influences and ignores minor ones even though they may have been important in their time. Where there is a choice of theorists to discuss we have chosen the one whose work we think epitomises the theory best. Where we discuss a theory it is just an overview of its major contribution to corporate theory and not a complete description. Additionally, as UK corporate theory has a distinct character we will discuss it in Chapter 16 rather than here.

15.11 As we discussed briefly in Chapter 8, the fact the state had the dominant role in the formation of companies through charter or statute led to the view that the company was a concession or privilege from the state. The concession theory (hereafter, concession) is also linked with the fiction theory (hereafter, fiction). Fiction theory similarly emphasises the law's key role in the creation of the corporation. It views the corporation as a legal person rather than a natural one thus it is a fiction. Concession and fiction theories are therefore bound together because the corporation in a concession analysis is simply a legal creation of the state and therefore, according to fiction theory, a legal fiction. They are also bound together because they have the same essential observation to make about company law, that is, that the state's role in the creation of corporations is central and therefore state intervention in corporate activity is more easily justified. The corporation, after all, is just a manifestation of the will of the state.

15.12   The weakness of concession and fiction theories is that they have little to say on the subject of the private individuals behind the corporation. Once registered companies arrived in the mid-19th century and incorporation became a simple matter of registration rather than requiring a charter or specific Act of Parliament, this weakness became very apparent. Other theories arose to challenge the dominance of concession and fiction theories which were better equipped to deal with the diminished role of the state in forming the company. These theories are known as the corporate realist and aggregate theories (hereafter, corporate realism and aggregate).

15.13   Aggregate theory drew on Roman law theory surrounding the Roman *Societas* (association) which had legal personality. The *Societas* was a particularly important influence in the evolution of the company as it directly influenced common law partnerships and the continental European *société en commandite*. These entities were formed by individuals who agreed to associate with each other for a common purpose. From this, aggregate theory emphasised the real persons behind the corporation. The law was not central to the formation of the company, rather the company was an aggregate of the individuals who had contracted for its formation. Therefore, the private individuals behind the aggregate are the focus of the corporation's rights and obligations. The corporation in an aggregate analysis has no independent existence and everything is explained by reference to the members of the corporation.

15.14   Aggregate theory had two significant claims to make about the operation of company law. First, as the company is formed by private contracting individuals state interference in what is viewed as essentially a private arrangement becomes very difficult to justify as it would be an interference with the individual's freedom to contract. Second, and perhaps most significantly, as everything to do with the corporation was only relevant by reference to the contracting individuals behind it, the theory served to justify the primacy that company law gives to shareholders as the key contracting individuals behind the corporation.

15.15   However, with the arrival of the managerial company aggregate theory began to struggle for influence. First, as shares became increasingly transferable and shareholders behaved more like speculators than owners the idea that a legally binding contract was behind the corporation started to lose its legitimacy. Second, the separation of ownership from control itself raised questions about relating the company only to its shareholders. Identifying the shareholders from a fluctuating dispersed group was difficult and they seemed uninterested in exercising control. At the same time managers had also emerged as a significant force within the corporation who exerted more power than the shareholders. Accompanying this decline in the shareholders' influence was the sense that the corporation was now a thing in itself which affected a much wider constituency than just its shareholders. In particular aggregate theory has great difficulty explaining corporate personality, specifically the fact that the company owns its own property and that fiduciary duties are owed to the company. Corporate realism emerged to offer an explanation better suited to the managerial company.

15.16 Corporate realism is the theory that probably seems the strangest to a 21st-century reader. It originated from 19th-century German theorists who considered the company to have a 'real' separate existence from its shareholders. Essentially it argued that once a collective is formed it takes on a life of its own which cannot be referenced back to its members. The sum of the individuals' interests does not in any way equate to the interests of the collective. The collective has interests and objectives which may not change even though the members of the collective may change many times over. As in aggregate theory the state is irrelevant to the existence of the collective. Its legitimacy is established by the coming together of its original members but once the collective is formed it continues on its own independent way without reference to individual members.

15.17 The theory offers some important insights into the nature of the managerial company. As the corporation is a real person with its own interests it can in no sense be owned by the shareholders. The shareholders have no primacy within the realist model; rather the company's interests and objectives as defined by its managers are paramount. This being so, corporate realism goes a long way to legitimising the manager-dominated companies that arose at the beginning of the 20th century. It did not however deal with the managerial accountability issue as it assumed a neutral disinterested management. This is something that aggregate theory solves by emphasising the primacy of the shareholders, i.e. the managers are accountable to the shareholders. Thus, corporate realism left a key question unanswered, that is, what are the interests of this real person if they are not equated with the shareholders? Additionally, corporate realism is somewhat malleable as far as the state is concerned. Some proponents of corporate realism considered the corporate person subject to state regulation as any powerful person who could affect the community would be. Others considered the corporate person as a purely private person and thus free from state control.

15.18 These deficiencies in corporate realism went largely unchallenged until the Great Depression in the 1930s. The first major challenge to it was the work of Berle and Means (1932), primarily their concern about unaccountable managers. However, while *The Modern Corporation and Private Property* was an important milestone in the corporate governance literature it was a debate between Adolf Berle and Merrick Dodd played out in the pages of the *Harvard Law Review* that was to shape the course of the corporate governance debate significantly.

15.19 Dodd (1932) sought to provide an answer to the key unanswered question of corporate realism: what are the interests of this real person if they are not equated with the shareholders? Dodd set out a corporate realist model where the company is a real person and not an aggregate of its members. Just as other real persons have citizenship responsibilities that require personal self-sacrifice a corporation has social responsibilities which may sometimes be contrary to its economic objectives. In turn, managers of this citizen corporation are expected to exercise their powers in a manner which recognises the company's social responsibility to employees, consumers, and the general public. In providing this pluralist formulation Dodd emphatically rejected the notion of shareholder primacy and provided a clear basis for the separation of ownership from control.

15.20   Berle (1932) in his response to Dodd's article opposed Dodd's solution. He believed that the Dodd answer was too vague. It would be practically unenforceable and lead to the furtherance of managerial dominance. Instead he sought to focus the company's accountability mechanism on just the shareholders. He proposed an aggregate theory in which managers are trustees for the shareholders not the corporation. Thus, the managers are accountable to the shareholders and shareholder wealth maximisation is the sole corporate interest.

15.21   The two views broadly shaped the debate over the period up to the 1960s. However, the apparent and tangible success of managerial companies after the Second World War caused the Berle thesis great difficulty. Despite the lack of any legislative intervention in the USA to promote the Dodd pluralist approach, managerial companies did indeed appear to be able to act like corporate citizens and balance the needs of shareholders, employees, and the general public. By 1959 just as evidence was emerging (see later) that supported Berle's claims of a lack of managerial accountability in a pluralist model, Berle gave up and adopted a pluralist approach.

The introduction of economic theory

15.22   However, by the early 1970s changes in the global economy began to affect the managerial company's ability to balance these different constituencies. In turn aggregate theories were redeveloped by economists and began to challenge corporate realism once again. In this section we deal largely with the economic theories that have influenced corporate legal scholarship.

15.23   Economic theory is concerned primarily with efficiency. Here we are talking about two types of efficiency, first, that resources are allocated efficiently and, second, that production is efficient, that is, output is maximised from a given input. Using these tools economic theory can test whether a company (firm) is operating efficiently or whether company law is promoting efficiency. While it may seem odd to company lawyers, traditional (neo-classical) economic theory did not recognise the firm in its analysis, viewing it purely as an individual capable of operating in a marketplace. The internal arrangements of the firm were irrelevant and so neo-classical economics had no real insight into the separation of ownership from control. The focus of neo-classical economics is instead on the market and its equilibrium mechanisms.

15.24   In studying markets it makes four key suppositions. The first is that the laws of supply and demand will determine price. That is, if the price of a good is higher in one market than another, sellers will move to the higher market until the price difference is eliminated. It is in essence the market that establishes the price. As the market is the key mechanism for price setting any state interference with this mechanism is unwelcome as it causes ineffi-ciency. Thus neo-classical economics provides a justification for limiting the state's role in regulating both markets and the firms operating in them.

15.25 The second assumption is that the market itself is perfectly competitive. That is, there are a large number of firms producing an identical product, with the same costs and no barriers to entering that market. The third assumption is that the firm has only one objective and that is profit maximisation in both the short and long term. Additionally the firm pursues this goal without reference to the response of other firms in the market-place. The fourth assumption is that the firm has perfect certainty about its activities. That is, it has complete information about all present and future events that would influence its activities. This allows the firm to act in perfect certainty and make a rational profit-maximising choice.

15.26 Therefore, in the neo-classical perfect marketplace the price is set by supply and demand and the rational firm operating in it in full knowledge of the present and future makes output decisions in order to maximise its profit without reference to the response of other firms. Critics of neo-classical economics have focused on the fact that it makes funda-mental assumptions that may not bear any relation to reality. The following should give a flavour of those criticisms. 'A neo-classical economist falls down a well. A passer-by rushes over to see if he is all right and looks down the well to see the economist standing at the bottom of the well looking up. The passer-by shouts down that he is going to get help but the neo-classical economist replies "No need, I'll assume a ladder".'

15.27 The managerial company in particular caused great difficulty for neo-classical theory as its very existence destroyed some of its key assumptions and therefore its predictive ability. First, the large size of these managerial companies meant they operated in markets with few other firms, in other words, an imperfectly competitive marketplace. Second, if management is purely responding to market stimulus in a rational profit-maximising way the separation of ownership from control has no significance. Management of the firm either is neutral or is purely an agent for the market's price mechanism—in this manage-ment has no discretion. An owner-controller will also be responding to market stimulus in a rational profit-maximising way. Therefore, the outcomes in a neo-classical market for a managerial company and an owner-managed firm are the same. As a result neo-classical theory had no way to explain the evident difference between owner-managed and manager-dominated companies.

15.28 By the 1930s, at the same time as Berle and Dodd were arguing about their solution to the managerial corporation, neo-classicists were re-evaluating the role of the firm in their theory. A revisionist group of economists directly attacked the underlying assumptions of neo-classicism by arguing that imperfect markets were the norm, firms did respond to one another, firms set prices not the market, and profit maximisation could not be assumed. By the 1950s mainstream economists were beginning to facilitate this revisionist view and a managerial theory of the firm arose.

15.29   The focus of managerial theory was the ability of the managerial firm to subvert the neo-classical model. As Williamson (1974) later put it '[t]he justification for the profit maximisation assumption is its usefulness, and whereas this may be substantial for some purposes, it may be less valuable for others'. Thus, the internal organisation of the firm became the focus of economic theory. Williamson (1964) for example considered that managerial discretion was used to benefit managers themselves, that self-interest was not just made up of salary but also included status and power. Williamson argued that managers favoured using their discretion in ways which directly enhanced their power and status. Interestingly, he argued that the key to managers being able to maximise their own self-interest was their ability to achieve profits above the level necessary to retain their position. This excess profit was in effect the amount they could spend on their own self-interest (see also Koopmans (1957)).

15.30   From a similar assumption of managerial maximisation of self-interest Marris (1964) argued that long-term growth was the main objective of managers. In a neo-classical model growth is a by-product of profit maximisation but in Marris's managerial model growth is the main objective. As Chandler (1977) later stated, 'in making administrative decisions, career managers preferred policies that favoured the long-term stability and growth of their enterprises to those that maximised current profits'. However, this pursuit of growth imposes a significant constraint. For a time shareholders may be tolerant of the pursuit of growth as it will enhance the long-term profitability of the company. Slowly over time, as it becomes apparent to shareholders that a return on their investment may never occur in a continuous growth cycle, they may sell their shares. This will depress the share price and make the company vulnerable to a takeover and the management being replaced. It follows from this that managers cannot achieve the maximum growth rate but rather have to ensure that some of the available capital for growth goes back to the shareholders.

15.31   Baumol (1959, 1967) however offered a narrower managerial model. He argued that sales revenue maximisation was the main objective of management, rather than profit maximisation. Sales revenue could maximise profits but this would only be by chance; it would not be a main objective. Managers' salaries, corporate rankings, and managerial prestige were often tied to sales revenue and therefore, he argued, sales revenue maximisation had become the primary goal of the managerial firm.

15.32   Baumol also recognised that there were internal and external constraints on the managers' discretion. Dispersed shareholders might leave managers to pursue their sales objectives as long as a certain amount of profit flowed back to them but if managers did not meet these expectations the shareholders might remove them and replace them with managers who would meet these expectations. Another constraint on managerial discretion was the threat of a hostile takeover. If the shareholders were unhappy with management policy they might sell shares and thus affect the share price. If that price was low enough another company might buy all the shares in the company, replace the management, and run it more efficiently or sell off its assets for a profit. Accordingly, managers had to exercise their discretion to achieve 'profit satisficing' for their share-holders, in other words providing the minimal amount of profit necessary to stop the shareholders exercising their removal power or selling their shares.

15.33 The power of managerial theory is that it provides plausible explanations for the internal motivations of the management of the firm. Therefore, it has some predictive power in imperfect markets. In general the overall effect of managerial theory with its demonstra-tion of managerial self-interest was detrimental to the claims of corporate realists and the citizen corporation. Crucially the evidence and analysis of managerial economists began to influence corporate theory. In a series of articles over the course of the 1960s Manne (1987) utilised a managerial market-oriented analysis to argue that managers were more accountable to shareholders than was assumed. He argued that managers have to behave if they are to tap capital markets in the future, if they are to enhance the firm's reputation and their own, and if they are to avoid being taken over.

15.34 By the 1970s, however, economic conditions had deteriorated and the managerial firm had become the focus of general discontent. No longer was it seen as fulfilling a corporate citi-zenship role, rather the very legitimacy of the managerial firm was increasingly questioned. At the beginning of the 1970s the work of Coase (1937) began to influence a number of economists. Coase had been writing on the nature of the firm during the Great Depression. He was concerned primarily with the failure of neo-classical economics to deal with the organisational nature of the firm. He had asked a very simple question, 'Why are there these islands of conscious power?' In other words, if the market is the price setter, how come the decision-making process in the firm comes before the market-price mechanism operates? Coase argued that operating in the marketplace had costs to the individuals who use it. Uncertainty was an inherent part of the process of contracting in the marketplace. Contrary to the neo-classical assumption of rationality they did not operate in perfect knowledge and so transaction costs arose because of that uncertainty. For example individuals had to spend money acquiring information and enforcing contracts, all because of market uncertainty.

15.35 The firm according to Coase was a solution to these uncertainties as it mitigated the effect of transaction costs. Inside the firm relationships were more certain because of the greater levels of cooperation. Individuals could come together to minimise costs within the firm under the direction of an entrepreneur who would coordinate the resources of the firm. The firm would continue to grow until the costs of coordination within the firm were equal to the cost of market coordination. The importance of Coase's work was in its recognition that firms were not individuals operating in the marketplace as neo-classical theory assumed, nor did market equilibrium forces simply flow through it. Firms did exist and had to be analysed differently. As Zingales (2000) noted:

> The link between theory of the firm and corporate governance is even more compel-
> ling . . . The word 'governance' implies the exercise of authority. But in a free-market

economy, why do we need any form of authority? Isn't the market responsible for allocating all resources efficiently without the intervention of any authority? In fact, Coase (1937) taught us that using the market has its costs, and firms alleviate these costs by substituting the price mechanism with the exercise of authority. By and large, corporate governance is the study of how this authority is allocated and exercised. But in order to understand how this authority is allocated and exercised, we first need to know why it is needed in the first place. We need, thus, a theory of the firm.

15.36 Alchian and Demsetz (1972) attempted to provide such a theory of the firm in taking issue with Coase's transaction cost theory by disputing the primary role of the entrepreneur (management) in the firm. They considered that Coase's coordinating entrepreneur had no legitimacy and went on to argue that the firm was in fact a marketplace (i.e. market forces did flow through it) within which management did not direct or authorise so much as constantly renegotiate the contracts within the firm. Taking the example of a worker in the firm they argue that it is deceptive to view the worker as simply subject to the will of management. The worker is indeed ordered to carry out tasks but the worker also orders the manager to provide payment. They describe the firm as a nexus of contracts (note the resonance with aggregate theory) in which there is equality of power and therefore no hierarchy. In the constant renegotiation process both sides are satisfied with the outcome.

15.37 Alchian and Demsetz did recognise one key difference between markets and the firm. That is that the firm operates as a non-hierarchical team of workers. As they work together there is opportunity for members of the team to become inefficient and so a monitoring agent is needed if the team is to be efficient. The shareholders are thus given this role in the firm. The shareholders are forced to carry out this role as they have the primary claim over the earnings of the firm once the creditors have been paid. In essence all the others within the team (employees and creditors) have contracted for a fixed sum. The shareholders have no such security, they might get nothing, and so have the incentive to monitor. In order to carry out the monitoring role the shareholders are able to change the membership of the team if necessary. The Alchian and Demsetz firm thus places the shareholders in the key role of monitor and directly attacks the managerial firm as being inefficient because it is unconstrained by shareholders. The implication of this is that the managerial firm does not contain the necessary mechanisms to focus managerial power on the goal of profit maximisation.

15.38 Jensen and Meckling (1976) added to the Alchian and Demsetz nexus of contracts analysis by arguing that the relationship between the shareholders and management was that of agent and principal. However, the manager of the firm knows more about the operation of that firm than the shareholders. In order for the shareholders to effectively ensure that the manager was making decisions in an efficient manner the shareholders incur 'agency costs', that is the cost of the shareholders acquiring enough information themselves about the firm's operation to be able to check on management. Shareholders will only bear these agency costs if the part of the firm's earnings that flows to them is greater than the cost of monitoring. Owner-managed firms have few or no agency costs but the agency cost increases as management's ownership decreases. In the managerial firm where management have no significant ownership the agency costs are highest.

15.39 However, the agency costs are diminished by a number of market-oriented factors, i.e. market forces do flow through the firm. First, as the managerial theorists have noted, the efficient operation of the market for corporate control (hostile takeovers) acts as a restraint on management. If agency costs are too high this will be reflected in a low share price and a takeover bid which will replace the inefficient management. Second, the levels of debt can also constrain management. High levels of debt increase the risk of the firm entering insolvent liquidation as a result of management failure. Debt therefore results in a lack of discretionary cash surplus for management to satisfy their self-interest and operates to keep management efficient. If the firm does generate a discretionary cash surplus this should therefore be returned to the shareholders to replicate the effect of debt on management. Third, management will be highly disciplined where the firm operates in a competitive marketplace. In such a marketplace the threat of insolvency is exacerbated because of the need to cut costs to remain competitive.

15.40 Agency cost theory did not have the field all to itself; others, notably Williamson (1975), were developing a different theory similarly dealing with the work of Coase. Williamson argued like Coase that transaction costs borne by those operating in the marketplace did indeed mean that markets were imperfect. The firm with its organisational hierarchy operated to mitigate the effect of market inefficiency for participants. Williamson (1984) further extended his analysis to justify shareholder primacy on the basis of the inability of shareholders to renegotiate their position. Shareholders buy their shares without any contractual assurance that management will maximise profits. Employees and creditors in contrast can seek assurances in their contracts and even renegotiate better protections over time. Shareholders are stuck with their deal for as long as they have their shares. For Williamson the organisational structure of the firm did not just provide a way of mitigating market inefficiencies but also was formed to protect the shareholders' risk and ensure their claims in particular.

15.41 The nexus of contracts theory, while largely a reformulation of aggregate theory, provided the additional tools based upon economic efficiency to attack the managerial firm and the pluralism of corporate realists such as Dodd. In a nexus of contracts analysis the firm is reduced to contracts and markets and thus the firm is not in any sense a real person. Therefore, it has no interests of its own into which one can place corporate social responsibility. Additionally, the allocation of resources by management to social issues would be inefficient as the monitoring mechanism within the firm in a nexus of contracts analysis ensures efficiency through a presumption that shareholders maximise their own self-interest.

15.42 As with aggregate theory, the nexus of contracts theory also diminishes the role of the state in regulating companies. As we have observed, if the company is viewed as a public creation then justifying state regulation of corporate affairs is relatively easy. If it is viewed as a private concern then state interference in its activities becomes more difficult to justify and the methods by which it is acceptable to interfere become more restrictive. Mandatory rules therefore, which override any private agreements between contracting parties, are not acceptable in a nexus of contracts analysis nor are any rules which interfere with the efficient operation of the marketplace. For example mandatory company law provisions which impede takeovers would offend both aspects of the theory. The state's role is therefore reduced to facilitating private contracting arrangements where possible by providing default rules which apply in the absence of any agreement to the contrary (e.g. the model articles) or enabling rules which provide a framework for private parties to carry out certain functions, for example winding up the company in an insolvency. In essence the strength of the nexus of contracts theory is its ability to provide clear certain answers to many aspects of corporate behaviour. In particular it can easily solve any managerial accountability issues. It also, as Cheffins (1999) has pointed out, woke company lawyers up by giving them something interesting to think about. It is not, however, without weaknesses—especially where corporate personality is concerned. Despite many attempts the theory has yet convincingly to accommodate the fact that the directors owe fiduciary obligations to the company and not the shareholders and that the company owns its own property. As we will see later, a team production analysis of the company may offer a convincing alternative to a contracts analysis.

15.43   Until the end of the 1980s shareholder theories, whether through a nexus of contracts analysis or a Williamson/Coaseian analysis, ruled the roost. In particular agency cost theory found a ready audience as institutional investors (pension funds, insurance companies, and investment funds) grew to become the largest shareholders in the USA and the UK. These institutional investors preferred market-oriented solutions because they minimised the monitoring costs they would otherwise incur. Shareholder-oriented accountability became the active focus of institutional investors with the promotion of agency cost-reducing monitoring mechanisms such as share options, non-executive directors, and hostile takeovers during the 1980s. Corporate realism with its idea of corporate citizenship declined in influence once the focus in the US and the UK Government and private sector was on the promotion of market-based solutions.

15.44   However, a growing disquiet over the excesses of the untrammelled market (in particular the takeovers market) and the resulting recession in the late 1980s provided a space in which this shareholder focus could be challenged. The disquiet revolved around the detrimental effect market-based solutions appeared to have on stakeholder constituencies such as employees, consumers, and the general public. Soon stakeholder efficiency arguments began to appear. Freeman and Evans (1990), while starting with a Williamson/Coaseian analysis, depart from it by arguing that stakeholders are risk-takers in a similar manner to shareholders and therefore the organisational structure of the firm should reflect this fact. Hill and Jones (1992), while starting with an agency cost theory analysis, went on to develop a 'stakeholder agency theory' to justify a wider focus for managerial discretion. In an important theoretical development Blair and Stout (1999) have argued against viewing the corporation through a principal–agent prism but instead as a vehicle for team production. As such they argue that the company provides a means through which shareholders, creditors, executives, employees, and other potential 'stakeholders', for their own benefit, jointly relinquish control over their resources to a professional board of directors. Bainbridge (2002) continued the board-centred proposition by arguing that board power is legitimised as the product of centuries of experimentation and evolution that resulted in a legal model of the corporation that focused corporate power on the board. In the aftermath of the financial crisis, models of the corporation focused on more representative stakeholder boards emerged (Greenfield (2008)). In turn Roe (2014), concerned about this direction of travel, cautioned against moving too far towards protecting boards from shareholder influence. In the UK, as we will explore in Chapter 16, a continuing theme within the corporate governance literature is a focus on the extent of corporate power itself as legitimising constraints on director power.

15.45 An interesting development of additional note is the work of Hansmann and Kraakman (2000) who, although adopting a nexus of contract approach as a starting point, emphasise the proprietary nature of firms. They point out that company law enables a company to own its own assets and go on to argue that it is not possible for contract, property, or agency law to achieve a key aspect of corporate behaviour they call 'affirmative' asset partitioning. Hansmann and Kraakman observed that not only does limited liability protect the shareholders from the company's creditors but that it can also serve to put the business assets of an individual out of reach of that individual's personal creditors. By forming a company and placing his business assets in the company in return for shares in it the individual no longer has any legal interest in the assets. This serves to partition the personal assets of the shareholder from his business assets. If the shareholder is insolvent the personal creditors can take the shares but cannot get at the assets of the company. The company can then, as it owns the assets, give other creditors priority over the business assets. The company itself can also partition its assets through subsidiaries in order to protect its assets. They claim that this can only be achieved through legislation. The importance of Hansmann and Kraakman's observation is that a nexus of contracts analysis is insufficient to explain this key part of corporate behaviour. It means that concession theory may make a comeback as the state has a larger role in a proprietary analysis than was assumed, with all the regulatory legitimacy implications that fact carries with it. Other scholars, notably Armour and Whincop (2004), have subsequently argued that the foundations of company law are proprietary in nature.

Global corporate governance

15.46 An important sub-set of the corporate governance debate has been introduced by high-profile studies by La Porta et al (1998, 1999, 2003) who have argued that forms of legal protection for shareholders are crucial in determining whether a market-based economy in which the Berle and Means corporation plays a crucial role will arise. The 'law matters' thesis on which it is based is however a relatively old one. The reconstruction efforts of the international institutions set up in the aftermath of the Second World War were premised not only on the 'law matters' but on the 'Western law matters' thesis. That is, developing countries seeking investment should pass through a clear set of stages as Western states have done in order to 'Modernise' and replicate the present Western form. By the 1960s 'Modernisation' theory had been adopted and adapted by the Law and Development movement to incorporate the ideas of Weber.

15.47   Weber's work had been at least partly driven by an attempt to understand why capitalism had materialised in European civilisation but not in others. As Perry (2001) states:

> *Weber concluded that the emergence of 'logically formal rational' decision making and the rule of law was in large part responsible for providing the environment necessary for capitalism to flourish in Europe by creating an environment of low governmental discretion and high 'calculability' or predictability, of laws.*

Over the course of the 1960s and early 1970s the investment programmes of public and private international organisations active in Asia, Africa, and Latin America were all premised on the Law and Development movement's Weber-inspired idea of transplanting Western legal concepts (in practice primarily US concepts) into developing countries. This had little success. In 1974 this underlying premise suffered a near-fatal blow when Trubek and Galanter (1974) criticised it for taking no account of the social, institutional, and cultural differences that exist between developed and developing states. They accused the Law and Development movement of being naive in its presumption that the West has achieved the ideal legal system upon which all else must naturally be modelled.

15.48   However, despite this discrediting of the theoretical framework, public international bodies led by the World Bank and the International Monetary Fund (IMF) continued their interest in Weberian law reform as a driver of development. Over the course of the 1980s and 1990s programmes aimed at encouraging good governance through law reform blossomed. At the same time these organisations moved their focus from a state-centred development model to a focus on the private sector as a driver of development through privatisation and market liberalisation. It was only a matter of time before these two themes merged and private sector governance, in other words corporate governance, became a focus for these organisations. The events that triggered this merger were the Asian and Russian crises in 1997 which created an interest for international organisations in minimum standards of corporate governance.

15.49   The IMF and the World Bank identified corporate governance failures in particular in Indonesia as having contributed to the Asian crisis and wanted minimum standards to be attached to their lending assessment criteria. In response to this the OECD, in partnership with the World Bank, developed a set of minimum standards of corporate governance based firmly on the UK and US corporate governance standards (the Cadbury Committee's work in particular) which have since been promoted by those organisations throughout the world (see Dignam and Galanis (1999), Dignam (2000), and http://ecgi. global/code/oecd-principles-corporate-governance).

15.50 The work of La Porta et al must be set against this backdrop of promoting private law solutions that facilitate the emergence of a market-based economy. In an influential set of articles they argued that the level of legal protection for shareholders present in a jurisdiction is the key factor in determining corporate governance outcomes. Examining a wide range of countries they found that where there is weak investor protection public companies have concentrated ownership patterns (families, banks, the state, and other companies hold the shares). Conversely, where there is strong legal protection the Berle and Means corporation with its dispersed ownership characteristic will emerge which is more likely to facilitate private sector investment. Weak investor protection, they suggest, has 'adverse consequences for financial development and growth'. The strong subtext here, or text in some of their later work, is that an insider corporate governance system (i.e. where concentrated ownership is present; the majority of systems) is underdeveloped and that the outsider system (i.e. where ownership is dispersed; a very small minority of systems) is the superior model and that movement to the superior model is possible by adopting UK/US shareholder protection provisions. In 2003 they went one step further and claimed that state-based regulation of securities markets was ineffective and that facilitating private regulation through disclosure and liability rules enforceable by shareholders were the key factors in developing a strong securities market.

15.51 Their highly controversial work with its strong Weberian echoes is open to the same criticisms levelled at the Law and Development movement in the 1970s that: (a) it pays little attention to social, institutional, and cultural differences (for example, Dignam and Galanis (2009) found that the introduction of shareholder oriented laws in Germany may have brought about further managerial entrenchment); and (b) it is naive in assuming that the ideal has been achieved in the UK/US model. Cheffins (2002a) for example, dealing with the inferences of the 'law matters' thesis and having examined the advantages and disadvantages of diffuse and concentrated ownership, concludes:

> [o]nce it is recognised that the trade-offs between diffuse and concentrated ownership mean it cannot be taken for granted that the Berle–Means corporation is inherently superior, the Darwinian inferences that can be drawn from the law matters thesis need to be recast . . . In sum while the law matters thesis seems to offer a clear and urgent message for policy-makers, the practical realities of corporate ownership mean that the true situation is considerably more complex.

Others such as Allen and Gale (2001) have pointed out that sweeping observations about insider corporate governance systems have little validity when the truth is that we simply do not know much about these systems at all. Still others, most notably what has become known as the 'Varieties of Capitalism' school led by Soskice and Hall (2001), argue that corporate governance systems with concentrated ownership patterns have a level of coordination between institutions in the economy that makes them both efficient and resilient to convergence.

15.52   The main criticism levelled at the La Porta thesis is that it is simply incorrect in that the authors have overstated the importance of minority protection in the emergence of out-sider systems. While there can be little doubt that the observation that outsider systems have strong investor protection is correct that does not mean that there is a causal link between the two. Coffee (2001) has suggested that La Porta et al have misunderstood their results and that they may actually reveal that developed markets are a precondition for the emergence of strong shareholder protection, rather than the other way round. Taking a snapshot of minority protection today could be misleading as this protection may have been introduced after the Berle and Means corporation emerged.

15.53   Coffee's point is certainly compelling given the experience of the emergence of the Berle and Means corporation in the USA and the UK. In both countries the Berle and Means corporation emerged without a protective legal environment for shareholders. In both countries the quality control function within the marketplace was fulfilled by the stock exchanges in New York and London and the brokers attached to them. These private in-stitutions promoted protective disclosure and self-dealing rules (the audit, for example, was a shareholders' initiative) which provided a certain integrity for the marketplace and those investing in it (see Cheffins (2002b)).

15.54   For example, the UK experience of formal legal protection for minority shareholders lends no help to the La Porta et al case. As we have observed in Chapter 10 common law rules such as the exceptions to *Foss v Harbottle* (1843) have always been very complex and difficult to use and legislative attempts to provide a remedy for oppressed minorities in the UK were largely ineffective until recently. It was only in 1980 that a useable statutory minority protection provision emerged. Even then it was not aimed at shareholders of public companies but rather at shareholders in private companies. Thus, by the time the UK had a direct formal legal protection for oppressed minorities the Berle and Means corporation had already emerged.

15.55   Legal shareholder protection, rather than being a precondition for the emergence of the Berle and Means corporation with its dispersed shareholding system, seems to follow on after the emergence of such a system. However, despite this the La Porta thesis was enormously influential until the financial crisis that unfolded in autumn 2008. Since then crucial organisations such as the World Bank and the IMF, who in the past based part of their conditions of lending on the questionable conclusions of the La Porta thesis, have stopped doing so as the legitimacy of the shareholder-oriented model of the corporation has been called into question in the aftermath of the financial crisis, and board-focused models, albeit from very different perspectives—such as Blair and Stout's (1999) team production theory, Bainbridge's (2006) director primacy model, and Greenfield's (2014) third way—have gained greater traction.

FURTHER READING

This chapter links with the materials in Chapters 8 and 11 of *Hicks and Goo's Cases and Materials on Company Law* (Oxford, OUP, 2011, xl +649p).

Allen and Gale, 'A Comparative Theory of Corporate Governance', Wharton Business School Financial Institutions Center Working Paper series 03–27 (2001).

Armour and Whincop, 'The Proprietary Foundations of Corporate Law' (September 2004), http://ssrn.com/abstract=665186.

Bainbridge, 'Director Primacy and Shareholder Disempowerment' [2006] *Harvard L Rev* 119: UCLA School of Law, Law-Econ Research Paper No 05-25, http://ssrn.com/abstract=808584.

Berle, 'For Whom Are Corporate Managers Trustees: A Note' [1932] *Harvard L Rev* 1365.

Berle and Means, *The Modern Corporation and Private Property* (New York, Harcourt, 1932; revised edn, 1968).

Blair and Stout, 'A Team Production Theory of Corporate Law' [1999] 85(2) *Virginia L Rev* 248, http://ssrn.com/abstract=425500.

Cheffins, *Company Law: Theory, Structure and Operation* (Oxford, OUP, 1997).

Cheffins, 'Using Theory to Study Law: A Company Law Perspective' [1999] *CLJ* 197.

Dignam, 'The Future of Shareholder Democracy in the Shadow of the Financial Crisis' (2013) 36 *Seattle University L Rev* 639, http://ssrn.com/abstract=2244897.

Dignam and Galanis, 'Australia Inside/Out: The Corporate Governance System of the Australian Listed Market' (2004) 28(3) *Melbourne University L Rev* 623.

Dignam and Galanis, 'Corporate Governance and the Importance of Macroeconomic Context' (2008) 28 *OJLS* 201.

Dignam and Galanis, *The Globalization of Corporate Governance* (Farnham, Ashgate, 2009). See xxiv, p 458.

Dodd, 'For Whom Are Corporate Managers Trustees?' [1932] *Harvard L Rev* 1145.

Greenfield, 'The Third Way: Beyond Shareholder or Board Primacy' (2014) 37 *Seattle University L Rev* 749, http://lawdigitalcommons.bc.edu/cgi/viewcontent.cgi?article=1727&context=lsfp.

Hansmann and Kraakman, 'The Essential Role of Organizational Law' [2000] *Yale LJ* 110.

Hill and Jones, 'Stakeholder-Agency Theory' [1992] *J of Management Studies* 131.

La Porta, Lopez-de-Silanes, and Shleifer, 'Corporate Ownership Around the World' (1999) 54 *J of Finance* 471.

La Porta, Lopez-de-Silanes, and Shleifer, 'What Works in Securities Laws?' (2003) NBER Working Paper No 9882, July, JEL No G15, G18, G3, G22, P5.

La Porta, Lopez-de-Silanes, Shleifer, and Vishny, 'Law and Finance' (1998) 106 *J of Political Economy* 1152.

Mizruchi, 'Berle and Means Revisited: The Governance and Power of Large U.S. Corporations' (2004) 33(5) *Theory and Society* 579.

Pettet, *Company Law*, 5th edn (Harlow, Longman, 2018), ch 3.

Roe, 'Corporate Short-Termism—In the Boardroom and in the Courtroom' (2013) 68 *Business Lawyer* 981; ECGI Law Working Paper No 210; Harvard Public Law Working Paper Nos 13–18, http://ssrn.com/abstract=2239132 or http://dx.doi.org/10.2139/ssrn.2239132.

Soskice and Hall, 'Introduction' in Hall and Soskice (eds) *Varieties of Capitalism: The Institutional Foundations of Comparative Advantage* (New York, OUP, 2001), 1–68.

Zingales, 'In Search of New Foundations' (2000) 55 *J of Finance* 1623.

SELF-TEST QUESTIONS

1 Explain concession theory.

2 What was the importance of the Berle and Means thesis?

3 Explain corporate realism.

4 How does economic theory aid company lawyers?

5 In your view does corporate law matter?

6 What are the alternatives to shareholder-oriented corporate law?

16 Corporate governance 2: the UK corporate governance debate

SUMMARY

Introduction
The background to the UK debate
A word on UK corporate theory
The corporate governance debate: the industry response
The corporate governance debate: the Government response
Corporate governance failure and the financial crisis
The Walker Report 2009
Ongoing reform

Introduction

16.1 In this chapter we examine the specific UK corporate governance debate and the responses by Government and industry. As we noted briefly in Chapter 15, although the Berle and Means corporation with its dispersed ownership system emerged in the UK, albeit at a later stage than in the USA, the character of the UK corporate governance debate has differed markedly from that in the USA.

The background to the UK debate

16.2 While persistent underperformance relative to other economies led to the same disillusionment with the managerial corporation as was evident in the 1970s in the USA, the UK reaction was somewhat different at first. A concern about unaccountable managers and underperformance resulted initially in a focus on industrial democracy as a solution to unaccountable managers. Unlike the USA where solutions were sought based on shareholder primacy the UK sought to constrain management discretion by increasing the power and participation in the firm of the employees. The high point in the industrial democracy debate came in the late 1970s with the report of the Bullock Committee (1977), *Report of the Committee of Enquiry on Industrial Democracy*, advocating the benefits of increased employee participation. At this point even the CBI accepted that a more inclusionary approach was needed.

16.3 Things changed rapidly with the election of the Conservative Government led by Margaret Thatcher in 1979. Margaret Thatcher's admiration for US free-market economists, particularly the work of Friedrich Hayek, soon had the UK engaging in wholesale reform of its public sector based upon market solutions. The privatisation of public sector industries (telecom, gas, water, electricity etc), reform of pension provision, healthcare, social welfare, the removal of barriers to capital inflow and outflows, and the removal of employment protection changed the nature of the corporate governance debate utterly within the course of a decade. Government policy changed from giving priority to creating employment to a focus on economic tools such as interest rate levels which could keep capital flowing into the UK. Industrial democracy was off the agenda to be replaced by shareholder-oriented, market-based solutions. Initially, a boom occurred but by the late 1980s the boom ran out of steam and recession followed by the beginning of the 1990s.

16.4 Paralleling the US situation this provided a gap in which the experience of the previous decade could be evaluated. General public concerns were expressed by the academic community and the media that market forces had a detrimental effect on employees and communities. Employment reform had made it easier and less costly for companies to dismiss employees. This was followed by post-privatisation employee rationalisation and a booming market in takeovers and mergers had resulted in further rationalisation of employees. Management in the UK also appeared to push higher proportions of wealth generated by the company to the shareholders as dividends rather than reinvesting it in the company. In effect companies seemed to be adopting a Jensen and Meckling (1976) model where discretionary surplus cash flow is distributed immediately to the shareholders. In effect this reduced the financial cushion that management might have had if there was a downturn in the economy. As a result the combined effect of market-based shareholder performance measures and employment reform made it the easy choice for management to cut costs by dismissing employees. In all, employee insecurity was rife. At the same time directors' salaries had increased enormously. Finally, the combination of these factors and the totally unexpected collapse of a number of high-profile companies turned corporate governance reform into a political issue. Before we turn to examine the Government and industry responses to these corporate governance issues we first consider UK corporate theory generally.

A word on UK corporate theory

16.5 As we have observed in Chapter 15, corporate theory was dominated in the 20th century by US theorists. It is not the case that UK academics were inactive over the 20th century but rather that corporate law as a separate area of study in the UK only emerged in the 1950s. Even then until recently it remained a largely black letter subject. To the extent that corporate governance was an issue for UK academic lawyers the major contributions were made by employment lawyers such as Lord Wedderburn (1982, 1993). However, by the early 1990s corporate governance was entering mainstream study, engaging the interest of political scientists, sociologists, and company lawyers.

16.6 Despite the boom in market-oriented solutions in the 1980s and the undoubted influence on the US debate by UK economists, economic theory has not until very recently been a feature of the UK corporate governance debate. In general both the message and the messenger are treated with suspicion. Ireland (2003) probably captured the majority view when he stated:

> [w]hile it would be churlish not to welcome a development with the potential to broaden the intellectual horizons of academic company law, it is difficult to be effusive about this particular theoretical turn. In the U.S., for example, the advent of corporate con-tractualism, buoyed in the 90s by the stock market bubble, the perceived strength of the American economy relative to its European and Japanese rivals and a growing belief in the superiority of Anglo-American governance mechanisms, has been characterised less by a blossoming of new avenues of inquiry than by a process of intellectual closure, albeit one distinguished by the intoxicated enthusiasm of born-again conversion. Indeed, a few sniffs of the contractual font have seen one or two rolling around the theoretical aisles on this side of the Atlantic too, though fortunately we have thus far been spared the boss-eyed inebriation which until recently characterised so much American corporate scholarship. With its slavish faith in the efficacy of 'the market', its yearning completely to privatise the public company and its uncritical commitment to 'shareholder value' as the overriding corporate goal, it is difficult to escape the conclusion that contractual theory has ideological qualities which render it ill-suited to sober, open-minded analysis.

16.7 Historically, moral philosophy rather than economics has been the dominant influence on the UK debate, centring on moral claims for participation and responsibility towards those affected by the actions of corporations (namely stakeholders), i.e. the employees, customers, creditors, the environment, and the general public. These arguments against the primacy UK company law gives to shareholders have been based on three general points. First, corporations are very powerful and therefore have an enormous effect on society. Thus a narrow accountability to shareholders is insufficient to protect society's interests. Second, some like Parkinson (1993) argue that the assumption that shareholders have a moral claim to primacy by virtue of their property rights is plainly incorrect. If shareholder primacy is to be justified it must be on other grounds. Third, the moral claims of others (stakeholders) either outweigh the shareholders' claims or are at least equal to them when it comes to allocating primacy.

16.8 However, these moral claims seemed overwhelmed by the efficiency-based arguments of government and private sector in the 1980s. In response, by the early 1990s a twofold approach was emerging in the corporate governance literature. First, it was still morally right to include stakeholders in the decision-making process and, second, it could be justified on competitive grounds. For example contented employees are more productive, the business entity benefits through lower transaction costs because of higher levels of trust and a greater sense of community, thus ultimately the economy and society benefit.

16.9   The most important work in the early 1990s was Parkinson's (1993) *Corporate Power and Responsibility Issues in the Theory of Company Law*. Parkinson establishes in the first chapter the view that shareholders have no moral entitlement to primacy in company law. He then went on to build the case for corporate social responsibility. The importance of the work is less in the case Parkinson builds for corporate social responsibility, which is in itself compelling, but that in doing so he actively engages with the contractarian model and seems to win, to the palpable relief of many company lawyers all over the UK.

16.10   Much of the post-1990 UK literature just tips a nod at the economic theory before returning to more familiar territory. As Cheffins (2003) observes:

> In the UK ... contractarian analysis does not currently constitute the mainstream or orthodox approach at the academic level. Instead, in British interdisciplinary corporate law scholarship, there is a tendency to acknowledge law and economics, cite its limitations and shift to a different theoretical ground. The most typical move UK academics currently make is to discuss the company by reference to its employees and others potentially having a 'stake' in the business, such as suppliers, customers and perhaps society at large. Those adopting a 'stakeholder' perspective often argue that company law should offer explicit protection to the various constituencies associated with companies. This argument is sometimes framed in economic terms, with the logic being that stakeholders need incentives to make firm-specific investments that are allegedly pivotal ingredients of long-term corporate success. In other instances, however, public scrutiny and control of corporate activity is justified on wider grounds. The thinking is that companies are too important to the economy to exist for the benefit of a single constituency, namely the shareholders. Regulation which secures fair treatment for potentially vulnerable stakeholder groups is therefore justified, even if the measures in question may reduce corporate profits.

Things have however been changing over the past two decades or so. In particular the publication of Cheffins (1997) *Company Law, Theory, Structure and Operation*, which provides an analysis of UK company law utilising economic theory to provide a conceptual framework, has done much to bring economic theory into mainstream UK company law analysis while more recent work such as Moore (2013) *Corporate Governance in the Shadow of the State*, represents a maturing of the UK theoretical debate where economic analysis is concerned. Reform bodies such as the Law Commission have increasingly utilised economic theory in their company law work and the Court of Appeal used economic analysis of the law in deciding *Item Software (UK) Ltd v Fassihi* (2004). Despite this however, the moral philosophy strand of the debate still represents the mainstream analysis.

The corporate governance debate: the industry response

16.11 The successive impacts of scandal and recession in the late 1980s and early 1990s led ultimately to reform of UK listed companies. The collapse of three companies (BCCI, Polly Peck, and the Robert Maxwell Group) all of whom had clean bills of health from their auditors, yet collapsed suddenly, dented market confidence in the accountability processes operating in UK listed companies which in turn fed into a general public distrust of large companies. While the Government vaguely threatened to legislate, ultimately it was industry itself coordinated by the Bank of England (BOE) that responded to these concerns.

The Cadbury Committee

16.12 The first response was the Cadbury Committee (1992) on the Financial Aspects of Corporate Governance. The remit of the Committee, established by the Financial Reporting Council, the London Stock Exchange, and the combined accounting bodies, was fairly narrow but its chairman, Sir Adrian Cadbury, took the view that the quality of financial reporting could only be ensured if boardroom accountability was also improved. Thus the Committee examined boardroom accountability issues, and produced solutions based upon the monitoring role of non-executives and wider disclosure regimes. It considered that:

> *Corporate governance is the system by which companies are directed and controlled. Boards of directors are responsible for the governance of their companies. The shareholders' role in governance is to appoint the directors and the auditors and to satisfy themselves that an appropriate governance structure is in place.*

The main recommendations were as follows:

(1)   The Committee emphasised the key role of the board in the company's decision-making process and recommended that major transactions should be decided by the board. *This may seem obvious but Cadbury was concerned that senior managers rather than the board were making these key decisions with the resulting diminishing of board responsibility.*

(2)   The key roles of managing director (sometimes called Chief Executive Officer) and Chairman of the Board should not be combined as to do so represented a dangerous concentration of power which could allow an individual to dominate a board. *This was a reflection of the lesson learned from the Maxwell collapse where Robert Maxwell held both key positions.*

(3)   The main board should have non-executive directors (NEDs) sufficient in number and quality to carry significant weight in board decisions. These NEDs should

be independent of the company. A committee structure should also be put in place to improve the accountability of the appointment of directors, the pay (remuneration) of directors, and the audit process.

Therefore a listed company should have three sub-committees of the board to cover appointments, remuneration, and audit. The accountability process would be ensured by having NEDs on each of the sub-committees. The remuneration committee in particular was to be made up wholly or mainly of NEDs and the audit committee should have at least three NEDs. The audit committee was crucial to the financial accountability of the company as it was to oversee the audit process and act as a primary reference point for the auditor in order to mitigate management influence over the audit. The committee would also monitor the amount of non-audit work the auditor was carrying out. The amount of income the auditor had from non-audit work was a concern for the integrity of the audit process as if it was significant it could allow management to affect the independence of the auditor. For example if the auditor discovered a discrepancy in the accounts management could threaten to give the lucrative non-audit work to another firm of accountants if the auditor revealed it. This type of pressure on the auditor was at the heart of many of the UK corporate collapses in the late 1980s and indeed the later US collapses (Enron and WorldCom: see para **16.25**) at the beginning of the 21st century.

16.13 The majority of the Cadbury Committee recommendations were implemented by the London Stock Exchange. However, they were not implemented as enforceable Listing Rules (see Chapter 5) but rather by the odd mechanism of appending them to the Listing Rules. Accordingly, there was no penalty for non-compliance but if a company did not comply it had to explain why it had not complied. That explanation should also be reviewed by the auditor. In essence it left it to companies to decide themselves what to do as there was no external scrutiny of the explanations for non-compliance (see Finch (1992) and Riley (1994)). The idea was that shareholders would punish non-compliant companies by selling their shares.

16.14 The NED was the Cadbury Committee's solution to accountability issues within the listed company. This was not, however, anything new. There had been a certain disquiet from the 1970s onwards about the ability of British industry to compete globally. The formation of PRONED by the BOE at the beginning of the 1980s to promote the virtues of NEDs was in many ways a precursor to the Cadbury Committee. Britain in the early 1980s was in recession and the BOE considered that non-executives offered a way forward towards a more accountable management style. The NED was supposed to provide an independent, objective check on the executive directors who might not put the shareholders' interests first.

16.15 In essence the NED is a neo-classical *ex ante* monitor designed to ensure the efficiency of management. PRONED was successful in some ways at raising the profile of NEDs but events soon overtook it. In the mid- to late 1980s the British economy was booming.

Pressure for change was easily resisted by arguing that the present system was working and serving the economy very well. The emergence of the Cadbury Committee during the recession in the early 1990s is significant. Britain was in recession and arguments that the present system works very well were ringing hollow. At the start of the 1990s the BOE in particular was once again concerned that there was some sort of malaise at the heart of British industry. The recession of the early 1990s gave the BOE the chance to build on the initial PRONED experiment.

16.16 Cadbury, while it provided the overall framework used to this day, was not big on implementation detail and left some key issues incomplete. First, it had never actually defined independence and so companies continued to appoint friends of management, ex-managers, and managers of other connected companies to the board as NEDs. Second, it did not specify that NEDs be a majority on the main board and allowed executive managers to sit on the sub-boards which made it very difficult for NEDs to be effective. This problem first manifested itself in the continuing upward spiral of directors' pay despite the new mainly non-executive remuneration committee.

The Greenbury Committee

16.17 By 1995 there was an enormous public outcry at large director pay increases generally but specifically for executives of the privatised utilities. The Prime Minister at the time, John Major, indicated that he disapproved and that the Government would introduce pay constraints. Again the industry response was to set up a committee headed this time by Sir Richard Greenbury (at that time the Chairman of Marks & Spencer) to examine the issue of directors' remuneration. The Greenbury Committee (1995) Report, *Directors' Remuneration, Report of the Study Group*, identified clearly the issue at the heart of directors' remuneration difficulties. That is, there is an inherent conflict of interest in directors deciding on their own pay.

The Committee thus recommended:

(1)   There should be no executives on the remuneration committee because of their inherent conflict of interest and remuneration committees should take account of the wider economic scene inside and outside the company when making executive salary decisions.

(2)   Share options should be replaced by long-term (i.e. three years') performance-related criteria, which are put to the shareholders. Share options were a problem because once granted it was impossible to tell how much they would be worth in the future, leaving the company open to criticism for overpaying its executives. Share price may also be an inappropriate measure of performance both encouraging directors to make short-term share-price-maximising decisions and giving only a general market view of the company's prospects, not the individual director's performance.

(3)   There should be higher levels of salary disclosure in the annual accounts. This would enable closer scrutiny of directors' salaries.

(4)   Ideally directors should have one-year rolling contracts but two years may be acceptable. This would allow directors to be dismissed more easily without the need to pay off the remainder of their long-term contracts.

As with Cadbury, the recommendations of the Greenbury Committee were adopted by the London Stock Exchange in the same non-binding manner.

16.18 While the Greenbury Committee was effective in identifying the problems inherent in remuneration issues the solutions the Committee provided, by using non-executive committees to consider directors' pay and wider disclosure of salaries in the accounts, were largely unsuccessful. Directors' pay has continued to climb and has been accelerated by the more open disclosure environment created by the Greenbury recommendations. Once directors were able to access the salary information of their equivalents in other companies salary negotiations started with a claim to be paid the same as if not more than the highest paid director of an equivalent company. Another factor in the continued rise of directors' salaries has been the widespread practice of boardrooms employing salary consultants to advise the remuneration committee. These consultants are not, however, independent of the company and tend to also provide other advice to management which opens them to accusations of conflicts of interests, i.e. they are more likely to retain and increase their non-salary consultancy work if they provide salary advice which results in higher salaries for management. Additionally, non-executives have found it hard to justify lower salaries on the wider economic scene criteria recommended by Greenbury (see Chapter 13 and paras **16.38–16.40** for more on directors' pay).

The Hampel Committee

16.19 The Cadbury Committee had recommended that a committee should be appointed to review the effect of its recommendations and perhaps update them. A committee was formed under the chairmanship of Sir Ronald Hampel in order to do just that. It reported in January 1998 and its findings mostly consisted of a review of Cadbury and Greenbury. Its main recommendations were:

(1)   That Cadbury, Greenbury, and its own recommendations be incorporated into one super code. This became known as the Combined Code and eventually the UK Corporate Governance Code.

(2)   Non-executives should have a leader. This in effect creates three power bases on the board, the managing director, the chairman, and the leader of the non-executives.

(3)   Institutional investors should consider voting at AGMs.

(4) Remuneration details should be even clearer and should include hidden costs to the company such as the full cost of pension provision.

(5) The Committee was of the view that directors should not have to give an opinion on the effectiveness of internal financial controls.

(This issue about the effectiveness of internal financial controls arose because of the work of an accountancy committee (the Turnbull Committee) that was examining whether directors should have to make some sort of risk-assessment statement about the company's internal financial controls. The Turnbull Committee disagreed with Hampel when it finally reported in 1999 recommending that directors maintain and have primary responsibility for a system of internal controls to evaluate and deal with both financial and non-financial risks (among other things, the risk that the directors may damage the company's reputation through their public statements). The London Stock Exchange implemented the Turnbull recommendations in the same manner as the other corporate governance codes.)

(6) Sometimes companies can have combined chairmen and managing directors.

Sir Ronald Hampel held such a combined role at ICI Plc at the time of his review.

16.20 The Hampel report rejected any consideration of two-tiered boards where the executives are supervised by an entire board of non-executives as in Germany and as the EU Draft Fifth Directive on Company Law proposed at the time. The reason for rejecting the idea was that they found no support for it among those they canvassed. They also rejected compulsory voting for institutional investors. They considered that stakeholders were best served by the board pursuing profit-maximising policies and that a permanent committee on corporate governance was unnecessary. In all the report was more active in rejecting ideas than it was at recommending positive improvements (see Dignam (1998)). The London Stock Exchange implemented its recommendations and now the recommendations of Cadbury, Greenbury, Hampel, Smith, and Turnbull form parts of the UK Corporate Governance Code.

16.21 While it is difficult to say whether there has been an improvement in board standards since the 1980s the fact that there were no post-Enron (see para **16.25**) collapses in UK listed companies may be an indication that audit committees may in a general sense be doing their job properly. Directors' pay however remained an issue as directors' salaries continued to increase after Greenbury and eventually the Government introduced the Directors' Remuneration Reporting Regulations 2002 (SI 2002/1986, and CA 2006, s 420) as well as more recent reforms in ss 79–82 of the ERRA 2013 requiring that the general meeting play a role in setting and monitoring board pay (see Chapter 13). The reforms require that directors' salaries be put to the shareholders for an advisory vote. The vote is non-binding but a negative vote is a powerful signal to the remuneration committee that they got things very wrong. The ERRA 2013 goes further and requires a binding vote on future board remuneration policy at least every three years. The independence of NEDs, as we will see, has continued to engage the reform process. The 2002 White Paper, although it deals directly with the duties of directors, proposes leaving the Combined Code as a self-regulating matter. The Government felt it was not a matter for legislation (White Paper (2002), Vol I, para 3.31) and that has remained the case under the CA 2006. Additionally as we observe later (paras **16.38–16.40**) both excessive pay and NED failure played a part in the financial crisis which is the subject of continuing reform.

The corporate governance debate: the Government response

16.22   The election of the Labour Government in 1997 brought a huge change of attitude to industry regulating itself. While the Conservative Government was content to stand by and allow industry to regulate itself the new Government was not. Within a few years the BOE was removed as primary financial regulator (it was viewed as being too closely tied to those it regulated) and a raft of self-regulating organisations in the financial sector including the London Stock Exchange were placed under the control of the Financial Services Authority. The corporate governance committees were also within the sights of the incoming administration. Tony Blair had identified himself with the concept of 'stakeholders' all through the 1997 election campaign and Margaret Beckett, who became the Minister at the Department of Trade and Industry (DTI) in 1997, was particularly committed to corporate governance reform (the DTI changed its name to the Department for Business, Enterprise and Regulatory Reform in June 2007 (DBERR), then to the Department for Business, Innovation and Skills (BIS) in 2009, and in July 2016 to the Department for Business, Energy & Industrial Strategy (BEIS)). (Yes, we agree they should stop messing about with this important department of Government.) She went to great lengths to harass Sir Ronald Hampel and his committee before the final report in 1998 and when she considered his report had failed to provide sufficient reform, the DTI included corporate governance reform firmly in the remit of its major company law review. In doing so the incoming Labour Government reflected the mainstream UK theoretical view and so brought a focus within corporate governance reform on the moral claims of stakeholders to inclusion in the corporate decision-making process.

16.23   Thus the CLRSG was formed to review the whole of company law in the UK with a specific committee to explore corporate governance reform. This was a sensitive area for the new Government as it had just engaged in an act of spectacular socialism with the windfall tax on the privatised industries clawing back £5.2 billion. As a result it did not wish to antagonise the business community much further. For a while things went well and the CLRSG corporate governance committee explored a wide range of ideas. However when Margaret Beckett was replaced by Stephen Byers as DTI minister this freedom was curtailed and the corporate governance committee focused only on 'enlightened shareholder value', a sort of vague encouragement to enlightened managers (for detail see later) who might have stakeholder concerns and that was pretty much as it stayed until the final report.

16.24 The CLRSG *Final Report* concluded that company law needed to 'think small first' and focus on small private companies as these were the greater in number (being described as 'the engine room of the economy'). These are not, however, the most economically important companies in the UK. This approach represented a significant change from the original function of company law in the UK and a move in focus away from the most important economic actors to those of lesser importance. Perhaps some re-balancing was needed but it was also convenient for the Government not to shake things up too much. The corporate governance section was the one exception to think small first. The Government welcomed the CLRSG *Final Report* but could find no time for it in its legislative agenda and it was beginning to look as if the *Final Report* might not ever translate into legislation. Instead discrete initiatives began to arise, the most important of which was the Treasury-sponsored Myners Report (2001), *Institutional Investment in the UK: A Review*. This review arose out of concerns that institutional investors (pension, insurance, and general professional investment funds) were too passive in terms of their ownership of the shares of large British companies. The report produced a range of recommendations in the form of a voluntary code of conduct aimed at more responsible investment decision making by trustees of these funds through training, clarity of objective, seeking advice, and the elimination of conflicts of interest (see http://www.icaew.com/en/library/subject-gateways/corporate-governance/codes-and-reports/myners-report).

16.25 However, events overtook matters and caused a reassessment of the Government's priorities. The collapse of US company Enron (see http://news.bbc.co.uk/1/hi/business/1780075.stm) in late 2001 caused the Government to launch a flurry of initiatives. Enron had collapsed without warning and at the heart of the collapse was a conflict of interest in the audit process. The auditors of Enron were earning enormous amounts of money from Enron in non-audit work which seemed to allow management to compromise the independence of the auditor and as a result a completely misleading picture of the company's financial position was produced. The audit committee of Enron also seemed to have failed to do its job. This was worrying as Lord Wakeham, a pillar of the UK establishment and the then Chairman of the Press Complaints Commission, was a member of the Enron audit committee. In quick succession the Government announced that it would find time for a Company Law Bill and that a review of the role of non-executives and audit committees would take place.

The White Paper and corporate governance

16.26 In July 2002 the Government published its White Paper in two volumes, the second volume containing a draft Companies Bill. The White Paper contained two significant proposals within it based on the recommendations of the CLRSG *Final Report* that are central to the corporate governance debate. The first was a change in the formulation of directors' duties to include other constituencies if directors feel so inclined. This was the so-called 'enlightened shareholder value' approach. The second initiative was to introduce a form of corporate constituency reporting. That is, the annual report from the directors should include a section on the impact of the company's activities on stakeholders. We will now consider each in turn.

Enlightened shareholder value

16.27 Schedule 1, para 2 to the draft Bill 2002 set out a codification of directors' duties formulated around a primary focus on the shareholders but with a strange formulation that
required the directors to take into account 'material factors' which in the notes included
stakeholders (employees, local community, environment, suppliers, and customers). A
great deal of time was then taken up by policy makers trying to define when something
was 'material' but eventually in the Companies Act 2006 the 'enlightened shareholder
value' formulation was changed. The 2006 Act as a result contains no mention of 'material
factors' instead using the more positive phrase 'have regard'. Additionally the stakeholder
issues were taken out of the notes and placed firmly in the section itself. The obligation is
now contained in s 172 of the CA 2006 and reads as follows:

> ### 172 Duty to promote the success of the company
>
> (1) A director of a company must act in the way he considers, in good faith, would be
> most likely to promote the success of the company for the benefit of its members as
> a whole, and in doing so have regard (amongst other matters) to—
>
> (a) the likely consequences of any decision in the long term,
>
> (b) the interests of the company's employees,
>
> (c) the need to foster the company's business relationships with suppliers, custom-
> ers and others,
>
> (d) the impact of the company's operations on the community and the environ-
> ment,
>
> (e) the desirability of the company maintaining a reputation for high standards
> of business conduct, and
>
> (f) the need to act fairly as between members of the company.
>
> (2) Where or to the extent that the purposes of the company consist of or include pur-
> poses other than the benefit of its members, subsection (1) has effect as if the refer-
> ence to promoting the success of the company for the benefit of its members were to
> achieving those purposes.
>
> (3) The duty imposed by this section has effect subject to any enactment or rule of law
> requiring directors, in certain circumstances, to consider or act in the interests of
> creditors of the company.

This reformulation is stronger than its predecessor from 2002. It is certainly less confusing
and seems to more accurately reflect the CLRSG's intention to encourage or legitimise
'enlightened' directors considering the interests of 'stakeholders' in their decision-making
process. It retains the primacy of the shareholders while also compelling directors to consider the company's stakeholders. In offering guidance on how the section will operate
the Government is of the view that:

The words 'have regard to' mean 'think about'; they are absolutely not about just ticking boxes. If 'thinking about' leads to the conclusion, as we believe it will in many cases, that the proper course is to act positively to achieve the objectives in the clause, that will be what the director's duty is. In other words 'have regard to' means 'give proper consideration to'. (Department of Trade and Industry (June 2007) Companies Act 2006: Duties of Company Directors: Ministerial Statements)

Obviously, in terms of its enforcement only shareholders have the ability to ensure directors are complying with the stakeholder provisions of s 172 (see Chapter 14) but given that many environmental groups and employees hold shares in companies the section may well have more bite than it seems. Whether it becomes an effective stakeholder provision may well depend less on 'enlightened' shareholders and directors but more on an 'enlightened' judiciary.

16.28 In general the response from company lawyers to the 'enlightened shareholder value' approach has ranged from apathy to disappointment. It has, however, particularly disappointed the non-governmental organisation (NGO) community, and as a result Amnesty International and Friends of the Earth proposed an alternative Corporate Responsibility Bill (see http://www.publications.parliament.uk/pa/cm200203/cmbills/129/03129.i.html). The alternative Bill is interesting as it does not displace shareholder primacy; rather it gives stakeholder issues a higher priority with strong disclosure and enforcement provisions. On the NGO views on the Companies Act 2006, see http://www.corporate-responsibility.org/.

The Business Review

16.29 The change in the formulation of the directors' core duty was accompanied in the 2002 White Paper by the introduction of an Operating and Financial Review (OFR) which would provide a narrative statement on the company's activities as it affects stakeholder constituencies. The Government at the time considered that:

> *A reporting requirement in these terms would also be a major benefit for a wider cross-section of a company's stakeholders. The new requirement to report, for example, on material environmental issues would be a major contribution to both corporate social responsibility and sustainable development initiatives. The Government has long recognised, and promoted, the business case for these and sees the OFR as the opportunity for directors to demonstrate their response to this business case. (Para 4.32)*

16.30 The auditors' role was also to increase to encompass the OFR, and the Government proposed that overseeing the operation of the OFR would be the responsibility of a new Standards Board—essentially an upgraded Accounting Standards Board (White Paper (2002), Vol I, paras 4.28–5.24). However, a serious question remained as to whether the auditor and an upgraded Accounting Standards Board were suitable to ensure a proper evaluation of stakeholder interests given that their primary skills lie in financial analysis.

16.31 In March 2005, the Companies Act 1985 (Operating and Financial Review and Directors' Report etc) Regulations 2005 (SI 2005/2011) were approved by Parliament. The Regulations amend the Companies Act 1985 reporting requirements and required directors of companies quoted on the stock exchange to prepare an OFR for financial years commencing on or after 1 April 2005. Large and medium-sized non-quoted companies were also covered by the 2005 Regulations as they were required to produce an enhanced directors' reporting regime for such companies. However, small companies were exempt from the enhanced regime. As the DTI guidance explained with regard to the 2005 OFR regime:

> *Directors are required to provide a balanced and comprehensive analysis consistent with the size and complexity of the business of:*
>
> • *the business's development and performance during the financial year;*
>
> • *the company's (or group's) position at the end of the year;*
>
> • *the main trends and factors underlying the development, performance and position of the company (or group) and which are likely to affect it in the future.*
>
> *This will include a company's (or group's) objectives, strategies and the key drivers of the business, focusing on more qualitative and forward-looking information than has traditionally been included in annual reports in the past. It must include a description of the resources available to the company (or group), of the principal risks and uncertainties facing the company (or group), and of the capital structure, treasury policies and objectives and liquidity of the company (or group). In fulfilling these general requirements, directors will need to consider whether it is necessary to provide information on a range of factors that may be relevant to the understanding of the business, including, for example, environment, employee and social and community issues. (DTI Guidance on the OFR and changes to the directors' report (2005))*

While this was a somewhat watered-down version of the CLRSG recommendations, particularly on the stakeholder reporting mechanism, the 2005 OFR proved extremely controversial. Quoted companies in particular expressed outrage at the lack of consultation before the Government pushed the OFR Regulations through Parliament. The main concern of listed companies was the potential increase in personal liability that directors may have had for forward-looking financial information. The Government's initial response to this criticism was to emphasise the importance and availability of professional indemnity insurance. However, in a spectacular *volte face*, having pushed the Regulations through Parliament during 2005 over these protests, the Chancellor at the time, Gordon Brown, announced on 28 November 2005 that the OFR Regulation would be repealed from 12 January 2006. (See the Companies Act 1985 (Operating and Financial Review) (Repeal) Regulations 2005 (SI 2005/3442).)

16.32 This poorly managed process was complicated further by the fact that the European Accounts Modernisation Directive (2003/51/EC) requires a fair business review (FBR) to take place. Under the Directive a business review:

> requires a balanced and comprehensive analysis of the development and performance of the company during the financial year and the position of the company at the end of the year; a description of the principal risks and uncertainties facing the company; and analysis using appropriate financial and non-financial key performance indicators (including those specifically relating to environmental and employee issues).
>
> Companies producing a business review must disclose information that is material to understanding the development, performance and position of the company, and the principal risks and uncertainties facing it. This will include information on environmental matters and employees, on the company's policies in these areas and the implementation of those policies. Moreover, key performance indicators must be used where appropriate (including those specifically relating to environmental and employee issues).
>
> Similarly, companies producing a business review will need to consider disclosing information on trends and factors affecting the development, performance and position of the business, where this is necessary for a balanced and comprehensive analysis of the development, performance and position of the business to describe the principle risks and uncertainties facing it, or to provide an indication of likely future developments in the business of the company.

Additionally, as a result of the repeal of the OFR, the NGO, Friends of the Earth (FOE), successfully sought judicial review of the Government decision to repeal the OFR because there had been no consultation period before the repeal. The Government then settled with FOE and agreed that a consultation would be held as part of the implementation of the Companies Act 2006. The Government then subsequently introduced a 'business review' (based on the Directive guidance just quoted) in s 417 of the CA 2006 which provides for a narrative statement on the company's activities as it affects stakeholder constituencies. In essence having repealed the OFR Regulations the Government was eventually forced to introduce a 'business review' (BR) which remains a watered-down version of the OFR.

16.33 On a more positive note, clearly the change in directors' duty and the BR are designed to operate in tandem. As the BR seems to encourage directors to report each year on how the company's activities have affected stakeholders it may serve to focus their minds on stakeholder issues. Further, the change in directors' duties will make it easier for those inclined to act in the interests of stakeholders to justify those decisions. In many ways the report of the CLRSG, the BR, and the Company Act 2006 codification of directors' duties are important because, although they may do little to really disturb the status quo, they do succeed in formally legitimising stakeholder issues in the business community.

The US Sarbanes-Oxley Act of 2002

16.34 The US Sarbanes-Oxley Act became law in the USA on 30 July 2002 in response to the Enron and WorldCom scandals and applies to all US and non-US companies that are required to file periodic reports with the US Securities and Exchange Commission (SEC). As a result it introduces much more extensive reporting requirements for UK companies listed on any US stock exchange or with registered debt securities in the USA (listed or otherwise). It also applies to UK subsidiaries of US companies and UK companies with 300 or more US shareholders. Under s 906 of the Act every periodic report containing financial statements filed by reporting companies must be accompanied by written statements by the company's CEO and CFO certifying that:

(1) the report fully complies with the requirements of s 13(a) or 15(d) of the Securities Exchange Act 1934;

(2) information contained in such periodic report fairly presents, in all material respects, the financial condition and results of operations of the reporting company;

(3) they have reviewed the report;

(4) the report does not contain any untrue statements of material facts or omissions of material facts.

Section 302 of the Act also provides that the CEO and the CFO of a company that files reports under the Securities Exchange Act certify in each annual and quarterly report that:

(1) the financial information in the report fairly presents, in all material respects, the financial condition, results of operations, and cash flows of the company;

(2) they are responsible for establishing and maintaining disclosure controls and procedures;

(3) they have evaluated the effectiveness of the disclosure controls and procedures within the last 90 days (with the results of the evaluation included in the report);

(4) they have disclosed to the auditors and the audit committee all 'significant deficiencies' and 'material weaknesses' in internal controls and any fraud involving management or other employees who have a significant role in the internal controls; and

(5) they have indicated in the report whether or not there were significant changes in internal controls or in other factors that could significantly affect internal controls, including corrective actions.

Failure to comply with these provisions is a criminal offence.

16.35 The Act also introduces independence criteria for NEDs on the audit committee broadly similar to those found in the Combined Code. Section 407 of the Act requires an additional statement disclosing whether the audit committee includes one person who is a 'financial expert' (and if not, why not). A 'financial expert' is an individual who has (through education and experience as a public accountant, auditor, CFO, comptroller, or principal accounting officer of an issuer or from a similar position) particular types of knowledge and experience. The extra compliance costs of Sarbanes-Oxley, estimated at $5 million for small companies and between $30–40 million per year for larger companies, has led to some dual UK/US listed companies delisting in the USA. Other UK companies without dual listings but with more than 300 US shareholders bought out their US share-holders to escape the compliance costs. In all the compliance costs and possibility of very serious criminal sanction for directors has led to significant problems for the US stock exchanges in attracting international companies to list in the USA. In response to these problems in May 2007 the SEC produced new guidance on interpreting the most prob-lematic parts of Sarbanes-Oxley, with the intention of making it less burdensome.

The Independent Review of Non-Executive Directors (the Higgs Review)

16.36 In April 2002 as a result of the collapse of Enron and the implication from that collapse that the NED was an ineffective monitor of management, the DTI announced a review of the non-executive with a view to strengthening the quality, independence, and effective-ness of UK NEDs. The review was carried out by Derek Higgs who consulted widely and produced a final report in January 2003. Its key recommendations were as follows:

(1) At least half the board excluding the chairman should be independent NEDs.

(2) The chairman has a crucial role in the effective operation of the board. Therefore the position of the chief executive officer (managing director) and chair should not be combined. Further their individual responsibilities should be defined and the chairman should meet the independence requirements below.

(3) The role of the non-executive director should cover four areas:

- **Strategy:** NEDs should constructively challenge and contribute to the develop-ment of strategy.

- **Performance:** NEDs should scrutinise the performance of management in meeting agreed goals and objectives and monitor the reporting of performance.

- **Risk:** NEDs should satisfy themselves that financial information is accurate and that financial controls and systems of risk management are robust and defensible.

- **People:** NEDs are responsible for determining appropriate levels of remuner-ation of executive directors and have a prime role in appointing, and where ne-cessary removing, senior management and in succession planning.

(4) NEDs should meet as a group once a year without the chairman or any execu-tives. The annual report should state whether they have done so.

(5) A senior independent director should be identified who meets the test of independence as set out in point (6). That senior independent director should be a further point of contact for the shareholders.

(6) The Review set out a definition of independence. A NED is considered independent when the board determines that the director is independent in character and judgement and there are no relationships or circumstances which could affect, or appear to affect, the director's judgement. Such relationships and circumstances arise where the director: is or has been an employee of the company; has or had a business relationship with the company; is being paid by the company other than a director's fee and certain other payments; has family ties to the company or its employees; holds cross-directorships or has significant links with other directors through involvement in other companies or bodies; represents a significant shareholder; has served on the board for ten years.

(7) The board should identify in its annual report the NEDs it determines to be independent. The board should state its reasons if a director is considered to be independent notwithstanding the existence of relationships or circumstances which may appear relevant to its determination.

Listed companies were not particularly happy with the conclusions of the Higgs Review but after quite a lot of difficult negotiations its main recommendations were implemented by the London Stock Exchange through the Combined Code (now the UK Corporate Governance Code).

16.37 The Higgs Review is partly in the tradition of the previous corporate governance committees in that Derek Higgs was (sadly he died of a heart attack in April 2008) a key insider in the financial services sector in the UK. For example he sat on the boards of a wide range of listed companies as well as operating at a senior level within a number of major financial institutions. However, despite his obvious credentials as a safe pair of hands the Higgs Review fleshes out many of the gaps left by the Cadbury Report and its successors. Key among that fleshing out is that it provides detailed guidance on the role of the NED, the number of independent NEDs on a main board, and crucially a good definition of independence. For that reason it made a significant positive contribution to UK corporate governance. Its weakness is perhaps that companies get to say who is independent or not according to the Higgs criteria without any additional external scrutiny. Only time will tell whether companies will abide by the spirit of the Review and attribute definitions of independence honestly. (See also the Tyson Report (2003) which followed up on some of the Higgs Recommendations as to implementation (http://www.icaew.com/en/library/subjectgateways/corporate-governance/codes-and-reports/tyson-report) and the Smith Report (2003) which amended the UK Corporate Governance Code to ensure the independence and integrity of the Audit Committee in the aftermath of Enron (https://www.icaew.com/en/library/subject-gateways/corporate-governance/codes-and-reports/smith-report).

Corporate governance failure and the financial crisis

16.38 In autumn 2008 extreme risk taking on the part of the world's major banks almost brought about the collapse of the global financial system. The UK, because of the importance of the banking sector to its economy, was particularly badly affected with the Government stepping in to save a number of major banks from collapse. UK Government financial commitment to the banking sector as a result of the financial crisis reached over 60 per cent of UK GDP in 2010 (BOE Data 2010); the biggest bailout of any Western nation at the time. While the trigger for the crisis related to lax lending practices and complex mortgage-backed securities, questions remained as to how shareholders and NEDs allowed and rewarded extreme risk taking by bank employees. To attempt to address these failings the Treasury in February 2009 asked Sir David Walker, a senior adviser to the US investment bank Morgan Stanley and a former director of the Bank of England 'to review corporate governance in UK banks in the light of the experience of critical loss and failure throughout the banking system'. Sir David's connection with Morgan Stanley created significant concern that the committee's report would not provide the governance shake up that the banking industry needed (see the Treasury Committee Report (2008/9) Banking Crisis: reforming corporate governance and pay in the City, http://www .publications.parliament.uk/pa/cm200809/cmselect/cmtreasy/519/519.pdf).

The Walker Report 2009

16.39 In November 2009 Sir David unveiled his report. Having reviewed the problems within the UK financial industry he considered that:

(a) the boards of big banks didn't understand the scale of the risks their organisations were running;

(b) that non-executives of big banks did too little to rein in the excesses of the executive directors;

(c) that shareholders in banks also failed to curb reckless gambling by financial institutions, that the owners didn't 'exercise proper stewardship';

(d) and that bankers were paid in a dangerous way which encouraged them to speculate imprudently.

His solutions to these significant problems were as follows:

(i) Financial institutions should form a risk committee, separate from the audit committee, to monitor all substantial transactions and stop the transaction if it is deemed too risky. The committee should be chaired by an NED.

(ii) Currently NEDs devote too little time to their role (20–25 days currently, often for pay of more than £100,000 a year). Bank and financial institution NEDs need to devote 30–36 days each year to the role. They also must be properly trained and scrutinised closely by the FSA to ensure they can hold executives to account.

(iii) The chairmen of banks or other financial institutions similarly devote too little time to their roles and should commit no less than two-thirds of their time to the business. The chairman should have significant and relevant 'financial industry experience' and should face re-election by shareholders every year.

(iv) The remuneration committee should set the pay of executive directors and 'high end' individuals below board level. 'High end' individuals are those 'who as executive board members or other employees perform a significant influence function for the entity or whose activities have, or could have, a material impact on the risk profile of the entity'. The pay of these 'high end' employees should be disclosed (anonymously) in the annual report in bands ranging from '£1 million to £2.5 million, in a range of £2.5 million to £5 million and in £5 million bands thereafter'.

(v) Bonuses or any element of performance pay should have time delays of several years, up to five years, or enough time to assess that the transactions that engaged the bonus or performance pay did indeed benefit the bank in the way intended.

(vi) The board and the FSA should monitor more closely the selling activities of major shareholders to understand what triggered the sales.

(vii) Institutional shareholders and fund managers should be more engaged with the companies they invest in. To encourage this they should comply or explain with the stewardship code overseen by the Financial Reporting Council in the same manner as the Combined Code.

16.40 Judged by the standards of the previous corporate governance reports Sir David's report is sensible and measured in its response. Unfortunately he was not reporting at a 'normal' time and given the public appetite for significant governance reform in the banks responsible for triggering the financial crisis (particularly on pay), 'sensible and measured' was never going to be received well. Indeed the combination of suspicion of conflict of interest because of his position with Morgan Stanley and the lack of any deep reforms meant the report was met with great disappointment. Specifically, many of the reforms he suggested were already present in UK banks before the crisis. Northern Rock had a risk committee, for example, but it failed to stop its collapse. Some bank remuneration committees already had responsibility for 'high end' employees with little effect on risk or pay inflation. Disclosure of executive pay in the Greenbury Committee Report had been one of the largest drivers of increased executive pay, so enhanced disclosure seemed unlikely to help. Away from the pay recommendations, the Walker Report recommendations on enhanced NEDs and shareholder stewardship are indeed a contribution to the development of corporate governance principles generally within UK listed companies but overall the sense that the review was incomplete led to a continuing set of reforms.

Ongoing reform

16.41 Between 2009 and 2018 a number of key reports and reforms took place related to the financial crisis and its aftermath. Following on from the Walker Report in June 2010 the Financial Reporting Council (FRC) produced a new version of the Combined Code renaming it the UK Corporate Governance Code. The new code emphasised ongoing communication and engagement between the board and shareholders, enhanced the NED role, recommended the annual re-election of directors, and announced that a new 'Stewardship Code' would be produced as a guide to all shareholders on responsible engagement with companies. In July 2010 the FRC produced its 'Stewardship Code'. Although the Code does not explicitly define what it means by 'Stewardship' the preface to the Code states:

> The Stewardship Code aims to enhance the quality of engagement between institutional investors and companies to help improve long-term returns to shareholders and the efficient exercise of governance responsibilities. Engagement includes pursuing purposeful dialogue on strategy, performance and the management of risk, as well as on issues that are the immediate subject of votes at general meetings.

The Code then goes on to outline core principles that institutional investors should:

- publicly disclose their policy on how they will discharge their stewardship responsibilities;
- have a robust policy on managing conflicts of interest in relation to stewardship and this policy should be publicly disclosed;
- monitor their investee companies;
- establish clear guidelines on when and how they will escalate their activities as a method of protecting and enhancing shareholder value;
- be willing to act collectively with other investors where appropriate;
- have a clear policy on voting and disclosure of voting activity.

The idea behind both the updating of the UK Corporate Governance Code and the emergence of a 'Stewardship Code' was to address wider corporate governance concerns revealed by the financial crisis focused on the short-term behaviour of shareholders and the ability of NEDs to monitor. The Code was updated again in 2012, 2014, 2016, and 2018 to improve issues such as audit and risk standards, enhance diversity, remuneration transparency, succession planning, and corporate culture. Similarly the Stewardship Code was updated to address criticisms that 'stewardship' was too vague. Importantly the Code has moved from an emphasis on 'comply or explain' to an evaluation of how the main principles are applied by companies. Over time compliance with the UK Corporate Governance Code by FTSE 350 companies has been patchy but is improving and by 2019 companies declaring compliance reached 73 per cent (a record high). Worryingly though, problems remained focused on key red-flag areas such as quality of reporting, succession, independent NEDs and chairs, risk reporting, as well as audit, remuneration, and shareholder engagement issues. (See https://www2.grant-thornton.co.uk/rs/445-UIT-144/images/Corporate%20Governance%20Review%20 2019%20%28LP1%29.pdf). Indeed the collapse of Carillion Plc in 2018 and Patisserie Valerie in 2019 has focused regulatory reform once again on corporate governance, audit, and regulatory failure. (See the Kingman Review on Financial Reporting (2018) https:// www.gov.uk/government/publications/financial-reporting-council-review-2018 and the Brydon Review on Audit reform (2019) https://www.gov.uk/government/publications/ the-quality-and-effectiveness-of-audit-independent-review).

16.42 At the EU level there have also been developments related to the financial crisis in 2008. First, in 2010 the Commission produced a *Green Paper on Corporate Governance in Financial Institutions*. In contrast to the UK's Walker Report the paper got to grips with some of the really dysfunctional aspects of bank corporate governance and proposed a range of potential solutions ranging from increased civil and criminal penalties, the prohibition of stock options and golden parachutes, and the introduction of a duty to depositors and stakeholders. Interestingly, and in complete contrast to the UK debate, the paper asks fundamental questions about whether shareholder governance works at all (see https://publications.europa.eu/en/publication-detail/-/publication/1788e830-b050-447c-8214-77ed51b13241/language-en/format-PDF/source-search). The second development was a flurry of initiatives on corporate governance and company law generally, culminating in the May 2017 amendment of the original Shareholders' Rights Directive ((EU) 2017/828). The revisions are aimed at enhancing and facilitating greater shareholder long-term engagement in monitoring management. As the Commission explained:

> Key elements of the proposal include stronger transparency requirements for institutional investors and asset managers on their investment and engagement policies regarding the companies in which they invest as well as a framework to make it easier to identify shareholders so they can more easily exercise their rights (e.g. voting rights), in particular in cross-border situations (44% of shareholders are from another EU Member State or foreign). Proxy advisors would also have to become more transparent on the methodologies they use to prepare their voting recommendations and on how they manage conflicts of interests.

Additionally the Directive includes an EU-wide version of 'say on pay' focused on a shareholder vote on remuneration policy very similar to the UK version.

16.43 In October 2010 BIS (now BEIS) launched a consultation called 'A Long-Term Focus for Corporate Britain: A Call for Evidence'. The review examined the role of directors and shareholders and in particular was concerned about shareholder engagement and market short-termism. The result of this review was the commissioning of a report in

June 2011 from John Kay on *Equity Markets and Long-Term Decision Making* to examine how investors, shareholders, regulators, and the boards of UK-quoted companies focus on the long-term interests of British business and the economy. In February 2012, Kay and his colleagues produced the interim review, which provided a wide range of evidence that British companies were subject to damaging short-term pressures, particularly from shareholders. It then went on to set out ideas for to how to correct this problem, including changes to long-term-focused directors' duties, dual-class voting, and tax incentives to encourage long-term shareholding, and reduced financial disclosure to encourage managers to plan for the longer term. However, of these interim suggested solutions the final report, when it appeared in July 2012, contained only a significant recommendation on removing quarterly disclosure. The report's other main focus, in terms of solving the short-termism problem, was to target the investment chain. This targeting focused on encouraging trust, providing long-term incentives for asset managers, and introducing fiduciary standards of care for those in the investment chain while also encouraging good practice focused on long-term investing. On remuneration for executives, the review refreshingly recommended ultra long-term share incentives to ensure a focus on the very long term. Again, these are significant recommendations, but where shareholders were concerned the final report focused on encouraging a form of enhanced shareholder 'stewardship' based on trust, respect, engagement, and understanding, which included not just engagement with matters of corporate governance but strategic issues as well. In 2014 as part of the Government exploring ways to address the Kay review's identification of short-termism in the investment intermediary chain the Law Commission produced a report and consultation on the fiduciary duties of investment intermediaries with the aim of potentially using fiduciary duties to enhance trust within the investment intermediary chain (see http://www.lawcom.gov.uk/project/fiduciary-duties-of-investment-intermediaries/).

16.44   The pay of executives of large companies has formed a problematic and irresolvable aspect of the UK's corporate governance debate, as we observed earlier in this chapter when we discussed the Greenbury Report. The collapse of the banks and the link between pay and risk observed by the Walker Report added another dimension, while the pay of the chief executives of the failed banks added pay for failure to the debate. In 2007, the year that led to the collapse of Royal Bank of Scotland (RBS), Halifax Bank of Scotland (HBOS), and Lloyds TSB, Fred Godwin (formerly Sir—his knighthood for services to banking was removed in 2012), the Chief Executive of RBS, was paid £4,190,000; Andy Hornby, HBOS Chief Executive was paid £1,926,000; Eric Daniels, Chief Executive of Lloyds TSB, was paid £2,884,000. As they each left their positions in the failed banks their severance packages proved extremely controversial. For leading RBS to collapse (Sir) Fred Godwin received a severance package worth £16.9 million (eventually he received a reduced amount). Eric Daniels, the Chief Executive of Lloyds TSB, left the bank in 2010 having been paid approximately £2.5 million in pay and bonus that year plus a £5 million pension. Andy Hornby, by far the youngest of the three, was paid £2.06 million in 2008, but did partly recognise the issue of reward for failure and waived his severance pay and pension rights. However he was also granted a consultancy post with the bank worth £720,000 a year, which proved extremely controversial and was terminated in 2009.

Excessive remuneration and reward for failure in the failed banks built and surpassed already existing public resentment at perceived rampant elite remuneration. As a result, an independent review on remuneration problems in the UK was undertaken by the High Pay Commission in 2011.

16.45   The High Pay Commission's final report 'Cheques With Balances: Why Tackling High Pay Is In the National Interest' concluded that excessive high pay, exemplified by some executive salaries increasing by 4,000 per cent over 30 years while average worker salaries increased modestly, was damaging companies, the economy, and society as a whole. In finding no evidence that a labour market for executives was driving this increase in pay the Commission recommended a number of solutions. These were: simplifying executive pay, placing employees on remuneration committees, publishing a company's top ten executive pay packages, requiring companies to publish a pay ratio between the highest paid executive and the company median, making firms reveal the total pay figure earned by executives, and the formation of a permanent national body to monitor high pay (see http://highpaycentre.org/).

16.46   Given the public concern and the seeming inability of companies themselves to control remuneration ss 79–82 of the ERRA 2013 introduced an enhanced version of the existing 'say on pay regime'. The director's remuneration report must now contain both the detail of payments to directors and the remuneration policy under which the payments were made. At least every three years the remuneration policy of the company must be put to the shareholders for a binding vote requiring a 50 per cent majority for approval. Payments can then not be made which will breach the policy without an additional shareholder vote to approve the payment. An advisory vote must also be held each year seeking shareholder approval for the payments made in the previous year. If the vote fails it then forces a binding vote on remuneration policy at the next AGM. Companies with over 250 employees have also been required under s 147 of the Small Business, Enterprise and Employment Act 2015 to publish information from 2017 on any differences in the pay of males and females within their organisations. The resulting disclosures have illustrated the sometimes enormous gulf between male and female salaries in companies (see https://www.gov.uk/guidance/gender-pay-gap-reporting-overview#mandatory-gender-pay-gap-reporting).

16.47   After the Brexit referendum in June 2016 and David Cameron's resignation as Prime Minister in July 2016, Theresa May was elected leader of the Conservative Party and became Prime Minister. Part of her campaign for that role and her subsequent general election campaign in April to July 2017 focused on a renewed British industrial strategy. As part of that her Government introduced a consultation that led to a Green Paper on corporate governance. The focus of the proposed reforms was executive pay, employee/customer/supplier voice, and corporate governance in large private businesses. From the consultation on these issues the Government invited the FRC to: revise the UK Corporate Governance Code to provide more specific advice on dealing with significant shareholder opposition to executive pay issues (there was a feeling that shareholder opposition could be easily ignored); enhance the role of the remuneration committee to include overseeing pay across the company; and explaining the alignment of executive pay to the wider workforce (executives had been increasingly avoiding board or full board roles in order to escape remuneration committee scrutiny of their salaries and so extending the remit to cover all workforce pay addresses that problem and also provides the remuneration committee with responsibility for explaining their decisions company-wide); extend the recommended minimum vesting period for executive share awards from three to five years (this provides a longer term focus); to introduce an employee voice provision within the Code, requiring a company to choose one of either a designated NED representing employees, an employee advisory council, or a director from the workforce (this potentially addressed a long-running issue about the importance of employee voice at board level); develop a set of corporate principles for large private companies (corporate governance issues are not just confined to listed companies and so it is hoped this development would encourage good practice outside the listed market). However the collapse of the listed construction company Carillion in January 2018 and its apparent range of corporate governance issues including audit and remuneration failure as well as the FRC's handling of it led to the recommendation by the Kingman Review that the FRC be replaced by an new independent statutory regulator called the Audit, Reporting and Governance Authority. Progress on the Corporate Governance Code is currently stalled as that transition has still to take place as we write in April 2020 and is likely to be further delayed by the wider impact of the Covid-19 pandemic (see the Kingman Review (2018), https://www.gov.uk/government/news/independent-review-of-the-financial-reporting-council-frc-launches-report).

16.48 However the Government itself has actioned its key concerns by introducing secondary legislation in the Companies (Miscellaneous Reporting) Regulations 2018 (SI 2018/860) where:

- Large companies are required to include a statement as part of their strategic report describing how the directors have had regard to the matters in s 172(1)(a)–(f) of the Companies Act 2006.

- Companies with more than 250 UK employees are required to include a statement as part of their directors' report summarising how the directors have engaged with employees, how they have had regard to employee interests, and the effect of that regard, including on the principal decisions taken by the company in the financial year.

- Large companies are required to include a statement as part of their directors' report summarising how the directors have had regard to the need to foster the company's business relationships with suppliers, customers, and others, and the effect of that regard, including on the principal decisions taken by the company during the financial year.

- Very large private and public unlisted companies are required to include a statement as part of their directors' report stating which corporate governance code, if any, has been applied and how. If the company has departed from any aspect of the code it must set out the respects in which it did so, and the reasons. If the company has not applied any corporate governance code, the statement must explain why that is the case and what arrangements for corporate governance were applied.

- Quoted companies with more than 250 UK employees are required to publish, as part of their directors' remuneration report, the ratio of their CEO's total remuneration to the median (50th), 25th, and 75th percentile full-time equivalent remuneration of their UK employees. Alongside this, companies have to publish supporting information, including the reasons for changes to the ratios from year to year and, in the case of the median ratio, whether, and if so how, the company believes this ratio is consistent with the company's wider policies on employee pay, reward, and progression.

- All quoted companies are required to illustrate, in the directors' remuneration policy within their directors' remuneration report, the effect of future share price increases on executive pay outcomes. Companies are also required to include a summary in their directors' remuneration report of any discretion that has been exercised on executive remuneration outcomes reported that year in respect of share price appreciation or depreciation during the relevant performance periods.

The Government has also asked the Investment Association to maintain a public register of shareholder opposition to pay awards and how the company says it will respond. This, it hoped, would allow problematic companies and their responses to be tracked over time (BEIS, Corporate Governance Reform: government response (2017), https://www.gov .uk/government/consultations/corporate-governance-reform#history).

16.49 The financial crisis also triggered a concern that gender played a role in the 'group think' that nearly destroyed the banking sector in the UK. As a result of this and wider equality issues BIS (now BEIS) commissioned Lord Davies to examine the issues surrounding gender at board level in UK companies. In February 2011 Lord Davies' report 'Women on Boards' was published. The report found that only 135 out of 1,076 (12.5 per cent) FTSE 100 board seats were held by women and 18 of those companies had no women on the board at all. In the wider FTSE 250, things were worse with nearly 50 per cent of firms having no women at all on their boards. The report noted that change was occurring but at a very slow pace, and at current rates of increase it would take 70 years to reach gender parity. The report considered lack of female representation on the boards to be a huge waste of talent and, while it did not feel that mandatory gender targets were appropriate, it recommended all FTSE 350 companies publish in aspirational terms the percentage of women they aimed to have on their boards by 2013 and 2015. FTSE 100 firms in particular were given a minimum aim of 25 per cent by 2015. It also recommended that all quoted companies be required to disclose each year the proportion of women on their board, women in senior executive positions, and female employees in the whole organisation; and as part of their corporate governance compliance companies should explain how diversity is catered for in their appointments processes and consider how to mentor aspiring female candidates for board membership. In 2012 a one-year review of the effect of the Davies report seemed to show evidence of an increase in women on the boards of both FTSE 100 and 250 companies sufficient to reach the minimum FTSE 100 minimum target of 25 per cent by 2015. The formal process of integrating the Davies recommendations into the UK Corporate Governance Code was completed in 2012, which seems to have had a further boosting effect on gender equality. In his 2014 review Lord Davies noted:

> Women's representation on FTSE 100 boards now stands at 20.7%, up from 12.5% in 2011, with only two all male boards remaining. The FTSE 250 have achieved 15.6%, up from 7.8% in 2011 - with 83 of the FTSE 250 all male boards in 2011 now having recruited one or more women onto their boards.

By 2015 representation hit 26.1 per cent made up of 31.4 per cent non-executive positions and 9.6 per cent women in executive roles. Additionally in 2011 there were 152 all-male FTSE 350 boards which has now reduced to just 15. Building on this progress in 2017 the Hampton-Alexander Review, *Improving gender balance in FTSE Leadership*, set a 33 per cent target of women on FTSE 350 boards and 33 per cent of women in FTSE 100 leadership teams by 2020. By 2018, FTSE 100 companies had over 30 per cent of their board positions filled by women for the first time and FTSE 350 companies had 26 per cent of their board positions filled by women (see https://ftsewomenleaders.com/wp-content/uploads/2020/02/HA-Review-Report-2018.pdf). However despite these gains the European Commission regards progress on board gender equality achieved by self-regulation across Member States as too slow and is considering introducing an EU Directive for Europe-wide quotas for women on boards (see http://ec.europa.eu/justice/gender-equality/files/documents/140303_factsheet_wob_en.pdf).

FURTHER READING

This chapter links with the materials in Chapters 8, 11, and 12 of **Hicks and Goo's Cases and Materials on Company Law** (Oxford, OUP, 2011, xl +649p).

All the corporate governance reports in their various incarnations are available at http://www.icaew.com/en/library/subject-gateways/corporate-governance/codes-and-reports.

The current Financial Reporting Council UK Corporate Governance Code, Stewardship Code, and related ongoing consultations can be found at https://www.frc.org.uk/Our-Work/Corporate-Governance-Reporting/Corporate-governance/UK-Corporate-Governance-Code.aspx.

The Stewardship Code can be found at https://www.frc.org.uk/Our-Work/Codes-Standards/Corporate-governance/UK-Stewardship-Code.aspx.

For an overview of current issues in Stewardship trends, see https://www.fca.org.uk/publications/feedback-statements/fs19-7-building-regulatory-framework-effective-stewardship.

BIS, 'A Long-Term Focus for Corporate Britain: A Call for Evidence' (2010), http://webarchive.nationalarchives.gov.uk/+/http://www.bis.gov.uk/Consultations/a-long-term-focus-for-corporate-britain.

Cheffins, *Company Law: Theory, Structure and Operation* (Oxford, OUP, 1997).

Company Law Reform (Cm 6456, 2005) (Consultative Document, March 2005), para 7B, http://webarchive.nationalarchives.gov.uk/+/http://www.dti.gov.uk/cld/WhitePaper.pdf.

Davies (2011) 'Women on Boards', https://www.gov.uk/government/uploads/system/uploads/attachment_data/file/31480/11-745-women-on-boards.pdf and https://www.gov.uk/government/uploads/system/uploads/attachment_data/file/482059/BIS-15-585-women-on-boards-davies-review-5-year-summary-october-2015.pdf.

Dignam, 'A Principled Approach to Self-Regulation? The Report of the Hampel Committee on Corporate Governance' [1998] *Co Law* 140.

Dignam and Galanis, *The Globalization of Corporate Governance* (Farnham, Ashgate, 2009), chs 5 and 6.

European Commission, *Green Paper on Corporate Governance in Financial Institutions* (2010), http://ec.europa.eu/internal_market/company/modern/corporate_governance_in_financial_institutions_en.htm.

Finch, 'Board Performance and Cadbury on Corporate Governance' [1992] *JBL* 581.

Hampton-Alexander Review, *Improving gender balance in FTSE Leadership* (2017), https://www.gov.uk/government/publications/ftse-women-leaders-hampton-alexander-review.

High Pay Commission, 'Cheques With Balances: Why Tackling High Pay Is In the National Interest' (2011), http://highpaycentre.org/.

Kay Review, *Equity Markets and Long-Term Decision Making* (2012), https://www.gov.uk/government/consultations/the-kay-review-of-uk-equity-markets-and-long-term-decision-making.

Moore, *Corporate Governance in the Shadow of the State* (Oxford, Hart, 2013).

Myners Report, *Institutional Investment in the UK: A Review* (2001), http://webarchive.nationalarchives.gov.uk/+/http://www.hm-treasury.gov.uk/media/1/6/31.pdf.

Parkinson, *Corporate Power and Responsibility: Issues in the Theory of Company Law* (Oxford, OUP, 1993).

Pettet, 'Towards a Competitive Company Law' [1998] *Co Law* 134.

Riley, 'Controlling Corporate Management: UK and US Initiatives' [1994] *LS* 244.

Wedderburn, 'The Social Responsibilities of Companies' [1982] *Melbourne University L Rev* 1.

Wedderburn, 'Companies and Employees: Common Law or Social Dimension?' [1993] *LQR* 220.

Wheeler, *A Reader on the Law of the Business Enterprise* (Oxford, OUP, 1995).

SELF-TEST QUESTIONS

1   Can industry-based solutions to corporate governance problems ever be effective?

2   Can directors' pay be restrained by law?

3   Will s 172 of the CA 2006 and the business review stakeholder provisions work in practice?

4   Who should directors be responsible to?

5   Have NEDs operated as an effective constraint on management?

17 Corporate rescue and liquidations in outline

SUMMARY

Corporate rescue
Liquidations
Voluntary winding-up
Compulsory winding-up
The consequences of a winding-up petition on dispositions of company property
Winding-up in the public interest
The duties and functions of the liquidator
Avoidance of transactions entered into prior to the liquidation
The personal liability of directors under the Insolvency Act 1986
Distribution of surplus assets
Dissolution
Reform

Corporate rescue

17.1 The current regime governing liquidations owes its antecedents to the *Report of the Review Committee on Insolvency Law and Practice* (Cork Committee Report (Cmnd 8558, 1982)) and the recommendations of the Cork Committee led to the Insolvency Act 1986 (IA 1986). A principal objective of the 1986 reforms was to facilitate a rescue culture, i.e. enable companies in financial difficulties to be rescued before sliding into insolvency. Indeed, this objective has been described as fundamental to much of the IA 1986 (*Powdrill v Watson* (1995), Lord Browne-Wilkinson). In essence, 'rescue' is 'a major intervention necessary to avert eventual failure of the company' (Belcher (1997)). As explained by the Cork Committee:

> a concern for the livelihood and well-being of those dependent upon an enterprise which may well be the lifeblood of a whole town or even a region is a legitimate factor to which a modern law of insolvency must have regard. The chain reaction consequences upon any given failure can potentially be so disastrous to creditors, employees and the community that it must not be overlooked. (Para 204)

Events surrounding the closure of MG Rover in Longbridge in 2005 illustrate the devastating consequences that the 'chain reaction' noted by Cork can cause (see the report of the National Audit Office, https://www.nao.org.uk/report/the-closure-of-mg-rover/).

17.2 Two procedures were introduced by the IA 1986 aimed at implementing the objective of corporate rescue: (i) the administration order; and (ii) the company voluntary arrangement (CVA), these are outlined later. The administration procedure was fundamentally reformed by the Enterprise Act 2002. More generally, liquidation law has been the subject of reforms introduced by the Enterprise Act 2002 (which inserted Sch B1 into the IA 1986), the Deregulation Act 2015, the Small Business, Enterprise and Employment Act 2015 (SBEEA 2015), and the Insolvency (England and Wales) Rules 2016 (SI 2016/1024) (IR 2016) which consolidated, with amendments, the secondary legislation in England and Wales (as from 6 April 2017). The reforms are aimed at reducing costs by streamlining and simplifying the law. Finally, in terms of taxonomy, it should be noted that 'liquidation' and 'winding-up' are merely labels that cover the procedure governing the way in which a company, whether solvent or insolvent, is dissolved.

(i) Administration

17.3 Section 8 together with para 3(1) of Sch B1 to the IA 1986, as substituted by s 248 of the Enterprise Act 2002 (see also Parts 3, 14–15, and 18 of the IR 2016, which cover operational matters), lay down the objective of administration in terms of the duty borne by the administrator. An administrator (who must be a qualified insolvency practitioner (IP), note that both the SBEEA 2015 and the Deregulation Act 2015 reform the system of regulation of IPs):

> must perform his functions -with the objective of:
>
> (a) rescuing the company as a going concern, or
>
> (b) achieving a better result for the company's creditors as a whole than would be likely if the company were wound up . . . ,
>
> (c) realising the property in order to make a distribution to one or more secure or preferential creditors.

17.4 The court may appoint an administrator on application by the company, the directors, or one or more creditors where the company is or is likely to become unable to pay its debts and the appointment is reasonably likely to achieve one of the three specified purposes listed above (see paras 11, 12, 14, and 22 of Sch B1 to the 1986 Act; see *Fliptex Ltd v Hogg* (2004); *Re Eco Link Resources Ltd* (2012); and *Bank of Scotland plc v Targetfollow Property Holdings* (2010)). One of the objectives of the reforms introduced by the Enterprise Act 2002 was to promote out-of-court entry routes into administration. This has the advantage of saving costs. Appointment of administrators can thus be made by the company or its directors or by a qualifying floating charge holder (QFCH) (see paras 14–21 of Sch B1 to the 1986 Act and rr 3.16–3.26 of IR 2016); for the issues that can arise by such appointments, see, for example, *Petit v Bradford Bulls (Northern) Ltd* (2016) and *Re BHS Ltd* (2016). Once appointed, the administrator has up to eight weeks to produce a report setting out proposals for the future of the company's business (para 49(5) of Sch B1). This must be put to the creditors for their approval. If the administrator's proposals are rejected, the company will generally be put into liquidation. If, on the other hand, the creditors accept the proposals, their rights can be restructured under a scheme of arrangement and the company will exit administration. The administrator must report the outcome to the court (para 53 of Sch B1). There is a 12-month fixed time limit for the completion of administrations, although it is possible to obtain time extensions (see IR 2016, r 3.54; and s 127 of SBEEA 2015).

During administration the company has the benefit of a moratorium on insolvency proceedings being initiated against it (paras 42–44 of Sch B1). The effect is to protect the company from hostile actions of its creditors. Thus, for example, the company cannot be wound up and no steps may be taken by charge holders to enforce any security over the company's property (s 10(1) of the IA 1986; paras 70–71 of Sch B1; see *Bristol Airport plc v Powdrill* (1990)). However, the moratorium can be displaced where the interests of justice so require. For example, in *Uniserve Ltd v Croxen* (2012), the court came down in favour of the rights of contractual lien holders to retain goods in their possession rather than allowing the claims of the administrators who wanted the moratorium continued (see also *Re UK Housing Alliance (North West) Ltd* (2013)).

17.5 The legislation confers a wide range of management powers on the administrator so that he 'may do all such things as may be necessary for the management of the affairs, business and property of the company' (s 14(1)). These include the power to remove and appoint directors (s 14 of IA 1986, Sch 1 and para 61 of Sch B1) and to dispose of property subject to a floating charge (para 70 of Sch B1) and, with the court's consent, property subject to a fixed charge (para 71 of Sch B1). Additional powers were given to administrators by s 117 of the SBEEA 2015 so as to enable them to bring proceedings for fraudulent and wrongful trading (see paras **17.64** and **17.71**). However, curiously administrators do not have a power of disclaimer and so the court in *Re Graico Property Co Ltd* (2016) had to place the company which was in administration into liquidation in order to enable the disclaimer of an onerous lease.

The approach that the court should take towards the administration process was explained by Neuberger J in *Re T & D Industries plc* (2000). Here the joint administrators of two connected companies applied for a direction under s 14(3) of the IA 1986 that no direction of the court was necessary before they could dispose of assets belonging to the companies even though the proposed sale had not been laid before the creditors. The judge, noting that administration proceedings were intended to be a cheaper and more informal alternative to liquidation, held that in the circumstances they did not require the court's leave. In his reasoning, he outlined the relevant principles which should guide administrators in the exercise of their powers. Neuberger J stated that although an administrator needs time to obtain the necessary information and advice before he can make his proposals, this should be done as speedily and efficiently as possible and it is desirable for administrators to call a meeting of creditors as soon as is reasonably feasible. Commercial and administrative decisions are for the administrator and not the court and an application for directions is only appropriate where there is a point of principle in issue or a dispute as to the appropriate course of action to be taken. Where an administrator needs to make an urgent decision he should have what consultation he can with the creditors (see further *Re Transbus International Ltd* (2004), in which Lawrence Collins J expressly adopted Neuberger J's statement of principles as applicable to the administration regime). References to creditors' meetings should now be read in the light of the recent reforms aimed at speeding up the process and cutting costs. A creditors' meeting is no longer the default requirement unless requested by 10 per cent of the creditors in value, or by 10 per cent of their number or by ten individual creditors (see ss 246ZE–246ZG and 379ZA–379ZC of IA 1986). Further, the SBEEA 2015 introduced the 'deemed consent' device and deregulated the procedures for the giving of notices to creditors. Where an office-holder writes to creditors with a proposal, and does not receive objections from 10 per cent of creditors in value, the proposal is deemed to be approved. This procedure is available unless the court or the insolvency legislation requires the use of a creditors' decision-making procedure (ss 246F and 379B of IA 1986; see the IR 2016, rr 15.6 and 15.7).

Pre-packaged sales in administration

17.6 The use of so-called 'pre-packaged' administrations as a strategic response to the onset of corporate difficulties are increasing. According to the Insolvency Service (see the *Report on the First Months' Operation of Statement of Insolvency Practice 16* (July 2009)), a pre-pack is:

> *any situation where the business of an insolvent company is prepared for sale to a selected buyer ('pre-packaged'), prior to the company's entry into formal insolvency proceedings. The agreed sale is carried out by an authorised insolvency practitioner acting as office holder within the proceedings, shortly following their appointment.*

Very often the pre-pack purchaser is one or more of the existing owner/managers of the insolvent company. Perhaps not surprisingly, therefore, pre-packaged sales have generated considerable controversy in the media and amongst politicians on the basis that all too frequently creditors are given insufficient information to be able to influence events or to determine whether or not the sale was in their best interests. This lack of transparency has given rise to allegations that the procedure has been used to benefit purchasers at the expense of creditors so that it is little more than a facet of the 'phoenix' syndrome. While it is beyond the scope of this book to examine the merits and disadvantages of the process (see the summary provided by HHJ Cooke in *Re Kayley Vending Ltd* (2009); see further Finch and Milman (2017: ch 10), suffice it to say that by way of response to the criticisms, the Association of Business Recovery Professionals (R3) issued the Statement of Insolvency

Practice (SIP) 16, which came into force in January 2009. SIP 16 is principally directed towards increasing the levels of information available to creditors in order to reinforce the transparency of the pre-pack process. More particularly, it introduces a requirement to provide creditors with key information regarding the (pre-pack) sale as soon as possible after its completion. Given the criticisms directed towards the lack of transparency in pre-pack sales, BIS (now BEIS) issued a statement on 31 March 2011 announcing that steps were being taken to 'improve transparency and confidence' in the process. The measures include:

1.   *in circumstances where there has been no open marketing of the assets, a requirement that administrators give notice to creditors when they propose to sell a significant proportion of the assets of a company or its business to a connected party,*

2.   *a requirement that administrators file with Companies House a detailed explanation of why a pre-pack sale was undertaken,*

3.   *a requirement that administrators confirm that the sale price represents best value for the creditors.*

In the light of the various calls for increased transparency, a new SIP 16 was issued which came into effect on 1 November 2013. The key aim is to provide clear, comprehensive, and timely explanations to creditors. Amongst other things, it gives emphasis to the importance of transparency in pre-pack administration sales. For example, principle 4 states that '[c]reditors should be provided with a detailed explanation and justification of why a pre-packaged sale was undertaken, to demonstrate that the administrator has acted with due regard for their interests'. It also contains provisions relating to disclosure. Administrators should provide creditors with a detailed narrative 'explanation and justification' of why a sale was undertaken, confirming that the sale price was the best reasonably obtainable in the circumstances. The objective is to demonstrate that the administrator acted 'with due regard' to the interests of creditors.

In July 2013, the Insolvency Service launched a review of pre-packaged administrations led by Teresa Graham which reported in June 2014 (see https://www.gov.uk/government/publications/graham-review-into-pre-pack-administration). The review encompassed the guidance and advice that is available to creditors and others who are affected by insolvencies. Its terms of reference were to assess:

- the long-term impact of pre-pack deals to form a view as to whether they encourage growth and employment; and whether they provide the best value for creditors as a whole;

- the usefulness of the pre-pack procedure in the context of business rescue generally, using international comparisons as and when appropriate;

- whether pre-packs cause harm to any particular groups of creditors and specifically whether unsecured creditors are disadvantaged;

- whether there are any practices associated with pre-packs that cause harm.

The review broadly supported self-regulation but with more control mechanisms. In this context, it is noteworthy that s 129 of the SBEEA 2015 amends Sch B1, para 60 of the IA 1986 and inserts para 60A which, subject to certain conditions, empowers the Secretary of State to make regulations to prohibit or impose conditions on sales, disposals, or hiring out of the assets of the company in administration to connected persons without obtaining approval from the court, the creditors, or other persons specified in the regulations.

(ii) Company voluntary arrangement (CVA)

17.7 As an alternative to the burdensome procedure laid down in s 425 of the CA 1985 for a statutory scheme of arrangement (see Chapter 5), ss 1–7 of the IA 1986, which are based on Cork Committee recommendations, provide for a company to enter into a voluntary arrangement with its creditors by way of a straightforward procedure that allows it to organise its debts. Section 1(1) defines a CVA as 'a composition in satisfaction of its debts or a scheme of arrangement of its affairs'. Directors may initiate a CVA by making a proposal to the company and its creditors for a voluntary arrangement. However, if the company is in liquidation or is subject to an administration order, the directors cannot make a 'proposal'; rather the liquidator or administrator may, albeit subject to a different procedure. The term 'proposal' is defined by s 1(1) as 'one which provides for some person (the "nominee" [who must be an insolvency practitioner]) to act in relation to the voluntary arrangement either as trustee or otherwise for the purpose of supervising its implementation'. The nominee has 28 days after being given notice of the proposal to submit a report to the court stating whether, in his opinion, the proposed CVA has a reasonable chance of being approved and implemented and whether meetings of the company and its creditors should be summoned to consider the proposal (s 2(2); see IR 2016, r 2.25(2) and r 15.3). The approval of the meeting (requiring 75 per cent by reference to the value of their claims of the creditors voting, and 50 per cent in value of the shareholders present at a shareholders' meeting, IR 2016, r 2.36) will bind everyone who was entitled to vote (ss 3–5). There are provisions designed to protect minorities (see, for example, s 6 which lays down the procedure for challenging decisions at the relevant meetings; see, for example, *Re Gatnom Capital & Finance Ltd* (2010)). As a result of reforms introduced by the Insolvency Act 2000, the CVA procedure now provides for a moratorium on enforcement by creditors (IA Act 1986, Sch A1, introduced by s 1 of the 2000 Act).

Liquidations

17.8 In almost all of the preceding chapters many of the company law cases we have examined concern failed companies. Company law by its very nature tends only to be tested where the company has failed and the ashes are raked over and knowledge of the main provisions dealing with failed companies is therefore essential.

17.9 A company ceases to exist when it is dissolved. It is the process leading up to its demise which is termed winding-up or liquidation. Winding-up obviously occurs where the company is unable to pay its debts, i.e. it is insolvent (IA 1986, s 122(1)(f): see later). However, a solvent company may also be wound up for a variety of reasons. For example, the member/managers of a quasi-partnership type of company may wish to retire; or they become deadlocked due to a dispute (*Re Yenidje Tobacco Co Ltd* (1916)); or because the venture which the business was originally incorporated to pursue has come to an end (*Re German Date Coffee Co* (1882): s 122(1)(g) of the 1986 Act, see Chapter 11). Whatever the reason for a company's liquidation, be it insolvent or solvent, the regime governing the process is to be found in the IA 1986 together with the IR 2016.

17.10 As commented earlier, the 1986 Act and its 1985 predecessor were passed in order to implement the recommendations of the Cork Committee which had undertaken a thorough review of insolvency law, including that relating to personal bankruptcy. With respect to the winding-up of companies, the overriding objectives of the 1986 corporate insolvency regime are: (i) to maximise the return to creditors where the company cannot be saved; (ii) to establish a fair system for the ranking of competing claims by creditors; and (iii) to provide a mechanism by which the causes of the company's failure can be identified and those guilty of mismanagement can be made answerable (see further Goode (2011)). The 1986 Act introduced a range of devices aimed at achieving these objectives. Further, reference must also be made to the Enterprise Act 2002 which has done much to recast insolvency law, particularly by removing the Crown Preference (for example, taxes owed by a company are now an unsecured debt). This reform impacts on the floating charge in a way that is designed to prevent such chargees enjoying a total windfall. The 1986 Act has also been amended by the Insolvency Act 2000 and the EC Regulation on Insolvency Proceedings (EC 1346/2000) which came into force in May 2002 and regulates cross-border insolvency proceedings.

17.11 In essence, companies may be wound up through three types of procedure:

- voluntary winding-up,
- compulsory winding-up, and
- on grounds of public interest.

Voluntary winding-up

17.12 A company can initiate its own winding-up. Section 84(1) of the 1986 Act provides that the company may be wound up voluntarily in three situations. First, when the period, if any, fixed for the duration of the company by the articles expires, or the event, if any, occurs for which the articles provide will result in the company being dissolved, and the general meeting has passed a resolution requiring it to be wound up voluntarily (this category is rare nowadays). Second, if the company resolves by special resolution that it be wound up voluntarily. Third, if the company resolves by extraordinary resolution to the effect that it cannot by reason of its liabilities continue its business and that it is advisable to wind up (this will result in a creditors' winding-up). A copy of the resolution must be sent to the Registrar of Companies within 15 days (s 84(3) of IA 1986). The company shall, within 14 days of the passing of the resolution, give notice of it by placing an advertisement in the *Gazette*.

The second and third categories specified in s 84 are, in practice, the more common. It is to these we now turn.

Members' voluntary winding-up

17.13 In a members' winding-up the directors swear a declaration of solvency to the effect that they have made a full enquiry into the company's affairs and that they have formed the opinion that the company will be able to pay its creditors in full, together with interest at the official rate, within such period, not exceeding 12 months from the commencement of the winding-up, as may be specified in the resolution (s 89(1) of IA 1986; see the IR 2016, Pt 5). The declaration must contain a statement of the company's assets and liabilities as at the latest practicable date before the making of the declaration. A director swearing a declaration of solvency must have reasonable grounds for his opinion that the company will be able to pay its debts in full, including interest, within the period specified in the declaration otherwise he will be liable to imprisonment or a fine, or both (s 89(4)). If the debts are not paid in full within the specified period it is presumed that the director did not have reasonable grounds for his opinion. If there is no such declaration of solvency the winding-up will be classified a 'creditors' voluntary winding-up' (s 90), and their debts may not be satisfied in full.

17.14 A voluntary winding-up is deemed to commence at the time of the passing of the special resolution by the general meeting declaring that the company be wound up voluntarily (ss 84(1) and 86). Henceforth the company will cease to carry on business except insofar as may be required for its beneficial winding-up (s 87(1)). Any transfer of shares without the sanction of the liquidator, and any alteration in the status of the company's members, will be void (s 88).

17.15 The general meeting appoints one or more liquidators for the purpose of winding up the company's affairs and distributing its assets. On the appointment of a liquidator all the powers of the directors cease, except insofar as the company in general meeting or the liquidator sanctions their continuance (s 91(1) and (2)). The principal role of the liquidator in a voluntary winding-up is to realise the company's assets and apply the company's property 'in satisfaction of the company's liabilities *pari passu* and, subject to that application' to distribute its property 'among the members according to their rights and interests in the company' (s 107). As soon as the company's affairs are fully wound up, the liquidator must call a general meeting of the company and lay before it an account of the winding-up showing how the process had been conducted and how the company's property had been disposed of (s 106). If, on the other hand, the liquidator is of the opinion that the company will be unable to pay its debts in full (together with interest at the official rate) within the period stated in the directors' declaration, he can change the members' winding-up into a creditors' winding-up provided he goes through the procedural conditions laid down in s 95.

Creditors' voluntary winding-up

17.16 Where a directors' declaration of solvency has not been made, the liquidation is a creditors' voluntary liquidation (s 90). As with a members' voluntary liquidation, this is also brought about by the company's members (see IR 2016, Pt 6). This is done either by passing a special resolution or by passing an extraordinary resolution to the effect that the company 'cannot by reason of its liabilities continue its business, and that it is advisable to wind up' (s 84(1)). Section 98(1) of the IA 1986 provides that the company must call a meeting of creditors within 14 days of the meeting at which the resolution for voluntary winding-up is to be proposed. The section also requires notices of the creditors' meeting to be sent by post to the creditors not less than seven days before the day on which that meeting is to be held and that the meeting be advertised in the *Gazette* and in at least two newspapers circulating in the locality where the company's principal place of business is situated. At that meeting the directors must lay before it a 'statement of affairs' showing particulars of the company's assets, debts, and liabilities; the names and addresses of its creditors; the securities held by them; and the dates when such securities were given (s 99). It was noted earlier (para **17.5**) that the SBEEA 2015 abolishes the s 98 requirement for a physical creditors' meeting (s 126). Creditors' views can now be sought by less expensive methods such as virtual meetings (see IR 2016, r 6.14; and Sch 9 to the 2015 Act). The 14-day requirement in s 98(1) of the IA 1986 continues to apply. It will be recalled that physical meetings are only required if 10 per cent of creditors (in number or in value) or ten creditors call for such a meeting (s 246ZE of IA 1986); for gazetting and the requirements governing notices, see IR 2016, Pt 1.

17.17 At the respective meetings of the company and the creditors, a person may be nominated to be liquidator for the purpose of winding up the company's affairs and distributing its assets (s 100). If different persons are nominated the creditors' decision takes priority. However, s 100(3) goes on to provide that in the event of there being different nominees, any director, member, or creditor may, within seven days of the creditors' nomination, apply to the court for an order either that the company's nominee shall become the liquidator or joint liquidator with the creditors' nominee, or that some other person shall be liquidator.

17.18 Upon the appointment of a liquidator all powers of the directors cease except to the extent sanctioned by the liquidation committee, or if there is no such committee, by the creditors (s 103). It is further provided that if 'from any cause whatever there is no liquidator acting' the court may appoint one; it also has jurisdiction to remove a liquidator 'on cause shown' and appoint another (s 108). In *AMP Music Box Enterprises Ltd v Hoffman* (2002) Neuberger J refused a creditor's application to remove the liquidators of a company where it had been alleged that they lacked independence. Although criticisms could be made of the liquidators' conduct with respect to their investigation of the claims of two supporting creditors, they had lacked time to deal with the matter and, in any case, had spent the preceding five weeks dealing with the present application. It would be unfair to the liquidators and, more significantly, unnecessary for the creditors' and company's interest as well as unnecessarily disruptive and expensive to remove them.

The liquidation committee

17.19 To encourage creditor participation (a key recommendation of the Cork Committee), the creditors may appoint a liquidation committee to liaise with the liquidator on behalf of them all. Appointing a liquidation committee has the advantage of facilitating efficient communication with the liquidator because it avoids the necessity of convening full meetings of the creditors and members. The committee may consist of at least three but not more than five creditors (s 101(2)). In a solvent winding-up, up to three contributories may also be members of the committee. In a creditors' voluntary winding-up, provided no objections are raised, up to five members of the company can sit on the committee. However, should the creditors object to the presence of company members they can be displaced and on any application to the court, the court may, if it thinks fit, appoint other persons to act as members in place of those specified in the resolution (s 101). Section 141 states that the purpose of the liquidation committee is to exercise the functions conferred on it under the Act. The primary role of the liquidation committee is to monitor the actions of the liquidator in his conduct of the winding-up process and to sanction the exercise of his powers (see further the IR 2016). The liquidator is under a duty to keep the liquidation committee informed of matters arising out of the winding-up and to supply it with information (r 17.21).

17.20 As seen earlier, as soon as the company's affairs are fully wound up the liquidator is under a duty to make up an account showing how the winding-up had been conducted and the company's property disposed of. In relation to a creditors' winding-up, it has been seen that the SBEEA 2015 and the IR 2016 have relaxed the requirements for creditors' meetings (see para **17.5**).

Compulsory winding-up

17.21 Although not all of the grounds for compulsory liquidation require a petition, in practice it will normally arise by way of court proceedings being brought against the company by an unpaid creditor. Technically, there are seven grounds on which the court may order a company to be wound up. These are set out in s 122(1) of the 1986 Act:

    (a) the company has by special resolution resolved that the company be wound up by the court;

    (b) being a public company which was registered as such on its original incorporation, the company has not been issued with a certificate under s 117 of the

Companies Act (public company share capital requirements) and more than a year has expired since it was so registered;

(c) it is an old public company, within the meaning of the Consequential Provisions Act;

(d) the company does not commence its business within a year from its incorporation or suspends its business for a whole year;

(e) the number of members is reduced below two;

(f) the company is unable to pay its debts;

(g) the court is of the opinion that it is just and equitable that the company should be wound up (see Chapter 11).

For present purposes we will focus upon corporate insolvency, ground (f) although such petitions also generally enlist ground (g) in support of the claim (*Re JE Cade & Son Ltd* (1992)).

The company is unable to pay its debts

17.22 By s 123(1) a company will be deemed to be insolvent if: (i) a creditor, to whom a sum exceeding £750 is owed, has served on the company at its registered office a written demand, in the prescribed form, requiring the company to pay the debt and the company has for three weeks thereafter neglected to pay; or (ii) an execution or other process issued on judgment in favour of a creditor of the company is returned unsatisfied in whole or in part; or (iii) the court is satisfied that 'the company is unable to pay its debts as they fall due' (s 123(1)(e), termed the cash flow test). In this latter case, a company will also be deemed unable to pay its debts if the court is satisfied that the value of the company's assets is less than the amount of its liabilities, taking into account its contingent and prospective liabilities (s 123(2), the 'balance sheet test'; see *Re Cheyne Finance plc* (2008)). The fact that the company is solvent will not of itself be a sufficient ground to have a petition struck out; the failure to pay an undisputed debt which has been repeatedly requested will be taken to mean that the company is unable to pay and the creditor can maintain a winding-up petition (*Taylor's Industrial Flooring Ltd v M & H Plant Hire (Manchester) Ltd* (1990); *Cornhill Insurance plc v Improvement Services Ltd* (1986)).

In *BNY Corporate Trustee Services Ltd v Eurosail-UK 2007-3BL plc* (2013) the Supreme Court considered the meaning of s 123(2) and the phrase a company being 'unable to pays its debts'. The case concerned the insolvency of the Lehman Brothers group which collapsed in September 2008. The particular issue arose out of the acquisition by the group of a portfolio of mortgage loans, most of which were sub-prime, funded by loan notes. Most of the notes were repayable in 2045. Lord Walker, delivering the leading judgment, said that it was unclear how s 123(1)(e) and s 123(2) interacted although the latter seems to be directed towards underlining that the cash flow test includes an element of futurity, but only with regard to the reasonably near future:

Despite the difference of form, the provisions of section 123(1) and (2) should in my view be seen . . . as making little significant change in the law. The changes in form served, in my view, to underline that the 'cash-flow' test is concerned, not simply with the petitioner's own presently-due debt, nor only with other presently-due debt owed by the company, but also with debts falling due from time to time in the reasonably near future. What is the reasonably near future, for this purpose, will depend on all the circumstances, but especially on the nature of the company's business . . . The express reference to assets and liabilities is in my view a practical recognition that once the court has to move beyond the reasonably near future (the length of which depends, again, on all the circumstances) any attempt to apply a cash-flow test will become completely speculative, and a comparison of present assets with present and future liabilities (discounted for contingencies and deferment) becomes the only sensible test. But it is still very far from an exact test, and the burden of proof must be on the party which asserts balance-sheet insolvency.

While the decision is to be welcomed, at least insofar as it clarifies the interrelationship between the two tests, no guidance is given on determining what is the 'reasonably near future'. It does, however, acknowledge that the determination of balance sheet insolvency is more difficult and requires a proper assessment of assets and liabilities. It is also clear that the balance sheet test becomes more difficult to apply as the liabilities falling due become more distant (which, on the facts of the case, fell some 30 years hence).

(See also *Carman v Bucci* (2013).)

17.23 The process for initiating a compulsory winding-up is set in motion by a petition, which must be served on the company, and other parties specified in the rules (see generally IR 2016, Pt 7). It must also be advertised. Section 124(1) specifies the parties who have *locus standi* for bringing an application for winding-up. The section states that a petition may be presented either by the company, its directors, any creditors (whether contingent or prospective), or by any contributories, i.e. members or certain former members (s 79), 'or by all or any of those parties, together or separately'. However, where directors wish to apply for winding-up they must do so as a board, so that the petition must be brought by one or more of the directors acting in accordance with a unanimous or majority resolution of their colleagues (*Re Instrumentation Electrical Services Ltd* (1988)). The right of a contributory to petition for winding-up cannot be limited or excluded by the articles of association (*Re Peveril Gold Mines Ltd* (1898)), but to have standing he must demonstrate that he possesses a tangible interest in the liquidation. Jessel MR in *Re Rica Gold Washing Co* (1879) considered the meaning of 'tangible interest' in relation to a petitioner who held 75 £1 fully paid shares:

He is not liable to contribute anything towards the assets of the company, and if he has any interest at all, it must be that after full payment of all the debts and liabilities of the company there will remain a surplus divisible among the shareholders of sufficient value to authorise him to present a petition . . . the petitioner must show the court by sufficient allegation that he has a sufficient interest to entitle him to ask for the winding-up of the company. I say 'a sufficient interest', for the mere allegation of a surplus or of a probable surplus will not be sufficient. He must show what I may call a tangible interest. I am not going to lay down any rule as to what that must be, but if he showed only that there was such a surplus as, on being fairly divided, irrespective of the costs of the winding-up, would give him £5, I should say that it would not be sufficient to induce the court to interfere in his behalf . . .

17.24   A contributory is not entitled to present a winding-up petition unless either the number of members is reduced below two (single-member private companies excepted), or the shares held by him, or some of them, either were originally allotted to him, or have been held and registered in his name for at least six months during the 18 months before the commencement of the winding-up, or have devolved on him through the death of a former holder (s 124(2)). This is a deterrent provision designed to prevent shares being purchased by individuals whose immediate aim is to launch a winding-up petition. However, whether the stipulated time period is sufficient to achieve this objective is open to doubt.

17.25   As we commented earlier, in practice most petitions are brought by creditors who cannot get paid. However, if the debt is disputed on bona fide grounds the company may apply to have the petition dismissed as an abuse of process without waiting for the substantive hearing (*Re A Company (No 0012209 of 1991)* (1992); *Coilcolor Ltd v Cantrex Ltd* (2015); and *Mulalley And Co Ltd v Regent Building Services Ltd* (2017)). The policy here was explained by Jessel MR in *Re London and Paris Banking Corpn* (1874), in which the petitioner had charged the company £267.00 for furniture. The directors considered the price to be exorbitant and, on the advice of two independent valuers, offered him £197.00. The Master of the Rolls said that the petition was presented:

> *to put pressure upon the company, perhaps by threat of the advertisements, or by some other means, to compel them to pay; in other words, to extort from them a sum larger than they bona fide believed to be due from them, and a sum which they had been advised by two valuers was excessive. I cannot encourage any such course of proceeding, and I therefore dismiss the petition with costs.*

(See also *Ebbvale Ltd v Hosking* (2013) PC.)

Thus, where the debt is disputed on genuine grounds the court will not entertain a winding-up petition. The position was explained further by Pumfrey J in *Re Ringinfo Ltd* (2002):

> *The processes of the Companies Court are not to be used in cases where there are issues of disputed fact. This court is not, for these purposes, a debt-collecting court, and matters of disputed fact must be resolved in actions. A debt disputed on genuine and substantial*

grounds cannot support a winding up petition, and an attempt to invoke the processes of the Companies Court in relation to a debt which is known to be disputed on genuine and substantial grounds is an abuse of the process of the court. The petition will be struck out if the petition has been presented, and an injunction will be granted to restrain its presentation if it has not.

(See *Tallington Lakes Ltd v Ancasta International Boat Sales Ltd* (2012).)

But where the company wishes to put forward a substantial defence to the sum claimed, or a cross-claim, 'it is incumbent upon it to show that the defence or the cross-claim is genuine, serious and of substance' (*Orion Media Marketing Ltd v Media Brook Ltd* (2002), Laddie J).

17.26 On the other hand, provided the creditor is able to show that he is owed a debt of £750 or more and has acted in accordance with the conditions laid down by s 123(1), it is irrelevant that he is motivated by malice or antagonism towards the company or its directors (*Bryanston Finance Ltd v De Vries (No 2)* (1976)). For small debts, s 131 of the SBEEA 2015 relaxes the rules relating to proof for debts of £1,000 or less by introducing a 'deemed proof' procedure (IR 2016, rr 14.1(3) and 14.3(3)). A creditor who is owed a sum in excess of the prescribed threshold is prima facie entitled to a winding-up order *ex debito justitiae*, although the court may refuse to make an order if the petition is not supported by the majority of creditors (s 195). In this respect Hoffmann J has stated that whether or not a winding-up order is granted is within the discretion of the court and that in exercising this discretion regard may be had to a range of factors, including: the number of opposing creditors, the value of the debts owed to them, their quality, their motives, and to general principles of fairness and commercial morality (*Re Lowestoft Traffic Services Ltd* (1986); see also the observations of Park J in *Re Lummus Agricultural Services Ltd* (2001); and see *Angel Group Ltd v British Gas Trading Ltd* (2013)).

17.27 Section 125 lays down the powers of the court on hearing a petition. The court may dismiss the petition, adjourn the hearing conditionally or unconditionally, or make an interim order or any other order that it thinks fit, but it cannot refuse to make a winding-up order on the ground that the company's assets have been fully mortgaged or that the company has no assets (s 125(1)).

17.28 When a winding-up order is made it operates in favour of all the creditors and contributories of the company as if made on the joint petition of a creditor and a contributory (s 130(4)). A liquidator will have to be appointed unless the court made a provisional appointment at some time after the petition was presented (s 135(1)). In this respect s 136(2) provides that on a winding-up order being made by the court the Official Receiver becomes the liquidator of the company and continues in office until another person is appointed. The Official Receiver in discharging his office as liquidator has the power to summon separate meetings of the company's creditors and contributories for the purpose of choosing a person to be liquidator of the company in his place (s 136(4)).

The consequences of a winding-up petition on dispositions of company property

17.29 The 'commencement of the winding-up' is deemed to relate back to the date when the petition was presented (s 129(2)), or exceptionally, where the company is already in a voluntary liquidation, the time of the passing of the resolution for voluntary winding-up (s 129(1)). The retroactive effect of a winding-up order assumes critical importance in relation to dispositions of company property. This is because s 127 provides that in a winding-up by the court, any disposition of the company's property, and any transfer of shares, or alteration in the status of the company's members, made after the commencement of the winding-up is void, unless the court otherwise orders. No court order is required because the sanction is applied automatically. Section 127 does not trigger to invalidate a disposition of property where it has no impact on the creditors, as would be the case where, for example, there has been a disposition by an administrator. But rather, its overall effect is designed to preserve corporate assets for the benefit of the general body of creditors by empowering the liquidator to 'claw back' company property which has been transferred by directors after a petition has been presented and liquidation is imminent (see *Coutts & Co v Stock* (2000), Lightman J; on the meaning of 'property', see *Akers v Samba Financial Group* (2017)).

17.30 A third party dealing with a company against which a winding-up petition has been brought should apply to the court for a validation order, otherwise he runs the risk that the court will refuse to validate the transaction and he will be ordered to transfer back the property that has passed to him unless he acquired it as a bona fide purchaser for value without notice (*Re J Leslie Engineers Co Ltd* (1976)). The court's authorisation can be sought in advance by either party to the transaction or proposed transaction. For example, in *Re AI Levy (Holdings) Ltd* (1964) the court consented to the company's proposed disposal of a lease prior to the petition hearing and a clause in the lease which provided for its forfeiture in the event of the company being wound up did not therefore take effect.

17.31 The court's jurisdiction to grant its consent to a disposition of property is discretionary. Some guidance as to how this discretion will be exercised was provided by Buckley LJ in *Re Gray's Inn Construction Co Ltd* (1980). He observed that it was a fundamental concept of insolvency law that the free assets of the company at the commencement of the liquidation should be distributed rateably among the unsecured creditors (that is, all creditors participate in the common pool of free assets in proportion to the size of their admitted debts, see later). He noted, however, that there may be times when it would be beneficial, both to the company and to its unsecured creditors, that the company be permitted to dispose of some of its property after the petition has been presented but before the winding-up order has been made. This would be the case where, for example, the company has the opportunity by acting speedily to sell an asset at an exceptionally good price. However, Buckley LJ stressed that in considering whether to make a validating order the court should ensure that the interests of the unsecured creditors are not prejudiced. He stated that where an application is made in respect of a specific transaction this may be susceptible of positive proof. On the other hand, whether or not the company should be permitted to carry on business generally is more speculative and will depend on whether a sale of the business as a going concern will be more beneficial than a break-up realisation of the assets.

17.32 Buckley LJ concluded that the court will normally validate a transaction entered into in good faith where the parties are unaware that a petition has been presented unless there are grounds for believing that the disposition involves an attempt to prefer a particular creditor over and above the rest. Accordingly, although the court will be disinclined to consent to any transaction which has the effect of preferring a pre-liquidation creditor nevertheless 'the court would be inclined to validate a transaction which would increase, or has increased, the value of the company's assets, or which would preserve, or has preserved, the value of the company's assets from harm which would result from the company's business being paralysed'.

Post-petition banking transactions

17.33 Whether or not payments into and out of a bank account constitute dispositions by a company for the purposes of s 127 has been a vexed issue. In the *Gray's Inn* case (see para **17.31**), Buckley LJ accepted the concessions offered by the bank's counsel to the effect that irrespective of whether the account in question is overdrawn or in credit: (i) payments out of the company's account to third parties constituted dispositions of the company's property; and (ii) they constituted dispositions of property which the bank was liable to make good. However, this reasoning has been criticised by Goode (2011). He convincingly argues that there was no disposition of company property in the case. The account was at all times overdrawn so that in relation to the payments made 'the bank used its own moneys to meet the company's cheques for what were presumably payments to suppliers and other creditors in the normal course of business, so that in relation to such payments the bank became substituted as creditor for the persons to whom they were made'. But where, on the other hand, a company credits its bank account with a cash payment this will constitute a disposition of property because the bank acquires ownership of the money and the company has a corresponding right to claim against the bank. Such a claim becomes an asset of the company and this holds true whether or not the account is in credit or is overdrawn.

17.34 Academic criticism aside, the decision in *Gray's Inn* has not been universally welcomed by the courts and subsequent case law has adopted an inconsistent approach to the issue of post-petition banking transactions. For example, in *Re Barn Crown Ltd* (1995) Judge Rich QC, sitting as a High Court judge, held that where a company deposits a cheque into its bank account which is in credit, no disposition of property arises because the bank collects it as the company's agent and it therefore acquires no interest of its own in the cheque.

On similar reasoning three Commonwealth cases (*Re Mal Bower's Macquarie Electrical Centre Pty Ltd* (1974); *Re Loteka Pty Ltd* (1989); and *Tasmanian Primary Distributors Pty Ltd v RC & MB Steinhardt Pty Ltd* (1994)) have held that when a bank pays a cheque drawn by a company in favour of a third party payee, a disposition of company property arises as against the payee but this does not constitute a disposition as far as the bank is concerned because it is acting merely as an intermediary or agent in the transaction. On the other hand, *Gray's Inn* was followed by the trial judge in *Hollicourt (Contracts) Ltd v Bank of Ireland* (2000), considered later.

17.35 The confused state of the authorities was further compounded by the decision of Lightman J in *Coutts & Co v Stock* (2000) in which the judge doubted, albeit correctly, the Court of Appeal's reasoning in *Re Gray's Inn*. The case is of particular interest because he sought to lay down fundamental principles which would serve to inject some coherence into the law governing the impact of s 127 on payments into and out of company bank accounts. It also presaged the Court of Appeal's view on the effect of s 127 on payments out of a company's bank account (see *Hollicourt (Contracts) Ltd v Bank of Ireland* (2000), later). The facts in *Coutts* were that the bank had granted a £200,000 overdraft facility to L Ltd, which was secured by a personal guarantee given by S, a director of the company. Shortly thereafter a winding-up petition was brought against the company. At this time its account was £500 in credit. However, at the time the petition was advertised the account was £121,875 in the red and by the time the winding-up order was granted its overdraft had increased to some £190,000. These increases were due to the bank having honoured cheques in favour of third parties, although most of the payments were in fact made to three companies either owned or controlled by S. Coutts sought to enforce S's guarantee. S responded by arguing that s 127 disentitled the bank from debiting L Ltd's account by honouring cheques after the presentation of the petition and that therefore the bank could not recover from him the amounts it had paid out.

17.36 Lightman J stated that two issues arose on the facts. First, whether the retrospective effect of s 127 operated to disentitle the bank from debiting the account after the petition had been presented (absent any validation order) and therefore prevented it from recovering the sums from S, as guarantor. Second, if the answer to the first question was in the affirmative, whether the guarantee agreement resulted in S being liable as principal debtor.

17.37 The judge noted that the invalidation under s 127 is limited to dispositions of property. It does not invalidate a company's assumption of liabilities and so the section does not preclude, for example, a company incurring liabilities for such things as utilities or employees' wages. Thus, an increase in a company's overdraft during the period between the presentation of the petition and the court's winding-up order is outwith s 127. Further, the provision does not impact upon a company's use or exhaustion of its assets. More particularly, the presentation of a winding-up petition does not invalidate the bank's mandate to honour the cheques of the company and the subsequent winding-up order does not operate to invalidate the loan made by the bank to the company through continuing to honour its cheques drawn on the overdrawn account. Significantly, Lightman J concluded:

> On principle . . . the acts of the bank in honouring cheques drawn on a company's over-drawn account constitute (i) loans of the sums in question by the bank to the company and (ii) payment by the bank as agent of the company of the sums loaned as moneys of the company to the party in whose favour the cheques are drawn. On this analysis, the loan by the bank to the company is not a disposition of the company's property (it is a disposition of the bank's money to the company) and is therefore outside s 127; but the payment by the bank as agent for the company does constitute a disposition to the payee by the company within s 127 and is recoverable by the liquidator from the payee [citing Millett J in Agip (Africa) Ltd v Jackson (1992)].

Preferring the Commonwealth approach and endorsing Goode's criticisms (see para **17.33**), the judge therefore held that the bank was entitled to the sum claimed by way of a debt from the guarantor and that s 127 had no impact on his liability.

17.38 It was against this uncertain state of the s 127 jurisprudence, the hallmark of which was described by Lightman J as 'confused', that the Court of Appeal in *Hollicourt (Contracts) Ltd v Bank of Ireland* (2000) had to decide whether the impact of s 127 operated to make the bank liable, on the application of the liquidator, to make restitution to the company of the amounts it had paid out to third parties. The decision arose out of an appeal against the decision of Blackburne J who had held, applying *Gray's Inn*, that the bank's honouring of company cheques after the date of the petition constituted dispositions of the monies standing to the credit of the company so that, therefore, the bank could not debit the account. The Court of Appeal, allowing the appeal, held that only the payees were liable to make restitution on the amount of the cheques to the company, not the bank. Mummery LJ observed that for s 127 to trigger, a disposition amounting to an alienation of the company's property had to be made. The bank in honouring the cheques obeyed as agent the order of its principal to pay out of the principal's money in its hands to the amount drawn in favour of the payee. The beneficial ownership of the property represented by the cheque was never transferred to the bank, to which no alienation of the company's property was made. Accordingly, the company could not recover the amounts from the bank, which had only acted in accordance with its instruction as the company's agent to make payments to the payees out of the bank account. Section 127 only avoided 'dispositions' of the company's property; it did not avoid all or any related transactions. Mummery LJ observed that this result carried the practical advantage of avoiding what in some cases could be complex analysis of whether payments were made out of an account which was in debit or in credit (see also *Re Tain Construction Ltd* (2004)).

From the perspective of company liquidators this decision will be unwelcome. The third parties that benefit from the dispositions are generally diffuse and difficult to trace. Banks, on the other hand, are readily identifiable targets to proceed against and they no doubt breathed a sigh of relief. That said, it is noteworthy that in *Express Electrical Distributors*

Ltd v Beavis (2016) although a case not involving a disposition of the company's property in favour of a bank, the Court of Appeal nevertheless took the opportunity to doubt the decision in *Re Gray's Inn Construction Co Ltd*, emphasising that unless there are obvious exceptional circumstances where a disposition is in the interests of the general body of creditors, a validation order should not be granted. For the future then, it may well become more difficult for a bank to obtain the court's validation for payments made into an overdrawn account once a winding-up petition has been presented and advertised.

Winding-up in the public interest

17.39 An increasing number of petitions are presented by the Secretary of State in the public interest under s 124A of the IA 1986. This provides an additional type of compulsory winding-up where, following a BEIS investigation or other official inquiry, it appears to the Secretary of State 'that it is expedient in the public interest that a company should be wound up if the court thinks it just and equitable for it to be so' (see *Re Millennium Advanced Technology* (2004); *Re Drivertime Recruitment Ltd* (2004); and *Secretary of State for Business, Innovation and Skills v PAG Management Services Ltd* (2015)). In *Re Corvin Construction Ltd* (2013) the court explained that part of its jurisdiction to wind up companies in the public interest is to assist in the maintenance of minimum standards of commercial behaviour and of probity. The protection of the public from inevitable loss, notwithstanding that the conduct in question is not unlawful, is a matter to which the court ought to have regard. It is not, therefore, necessary to prove insolvency and the provision adds to the power of the Secretary of State to intervene where it is apparent that a company is defrauding a large number of creditors. For example, in *Re Alpha Club (UK) Ltd* (2002) the company operated a 'pyramid' selling scheme which the deputy judge roundly condemned: 'The reality is, as with all pyramid selling schemes of which this is a classic example, a time comes when there is a saturation point and the members who joined later have no real prospect of ever making profits, or ever recovering their investment, let alone making profits'. The Secretary of State brought an action under s 124A despite the fact that the company had been voluntarily wound up. The court granted the order on the basis that the scheme was 'pernicious and inherently objectionable' because it 'put at risk those who came later into the scheme and therefore is something of which this court should disapprove'. The deputy judge concluded that although the court was not a court of morals it had a statutory function under the companies legislation and it was in the public interest that the public should be made aware that the Secretary of State had investigated a company and had concluded that it ought to be wound up. Similarly, in *Re Supporting Link Ltd* (2004) the Secretary of State's petition was granted against a company which, by making unsolicited telephone calls, sold advertising space in publications produced and distributed by it. The court found that the company had taken money from potential advertisers by misrepresenting the extent of its donations to charity, the nature of its publications, and their geographical distribution. Sir Andrew Morritt V-C explained that the company's operations had been founded and continued upon deception. It would, therefore, be just and equitable to wind the company up. In *Re UK-Euro Group plc* (2006), the deputy judge found that the managing director of the company had misinformed and deceived investors to such an extent that he could be considered a danger to the public. There being a total lack of commercial probity in the company's dealing with both its shareholders and the FSA, a winding-up petition was granted. The Secretary of State was also directed to approach the prosecuting authorities with a view to considering whether criminal charges might be brought against him. (See also *Re PGMRS Ltd* (2011).)

17.40 Where the court grants an order the Secretary of State will normally recover costs from the company (*Re Xyllyx plc (No 2)* (1992)) and the Court of Appeal has held that costs may be recovered from a controlling director personally (as opposed to the company) where the costs of defending a petition were expended in the director's individual interests and the company was essentially his alter ego (*Re North West Holdings plc* (2001); see also *Secretary of State for Trade and Industry v Aurum Marketing Ltd* (2002), Mummery LJ).

By way of an alternative to ordering a company to be wound up on this ground, the court may address public concerns by requiring undertakings from either the company or its board of directors. For example, in *Bell Davies Trading Ltd v Secretary of State for Trade and Industry* (2004) the Court of Appeal upheld the decision of the trial judge who dismissed the winding-up petition on condition that the companies in question offer binding undertakings (see also *Secretary of State for Business, Enterprise and Regulatory Reform v Amway (UK) Ltd* (2008)).

The duties and functions of the liquidator

17.41 As we discussed earlier, the winding-up order terminates the management powers of the company's directors (*Measures Bros Ltd v Measures* (1910)). Their powers are transferred to the liquidator together with their fiduciary duties, and so a liquidator must act in good faith, avoid a conflict of interests, and not make a secret profit (*Silkstone and Haigh Moore Coal Co v Edey* (1900)). Absent a special relationship, it seems that liquidators do not owe a general tortious duty of care to creditors (see *Peskin v Anderson* (2001) and *Oldham v Kyrris* (2003)). A liquidator is not a trustee for the individual creditors and contributories for if such were the position 'his liability would indeed be onerous, and would render the position of a liquidator one which few persons would care to occupy' (*Knowles v Scott* (1891), Romer J). In *Re Silver Valley Mines* (1882) Cotton LJ described the position of liquidator thus:

> he is not in the ordinary sense a trustee. He is a person appointed by the court to do a certain class of things; he has some of the rights and some of the liabilities of a trustee, but is not in the position of an ordinary trustee. Being an agent employed to do business for a remuneration, he is bound to bring reasonable skill to its performance.

It is now provided by s 230(3) of the 1986 Act that a company liquidator must be a qualified insolvency practitioner. The person must be an 'individual', not a corporate body. He acts in the name of the company and therefore will not be personally liable on contracts made by him on the company's behalf (*Stead, Hazel & Co v Cooper* (1933)). Nor will he be personally liable for the professional costs of a solicitor instructed by him to undertake company business (*Re Anglo-Moravian Co* (1875)).

17.42   The principal functions of a liquidator in compulsory liquidations are specified in s 143 which provides that he is 'to secure that the assets of the company are got in, realised and distributed to the company's creditors and, if there is a surplus, to the persons entitled to it'. In the discharge of his functions the liquidator is an officer of the court and is subject to its control. Section 144 goes on to state that the liquidator is to take into his custody or under his control all property and things in action to which the company appears to be entitled. In this regard, he can require any person who has in his possession or control any property, books, papers, or records to which the company appears to be entitled to pay, deliver, convey, surrender, or transfer the same to him (s 234). If the liquidator mistakenly seizes or disposes of any property which is not the property of the company, then provided at that time he had reasonable grounds for believing that he was entitled to seize or dispose of the property, he will not be liable to any person in respect of any loss or damage suffered unless such loss was caused by the liquidator's negligence (s 234(3) and (4)). However, and as with directors, on the application of a creditor or contributory the court can compel the liquidator to account under s 212 of the 1986 Act if he has misapplied or retained, or become accountable for, any money or other company property, or has been guilty of any misfeasance or breach of any fiduciary duty or other duty owed to the company.

17.43   Historically, the powers of a liquidator were laid down in ss 165–168 of and Sch 4 to the 1986 Act. With respect to winding-up by the court the governing provision was s 167 which divided the liquidator's powers into two categories: those that may be exercised only with the sanction of the court or the liquidation committee; and those which are exercisable without the need to obtain such sanction. For example, the liquidator had to obtain the appropriate sanction before exercising his power to bring or defend proceedings in the name and on behalf of the company and to carry on the business of the company so far as was necessary for its beneficial winding-up (s 167(1)(a), Part II, Sch 4). No such sanction was required for the liquidator to sell company property or to raise money by providing security on company assets (s 167(1)(b), Part III, Sch 4). Now, however, s 120 of the SBEEA 2015, by amending ss 165, 167, 169, and Sch 4, removes the sanction requirement on liquidators (it did not apply to administrators) so as to speed up the winding-up process.

17.44   In a members' voluntary winding-up, the requisite sanction is provided by obtaining an extraordinary resolution of the company. For a creditors' voluntary winding-up, sanction is obtained by the same means outlined in relation to compulsory winding-up, except that if there is no liquidation committee the consent of a meeting of creditors will need to be obtained (note the changes made to the requirements for formal creditors' meetings by the SBEEA 2015 (see para **17.5**)).

17.45 It was seen in *Re Gray's Inn Construction Co Ltd* that Buckley LJ stated that it was a basic concept of insolvency law that the free assets of the company in liquidation should be distributed rateably among the company's unsecured creditors (see also *Express Electrical Distributions Ltd v Beavis* (at para **17.38**)). This is the *pari passu* principle of distribution which is founded upon the anti-deprivation principle (see *British Eagle International Airlines Ltd v Compagnie Nationale Air France* (1975)). It governs both types of voluntary liquidation (see s 107), whereby all creditors participate in the common pool of free assets in proportion to the size of their admitted debts. For compulsory liquidations the principle is embodied in IR 2016, r 14.12 which states: '[d]ebts other than preferential debts rank equally between themselves in the winding-up'. Although a creditor cannot by contract seek to exclude the *pari passu* principle in order to gain priority over other claims (*British Eagle International Airlines Ltd v Compagnie Nationale Air France* (see earlier); and *Belmont Park Investments Pty Ltd v BNY Corporate Trustee Services Ltd and Lehman Brothers Special Financing Inc* (2011)), he can agree to defer his debts to the claims of other creditors (*Re Maxwell Communications Corpn plc (No 2)* (1994) and *Perpetual Trustee Co Ltd v BNY Corporate Trustee Services Ltd* (2009)). The Cork Committee (see earlier) criticised the *pari passu* principle on the basis that the existence of preferential debts frustrated the operation of such distribution (see para **17.50**). Preferential debts are 'unsecured debts which, by force of statute, fall to be paid in a winding-up in priority to all other unsecured debts (and to claims for principal and interest secured by a floating charge)' (Finch and Milman (2017)).

17.46 Creditors having rights *in rem* are not affected by the *pari passu* principle. For example, corporate property, which is subject to a fixed charge, must be used first to redeem the secured loan to which the charge relates. Similarly, where a supplier of goods has reserved title until payment, ownership will not have passed to the company and so the liquidator cannot incorporate these goods into the common pool of assets. Problems can, of course, arise where such goods have been mixed. A practical solution, however, was crafted by the court in *Re CKE Engineering Ltd* (2007), in which it was held that zinc, which had been supplied on title retention terms to a company which had subsequently gone into administration, and which had been melted down in a tank together with zinc from another supplier, could be given a notional valuation in order to give the supplier a proportionate part of the value of the molten metal.

17.47 If there are insufficient assets left over after taking account of any fixed charges together with preferential debts to satisfy the unsecured creditors, their debts abate equally. Section 175 IA 1986, which is of general application, provides:

> (1) In a winding up the company's preferential debts shall be paid in priority to all other debts.
>
> > (1A) Ordinary preferential debts rank equally among themselves after the expenses of the winding up and shall be paid in full, unless the assets are insufficient to meet them, in which case they abate in equal proportions.

> (1B) *Secondary preferential debts rank equally among themselves after the ordinary preferential debts and shall be paid in full, unless the assets are insufficient to meet them, in which case they abate in equal proportions.*
>
> (2) *Preferential debts—*
>
>   . . .
>
> (b) *so far as the assets of the company available for payment of general creditors are insufficient to meet them, have priority over the claims of holders of debentures secured by, or holders of, any floating charge created by the company, and shall be paid accordingly out of any property comprised in or subject to that charge.*

In summary, the order in which debts are to be satisfied in a liquidation after repayment of fixed chargees is as follows (see ss 107 and 115 (voluntary liquidations) and ss 143 and 156 (compulsory liquidations)):

(i)   *all expenses properly incurred in the winding-up, including the remuneration of the liquidator;*

(ii) *preferential debts;*

(iii) *floating charges;*

(iv) *ordinary debts;*

(v)   *deferred and subordinated debts;*

(vi) *any balance remaining is distributed to members in accordance with their entitlements under the company's [constitution].*

(For a summary of the priority list, gleaned from the legislation and Insolvency Rules, see Lord Neuberger's speech in *Re Nortel Companies; Bloom v Pensions Regulator* (2013).)

17.48 Preferential debts rank equally among themselves after the expenses of the winding-up are paid unless the 'assets' are insufficient to meet them, in which case they abate in equal proportions (s 175(2)(a) and (b)). However, as seen above, they take priority over the claims of holders of debentures secured by floating charges even if the charge crystallised before the commencement of the winding-up (s 175(2)(b); see *Re Portbase Clothing Ltd* (1993), Chadwick J). The references in s 175 to 'ordinary preferential debts' and 'secondary preferential debts' were inserted by the Banks and Building Societies (Depositor Preference and Priorities) Order 2014 (SI 2014/3486), applicable to insolvent financial institutions. The latter category relate to sums due to depositors over and above those recoverable under the Financial Services Compensation Scheme.

The vulnerability of floating chargees was compounded by the first instance decision in *Re Leyland Daf Ltd* (2001) in which Rimer J held that expenses properly incurred by a liquidator in a creditors' winding-up are payable out of the assets comprised in a crystallised floating charge in priority to the claims of the chargee (affirmed by the Court of Appeal, *Re Leyland Daf Ltd* (2003)). This was an application of the decision in *Re Barleycorn Enterprises Ltd* (1970), in which the floating charge had crystallised into a fixed charge when the company was ordered to be wound up. The Court of Appeal there held, viewing the issue as one of priority, that expenses incurred by the liquidator in the winding-up process ranked ahead of preferential creditors which, in turn, had priority over floating chargees. In the view of the court, this was the intent behind s 175. Both Lord Denning MR and Phillimore LJ explained that the term 'assets' in s 175 did not mean 'free assets' as it did in earlier legislation, but rather assets which include those within the scope of the charge. However, the House of Lords in *Leyland Daf* unanimously overruled *Barleycorn* (see, in particular, the speeches of Lord Hoffmann and Lord Millett), holding that once a floating charge crystallises into a fixed charge it no longer forms part of the company's free assets and so liquidators could no longer look to the fund of floating charge assets to cover their remuneration and expenses. This clearly reinforced the value of the floating charge. The implication of Lord Hoffmann's and Lord Millett's approach, therefore, was that a crystallised floating charge was no longer part of the company's property. From the perspective of liquidators, the decision left them in a particularly vulnerable position. In an interesting but highly complex case involving an unjust enrichment action (decided just three weeks before *Leyland Daf* went to the House of Lords), it was held that the liquidator of a company cannot recover against a floating chargee where an administrative receiver had not accounted to the preferential creditors. Prospective litigation costs are not payable out of assets subject to a floating charge (*Re Demaglass Ltd* (2003)).

The House of Lords' decision in *Leyland Daf* generated considerable controversy and s 1282 of the CA 2006 (inserting s 176ZA into the IA 1986) reverses it by allowing assets subject to a floating charge to be available to fund general expenses of a liquidation.

The effect is that where the assets available to the general creditors are insufficient to meet the expenses of a winding-up, such expenses have priority over floating charges and also preferential creditors (see also the Insolvency (Amendment) Rules 2008 (SI 2008/737), rr 4.218A–4.218E).

17.49   Prior to the Enterprise Act 2002, preferential debts were defined by s 386 as debts listed in Sch 6 to the 1986 Act: i.e. debts owed to the Inland Revenue in respect of PAYE deductions during the previous 12 months but not remitted to the Revenue; debts due to Customs and Excise in respect of six months' VAT; debts owed to the Department of Health and Social Security in respect of employers' national insurance contributions (NICs); debts owed by way of unpaid wages to employees and former employees for the four-month period before the commencement of the winding-up (maximum of £800) together with unpaid holiday pay and outstanding contributions to pension schemes. Corporation tax liabilities which accrue after the commencement of a winding-up are a 'necessary disbursement' of the liquidator and are therefore expenses of the winding-up payable before preferential debts (*Re Toshoku Finance (UK) plc, Kahn v Inland Revenue* (2002)).

17.50 In a reform which was partially reversed in 2020 (see below), the Enterprise Act 2002, s 252, abolished Crown preferential debts, i.e. debts due to the Inland Revenue, Customs and Excise, and social security contributions. The intention was to benefit unsecured creditors. However, to offset the advantage which the abolition gave to floating chargees, s 252 of the Enterprise Act, inserted s 176A into the 1986 Act, requiring, for the benefit of unsecured creditors a ring-fenced fund (the 'prescribed part') to be created out of the realisations of floating charges (applying to floating charges created after 15 September 2003). The amount to be transferred to the prescribed fund for transmission to unsecured creditors is calculated according to the following: 50 per cent of the first £10,000 plus 20 per cent of available funds above £10,000 up to a maximum of £600,000—in March 2020, the maximum was increased by the Government to £800,000 (see the Insolvency Act 1986 (Prescribed Part) (Amendment) Order 2020 (SI 2020/211)), applicable to floating charges created after 6 April 2020, although the reform will apply to a floating charge created before 6 April 2020 if a later floating charge (over any of the company's assets) ranks equally or in priority. When the increase was proposed in 2018, the Government explained that 'while prescribed part payments very rarely reach the current cap, in the small number of cases that do, it will mean that unsecured creditors will benefit from increased payments'. In practice, however, the change will make the floating charge less attractive to lenders who are likely to suffer a corresponding decrease in their recoveries.

Further, in the Government's autumn 2018 budget, it was announced that HMRC would be restored as a preferential creditor as from April 2020 (now postponed until 1 December 2020) in the recovery of certain debts, including VAT, PAYE, Employee NICs, and Construction Industry Scheme deductions (but not corporation tax)—thus restoring HMRC's priority ahead of the 'prescribed part', floating chargees, and unsecured creditors. It is estimated that the return to preferential status will deliver a £185 million increase in taxes for the Government. This reinstatement of preferential treatment has proved controversial, not least because of the significance of inventory-based lending in the UK secured by floating charges (some £3 billion to SMEs). In terms of risk, lenders will need to make greater provision to cover VAT and PAYE preferential payments, but a difficulty here lies in calculating this risk and so the use of fixed charges and personal guarantees could increase. Lenders have warned that the reform may result in reduced funds being available which could, therefore, have a negative impact on business growth.

The question as to whether or not a secured creditor which had exhausted its security but whose debt had nevertheless remained unsatisfied could have access to the ring-fenced fund has now been answered in the negative by the courts. In *Re Permacell Finesse Ltd* (2007), it was held that a secured creditor with a floating charge shortfall could not participate in the prescribed fund allocated to unsecured creditors unless, of course, the fund exceeds the amount needed to satisfy unsecured debts. Further, in *Re Airbase (UK) Ltd* (2008), Patten J held that this exclusion applied to all secured creditors (including fixed and floating chargees) who suffer a shortfall on security realisation. However, it should be noted that the prescribed fund can be disapplied in circumstances where the cost of making a distribution to unsecured creditors would be disproportionate to the benefits (see s 176A(5)). In *Re Hydroserve Ltd* (2007), Rimer J granted the request of the administrators to disapply the prescribed fund requirement where there was a mere £5,000 to be shared out proportionately between 122 creditors (for an example where the court refused the application to disapply the fund under s 176A(5), see *Re International Sections Ltd (in liquidation)* (2009)).

17.51 Section 74(2)(f) provides that a sum due to any member of the company by way of dividends, profit, or otherwise is not deemed to be a debt of the company, payable to that member in a case of competition between himself and any other creditor who is not a member, but such sum may be taken into account for the purpose of the final adjustment of the rights of contributories among themselves. Put simply, this is a deferred debt and cannot be paid until all other company debts are satisfied. In *Soden v British and Commonwealth Holdings plc* (1998) the House of Lords held that the damages claimed by a member in an action for misrepresentation against the company which he claimed had induced him to buy his shares did not fall under the statutory contract contained in s 14 of the Companies Act 1985 (see now s 33(1) of CA 2006), and were not sums due to him qua member. The claim was not therefore deferred to other creditors.

Avoidance of transactions entered into prior to the liquidation

17.52 We have seen that the principal function of a liquidator is to maximise returns for creditors and this objective is underpinned by a range of provisions contained in the 1986 Act that empower the liquidator to revitalise the assets of an insolvent company by challenging dubious transactions entered into by the company or its directors (see also s 127 (earlier) and s 245 (Chapter 6)). Before we turn to consider these provisions, it should be stressed that a liquidator should not be overzealous in launching litigation because the assets of the company may not be sufficient to cover the costs. Further, in a number of cases the courts have made it clear that a liquidator who proposes to bring proceedings, for example under s 214 (wrongful trading) or for preferences under s 239, has no automatic right to have the costs paid as a liquidation expense under s 115 (see the remarks of Millett J in *Re MC Bacon Ltd (No 2)* (1990); and Peter Gibson LJ in *Re Floor Fourteen Ltd, Lewis v IRC* (2001), applying *Mond v Hammond Suddards* (2000)). From a practical perspective, this restrictive approach towards costs clearly undermines the threat of a liquidator's action as a deterrent against directorial abuses of the corporate form. Liquidators are therefore likely to look to state creditors such as the Inland Revenue to run the risk of such litigation although, with the abolition of its status as a preferential creditor, there is little incentive for the Revenue to do this. On a more positive note, in *Official Receiver v Doshi* (2002) the liquidator was able to 'piggy-back' a successful wrongful trading action on state-funded CDDA proceedings (on the disqualification regime, see Chapter 13). On a procedural issue, s 253 of the Enterprise Act 2002 now requires liquidators to seek the sanction of the creditors' liquidation committee before instituting certain proceedings under the 1986 Act (Insolvency (Amendment) (No 2) Rules 2002 (SI 2002/2712), r 23).

We now turn to consider the avoidance provisions.

Transactions at an undervalue

17.53   Section 238 empowers the liquidator to apply to the court for an order where the company has 'at a relevant time' entered into a transaction at an undervalue. The court can make such order as it thinks fit for restoring the position to what it would have been had the company not entered into the transaction (s 238(3)). The 'relevant time' is defined as two years ending with the onset of insolvency provided that at the relevant time the company is unable to pay its debts within the meaning of s 123 (see paras **17.22** *et seq*), or it becomes unable to pay its debts within the meaning of s 123 as a consequence of the transaction. This requirement is presumed to be satisfied, unless the contrary is shown, in relation to any transaction at an undervalue which is entered into by the company with a person who is connected with the company (s 240(2)). The onset of insolvency is defined as the date of the commencement of the winding-up (s 240(3)). It should be noted that fraud is not required. The action can be defended if the party receiving the asset at an undervalue can prove that the company was solvent at the time (a burden not discharged in *Re Husky Group Ltd* (2014)).

Section 238(4) provides that a company enters into transaction with a person at an undervalue if:

   (a)   the company makes a gift to that person or otherwise enters into a transaction with that person on terms that provide for the company to receive no consideration; or

   (b)   the company enters into a transaction with that person for a consideration the value of which, in money or money's worth, is significantly less than the value, in money or money's worth, of the consideration provided by the company.

In *Hunt (Liquidator of Ovenden Colbert Printers Ltd) v Hosking* (2013), the Court of Appeal stressed that the requirement that the company had itself entered into a transaction was an essential element of a s 238 claim. Kitchin LJ explained that:

> to focus unduly on the term 'transaction' risks obscuring the need for the second and vital element, namely the requirement that the transaction be something that the company has 'entered into'. This expression connotes the taking of some step or act of participation by the company. Thus the composite requirement requires the company to make the gift or make the arrangement or in some other way be party to or involved in the transaction in issue so that it can properly be said to have entered into it, and of course it must have done so within the period prescribed by s.240.

17.54   The scope of s 238(4)(b) and, more particularly, the meaning of 'consideration' for its purposes, was considered by Millett J in *Re MC Bacon Ltd* (1990). The company had given a debenture to its bank at a time when it was of doubtful solvency and could not have continued business without the bank's support in not calling in the company's overdraft. Millett J held that this was not a transaction at an undervalue because the security had neither depleted nor diminished the value of the company's assets. The judge observed that the consideration consisted of the bank's forbearance from calling in the overdraft, honouring the company's cheques, and making fresh advances:

> The mere creation of a security over a company's assets does not deplete them and does not come within the paragraph. By charging its assets the company appropriates them to meet the liabilities due to the secured creditor and adversely affects the rights of other creditors in the event of insolvency. But it does not deplete its assets or diminish their value. It retains the right to redeem and the right to sell or remortgage the charged assets. All it loses is the ability to apply the proceeds otherwise than in satisfaction of the secured debt. That is not something capable of valuation in monetary terms and is not customarily disposed of for value.

(Millett J also held that this was not a voidable preference within s 239, see later.)

17.55 The provision will lead to a successful challenge by a liquidator where a company gratuitously gives away assets prior to its liquidation (*Re Barton Manufacturing Co Ltd* (1999); see also *Whalley v Doney* (2003)); or where it sells assets for a consideration less than their true worth (*Phillips v Brewin Dolphin Bell Lawrie Ltd* (2001)). In *Brewin Dolphin* the House of Lords laid down guidelines for valuing the consideration given in return for an asset. Lord Scott, delivering the leading speech, stressed that speculative values were not to be taken into account: '[f]or the purposes of section 238(4) . . . and the valuation of the consideration for which a company has entered into a transaction, reality should . . . be given precedence over speculation'. The court will therefore have regard to events occurring after the agreement was concluded provided they impact on the value of the consideration given (see also *Re Sonatacus Ltd; CI Ltd v Liquidators of Sonatacus Ltd* (2007); *Re Bangla Television Ltd; Valentine v Bangla Television Ltd* (2009); *Stanley v TMK Finance Ltd* (2010); and *Global Corporate Ltd v Hale* (2017)).

17.56 Section 241 provides for a wide range of orders available to the court for the purpose of restoring the position to what it would have been had the company not entered into the transaction. For example, the court may require any property transferred as part of the transaction to be vested in the company; release or discharge any security given by the company; require any person to pay to the liquidator sums received by him from the company; provide for a surety or guarantor whose obligations have been released or discharged to be under new or revived obligations; provide for security to be given for the discharge of obligations imposed by the order; and provide for the extent to which any person whose property is vested by the order in the company, or on whom obligations are imposed by the order, is to be able to prove in the winding-up.

Further, s 238(5) provides that the court will not make an order if it is satisfied: (i) that the company which entered into the transaction did so in good faith and for the purpose of carrying on business; and (ii) that at the time it did so there were reasonable grounds for believing that the transaction would benefit the company. This defence would presumably cover an expeditious sale of assets at an undervalue which was entered into with the intention of keeping the company afloat.

Transactions defrauding creditors

17.57 Section 423 of the IA 1986 aims to protect creditors and potential creditors from fraud, its object being to remedy the avoidance of debts (*Chohan v Saggar* (1994) CA). In terms similar to those seen in s 238(4), it provides:

> (1) *This section relates to transactions entered into at an undervalue; and a person enters into such a transaction with another person if—*
>
> (a) *he makes a gift to the other person or he otherwise enters into a transaction with the other on terms that provide for him to receive no consideration; . . . or*
>
> (c) *he enters into a transaction with the other for a consideration the value of which, in money or money's worth, is significantly less than the value, in money or money's worth, of the consideration provided by himself.*

It will be recalled that under s 238 the power of the court to make an order in relation to a transaction at undervalue is limited by the requirement that it must have been entered into at a 'relevant time'. Section 423 contains no such temporal restriction. Rather, the restriction is contained in s 423(3) which provides that with respect to a person entering a transaction at undervalue, the court will make an order if it is satisfied that it was entered into by him for the purpose:

> (a) *of putting assets beyond the reach of a person who is making, or may at some time make, a claim against him, or*
>
> (b) *of otherwise prejudicing the interests of such a person in relation to the claim which he is making or may make.*

In *IRC v Hashmi* (2002) the Court of Appeal held that putting the assets in question beyond the reach of a creditor, on the facts, HMRC, need not be the dominant purpose of the transaction. Looking to the objective of the provision, Arden LJ said: 'Section 423 plays an important role in insolvency law. It can moreover apply even though the debtor is not in a formal insolvency . . . Section [423] is a carefully calibrated section forming part of a carefully calibrated group of sections.' She concluded by observing that the provision should be construed as permitting the court to set aside a transaction that may have been entered into for a number of purposes, provided that a 'real substantial purpose' was to put assets beyond the reach of the creditor (HMRC). She concluded by stating that it would have frustrated the purpose of the provision to permit the defendant to avoid an order merely because other purposes could be demonstrated.

(See also *JSC BTA Bank v Ablyazov* (2018).)

Although 'dishonesty' is not a prerequisite under s 423, Russell LJ explained in *Lloyd's Bank Ltd v Marcan* (1973) that where a person 'disposes' of an asset which would otherwise have been available to his creditors 'with the intention of prejudicing them by putting it [or its value] beyond their reach' such a person is 'in the ordinary case acting in a fashion not honest in the context of the relationship of the debtor-creditor'. As with ss 238 (see earlier) and 239 (see later), s 423(3) provides that where a transaction has been entered into at an undervalue, 'the court may ... make such order as it thinks fit for: (a) restoring the position to what it would have been if the transaction had not been entered into, and (b) protecting the interests of persons who are victims of the transaction'. Accordingly, a director who disposes of company property within the terms of s 243 will be in breach of his duties owed to the company and will therefore be liable to compensate it for any loss if it is not restored, and such compensation will include the amount of undervalue. In *BTI 2014 LLC v Sequana SA* (2019), (discussed at **7.15** and **14.41**), the Court of Appeal accepted that the payment of dividends that are otherwise lawful could be caught by s 423 as a 'transaction' for no consideration. Although 'transaction' normally denotes a bilateral activity it can also encompass an activity in which a single person is engaged, such as a gift, and so the court concluded that there was no legitimate policy reason for restricting the scope of s 423 to exclude dividend payments or any other unilateral act. David Richards LJ held:

> In my judgment, it cannot be said that the company receives consideration for the payment of a dividend. It is not enough to say that the dividend is paid in accordance with the rights attached to the shares, where those rights are quite different from, for example, the right to receive interest payments on loan notes or the right to be considered for bonus declarations on a with-profits fund. If and when a company pays a dividend to shareholders, the terms of the dividend do not provide for the company to receive any consideration nor will it receive any consideration.

The judgment of the Supreme Court is awaited.

Voidable preferences

17.58   In order to prevent companies preferring a particular creditor or group of creditors over and above the general body of creditors, s 239 enables the liquidator to apply to the court for an order, on such terms as it thinks fit, for restoring the position to what it would have been had the company not given the preference. A company gives a preference to a person if:

(a)   that person is one of the company's creditors or a surety or guarantor for any of the company's debts or other liabilities; and

(b)   the company does anything or suffers anything to be done which (in either case) has the effect of putting that person into a position which, in the event of the company going into insolvent liquidation, will be better than the position he would have been in if that thing had not been made (s 239(4)).

It is further provided that the court shall not make an order in respect of a preference given to any person unless the company which gave the preference was *influenced* in deciding to give it by a *desire* to place that person in a better position he would otherwise have been in (s 239(5), emphasis added). The emphasis is therefore upon the motivation underlying the transaction rather than upon its effect.

17.59 In *Re MC Bacon Ltd* (earlier), Millett J stressed that it is no longer necessary to enquire whether there was 'a dominant intention to prefer' (as was the case under the pre-existing law), but whether the company's decision was 'influenced by a desire to produce the effect mentioned in subsection (4)'. The provision obviously covers the case where, for example, the company pays off a loan which a director has personally guaranteed just as insolvency becomes inevitable. Similarly, the section would apply where a creditor has been paid before others in order to ensure that he does not join the general body of creditors who are looking to the pooled assets for payment. But, as we have seen, in *Re MC Bacon Ltd*, Millett J held that the debenture could not be challenged as a preference because the directors had not been motivated by a desire to prefer the bank but only by the wish to carry on trading by avoiding the calling in of the company's overdraft. Construing the key words in s 239(5) namely, 'influenced' and 'desire', Millett J noted that it is no longer necessary to prove an intention to prefer but rather a *desire* to prefer. He concluded:

> *Intention is objective, desire is subjective. A man can choose the lesser of two evils without desiring either. . . . A man is not to be taken as desiring all the necessary consequences of his actions. Some consequences may be of advantage to him and be desired by him; others may not affect him and be matters of indifference to him; while still others may be positively disadvantageous to him and not be desired by him, but be regarded by him as the unavoidable price of obtaining the desired advantages. It will still be possible to provide assistance to a company in financial difficulties provided that the company is actuated only by proper commercial considerations.*

(See also *4Eng Ltd v Harper* (2009), Sales J; cf *Re Sonatacus Ltd; CI Ltd v Liquidators of Sonatacus Ltd* (2007).)

It therefore seems that the provision will not apply where it is apparent that the company made the preference in order to stay in business but it will bite in circumstances where the preferred creditor is a connected person. In such a case there is a presumption under s 239(6) that the payment was influenced by the necessary desire to prefer (see *Re Brian D Pierson (Contractors) Ltd* (2001); *Re Cityspan Ltd* (2007)).

17.60 We observed earlier that the effect of the commencement of liquidation is that all assets then held by the company become subject to a statutory trust in favour of the unsecured creditors. This statutory trust will also encompass assets recovered by the liquidator under s 239 (*Re Oasis Merchandising Services Ltd* (1997); see also *Re Floor Fourteen Ltd* (earlier)).

17.61 A preference can be avoided only if it was given at a relevant time. As with transactions at an undervalue (see earlier), this is defined by s 240. For the purposes of s 239 'relevant time' means a period of two years ending with the onset of insolvency where a preference is given to a person who is connected with the company (otherwise than by reason only of being its employee). In other cases, i.e. where the beneficiary of the preference is not a connected person, the relevant time is six months ending with the onset of insolvency. In either case, the relevant time only triggers if the company is unable to pay its debts within the meaning of s 123 when the preference is given or becomes unable to pay its debts as a result of giving the preference. In contrast to transactions at an undervalue, this requirement is not presumed even where the preference is given to a connected person. In *Wills v Corfe Joinery Ltd* (1997) it was held that the relevant date for determining whether loan payments made to directors of a company about to go into voluntary liquidation were preferential payments was the date on which such payments were actually made, not the date when payment was originally due. Further, because the directors were connected persons within s 239(6), the burden of proof was on them to rebut the statutory presumption that the company's actions were motivated by a desire to give preferential treatment to them (see also *Re Transworld Trading Ltd* (1999); *Re Stealth Construction Ltd* (2011); and *Green v El Tai* (2015)). In *Re Conegrade Ltd* (2003) the company operated a loan account which covered loans made by the defendant directors. At a board meeting attended by all those entitled to vote, it was agreed that a property belonging to the company, valued at £125,000, would be sold to the defendants and leased back to the company. The defendants paid only £64,808, being the amount of the balance in the loan account. The company became insolvent within the relevant time and the liquidators successfully argued that the transaction was a preference under s 239. There was no compelling reason for the transaction other than a 'desire', which was presumed, to place the defendants in a better position. The liquidators had also argued that this was a 'substantial property transaction' (see para **14.94**), which requires a shareholders' resolution. Lloyd J rejected this claim on the basis that all those entitled to vote had attended the board meeting.

Extortionate credit bargains

17.62 Under s 244 the liquidator may apply to the court for an order setting aside or varying a transaction for, or involving, the provision of credit to the company where the transaction is extortionate and was entered into within three years of the date when the company went into liquidation. A credit transaction is extortionate if, having regard to the risk accepted by the person providing the credit:

(a) the terms of it are or were such as to require grossly exorbitant payments to be made (whether unconditionally or in certain contingencies) in respect of the provision of the credit; or

(b) it otherwise grossly contravened ordinary principles of fair dealing (s 244(3)).

There is a rebuttable presumption that a transaction with respect to which an application is made under the section is extortionate. The provision mirrors ss 137–139 of the Consumer Credit Act 1974. It must be demonstrated that the transaction was oppressive, not merely unfair or unwise, reflecting 'a substantial imbalance in bargaining power of which one party has taken advantage' (*Wills v Wood* (1984), Sir John Donaldson MR).

The personal liability of directors under the Insolvency Act 1986

17.63   Directors may be held personally liable to compensate creditors where they have been guilty of fraudulent trading, wrongful trading, or some misfeasance. Before turning to these issues, it is noteworthy that personal liability is also triggered by ss 216 and 217 of the 1986 Act which are designed to address the so-called 'phoenix syndrome'. These provisions prohibit a director of a company that has gone into insolvent liquidation from being involved for five years in the management of a company using either the same name as the insolvent company or a name that is so similar as to suggest an association with it. The prohibition also applies to a director who left the company within 12 months of its liquidation. Breach of the rule renders the director criminally liable although he may apply to the court for leave to act as a director of a similarly named company. In addition to criminal penalties, a director who is in breach of s 216 has unlimited liability for the debts of the company incurred after he became director (s 217).

Fraudulent trading

17.64   As we discussed briefly in Chapter 2, a director will not be able to hide behind the corporate veil and avoid personal liability for the company's debts where he has used the company for fraudulent trading (or for wrongful trading, see later). Civil liability is imposed by s 213 of the 1986 Act which provides that if in the course of the winding-up of a company it appears that any business of the company has been carried on with intent to defraud creditors of the company or creditors of any other person, or for any fraudulent purpose, the court, on the application of the liquidator, may declare that any persons who were knowingly parties to the carrying on of the business in that manner are to be liable to make such contributions (if any) to the company's assets as the court thinks proper. In *Jetivia SA v Bilta UK Ltd* (2015), the Supreme Court held that fraudulent trading had extra-territorial effect because the term 'any person' as used in the provision is unqualified and so a contribution order could be made against a Swiss national. It was noted that the effect of a winding-up order is world-wide and so limiting the effect of s 213 to the UK would severely curtail its effectiveness.

Knowledge of the fraud includes blind-eye knowledge, which requires a suspicion of the relevant facts existing coupled with a deliberate decision to avoid confirming that they did exist (*Morris v State Bank of India* (2005), CA; *Re Overnight Ltd (In liquidation) (No 2)* (2010)). In *Pantiles Investments Ltd v Winckler* (2019) the judge, having reviewed the case law, accepted that 'knowledge' requires 'dishonesty' and adopted the criminal law test. ICC Judge Mullen said:

> The test for dishonesty in the criminal context was recently considered by the Supreme Court in Ivey v Genting Casinos (UK) Ltd (trading as Crockfords Club) [2018]. Lord Hughes JSC said at 416:
>
> > 'The test of dishonesty is as set out by Lord Nicholls in Royal Brunei Airlines Sdn Bhd v Tan *and by Lord Hoffmann in* Barlow Clowes International Ltd v Eurotrust International Ltd. . . . When dishonesty is in question the fact-finding tribunal must first ascertain (subjectively) the actual state of the individual's knowledge or belief as to the facts. The reasonableness or otherwise of his belief is a matter of evidence (often in practice determinative) going to whether he held the belief, but it is not an additional requirement that his belief must be reasonable; the question is whether it is genuinely held. When once his actual state of mind as to knowledge or belief as to facts is established, the question whether his conduct was honest or dishonest is to be determined by the fact-finder by applying the (objective) standards of ordinary decent people. There is no requirement that the defendant must appreciate that what he has done is, by those standards, dishonest.'
>
> Again, this approach to the test has been applied in the context of accessory liability in civil proceedings (see Group Seven Ltd v Notable Services LLP [2019]). I accept that this is the test that I must adopt.

The Court of Appeal has held that there is no power to make a punitive award in assessing the amount of any contribution (see *Morphitis v Bernasconi* (2003), discussed later). However, criminal liability for fraudulent trading is imposed by s 993 of the CA 2006, the wording of which is virtually identical to s 213. A person who uses a company for fraudulent trading is liable to be prosecuted whether or not the company is being wound up and, on conviction, is liable to a fine, imprisonment, or both.

17.65 The meaning of fraud for the purposes of s 213 has been defined as requiring 'real dishonesty involving, according to current notions of fair trading among commercial men at the present day, real moral blame' (*Re Patrick and Lyon Ltd* (1933), Maugham J; see also *Re Sobam BV* (1996)). Actual dishonesty must be proved (*Welham v DPP* (1961); *Bernasconi v Nicholas Bennett & Co* (2000); and *Aktieselskabet Dansk Skibsfinansiering v Brother* (2001)), although allowing a company to trade knowing that it is unable to meet all of its debts as they fall due may amount to sufficient evidence of dishonest intent (*R v Grantham* (1984)). Similarly, accepting advance payment for the supply of goods from one creditor where the directors knew that there was no prospect of the goods being supplied and the payment returned has also been held to amount to fraud committed in the course of carrying on business (*Re Gerald Cooper Chemicals Ltd* (1978)). It is therefore not necessary to show that all of the company's creditors have been defrauded. Given the stringent conditions required for establishing fraudulent trading it is used by liquidators only in extreme cases.

17.66 The difficulty of establishing fraud is illustrated by *Re Augustus Barnett & Son Ltd* (1986). An off-licence chain was the wholly owned subsidiary of a Spanish company. The off-licences traded at a loss for some time but the parent company repeatedly issued statements that it would support its subsidiary. Such statements had been made via 'comfort letters' to the subsidiary's auditors and were published in its accounts for three successive years. When eventually the parent company withdrew its support and allowed the subsidiary to go into liquidation it was alleged that the parent company was guilty of fraudulent trading. It was held that the facts did not disclose the requisite intent to defraud the creditors. Indeed, they were consistent with the parent company having an honest intent, at the time it made the statements, to support its subsidiary. The fact that it later changed its mind did not prove that its original intent was fraudulent. On the other hand, a clear example of fraudulent intent appears from the facts of *Re William C Leitch Brothers Ltd* (1932), in which the liquidator sought declarations that the director of the company had been knowingly a party to carrying on the business of the company with intent to defraud its creditors and that he was therefore personally liable for all the company's debts. The company had owed some £6,500 for goods on 1 March 1930 and it lacked the means to pay off these debts. Subsequently, the director ordered goods worth £6,000. These became subject to a charge contained in a debenture held by him. He also lent sums of money to the company after this date, which were paid off in part by the company. Later, he appointed a receiver on the ground that the company had defaulted on interest payments. The company's bank account with the Midland Bank was overdrawn by some £800. He had guaranteed this sum and had deposited title deeds with the bank. Between April and June 1930 some £684 of the overdraft was paid off. It also emerged that the goods which the director had ordered were greatly in excess of the company's requirements. In holding the director liable, Maugham J observed:

> if a company continues to carry on business and to incur debts at a time when there is to the knowledge of the directors no reasonable prospect of the creditors ever receiving payment of those debts, it is, in general, a proper inference that the company is carrying on business with intent to defraud . . .

17.67 Given the difficulties of establishing fraud, the wrongful trading provision contained in s 214 of the 1986 Act (see later) is generally the preferred route for liquidators seeking recovery. Opportunities are therefore scarce for the courts to examine the scope of the civil liability imposed for fraudulent trading. However, the Court of Appeal has pronounced on a range of questions concerning liability under s 213. In *Morphitis v Bernasconi* (see earlier), the fortunes of a haulage company which had operated profitably for a number of years declined largely as a result of a number of onerous leases on warehouse premises. On counsel's advice, a restructuring scheme was devised whereby the business would be transferred to a new company. The new company started to trade on 1 January 1993. As part of this scheme, the company's trade creditors, other than the landlord, were paid off in order to avoid criminal liability under s 216 of the 1986 Act if a winding-up petition were to be presented within 12 months of the company ceasing to trade (s 216 prohibits a director of a company that has gone into insolvent liquidation from being involved for five years in the management of a company using either the same name as the insolvent company or a name that is so similar as to suggest an association with it). The landlord, having threatened to present a winding-up petition within that critical time frame, was persuaded by the company's solicitors to accept payment of rent by instalments. The last payment which had been promised for 23 December 1993 was not made. Indeed, it had never been the company's intention to make that payment given that the intended objective of averting a petition during that critical year had been achieved. The landlord finally served a statutory demand for rent in September 1994 and the company was wound up on 20 December 1994.

The liquidator disclaimed the leases and sought a declaration under s 213 that the two former directors of the company together with the company's firm of solicitors were knowingly parties to the carrying on of the business with intent to defraud creditors and for other fraudulent purposes and that, therefore, they were liable to make such contributions to the company's assets as the court thought proper. The liquidator accepted a payment into court of £75,000 made by the solicitors. At first instance it was held that the directors were guilty of fraudulent trading. The defendants successfully appealed. Although the Court of Appeal endorsed the judge's finding that liability under s 213 can arise though only one creditor had been defrauded by a single transaction (applying *Re Gerald Cooper Chemicals Ltd* (see earlier)), it emphasised that what must be established is that the company's business has been carried on with intent to defraud its creditors. Thus, liability will not necessarily trigger where, as on the facts, the business was carried on throughout 1993 not with a view to defrauding the landlord, but with the objective of protecting the directors, Monti or Bernasconi, from the penalties imposed by s 213. Chadwick LJ, delivering the only reasoned judgment of the court, stressed that although the promise to the landlord to pay by instalments was intended to mislead:

> [I]t has not been shown that, by carrying on of the business of the company during the period that Ramac [the landlord] was so misled, Mr Monti or Mr Bernasconi intended to defraud Ramac; or, indeed, that the carrying on of the business of the company did defraud Ramac—in the sense that Ramac's claim as a creditor in the liquidation was prejudiced by the carrying on of the business.

17.68 Although it was held that the directors were not liable, Chadwick LJ nevertheless took the opportunity to comment upon the issue of liability under s 213 which, it will be recalled, confers discretion on the court in this regard. The judge took the view that in determining the measure of contribution to be made to the company's assets there must be:

> some nexus between (i) the loss which has been caused to the company's creditors generally by the carrying on of the business in the manner which gives rise to the exercise of the power and (ii) the contribution which those knowingly party to the carrying on of the business in that manner should be ordered to make to the assets in which the company's creditors will share in the liquidation.

By way of example, Chadwick LJ stated that a clear case where contribution would be ordered would be where the carrying on of business with fraudulent intent had led to the misapplication, or misappropriation, of the company's assets. In his view, an appropriate order in such a situation might be that those who knowingly participated should 'contribute an amount equal to the value of assets misapplied or misappropriated'. He also went on to add that where the carrying on of business with fraudulent intent had led to claims against the company by those defrauded, the appropriate order might be that those:

> knowingly party to the conduct which had given rise to those claims in the liquidation contribute an amount equal to the amount by which the existence of those claims would otherwise diminish the assets available for distribution to creditors generally; that is to say an amount equal to the amount which has to be applied out of the assets available for distribution to satisfy those claims.

17.69   Having laid down guidelines which should inform the court in the exercise of its statutory discretion, Chadwick LJ concluded that there was no scope under s 213 for a punitive element in the amount of any contribution. Perhaps surprisingly this point had by no means been certain. For example, in *Re William C Leitch Brothers Ltd* (see earlier), Maugham J stated that s 213 carries a punitive element and a director may thus be ordered to pay more under the provision than is actually owed to the creditors who have been defrauded. However, noting that the power to punish a person who is knowingly a party to fraudulent trading is contained in s 458 of the CA 1985, Chadwick LJ added that:

> It could not have been Parliament's intention that the court would use the power to order contribution under section 213 of the 1986 Act in order to punish the wrongdoer. In my view, had the judge been right to find fraudulent trading in the present case, he would, nevertheless, have been wrong to include a punitive element in the amount of contribution which he ordered.

For the reasons noted earlier, there is a dearth of authority on s 213 of the 1986 Act. The decision in *Morphitis v Bernasconi* is therefore significant insofar as it both resolves a number of issues relating to the conduct which will support a finding of fraud (in this respect it seems to have been material that the restructuring scheme was devised by counsel) and, importantly, provides clear guidance on how any order for contribution should be measured. It now seems clear that in assessing the amount to be contributed by the guilty parties there must be a causative connection between the sum ordered and the loss suffered by the creditors.

17.70   The term 'parties to the carrying on of the business' contained in s 213 is expansive in effect so that *any person* who takes a positive step in the fraudulent trading can be liable (*Re BCCI SA* (2002); cf s 214 later, the scope of which is limited to directors and shadow directors). The failure of a company secretary to advise the directors that the company is insolvent is not sufficient to render him a party to the carrying on of the business in a fraudulent manner (*Re Maidstone Building Provisions Ltd* (1971)). But it has been held that a creditor who knowingly accepts money fraudulently obtained by the company is a party to the carrying on of the business in a fraudulent manner (*Re Gerald Cooper Chemicals Ltd*, earlier).

The decision of the Supreme Court in *Jetivia SA v Bilta (UK) Ltd* (2015) is very significant in this context because it removes a potentially important defence that could operate particularly in the context of small companies. The court held that a liquidator of a small company is not prevented from bringing a fraudulent trading action against the controllers of the company by them arguing that the company itself was tainted by their fraud, thereby blocking the claim by virtue of *ex turpi causa non oritur actio*. The Supreme Court also held that s 213 of the IA 1986 had extra-territorial application (see also *Erste Group Bank AG v ISC 'VMZ Red October'* (2015)).

Wrongful trading

17.71 It has been seen that s 213 requires proof of dishonest intent so that directors who carry on business negligently do not fall within its scope. To address this loophole, and following the recommendations of the Cork Committee (see earlier), s 214 of the IA 1986 introduced the concept of 'wrongful trading'. As with fraudulent trading, s 214 only applies where the company is in liquidation. The section provides that a liquidator of a company in insolvent liquidation can apply to the court to have a person who is or has been a director of the company declared personally liable to make such contribution (if any) to the company's assets as the court thinks proper for the benefit of the unsecured creditors. The term director for the purposes of s 214 encompasses 'shadow-directors' and *de facto* directors (*Re Hydrodam (Corby) Ltd* (1994)). Where the director has died the liquidator can maintain the claim against his estate (*Re Sherborne Associates Ltd* (1995)). The liquidator must prove that the director in question allowed the company to continue to trade, at some time before the commencement of its winding-up, when he knew or ought to have concluded that there was no reasonable prospect that the company would avoid going into insolvent liquidation (see, for example, *Rubin v Gunner* (2004); and *Singla v Hedman* (2010)). In *Re Continental Assurance Co of London plc* (2001) Park J stressed that '[t]he continued trading—albeit wrongful—has to make the company's position worse, so that it has less money available to pay creditors, rather than leave the company's position at the same level' (see also *Liquidator of Marini Ltd v Dickenson* (2003)). An awareness that creditors are exerting pressure for payment or refusing to make further deliveries will be sufficient (*Re DKG Contractors Ltd* (1990)).

In determining whether a director ought to have concluded that an insolvent liquidation was unavoidable s 214(4) provides:

> *the facts which a director of a company ought to know or ascertain, the conclusions which he ought to reach and the steps which he ought to take are those which would*

be known or ascertained, or reached or taken, by a reasonably diligent person having both—

(a) *the general knowledge, skill and experience that may reasonably be expected of a person carrying out the same functions as are carried out by that director in relation to the company, and*

(b) *the general knowledge, skill and experience that that director has.*

17.72 The first reported case under s 214 was *Re Produce Marketing Consortium Ltd* (1989) in which two directors were each held liable to contribute £75,000 to company's assets. Knox J held that the time at which they ought to have realised that the company's liquidation was unavoidable was the latest possible date on which the annual accounts for that year ought to have been delivered. The fact that the directors had not seen them was irrelevant and, in any case, they had acquiesced in the delay of their delivery. Construing s 214(4), Knox J took the view that its objective and subjective elements required each director to be judged not only on the facts actually known to them but also according to those facts which should have been known had the accounts been duly delivered as required by the Companies Act. The judge, accepting counsel's submission that the requirement to have regard to the functions to be carried out by the particular director in relation to the company in question which involves having regard to the particular company and its business, stated:

> *It follows that the general knowledge, skill and experience postulated will be much less extensive in a small company in a modest way of business, with simple accounting procedures and equipment, than it will be in a large company with sophisticated procedures. Nevertheless, certain minimum standards are to be assumed to be attained. Notably there is an obligation laid on companies to cause accounting records to be kept which are such as to disclose with reasonable accuracy at any time the financial position of the company at that time.*

Knox J concluded that the knowledge to be imputed to directors in testing whether or not they knew or ought to have realised that there was no reasonable prospect of the company avoiding insolvent liquidation is not limited to the documentary material available at the given time. This, he thought, was evident from the wording of s 214(4) which refers to those facts which he ought to ascertain, 'a word which does not appear in subsection (2) (b)'. Accordingly, there is to be included not only the factual information available to the directors but also what with 'reasonable diligence and an appropriate level of general knowledge, skill and experience, was ascertainable'. It should be noted that it is no defence for directors of a small family-run incorporated business that they lacked the basic financial and accounting knowledge necessary to fulfil their obligations (*Re DKG Contractors Ltd* (see earlier)). The failure to seek professional advice in times of difficulty is no excuse. Nor is it a defence that the director did not play an active part in the management of the company. In *Re Brian D Pierson (Contractors) Ltd* (2001) Hazel Williamson QC, sitting as a deputy High Court judge, observed that: '[o]ne cannot be a "sleeping director"; the function of "directing" on its own requires some consideration of the company's affairs to be exercised'.

17.73 Directors may be able to avoid liability if the conditions set out in s 214(3) are satisfied, namely, that if after the time when they first knew or ought to have concluded that there was no reasonable prospect that the company would avoid going into insolvent liquidation, they took every step with a view to minimising the potential loss to the company's creditors. In *Brooks v Armstrong* (2015) the court stressed that the burden of proof is squarely on the director to demonstrate that he 'took every step' to minimise loss to creditors once the collapse of the company became apparent. The onus is not on the liquidator to prove that every step was not taken. The court noted that what is 'every step' which a reasonably diligent person with the knowledge of or attributed to the director will depend upon the facts. As a matter of guidance the following factors fall to be considered by directors and kept under review both generally and when considering specific financial decisions assuming the business remains sustainable:

> *Ensuring accounting records are kept up to date with a budget and cash flow forecast; preparing a business review and a plan dealing with future trading including steps that can be taken (for example cost cutting) to minimise loss; keeping creditors informed and reaching agreements to deal with debt and supply where possible; regularly monitoring the trading and financial position together with the business plan both informally and at board meetings; asking if loss is being minimised; ensuring adequate capitalisation; obtaining professional advice (legal and financial); and considering alternative insolvency remedies.*

A decision to carry on business may in the particular circumstances be an acceptable course of action to follow, but the court will no doubt take a dim view if this involves increasing the company's indebtedness. On the one hand, realising the company's assets at a reasonable price in order to begin the process of discharging the company's debts may bring the directors within s 214(3). But resigning from the board and seeking opportunities elsewhere will not be an acceptable course of action (*Re Purpoint Ltd* (1991)). The best course of action for the purposes of s 214(3) is probably to seek professional advice at the earliest opportunity possible (as in *Re Continental Assurance Co of London plc* (earlier)), especially since liability for wrongful trading can lead to disqualification (see Chapter13); the absence of warnings from advisers will not relieve directors from their responsibility to review the company's position critically (*Re Brian D Pierson (Contractors) Ltd* (2001)). Relief under s 1157 of the CA 2006 (see Chapter 14) is not available in wrongful trading proceedings (*Re Produce Marketing Consortium Ltd* (1989)).

17.74 For the purposes of an order under s 214 whereby a director will be required to contribute to the company's assets, the court will assess the sum payable by reference to the amount by which the company's assets were reduced by the conduct in question. For example, in *Valentine v Bangla Television Ltd* (2009), the court ordered the directors to contribute £250,000 to the assets of the company on the basis that this sum represented the increase in the net deficiency caused by the transfer of company assets at an undervalue (for earlier proceedings involving the issue of the transaction at undervalue, see para **17.55**). Where the company has kept inadequate records the court, in its discretion, may determine the period of wrongful trading (*Re Purpoint Ltd* (1991)). Interest will be payable from the date of the winding-up (*Re Produce Marketing Consortium Ltd (No 2)* (1989)). In *Re Continental Assurance Co of London plc* (earlier), Park J observed, by way of obiter, that if liability is proved it is several liability for each individual director so that, therefore, the position of each director has to be assessed by the court.

The evidential hurdle confronting a liquidator or administrator seeking a wrongful trading order is considerable and, in the light of the decision in *Re Ralls Builders Ltd (In Liquidation); Grant v Ralls* (2016), proceedings may become a route so beset with risks, including those relating to costs, as to make misfeasance proceedings the default action (see para **17.75**). The company had made trading losses in the financial year to 31 October 2009, and on 13 October 2010 the directors put the company into administration (conduct which would satisfy the statutory defence in s 214(3)). In January 2011 it slid into insolvent liquidation. The liquidators applied for an order under s 214, contending that the directors knew or ought to have realised by 31 July 2010 (the relevant date) that the company had no reasonable prospect of avoiding liquidation. They sought a contribution of £1.5 million to the company's assets. The court, finding that the relevant date was 31 August 2010, not 31 July 2010 as claimed, held that the directors had failed to take the steps they ought to have taken to reduce the risks to creditors because they had increased the indebtedness of the company and were therefore outwith the s 214(3) defence. However, the court refused to order the directors to make a contribution to the company's assets under s 214(1) because it had not been proved that the net deficiency of the company had increased between 31 August 2010 and the date when the company entered into administration. In his reasoning, Snowden J implied into the statutory language of the provision a causation requirement: there must be a link between the alleged wrongful trading and any resulting loss to creditors. In subsequent proceedings, *Re Ralls Builders Ltd (No 2)* (2016), Snowden J, applying settled rules that restrict the recoverability of professionals' time-costs as damages in contract and tort actions, rejected the liquidators' contention that the directors should be ordered to contribute to the costs of investigating and pursuing the wrongful trading action. A consequence of this decision is that even if a s 214 action is successful, the recovery for creditors may be wiped out by the costs and expenses of pursuing the wrongful trading action.

(The causation point in *Re Ralls Builders Ltd* was applied by the court in *Brooks v Armstrong* (2016), where it was also stressed that directors should be permitted a proper amount of time to assess the options that are available to them.)

Misfeasance proceedings

17.75 We have seen that when a company is a going concern any breaches of duty by the directors is actionable by the company only, unless, exceptionally, an action can be brought by a shareholder with respect to such breaches amounting to unfairly prejudicial conduct (see Chapters 10 and 11). In a winding-up, typically it will be the liquidator, not the company, who will bring an action against the directors for any breaches of duty committed by them. Section 212 of the 1986 Act provides a summary remedy in such circumstances.

The provision states that if in the course of the winding-up it appears that an officer of the company (a term that encompasses a director, secretary, or manager or, inter alia, a promoter or liquidator of a company) has misapplied or retained or become accountable for any money or other property of the company, or has been guilty of any misfeasance or breach of any fiduciary duty or other duty in relation to the company the court may, on the application of the Official Receiver, the liquidator, or any creditor or contributory, examine the conduct in question and compel the person to repay or restore or account for the money or property or to contribute such sum to the company's assets by way of compensation as the court thinks just (see, for example, *Re MDA Investment Management Ltd* (2005); and *Swan v Sandhu* (2005)). A contributory can only bring proceedings under s 212 with the leave of the court. The burden of proof is on the claimants to establish misfeasance on the part of a director; it is not for the director in question to justify his conduct (*Mullarkey v Broad* (2008)).

17.76 Misfeasance covers the entire spectrum of directors' duties (*Re Westlowe Storage and Distribution Ltd* (2000); *Re HLC Environmental Projects Ltd* (2013), para **14.39**). Although, as has been seen, ratification by the company in general meeting can excuse the director from liability (see CA 2006, s 239), it is doubtful whether such ratification will be effective when the company's fortunes have declined to such an extent that liquidation has become inevitable (*West Mercia Safetywear Ltd v Dodd* (1988)).

In the performance of their duties liquidators, as officers of the court, are vested with extensive powers; however, they may also find themselves liable in misfeasance. In *Re Centralcrest Engineering Ltd* (2000) the Inland Revenue brought proceedings against the liquidator under s 212. The liquidator had allowed the company to continue to trade for 27 months after it had gone into compulsory liquidation. At the time of the liquidation the shortfall for creditors was £25,000. Following the trading the liquidator sold the company's assets to its directors for £6,500. As a result of the trading £73,230 was left owing to the Inland Revenue. It was held that the liquidator's misfeasance had two elements: first, allowing the company to continue to trade without the sanction of the court or liquidation committee (see s 167 at para **17.43**); second, allowing the company to continue to trade when it was apparent that she should have realised its assets soon after her appointment. The liquidator was therefore liable to compensate the company for its losses of £120,826 incurred during the trading period.

Distribution of surplus assets

17.77 As we have seen time and again, the key function of a liquidator is to maximise the funds available in the corporate pot in order to meet the claims of creditors who have submitted a valid proof of debt. The procedure for proving debt is set out in IR 2016, Pt 14. In order to save costs, it is better for a liquidator to reject a proof of debt thereby leaving the onus on the creditor to prove its validity (under IR 2016, rr 14.8–14.9), than for a liquidator to apply to the court to determine its enforceability (*Bellmex International Ltd v Green* (2001),

Evans-Lombe J). Even if a liquidator has admitted proof of a debt he can still change his mind. In *Re Allard Holdings Ltd* (2001) the liquidator became suspicious of proofs he had earlier admitted. It was held that the liquidator need only show on a balance of probabilities that he had made a mistake. In *Re Globe Legal Services Ltd* (2002) the liquidators admitted a disputed proof of debt of £30,000 and subsequently implied that they would increase the proof to £173,000. The debt in question related to the costs of the company's landlords, a firm of solicitors, enforcing a debt of rent. Two weeks later the liquidators wrote to the landlords notifying them that they could not agree to the sum of £173,000. The liquidators then applied to the court under IR 2016, r 14.11 to expunge the admission of proof for £173,000 or to reduce it to £30,000. The judge expunged the entire proof. Neuberger J stated that the proper test to have a debt admitted by mistake expunged was a balance of probabilities rather than the criminal onus of proof of beyond all reasonable doubt.

In the rare event of there being a surplus of assets after the expenses and costs of the liquidation have been met and the company's liabilities have been satisfied, the liquidator will distribute the remaining property among the members according to their rights as laid down in the *company's constitution*.

17.78 Typically a company's constitution will provide that the sum paid on preference shares must be repaid before any amount is returned to the holders of ordinary shares or deferred shares in the company. Unlike ordinary shareholders, however, preference shareholders do not have the right to participate in any remaining surplus after all capital has been repaid (see *Scottish Insurance Co v Wilsons and Clyde Coal Co* (1949), Lord Simonds). Such surplus will be distributed to the shareholders by reference to the nominal amount of share capital held by them and not in proportion to the amount paid up on their shares. In this regard Lord Macnaghten observed in *Birch v Cropper* (1889) that in a winding-up:

> The assets have to be distributed. The rights arising from unequal contributions on shares of equal amounts must be adjusted, and the property of the company, including its uncalled capital not required to satisfy prior claims, must be applied for that purpose. But when those rights are adjusted, when the capital is equalised, what equity founded on inequality of contribution can possibly remain. The rights and interests of the contributories in the company must then be simply in proportion to their shares.

Dissolution

Voluntary winding-up

17.79 Section 201 of the IA 1986 provides where the liquidator has sent to the Registrar of Companies his final account and return under s 94 (members' voluntary winding-up) or s 106 (creditors' voluntary winding-up), the Registrar shall forthwith register them, and on the expiration of three months from the registration of the return the company is deemed to be dissolved. However, the court may, on the application of the liquidator or any other person who appears to the court to be interested, make an order deferring the date at which the dissolution of the company is to take effect (s 201(3)).

Compulsory winding-up

17.80 Section 202 provides that where the Official Receiver is the liquidator of the company, and it appears to him that the realisable assets of the company are insufficient to cover the expenses of the winding-up and that the affairs of the company do not require further investigation, he may at any time apply to the Registrar of Companies for the early dissolution of the company. Such an application is then registered by the Registrar and at the expiry of three months from the date of the registration of the notice the company is dissolved.

Where such notice is given by the Official Receiver, any creditor or contributory of the company may apply to the Secretary of State for directions. The grounds for such an application are:

(a) that the realisable assets of the company are sufficient to cover the expenses of the winding-up;

(b) that the affairs of the company do require further investigation; or

(c) that for any other reason the early dissolution of the company is inappropriate (s 203(2)).

The Secretary of State may issue such directions as he thinks fit for enabling the winding-up of the company to proceed as if the Official Receiver had not applied for early dissolution. He may also, in his discretion, direct that the dissolution of the company be deferred.

17.81 Where no application is made by the Official Receiver for an early dissolution, s 205 provides that when the liquidator has filed his final returns or the Official Receiver has filed a notice stating that he considers the winding-up to be complete, the Registrar of Companies shall register those returns or the notice forthwith. At the end of the period of three months beginning with the day of that registration the company is dissolved (s 205(2)).

Reform

17.82 As has been seen in this chapter, the regime governing corporate rescue mechanisms and liquidations of companies has been the subject of intense reform in recent years. This reformist zeal continues: the aim being to maintain the UK's position at the forefront of insolvency best practice. On 25 May 2016 the Insolvency Service (IS) began a consultation exercise on options for reforming corporate insolvency law (*A Review of the Corporate Insolvency Framework: A consultation on Options for Reform* (https://www.gov.uk/government/consultations/a-review-of-the-corporate-insolvency-framework)). In late September 2016 IS published its comments to the responses received. Despite its title, the focus of the exercise lies with corporate rescue rather than on winding-up procedures. There are a number of recommendations for reform covering the protection of essential supplier contracts; ensuring restructuring plans bind both secured and unsecured creditors; and developing the rescue financing market. The key proposal is the creation of a new pre-insolvency moratorium period for financially distressed companies. The objective is to facilitate successful restructuring by reducing costs, improving the prospects of reaching agreement with creditors, and encouraging directors to take action early. The recommended moratorium period is three months, with the possibility of an extension subject to creditor approval. During the moratorium creditors would not be able to take action against the company while it is preparing to restructure. The directors would remain in place, subject to oversight by a supervisor whose primary role will be to protect creditor interests. The directors would continue to be subject to their usual duties to the company, but they would be relieved from any liability under s 214 of the IA 1986 while the moratorium period is running. There is every chance that these proposals will reach the statute book in some form in the light of the World Bank Survey at that time that saw the UK fall in the league tables because of the lack of debtor-led processes.

17.83 Yet another insolvency law consultation paper was launched by BEIS on 20 March 2018, the focus of which is on the governance of companies when they are approaching insolvency (the consultation closed on 11 June 2018). It is stated that the aim of the proposals is to reduce the risk of major company failures occurring through shortcomings of governance or stewardship, and to strengthen the responsibilities of directors of companies when they are in or approaching insolvency. There are four key proposals. In summary:

    (i)   Sales of businesses in distress: the Government is proposing to introduce a new offence under which directors of group companies are held accountable where they approve the sale of an insolvent subsidiary and the sale results in harm to the subsidiary's stakeholders, such as its employees and creditors.

    (ii) Reversal of value extraction schemes: the Government states that the law does not deal adequately with the situation where a company, which is not yet in administration or liquidation, has been 'rescued' by new investors who then go on to extract value to return at least part of their investment and reduce their potential loss should the company become insolvent. Insolvency practitioners' powers should be increased so that they can challenge excessive management fees, excessive interest charges on loans, the grant of charges over company property, and the sale and leaseback of assets.

    (iii) Investigating the actions of directors of dissolved companies: the Government states that there is a concern that dissolution of companies, as an alternative to putting a company into a formal insolvency process, is being used by share-holders/managers to 'shed' the company's liabilities and that management frequently continue to run the same business via a new company. It is therefore proposed to introduce increased investigative powers to allow for investigation into the conduct of individuals who were directors of companies which have been dissolved.

(iv) Strengthening corporate governance in pre-insolvency situations: there are a number of proposals which focus on stronger corporate governance and transparency measures, shareholder responsibilities, payment of dividends, the use of professional advisers, and measures for protecting companies in the supply chain.

In August 2018 the Government published its response, *Insolvency and Corporate Governance*, to the 2016 and March 2018 recommendations for reforming the UK insolvency framework. One of the key proposals put forward is the introduction of a new restructuring moratorium to help business rescue in order to 'give those financially distressed companies which are ultimately viable, a period of time when creditors . . . cannot take action against the company, allowing it to make preparations to restructure or seek new investment'. Modelled on administration (see paras **17.3–17.6**), it is intended to introduce a debtor-in-possession pre-insolvency moratorium, lasting 28 days, for the majority of companies (finance and insurance sector companies are excluded as are those listed in paras 4A–4J of Sch A1 to the IA 1986). The objective is to protect a company from creditor actions while the moratorium is in place unless the company consents or the court grants leave. The company's management will remain in place. The idea is to smooth the path to a number of outcomes such as agreeing an informal restructuring plan with creditors or entering into insolvency as a precursor to rescue or liquidation. The proposed moratorium is designed to supplement existing processes rather than replace them. Subject to conditions, it can be extended by a further 28 days without the need for creditor or court consent. Entry into the moratorium is for those companies which will 'become insolvent if action is not taken' rather than the requirement that the company be 'already, or imminently in financial difficulty or insolvent'. Companies that are insolvent are therefore excluded given the requirement that a company must have sufficient funds to satisfy 'current obligations as and when they fall due as well as any new obligations that are incurred in the moratorium'. Overseeing the moratorium will be a qualified insolvency practitioner, termed a 'monitor', who will be an officer of the court, charged with, amongst other things, protecting the interests of creditors and preventing abuse of the new moratorium. It remains to be seen when parliamentary time is found for the implementation of these reforms.

17.84 At the EU level, in December 2012 the European Commission announced its plans for the reform of insolvency law at EU level. In *A new European approach to business failure and insolvency* (COM(2012) 742 final), the Commission states that it has adopted a proposal for the reform of insolvency law based on giving businesses a second chance.

The modernisation of EU insolvency laws so as to facilitate the survival of businesses and to give entrepreneurs a second chance is viewed as crucially important in terms of improving the functioning of the internal market and supporting economic activity in the aftermath of the global financial crisis. Public consultation began in July 2013 and the final text of the EC Insolvency Regulation was published on 5 June 2015. Regulation (EU) 2015/848 entered into force on 26 June 2017.

FURTHER READING

This chapter links with the materials in Chapter 19 of *Hicks and Goo's Cases and Materials on Company Law* (Oxford, OUP, 2011, xl +649p).

Campbell, 'Protection by Elimination: Winding up of Companies on Public Interest Grounds' [2001] *IL & P* 129.

Cooke and Hicks, 'Wrongful Trading– Predicting Insolvency' [1993] *JBL* 338.

Finch, 'Re-invigorating Corporate Rescue' [2003] *JBL* 527.

Finch, 'Pre-Packaged Administrations: Bargains in the Shadow of Insolvency or Shadowy Bargains?' [2006] *JBL* 568.

Finch, 'Corporate Rescue: Who is Interested?' [2012] *JBL* 190.

Fox et al, 'A Review of the Corporate Insolvency Framework: A Lawyers' Perspective' [2016] *ICR* 300.

Keay, 'What Future for Liquidation in Light of the Enterprise Act Reforms' [2005] *JBL* 143.

McCormack, 'Super-Priority New Financing and Corporate Rescue' [2007] *JBL* 701.

Oditah, 'Wrongful Trading' [1990] *LMCLQ* 205.

Oditah, 'Assets and the Treatment of Claims in Insolvency' [1992] LQR 459.

Pugh, '*Hollicourt* to Reduce Banks' Exposure under Section 127' [2001] *IL & P* 53.

Rajak, 'The Challenges of Commercial Reorganisation in Insolvency: Empirical Evidence from England' in Ziegel (ed) *Current Developments in International and Comparative Corporate Insolvency Law* (Oxford, Clarendon Press, 1994).

SELF-TEST QUESTIONS

1 What is meant by: (i) a transaction at an undervalue; (ii) a voidable preference; (iii) fraudulent trading; and (iv) wrongful trading?

2 What are the consequences of a winding-up petition on dispositions of corporate property?

3 On 1 June 2019 Charlie, an unpaid creditor of Acme Ltd, petitioned the court to wind up the company. Acme Ltd has two directors, Able and his wife. Able's wife has been content

to leave the management of the company to him and she has played no active part in its affairs.

A liquidator is appointed on 1 July 2019. He has discovered the following events:

(a) On 1 March 2019 Z Bank lent £80,000 to Acme Ltd to cover three months' wages owed to Acme Ltd's employees. The loan is secured by a floating charge.

(b) On 30 April 2019 Able successfully negotiated an unsecured loan of £75,000 from Z Bank. He told the bank that the money was needed to help the company trade out of its financial difficulties. In fact, Able used part of the sum to satisfy a debt of £5,000 owed to Derek, a trade creditor, which Able had personally guaranteed. As a consequence of the company continuing to trade, its indebtedness to creditors is increased by £50,000.

(c) On 1 July 2018 the board of Acme Ltd declared a dividend. The shareholders have not been paid and are now pressing for payment.

(d) The company's employees have not been paid since 1 June 2019.

Advise the liquidator.

Select bibliography

1 Introduction to company law

Company Law Review Steering Group (CLRSG) *Modern Law for a Competitive Economy—The Strategic Framework* (London, DTI, February 1999).

CLRSG *Modern Law for a Competitive Economy—Developing the Framework* (London, DTI, March 2000).

CLRSG *Modern Law for a Competitive Economy—Completing the Structure* (London, DTI, November 2000).

Davies and Worthington *Gower's Principles of Modern Company Law* 10th edn (London, Sweet & Maxwell, 2016), chs 1–4.

Finch and Freedman 'The Limited Liability Partnership: Pick and Mix or Mix-up?' [2002] *JBL* 475.

Freedman 'Small Businesses and the Corporate Form: Burden or Privilege?' [1994] *MLR* 555.

Henning 'Limited Liability Partnerships, Limited Partnerships, and Limited Liability Partnerships' [2000] *Co Law* 165.

Extracts from the economics literature, specifically selected for company law students, can be found in Romano (ed) *Foundations of Corporate Law* (Oxford, OUP, 1993).

2 Corporate personality and limited liability

CLRSG *Developing the Framework* (March 2000) and *Completing the Structure* (November 2000), paras 4.11–4.22.

Davies and Worthington *Gower's Principles of Modern Company Law* 10th edn (London, Sweet & Maxwell, 2016), chs 8 and 9.

Gallagher and Zeigler 'Lifting The Corporate Veil in The Pursuit Of Justice' [1990] *JBL* 292.

Grantham and Rickett 'The Bootmaker's Legacy to Company Law Doctrine' in Grantham and Rickett (eds) *Corporate Personality in the 20th Century* (Oxford, Hart Publishing, 1998).

Henning 'Limited Liability Partnerships, Limited Partnerships, and Limited Liability Partnerships' [2000] *Co Law* 165.

Home Office consultation document 'Reforming the law on involuntary manslaughter: the Government's proposals' (May 2000).

3 Lifting the veil

Bromilow '*Creasey v Breachwood Motors*: Mistaken Identity Leads to Untimely Death' (1998) 19 *Co Law* 198.

Cheffin *Company Law: Theory, Structure and Operation* (Oxford, OUP, 1997), pp 497–508.

Davies and Worthington *Gower's Principles of Modern Company Law* 10th edn (London, Sweet & Maxwell, 2016), chs 8 and 9.

Hare 'Family Division 0; Chancery Division 1: Piercing the Corporate Veil in the Supreme Court (Again)' [2013] *CLJ* 72.

Home Office 'Reforming the law on involuntary manslaughter: the Government's proposals' (consultation document) (London, Home Office, May 2000).

Lim '*Salomon* Reigns' (2013) 129 *LQR* 480.

4 Promoters and pre-incorporation contracts

Green 'Security of Transaction after *Phonogram*' (1984) 47 *MLR* 671.

Griffiths *Contracting with Companies* (Oxford, Hart Publishing, 2005).

Green 'Security of transaction after Phonogram' (1984) 47 *MLR* 671.

Gross 'Who is a Company Promoter?' (1970) 86 *LQR* 493.

Gross 'Pre-incorporation Contracts' (1971) 87 *LQR* 367.

Savirimuthu 'Pre-Incorporation Contracts and the Problem of Corporate Fundamentalism' [2003] *Co Law* 196.

Worthington *Sealy and Worthington's Text, Cases, & Materials in Company Law* 16th edn (Oxford, OUP, 2016), pp 498–504.

5 Raising capital: equity and its consequences

Baxter 'The Role of the Judge in Enforcing Shareholder Rights' [1983] *CLJ* 96.

Campbell 'Note: What *is* Wrong with Insider Dealing?' [1996] *LS* 185.

Davies 'Control Shifts via Contracting with Shareholders' in G Ringe and J Gordon (eds) *The Oxford Handbook of Corporate Law and Governance* (Oxford, OUP, 2017).

Davies and Worthington *Gower's Principles of Modern Company Law* 10th edn (London, Sweet & Maxwell, 2016), chs 24–26 and 28–30.

Davies, Hopt, and Ringe 'Control Transactions' in R Kraakman et al (eds) *The Anatomy of Corporate Law*, 3rd edn (Oxford, OUP, 2016).

Eisenberg 'The Structure of Corporation Law' (1898) 89 *Colum L Rev* 1461.

Gale, Gale, and Scanlan 'Fraud and the Sale of Shares' [2001] *Co Law* 98.

Goldberg 'The Enforcement of Outsider Rights Under Section 20(1) of the Companies Act 1948' [1972] *MLR* 363.

Goldberg 'The Controversy on the Section 20 Contract Revisited' [1985] *MLR* 158.

McVea 'What's Wrong With Insider Dealing?' [1995] *LS* 390.

Wilks 'The Amoral Corporation and British Utility Regulation' [1997] *New Political Economy* 280.

Worthington *Sealy and Worthington's Text, Cases, & Materials in Company Law* 16th edn (Oxford, OUP, 2016), ch 9.

6 Raising capital: debentures: fixed and floating charges

Ferran and Ho *Principles of Corporate Finance Law* (Oxford, OUP, 2014).

Gough *Company Charges* (London, Butterworths, 1996).

Gullifer (ed) *Goode on Legal Problems of Credit and Security* (London, Sweet & Maxwell, 2013).

McCormack 'Extension of Time for Registration of Company Charges' [1986] *JBL* 282.

Worthington 'Fixed Charges over Book Debts and Other Receivables' [1997] *LQR* 562.

Worthington *Personal Property Law: Text, Cases and Materials* (Oxford, Hart Publishing, 2000).

Worthington *Sealy and Worthington's Text, Cases, & Materials in Company Law* 16th edn (Oxford, OUP, 2016), ch 12.

7 Share capital

Davies and Worthington *Gower's Principles of Modern Company Law* 10th edn (London, Sweet & Maxwell, 2016), chs 11–13.

Ferran and Ho *Principles of Corporate Finance Law* (Oxford, OUP, 2014).

Sykes 'Financial Assistance' [2000] *Co Law* 65.

Worthington *Sealy and Worthington's Text, Cases, & Materials in Company Law* 16th edn (Oxford, OUP, 2016), ch 10.

8 The constitution of the company: dealing with insiders

Barc and Bowen (eds) *Tolley's Company Law*, Vol I (Croydon, Tolley, 1988), p 126.

Cheffins 'Corporate Theory' in *The Oxford Handbook of Legal Studies* (Oxford, OUP, 2003), ch 23.

Drury 'The Relative Nature of a Shareholder's Right to Enforce the Company Contract' [1986] *CLJ* 219.

Goldberg 'The Enforcement of Outsider Rights under Section 20(1) of the Companies Act 1948' [1972] *MLR* 362.

Goldberg 'The Controversy on the Section 20 Contract Revisited' [1985] *MLR* 158.

Gregory 'The Section 20 Contract' (1981) 44 *MLR* 526.

Posner *Economic Analysis of the Law* (Boston, MA, Little Brown, 1986), p 386.

Prentice 'The Enforcement of "Outsider" Rights' [1980] 1 *Co Law* 179.

Stokes 'Company Law and Legal Theory' in Twining (ed) *Legal Theory and the Common Law* (Oxford, Blackwell, 1986).

9 Classes of shares and variation of class rights

Pennington *Company Law* (London, Butterworths, 2001), ch 7.

Worthington *Sealy and Worthington's Text, Cases, & Materials in Company Law* 16th edn (Oxford, OUP, 2016), ch 11.

10 Derivative claims

Baxter 'The Role of the Shareholder in Enforcing Shareholder Rights' [1983] *CLJ* 96.

Baxter 'The Role of the Judge in Enforcing Shareholder Rights' [1987] *NILQ* 6.

Beck 'The Shareholders' Derivative Action' (1974) 52 *Can Bar Rev* 159.

Boyle *Minority Shareholders' Remedies* (Cambridge, CUP, 2002).

Davies *Introduction to Company Law* (Oxford, OUP, 2010).

Davies and Worthington *Gower's Principles of Modern Company Law* 10th edn (London, Sweet & Maxwell, 2016), ch 17.

Hirt 'The Company's Decision to Litigate Against its Directors: Legal Strategies to Deal with the Board of Directors' Conflict of Interest' [2005] *JBL* 159.

Sullivan 'Restating the Scope of the Derivative Action' [1985] *CLJ* 236.

Wedderburn 'Shareholders' Rights and the Rule in *Foss v Harbottle*' [1957] *CLJ* 154 and [1958] *CLJ* 219.

11 Statutory shareholder remedies

Boyle 'Judicial Interpretation of Part XVII of the Companies Act 1985' in *Company Law in Change* [1987] *Current Legal Problems* 26.

Boyle *Minority Shareholders' Remedies* (Cambridge, CUP, 2002).

Company Financial and Insolvency Law Review Special issue, Autumn 1997.

Company Lawyer Special issue [1997] 18(8).

CLRSG *Modern Company Law For a Competitive Economy: Developing the Framework* (London, DTI, March 2000).

CLRSG *Modern Company Law For a Competitive Economy: Completing the Structure* (London, DTI, November 2000).

Ferran 'Shareholder Remedies: The Law Commission Report' [1998] *CfiLR* 235.

Griggs and Lowry 'Minority Shareholders' Remedies: A Comparative View' [1994] *JBL* 463.

Law Commission Consultation Paper No 142 *Shareholder Remedies* (1996).

Law Commission Report No 246 *Shareholder Remedies* (1997).

Lowry 'Stretching the Ambit of Section 459 of the Companies Act 1985: The Elasticity of Unfair Prejudice' [1995] *LMCLQ* 337.

Lowry 'The Pursuit of Effective Minority Shareholder Protection: Section 459 of the Companies Act 1985' [1996] *Co Law* 67.

Prentice 'Minority Shareholder Oppression: Valuation of Shares' (1986) 102 *LQR* 179.

Prentice 'The Theory of the Firm: Minority Shareholder Oppression: Sections 459– 461 of the Companies Act 1985' (1988) 8 *OJLS* 55.

Riley 'Contracting Out of Company Law: s 459 of the Companies Act 1985 and the Role of the Courts' [1992] *MLR* 782.

Worthington *Sealy and Worthington's Text, Cases, & Materials in Company Law* 16th edn (Oxford, OUP, 2016), ch 13.

Womack 'Winding Up on the Just and Equitable Ground—Stay of Winding-Up Order' [1975] *CLJ* 209.

12 The constitution of the company: dealing with outsiders

Davies and Worthington *Gower's Principles of Modern Company Law* 10th edn (London, Sweet & Maxwell, 2016), ch 7.

DTI Consultation Document *Reform of the Ultra Vires Rule* (the Prentice Report) (1986).

DTI Consultation Document *Political Donations by Companies* (March 1999).

Worthington *Sealy and Worthington's Text, Cases, & Materials in Company Law* 16th edn (Oxford, OUP, 2016), ch 3.

13 Corporate management

Davies and Worthington *Gower's Principles of Modern Company Law* 10th edn (London, Sweet & Maxwell, 2016), chs 10 and 14.

Drake 'Disqualification of Directors—the "Red Card"' [1989] *JBL* 474.

Griffin *Personal Liability and Disqualification of Company Directors* (Oxford, Hart Publishing, 1999).

Hicks *Disqualification of Directors: No Hiding Place for the Unfit?*, ACCA Research Report 59 (1998).

MacKenzie '"Who Controls the Company?"—the Interpretation of Table A' [1983] *Co Law* 99.

Milman 'Personal Liability and Disqualification of Company Directors: Something Old, Something New' [1992] *NILQ* 1.

Study Group on Directors' Remuneration Report (the Greenbury Report) (London, Gee, 1995).

Villiers 'Executive Pay: Beyond Control?' [1995] *LS* 260.

14 Directors' duties

Armour and Conaglen 'Directorial Disclosure' [2005] *CLJ* 48.

Austin 'Fiduciary Accountability for Business Opportunities' in Finn (ed) *Equity and Commercial Relationships* (Sydney, Law Book Company of Australia, 1987), ch 6.

Beck 'The Quickening of the Fiduciary Obligation' [1975] *Can Bar Rev* 771.

Berg 'The Company Law Review: Legislating Directors' Duties' [2000] *JBL* 472.

Chambers 'Constructive Trusts and Breach of Fiduciary Duty' [2013] *Conv* 73.

CLRSG *Modern Company Law For a Competitive Economy: Developing the Framework* (London, DTI, March 2000).

Copp 'Section 172 of the Companies Act 2006 Fails People and Planet' [2010] *Co Law* 406.

Developing Directors' Duties [1999] *CfiLR* (special edition devoted to the Law Commission's and Scottish Law Commission's reports on directors' duties (Nos 261 and 173) and the DTI's fundamental review of core company law).

Edelman 'When do Fiduciary Duties Arise?' [2010] *LQR* 302.

Hicks 'Directors' Liability for Management Errors' [1994] *LQR* 390.

Ho and Lee 'Reluctant Bedfellows: Want of Authority and Knowing Receipt' [2012] *MLR* 91.

Jones 'Unjust Enrichment and the Fiduciary's Duty of Loyalty' [1968] *LQR* 472.

Keay 'The Duty of Directors to Take Account of Creditors' Interests: Has it Any Role to Play?' [2002] *JBL* 379.

Kershaw *Company Law in Context* (Oxford, OUP, 2012).

Law Commission and Scottish Law Commission *Company Directors: Regulating Conflicts of Interests and Formulating a Statement of Duties* (Nos 261 and 173, respectively).

Lowry 'Poison Pills in US Corporations—A Re-examination' [1992] *JBL* 337.

McGhee (ed) *Snell's Equity* (London, Sweet & Maxwell, 2017).

Lord Millett 'Bribes and Secret Commissions' [2012] *CLJ* 583.

Payne 'A Re-examination of Ratification' [1999] *CLJ* 604.

Sealy '"Bona fides" and "Proper Purposes" in Corporate Decisions' [1989] *Monash Univ LR* 265.

Sealy 'Personal Liability of Directors and Officers for Debts of Insolvent Corporations: A Jurisdictional Perspective' in Ziegel (ed) *Current Developments in International and Comparative Corporate Insolvency Law* (Oxford, Clarendon Press, 1994).

Smith 'Deterrence, Prophylaxis and Punishment in Fiduciary Obligations' [2013] *J of Equity* 87.

Walters 'Directors' Duties: The Impact of the Company Directors Disqualification Act 1986' [2000] *Co Law* 110.

Worthington 'Corporate Governance: Remedying and Ratifying Directors' Breaches' [2000] *LQR* 638.

Worthington 'Fiduciary Duties and Proprietary Remedies: Addressing the Failure of Equitable Formulae' [2013] *CLJ* 720.

15 Corporate governance 1: corporate governance and corporate theory

Alchian and Demsetz 'Production, Information Costs, and Economic Organization' [1972] *American Economic Review* 777.

Baumol *Business Behaviour, Value and Growth* (New York, Macmillan, 1959), p 27.

Baumol *Business Behaviour, Value and Growth* (New York: Harcourt, Brace & World, 1967).

Berle *Power without Property* (New York, Harcourt, Brace, 1959).

Chandler *The Visible Hand: The Managerial Revolution in American Business* (Cambridge, MA, Harvard University Press, 1977).

Chandler *Scale and Scope: The Dynamics of Industrial Capitalism* (Cambridge, MA, Belknap Press of Harvard University Press, 1990).

Cheffins (2002a) 'Corporate Law and Ownership Structure: A Darwinian Link? Contemporary Issues in Corporate Governance' [2002] *University of New South Wales LJ* 378.

Cheffins (2002b) 'Comparative Corporate Governance and the Australian Experience' in Ramsay (ed) *Key Developments in Corporate Law and Trusts Law* (Sydney, Butterworths, 2002), p 26.

Coase 'The Nature of the Firm' (1937) 4(4) *Economica* 386.

Coffee 'The Rise of Dispersed Ownership: The Roles of Law and the State in the Separation of Ownership and Control' [2001] 1 *Yale LJ* 25.

Dignam 'Exporting Corporate Governance: UK Regulatory Systems in a Global Economy' [2000] *Co Law* 70.

Dignam and Galanis 'Governing the World: The Development of the OECD's Corporate Governance Principles' [1999] *European Business L Rev* 396.

Easterbrook and Fischel *The Economic Structure of Corporate Law* (Cambridge, MA, Harvard University Press, 1991).

Freeman and Evans 'Corporate Governance: A Stakeholder Interpretation' [1990] *J of Behavioral Economics* 337.

Friedman *Capitalism and Freedom* (Chicago, IL, University of Chicago Press, 1962).

Keynes 'The End of Laissez-Faire' in *Essays in Persuasion* (London, Macmillan 1931).

Koopmans *Three Essays on the State of Economic Science* (New York, McGraw-Hill, 1957), pp 140–141.

La Porta, Lopez-de-Silanes, and Shleifer 'Corporate Ownership Around the World' [1999] *J of Finance* 471.

La Porta, Lopez-de-Silanes, Shleifer, and Vishny 'Law and Finance' [1998] *J of Political Economy* 1113.

Manne 'Intellectual Styles and the Evolution of American Corporate Law' in Radnitzky and Bernholz (eds) *Economic Imperialism: The Economic Approach Applied Outside the Field of Economics* (New York, Paragon House Publishers, 1987), pp 219–241.

Marris *The Economic Theory of Managerial Capitalism* (London, Macmillan, 1964).

Mintzberg *Power in and Around Organisations* (Upper Saddle River, NJ, Prentice Hall Inc, 1983).

Perry *Legal Systems as a Determinant of FDI: Lessons from Sri Lanka* (London, Kluwer Law International, 2001) 48.

Trubeck and Galanter 'Scholars in Self-Estrangement: Some Reflections on the Crisis in Law and Development Studies in the United States' [1974] *Wisconsin L Rev* 1062.

Williamson *The Economics of Discretionary Behavior: Managerial Objectives in a Theory of the Firm* (Chicago, IL, Markham, 1964).

Williamson *The Economics of Discretionary Behaviour: Managerial Objectives in a Theory of the Firm* (London, Kershaw Publishing Co Ltd, 1974).

Williamson *Markets and Hierarchies: Analysis and Antitrust Implications. A Study in the Economics of Internal Organization* (London, Collier Macmillan, 1975).

Williamson 'Corporate Governance' [1984] *Yale LJ* 1197.

16 Corporate governance 2: the UK corporate governance debate

Cheffins 'Corporate Theory' in *The Oxford Handbook of Legal Studies* (Oxford, OUP, 2003), ch 23.

Committee of Enquiry on Industrial Democracy (the Bullock Committee) *Report of the Committee of Enquiry on Industrial Democracy* (London, HMSO, 1977).

Confederation of British Industry *Responsibilities of the British Public Company; Final Report of the Company Affairs Committee* (London, CBI, 1973).

Elmagrhi, Ntim, Collins, and Wang 'Antecedents of Voluntary Corporate Governance Disclosure: A Post-2007/08 Financial Crisis Evidence from the Influential UK Combined Code' [2016] *Corporate Governance: The international journal of business in society*, https://ssrn.com/abstract=2753919.

Etzioni *The Spirit of Community: Rights, Responsibilities and the Communitarian Agenda* (New York, Crown Publishers, 1993).

Hadden *Company Law and Capitalism* (London, Weidenfeld & Nicolson, 1977), p 75.

Ireland 'Property and Contract in Contemporary Corporate Theory' [2003] *LS* 453.

Jensen and Meckling (1976) 'Theory of the Firm: Managerial Behaviour, Agency Costs, and Ownership Structure' (1976) 3 *J of Financial Economics* 305.

Kelly and Parkinson 'The Conceptual Foundations of the Company: A Pluralist Approach' in Parkinson, Gamble, and Kelly (eds) *The Political Economy of the Company* (Oxford, Hart Publishing, 2001).

Minhat, Marizah, and Dzolkarnaini 'Is Executive Compensation a Substitute Governance Mechanism to Debt Financing and Leasing?' (2015) 48(14) *Applied Economics* 1293, https://ssrn.com/abstract=1650298.

Plender *A Stake in the Future—The Stakeholding Solution* (Sonama, CA, Nicholas Brealey Publishing, 1997), pp 23–24.

17 Corporate rescue and liquidations in outline

Campbell 'Protection by Elimination: Winding up of Companies on Public Interest Grounds' [2001] *IL&P* 129.

Finch and Milman *Corporate Insolvency Law: Perspectives and Principles* (Cambridge, CUP, 2017).

Fletcher and Crabb *Insolvency Act 1986* (Current Law Statutes Annotated Reprints) (London, Sweet & Maxwell, 1986).

Goode *Principles of Corporate Insolvency Law*, 4th edn (London, Sweet & Maxwell, 2011).

Oditah 'Misfeasance Proceedings against Company Directors' [1992] *LMCLQ* 207.

Review Committee on Insolvency Law and Practice (the Cork Committee) *Report of the Review Committee on Insolvency Law and Practice* (Cmnd 8558, 1982).

Index